INFANTICIDE

Comparative and Evolutionary Perspectives

INFANTICIDE

Comparative and Evolutionary Perspectives

Glenn Hausfater

Sarah Blaffer Hrdy

Editors

ALDINE
Publishing Company
New York

ABOUT THE EDITORS

Glenn Hausfater is Professor, Division of Biological Sciences, The University of Missouri-Columbia. He is the author (with J. and S. A. Altmann) of: *Guidebook for the Long-Term Monitoring of Amboseli Baboons and Their Habitat; Dominance and Reproduction in Baboons;* and *Early Vegetation of the Illinois Valley.*
Sarah Blaffer Hrdy was Associate in Biological Anthropology, Peabody Museum, Harvard University and presently is Professor, Department of Anthropology, University of California, Davis. She is the author of: *The Woman That Never Evolved; The Langurs of Abu;* and *The Black-man of Zinacantan.*

Copyright © 1984 by Wenner-Gren Foundation for Anthropological Research Incorporated

Aldine Publishing Company
200 Saw Mill River Road
Hawthorne, N.Y. 10532

Library of Congress Cataloging in Publication Data
Main entry under title:
Infanticide: comparative and evolutionary perspectives.
   (Biological foundations of human behavior)
   Bibliography: p.
   Includes index.
   1. Infanticide in animals—Congresses.   2. Infanticide
—Congresses.   3. Behavior evolution—Congresses.
I. Hausfater, Glenn.   II. Hrdy, Sarah Blaffer, 1946–
III. Series.
QL762.5.I54   1984   591.51   84–6386
ISBN 0–202–02022–3

Printed in the United States of America
10 9 8 7 6 5 4 3 2 1

"Natural selection can honestly be described as a process for the maximization of short-sighted selfishness. T. H. Huxley's term 'moral indifference' might aptly characterize the physical universe. For the biological world, a stronger term is needed."

George Williams, 1980

CONTENTS

III. INFANTICIDE IN RODENTS: QUESTIONS OF PROXIMATE AND ULTIMATE CAUSATION

IV. INFANTICIDE IN HUMANS: ETHNOGRAPHY, DEMOGRAPHY, SOCIOBIOLOGY, AND HISTORY

PREFACE

This volume—one product of a 1982 Wenner-Gren Foundation conference on "Infanticide in Animals and Man" held at Cornell University—marks the end of a transition period. Over the past decade, the intellectual pendulum in behavioral biology and related disciplines has swung from an earlier view that infanticide could not possibly represent anything other than abnormal and maladaptive behavior to the current view that in many populations infanticide is a normal and individually adaptive activity. Reflecting this change of perspective and exemplified by the papers in this volume, researchers have begun to interpret an ever expanding list of behaviors as subtle forms of infanticide or counterstrategies to infanticide.

Quite possibly, readers ten years from now may take for granted the occurrence of infanticide in various animal species and may even be unaware of the controversies and occasionally heated debate that have marked the last decade of research on this topic. Such readers will thus most likely be puzzled by the obsessive reiteration in this volume of the theme that infanticide is a natural and not necessarily pathological behavior. However, it is well to remember that no book can be free from its historical context and the present volume is no exception.

By and large, then, the chapters in this volume stress the widespread or frequent occurrence of infanticide as well as the adaptive nature of this behavior for at least some of the individuals concerned. Repeated emphasis of these points, however, should not be taken as an indication that either our coauthors or ourselves believe infanticidal behavior to be omnipresent in the animal kingdom. Rather, this emphasis reflects the degree to which we consider the evolutionary importance of infanticide and related phenomenon to have been heretofore overlooked.

There is also a second point that should be emphasized, a point unnecessary perhaps for most biologically oriented readers, but essential for many others if we wish to avoid misunderstandings. Years of awkward arguments with friends in the humanities have taught us that researchers who study animals tend to view the world in a slightly different way from those who study people. Our aim in this volume has been to describe and understand the natural world. It is important to recognize, however, that this is a separate process from deciding what one's own values are, and what we are willing to sanction or not sanction in the societies in which we live. For guidance in these matters we must attend at least as strongly to the insights of philosophy and ethics as to the workings of the natural world.

Many—perhaps all—of those who participated in the infanticide symposium felt that our sense of satisfaction at having obtained, at least to some extent, an increased understanding of the way in which nature operates was tempered by our focus on what is after all a somber topic. But there was also a great deal of intellectual excitement generated by bringing together researchers from such diverse backgrounds as anthropology, psychology, zoology, demography, public health, and history. Neither the conference itself, nor this volume, would have been possible without the support and assistance of the Wenner-Gren Foundation for Anthropological Research. We are very grateful both to its Board of Trustees and especially to its Director of Research, Mrs. Lita Osmundsen.

Administrative details of the conference and of the preparation of this volume, and a small mountain of paperwork in their wake, fell into the capable hands of Stacey Coil. Only her cheerful assistance kept a two-year long undertaking within manageable bounds. Kathy Horton prepared the consolidated bibliography which we hope readers of this volume will find both useful and convenient, and Carol Saunders carefully checked all of the references therein against the original manuscripts. Special thanks are also due to symposium co-organizers Mildred Dickemann and Christian Vogel for lending their expertise, advice, and support to this project at all stages, and to Mel Konner and Richard Wrangham, Editors of the series "Biological Foundations of Human Behavior," for giving us free rein in preparing this volume. Finally, we wish to thank Kyle Wallace of Aldine for sharing our vision of such a high-quality book and for working with us in such a congenial way to make that hope a reality.

Sarah Blaffer Hrdy
and
Glenn Hausfater

Comparative and Evolutionary Perspectives on Infanticide: Introduction and Overview

Sarah Blaffer Hrdy
Glenn Hausfater

INTRODUCTION

Infanticide has only recently come to be regarded as a biologically significant phenomenon. The fact that infanticide is considered an abhorrent practice in our own society is only a part of the reason why researchers for so long failed to realize how widespread infanticide is in the natural world. A second reason had to do with evidence. Early field reports of infanticide among langur monkeys and lions were sketchy; data were even sparser for other wild mammals. In the case of birds, researchers knew that egg destruction by conspecifics and siblicide occurred but the true frequencies of these acts was unknown and they were generally considered to be isolated phenomena. Eventually, detailed information emerged from laboratory studies of rodents, but infanticide and cannibalism in these species was typically attributed to overcrowding or to other features of captivity itself.

Yet a third reason why the importance of infanticide was so long unrecognized was that reigning intellectual traditions in the biological and social sciences evaluated behaviors according to their contributions to survival of the species and the group. From this perspective there could be only two explanations for infanticide: either the behavior was pathological or else it functioned adaptively to regulate population size through prevention of overcrowding (Calhoun, 1966; Christian *et al.,* 1963). Any behavior which resulted in death or injury to offspring was by definition "abnormal" (see for example King, 1963: 85–6).

According to classical ethology, animals (with the notable exception of humans) rarely kill members of their own species under natural conditions (Lorenz, 1966). Nevertheless, it was widely accepted that if sufficiently stressed, as through crowding, animals might become infanticidal or cannibalistic (Calhoun, 1962); such behavior was considered maladaptive. By the late 1970's however, intraspecific killing, including infanticide, had become more widely documented. In many cases there was no indication of either crowding or "abnormal" conditions. The focus of research shifted from *whether* infanticide occurred under natural conditions to *why* it occurred, and *how* frequently. Some researchers even began to ask if there were circumstances under which infanticide might be reproductively advantageous for one or more of the individuals involved.

This shift in thinking about infanticide can be traced in large part to Williams' influential critique of current evolutionary thinking (1966) and to seminal writings on kin selection and sexual selection by W. D. Hamilton (1964a) and Robert Trivers (1972). Once infanticide began to be explained in evolutionary terms (Hrdy 1974), published reports of infanticide in mammals increased dramatically. Ethologists began to recognize how widespread intraspecific killing, infanticide, and cannibalism—behaviors long considered "unnatural"—actually were. As several papers in this volume amply demonstrate, infanticide and cannibalism are for many animals everyday occurrences during those seasons when infants are present (Dominey and Blumer, Chapter 3, this volume; Polis, Chapter 5, this volume). Likewise, in certain species of birds, the first-hatched chick inevitably kills its younger sibling (Mock, Chapter 1, this volume). For many other species, infanticide is far less common than in the cases just cited, but it nevertheless plays an important role in shaping reproductive biology and social behavior.

DEFINITIONS

According to a conventional definition, such as the one used by Mock (Chapter 1, this volume), *infanticide* is any behavior that makes a direct and significant contribution to the immediate death of an embryo or newly hatched or born member of the perpetrator's own species. This definition has the merit of being easily comprehended across a spectrum of disciplines. However, as Mildred Dickemann points out in the introduction to Section IV of this volume, the decision to focus only on elimination of an embryo or newborn is somewhat arbitrary. In agreement with Dickemann, we feel that from the standpoint of development of theory, it may be useful to formulate a single broad definition that includes any form of lethal curtailment of parental investment in offspring brought about by conspecifics. Included in this definition would be curtailment of parental investment through destruction of gametes (see Charnov, Chapter 7, this volume) or reabsorption of a foetus. Because this definition applies throughout the period of offspring dependence (Hayssen, Chapter 6, this volume) no distinction between infanticide or pedicide (killing of children) is implied unless specified. In some species (such as humans) parental investment continues well after weaning and the decision by a parent to terminate investment may occasionally take place late in the overall reproductive process. At this level of generality, contraception, abortion, direct killing of an infant, or nutritional neglect of a child are seen as related phenomena, differing only in the stage of the reproductive continuum at which curtailment of parental investment occurs. Furthermore, as Dickemann stresses, only by viewing foeticide-infanticide-pedicide in the context of the whole range of possible manipulations of the reproductive continuum can we make meaningful statements about the selective value of infanticidal behavior in cost-benefit terms.

Our chief concern in recommending the use, at least over the next few years, of such a broad definition is to avoid at this early stage in research narrowing our focus to the point that we arbitrarily exclude from consideration any of the remarkably diverse array of intraspecific social behaviors which lead to decreased survival of immatures. This point may be particularly pertinent in the case of humans where so-called *deferred infanticide* takes many forms and where reduced investment by parents in unwanted children may continue long after weaning (Scrimshaw, Chapter 22, this volume).

FUNCTIONAL CLASSES OF INFANTICIDE AND ULTIMATE CAUSATION

The above definition reflects our view that infanticide is a protean phenomenon. Between and within taxa, patterns of infanticidal behavior exhibit wide variation. Adults of either sex, and even other immatures, have been implicated in infanticide and the perpetrator may be either a close or distant relative of the victim, or not related at all. About the only consistent feature in all cases of infanticide, as broadly defined, is the relative vulnerability of the victim and the fact that offspring, with a few exceptions, represent a costly accumulation of resources contributed either by one or both parents. Where parents themselves are implicated in the elimination of offspring, it is often because continued demands by the offspring on scarce resources are anticipated.

Among the many surprising forms of infanticide described in the following chapters are the cases of siblicide in birds, a phenomenon that parents themselves facilitate by laying eggs at intervals so that the first-hatched chick is typically larger and stronger than the second. Furthermore the parents generally do not intervene when the older chick attacks the younger (Mock, Chapter 1, this volume). Sand sharks provide another striking example: siblings begin to devour one another while still squirming inside the mother's oviduct, a hitherto undreamed of hazard of viviparity (Dominey and Blumer, Chapter 3, this volume). Here, as in the avian cases, the individual gain to the surviving sibling apparently overrides losses in inclusive fitness incurred by itself and its parents from the death of close kin. In other fish species, and in many vertebrates, cannibalism by relatives may be an occasional by-product of the way that these organisms obtain food, e.g., through filter feeding (Fox, 1975a; Dominey and Blumer, Chapter 3, this volume; Polis, Chapter 5, this volume).

For most mammals, however, with the exception of humans and other species where mothers in certain circumstances may opt to abandon offspring, infants tend to be killed by unrelated individuals who either exploit the infant as a resource (i.e., cannibalism) or who thereby gain access to physical resources (such as food or a nest site) or to the breeding capacity of one of the infant's parents. The death of an unrelated infant also reduces the net reproductive success of a competitor of the infanticidal individual.

In organizing our thinking about the range of behaviors which fall under our broad definition of infanticide, we have found it helpful to use Hrdy's (1979) five functional categories of infanticide: (1) *exploitation* of the infant as a resource, usually cannibalism; (2) *competition for resources* where death of the infant increases resources available to the killer or its lineage; (3) *sexual selection,* where individuals improve their own opportunities to breed by eliminating dependent offspring of a prospective mate; and (4) *parental manipulation* of progeny, where parents on average increase their own lifetime reproductive success by eliminating particular offspring. Obviously, though, not all cases of infanticide are adaptive for the killer. Thus we have reserved the term (5) *social pathology* for cases where infanticide on average decreases the fitness of the infanticidal individual. It is also possible that researchers may eventually document cases in which infanticide is selectively neutral, but for a variety of reasons, this is highly problematic.

Several earlier theories emphasized the role of infanticide in population regulation. Not surprisingly, this emphasis was most strong in studies of infanticide in rodents, since many species are characterized by marked fluctuations in population density and associated density-dependent changes in behavior, but population regulation has also been invoked to explain infanticide among primates (Ripley, 1980). There is little question that under circumstances of high population density infanticide-foeticide not only occurs with increased frequency, but also has the effect of reducing recruitment to the population through births. However, as Brooks (Chapter 17, this volume) points out, in many cases the population has already begun to decline well before the increase in infanticide is observed. Although it is theoretically possible that infanticide might serve as an adaptive mechanism to regulate population size, this would be limited to cases of isolated populations characterized by low migration and high rates of extinction. Hence, the conditions permitting such group selection would be rare among most vertebrates. More often, population regulation will be a secondary consequence of infanticide. By and large then, one should look for benefits to individuals rather than groups for the primary selection pressure in infanticide (Williams, 1966; Bates and Lees, 1979).

Available evidence on infanticide from wild populations is not nearly as complete or as precise as one might wish. For no single animal population have the costs and benefits of infanticidal behavior been determined for all parties involved. Nevertheless, even at this early stage, there is sufficient evidence to allow us to evaluate roughly the relative frequency of different types of infanticide in various taxa.

Not surprisingly, exploitation of immatures as a resource, usually through cannibalism, turns out to be most common among predatory species, particularly insects, spiders, amphibians, and fishes where there are substantial size differences between adults and immature forms, and where there is often little parental protection (see Simon, Chapter 4, Dominey and Blumer, Chapter 3, and Polis, Chapter 5, this volume). Sometimes infants are eaten by close relatives, and occasionally even by their own parents. However, most species where this might otherwise be a problem appear to have evolved specific mechanisms to reduce its chance occurrence, e.g., parents and offspring occupy separate feeding niches.

Of all classes of infanticide, the most difficult to document convincingly is resource competition since one must first demonstrate that some resource is actually limiting, and, second, that infanticidal individuals thereby gain increased access to the resource (cf. Leland *et al.,* Chapter 8, this volume). Conversely, it could be argued—admittedly at a fairly high level of abstraction—that virtually all classes of infanticide ultimately relate to competition for resources. At present, the best documented cases of infanticide due to resource competition seem to be among birds (Mock, Chapter 1, this volume) and ground squirrels (Sherman, 1981). Infanticide is a major source of infant mortality among ground squirrels and adult females turn out to be the primary killers. Mothers whose infants are killed often vacate their "unsafe" burrows, leaving an available nest site for subsequent use by the infanticidal female.

In sexually selected infanticide, breeding opportunities rather than ecological resources are at issue. This form of infanticide appears to be most prevalent among polygynous mating systems where breeding occurs throughout the year, and where male tenure of access to females is on average short (Hrdy, 1977; Chapman and Hausfater, 1979). Typically infanticide follows male takeovers when a male from outside the troop usurps the resident male. However, cases are known in which a male currently residing in a troop kills infants after rising from non-breeding to breeding status in the troop hierarchy (Wolf, 1980 for wild *Presbytis cristata;* Busse and Gordon, 1983 for captive *Cercocebus atys;* and Leland *et al.,* Chapter 8, this volume for wild *Colobus badius*). In either event males are "entering" a breeding system from which they were previously excluded and hence are unlikely to be the fathers of infants killed. Relatives of the infants, including the mother and probable father defend the infant [see Chapters by Leland *et al.* (8); Crockett and Sekulic (9); Collins *et al.* (10), and Fossey (11), in Section II of this volume].

Infanticide by immigrant males was first observed by scientists among Hanuman langur monkeys at Dharwar in South India (Sugiyama, 1965b, and this volume, Chapter 15). Unweaned infants were attacked by males from all-male bands which had invaded the one-male harem groups (the basic breeding unit in this population) and evicted the resident male. Similar take-overs followed by attacks on unweaned infants have now been reported among langurs at Jodhpur (Mohnot, 1971a; Vogel and Loch, Chapter 12, this volume) and Mount Abu (Hrdy, 1977b), but not at certain other study sites in both Nepal and India (Curtin and Dolhinow, 1978; Boggess, Chapter 14, this volume). This within-species variation has led to considerable controversy concerning the causes and adaptive significance of langur infanticide (Dolhinow, 1977; Curtin, 1977; Curtin and Dolhinow, 1978, 1979; Boggess, 1979, 1980, and this volume Chapter 14; Vogel, 1979; Schubert, 1982; Harraway, 1983) and viewpoints voiced in this controversy have become part of the intellectual background for subsequent studies of infanticide in other animal species.

In contrast to other primates, infanticide as practiced in traditional human societies appears to be primarily a form of parental manipulation of their progeny (Alexander, 1974; Dickeman, 1975, and this volume). The death of an infant and termination of parental investment will sometimes improve the chances for survival of either the mother or her older offspring or will otherwise lead to greater net reproductive fitness for the mother of the infant, the father, or both. The circumstances surrounding infanticide in humans include the existence of older offspring whose chances for survival might be diminished if resources were diverted to a new infant, illegitimacy, deformity, poor ecological conditions, or economic patterns that give one sex lower breeding or resource accrual potential than the other, or else make one sex more expensive than the other. A woman confronted with stressful conditions (including the prospect of little or no paternal support) may spontaneously lose her infant prior to birth (Baird, 1945; Berle and Javert, 1954) Roberts and Lowe, 1975; Bernds and Barash, 1979). Interestingly, sonograms of women in the first trimester of pregnancy reveal that twins are conceived two to four times more often than they are born; in the majority of cases, the smaller of the two foetuses disappears by the third trimester and is apparently reabsorbed by the mother (Robinson and Caines, 1977; Varma, 1979). Even where parental investment is not terminated outright through abortion or infanticide, nurturance may be reduced and offspring neglected or abused (Daly and Wilson, 1978).

In sum, from the standpoint of understanding the evolution of infanticide, it is critical to recognize that many different kinds of social, ecological, and parental interactions can reduce an infant's chances of survival or reflect a parental decision to terminate further investment in an offspring. There is no unitary mechanism across species, and the infanticidal individual may gain a reproductive advantage in any of a number of different ways. Nevertheless, it is possible to restate each of the above functional classes of infanticide as an explanatory hypothesis which in turn leads to its own set of testable predictions. In the case of sexually selected infanticide among primates, for example, it is predicted that (1) infanticidal behavior is heritable; (2) that an infanticidal male will typically not be the father of any infant he kills; (3) that on average the killer will gain sexual access to the mother sooner than if the infant had lived; and (4) that the reproductive gain to the killer will be a function of the average tenure length and age of the infant at death. These predictions as well as those generated for other functional classes of infanticide are summarized in Table I.

Although for various reasons the most sustained thought has been given to deriving predictions suitable for testing the first four functional categories of infanticide listed above, Glass (1983) has recently suggested several novel ways of testing both the social pathology hypothesis and the idea that infanticide is brought about by high levels of social stress. Clearly, considerable overlap exists in the specific predictions drawn from these various hypotheses. Thus, nearly all hypotheses—except the sexual selection hypothesis—predict that both sexes should engage in killing of unrelated infants where possible. Nevertheless Table I suggests that the possibility of distinguishing between these

Table I. Predictions generated by five explanatory hypotheses for infanticide[a]

Class of infanticide	Degree of relationship	Age of infant	Age and sex of killer	Nature of gain
1. Exploitation as resource	Distant	Size and vulnerability more important than age	Either sex at any age large enough to subdue victim	Nutritional gain by killer
2. Competition for Resources	Distant	Vulnerability more important than age	Either sex usually (but not always) adults	Increased availability of resources for killer and killer's kin
3. Sexual selection	Distant	Unweaned (but specifically younger than age at which ovulation resumes or amenorrhea terminated)	Adult of sex investing least in offspring, typically male	Additional breeding opportunity
4. Parental manipulation	Close (~.5)	Just after birth (but any age possible depending on time-course of parental investment)	Either sex, but most likely an individual of the sex investing most in offspring, typically female	Increased inclusive fitness for one or both parents
5. Social pathology	Relationship not critical for this hypothesis	Size, proximity, and vulnerability more important than age	Adult of sex most likely to respond to social disturbance with increased aggressiveness	None for the killer directly, although decrease in population density may eventually result

[a] Specific predictions concern the degree of relationship between the infanticidal individual and the infant, age of the infant killed, sex of the killer, and the nature of the gain accruing to the infanticidal individual.

XX

five explanatory hypotheses, as applied to any given case of infanticide, does exist.

INFANTICIDE AS A SELECTIVE PRESSURE

Zoologists have long taken it for granted that predation was a significant pressure selecting for a variety of morphological and behavioral attributes, such as, the large body size of terrestrial primates (relative to arboreal ones), their retreat at night to sleeping trees, or their social traits like gregariousness or alarm calling. However few field workers (mainly terrestrial and diurnal) have actually witnessed predators (mainly aerial or nocturnal) kill and eat a monkey. Nevertheless, comparisons with other taxa, the occasional disappearance of healthy animals, the obvious alarm exhibited by monkeys confronted by a leopard or other potential predator, as well as the complex of adaptations mentioned above, have been sufficient to convince virtually all primatologists that predation has been an important factor in primate evolution.

As with predation, eyewitness observations of infanticide are uncommon except among laboratory rodents and certain species of birds, fish, and invertebrates. Except for a few groups, infanticide tends to be only sketchily documented among wild mammals. Nevertheless, the majority of scientists present at the Wenner-Gren symposium at Cornell University—admittedly not a random sample—now take for granted that the destruction of infants by conspecifics is a chronic hazard in the lives of many animals and, in some cases, even the major source of infant mortality. This assumption has radically altered the way that we interpret certain well-known behaviors.

In his review of infanticide among amphibians, Simon (this volume, Chapter 4) notes the high correlation between the occurrence of egg cannibalism and the existence of parental care, and asks the question: Is this correlation due to the need of brooding parents to supplement their energy intake during the long period of egg attendance, or might parental care itself have evolved in these species as a defense against cannibalism? It is an easy enough idea to test. The first hypothesis predicts that a male will eat eggs that he himself has fertilized, while the second predicts that he will not do so.

The more important point, however, is that if one accepts infanticide as a frequent occurrence in the social life of a species, an occurrence more costly to one sex than the other, it then becomes reasonable to look for evolved counterstrategies to infanticide. Thus, adult male baboons who carry infants on their ventrum during fights, were believed to be using the infants as "agonistic buffers" to shield themselves from attack by more dominant males. However, according to a more recent interpretation, some adult males in such situations are carrying infants in order to protect them from infanticidal attacks by unrelated, immigrant males (Busse and Hamilton, 1981; Collins *et al.,* Chapter 10, this volume).

Preventive measures may have been taken even further in the case of tree hole-dwelling mosquitoes of the genus *Toxorhynchites* (reviewed by Polis, Chapter 5, this volume). Just before pupation, a highly vulnerable quiescent phase in the life cycle of these insects, the larvae embark on a "killing frenzy," cannibalizing all accessible conspecifics. The apparent selection pressure behind this massacre is the *prospect* of infanticide: if even one younger larva survives, it would consume the negligent killer once pupation rendered it vulnerable. A primary selective pressure for the killing frenzy can thus be thought of as an infanticidal act which has not yet occurred and which will rarely ever be seen!

Another example of how the recent awareness of infanticide has led to reinterpretation of well known phenomena is the case of the "Bruce effect" (Bruce, 1960). Among a wide array of wild and laboratory-housed mice and voles (*Mus, Peromyscus, Microtus, Clethrionomys*) a recently inseminated female who is exposed to a strange male, other than her mate, spontaneously terminates her pregnancy. Recently, Wilson (1975) and others have pointed out that reproductive advantages would accrue to the strange male who caused a female to divert investment from the offspring of competitors. But as Wilson aptly queried, how could such an ostensibly wasteful and disadvantageous trait evolve among females? However once the possibility was considered that strange males present a threat to the survival of the female's impending litter, a number of researchers simultaneously arrived at the same answer. Faced with a potentially infanticidal male it might well be advantageous for a female to terminate further investment in an ill-fated reproductive venture until she could conceive a litter under more stable social conditions conducive to the infants' survival (Schwagmeyer, 1979; Hrdy, 1979; Labov 1980; 1981b; Huck, Chapter 18, this volume).

Such an interpretation is very new, and its acceptance will depend in large part upon the demonstration that both the Bruce effect and infanticide by strange males do indeed occur in the wild; at present both phenomena have only been observed among captive animals. Alternative interpretations, namely that reabsorption of litters is brought about through crowding and serves to reduce population growth (Chipman *et al.,* 1966), that the Bruce effect is an artifact of laboratory conditions and handling (Bronson, 1979; and others), or that the Bruce effect is an artifact of endocrine process which evolved for reason unrelated to either strange males or infanticide (Keverne and de la Riva, 1982), can not currently be ruled out.

The hypothesis that the Bruce effect evolved as a female counter-strategy to infanticide by males has in turn led to additional speculation about the adaptive significance of spontaneous abortions in animals other than rodents. Hence researchers who have recorded pregnancy termination at the time of male invasions among wild horses, baboons, and lions (Berger, 1983; Pereira, 1983; Packer and Pusey, Chapter 2, this volume) have wondered if a tendency to abort at such times might not sometimes be adaptive. No doubt, some will see these speculations as the construction of sand turrets upon sand castles but it is our opinion that there do exist substantial grounds for taking such ideas seriously, and that they merit considerable further investigation.

Along these lines, Huck (Chapter 18, this volume) designed a series of investigations to test the idea that infanticide has been a selective pressure in the evolution of an analogue of the Bruce effect among hamsters. Taking advantage of the fact that among hamsters females are dominant to males and also infanticidal, he predicted that a strange female should be more likely than a strange male to induce abortion. As predicted, pregnancy was blocked in nearly one-half of the recently mated subordinate female hamsters who were exposed to near-term dominant females.

The realization that infanticide may be a chronic hazard for many species has far-reaching implications for the likelihood that female counterstrategies to infanticide have also evolved. Because female mammals typically invest more care and resources in offspring than do males, maternal counterstrategies to infanticide should be selected for at the level of morphology, reproductive physiology, and temperament. Paternal counterstrategies ought to evolve also and may be manifested in the protection by males of particular infants likely to be their own progeny, as well as in general defense by males of females or territories (Hrdy, 1979). However, the issue of counterstrategies is a complex one and raises questions such as why females have not been *more* successful in eliminating behavior patterns so detrimental to their fitness (Hrdy, 1981; Hausfater, Chapter 13, this volume).

The capacity of females to conceive again soon after losing an infant is, of course, a crucial precondition for sexual selection to favor infanticide in males. Mathematical models presented by Hausfater (Chapter 13, this volume) illustrate that a lag of even relatively short duration between death of a female's offspring and her next conception can make infanticide untenable as a male reproductive strategy. Hence, we predict that sexually selected infanticide will rarely be found among seasonal breeders or in any other setting where environmental or social cues preclude an immediate return to breeding condition by females following the death of their most recent offspring. Nevertheless, even in the case of strictly seasonal breeders infanticide might still confer on males a limited reproductive advantage were it the case that a female who loses her litter in one season is more likely to breed successfully or to produce a larger litter in the subsequent breeding season (H. Hoeck, personal communication; Andelman, 1984).

PROXIMATE CAUSATION

Whereas field researchers have tended to focus on questions about the ultimate causation of infanticide, laboratory scientists, primarily working with rodents, have focused most closely on questions about proximate mechanisms. *How* are infanticidal behaviors elicited or inhibited? What makes some individuals, but not others, kill young? Why are some offspring but not others killed and by what means do infanticidal individuals avoid killing their own offspring?

As in sexual behavior and aggression, male and female rodents exhibit quite different patterns of infanticidal behavior. For this reason, many of the early hormonal studies of infanticide focused on the role of testosterone (reviewed in Svare *et al.,* Chapter 20, this volume). In certain strains of mice for example, pup-killing behavior begins in males at about 1 month of age, approximately the same time that levels of circulating testosterone show a sharp increase. Furthermore, castration reduces infanticide in mice and hormone replacement therapy with testosterone restores infanticide in males and elicits it in females.

Clearly, the evidence is compelling that testosterone is implicated in infanticide by males and females, but it is only part of the story. The effects of gonadal hormones may vary from strain to strain and in some wild strains females are far more infanticidal than males (Jakubowski and Terkel, 1982; Labov, this volume, see Introduction to Part III). Furthermore, adult sensitivity to steroid hormones may be influenced by hormonal levels during prenatal and neonatal life. For example, vom Saal (Chapter 21, this volume) has shown that positioning *in utero* and the sex of adjacent foetuses affect embryonic levels of circulating testosterone which, in turn, appear to influence infanticidal tendencies in adulthood. Since uterine placement of embryos is presumably dictated by chance, vom Saal's findings underscore the existence of stochastic components in the production of infanticidal and noninfanticidal phenotypes.

Other factors influencing infanticide include timing and the nature of social encounters. Hence, when a male mouse is introduced into a cage containing a female and her newborn pups, one of three things happens: the male ignores the pups, attacks them, or engages in caretaking behaviors such as retrieving the pups and keeping them warm. Whether a male kills the pups or cares for them depends both on his recent mating experience, particularly whether or not he mated at about the time the pups might have been conceived (vom Saal and Howard, 1982; vom Saal, this volume), and on his familiarity or past consort relationships with the mother (Labov, 1980; Huck et al., 1982). In the case of monogamously mated gerbils, the situation may be more nearly deterministic. Pup-killing is permanently inhibited in males that have been previously pair-bonded with a breeding female (Elwood and Ostermeyer, Chapter 19, this volume).

Dominance status is another mediating variable in rodent infanticide. Among mice, the achievement of dominant status by a male apparently facilitates infanticide, although this effect may be overridden by prior sexual experience (vom Saal, Chapter 21, this volume). Social rank is also important in infanticide by females though its precise role is not yet well understood (Wasser, 1983a; Fossey, Chapter 11, this volume).

In marked contrast to many invertebrates and nonmammalian vertebrates (Dominey and Blumer, Chapter 3, this volume; Polis, Chapter 5, this volume), there apparently exist among most mammals mechanisms which ensure that parents avoid killing their own offspring. For mothers, endocrinological changes during pregnancy, and the inviolability of young within particular locales (e.g., near the nest, within the group) make it unlikely that mothers would kill or eat their own progeny.

Fathers are more problematic, especially when they have not been paired with the mother in a monogamous arrangement. Although technically it might sometimes be feasible for fathers to identify phenotypes of probable offspring (Holmes and Sherman, 1983), such powers have not yet been documented for progenitors in any species (Labov, 1980). More commonly, one finds that males show a generalized inhibition that forestalls them from killing any infant which they might possibly have fathered, even though this may sometimes result in their being tolerant of infants sired by other males (see McLean, 1983). Given that males who killed their own offspring would usually be drastically selected against, it makes sense for males to be conservative when confronted with uncertain paternity. As vom Saal (Chapter 21, this volume) shows, males in some strains of mice are inhibited from killing *all* infants, regardless of paternity, for a period of weeks after they have mated. Such males do not resume killing infants until after all offspring potentially resulting from this prior episode of mating would be past the age of weaning.

In situations where the targeting of victims is more specific, it appears that males use the mother rather than the infant itself as the cue either to attack or tolerate it. This suggestion, originally proposed for wild langur monkeys (Hrdy, 1977b), has only been systematically tested in the case of rodents (Labov, 1980; Huck *et al.,* 1982). Prior mating experience with an individual scented with the urine of a pregnant female reduced the likelihood that a male would subsequently kill off-spring of a female with the same scent. Conversely, males can be "tricked" into killing their own offspring by placing them in the nest of a strange female (Huck, Chapter 18, this volume).

Nevertheless, the detailed workings of most infanticidal mating systems are far from understood. For example, are males generally tolerant of infants and only incited to infanticidal behavior by a particular sequence of stimuli, such as those that might occur in the nest of an unfamiliar female or in an unfamiliar group? Or, as in the case of the monogamous gerbils studied by Elwood and Ostermeyer (Chapter 19, this volume), do generally infanticidal individuals *become* tolerant in the course of a prolonged consortship with a pregnant female? The confounding effects of female counterstrategies and female behaviors which confuse paternity must also be taken into account (Hausfater, Chapter 13, this volume). In the case of higher primates it also seems likely that individuals are making sophisticated evaluations about the risk of retaliation by other group members (Collins *et al.*, Chapter 10; Leland *et al.*, Chapter 8, both this volume), evaluations that may border on conscious decisions (Fossey, Chapter 11, this volume). Whatever the answers to such questions, they will be rooted in the ecology and evolutionary history of the particular species, and pursuit of these answers is likely to be a focus of research in behavioral biology for some years to come.

HUMAN INFANTICIDE VIEWED IN EVOLUTIONARY PERSPECTIVE

Infanticide in Traditional Societies

Virtually every category of infanticide which has been described for other animals can be documented anecdotally for the human species. Given the apparent prevalence of infanticide by alien males in other higher primates, it is plausible that this nonparental form of infanticide may have been important in the course of hominid evolution (Alexander, 1974), but this will be almost impossible to prove. For contemporary western societies there does exist some evidence indicating that infants with alien males living in the same household run an elevated risk from child abuse and even death (Daly and Wilson, 1978 and this volume, Chapter 24), but we doubt that it will ever be possible to conclusively demonstrate *sexually selected* infanticide among humans. Not least among the problems would be the need to discover a genetic component underlying infanticidal behavior (Lenington, 1981). Furthermore, the contemporary data fail to show that males benefit reproductively from child abuse, child homicide or infanticide, and indeed, the opposite could be argued more forcefully.

Whether or not infanticide is sanctioned by a particular society, such practices are rarely recorded. Infanticide must therefore be derived primarily from interviews with individuals who recount—with varying degrees of reliability—personal experiences or village hearsay (Shostak, 1981). Bugos and McCarthy (Chapter 25, this volume) describe from firsthand experience informant evasiveness and other difficulties encountered by researchers attempting to collect information about infanticide. Ironically, only when infanticide is outlawed in societies with centralized governments do we begin to have fairly extensive documentation of infanticide in the form of sex ratio data derived from censuses (Miller, 1981 for India) and court records (Sauer, 1978 for Great Britain). Even with such data, analysis must often be inferential or indirect so that, for example, female preferential infanticide is inferred from censuses showing a preponderance of males at different ages. It should be noted that these problems are as serious for conventional historical demography (Johansson, Chapter 23, this volume) as they are for more controversial sociobiological analyses (Daly and Wilson, this volume), and that the methods used to cope with them are not substantially different.

In reviewing ethnographic and historical sources Dickeman (1975) Scrimshaw (Chapter 22, this volume), and others, have all reached the same conclusion: the most reliably documented cases of infanticide in humans involve parents and are best described as parental manipulation of their progeny (Alexander, 1979). In contrast to all other primates, but similar to some birds (Mock, Chapter 1, this volume) and fish (Dominey and Blumer, Chapter 3, this volume) close relatives tend to be the perpetrators. Among humans one or both parents appear to make a conscious or unconscious calculation concerning the cost of the infant, probable current and future demands on parental resources, alternative uses to which those resources might be used as well as the future breeding options that the parents might have. The infant's own future survival and breeding or marriage prospects may also be taken into account.

Although it is rare to have firsthand information from parents who have decided to commit infanticide, when parents do talk about it they can be quite explicit about the practical imperatives. Diamond Jenness (1922:166) an ethnographer who worked among the Copper eskimo of the Canadian Arctic describes the rationale for a young couple who decide, for the second time in a row, not to keep an infant daughter: the timing was bad, they were confident they would have other children and hoped that they would have a son who could hunt and care for them in their old age. However, whether such decisions represent parental efforts to maintain their social and economic status and quality of life or whether they represent an effort to maximize the inclusive fitness of the family or lineage remains unresolved (Scrimshaw, Chapter 22, this volume). Such questions will be answerable only when we have precise information on the life historical context within which decisions are made and data on long-term reproductive success of lineages which permits us to test subtle differences between these two closely related hypotheses. Not the least of the problems is the likelihood that the long-term success of lineages has typically been linked in human history with socioeconomic status.

A recent study of infanticide among the Ayoreo indians of Bolivia and Paraguay by Bugos and McCarthy (Chapter 25, this volume) is a first effort toward analysis of the maternal decision-making process. They provide a unique and important body of marital and reproductive histories which illustrate the close link between infanticide and environmental and social conditions, particularly scarce resources and lack of paternal support. From their data, Bugos and McCarthy are able to document a decreased probability of infanticide with maternal age, a finding that is clearly in line with the hypothesis that these mothers are taking into account their own "reproductive value" (i.e., likely future reproduction) as well as prevailing environmental conditions when they decide to terminate investment in a particular infant. At present, however, it is not possible to differentiate between the two most likely explanatory models, namely the hypothesis that mothers are attempting to maintain their own quality of life, or alternatively that they are striving to enhance their inclusive fitness over the course of a lifetime, even at the expense of a particular infant (Alexander, 1979).

As Scrimshaw (Chapter 22, this volume) describes in some detail, parental elimination of unwanted infants tends to be carried out with a minimum of violence; rarely are wounds inflicted. In this respect, humans appear to be unusual among primates but scarcely unique among vertebrate animals generally since abandonment of young is known to occur in many birds and mammals (e.g. lionesses during food shortage may abandon a litter; a mother kangaroo pursued by a predator may jettison her joey). Insofar as humans articulate conscious rationales for infanticide, however, they are unique.

Several recent studies aimed at evaluating causes and frequency of infanticide in human societies have drawn on ethnographies encoded in the Human Relations Area Files. In addition to the analyses carried out by Scrimshaw and by Daly and Wilson (Chapters 22 and 24, respectively), Whiting *et al.* (1977) examined infanticide for 84 societies in which reliable data on the presence of the behavior were available. For fully one-third of the societies in the Whiting study infanticide was reported as a means of eliminating defective offspring. Birth spacing was another frequently cited reason for infanticide. In 72 societies for which it was possible to make a judgement, 36% reported the practice of killing an infant born too soon after its older sibling. Interestingly, the likelihood was greatest in hunting-gathering-fishing societies, which tend to be nomadic, and relatively lower in pastoral and agricultural ones (but see also the discussion in Howell, 1976b, suggesting that due to lactational amenorrhea and consequent long birth intervals the rate of infanticide among hunter gatherers like the !Kung would have been very low, on the order of 2% of births). Such cross-cultural findings have led to a fairly general consensus among anthropologists that as originally suggested by Birdsell (1968), infanticide by parents has deep roots in human history, and has probably been part of our adaptive repertoire since Pleistocene times.

Infanticide may entail intentional destruction of the infant soon after birth, or take a less direct form (see Scrimshaw, Chapter 22, and Johansson, Chapter 23, this volume). There are a wide range of human behaviors which may decrease the likelihood of infant survival. Such practices are extraordinarily elaborate and include neglect and nutritional discrimination (Cassidy, 1980; McKee, 1982); sending the infant away to be suckled by hired, often inadequate wet nurses (Sussman, 1975; 1977; Badinter, 1980); sending infants away to foster homes for a period of harsh apprenticeship associated with lower than average rates of survival (Bledsoe, 1983); or abandonment. The latter may take the form of either exposing the infant to the elements or of deserting it in a location where there is some possibility that others will adopt and care for it (Scrimshaw, this volume, Chapter 22; Balikci, 1967; Trexler, 1973a).

It should be clear from this discussion that infanticide as most often documented for humans differs markedly from its occurrence among other primates. While human infanticide appears to be most often perpetrated by the biological parents, among nonhuman primates infants tend to be killed by unrelated males or by females belonging to a matriline different from the infant's mother. We know of no case among wild monkeys where a mother has been observed to kill her own offspring. Although occasionally inexperienced, primiparous mothers will handle infants roughly, such treatment typically improves within days after birth (Hrdy, 1976). Murderous abuse by mothers is only reported among captive primates, most often among animals which have been socially isolated (e.g. Harlow *et al.*, 1966) but not always (e.g. Troisi *et al.*, 1982). Such abuse has never been reported among wild monkeys and apes. Because distinctions between naturalistic and captive behaviors are often ignored, considerable confusion has emerged in both the popular (Herbert, 1982) and technical literature (Caine and Reite, 1983) concerning "the evolution" of child abuse. It may well be true that simian and human mothers respond to stress in the same way and thus that social isolation results in offspring abuse by both human mothers and monkey mothers (Suomi and Ripp, 1983), but it is extremely unlikely that adaptation could be at issue since no monkey or human ever evolved in social isolation.

Sociobiological Analyses and Contemporary Child Abuse

From a sociobiological perspective, humans are viewed as "strategists" whose ultimate goal is to increase inclusive fitness (that is, the sum of individual fitness plus the fitness of his or her relatives weighted according to their degree of genetic relatedness). Because long-term rather than immediate reproductive success is at issue, an infant may be eliminated if the parent or step-parent thereby enhances overall reproductive prospects. It is assumed that individuals have at their disposal limited resources which can be translated into reproductive effort (Alexander, 1979; Daly and Wilson, Chapter 24, this volume). Just how individuals allocate such resources among offspring in their charge should depend on their assessment of (1) degree of relatedness to the offspring; (2) worth of the offspring in terms of its ability to translate parental investment into subsequent reproduction; and (3) alternative uses to which the parent could devote the resources, such as diverting the same resources to an older or stronger child, or delaying reproduction until conditions are more favorable. To what extent can such an evolutionary approach elucidate the problem of contemporary child abuse?

Infanticide occurs when conspecifics bring about an infant's death, but "abuse" is much more difficult to ascertain since species and cultures differ greatly in respect to caretaking. For example, many societies might find it cruel that Western mothers force infants to sleep in separate cribs, whereas we find repugnant the "circumcision" of young girls to make them marriageable. Hence, some anthropologists would define abuse and neglect as "harsh treatment of children unrelated to purposeful socialization and unsupported by cultural norms" (Poffenberger, 1981). However, while very useful in considering contemporary child abuse in the West, this definition excludes institutionalized forms of mistreatment obviously detrimental to fitness of the victims (e.g., harsh treatment of adopted daughters in traditional Chinese culture, described in Wu, 1981). Furthermore, many behaviors which cultures rationalize as "good" for children (e.g., the practice of denying infants colostrum) are almost certainly detrimental. Hence, we concur with Korbin (1981:205) that it would be virtually impossible to set up cross-culturally valid standards for either optimal child rearing or for behavior which is abusive. Hence in a rural Indian community where female infanticide is probably still practiced with at least passive support from the community a father can nevertheless frown upon corporal punishment of surviving children: "When we work so hard to provide food for children to become strong, should we beat them and make them weak?" (cited in Poffenberger, 1981). Balikci (1970:150) makes a similar point. Infanticide among the eskimoes he studied can not be considered as "callousness" toward children. Children allowed to live were dearly loved.

Yet, by any standards, the bizarre pattern found in some contemporary cases (and perhaps earlier cases, deMause 1974) where chronic mistreatment and even torture of young by a biological parent alternates with ambivalent expressions of solicitude by that same parent must be considered maladaptive. Nevertheless, some portion of the cases of contemporary child abuse may be attributed to emotions which might well have been adaptive at one time. Indeed, as Scrimshaw suggests, some victims of child abuse might—in some other era—have been eliminated at birth. This is the dimension of child abuse currently being explored by sociobiologists (Daly and Wilson 1980; 1981a; 1981b; Chapter 24, this volume; Lenington, 1981; Lightcap *et al.,* 1982).

In line with predictions generated by a sociobiological model of child abuse the children in contemporary western societies who appear to be most at risk from neglect or abuse tend to be those born to families with scarce resources, children with birth defects, children later in the birth order, and children with unrelated males in the home. However, as Lenington (1981) points out, the same findings would be predicted by alternative, nonevolutionary hypotheses. For example, if child abuse were a pathological response brought about through stress, we would still expect a higher incidence among families with few resources or many children. The majority of cases of child abuse and child homicide involve the biological parents and many of these can be explained by economic and developmental factors in the lives of the adults involved. In particular, parents who were themselves abused as children are most likely to abuse their own children (Kempe and Kempe, 1978). As Lenington cautions, then, evolutionary models will at best explain only a portion of cases of violent mistreatment of human immatures.

In a society where stringent legal sanctions against child abuse exist and where children abandoned to institutions have fair prospects for survival, it would virtually never be advantageous for a parent to inflict injuries on his or her own child. Accordingly, if one invokes evolutionary models (as opposed to social pathology) to explain contemporary child abuse, one must either assume that violence toward immatures is vestigial, evolved in some different era and no longer adaptive or else argue, as do Daly and Wilson (Chapter 24, this volume) that abuse patterns can be traced back to differential parental solicitude and reflect an evolved intolerance or reduced solicitude toward particular kinds of infants (e.g., unrelated; poor quality), or toward infants under certain conditions (e.g., insufficient resources) rather than selection for abusive behavior per se. Were societal norms different, psychological motivations causing parents to discriminate against certain children might—however cruel—nevertheless enhance the inclusive fitness of parents.

Sex-Biased Infanticide

Evolutionary biology has produced a body of sophisticated theories to explain parental preferences for one sex or the other in nonhuman species (Charnov, 1982; Chapter 7, this volume) but currently, only a few such models are applicable to humans (Williams, 1979) and efforts by anthropologists to apply them are still very preliminary. One of the few models that theoretically ought to apply to humans is the *Trivers-Willard hypothesis*. According to Trivers and Willard (1973), a parent in good condition should bias investment toward sons among polygynous species whenever males in good condition enjoy better than average reproductive success (e.g., Clutton-Brock *et al.*, 1982; Dittus, 1979; McClure, 1981); a parent in poor condition, however, should preferentially produce daughters.

Under different social and ecological conditions, however, other models would be needed. Where daughters inherit their status from their mothers, and where high female status is correlated with better than average reproductive success for daughters (but not sons), one would expect high-status mothers to prefer daughters and low-status mothers to prefer sons. In fact, high-ranking mothers in some monkey species produce up to twice as many daughters as sons (Simpson and Simpson, 1982; Silk, 1983; Altmann, 1980). This model has only been tested among animals, but it ought also to apply in human societies with the appropriate marriage and mating systems—although it must be noted that humans, unlike the monkey and deer examples cited above, appear to lack the capacity to bias their sex ratios *in utero* and must rely on the more physiologically wasteful practice of infanticide after birth.

In our view, the work of Dickemann (1979a; 1981) provides the only compelling application to date of the Trivers-Willard or, in fact any such model, to human societies. Dickemann's analysis focuses on the widespread occurrence of preferential female infanticide among high-status families living in stratified social systems where the marriage system is hypergynous and the access to an unpredictable resource base is determined by status. Drawing on ethnographic studies from North India and Imperial China—both societies characterized by intense competition for scarce resources and extreme variance in male reproductive success—Dickemann (1979a:323) pointed out that "men of high rank [acquire] access to a disproportion of females through polygyny, and in addition [enjoy] greater health and earlier entry into reproduction, while those at the bottom are disproportionately excluded from reproduction through delayed marriage, heavy mortalities and the imposition of celibate roles, [and] their reproductive success is further reduced through heavy mortalities among their progeny."

These societies were also hypergynous, that is, a significant proportion of women are able to marry "up" the social scale into families of higher standing than their own. Such a marriage benefits not only the bride but her entire family. Her parents can look forward to grandchildren born into a world of improved opportunities. But marriage prospects for these daughters from high-status families entailed high costs in the form of dowries which their families must provide. To avoid these costs, daughters would be eliminated at birth, yielding the extraordinarily high sex ratios characteristic of many groups in North India in the nineteenth century (Miller, 1981). Parental investment, and the wealth that otherwise would have been diverted to daughters, was directed exclusively toward sons.

However, direct infanticide as traditionally practiced in North India is only one of several ways of biasing sex ratios. Recently, attention has been directed toward the allocation of food among family members. Sons are nursed for up to twice as long as daughters in societies as distant in space and time as peasants from ninth century France (Coleman, 1974), contemporary Equador (McKee, 1982), and modern India (Miller, 1981). Indirect evidence on this same point is provided by the finding that birth intervals in many cultures tend to be longer after the birth of a son than a daughter (Haldar and Bhattacharyya, 1969; Khan, 1973). Current explanations for preferring offspring of one sex over the other (e.g. greater valuation of male labor, marriage patterns that make sons more valuable) are discussed in some detail in the chapters by Johansson (Chapter 23) and Scrimshaw (Chapter 22). With only a few exceptions (Hartung, 1976; 1982; Dickemann, 1979a; 1979b), little attention has been paid to the evolutionary dimensions of parental sex preferences.

Whatever the ultimate cause of sex preferences, infanticide as a means of biasing parental investment toward either sons or daughters probably has a long history. It is widely accepted that a hunting-gathering-fishing way of life has characterized human existence for more than 90% of the history of our species. The majority of such societies are known to practice infanticide as a means of birth spacing. Hence, as Jane Lancaster noted during symposium discussions, once conditions arose which made one or the other sex offspring more desirable, parents might have viewed the preexisting mechanism of control over the reproductive process, that is, infanticide, as a natural and quite acceptable means for biasing family sex ratios.

A NOTE ON THIS VOLUME

The chapters that follow explore in some depth topics outlined in this Introduction. In Part I, taxonomic reviews of infanticide among birds (Mock), carnivores (Packer and Pusey), fishes (Dominey and Blumer), amphibians (Simon), and invertebrates (Polis) are followed by two theoretical review papers, a description of phylogenetic constraints on the evolution of infanticide (Hayssen), and a précis of both new and previously published work which bears on the question of why parents would invest preferentially in offspring of a particular sex (Charnov). In Section II new data on infanticide among Old World cercopithecine monkeys (LeLand *et al.*; Collins *et al.*) and New World howler monkeys (Crockett and Sekulic) are presented along with a review of infanticide among the great apes (Fossey). New observations of infanticide among the langurs at Jodhpur (Vogel and Loch) serve as an introduction to the use of such langur data to test theoretical models with computer simulations (Hausfater). Finally some longstanding controversies concerning interpretation of langur field studies are reviewed (Boggess, Chapter 15, and Hausfater, in his introduction to the primate section).

In the introduction to Section III, Labov briefly contrasts the merits and disadvantages of performing experiments with laboratory rodents with those of studying wild primates. Labov stresses the need for more information concerning the natural history of wild mice. The rodent section begins with a review article by Brooks on the cause and consequences of infanticide among natural populations of rodents which provides the essential (if still sketchy) framework for interpreting experimental results. Such studies have involved a variety of rodent species (hamsters, mice and gerbils) and are described in detail in papers by Huck, vom Saal, Elwood and Ostermeyer, and Svare *et al.*

The introduction to the human section provides a critique of some current thinking about infanticide in our own species (Dickemann). This discussion is followed by a review of the ethnographic and historical literature on infanticide in humans (Scrimshaw). The remainder of the volume is devoted to the analysis of data. Johansson provides an historical and demographic case study of deferred infanticide in pre-modern Europe; Daly and Wilson provide a sociobiological analysis of cross-cultural data from traditional human societies as well as child homicide data from Canada; and Bugos and McCarthy provide a case study of infanticide among a lowland South American population which is in transition between its traditional culture and incorporation into the modern world.

Most of these chapters grew out of papers presented at the Wenner-Gren Symposium on "Infanticide in Animals and Man" which was held at Cornell University between August 16 and 22, 1982. Several papers presented at this conference were deleted, while several others were added later (in fact, the last chapter by Bugos and McCarthy was added after the book was in press).

During the conference, participants were assigned particular papers to comment on both in writing and during panel discussions. Several of these commentaries are published following the original contribution (Sugiyama, Hrdy) but, by and large, the most useful portions of the commentaries were either incorporated into the relevant chapter or else were summarized in the three section introductions. Hence, we believe we speak for most authors when we state that contributors to this volume were mutually indebted to one another for the final versions of their papers; this is certainly true of this introduction.

As with any symposium volume there are a few holes in our coverage of comparative and evolutionary perspectives on infanticide. In retrospect, it would have been useful to include a chapter on kin recognition and certainly it would have been valuable to have more historically oriented reviews of infanticide in human populations. Nevertheless, we believe that the volume fairly represents the "state-of-the-art" with regard to research on infanticide and should provide readers a broad, and occasionally deep, perspective from which to view an astonishingly widespread complex of behaviors which characterizes so many animals, including humans.

ACKNOWLEDGMENTS

We thank M. Dickemann, D. B. Hrdy, U. W. Huck, J. Labov, J. Lancaster, D. Mock, J. Moore, B. Smuts, and G. C. Williams for critical readings of this introduction.

LIST OF CONTRIBUTORS AND SYMPOSIUM PARTICIPANTS

Wenner-Gren Symposium on "Infanticide in Animals and Man" Cornell University, Ithaca, New York, August 16–22, 1982.

Lawrence S. Blumer, *Museum of Zoology and Division of Biological Sciences, University of Michigan, Ann Arbor, Michigan 48109*

Jane E. Boggess, *Department of Anthropology, University of California, Berkeley, California 94720*

John Broida, *Psychology Department, State University of New York, Albany, New York 12203*

Ronald J. Brooks,* *Department of Zoology, University of Guelph, Guelph, Ontario, Canada N1G 2W1*

Paul E. Bugos, Jr., *Department of Anthropology, Northwestern University, Evanston, Illinois 60201*

Curt Busse,* *Yerkes Regional Primate Center, Emory University, Atlanta, Georgia 30322*

Thomas Butynski, *Kibale Forest Project, P.O. Box 409, Fort Portal, Uganda, Africa*

Carol Sue Carter,* *Department of Psychology, University of Illinois, Champaign, Illinois 61820*

Eric Charnov,* *Departments of Biology, Anthropology and Psychology, University of Utah, Salt Lake City, Utah 89112*

D. Anthony Collins, *Zoology Department, University of Edinburgh, Edinburgh, U.K. EH9 3 JT*

Carolyn Crockett,* *Department of Zoological Research, U.S. National Zoological Park, Smithsonian Institution, Washington, D.C. 20008*

Martin Daly, *Department of Psychology, McMasters University, Hamilton, Ontario, Canada L8S 4K1*

Mildred Dickemann* *(Conference Coorganizer), Department of Anthropology, Sonoma State University, Rohnert Park, California 94928*

Wolfgang Dittus,* *Smithsonian Primate Project, 4/4 Galkande Road, Anniewatte, Kandy, Sri Lanka*

* *Indicates attendance at Ithaca Conference.*

Wallace J. Dominey, *Museum of Zoology and Division of Biological Sciences, University of Michigan, Ann Arbor, Michigan 48109*

Robert Elwood,* *Department of Zoology, The Queen's University of Belfast, Belfast, Northern Ireland, BT7 1NN, U.K.*

Dian Fossey,* *Karisoke Research Centre, B.P. 105, Ruhengeri, Rwanda, Africa*

Jane Goodall, *P.O. Box 727, Dar Es Salaam, Tanzania, Africa*

Glenn Hausfater* (*Conference Host and Coorganizer*), *Division of Biological Sciences, University of Missouri, Columbia, Missouri 65211*

Virginia Hayssen,* *Neurobiology and Behaviour, Cornell University, Ithaca, New York 14850*

Sarah Blaffer Hrdy* (*Conference Coorganizer*), *Department of Anthropology, University of California, Davis, California 95616*

U. William Huck,* *Department of Biology, Princeton University, Princeton, New Jersey 08544*

Sheila Johansson,* *Graduate Group in Demography, Program in Population Research, 2234 Piedmont Avenue, Berkeley, California 94720*

Craig Howard Kinsley, *Department of Psychology, State University of New York, Albany, New York 12203*

Jay Labov,* *Department of Biology, Colby College, Waterville, Maine 04901*

Jane Lancaster,* *Department of Anthropology, University of Oklahoma, Norman, Oklahoma 73019*

Lysa Leland, *New York Zoological Society, Bronx, New York 10460*

Hartmut Loch,* *Institut fur Anthropologie, Universität Göttingen, 3400 Göttingen, Federal Republic of Germany*

Lorraine M. McCarthy, *Department of Anthropology, Northwestern University, Evanston, Illinois 60201*

Lauris McKee,* *International Population Program, Cornell University, Ithaca, New York 14853*

Ian McLean,* *Institute of Animal Resource Ecology, University of British Columbia, Vancouver, British Columbia, Canada V6T1W5*

Frank Mallory,* *Department of Biology, Wilfred Laurier University, Waterloo, Ontario, Canada N2L 3C5*

Martha Mann, *Department of Psychology, University of Texas at Arlington, Arlington, Texas 76019*

Douglas Mock,* *Department of Zoology, University of Oklahoma, Norman, Oklahoma 73019*

S. M. Mohnot,* *Department of Zoology, University of Jodhpur, Jodhpur, Rajasthan, 342001, India*

Malcolm Ostermeyer, *Department of Zoology, The Queen's University of Belfast, Belfast, Northern Ireland BT7 1NN*

Craig Packer,* *Department of Ecology and Behavioral Biology, University of Minnesota, Minneapolis, Minnesota 55455*

Gary Polis, *Department of Biology, Vanderbilt University, Nashville, Tennessee 37235*

Anne Pusey,* *Department of Ecology and Behavioral Biology, University of Minnesota, Minneapolis, Minnesota 55455*

Suzanne Ripley,* *3 Howard Place, Englewood, New Jersey 07631*

Rasanayagam Rudran,* *Department of Zoological Research, U.S. National Zoological Park, Smithsonian Institution, Washington, D.C. 20008*

Susan Scrimshaw,* *School of Public Health, University of California, Los Angeles, California 90024*

Ranka Sekulic,* *9753 S.W. Appaloosa Place, Beaverton, Oregon 97005*

Martin Simon, *Department of Zoology, University of California, Davis, California 95616*

Thomas Struhsaker, *New York Zoological Society, Bronx Park, Bronx, New York 10460*

Yukimaru Sugiyama,* *Primate Research Institute, Kyoto University, Inuyama, Aichii, Japan 484*

Bruce Svare, *Department of Psychology, State University of New York, Albany, Albany, New York 12222*

Richard Trexler,* *Department of History, State University of New York, Binghamton, New York 13901*

Christian Vogel* (*Conference Coorganizer*), *Institut für Anthropologie, Universität Göttingen, 3400 Göttingen, Federal Republic of Germany*

Margo Wilson, *Department of Psychology, McMasters University, Hamilton, Ontario, Canada L8S 4K1*

Fred vom Saal,* *Division of Biological Sciences, University of Missouri, Columbia, Missouri 65211*

I BACKGROUND AND TAXONOMIC REVIEWS

1 Infanticide, siblicide, and avian nestling mortality

Douglas W. Mock

Cain slew Abel (Gen. 4:8) for reasons of petty jealousy: siblicide. Later God ordered Abraham to sacrifice his son Isaac as a test of faith (Gen. 22:2): infanticide. These biblical legends gained a measure of ecological complexity when the twin sons of Isaac and Rebekah battled *in utero* for the all-important first position: brawny Esau won the battle but lost the war (and his birthright) when the astute Jacob caught him short of critical resources (food) and struck a hard bargain.

Despite these and many similar traditional literary sources, the biological study of intrafamily strife has emerged only recently as a topic worthy of scientific pursuit. The theoretical excitement generated by Hamilton's (1964a,b) concept of *inclusive fitness* has focused primarily on explanations of apparently altruistic behavior, especially on how individuals can promote copies of their own genes that are carried by relatives. More recently, researchers have begun to regard selfishness in this same evolutionary perspective: in many circumstances, selection favors behavior that promotes the performer's direct fitness, even at the expense of close kin.

The theoretical analysis of selfishness is especially relevant to an understanding of infanticidal behavior in birds, because in that taxon a significant portion of the killing is perpetrated by kin, namely, parents and siblings. Ironically, the only extant review of avian infanticide (Wynne-Edwards, 1962: Chapter 22) presented it as a model of behavioral evolution via group selection. When the perspective of group selection fell from favor (see Lack, 1966; Williams, 1966), the topic of avian infanticide lapsed back to the level of anecdote and, with the exception of Stinson's 1979 review on raptors, has not been reviewed thoroughly since. In fact, the most comprehensive review on sources of avian nestling mortality (Ricklefs, 1967) does not even mention infanticide explicitly. In this chapter, an overview of the literature on avian infanticide is presented with an eye to organizing and evaluating proposed hypotheses for the adaptive significance of such behavior. In the process, it is shown how various fundamental attributes of birds might have shaped the patterns observed, and some needed directions for future research are indicated.

It is hoped that this chapter will encourage field workers to make the lengthy observations necessary to document avian infanticide more fully in the field and to test specific hypotheses. Because the infanticidal event itself is usually extremely brief, it is subject to substantial sampling problems (Hrdy, 1979; Trail *et al.,* 1981). Only vigilance and sensitivity to the issue will lead to greater understanding of the nature and frequency of socially induced mortality in birds. Survivorship data alone, collected during intermittent visits to nests, simply cannot reveal the relative importance of intraspecific killing, such as siblicide, compared with other sources of mortality.

DEFINITIONS

Throughout this chapter, the following general definition of infanticide is used: *behavior that makes a direct and significant contribution to the immediate death of an embryo or newly hatched (or born) member of the performer's own species.* This definition incorporates several key features

1. "Direct contribution" indicates that overt aggression and/or abusive neglect is involved. However, the death need not be caused by any particular blow(s). For example, the aggressive intimidation of a nestmate as an infanticidal (i.e., siblicidal) act would be included if the victim consequently starves to death, but the starvation would not count as infanticide if it resulted from nonaggressive sibling competition. Similarly, a parent would have to avoid feeding the starving victim (selectively, by its own actions) to meet this criterion. Finally, the definition is not intended to include remote parental manipulations (e.g., commencing incubation prior to clutch completion), although such actions undoubtedly contribute indirectly to infant death.

2. "Immediate death" specifically excludes all greatly protracted effects that might expedite the victim's demise far in the future. Basically, the animal must die as an infant.

3. "Embryo" is included to allow the various forms of foetal death,

which are detected relatively easily in oviparous animals. Ovipary affords significant flexibility in subsequent parental investment strategies, roughly comparable to that enjoyed by marsupials relative to placental mammals (Low, 1978; see also Hayssen, Chapter 6, this volume).

4. "Newly hatched" is admittedly a vague upper time limit for what is considered an infant. Typically, ornithologists distinguish prefledged young, which cannot fly well, from fledged young, which can. Here, infanticide refers to prefledged young only because their limited mobility reflects the higher vulnerability normally associated with infancy. An alternative cutoff point, the transition from reliance on parents to full independence, is much harder to identify in the field and may not occur until many months after hatching (e.g., in seabirds: Nelson, 1978; Burger, 1978). The other obvious advantage of using fledging as the criterion results from the fact that ornithologists cannot fly: The overwhelming bulk of their empirical data thus concerns nestling mortality (see Ricklefs, 1967).

A set of infanticide subcategories is also proposed based on the identity of the perpetrator(s). The fundamental separation of *nonkin infanticide* from *kin infanticide* puts emphasis on the interesting fact that the latter involves sacrificing shared genes for some presumed compensating benefit(s) to the perpetrator's inclusive fitness (see O'Connor, 1978). Kin infanticide can be subdivided further into *parental infanticide* and *siblicide.* Siblicide refers to the subset of infanticide known to be carried out by full- or half-sibs. Although this is a useful distinction for birds, the incidence of siblicide in other taxa is unknown (but see O'Gara, 1969; Wourms, 1981; Wourms *et al.,* 1981). The term *siblicide* (Braun, 1981; Braun and Hunt, 1983; Gould, 1982) is preferred over its widely used predecessors (*fratricide, cainism,* or *Cain and Abel struggle*) because the victim's gender is seldom specified in the literature.

With respect to the compensating benefits accruing to infanticidal individuals, this discussion is organized around the four functional hypotheses proposed by Hrdy (1979; see also Introduction, this volume). Briefly, Hrdy suggested that perpetrators of infanticide may profit from one or more of the following types of payoffs: (1) *exploitation* of the infant, especially as food (i.e., cannibalism); (2) *resource competition* either with the infant or with its parents; (3) *parental manipulation* (i.e., where parents truncate investment in one offspring so as to maximize their lifetime reproductive success); and (4) *sexual selection* wherein infanticide enhances the perpetrator's success in intrasexual competition (i.e., for mates). As shown presently, the study of avian infanticide involves considerable use of the first three of these (mutually compatible) explanations, touching only rarely on the fourth. By contrast, the study of infanticide in mammals has emphasized sexual selection to the near exclusion of the first three hypotheses (see Hrdy, 1979; Hausfater, Chapter 13, this volume).

BIOLOGICAL ATTRIBUTES OF BIRDS PERTAINING TO INFANTICIDE

Three phylogenetic constraints on cannibalistic infanticide in birds are rapid growth, determinate growth, and (in most species) the practice of swallowing food whole. Because most birds are thus "gape-limited predators" (Zaret, 1980), the period when chicks are subject to intraspecific predation is rather brief: There are no spectacularly large elderly individuals, as in many ectothermic taxa, capable of swallowing adolescent-sized birds whole. Only raptors (hawks and owls) and a few other predatory birds that dismember prey with their bills (e.g., skuas, shrikes) are exempt from gape-limitation.

Furthermore, in comparison with many other taxa, birds have "expensive" offspring, which Hrdy (1979) proposed as an important precondition for infanticide. Even though few birds exhibit the demographic and social features required by the sexual selection hypothesis for infanticide (see below), the sizeable parental care given to each avian offspring imposes real limits on the parents' ability to invest in other progeny (Trivers, 1972). To the extent that ovipary separates mother from zygote at an early stage, the mother's options for secondary adjustments in parental investment (including fatal termination) are broadened.

By contrast, the preponderance of monogamy among avian mating systems (an estimated 91% of all birds: Lack, 1968), places two major constraints on the evolution of infanticide. First, it erodes the potential for sexually selected infanticide, which is generally associated with polygynous mating systems. That is, a male bird is unlikely to secure an additional mate by performing infanticide on that female's progeny. A variety of ecological factors makes biparental care obligatory in most birds, which automatically establishes a selection pressure for females to require full-time assistance from monogamous males. Thus, a victimized mother bird is likely to mate with the male that kills her first brood only if she has no reproductive alternatives. Second, the prevalence of monogamy means that in many species two parents are involved in protecting the young from attack. Even in avian species where sexual size dimorphism gives a physical advantage to males (a pattern not particularly widespread in birds and frequently reversed, as in virtually all raptors), the hypothetical infanticidal male would have to contend with an equally large guarding male in addition to the female. The probability of successfully killing the progeny, much less obtaining the resident female, is diminished accordingly.

Class Aves also exhibits a higher incidence of polyandry (one female mating with two or more males) than any other class of terrestrial animals. This mating system raises the possibility of "reversed" patterns of sexually selected infanticide, with females performing the act in order to acquire additional males. Intriguingly, Stephens (1982, 1983) reported one such event in northern jacanas (*Jacana spinosa*): A polyandrous female apparently killed the brood of a neighboring male and immediately gained him as a member of her harem. Thus, the diversity of avian mating systems provides the opportunity for elegant comparative testing of the sexual selection and other hypotheses concerning infanticide in animals.

PATTERNS OF AVIAN INFANTICIDE

Infanticide in birds is most common in the four broad contexts of brood reduction, desertion, coloniality, and communal nesting. Contrary to Hrdy's (1979:20) assertion that infanticide is never common, ornithological field data demonstrate that it is regularly the most important source of nestling mortality in certain avian species. As such, it is expected to have been a major selective pressure and to have spawned an assortment of specific adaptations, which are discussed by context.

Context 1: Infanticide in Brood-Reduction Systems

In the huge literature on avian clutch size (see reviews by Lack, 1968; Klomp, 1970), special attention has been given to cases where females consistently lay more eggs than are successfully fledged on average. The regular loss of one or more members of the brood ("brood reduction") is regarded as a density-dependent system for maximizing parental reproductive success. Experimental additions of eggs usually (but not always: e.g., Nelson, 1978; DeSteven, 1980) show that the mean population clutch size is well matched to the maximum number of young that parents can rear to fledging (e.g., Lack, 1954; Crossner, 1977). Although this appears to be simple, brood reduction generates numerous and complex mixtures of parental manipulation and sibling resource-competition strategies that seem associated with ecological uncertainties—especially about food (Lack, 1968) and predation (Clark and Wilson, 1981).

One widespread parental strategy for dealing with the unpredictability of food resources—due to fluctuations either in food-abundance levels or in factors affecting foraging efficiency (e.g., poor weather: Stinson, 1980)—is the production of one or more "extra" eggs that produce surviving offspring only when food turns out to be particularly bountiful. In poor seasons, this extra reproductive effort is terminated early enough to avoid jeopardizing the other offspring or parental survivorship (Charnov and Krebs, 1974). Probably the most common tactic used in such parental manipulation (sensu Alexander, 1974:337) is beginning effective incubation prior to the completion of egg laying. The attending parents can thus give a developmental head start to the first-laid eggs, which translates into an asynchronous hatch pattern with age disparities approximating the laying intervals. Lack (1947, 1954) hypothesized that stronger and larger first chicks would out-compete their younger siblings if and when parental care becomes limiting. Thus, by creating initial asymmetries in the competitive abilities of broodmates, parents can hedge their bet, forestalling the final commitment to a given brood size until the ecological conditions are better known.

Many studies have shown that nidicolous species (those whose young remain in the nest) exhibit hatch asynchrony and, subsequently, brood reduction that starts with the youngest sib (Ricklefs, 1965; O'Connor, 1978). For example, Siegfried (1972) found that 85% of all nestling mortality in cattle egrets (*Bubulcus ibis*) is concentrated on the youngest (in this case, the third-hatched or *c*) chick and that two-thirds of those young display retarded growth. Death of the youngest chick by starvation has similarly been reported in many asynchronously hatching birds, including swifts (*Apus apus*) (Lack and Lack, 1951; Lack, 1956), corvids (Lockie, 1955), ploceids (*Quelea quelea*) (Ward, 1965), herons (Jenni, 1969), blackbirds (*Turdus merula*) (Snow, 1958), cormorants (Snow, 1960; Williams and Burger, 1979), thrashers (*Toxostoma curvirostre*) (Ricklefs, 1965), tawny owls (*Strix aluco*) (Southern, 1970), terns (Nisbet, 1973), and several gulls (Parsons, 1975; Lundberg and Väisänen, 1979; Hahn, 1981). Unfortunately, none of these studies provides any information about whether or not social behavior directly affected the mortality, usually because extensive direct observations of the broods were not made. Additional examples of avian brood reduction are reviewed in Lack (1954, 1968), O'Connor (1978), Howe (1978), and Hahn (1981).

In addition to the manipulation of asynchronous hatch, females sometimes create different-sized eggs. These differences reflect true disparities in nutrient (yolk) and energy (lipid) content of the eggs, and not merely water content (Romanoff and Romanoff, 1949; Parsons, 1970; Nisbet, 1978; Howe, 1978). When the effects of asynchronous hatch are reduced experimentally, egg-size differences have been shown to produce differential growth rates (Howe, 1976, 1978) and mortality (Parsons, 1975; Nisbet, 1978; see also Warham, 1975; Lundberg and Väisänen, 1979) in the chicks.

Parent and offspring roles in siblicide. Social behavior mediating intrabrood mortality is performed largely by the chicks themselves, although parents are also potentially important (O'Connor, 1978; Macnair and Parker, 1979; Parker and Macnair, 1979). The elder chicks, in addition to exercising their size and motor-skill advantages, may use physical aggression to enhance their own chances for survival. Parents presumably have the option of secondarily adjusting competitive asymmetries through differential allocation of parental care after hatching (e.g., by selectively feeding the runt).

Theoretically, siblicidal behavior reflects an evolutionary compromise between the direct and indirect components of the elder sib's fitness (Brown and Brown, 1981): the attacker effectively trades some of its indirect fitness so as to improve its own chances of surviving and reproducing. So long as it increases its probability of surviving by 0.50 times its full-sib's reproductive value (RV) (or 0.25 times its half-sib's RV, etc.), selection should favor this form of selfishness (Eickwort, 1973). Thus, if the intended victim has a fairly low probability of fledging—as is the case for many nidicolous birds—the rewards to the elder sib need not be particularly great. Furthermore, inasmuch as parents and their progeny do not share perfectly congruent genetic interests, theoretical arguments have been advanced predicting "parent–offspring conflict" over the apportionment of parental investment (Hamilton, 1964a,b; Trivers, 1974). The parent is expected to view each young as equally valuable to its own inclusive fitness, while each individual offspring, being twice as "related" to itself as to even a full sibling, strives to garner more than its fair share of parental investment.

Applying the foregoing logic to the issue of avian brood reduction, O'Connor (1978) predicted that there should be situations in which parents and their elder offspring "disagree" over the timing of brood reduction. To date, the only report of parental intervention during siblicidal brood reduction is that of Spellerberg (1971a) on South Polar skuas (*Catharacta maccormicki*). Spellerberg (1971a) reported that parents in a highly siblicidal population of skuas commonly intercept the attacking chick and/or brood fighting chicks, effectively squelching hostilities. Sometimes, each parent specializes in feeding one chick, which temporarily separates them. Finally, parents were described as sometimes giving (false?) alarm calls that elicit immediate crouching responses, thereby interrupting fights. The relatively simple practice of separating brood members may be a common parental tactic in various ground-nesting birds such as sandhill cranes (*Grus canadensis*) (Harvey *et al.*, 1968) and some ground-nesting owls (Ingram, 1959, 1962; Parmelee *et al.*, 1967). With regard to a recent exchange on which party should "win" in such cases of parent–offspring conflict (Alexander, 1974; Dawkins, 1976; see also Parker and Macnair, 1979; Macnair and Parker, 1979; Stamps and Metcalf, 1980), it should be noted that offspring seem to win in these avian cases. For example, the skua *a*-chick almost always succeeds in killing the *b*-chick (E. Young, 1963; Spellerberg, 1971a; Procter, 1975).

A cost–benefit analysis of avian siblicide is presented schematically in Fig. 1. Though the main cost to the elder chick must usually be the loss of a sibling's genes, considerable energetic output and possible risk of injury are probably important in some species. It can take many hours of laborious fighting to establish and maintain an effective dominance relationship. Indeed, there is significant risk of reversals in many species, even skuas (Spellerberg, 1971a; Procter, 1975), although this point needs further attention in the field. An additional direct-fitness cost is increased risk of predation, resulting from: (1) reduced number of sibling codefenders (which can be important if the predator is not substantially larger than the chicks [e.g., an adult conspecific]) and/ or (2) reduced number of alternative prey targets in the nest (Hamilton, 1971). Most commonly the benefits are in the form of reduced competition from broodmates. According to the literature, cannibalism among siblings is relatively rare (Stinson, 1979).

Presumably, the cost–benefit ratio reaches 1.0 at some point (Zone II in Fig. 1), after which siblicidal attacks are expected to decline. In

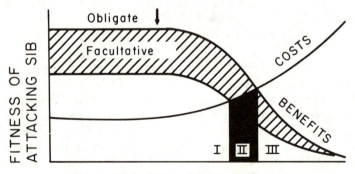

AGE OF VICTIM SIB

Figure 1. Schematic model of siblicidal aggression's net effects on the inclusive fitness of the attacking sib as a function of the victim's age. The initially high benefits from reducing "lifeboat-dilemma" competition drop after peak energy demands have been met. The costs, both in terms of lost indirect fitness and difficulty in killing the victim, increase as the "victim" ages. Zone I represents the time during which aggression pays the attacker. Zone II represents the transition in profitability (placement depends primarily on the shape of the Benefits curve). Zone III represents the period of declining aggression.

most siblicidal species, there is a decreased rate of fighting if the victim survives beyond a certain age (e.g., Ingram, 1959).

In general, parent birds seem to be passive during the brood-reduction process, whether that involves siblicide or merely nonaggressive competition (e.g., Matray, 1974; Newton, 1977; Werschkul, 1979; Safriel, 1981). During sib-fighting of great egrets (*Casmerodius albus*) in Texas, the attending parent typically preens or loafs, frequently not even watching as the victim is pummeled (Mock: unpublished data). Though there is a general impression that parents preferentially feed the smallest chick, there are few, if any, published data to that effect (Ryden and Bengsston, 1980). Clark and Wilson (1981) referred to unpublished data of such preferential feeding by budgerigar (*Melopsittacus undulatus*) parents, but Ryden and Bengsston (1980) found no evidence of preference in a film analysis of parental feeding in three passerine species: feeding priority was gained by the larger sibs taking positions closest to the parent. Clearly, this topic needs further attention.

Proximate and ultimate causes of avian siblicide. Siblicidal aggression is governed at the proximate level (sensu Alcock, 1979) by different factors in different bird species. The literature includes mention of: (1) *food amount,* relative to brood's total needs; (2) *size disparities* among siblings, affecting the ease with which a nestmate can be intimidated and, in some species, the risk of return injury (Spellerberg, 1971a,b; Edwards and Collopy, 1983); (3) *food size,* specifically, the degree to which parental offerings can be monopolized; (4) *parental interference;* (5) *intimidation by threat alone;* and (6) *opportunity for escape by victimized sib,* as in tree- versus ground-nesting species. It is not clear how these variables interrelate. For example, introducing size-matched "siblings" in lesser spotted eagle (*Aquila pomarina*) nests [to nullify factor (2)] did not promote brood harmony, as expected. Instead, a stable dominance relationship, the "acceptance of intimidation" by one chick, developed quickly—usually within a few minutes— and invariably led to siblicidal brood reduction (Meyburg, 1974, 1977).

As previously mentioned, the ultimate factor responsible for the evolution of most siblicide is probably competition for parental food (e.g., Stinson, 1979). The situation is a "lifeboat dilemma" (Hahn, 1981), although restrictions on food amount need not also be the proximate cause. The apparent paradox of vicious sib-fighting amidst a surfeit of food has led a number of workers (e.g., Wynne-Edwards, 1962; Skutch, 1967; Brown *et al.,* 1977; Gargett, 1977) to the erroneous conclusion that food must not be limiting. At second glance, however, it should not be surprising for an *a*-chick that can reliably expect to face a time of food shortage (e.g., when the sibs' collective growth requirements peak) to preempt the survivor's role as early as possible, while its size advantage is maximal (O'Connor, 1978; Stinson, 1979). If so, then there is no specific predicted relationship between the timing of sibling aggression and subsequent food shortages, which may or may not materialize in a given season. In general, sib attacks do not seem to be restricted to moments of parental feeding (Meyburg, 1977: personal observation).

It also follows that obligate siblicidal species may never show waning aggression (Zone III in Fig. 1) simply because that stage is normally never reached. Such birds would have had little or no opportunity to evolve a "switch-off" mechanism. Interestingly, Gargett (1978) reported that black eagles (*Aquila verreauxi*) continually *increase* their siblicidal intensity, even when presented with a "sib" after 6 weeks. (There may, of course, be other problems with the experimental introduction of alien chicks.)

Experimental tests of the ultimate causes of siblicide are difficult because they must be conducted at the proximate level; their results may or may not reflect selective forces. For example, to test the hypothesis that food amount is ultimately responsible for brood size, per-capita food availability can be manipulated proximally (by altering either the food itself or the brood size) and effects on chick survival, growth rates, and/or sibling competition tactics can be looked for. Extrapolating from short-term, single-season results to the parents' lifetime fitnesses, however, often requires the assumption that successive seasons are independent of one another (Williams, 1966; Trivers, 1972; Charnov and Krebs, 1974). For example, Nelson's (1966, 1978) "twinning" experiments with northern gannets (*Sula bassana*) seemed to demonstrate that the normal one-egg clutch was maladaptive because parents successfully raised two healthy young with apparent ease. The problem with that interpretation is that the effects on parental lifetime fitness were not measured. Admittedly, that is an extremely difficult measure to obtain (see DeSteven, 1980), so cautious interpretation of the experimental design may be the only practical recourse.

Similarly, if a species is believed to have evolved siblicidal aggression under conditions of "pending competition" (Stinson, 1979), the results of proximate-level experiments designed to "turn off" the aggression can be extrapolated to ultimate causation only with great caution. Basically, they must be regarded as testing only one of several possible proximate mechanisms. For example, food availability may be an important cause of siblicide at both the ultimate and proximate levels. Experimental provisioning of broods only tests whether or not the possible proximate mechanism ("hunger" as a trigger) is operating (e.g., Procter, 1975). In great egrets, such provisioning does not terminate sib-fighting (Mock: unpublished data), but alternative proximate mechanisms exist by which food shortages might still lead to adaptive siblicide (i.e., by lowering the threshold at which beaten chicks succumb to the cumulative effects of injury and starvation).

Obligate siblicide: examples and hypotheses. Obligate siblicide is a highly developed mechanism of brood reduction in at least two avian taxa: eagles (Accipitridae, especially *Aquila*) and boobies (Sulidae). The best raptor data have been gathered on the black eagle in southern Africa (Siegfried, 1968; Gargett, 1977, 1978; Brown *et al.*, 1977). Out of more than 200 records of two-egg clutches (notated as "c/2") in this species, there is only one record of both siblings surviving to fledge (Brown, 1974; Gargett, 1977). When two eggs are produced (76% of all clutches), the *a*-egg is considerably larger than the *b*-egg (Gargett, 1977). Interestingly, c/1 eggs are intermediate in size between the *a*- and *b*-eggs of c/2 clutches (Gargett, 1977), suggesting that c/2 mothers may be both increasing investment in *a*-eggs and decreasing investment in *b*-eggs. Asynchronous hatch gives the *a*-chick a several day growth headstart, such that it may be double or triple the weight of *b* when the latter hatches.

The most detailed actual account of a raptor siblicide (Gargett, 1978: 58–60) is paraphrased here to summarize and dramatize the behavioral events:

> *Day 1:* The *b*-chick hatched without mishap while the 4-day-old *a*-chick ignored it. Five hyrax carcasses, weighing a total of 5.7 kilos, were in the nest. When *b* was 15.5 hr old, it lunged toward *a*, presumably in an attempt to reach the female parent on *a*'s far side, and *a* pecked *b* in the face, toppling it. By nightfall, *a* had bloodied *b* with many attacks of about 30 blows per bout, totalling 287 blows, but *b* remained unintimidated. The mother offered food to both, but *b* managed to eat only once. After 24 hr, *a* weighed 163 g; *b*, 84 g.
>
> *Day 2:* The attacks intensified. Not only did *b*'s movements elicit aggression, but *a* attacked when *b* was still. Thoroughly intimidated, *b* no longer faced *a* and could not hold its head up. *a* even pulled *b* out from under the brooding female and pecked it. No food went to *b*, which lost 8 g while *a* gained another 40 g. On that day, the *b*-chick was pecked a total of 632 times.
>
> *Day 3:* Even though *b* could hardly move, *a* continued the attacks until *b* was dead, a total of 659 new blows. By the end of *b*'s 72-hr life, it weighed just 66 g. Meanwhile, *a* gained just 10 g the third day, for a total of 213 g. In all, *b* was pecked more than 1569 times in 38 bouts lasting a total of 187 minutes of active fighting.

Several interesting points, echoed in reports on other species, emerge from this description. First, there was a surplus of food. Second, the attending parent did not interfere with the attacks. Third, the *a*-chick paid a sizeable energetic price (apparently even retarding its own growth) for its hostility. Gargett made it clear that the mother offered food repeatedly to both chicks, but the *b*-chick became too intimidated to feed, and *a* frequently ignored the food while pummeling its sibling.

Collectively, the evidence is very strong that first-hatched black eagles do whatever is necessary to obtain all present and future parental care. Similar extremes are found in at least three other congeners: the lesser spotted eagle (*A. pomarina*) in Slovakia (Meyburg, 1974, 1977), the hawk eagle (*A. fasciata*) in the Transvaal, and the golden eagle (*A. chrysaëtos*) in Montana (see references in Gargett, 1978). There are no records for both nestlings of *A. pomarina* surviving to fledge (Meyburg, 1974, 1977; Gargett, 1978).

The adaptive significance of the second egg seems to be primarily as insurance against early demise of the first, not as a parental tactic for raising two young (Ingram, 1959; Dorward, 1962). The black eagle data show that eggs are sometimes stolen ($N = 32$, 8.8%) or infertile ($N = 19$, 5.2%) (Gargett, 1978), and many factors can kill or weaken the primary chick before the second egg hatches. Using Gargett's data for success in c/1 and c/2 black eagle clutches, Stinson (1979) showed that per-egg hatching-failure rates were comparable, but c/2 nests produced a fledged chick 76.4% of the time, while c/1 nests succeeded in only 49.0% of the attempts—a highly significant difference. It seems reasonable to assume that another egg is not particularly expensive for the female to produce: in this species, it weighs only 2.0–2.5% of the female's body weight (Brown *et al.*, 1977). Although relatively few records are available on exactly which chick survives, Gargett (1977) cites 5 *b*-chick survivors in a sample of 22 c/2 nests, or 22.7% in which the insurance paid off after the *a*-chick died.

The "insurance hypothesis" has also been applied convincingly to the obligate-siblicide system of masked boobies (*Sula dactylatra*). Kepler (1969) presented comparative data for typical c/2 and c/1 broods, showing that only 2 of 10 c/1 nests fledged a chick, while 57 of 90 (63%) of c/2 nests did so. In this species, the two eggs are laid about 5.5 days apart and, because of early incubation, hatch 4 days apart (Nelson, 1978). The *a*-chick usually pushes *b* out of the ground nest as soon as it hatches (Dorward, 1962); less commonly, it stomps *b* to death in the nest (Gould, 1982). However, sufficient *a*-chicks perish early to allow a sizeable fraction (22% in Kepler's sample) of *b*-chicks to survive and fledge. Similarly, Braun and Hunt (1983) reported that in 6 (of 132) c/2 black-legged kittiwake (*Rissa tridactyla*) nests, the elder sibling died in the egg or shortly after hatching and was survived by its *b*-sibling, which fledged.

Similar systems of obligate siblicide have been reported for pelicans (Vesey-Fitzgerald, 1957; Knopf, 1979; Cooper, 1980) owls (Ingram, 1959, 1962), and cranes (Miller, 1973). In general, the "insurance hypothesis" seems to be well supported by the few data that exist. Logically, it seems irresistible as a contributing advantage, if not necessarily the only selective advantage for larger clutch sizes. The most direct attempt to falsify the "insurance hypothesis" involved a comparison of fledging output from the nests of c/1 eagle species and siblicidal c/2 species

(Brown *et al.*, 1977). As Stinson (1979) pointed out, this is an inappropriate between-species comparison because it does not control for many of the species' differences that are unrelated to brood reduction. It could be quibbled that Stinson's intraspecific comparison of c/1 and c/2 success (presented previously for the black eagle data) might be biased if "less competent" pairs tend to produce the smaller clutches—although Gargett (1977) provided indirect evidence that the same pairs produce both c/1 and c/2 clutches in different years. It seems that nobody has attempted the obvious experiment of removing one egg from a sample of c/2 nests and comparing the resulting survivorship with natural c/2 controls of the same species. This may be most easily done in an abundant, colonial species that exhibits obligate siblicide (e.g., the masked booby or various pelicans).

Although the "insurance hypothesis" is reasonably secure as a causal explanation for the production of extra eggs and, indeed, as an "automatic" contributing factor in all brood-reduction systems (e.g., Braun and Hunt, 1983), other hypotheses have been proposed. Rowe (1947) suggested what may be called the "gluttony hypothesis," wherein the b-chick's brief presence supposedly stimulates a to eat more than it would otherwise and therefore to grow more robust. This essentially proximate-level idea (such a behavioral dependency by the a-chick would not be evolutionarily stable relative to the tendency to eat a lot regardless of brood size) was based on a single observation that one c/2 a-chick grew faster than one c/1 chick. Opposing cases have been reported since (e.g., Brown *et al.*, 1977), and this hypothesis is not regarded seriously today.

A third idea, the "icebox hypothesis" (Alexander, 1974), suggests that the b-chick may serve as a useful meal for a when food becomes scarce. As such, it could be viewed as a means by which the female "preserves" some nutrients during a time of relative plenty (laying and early nestling phases) for use later. There are few field data consistent with this hypothesis (e.g., Scharf and Balfour, 1971), and most studies report specifically that b-chicks are not eaten after siblicide (Meyburg, 1974; Gargett, 1978; Stinson, 1979).

Finally, mention must be made of the four or five species of crested penguins (*Eudyptes*). Their unique system of egg dimorphism and its consequences is best classified as "obligate brood reduction," at least until the precise causes of egg loss are determined. The general pattern is for the female to lay a small (but viable) a-egg (average wet weight about 100 g), then, about 3 days later, a larger b-egg (average about 150 g) (Lack, 1968; Warham, 1975). Incubation begins after the clutch is complete. It is not clear what happens next, except that most a-eggs vanish during the incubation. There is a rather widely held view that the parents actually evict the a-egg, but there are "no recent and authenticated reports of these birds deliberately ejecting fertile eggs before hatching has begun [Warham, 1975]." When both eggs hatch almost simultaneously as they commonly do in *E. crestatus* (Lack, 1968), the parents ignore the *a*-chick until it dies. There are no records of both chicks fledging for any *Eudyptes* species!

Crested penguin chicks hatching from *a*-eggs are proportionally smaller than those from *b*-eggs, but that difference can be made up in 2 days of parental feeding if *b* does not hatch. It is not known if sibling aggression occurs in two-chick broods. It is also unclear why the egg dimorphism in these birds favors the second offspring, although intense early-season male aggression (causing many first eggs to be lost or broken) is suspected (Warham, 1975). It would be most interesting to know more about the mechanism(s) of obligate brood reduction in these penguins, which may include poor incubation of the smaller egg, deliberate parental infanticide of eggs, accidental destruction during neighbor disputes (especially in the most densely colonial species), and/or posthatching persecution of *a* by its sibling and/or parents. Whatever the causes of its unusual demise, the *a*-egg is currently regarded as insurance against the loss of *b* (Lack, 1968; Warham, 1975).

Another type of obligate brood reduction has been reported in asynchronously hatching hooded grebes (*Podiceps gallardoi*). In this system, the parents lead the freshly hatched *a*-chick away from the nest immediately, thereby deserting the unhatched *b*-egg (Nuechterlein and Johnson, 1981). Though this system has not been carefully studied, the early desertion is believed to be invariant.

Facultative siblicide: examples and hypotheses. Facultative siblicide is expected in brood-reduction situations where the elder chick can sometimes enhance its own survival without necessarily killing siblings. For convenience, a distinction is made between conditional and probabilistic forms. *Conditional siblicide* refers to systems in which one or more ecological variables seem to trigger a wave of lethal aggression. *Probabilistic siblicide* is a more generalized strategy by which sibling aggression is used to vouchsafe priority to potentially inadequate resources, forcing junior sibs to get by on whatever remains; it is essentially a social means of exaggerating the elder sib's competitive superiority. Combinations of these two general strategies are likely to be very common.

All facultative siblicide features the chance for indirect fitness benefits for the perpetrator, should the lesser siblings survive, while minimizing risk to the direct component of fitness. This category shows similarities to obligate siblicide in being: (1) anticipatory (aggression starting before resource limitation); (2) variable in actual cause of death; and (3) variable in relationship to immediate food conditions. All existing reports of conditional siblicide implicate food amount as the key trigger (e.g., Procter, 1975; Braun and Hunt, 1983). The participants seem to behave according to the simple rule—"if hungry, fight."

The family of diurnal raptors (Accipitridae), shows a full spectrum of brood-reduction strategies (Newton, 1977), from obligate siblicide (some c/2 eagles) to conditional facultative siblicide (other eagles plus medium-sized *Buteo* and *Accipiter* spp.) to a total absence of fighting among the smallest raptors, even when their large broods face starvation. Mebs (1964), for example, reported that cannibalism in the common buzzard (*Buteo buteo*) was directly related to food shortages and occurred more often in c/4 nests than c/3 or c/2 nests (see also Pilz and Siebert, 1978). Newton (1977) found no cases of serious sibling aggression in the true falcons (*Falco*) or osprey (*Pandion*). However, Poole (1979, 1982) recently reported sib-fighting in Florida and New York osprey broods and noted that the aggression leads to effective intimidation and food monopolization by the dominant siblings. Suggestively, the aggression was greater in the low-latitude (Florida) population, where parental food provisioning was constrained by 25% less daylight for hunting.

In South Polar skuas, sibling aggression often forces the younger chick out of the nest (Procter, 1975), where it wanders about trying to solicit adoption in neighbors' nests but frequently is cannibalized instead (E. Young, 1963). Procter (1975) concluded that this sibling aggression is linked directly to food amounts at the home nest. Actually, the skua case is quite complex, making it difficult to categorize as to siblicide type. The published data show only one case of double fledging from 90 c/2 broods (E. Young, 1963), but there are numerous unpublished records of double fledgings during high-food seasons at Palmer Station, Antarctica (P. Pietz: personal communication). Furthermore, at Palmer very little sibling aggression was observed, suggesting that siblicide in this species may be both conditional and probabilistic.

A highly provocative conditional siblicide system is found in the blue-footed booby (*Sula nebouxii*). When food is abundant, the asynchronously hatched two or three young coexist peacefully, but when food is scarce, the *a*-chick pushes its sib beyond the white ring of guano created (and defended as a territory) by the parents. Thereafter, it is the parents' inflexible refusal to allow anything to enter the guano ring that causes the evicted sib's death (Nelson, 1978; Gould, 1982). (It could be argued that this is more properly classified as parental infanticide than conditional siblicide, but the implications for parent–offspring conflict are intriguing.)

Similarly, black-legged kittiwake *a*-chicks evicted more than one-half their *b*-siblings, usually when adverse weather reduced the amount of food delivered by the parents. Because kittiwakes nest on cliff ledges, such evictions are usually instantly fatal; but even when the victim managed to avoid falling into the sea by taking refuge on an adjacent rock shelf, it was ignored by its parents and died from exposure (Braun and Hunt, 1983).

Probabilistic siblicide features anticipatory aggression from one or more elder siblings that substantially retards development of the younger chicks but causes death only if food is insufficient in the long run. This has been the focus of this author's research on great egrets since 1979. All broods of this species observed in Texas have shown escalated sibling aggression, with the youngest (usually c) chicks growing more slowly and dying frequently. Sometimes the c-chick dies as the direct result of assaults when it is forced out of the nest and falls to its doom. Other times, c slowly starves to death in the nest. Usually, however, it survives to fledge. Food availability seems ineffective as a proximate inhibiting mechanism: Wild broods provisioned with 33% extra food per day and captive broods fed ad lib continued to exhibit high fighting levels (Mock: unpublished data). Overall, the aggression guarantees first access to food for the elder sibs yet does not prevent the c-chick from eating enough surplus food (if it exists) to withstand the physical beatings it invariably receives. On the occasion of premature death to the a- or b-chicks, c recovers more quickly.

A similar system seems to operate in cattle egrets (Blaker, 1969; Weber, 1975; Werschkul: unpublished data; Mock and Ploger: unpublished data), reddish egrets (*Egretta rufescens*) (R. Paul: personal communication), little blue herons (*Florida caerulea*) (Werschkul, 1979), grey herons (*Ardea cinerea*) (Owen, 1960), American white pelicans (*Pelecanus erythrorhynchos*) (R. Evans: personal communication), and pink-backed pelicans (*P. rufescens*) (Din and Eltringham, 1974). It may be very widespread in the many species that have asynchronous hatching and brood reduction but for which there are no observational data on the possible role of sibling aggression.

Sib-fighting leading to effective intimidation of younger chicks can be less conspicuous than the obvious physical abuse reported in the preceding species. In western grebes (*Aechmophorus occidentalis*), for example, Nuechterlein (1981) was able to detect intimidation of younger sibs under experimental conditions but not readily during field observations. Young grebes (dabchicks) travel about on the parent's back, which makes detailed observation difficult. Using a blindfolded adult under the chicks in the lab, however, Nuechterlein showed that the older chick beats and intimidates its younger sibling in response to a taped recording of the parental "food call."

Sib-fighting species are also well suited to tests of what Hahn (1981:425) called "sibling rivalry reduction hypothesis," based on Hamilton's (1964a,b) reasoning that "fierce competition will waste the energies of the brood and . . . behaviour of the adult(s) should tend to evolve so as to minimize this wastage which spells a lowering of total surviving progeny." That is, while parents should manipulate sibling asymmetries so as to facilitate occasional brood reduction, their differential investment is also constrained by the brood's overall developmental efficiency. Thus, the upper limit on hatch intervals may be set by the reproductive value of the youngest chick (which must not be so far behind as to be eliminated too early) and the optimal lower limit by sibling rivalry (a brood with evenly matched chicks may expend "too much" energy fighting to establish a stable dominance hierarchy). These predictions are currently being tested in field experiments on cattle egret hatch asynchrony (Mock and Ploger: unpublished data).

There are no data on how brood reduction may influence sex ratios in birds and certainly no known cases of parental bias in sex of surviving young, as has been shown for wood rats (McClure, 1981). However, recent discoveries of laying-order biases in brood sex ratios of geese (Ankney, 1982) and gulls (Ryder, 1983) make such possibilities all the more likely (but see Cooke and Harmsen, 1983).

Other hypotheses on differential investments. It must not be supposed from the emphasis placed on infanticide in the preceding account that all parental manipulations (including egg-size disparities and hatch asynchrony) of nestling birds necessarily evolved to facilitate brood reduction. First, there is the possibility that such manipulations are not adaptations per se but are merely the effects or consequences of something else (e.g., Williams, 1966). Bryant (1978), for example, has shown that decreasing egg size with hatching order may be simply an artifact of dwindling energy reserves in the female. The fact that it significantly influences the survival of the last offspring (as demonstrated experimentally by Parsons 1970, 1975) could be an epiphenomenon. However, in herring gull (*Larus argentatus*) experiments, immediate removal of the *b*-egg can lead to increased size of the *c*-egg, suggesting a strong relationship between parental investment and position in the clutch (Parsons, 1976; see also Lundberg and Väisänen, 1979). Interestingly, the reverse pattern, egg size increasing with laying order, has been reported in a few other asynchronously hatching species, where it has been proposed as a secondary parental manipulation to prolong the disadvantaged last chick's life as long as possible prior to brood reduction (Howe, 1978). This interpretation has been disputed (Clark and Wilson, 1981).

There is little or no controversy over hatch asynchrony being a parental reproductive strategy, even from traditional opponents of selectionist reasoning (Gould, 1982), but there is debate over which benefits to the parents are most important. Because only the "brood reduction hypothesis" implicates infanticide (and accommodates most observations of that phenomenon), it has been the focus of the preceding sections. As the first and most widely accepted explanation, it enjoyed many years of unequivocal support. However, mention must also be made of two relatively recent alternative hypotheses.

According to the "peak load reduction" hypotheses (e.g., Ingram, 1959; Hussell, 1972), asynchrony is a means of stretching limited amounts of parental care (especially food) over a longer period to avoid a deleterious squeeze. The other alternative model essentially substitutes predation pressure for food shortages. In their "nest failure hypothesis" model, Clark and Wilson (1981) showed that high predation rates could select for parental behavior that enables at least one chick to fledge as quickly as possible, lest the parents suffer total reproductive ruin. Clearly, more than one advantage may accrue to parents that produce asynchronous hatching, and it is misleading to assume that brood reduction alone accounts for the practice throughout Aves.

Context 2: Parental Infanticide

Parental manipulations need not be so subtle or indirect as those previously described: sometimes parents destroy their eggs and nestlings outright. This can take the form of physical attack (with or without cannibalism) or simple desertion. Overt attack is not widespread, but Schüz (1957) reported that first-breeding male white storks (*Ciconia ciconia*) sometimes kill their own offspring (a practice he called "kronism," after the mythical titan *Kronos* who ate his own children). The age-bias is provocative, since inexperienced birds are often less successful hunters and, therefore, believed to be more marginal as reproductives in species with complex hunting methods (Orians, 1969; Recher and Recher, 1969). The reported gender bias is more mystifying. It is particularly puzzling that the young are not subsequently eaten (Schüz, 1957), leaving one to wonder why the parent does not simply desert. A similar paradox is presented by egg-puncturing behavior of the presumed father in long-billed marsh wrens (*Telmatodytes palustris*) (Picman, 1977). In captive breeding programs, American kestrel (*Falco sparverius*) parents sometimes devour their own young, but this habit apparently can be corrected by changing the adults' diet (Porter and Wiemeyer, 1970). It is not known if diet affects "kronism" in wild birds.

By contrast, in many bird species desertion of offspring may be a common practice under certain circumstances. Desertion, too, seems to be more prevalent among inexperienced than experienced breeders (e.g., Coulson and White, 1958; Richdale, 1957; Knopf, 1979). Desertion of eggs and/or nestlings occurs mainly in response to intense local predation, human (and other potential predator?) traffic, and low food conditions. In general, desertion can be viewed as a parental strategy for maximizing lifetime reproduction by giving up on a lost cause. Field workers have noticed that desertion is most likely if the breeders are disturbed early in the season. Although such increasing tenacity has been interpreted classically as protection of a growing cumulative investment, it is more parsimoniously explained in terms of the diminishing residual investment needed to produce independent fledglings (Dawkins and Carlisle, 1976; Boucher, 1977).

Many Procellariiformes exhibit an intermediate parental strategy called "egg neglect," in which the eggs may be deserted for several days at a time while the adults pursue ephemeral food at sea (Boersma and Wheelwright, 1979; Murray et al., 1983). The embryos of these species are well adapted to withstand chilling and intermittent development but only within limits. For example, the fork-tailed storm-petrel (Oceanodroma furcata) egg needs 38.6 days of incubation in order to hatch, but that incubation can be spread successfully over as many as 71 days. The average total neglect is 9.1 days, and eggs neglected for 10 or more days experience significantly higher failure rates than those neglected fewer than 10 days (Boersma and Wheelwright, 1979).

Complete desertions in time of food shortage may also be quite common. Southern (1970) reported that 51% of tawny owl eggs fail to hatch, primarily because females quit incubating when their mates did not provide sufficient food. Similarly, by making food gathering more difficult for the adults, stormy weather can lead to the fatal desertion by skuas (E. Young, 1963) and kittiwakes (B. Braun: personal communication) chicks.

The response of American wood storks (Mycteria americana) to unseasonal rainfall provides an especially dramatic example of prudent desertion. Kahl (1964) showed that massive, colony-wide desertions of eggs and young occur if sustained rains interrupt the Everglades dry season. Stork breeding is tied closely to a dropping water table, which effectively concentrates aquatic prey into shrinking pools. High concentrations are essential for these tactolocating predators to meet the high food demands of their young, so rain spells disaster. Because adults live and breed for many years, it may pay to jettison a given breeding effort quickly when ecological conditions deteriorate.

Many studies that include desertion rates do not specify the suspected stimulus, but the data indicate that this form of infanticide can be a significant and regular source of mortality (e.g., Pettingill, 1939; H. Young, 1963; Kepler, 1969; Nelson, 1978; Werschkul, 1979; Knopf, 1979) and/or an episodic catastrophe (e.g., Van Someren and Van Someren, 1945; Kahl, 1964). In the first category, Ricklefs (1967) cited several passerine studies for which the average desertion rates were 4.2% for eggs and 1.7% for chicks (see also H. Young, 1963).

If the hatch intervals are long enough and/or the offspring sufficiently precocial, parental desertion can even function as a brood-reduction system (e.g., Nuechterlein and Johnson, 1981). Vesey-Fitzgerald (1957) reported that African white pelican (*Pelecanus onocrotalus*) *a*-chicks hatch "several days" before *b*. If an *a*-chick goes to join a "school" of youngsters before its sibling hatches, the parents desert the remaining egg. Otherwise, *a* kills *b* outright when the latter hatches. Miller (1973) described the same pattern for whooping cranes (*Grus americana*) and sandhill cranes (*G. canadensis*).

Context 3: Infanticide in Colonies

Because dense breeding colonies juxtapose vulnerable offspring and unrelated adults, they are hotbeds of infanticide. The density of conspecifics automatically intensifies competition for any limited resources (especially nest sites and building materials) and increases opportunities for cannibalism by adults and for risky food-stealing attempts by ambulatory chicks. For these reasons alone, it might be expected that the avian infanticide literature would be colony-biased, but there is more: many ornithologists have discovered the logistic advantages of being able to observe many nests at once. Thus, colony researchers studying other topics often publish anecdotal notes on infanticide as well. This vigilance helps compensate for some of the sampling problems caused by the brevity of the infanticidal act (Hrdy, 1979) and occasionally allows a choice between competing interpretations of mortality (e.g., cannibalism versus scavenging of already dead chicks). However, because bird colonies are often densely packed, problems associated with observer disturbance are particularly acute. A seemingly simple task like marking individual chicks in their nests can trigger mass panic among hundreds of adults and mobile young. This chaos can easily inflate estimates of predation mortality, cannibalism, and even adoptions. It is seldom possible to be absolutely confident that frequency data presented are free from such biases, but increasing awareness of this problem is generating greater caution in the field (e.g., Fetterolf, 1983). In any case, the general picture of relatively high levels of infanticide in bird colonies seems inescapable.

Cannibalism. As a food source for conspecifics, eggs and young chicks are both rich in essential nutrients (Polis, 1981) and remarkably free of chemical defenses (Orians and Janzen, 1974). As mentioned earlier, because the great majority of birds must swallow fresh food whole, cannibalism in most avian taxa is restricted to eggs and very young chicks.

Davis and Dunn (1976) reported that cannibalism, mostly performed by opportunistic neighbors that had recently lost their own progeny, was the single most important cause of egg mortality in a colony of lesser black-backed gulls (*Larus fuscus*). However, they suggested that this finding might have been due to extraordinarily high densities caused by a sustained population explosion. That is, the high rate of cannibalism observed might have been due largely to an unusual supply of food (chicks) and a "snowballing" effect as victims' parents became additional cannibals. It is not known to what extent cannibalism is a naturally important part of the behavioral repertoire of this species (see also Polis, 1981).

Parsons (1971) reported a high rate of cannibalism (23.3% of the eggs and chicks in a colony of 900 herring gulls) without reference to historical population changes. Of particular interest is his discovery that one-half of all cannibalism was performed by only four breeding individuals. Parsons regarded cannibalism as simple predatory opportunism and not as an aberrant response to famine conditions.

Though E. Young (1963) reported a rate of only 8% for observed cannibalism (by breeding adults) in a South Polar skua colony, another 54% of the offspring simply vanished, and many of these were believed to have been cannibalized also. Again, only a few cannibalistic individuals were involved (see also Pettingill, 1939; Polis, 1981). A few intriguing observations were made of parent skuas eating their own chicks, but Young conceded that those chicks might have been dead already. It is quite possible that reports of high levels of chick losses in other species (e.g., Vermeer, 1970) may include substantial unobserved cannibalism also.

Aside from the gulls and skuas, quantitative data on cannibalism are scarce, though some reports exist for colonial terns (Pettingill, 1939; Cullen, cited in Nelson, 1966) and frigatebirds (*Fregata aquila*) (Dorward, 1962). In noncolonial species, sample sizes plummet to anecdote level (e.g., bullfinch cannibalism is mentioned in Welty, 1975, without a cited reference), with a few notable exceptions. Yom-Tov (1974) made the potentially general observation that food dispersion may force parent carrion crows (*Corvus corone*) to leave eggs and nestlings unprotected; nests with relatively good nearby food supplies suffered lower cannibalism than nests farther from food. He estimated that up to 75% of all eggs and young are taken by conspecifics. Trail *et al.* (1981) observed cannibalistic infanticide in Mexican jays (*Aphelocoma ultramarina*), which they associated with reproductive competition (see Context 4). Finally, as discussed earlier, many raptor researchers consider cannibalism to be rare and incidental to siblicidal brood reduction (e.g., Meyburg, 1974; Stinson, 1979).

Noncannibalistic infanticide in colonial birds. With nutritional gain set aside, the motives for killing young colony neighbors become more complicated, but the fact that such behavior is commonly cited as a primary cause of death makes it very important. In general contrast to cannibalism, strikingly few other reports of colony infanticide describe intrusions by adult killers. Except for thefts of nesting material that cause eggs or young to fall and die (e.g., Siegfried, 1972), the fatal encounters between adults and chicks stem mainly from chick movements about the colony.

Unless bipedal mobility is environmentally constrained by cliffs (Cullen, 1957) or watery habitats (Burger, 1974), unfledged chicks of many gull species do considerable wandering, often with lethal consequences. In an article titled "Why do herring gulls kill their young?" Ward (1906) reported a high incidence in infanticide but did not answer his own question. In the years since, many authors have offered similar observations of killing by other gulls (e.g., Strong, 1914; Emlen, 1956; Nelson, 1966; Fordham, 1970; Vermeer, 1970; Hunt and Hunt, 1975, 1976), terns (Sprunt, 1948; Gauzer, 1981a,b), gannets (Nelson, 1966), and herons (Owen, 1960; Blaker, 1969). Ward's original question has still not been given a satisfactory answer, though it now seems clear that the extreme degree of territorial aggression found in colonies is often a significant proximate factor (e.g., Nelson, 1966; Hunt and Hunt, 1975, 1976). For some reason(s), chicks risk death to wander away from the relative safety of home.

Although some of the chicks' movements may be an artifact of human (observer) disturbances (e.g., Pierotti, 1981), natural incentives for wandering probably involve access to additional food supplies. The evidence is piecemeal but involves four tantalizing points: (1) "adoptions" of wanderer chicks have been reported in several colonial species; (2) chick kleptoparasitism of food has been observed; (3) a disproportionate share of these food-seeking wanderers are known to be on the bottom of their family's feeding hierarchy; and (4) both parents and siblings of many species have evolved elaborate, but not foolproof, kin-recognition abilities. Taken together, these suggest the plausible and testable hypothesis that subordinate colonial chicks wander in order to seek food when their chances of surviving at home are low (see also Graves and Whiten, 1980). That many of them are executed abroad for their efforts may not outweigh the fact that wandering can be the better of two bad options. Perhaps depending on the amount of parental care they need to fledge, such vagrants have the major options of trying to survive on their own (by scavenging or stealing opportunistically) or trying to establish themselves in a new brood. The latter can be viewed as a type of brood parasitism practiced by the chicks themselves and, as in other forms of parasitism, selection probably favors host refusal to some degree (Dawkins and Krebs, 1979).

For example, adoption of wandering young has been reported as "common" in South Polar skuas (Spellerberg, 1971a,b), and many of these cases are known to be otherwise doomed b-chicks (E. Young, 1963). In one case, the intruder was accepted into a nest that already had two smaller chicks, which it promptly killed. It was raised successfully by the new parents (E. Young, 1963). Similarly, spontaneous chick intrusion–adoptions have been reported as quite common (often 20–40% of study pairs) in several gull species (e.g., Hunt and Hunt, 1975; Graves and Whiten, 1980; Conover et al., 1980; Holley, 1980). In one sample of 10 herring gull adoptions, 6 led to successful fledging (Graves and Whiten, 1980).

While some wandering chicks may scavenge for dropped scraps, others definitely steal food from unrelated broods (Mock: personal observation). In this vein, Hunt and McLoon (1975) showed that gull chicks unsuccessful at obtaining food from their parents tend to wander significantly farther than successful chicks, and that only the wanderers were killed by neighbors. They added that being underfed probably contributes to such chicks' likelihood of succumbing when attacked. Parsons (1971) reported that vagrant c-chicks (of b/3 broods) are the most common victims of herring gull cannibalism. Likewise, the smallest chicks in common tern (Sterna hirundo) broods have been observed food-stealing, especially when food is short at their home nests (Stoeckle, 1974; Nisbet et al., 1978). This author's own recent observations of cattle egrets revealed that most attempts at food kleptoparasitism (which involve springing into a brood and trying to scissor the adult's bill as a bolus is regurgitated) involved chicks whose napes had been pecked bald, a condition found only at the bottom of brood dominance hierarchies. Some of these attempts were successful, though most were resisted actively by the chicks and/or parents of the invaded nest.

Finally, there is an extensive literature demonstrating the abilities of colonial bird parents to recognize their own young and reject other chicks. Furthermore, this discrimination reportedly is acquired at just the moment when chick mobility makes brood-mixing a significant problem and is generally regarded as a parental defense against intraspecific parasitism of parental investment (e.g., Tinbergen, 1953; Beecher et al., 1981a,b). Interestingly, in species where brood-mixing is not possible (e.g., solitary-nesting eagles), parents show no resistance to experimentally introduced chicks (Meyburg, 1977). Even in species that typically exhibit parental recognition of offspring, pairs nesting in habitats that preclude chick mobility (e.g., herring gulls on cliff ledges) show less perfect discrimination (Berens von Rautenfeld, 1978).

Relatively little is known about the behavioral tactics used by ambulatory young in overcoming the recognition and/or resistance of parents (two potentially separate attributes), but Graves and Whiten (1980) suggested that aspects of site specificity may reduce initial parental aggression. In particular, they showed that intruding herring gull chicks spent a disproportionate fraction of their earliest hours in a new territory very close to the nest, where the resident adults were significantly less likely to attack them. After about 3 days (during which the intruders typically received little food), the "parents" seemed to stop discriminating entirely and treated the alien young as their own (see also Conover *et al.,* 1980). Thus, despite probable selection pressures to avoid adopting unrelated chicks, parents may remain partially vulnerable to chick tactics that negate normal resistance, perhaps until the adults no longer can discriminate among the young on their territory. Apparently other birds also have strong inhibitions against attacking young in and about their nests (Yom-Tov, 1976; Graves and Whiten, 1980). Parsons (1971) reported that cannibalistic herring gulls sometimes actually adopt victims that survive being carried home as prey.

Chicks may also have an advantage in being able to distinguish parents from other adults before parents can recognize them (see Pierotti, 1980). For example, ring-billed gull (*Larus delawarensis*) chicks have parent-recognition ability at age 4 or 5 days (Evans, 1970), but parents do not acquire the converse until 7–9 days posthatching (Emlen and Miller, 1975; Conover *et al.,* 1980). Parents of this species are believed to rely on site defense during this early period, a system liable to infiltration.

Common terns in Massachusetts exhibit many features of the "vagrant chick" hypothesis (Stoeckle, 1974; I. C. T. Nisbet: personal communication). In this typically b/3 population, Nisbet has "quite often seen starving c-chicks wandering around from nest to nest, pushing into broods" [personal communication]. Stoeckle (1974) actually witnessed an acceptance of one such wanderer. Nisbet has a total of 10 records of successful adoptions (to fledging) out of about 300 closely monitored broods of marked chicks. Successful adoptions always occurred while the adoptee was young (up to a maximum of 8 days old, but usually under 5 days) and the invaded brood was in the process of hatching. The great majority of adoptees (6 of the 7 known-chick cases) were c-chicks, but all 10 became functional "a-chicks" in their adoptive broods. Parents that accepted adoptees suffered considerable reproductive losses: Resident c-chicks died in all 10 adopting broods, with b-chicks dying in 6 broods and a-chicks dying in 2 or 3 broods also. By contrast, the adoptee's genetic siblings showed elevated fledging success: only one a-chick died in all 10 of these broods. Thus, parents whose marginal c-chicks effected successful transfer seem to have accrued double fitness benefits. Though it is not known what fraction of vagrant c-chicks in this species die in unsuccessful attempts at getting adopted, their chances of survival at home seem to be very low (Nisbet and Cohen, 1975; Nisbet: personal communication).

Context 4: Cooperative and Communal Birds

Recent research on complexly social birds has deepened the understanding of cooperative behavior, but it has also underscored the pervasiveness of selfish tendencies. Infanticide by adult members of the local population—and even the same "cooperative" group—has now been reported for at least five communally nesting bird species, where it is regarded as a form of intragroup reproductive competition.

Vehrencamp (1977) described "egg-tossing" by communally nesting monogamous groove-billed anis (*Crotophaga sulcirostris*). The socially dominant female lays last after rolling some of the subordinates' eggs out of the shared nest. Even the dominant female seems to be under a laying time constraint imposed by asynchronous hatching and consequent brood reduction. Thus, the early females suffer infanticidal egg losses but produce relatively advantaged elder offspring. A similar system has been found in smooth-billed anis (*C. ani*) by Loflin (1982) in Florida, where, instead of egg-tossing, the dominant female buries some of the early eggs under nesting material before laying her own eggs.

Two to seven female ostriches (*Struthio camelus*) lay up to 13 eggs apiece in a shared nest, but only one "major hen" incubates with the single male. This produces more eggs than can be incubated effectively but, because all females lay concurrently, the option of evicting several "early" eggs is not open as a selfish tactic. Instead, Bertram (1979) reported that the major hen is able somehow to distinguish her own eggs from those laid by the minor hens and rolls many of the latter into a neglected ring around the nest, where they may serve as "buffers" against predation.

In Mexican jays, a few group members have been seen pilfering eggs and eating them (Trail et al., 1981). Though the attacks involved only 8 of 162 (5%) nests, they argued that this is probably a very low estimate. There is some evidence that this egg robbing occurs primarily in low-relatedness groups and at a time when the killers are breeding on the shared territory too. Trail et al. (1981) offered four tentative explanations: (1) infanticide reduces competition for local food for the young; (2) it reduces the very tight competition for reproductive "slots" in the local population; (3) it increases the amount of assistance the killers' own broods will receive from the shared force of "helpers"; and/or (4) it is not a social adaptation at all but just a manifestation of corvid egg-predation habits.

Finally, female acorn woodpeckers (*Melanerpes formicivorus*) have been observed performing egg-tossing from their own shared nests

(Koenig *et al.*, 1983; Mumme *et al.*, 1983). Unlike anis, communally nesting woodpeckers are usually close relatives; indeed, in 15 cases, the tosser was known to be a sister of the female whose egg was evicted, and in 3 cases the tosser was one of the groups' breeding males (Koenig *et al.*, 1983; Mumme *et al.*, 1983). Thus, as in the case of siblicide, the effects of kin selection seem to have been swamped by selfish interests. In two additional cases, newly immigrated female acorn woodpeckers seem to have killed young so as to gain use of the nest/territory for their own breeding effort (Stacey and Edwards, 1983).

CONCLUSIONS

From this survey, it appears that infanticide in birds may be more diverse, more common, and more readily observable than in other terrestrial vertebrates. In large part, this may be due to ovipary and the relationship between offspring growth patterns and parental care. Because avian embryos are separated from the mother early in the reproductive process, they can be considered as discrete units of parental fitness. Thus, they are individually more negotiable (specifically, more subject to forfeiture) than in viviparous species, where partial litter reduction prior to birth is seldom possible (but see O'Gara, 1969; Wourms, 1981; Wourms *et al.*, 1981).

Because infanticide can serve the fitness interest of parents, birds exhibit a comparatively wide range of parental options. During the *laying phase*, nutrients can be allocated unevenly among the brood members (variable egg size), causing significant effects on the future competitive balance among the nestlings. During the *incubation phase*, parental choice of when to initiate embryonic development often establishes further intrabrood competitive asymmetries. Parents also have opportunities to reduce clutch size before hatching, if that is advantageous (e.g., perhaps the *Eudyptes* penguins). In the *nestling phase*, parents are free to abandon the whole brood, to jettison part of the brood (e.g., by leading the first-hatched chick away from its unhatched sib), or to let any competitive asymmetries run their course. Where intrabrood competition is heightened by siblicidal aggression, parents theoretically have the option of "fine-tuning" it by directly interrupting fights, by preferentially feeding certain young, and by physically separating the chicks. At present, it is not understood clearly what conditions are associated with parental deployment of these options or how potential counterstrategies by the chicks (parent-offspring conflict) affect the options used.

In keeping with the reasoning that avian infanticide is most frequently a means of maximizing parental fitness, it seems that altricial (nidicolous) species generally are more subject to infanticide than are precocial (nidifugous) species. In altricial birds, the residual investment needed to produce independent young is relatively high; consequently, parents benefit more by cutting their losses when prospects for success deteriorate. Intriguingly, there are intermediate species (seminidifugous, in which young are mobile but rely on adults for focd) that show many of the same infanticide patterns as altricial species (e.g., cranes, grebes, and oystercatchers). In colonies, seminidifugous chicks may have the recourse of striking out on their own and trying to survive by freelancing or brood-crashing (e.g., gulls, terns, and skuas).

The recurring theme of avian infanticide as primarily a parental strategy differs qualitatively from the picture for other taxa. For example, compared with primates, there is relatively little ornithological documentation for Hrdy's (1979) sexual selection hypothesis of infanticide. To date that argument has only been raised for cooperative/communal species (Vehrencamp, 1977; Bertram, 1979; Loflin, 1982; Koenig et al., 1983; Stacey and Edwards, 1983), one polyandrous species (Stephens, 1982), one polygynous species (Picman, 1977), and one monogamous species, the barn swallow studied by Crook and Shields (1983). In the communal/cooperative species, Hrdy's resource competition category seems a more appropriate explanation for infanticide. The incentives for sexually selected infanticide may be constrained by the overwhelming prevalence of monogamy in birds. Hrdy's exploitation hypothesis is substantially supported in the colonial bird literature, but it is not clear that cannibalism is a significant mortality factor in most noncolonial birds.

Hrdy's parental manipulation and resource competition hypotheses are not clearly separable in the complex brood-reduction systems of birds. Sibling aggression plays a central role in many species and must be viewed simultaneously as serving the interests of both the parents (which established the size discrepancies) and the dominant siblings (O'Conner, 1978). Although siblicide has been reported for other vertebrates (e.g., pronghorns: O'Gara, 1969; sharks: Wourms, 1981; Wourms et al., 1981), it apparently reaches its highest development in predatory birds (raptors, skuas, pelicans, boobies, cranes, herons, etc.). Many cases of colony infanticide may also be related to competition for parental care, but on an interbrood level. Connections between intrabrood dominance hierarchies, food stealing from neighbors, "adoptions," and kin recognition may be found in many colonial bird species.

Finally, a distinction is made between obligate and facultative siblicide to draw attention to the variability exhibited by birds. Obligate siblicide is best understood as a parental hedge against hatching failure in extremely small clutches: By producing an inexpensive extra egg, total reproductive failure is avoided. In addition to that "insurance" benefit, facultative siblicide allows a late decision on final brood size without rigidly sacrificing indirect fitness.

ACKNOWLEDGMENTS

Many colleagues helped in the preparation of this chapter by contributing references, different perspectives, and/or criticisms of an earlier draft. I thank Barbara Braun, Michael Erwin, Roger Evans, Patricia Gowaty, Glenn Hausfater, Sarah Blaffer Hrdy, George Hunt, Michael Hutchins, Ian Nisbet, David Parmelee, Ray Pierotti, Pamela Pietz, Bonnie Ploger, Jim Quinn, Lynn and John Ryder, P. L. Schwagmeyer, Linda and Bill Southern, and Martin Stephens. In addition, Barbara Braun, Rob Loflin, Richard Paul, Pamela Pietz, David Werschkul, and especially Ian Nisbet generously provided unpublished information from their field studies.

Financial aid for my own research and writing was provided by the National Science Foundation (BNS 79-06059 and DEB 82-01252) and a University of Oklahoma Summer Research Fellowship. I thank them and the Wenner-Gren Foundation for sponsoring both the conference and publication of this volume.

2 | Infanticide in carnivores

Craig Packer
Anne E. Pusey

INTRODUCTION

There are inherent difficulties in reviewing the sources of mortality in wild carnivores. Besides the fact that mortality has often been inflicted by fieldworkers themselves, most carnivores are nocturnal, solitary, and wary of human observers. Consequently, ecological studies often consist solely of analyses of feces, and ranging studies are often based on the movement patterns of radio collars worn by unseen animals. Furthermore, even intensive direct observations do not always provide good data on cub mortality because female carnivores keep their young hidden for the first few weeks or months of life. Most cub mortality, therefore, must be inferred from disappearance, and the causes of death remain unknown. Finally, attributing death to infanticide presents special difficulties in carnivores. An observation of a carnivore eating a conspecific is not conclusive evidence of intraspecific predation: carnivores are usually scavengers as well as predators.

However, because of their carnivorous habits and because most bear altricial young, carnivores are more likely to exhibit infanticide than any other mammalian order. Infanticide can occur in several contexts, and examples of the phenomenon are discussed according to the identity of the perpetrator:

1. Infanticide by males
2. Extragroup infanticide

3. Intragroup infanticide by females
4. Intralitter infanticide

Infants are defined as immatures dependent on their mothers and *infanticide* as any behavior that directly induces infant mortality. Thus, as well as the infliction of mortal wounds on infants, infanticide includes harassment of the mother until she can no longer care for her young and apparently deliberate abandonment of young. Cases of infanticide in captivity that appear to be the consequence of an artificial environment are excluded (e.g., during group formation: Rabb *et al.*, 1967; or during an experiment in extreme crowding: Rasa, 1979). Inferences drawn from observations on captive animals are explicitly noted.

INCIDENCE OF INFANTICIDE IN CARNIVORES

Infanticide by Males

Lions. The most extensive data on infanticide by males come from the studies of the African lion (*Panthera leo*) in the Serengeti and Ngorongoro Crater, Tanzania. Between 1966 and 1973, four cases were found of newly arrived males killing one or more cubs in prides that they had just taken over (Bertram, 1975a). Published details are available for only one of these cases. Two males resident in the Kamarishe pride entered the Seronera pride's range and killed three small cubs while their mother was elsewhere (Schaller, 1972). The two Kamarishe males then evicted the resident male of the Seronera pride and later returned to the corpses of the dead cubs. One male ate the viscera of one of the cubs. The Kamarishe pride then shifted its range for 5 months, and the Kamarishe males were not seen mating with females of the Seronera pride until 6 months after killing the cubs.

In 1980, we made a fifth observation of infanticide by male lions. We heard sounds of a fight, and arrived to find a male eating what appeared to be the remains of a small cub. The male then approached the mother, she snarled at him, and he plunged his head into the grass beside her. The mother and a second female both attacked him. When the male withdrew, the mother picked up from the same spot in the grass a dead, 2-month-old cub, still bleeding from bite wounds. A third cub, seen escaping into the bushes during the fight, disappeared within 2 weeks. The infanticidal male was one of a group of four males that were simultaneously resident in two adjacent prides. His three companions started to associate with this third pride 6 months before the infanticide, but the infanticidal male was not seen with the pride until 6 weeks after the mother had conceived and was not observed with the female again until the day he killed the cubs. During the period in which the mother had conceived, a second male group was also observed mating with these females. Several weeks after killing her cubs, the infanticidal male was observed consorting with the female.

Finally, in July 1982, S. J. Cairns (personal communication) observed a nomadic male kill a small cub that was following 100 m behind two females and two other cubs. The females were not the mothers of any of the cubs and retreated from the male. The male had taken the cub's body into thick vegetation in the morning and was again seen carrying a dead cub that night. It is not known whether he was still carrying the corpse of the first cub or had killed a second cub because none of these cubs was seen again. The male had not associated with the pride before, and there is evidence that a male take-over was in progress.

In a separate study at the northern end of the Serengeti ecosystem, Jackman and Scott (1982) observed one of three newly arrived males kill two small cubs. The new males became resident in the pride, and the infanticidal male might have fathered the female's next litter.

In addition to these seven observations, there is circumstantial evidence that infanticide occurs almost every time a new coalition of males takes over a pride. A _male take-over_ is defined as the complete replacement of one coalition of males by another. Bertram (1975a) showed a significant increase in mortality of cubs less than 2 years old in the first 4 months after a take-over. In our study, there was a significant increase in the mortality of cubs whose fathers were replaced by a new coalition of males before the cubs were 4 months old (Table I), and all the older cubs (belonging to seven females) were evicted within 3.5 months of the take-over (Packer and Pusey, 1983a,b). Small cubs almost always disappeared within the first 2 months after

Table I. Mortality of lion cubs[a]

	Fathers replaced in first 4 months (%)[b]	Fathers remain in pride for first 6 months (%)[c]
All cubs in litter die before 6 months of age	89.5	40.8
At least one cub in litter survives to 6 months of age	10.5	59.2

[a] Mortality of lion cubs when their fathers were replaced by a new coalition of males (based on 10 take-overs) is contrasted with mortality of cubs when their fathers remained in the pride. Because cubs are unable to survive on their own until at least 18 months of age (Bertram, 1975a), mortality also includes cubs that disappeared. Chi-square $= 13.20$, $p < 0.001$.

[b] $N = 19$ litters.

[c] $N = 98$ litters.

a take-over. The only take-over in which small cubs survived involved "new" males returning to their natal pride. One of the two females whose cubs survived was a full sibling of all three incoming males. In all other cases, the incoming males were not close relatives of the infants and had not been seen associating with the females before.

We also had evidence of infanticide during an attempted take-over. An alien group of males was seen well within the pride range of a group of two lactating females with six cubs. On the same day, one female and two cubs disappeared, and the surviving female was wounded. The missing cubs were 4 months old and were the offspring of the surviving female, so the disappearances do not indicate a splitting up of the pride. In another case, we observed a male coalition chase away the resident males of a neighboring pride, then return to where the three females were keeping their cubs. The mothers attacked the intruding males, all three females were wounded, but no cubs were lost, and the intruders returned to their own pride. Two years later, yet another male group intruded into the range of the same three females. Coincident with this intrusion, one lactating female disappeared, and the others were wounded (though again no cubs were lost). We, therefore, assume that the missing mothers in this and the first case died while defending their cubs.

Although there are a number of direct observations of males killing infants in these studies, many more cases are inferred from the coincident disappearance of cubs at the take-over. It is also possible, as Bertram (1975a) pointed out, that females sometimes abandon their cubs at a take-over or are kept from their cubs by the new males until the cubs die of stravation; but this is difficult to determine. From our observations of attempted take-overs, we suspect that females more often defend their cubs than abandon them. Bertram (1975a) also suggested that females might abort upon exposure to new males. However, we found a number of cases where pregnant females did not abort at a take-over (Table I includes nine females that were pregnant at a take-over and gave birth to live young) (see Packer and Pusey, 1983a,b).

In summary, infanticide appears to be a regular feature of male take-overs in lions in Northern Tanzania and as such appears to be a reproductive strategy by males (Hrdy, 1974; Bertram, 1975a). Females with surviving offspring remain anestrus until their cubs are about 1½ years old but resume mating activity within days or weeks of losing their cubs (lions in East Africa do not breed seasonally) (Schaller, 1972; Bertram, 1975a; Packer and Pusey, 1983a). Since the infanticidal males nearly always remain with the pride after the take-over, the females mate with the infanticidal males.

Females that lose small cubs at a take-over conceive again an average of 134 days after the loss, whereas females whose cubs survive show an average postpartum amenorrhea of 530 days and then conceive about 1 month later (Packer and Pusey, 1983a). Because there is considerable cub mortality even in the absence of male take-overs (Bertram, 1975a; and Table I), it is probably more appropriate to include females whose dependent cubs died under other circumstances than a take-over with females whose cubs survived to independence. Over all these females, average postpartum amenorrhea is 345 days, and conception occurs about 1 month later (Packer and Pusey, 1983a). Thus, by killing small cubs when they first take over a pride, males sire cubs about 8 months sooner on average than they would if they allowed the cubs of the previous males to survive. The average tenure length of males is only 2 years (Bygott et al., 1979) and males might sometimes fail to breed if they did not speed up the return to receptivity of the females of their new pride. Furthermore, cub mortality is higher if there are older cubs present in the pride, and by removing the cubs of the previous males, incoming males enhance the survival of their own cubs (Bertram, 1975a).

In other parts of East Africa, there is only anecdotal evidence of infanticide by incoming males (Adamson, 1968; Cullen, 1969). However, male take-overs occur at a much lower frequency in the smaller parks because they contain only small isolated lion populations, and migrating males suffer high mortality outside protected areas (Van Orsdol, 1981).

Other species. In all other carnivore species, evidence of infanticide by males is largely anecdotal. Besides listing examples of infanticide, information is also included on the relevant reproductive parameters of females that determine whether or not males would gain a reproductive advantage from killing young.

Schaller (1967) cited two cases reported by hunters of male tigers (*Panthera tigris*) apparently killing cubs. There are also a number of suspected cases of infanticide from a detailed study of tigers (J. L. D. Smith, in preparation). Tigers are solitary, and the range of each territorial male overlaps those of several females (Sunquist, 1981). A territorial male died whose range included seven females. Three 6- to 13-month-old male cubs belonging to three females were found dead shortly after new males had replaced the territorial male (Smith, in preparation). In three other cases, litters disappeared coincident with male replacements. The new males could not have been the fathers of the cubs, and several were subsequently resident in the area long enough to have fathered the females' next litters. Tigers are not seasonal breeders, and the interbirth interval is about 2 years (Sankhala, 1967). Thus, a male would probably father cubs more quickly if he were to kill the small cubs in his new territory.

In pumas (*Puma concolor*), there are three reports of males killing cubs. The only details available on the first are that two cubs of a single litter were killed (Hornocker, 1970). In the second, on two occasions a hunter found cubs that had been "apparently killed by mature males" but were uneaten (Robinette *et al.*, 1961). In the third, a male killed and ate the cubs of a female that had been shot by a hunter (Young, 1927). In the last case, the infanticidal male was assumed by the author to have been the father of the cubs, because after the shooting his range included the site of the shot female's den. However, there was no information on associations between the male and the female prior to the shooting.

Pumas tend to breed seasonally (Robinette *et al.*, 1961; Hemker, 1982), and the interbirth interval is usually about 2 years (Robinette *et al.*, 1961; Hornocker, 1970). The loss of small cubs is likely, therefore, to cause the females to resume breeding 1 year earlier than if their cubs survived. However, there are no data on the subsequent reproductive activity of infanticidal males in pumas or is it known if the infanticidal males were unrelated to the cubs they killed.

In cheetah (*Acinonyx jubatus*), infanticide by males appears to be rare, although there is one case in Masai Mara, Kenya where a male was suspected of killing a female's 1-week-old cubs (Burney, 1980). In 1978, a male was seen fighting with a mother of newborn cubs near where the cubs were hidden. The male appeared to be searching for the cubs, but the cubs survived the incident. In 1979, a second male was seen fighting with the same female near the lair of a new set of cubs on the day that two of the cubs disappeared. Since the male had previously associated with the female, he might have been the father of the second litter (D. and L. Burney: personal communication).

In the adjacent Serengeti, females with cubs of several months of age have been seen to be "pinned down" temporarily by coalitions of males that are probably not related to the cubs, but little overt aggression is directed at the cubs, and the behavior of the males is not believed to cause cub mortality (T. M. Caro, personal communication). No infanticide has been observed in nearly 6 years of intensive study of cheetah in the Serengeti (G. W. Frame and T. M. Caro, personal communication).

In the Serengeti, cheetah do not breed seasonally and have an interbirth interval of about 18 months (Frame, 1980; G. W. Frame, personal communication). The ranges of females are much larger than those of males (Frame, 1980), and thus females must frequently encounter males that are not the father of their cubs. Because the loss of small cubs would speed up the reproduction of females, the apparent rarity of infanticide by male cheetah is an anomaly.

Infanticide by males is believed to be common in brown bears (*Ursus arctos*). Troyer and Hensel (1962) reported two cases of male brown bears killing and eating cubs and a third case of a male having eaten a cub. They suggested that males frequently kill small cubs during the mating season. Perry (1966) reported two cases in polar bears (*Ursus maritimus*) where males killed but did not eat cubs. However, in both cases the cubs' mothers had recently been shot by hunters. The cubs were killed only a short time after their mothers' deaths by males that had not been present at the shootings. Jonkel (1970) reported one case where a male was found eating a freshly killed female and her two cubs. He inferred from signs of fighting that the male had killed them. Because females and cubs can run much faster than males, Stirling (1974) stated that it is "unlikely that intraspecific predation occurs at more than an incidental level" in polar bears. But Stirling also reported that "cubs were extremely nervous in meetings with any unrelated bear."

Both species of bears breed seasonally but have a 2-year interbirth interval (Ewer, 1973), thus infanticide would have a similar effect on the reproduction of females as in pumas. However, as in pumas nothing is known of the relationships between the infanticidal males and the females and her cubs.

Russell (1981) observed one case of infanticide by an alien male in coatis (*Nasua narica*) and presented evidence that such killings are common, and that they were made by males that were not close relatives of the infants. However, infanticide does not appear to be a male reproductive strategy in this species. Since coatis only breed seasonally and females apparently breed each year, infanticide does not speed up the reproduction of the females. Also, the infanticidal male does not remain to breed with the females. Russell suggested that males utilize conspecific young as prey during times of food shortage (also see Sherman, 1981).

Although we know of no other carnivore species where infanticide by incoming males has been recorded, there are few other studies where immigration of males has been observed. In dwarf mongooses (*Helogale parvula*), breeding is seasonal and annual, and most take-overs by males occur at the mating season when the preceding year's young are no longer so vulnerable to predation (J. P. Rood: personal communication).

Although infanticide by males has not been observed in spotted hyenas (*Crocuta crocuta*), Kruuk (1972) made several comments that merit attention. A spotted hyena den is largely excavated and maintained by the cubs, with the result that they are inaccessible to adults. Kruuk attributed both this and the fact that females are larger than males to the danger that males pose to cubs. Females are dominant to males as a result of their greater size, and the nature of the den results in the cubs being protected from males during their mothers' absence. Little is known of the social dynamics of a clan, but males do often move into the ranges of other clans (Kruuk, 1972; van Lawick and van Lawick-Goodall, 1971) and are therefore likely to contact dens where they are unrelated to the cubs. Because female spotted hyenas show a long interbirth interval and do not breed seasonally (Kruuk, 1972), infanticide would be likely to cause them to resume breeding more quickly.

Extragroup Infanticide

There are several examples of individuals of one breeding group killing the young of another group. Camenzind (1978) had evidence of two cases where invading packs of coyotes (*Canis latrans*) killed the pups of neighboring packs. P. Moehlman (personal communication) came upon an invading family of golden jackals (*Canis aureus*) feeding on the pups of the resident family. However, the jackal pups might have died of other causes prior to being found by the invading pair. Frame and Frame (1981) observed an invading pack of wild dogs (*Lycaon pictus*) chase and scatter a resident pack, and one 15-week-old pup of the resident pack was never seen again. However, the missing pup might have disappeared because it was unable to relocate the rest of its family.

Schaller (1972) observed a nomadic female lion stalking the 7- month-old cub of another female, and the next morning the nomad was found eating the freshly killed cub. Schaller also saw a female kill two small cubs of another pride. J. D. Bygott and J. P. Hanby (personal communication) made two similar observations. First, a female from one pride entered the hiding place of the small cubs of an adjacent pride, and the cubs were never seen again. Second, one 9-month-old cub and one 15-month-old cub were killed in an interpride encounter that apparently involved no males.

In many of these cases, the young died when their parents were not in the immediate vicinity. Camenzind (1978) saw coyote packs successfully defend dens against invaders on five occasions.

Intragroup Infanticide by Females

Infanticide by the mother. In a few species, there are observations of deliberate abandonment of healthy young by their mothers (see Carlisle, 1982, for review). In lions, there is a striking tendency for females to abandon their litters when only one cub remains. Rudnai (1973) reported three cases of wild females abandoning healthy, single surviving cubs of less than 3 months of age, three cases by George Adamson's free-ranging females, and five cases by captive females. In the Serengeti, we twice observed mothers abandoning their single cubs of only a few weeks of age. Each mother carried her cub into an open area. In both cases, the cub was too small to move to cover and disappeared on the same day. Both cubs appeared to be in excellent health and both were males. Tait (1980) cited two cases of female grizzly bears (*Ursus horribilis arctos*) abandoning single cubs. Average litter size in lions and grizzly bears is between two and three, and both Rudnai and Tait calculated that females in these species would increase their lifetime reproductive success by abandoning single cubs and investing exclusively in larger litters.

Schaller (1972) observed a female lion abandon one of three healthy cubs but believed that she had not done so intentionally. We observed a female lion abandon two of her three starving cubs during a period of extreme prey scarcity: the mother and two of her pridemates were leading their cubs to a new location, and when her two weakest offspring fell behind, she called to them but did not return for them.

Infanticide by females other than the mother. A common feature of carnivore social structure is the presence of only one breeding female within a group. This is typical of canids (Kleiman and Eisenberg, 1973) and is also found in dwarf mongooses (Rood, 1980) and European badgers (*Meles meles*) (Kruuk, 1978).

In species where there is only one breeding female but more than one adult female present in the group, there is sometimes evidence of infanticide by the breeding female of the offspring of subordinate females. The dominant female was observed to kill a subordinate female's pups in wild dogs (van Lawick, 1974) and was suspected of having done so in captive wolves (*Canis lupus*) (Altmann, 1974). In captive red foxes (*Vulpes vulpes*), harassment of a subordinate female by the dominant female resulted in the death of the subordinate's cubs (Macdonald, 1979). In wild dogs, there are other examples of subordinate females giving birth, but the pups almost never survive (Frame et al., 1979). In dwarf mongooses, subordinate females regularly mate but fail to become pregnant, and if they do conceive, their litters regularly disappear (Rood, 1980). Although there is no direct evidence of infanticide, Rood suggested that the cubs might be killed by the dominant female.

Brown hyenas (*Hyaena brunnea*) show an interesting parallel to these species. Clans of brown hyenas contain more than one breeding female and share communal dens (Owens and Owens, 1979), but the births within the group are so widely spaced that only one female in the clan has small cubs at a time (D. D. Owens: personal communication; also see Mills, 1978). In the only observation of two females giving birth synchronously, the dominant of the two females harassed the subordinate to an unusual extent, and within a few days the subordinate had lost her cubs (D. D. Owens, in preparation).

An important consequence of the behavior of the dominant female in all these cases is that the subordinate female ended up helping to rear and (except in the wolves) even to suckle the offspring of the dominant female. It is likely that this form of infanticide represents an adaptive strategy by the dominant female: the infanticidal female both enforces her position as the only breeding female within the group and also ensures that her offspring receive additional care (also see Emlen, 1982; Macdonald and Moehlman, 1982). If the subordinate female were able to breed, her offspring would be in competition with the young of the dominant female, and the subordinate female would be expected to care for her own young rather than act as a helper for the dominant female. In all cases except the brown hyenas (where kinship was unknown), the "exploited" subordinate female was a close relative of the breeding female and, consequently, so were the victims of the infanticide.

There is one possible case of a female helper killing her younger siblings in golden jackals (van Lawick and van Lawick-Goodall, 1971). A young female was found eating a small pup at her mother's den, but the pups had been in poor health on the previous day. Although they mention that the helper might have killed it, the authors suspected that the pup had already died before the helper had found it. Detailed studies of the effects of helpers on pup survival in silverback jackals (*Canis mesomelas*) (Moehlman, 1979) and golden jackals (Moehlman, 1982) suggest that helpers usually increase pup survival rather than act as a source of mortality.

Intralitter Infanticide

Although siblicide is a common phenomenon in newly hatched birds (see Mock, Chapter 1, this volume), evidence in carnivores is extremely difficult to collect because most cubs are kept in dens and most observers are unwilling to destroy or disturb a den in order to observe them. However, Macpherson (1969) found a den of arctic foxes (*Alopex lagopus*) in which six of nine pups had been killed by a bite at the base of the skull. After taking two of the survivors into captivity, one killed the other in a fight over food, inflicting a wound similar to those found in the six dead pups at the den. Macpherson suggested that siblings often kill each other during times of food shortage.

Relevant to this section is a bizarre case in spotted hyenas in which two three-quarters-grown cubs were each found strangling 2-month-old cubs during the excavation of a den by Watson (1965). The two sets of cubs had been sharing the den and entered it on this occasion to avoid the scientists. The killings were presumably elicited by the panic of the young in response to the disturbance of the excavation: young spotted hyenas commonly survive the experience of sharing a den with older cubs (Kruuk, 1972).

DISCUSSION

It is almost impossible to estimate accurately how commonly infanticide occurs in carnivores. Evidence in most species is only anecdotal but, as pointed out at the beginning of this chapter, it is extremely difficult to collect good data on most species of carnivores. It is worth stressing that causes of cub mortality in carnivores almost always have to be inferred. For example, Schaller (1972) estimated that the most frequent cause of death in lion cubs was starvation, and although he provided compelling evidence in support of this, he did not mention ever having observed the moment of death in a starving cub. We have also seen many cubs that were obviously starving but have observed the death of only one starving cub.

Most carnivores will eat almost any small mammal that they can easily capture and kill, including a conspecific. In several species, adults have even been known to kill and eat large subadult and adult conspecifics (e.g., pumas: Lesowski, 1963; lynx (*Lynx canadensis*): Elsey, 1954; polar bears: Jonkel, 1970; and hyenas: Kruuk, 1972).

Because of the difficulties, therefore, in determining whether a specific case of infanticide constitutes an example of "spite," intraspecific competition, or simply of predation, we are reluctant to discuss all possible ways in which infanticide may be of adaptive significance in carnivores (instead, see Hrdy, 1979; Sherman, 1981). Here we concentrate on the following adaptive interpretations:

1. Infanticide is a female reproductive strategy by which a dominant female ensures that she is the only female in the group to breed at that time and also that her offspring receive care from the subordinate female. Furthermore, the dominant female's offspring are consequently not subject to competition for resources from the offspring of the subordinate (Hrdy, 1979). There are only a few examples of this behavior in any one species, but evidence comes from several species: wild dogs, red foxes, wolves, dwarf mongooses, and brown hyenas.

2. Infanticide is a reproductive strategy whereby males terminate the female's investment in the offspring of other males and stimulate a rapid resumption of receptivity (Hrdy, 1974; Bertram, 1975a). Although there are numerous examples of males killing infants, the existence of infanticide as a male reproductive strategy can only be confirmed in lions and possibly in tigers.

Most carnivores are solitary (Ewer, 1973), and even most "social" carnivores live in groups composed of only one breeding female. Only a few species (lions, some mongooses, and spotted hyenas) typically form social groups where more than one female breeds simultaneously.

Female carnivores, therefore, may be viewed as typically intolerant of the proximity of other breeding females. However, the existence of even a few species that form groups containing multiple breeding females and the more common existence of groups containing non-breeding female "helpers" as well as the single breeding female suggest that shifts in ecological variables (Macdonald, 1979; Waser, 1981) or hunting styles (Kleiman and Eisenberg, 1973; Kruuk, 1975) can lead to a change in social structure.

Therefore, there are likely to be conditions that result in conflict between females of the same group over whether the subordinate female also breeds or only helps rear the young of the dominant female, and infanticide by dominant females may be a manifestation of such conflict. (Note that the females are usually close relatives in these cases.) Ordinarily, the reproduction of the subordinate is suppressed by the behavior of the dominant (e.g., wolves: Zimen, 1976; red foxes: Macdonald, 1978; and dwarf mongooses: Rood, 1980), and infanticide in these species is an extension of this suppression (see Kleiman, 1980; McClintock, 1983).

The wide dispersion of females, together with strict seasonal and annual breeding, probably prevent infanticide as a male reproductive strategy from being ubiquitous in carnivores. Most monogamous species appear to be bonded for life, so that male tenure length is typically long, and male–male competition is not so severe as it is in highly polygynous species. Males in these species invest their reproductive effort in helping to rear offspring rather than in maximizing their number of mating partners (Trivers, 1972).

Because of the enormous difficulties of studying nocturnal and solitary species, relevant data on them are not available in proportion to the frequency of this type of social organization across species of carnivores. Like tigers, most solitary species are polygynous: males have territories that overlap those of several females (Ewer, 1973). Thus, infanticide as a male reproductive strategy may be confirmed eventually in many solitary carnivore species where the female's reproduction is accelerated by the death of her young.

ACKNOWLEDGMENTS

We would like to thank Glenn Hausfater and Sarah Blaffer Hrdy for inviting us to the conference and providing the motivation for writing this chapter. We are very grateful to D. and L. Burney, J. D. Bygott, S. J. Cairns, T. M. Caro, G. W. and L. H. Frame, J. P. Hanby, P. Moehlman, D. D. Owens, J. P. Rood, and J. L. D. Smith for valuable information. S. A. Altmann, T. M. Caro, C. Crockett, G. W. Frame, and J. P. Rood made many useful comments on the manuscript. We thank the Government of Tanzania for permission to conduct research and the Serengeti Wildlife Research Institute for facilities.

Field work has been supported by grants from the H. F. Guggenheim Foundation, the National Geographic Society, the Royal Society of Great Britain (A.E.P.), National Institute of Mental Health grant 15181 (C.P.), and the Eppley Foundation (A.E.P.).

3 Cannibalism of early life stages in fishes

Wallace J. Dominey
Lawrence S. Blumer

INTRODUCTION

Intraspecific predation or cannibalism is a common phenomenon among both invertebrates (Fox, 1975a; Polis, 1981) and vertebrates (Chapters 2 and 4, this volume). Among fishes, intraspecific predation and cannibalism of eggs (embryos), larvae, and juveniles are very common in nature and have been frequently reported, albeit in a very scattered literature. In this chapter, a survey of infanticide and cannibalism of early life stages in fishes is provided and the important behavioral consequences of these phenomena are described.

We consider infanticide to have occurred when an individual kills a conspecific egg (embryo), larva, or juvenile. In fishes, all infanticide is also cannibalism, because killing always involves consumption. The early life stages of fishes are not commonly termed *infants*. Thus, in this chapter, *cannibalism* refers to the killing and consumption of early life stages of conspecifics. This chapter also refers to *filial cannibalism*, cases in which the killer is the parent of the victim; *heterocannibalism*, cases in which the cannibal is not related to the victim (DeMartini, 1976; Rohwer, 1978); and *sibling cannibalism*, cases of fratricide which result in cannibalism. These latter terms permit us to focus on the important difference (in terms of inclusive fitness [Hamilton, 1964a,b]) between killing genetically unrelated versus related individuals.

Hrdy (1979) and Sherman (1981) proposed different but complementary classification schemes for infanticide. Sherman (1981) focused on the effects of infanticide on the reproductive success of the parents whose offspring were killed. The lifetime reproductive success of parents may either increase or decrease as a result of infanticide, and the behavior of parents and killers may differ accordingly.

In contrast, Hrdy (1979) categorized infanticide on the basis of potential benefits to the killer. An individual could gain from infanticide in the following contexts: (1) exploitation: the killer directly benefits (as by consumption); (2) resource competition: the killer gains access to resources; (3) parental manipulation: the killer ends parental care to improve the survivorship of itself or other offspring; and (4) sexual selection: the killer gains in competition among members of its own sex for the reproductive investment of members of the other sex. Although these categories are not mutually exclusive, they do provide a framework for examining the diversity of infanticide and intraspecific predation on early life stages observed in nature.

Our analysis of cannibalism begins with a brief discussion of fish reproductive biology and then focuses on reproductive features that favor cannibalism in this group. A selective review of the literature on cannibalism follows, including detailed information on species in five families in which filial cannibalism is known or suspected. Finally, the effect of cannibalism on demography and on parental care and reproductive patterns is considered, as is the adaptive significance of cannibalism.

REPRODUCTIVE BIOLOGY OF FISHES

Fishes are the most diverse of all vertebrates. Among four extant classes, jawless fishes (two classes in the Agnatha), cartilaginous fishes (Chondrichthyes), and bony fishes (Osteichthyes), there are approximately 450 families (Nelson, 1976) accounting for about 50% (18,818) of all living species of vertebrates. Reproductive modes in fishes are extremely diverse and include such oddities as parthenogenesis, gynogenesis, hermaphroditism, and parasitic dwarf males (Breder and Rosen, 1966).

The prevalence of external fertilization is one of the primary differences between fishes and terrestrial vertebrates. Although both internal and external fertilization occur in fishes, fertilization is external in most families of the phylogenetically diverse bony fishes (402 of 424). Eggs (or embryos) that are released by a female may be either demersal (density greater than water) or pelagic (density less than water). Demersal eggs, most common in freshwater groups, are frequently attached to objects on the substrate, such as rocks or vegetation (Balon, 1975a).

Pelagic eggs are most common in marine fishes, due to the stability and homogeneity of the marine environment (Baylis, 1981), and in reef-dwelling marine fishes, due to the necessity of dispersal (Barlow, 1981).

Among fishes with external fertilization and demersal eggs, success in reproduction depends on the choice and maintenance of oviposition sites (Balon, 1975a; Loiselle and Barlow, 1978). In both marine and freshwater fishes with demersal eggs, territoriality (e.g., Pomacentridae: Ebersole, 1977; Hexagrammidae: DeMartini, 1976; Salmonidae: Needham, 1961; Cottidae: Downhower and Brown, 1980) or varying degrees of colonialism (Centrarchidae: Breder, 1936; Cichlidae: Breder and Rosen, 1966) occur at oviposition sites. Male territoriality and sequential fertilization of the eggs of several mates are the likely antecedants of male parental care in fishes (Barlow, 1964; Loiselle, 1978; review in Blumer, 1979).

Parental care characterizes only 21% (89 families) of the approximately 424 families of bony fishes (Blumer, 1982a). In most terrestrial vertebrates, females alone provide care or are the principal caregivers, with the male furnishing supplemental aid (Lack, 1968; Daly and Wilson, 1978). In contrast, among bony fishes, males are commonly the principal caregivers (Baylis, 1981; Blumer, 1979; Perrone and Zaret, 1979; Ridley, 1978). In many groups, males alone attend offspring while females leave the oviposition site immediately after egg deposition (spawning). Among most caregiving bony fishes, eggs are demersal and deposited in a discrete mass on substrate materials (Breder and Rosen, 1966). In the cartilaginous fishes, species in 18 of the 24 families have internal gestation, a form of parental care; other forms of care are not well substantiated (reviewed by Wourms, 1977). Parental care in the jawless fishes is limited to nest construction by either the male or female (reviewed by Keenleyside, 1979).

In addition to the predominance of external fertilization, fishes differ from terrestrial vertebrates in both fecundity and relative offspring size. Fishes can produce clutches of up to hundreds of thousands. In general, fishes produce several orders of magnitude more zygotes than do birds, mammals, or reptiles (Altman and Dittmer, 1972). This high fecundity leads necessarily to the production of small offspring. In most terrestrial vertebrates, offspring are produced at a size that in comparison to adults is at most one or two orders of magnitude smaller; birds and reptiles release large eggs, and placental mammals give birth to large well-developed young. In contrast, the eggs of bony fishes are typically four to six orders of magnitude smaller than adults (Cushing, 1974; Loiselle and Barlow, 1978). Due to these differences in size, the early life stages of fish may feed on different prey items and indeed may occupy different ecological niches from adults (Keast, 1978; Helfman, 1978).

Reproductive Features Promoting Cannibalism

The extreme fecundity of fishes, compared with other vertebrates, is a major factor promoting cannibalism. The small offspring that result from high fecundity are often similar to the normal prey items taken by adults and juveniles. In addition, offspring are often found in the same habitats as adults at least during some of their developmental stages. We suspect that heterocannibalism occurs in virtually all fishes under natural conditions; hence, the absence rather than presence of cannibalism is the exceptional case.

A second feature promoting cannibalism in fishes is external fertilization. External fertilization results in the deposition of undeveloped, usually defenseless zygotes in a potentially hostile environment. In addition, many fishes with external fertilization produce clumps of demersal eggs, and in some species large numbers of eggs are concentrated in one area. The presence of many breeding and nonbreeding adults and juveniles at these breeding sites, coupled with the high caloric value of eggs and their desirability as prey, also favor cannibalism.

Among fishes, paternal care promotes a special type of cannibalism, filial cannibalism, in which parents consume their offspring. Filial cannibalism is promoted by paternal care because males invest little in gametes and because by cannibalizing some offspring, males may be able to remain longer at breeding sites.

Guardian males are provided with an energy-rich resource (eggs) at a time when they may have invested little in the offspring and when they are about to incur the energetic costs associated with giving care. In contrast, females make an enormous energy investment in eggs (Baylis, 1981). As Dawkins and Carlisle (1976) correctly pointed out, the amount of past reproductive investment does not necessarily predict the tendency for future investment. However, when past investment is correlated with the amount of future investment necessary to replace the current offspring, prior investment can be predictive. Usually past investment will be correlated with the amount of future investment needed to replace the current offspring (though not always, see Dawkins and Brockmann, 1980). In fishes, we believe that the high replacement cost of gametes should predispose females not to cannibalize their young in cases where they give care. Some adjustment of investment in offspring may occur as filial cannibalism, but egg resorption prior to oviposition should be a more energetically efficient means of terminating investment (DeMartini, 1976). In species in which females are normally prevented access to embryos by males, females may not show any inhibition of cannibalism.

In contrast to females, males have probably not made as large a prior investment in gametes. Whatever other investments males may make (such as in the acquisition of nest sites, construction of nests, or acquisition of mates) may increase their total parental investment, but such investment need not be lost following cannibalism of offspring. In fact, partial or even complete cannibalism of current offspring may actually help preserve a male's prior investment by enabling the male to retain ownership of his current nest site. Cannibalizing offspring is thus much less likely to be advantageous for females, which have made the bulk of their investment in gamete production, than for males.

In addition to the relatively small gametic investment made by males, the sequential acceptance of mates by caregiving males also promotes filial cannibalism. In many species of caregiving fishes, it is advantageous for males to remain for long periods of time on territories that are not primarily feeding sites (Loiselle and Barlow, 1978). By offsetting the considerable energetic costs associated with fasting and caregiving that territorial males often incur (Pedersen, 1979), filial cannibalism may increase not only the time males remain on territories but also their chances of attracting additional mates (DeMartini, 1976; Rohwer, 1978).

THE OCCURRENCE OF CANNIBALISM IN FISHES

In the sections that follow, we focus on field studies in which conspecific killing of eggs (embryos), larvae, or juveniles is reported. This review is not exhaustive, but its purpose is to demonstrate the diversity of groups in which cannibalism occurs and to describe the ecological and behavioral background for the phenomenon. Cannibalism of early life stages occurs in fishes from at least 30 families from four classes (Table I). These species include both marine and freshwater groups, fishes with internal and external fertilization, and fishes with demersal and pelagic eggs. Cannibalism occurs in a wide variety of habitats and in species with and without parental care.

Heterocannibalism

Heterocannibalism is an important source of early offspring mortality in natural populations of yellow perch (Alm, 1952), walleyes (Chevalier, 1973), orange chromide cichlids (Ward and Samarakoon, 1981), and three-spined sticklebacks (Kynard, 1978). Cannibalism of young by adults in nature occurs regularly in pike (19% of 203 stomachs had evidence of cannibalism; Hunt and Carbine, 1951), cavefishes (83% of 146 stomachs contained conspecifics; Hill, 1969), three-spined sticklebacks (51.7% of 760 stomachs contained conspecific eggs; Semler, 1971), painted greenlings (more than 50% of 247 stomachs contained conspecific eggs; DeMartini, 1976), and yellow bass (75% of 142 stomachs

Table I. The occurrence of cannibalism in fishes[a]

Family and species	Type of cannibalism	Victim	References
(Agnatha) Cephalaspidomorphi			
Petromyzonidae (lampreys)			
Lampetra minima	H?	J, A	Kan and Bond, 1981
Petromyzon marinus	H?	J	Davis, 1967
Chondrichthyes			
Odontaspididae (sand sharks)	S	E, L	Wourms, 1977
Odontaspis tauris	S	E, L	Springer, 1948
Lamnidae (mackerel sharks)	S	E, L	Wourms, 1977
Alopias superciliosus	S	E	Gruber and Campagno, 1981
Sphyrnidae (hammerhead sharks)	H	J, A	Coles, 1919
(Holocephali)			
Delphyodontos dacriformes	S?	E, L	Lund, 1980
Osteichthyes			
Clupeidae (sardines)			
Sardinops caerulea	H	E, L	Radovich, 1962
Engraulidae (anchovy)			
Engraulis mordax	H	E, L	Hunter and Kimbrell, 1980b
Esocidae (pike)			
Esox lucius	H	J	Frost, 1954; Hunt and Carbine, 1951; Kipling and Frost, 1970*; Lagler, 1956; Mann, 1982
Salmonidae (salmon and trout)			
Salmo gairdnerii	H	E	Greeley, 1932; Metzelaar, 1929
Salvelinus fontinalis	H	E	Greeley, 1932; White, 1930
Salvelinus namaycush	H	E	Rawson and Elsey, 1950; Royce, 1951
Salvelinus alpinus	H	J, A	Skreslet, 1973
Osmeridae (smelt)			
Osmerus eperlanus	H	J	Nikolsky, 1963; Scott and Crossman, 1973
Characidae (characins)			
Astyanax mexicanus	F, S	E, J	Breder, 1943*
Astyanax ruberrimus	H	A	Breder, 1943

48

Taxon			Reference
Ictaluridae [North American catfishes]			
Ictalurus nebulosus	H	E	Blumer, 1982b
	F	E	Fowler, 1917*
	F	J	Smith and Harron, 1904*
Ictalurus punctatus	F	E	Brown, 1942*; Nelson, 1957*
Noturus exilis	F?	E	Mayden and Burr, 1981
Clariidae (air-breathing catfishes)			
Clarias mossambicus	H, S?	J	Christensen, 1981*
Amblyopsidae (cavefishes)			
Amblyopsis rosae	H	J	Poulson, 1963
Amblyopsis spelaea	H	J	Poulson, 1963
Chologaster agassizi	H	J	Hill, 1969
Gadidae (cod and haddock)			
Gadus morhua	H	J	Nikolsky, 1963; Patriquin, 1967
Eleginus navaga	H	J	Nikolsky, 1963
Poeciliidae (live-bearers)	S?	E	Turner, 1947
Lebistes reticulatus	F	J	Breder and Coates, 1932*
			Rose, 1959*
Poeciliopsis monacha	F, H	J	Thibault, 1974
Gasterosteidae (sticklebacks)			
Gasterosteus aculeatus	H, F?	E	Assem, 1967*
	H, F?	E, L	Hynes, 1950; Kynard, 1978
	H	E, L	Li and Owings, 1978*; Semler, 1971;
			Wootton, 1971
Pygosteus pungitius	H	E, L	Hynes, 1950
Hexagrammidae (greenlings)			
Hexagrammos decagrammus	H	E	DeMartini, 1976
Oxylebius pictus	F?, H	E	DeMartini, 1976
Ophiodon elongatus	H	E	Hart, 1973
	F?, H	E	Jewell, 1968

continued

49

Table I. (*Continued*)

Family and species	Type of cannibalism	Victim	References
Cottidae (sculpins)			
Cottus bairdi	H	E, J	Bailey, 1952; Koster, 1936
	H	A	Downhower and Brown, 1980
	H	E	Staples, 1980
	H	J	Zarbock, 1951
Artedius fenestralis	H	E	DeMartini, 1976
Enophrys bison	H	E	DeMartini, 1976
Scorpaenichthys marmoratus	H	E	DeMartini, 1976
Percichthyidae (basses)			
Morone mississippiensis	H	J	Bulkley, 1970
Morone saxatilis	H	L, J	Rhodes and Merriner, 1973[*]
Serranidae (sea basses)			
Serranus subligarius	H	J?	Hastings and Bortone, 1980
Centrarchidae (sunfishes)			
Arcoplites interruptus	H	J	Imler, Weber and Fyock, 1975
Micropterus dolomieui	H	J	Clady, 1974
Micropterus salmoides	H	J	Clady, 1974; Cooper, 1936[*];
			DeAngelis, Cox, and Coutant, 1980[*]
Lepomis macrochirus	F, H	E, L	Dominey, 1981a, b
Lepomis megalotis	H, F?	E	Keenleyside, 1972
Percidae (perch and darters)			
Etheostoma barbouri	H	E, L	Flynn and Hoyt, 1979
Etheostoma olmstedi	H	E, L	Constanz, 1979[*]
Perca fluviatilis	H	J	Alm, 1952; Holcik, 1977; McCormack, 1965, 1970;
			Nikolsky, 1963; Smyly, 1952
Perca flavescens	H	J	Clady, 1974; Tarby, 1974
Stizostedion canadense	H	J	Swenson and Smith, 1976
Stizostedion lucioperca	H	J	Popova and Sytina, 1977
Stizostedion vitreum	S?, H	L, J	Chevalier, 1973; Forney, 1974, 1976
			Cuff, 1977[*], 1980[*]

50

Sparidae (porgies)			
Acanthopagrus cuvieri	H	L	Hussain, Akatsu and El-Zahr, 1981*
Cichlidae (cichlids)			
Cichla ocellaris	H	J	Zaret, 1977
Cichlasoma citrinellum	H	J	Barlow, 1976; McKaye and Barlow, 1976b
Etroplus maculatus	H	E	Ward and Samarakoon, 1981
Herotilapia multispinosa	F	E, J	Keenleyside, 1978*
Tilapia galilaea	F?	E	Liebman, 1933
Tilapia grahami	H	L, J	Coe, 1966
Tilapia leucosticta	F?	E, L	Welcomme, 1967
Tilapia nilotica	F?	E, J	Liebman, 1933
Blenniidae (combtooth blennies)			
Blennius incognitus	H	E	Goldschmid and Kotrschal, 1980
Blennius pholis	F, H	E	Qasim, 1956*, 1957
Eleotridae (sleepers)			
Gobiomorus dormitor	H	J	McKaye, Weiland and Lim, 1979
Gobiidae (gobies)			
Glossogobius giuris	H	J	Shrivastava and Desai, 1979
Scombridae (tuna and mackerel)			
Scomber japonicus	S	L	Hunter and Kimbrell, 1980a*
Anabantidae (climbing gouramies)			
Anabas testudineus	S	L, J	Banerji and Prasad, 1974*
Belontiidae (gouramies)			
Trichogaster trichopterus	F?, H	E	Chang and Liley, 1974*
	H	E	Wright, 1976; Miller, 1964*

[a] The families and species exhibiting cannibalism are listed with the type (S = sibling cannibalism; F = filial cannibalism; H = heterocannibalism), the victims (E = eggs or embryos; L = larvae; J = juveniles; A = adults), and references. A question mark indicates that a designation is uncertain and an asterisk indicates an aquarium or culture pond study. Families are listed in the phylogenetic sequence presented in Nelson (1976). The terminology for the developmental stages of victims follows that presented by Balon (1975b).

contained conspecific young; Bulkley, 1970). As shown by these few examples, cannibalism is neither rare nor is it explicable as an artifact of aquarium studies.

Although cannibalism is extremely common in fishes, at least two piscivorous species show inhibition of cannibalism: a cichlid and a leaf fish. *Cichla ocellaris* has a conspicuous caudal ocellus that was found to inhibit cannibalism (Zaret, 1977). The ocellus develops just after juveniles leave the protection of their parents and is lost in larger individuals. During the intervening time when the fish are vulnerable to intraspecific predation, the ocellus effectively inhibits cannibalism. Of 152 stomachs containing identifiable prey fishes, none contained conspecifics. The adults of the highly piscivorous leaf fish, *Polycentrus schomburgkii,* were never seen (in aquariums) to eat free-swimming young. Rather the adults would approach the young as if about to feed and then pause, often biting down repeatedly as if to engulf prey without actually attacking (Barlow, 1967).

Various observations have been reported concerning the relationship between food availability and cannibalism. Aquarium experiments with pike showed that cannibalism among juveniles occurred more frequently when alternate foods were unavailable (Kipling and Frost, 1970). Similar observations have been made for other species (Breder, 1943; Forney, 1974; Smyly, 1952). In contrast, some researchers have suggested that food availability does not affect cannibalism (Rose, 1959; Thibault, 1974). These discrepant findings parallel data on avian siblicide in relation to food availability (Mock, Chapter 1, this volume).

In *Poeciliopsis* (live-bearers), cannibalism has been suggested to have a "genetic" basis (Thibault, 1974). Laboratory crosses and backcrosses between a cannibalistic species and a noncannibalistic species resulted in five unisexual–bisexual *Poeciliopsis* "species" having different amounts of the two parental species genomes. The tendency to cannibalize offspring, like morphological features including dentition (which may affect the tendency to cannibalize), was correlated with genome dosage.

Finally, the incidence of cannibalism in fishes may sometimes correspond with the genetic relatedness between individuals. Bry and Gillet (1980) showed that full-sib groups of pike (*Esox lucius*) juveniles have a higher survivorship than do juveniles reared in mixed sibling groups. They attributed the higher survivorship of juveniles in full-sib groups to the somewhat lower variation in growth among individuals resulting in a reduction in cannibalism. In view of the ability of the young of some lower vertebrates to recognize siblings (Waldman and Adler, 1979), however, the avoidance of cannibalism by related individuals should also be considered. More work in this area is needed.

Filial Cannibalism: Case Studies

In the paragraphs that follow, brief accounts are given of species in five families in which cannibalism occurs and filial cannibalism is known or suspected. Because cannibalism has been defined as the killing and subsequent consumption of conspecifics, the many cases reported in which guardian parents remove and eat dead offspring have not been considered or reviewed. Instead, this discussion of filial cannibalism has been limited to cases in which parents apparently kill and eat otherwise healthy offspring.

Greenlings. The painted greenling, *Oxylebius pictus* (Hexagrammidae), is a North American Pacific coastal marine fish that is 25 cm or less in total length (Hart, 1973). In nature, males establish territories on rocky substrates upon which females deposit adhesive eggs. Males frequently mate sequentially with more than one female at a single spawning site. Males alone guard eggs (embryos) until hatching (De-Martini, 1976). DeMartini (1976) documented cannibalism of demersal embryos by both adult males and females. In general, males more frequently cannibalize young than females. Both guarding and nonguarding males cannibalize eggs, but cannibalism occurs most frequently among caregiving males. By showing that the developmental stage of eggs in the stomachs of caregiving males is different from that of their offspring, DeMartini demonstrated that heterocannibalism occurs. Filial cannibalism is also suspected, however, since guarding males are found to cannibalize eggs at the same developmental stage as their own offspring more frequently than expected if none of their own eggs were consumed.

Sticklebacks. The three-spined stickleback, *Gasterosteus aculeatus* (Gasterosteidae), is a common species in the marine and freshwaters of the northern hemisphere (Hart, 1973) and it has been used extensively for behavioral studies (Wootton, 1976). Adults are less than 10 cm total length. In freshwaters, where their reproduction has been well studied, males establish breeding territories and construct tube-shaped nests with pieces of vegetation. Males may obtain eggs from more than one female, and males alone guard and fan the eggs (embryos) and larvae (Wootton, 1976). In nature, adult males and females cannibalize eggs and larvae, but males are the most frequent cannibals (Kynard, 1978; Semler, 1971). Foraging schools of females and nonnesting males have been observed to attack and destroy nests and to eat entire clutches (Kynard, 1978). There is a negative correlation between the stage of eggs eaten and those in the cannibal's nest, suggesting that nesting males are not filial cannibalistic (Kynard, 1978). However, in 65% of 260 males that had cannibalized eggs, at least some of these were at the same developmental stage as the eggs in that male's nest

(Kynard, 1978). Thus filial cannibalism as well heterocannibalism might have occurred. Filial cannibalism in this species has also been suggested in another field study (Hynes, 1950) and in aquaria (Assem, 1967).

Gouramis. The blue gourami, *Trichogaster trichopterus* (Belontiidae), is a tropical freshwater species native to the Indo–Australian Archipelago, the Malayan peninsula, and Southeast Asia (Wheeler, 1975). Adults of this species are approximately 15 cm long. In nature, males establish nesting territories in colonies of 20–30 individuals. Some males receive eggs from more than one female, perhaps depending on position in the colony (Wright, 1976, as cited in Loiselle and Barlow, 1978). Females are chased from the nest immediately after spawning. Parental care in this species was intensively studied in aquariums (Chang and Liley, 1974). In both nature and in captivity, the male alone builds a floating-bubble nest and guards and retrieves eggs and larvae until the offspring reach the juvenile stage of development. In aquariums, both females and nonguarding males are cannibalistic on eggs and larvae (Chang and Liley, 1974). In nature, females readily cannibalize eggs (Wright, 1976, as cited in Loiselle and Barlow, 1978). An experimental study on brood adoption in the blue gourami indicated that males respond to variation in egg number, cannibalizing small clutches while exhibiting normal parental care for relatively large clutches (Chang and Liley, 1974). These results suggest that filial cannibalism may occur in nature (see section on Filial Cannibalism as Parental Manipulation).

Sunfishes. Bluegill sunfish, *Lepomis macrochirus,* and longear sunfish, *Lepomis megalotis* (Centrarchidae), are North American freshwater fishes. Adult bluegills are usually 17–20 cm total length, and longears are approximately 15 cm in total length (Scott and Crossman, 1973). In both species, males establish breeding territories and make bowl-shaped depressions (nests) in the substrate. Nesting occurs in discrete aggregations (colonies), and males may receive eggs from more than one female (Breder, 1936). Males alone guard the eggs and larvae until they disperse.

Heterocannibalism in nature was documented in longear sunfish by Keenleyside (1972). Females practice pseudocourtship as an egg-eating tactic. Filial cannibalism may also occur since some nesting males were found to have eggs in their stomachs, but nesting males were seldom seen to eat eggs when intruding into neighboring nests. Heterocannibalism by females adopting pseudocourtship also occurs in bluegill sunfish. In addition, foraging schools of male and female bluegills overrun nesting males and consume eggs (Dominey, 1981a). Filial cannibalism also occurs in bluegills. Males that receive relatively few eggs during spawning frequently consume their eggs. These males were observed to move to other sites where they established new nests and had the opportunity to obtain larger broods (Dominey, 1981b).

Cichlids. The cichlids (Cichlidae) are a very diverse group of brackish and freshwater fishes native to Africa, Asia, and South and Central America (Nelson, 1976). Members of this family have been the subjects of extensive behavioral research (Baerends and Baerends-van Roon, 1950). Reproduction in this family is characterized by territoriality and parental care, but interspecific variation in these features is extreme (Breder and Rosen, 1966). Nesting territories may be established by either the male or female or both together, and spawning occurs within the territory. Parental care can include nest construction, guarding eggs, larvae, and juveniles, fanning and manipulating offspring, feeding offspring (Noakes and Barlow, 1973), and in many species, oral brooding (reviewed in Oppenheimer, 1970). In oral brooding, one or both sexes carry the eggs, larvae, and (in some species) juveniles in the buccal cavity during their development. This form of caregiving by the parent involves a fast, sometimes for periods of weeks (Fryer and Iles, 1972; Oppenheimer, 1970).

Heterocannibalism is well documented in the Cichlidae (Table I); one example is detailed here. The orange chromide, *Etroplus maculatus,* is native to brackish waters in Sri Lanka. Pairs nest colonially (groups as large as 30 or more) in shallow waters (Ward and Samarakoon, 1981). Eggs are deposited in a substrate nest, and both sexes remain to guard the eggs and larvae (biparental care).

The major predators on *E. maculatus* eggs and larvae are conspecifics. As in sticklebacks and sunfishes, schools of nonbreeding adults of both sexes "raid" nests and cannibalize eggs and larvae. A congener, the green chromide (*Etroplus suratensis*) nests in similar habitats and at the same time of year as the orange chromide, but in contrast each biparental pair has an isolated nest, and heterocannibalism has not been observed (Ward and Samarakoon, 1981).

Among oral-brooding cichlids, such as *Tilapia nilotica,* adults collected in nature sometimes have conspecific eggs or larvae in their stomachs as well as brooded offspring in the buccal cavity (Liebman, 1933). This is not proof of filial cannibalism because offspring may have been swallowed during collection, but it is suggestive. In several cichlids, the number of offspring carried in the mouth gradually diminishes during the brooding period (Liebman, 1933; Welcomme, 1967). Some of these offspring may be consumed by the oral-brooding parent.

Finally, several members of the diverse assemblage of cichlids found in the Great Lakes of Africa prey almost exclusively upon the embryos and larvae contained in the mouths of brooding females of other cichlids (Fryer and Iles, 1972). Aquarium observations suggest that the mouth of a female is engulfed by these predators until the brood is jettisoned

(Greenwood, 1981). Such behavior would only be considered cannibalism if conspecific females were attacked. The opportunistic attack by conspecifics of young protruding from the mouths of brooding females does occur in *Tilapia grahami* (Coe, 1966). Similar behavior might have been the evolutionary antecedent to the behavior of the more specialized embryo predators (paedophages).

THE ADAPTIVE SIGNIFICANCE AND EFFECT OF CANNIBALISM

Heterocannibalism as Exploitation

As documented in the preceding sections, heterocannibalism is extremely common in fishes, more so than in other vertebrates. Most of the observed heterocannibalism is simply intraspecific predation and is best categorized as exploitation; the young are exploited as a food resource. Because of its common occurrence, cannibalism of embryos, larvae, or juveniles in some species may have important demographic effects. Cannibalism may be the principal factor limiting population size or density in many fishes (Kluchareva, 1956; Nikolsky, 1963; Ricker, 1954). Some researchers have actually measured the impact of cannibalism on early mortality. As much as 32% of the natural embryo mortality in the northern anchovy (*Engraulis mordax*) may be due to cannibalism (Hunter and Kimbrell, 1980b). Patriquin (1967) estimated that one-third of the standing crop of juvenile cod (*Gadus morhua*) are cannibalized annually in a landlocked population. In addition, cannibalism may account for the occurrence of dominant adult age-classes that persist for many successive years (Alm, 1952). Persistant dominant age-classes have been observed in perch (*Perca fluviatilis*) in populations in which adults were cannibalistic on younger age–classes (Holcik, 1977; McCormack, 1965), suggesting that cannibalistic adults kept younger age-classes in check by consuming them (Holcik, 1977; but see Tarby, 1974). Variations in age-class abundance and population size might have resulted from cannibalism in walleyes (*Stizostedion vitreum*) (Forney, 1976), pike *(Esox lucius)* (Kipling and Frost, 1970), and Pacific sardine (*Sardinops caerulea*) (Radovich, 1962).

Another potential effect of cannibalism is the ease with which some species invade new habitats or persist in habitats that are devoid of normal prey. For example, perch are sometimes found in lakes that do not contain other fish species. Adults cannibalize younger age-classes that are able to subsist on plankton in these lakes (Nikolsky, 1963). Cannibalism may also select for rapid growth rates in juveniles that are susceptible to intraspecific predation only at small sizes (Patriquin, 1967).

In addition to demographic effects, heterocannibalism may directly affect the reproductive behavior of fishes. For instance, parental care (guarding) of offspring in fishes has been suggested to evolve in response to interspecific predation. In many species in which heterocannibalism is common, heterocannibalism may be an even stronger selective pressure than interspecific predation. This may be particularly important, for example, in fishes such as sticklebacks (Kynard, 1978), orange chromides (Ward and Samarakoon, 1981), and bluegill sunfish (Dominey, 1981a) in which foraging schools of conspecifics raid nests. In many other species, large numbers of adults and juveniles are present during reproductive activities and could cannibalize young opportunistically. Generally the effect of heterocannibalism on breeding biology may be indistinguishable from and synergistic with the effect of interspecific predation.

In addition to parental care, biparental care may occur in response to heterocannibalism, as perhaps seen in the strongly heterocannibalistic, biparental orange chromides (Ward and Samarakoon, 1981). Two adults are sometimes necessary for successful brood defense under conditions of extreme predation pressure (Barlow, 1974; Baylis, 1981). In some species the cumulative offspring losses due to heterocannibalism and interspecific predation may make remaining to give care more advantageous for the second parent than any alternative activity would be. Similarly, the unusual phenomena of communal care and "kidnapping" observed in some fishes (McKaye and McKaye, 1977) may be responses to intense intra- or interspecific predation.

The effect of heterocannibalism on parental care patterns may not be limited to fishes. Simon (Chapter 4, this volume) found a correlation between species that provide parental care and egg cannibalism among amphibians. Although filial cannibalism may explain some of this correlation, filial cannibalism in amphibians is not commonly observed (Simon, Chapter 4, this volume) and may be rare. This correlation between parental care and egg cannibalism in amphibians may result primarily from heterocannibalism acting as a selective pressure much as has been suggested for fishes.

Like parental guarding, the degree of aggregation and synchrony during breeding may evolve in response to heterocannibalism. In species in which parents guard their offspring in nests, nesting synchronously and in colonies can serve an antipredator function. The offspring in nests in high-density areas are better protected against predators than those in nests in low-density areas (Dominey, 1981a; Loiselle, 1977; Ward and Samarakoon, 1981). Thus, in species in which heterocannibalism is prevalent, nesting synchronously and colonially may be favored. Such heterocannibalism has been suggested to be responsible for the breeding synchrony and nest aggregation observed in sticklebacks (Kynard, 1978).

Interestingly, in two well-documented cases of extreme colonialism (a sunfish and a cichlid), in which congeners in the same habitat were less colonial or nested singly, the strongly colonial forms were also strongly heterocannibalistic. Members of the strongly colonial species were the most frequent egg predators observed on both their own offspring and on the offspring of the related noncolonial species (Dominey, 1981a; Ward and Samarakoon, 1981). In both cases, the heterocannibals were present in mixed foraging schools of nonbreeding males and females. Because of their prevalence and success at attacking nests and cannibalizing eggs, bluegill sunfish were suggested to be their "own worst enemies." The strong tendency of bluegills to nest colonially may result from this selective pressure.

In cases in which neighboring guardian males raid nests, as in sticklebacks (Kynard, 1978) and greenlings (DeMartini, 1976), counterselection against extreme nesting aggregation should occur. Bluegills do not cannibalize the eggs of neighboring males (Dominey, 1981a), and in the highly colonial longear sunfish, nesting males do so only infrequently (Keenleyside, 1972). It would be interesting to know whether strongly colonial cichlids only infrequently cannibalize eggs or fry of neighboring pairs.

In addition to caregiving and the degree of aggregation during breeding, other behavioral features may evolve in response to heterocannibalism. For instance, guardian parents are typically most aggressive toward conspecifics. Such aggression may be in response to the threat of heterocannibalism. Other explanations, such as, sexual or social competition must also be considered. Even the approach of a female, gravid and ready to spawn, should be challenged by a nesting male since such females are known to cannibalize eggs. This conflict between courtship and defense of young might have contributed to the "aggressive" nature of courtship, especially in species in which guardian males accept mates sequentially and thus may already have offspring present.

In some cases, guardian males may not only repel but also cannibalize intruding conspecifics. In such cases (e.g., sculpins), the dispersal patterns of females and juveniles may relate to heterocannibalism (Downhower and Brown, 1980).

Filial Cannibalism as Parental Manipulation

Parents manipulate their investment in offspring in a variety of ways to improve their lifetime reproductive success (Alexander, 1974). One way for a parent to adjust its parental investment is by killing and consuming its own offspring: filial cannibalism. Although both male and female parents may consume their offspring in aquariums, in nature most filial cannibalism is by caregiving males. This is probably because males, as the typical caregiving sex, have access to the young and have made little gametic investment. Also, males may cannibalize a portion of their offspring in order to remain for long periods at breeding sites. In contrast, females should gain an energetic advantage by resorbing rather than cannibalizing their eggs as a way of adjusting parental investment.

Liebman (1933) first suggested that oralbrooders might cannibalize a portion of their offspring to compensate for reduced foraging during caregiving. Based on the presence of clumps of undifferentiated eggs in ripe females, Gunter (1947) suggested that females of a marine catfish might provide a nuptial feeding for males prior to the oralbrooding male's long parental fast. Obviously oralbrooding must limit foraging [although some foraging may occur (Coe, 1966)], but even when parents only guard nests, or are restricted to breeding sites, they may still have severe limitations on foraging.

In many species that defend territories, remaining at breeding sites for long periods is advantageous because additional matings can be acquired. Males in these species may be unable to forage efficiently or at all, often remaining in very confined areas, especially when offspring are present. Guarding itself may be energetically costly since males in some species must defend their nests against egg predators almost constantly (Dominey, 1981a). To compensate for these energetic costs, males can cannibalize a portion of their offspring; this type of parental manipulation is probably widespread in fishes (DeMartini, 1976).

In species in which eggs are acquired over time and do not complete development simultaneously, Rohwer (1978) has suggested that late-received eggs should be cannibalized preferentially as an investment in future clutches. This argument is plausible in cases in which males can remain on their territories and attract new mates. A corollary to this argument is that males with small clutches, in cases in which males are unlikely to receive additional eggs until the present offspring leave the nest, may gain by cannibalizing the entire clutch and attempting to attract new mates (Rohwer, 1978). Such complete cannibalism of small clutches occurs in sticklebacks (Assem, 1967) and apparently in painted greenlings (DeMartini, 1976).

Complete cannibalism of small clutches is predicted in cases in which the costs and benefits (in terms of inclusive fitness) of guarding are nearly balanced for typical-sized clutches. Nest abandonment is also predicted in these cases if males do not gain an advantage (such as the opportunity to remate) by retaining the spawning site. Two examples are relevant. First, male bluegills with small clutches abandon and cannibalize their offspring much more frequently than males with large clutches (Dominey, 1981b). Second, male gouramis respond to the presentation of large numbers of eggs with parental egg-retrieving behavior but frequently cannibalize small numbers of eggs (Kramer, 1973; Kramer and Liley, 1971; Chang and Liley, 1974). Both these species show dense and ephemeral aggregations of nesting males in nature (Wright, 1976, as cited in Loiselle and Barlow, 1978; Dominey, 1981a), in which males are unlikely to immediately renest at the same site.

Since many fishes have males that "sneak" or "steal" fertilizations (Morris, 1952; Barlow, 1967; Warner, Robertson, and Leigh, 1975; Constanz, 1975; Kodric-Brown, 1977; Wirtz, 1978; Dominey, 1980), guardian males may reduce the genetic cost of cannibalizing the eggs in their nests by selectively cannibalizing the offspring fertilized by "sneak" males rather than their own offspring. Recognition of one's own versus alien offspring has been shown in cichlids (McKaye and Barlow, 1976a), and selective filial cannibalism has been shown experimentally in a pupfish, *Cyprinodon macularius californiensis* (Loiselle, 1983). Selective cannibalism would reduce and perhaps eliminate the genetic costs of egg eating by guardian males if sufficient unrelated eggs were present.

Effects of Filial Cannibalism. Obviously, if filial cannibalism by guardian males is common, females should select those males that are least likely to consume their offspring. But how can they choose? The following factors may be important. First, males in generally good health and condition should be chosen. A weak, emaciated, or otherwise unfit male would be a poor choice because he may need to consume greater numbers of eggs and because he may abandon the offspring with a higher frequency. The aggressive nature of courtship in many species with guardian males may represent a test of a male's condition and "willingness" to guard the offspring.

Second, it may be advantageous for females to choose smaller males who have smaller energy requirements. Rohwer (1978) and DeMartini (1976) hypothesized that this selective pressure has acted against large male size in greenlings, in which males are smaller than females. Alternatively, however, one could argue that larger males should be able to store or obtain more energy reserves and thus would need to consume fewer eggs to stay in equal condition to smaller males. If smaller males are less likely to attract additional mates, they may be the best choice for females because the value of current offspring to these males would be high (Blumer and Dominey, in manuscript), and they are thus less likely to cannibalize them. However, this situation is complicated. When small males become the "best choices" for females, their likelihood of receiving additional mates should increase, and thus the value of their current offspring would decrease.

Third, females may gain by avoiding males with late-stage eggs because these males may cannibalize any newly laid eggs as an investment in a complete future brood cycle. Rohwer (1978) suggested female avoidance of males with late-stage eggs as an explanation for the mating and brooding "phases" shown by male fishes. Females should not deposit eggs in a nest with advanced embryos but may cannibalize any embryos already present. Thus, as their offspring develop, males should reach a point at which they no longer accept additional females on the nest, hence the observed behavioral change from mating to brooding.

Aside from avoiding particular males, it may generally be advantageous for females to preferentially deposit their eggs in nests that have, or are likely to receive, additional eggs. Males receiving abundant eggs are less likely to abandon their nests or cannibalize entire clutches (Dominey, 1981b; Assem, 1967). Furthermore, if partial filial cannibalism occurs indiscriminately, there will be a proportional "dilution" effect with fewer of each female's offspring being cannibalized as additional clutches are added (Rohwer, 1978). Many fishes deposit eggs synchronously, and some prefer to deposit eggs in nests where eggs (embryos) are already present. Although synchronous breeding and clumping can also have antipredator functions in fishes (Dominey, 1981a), even in fishes in which an antipredator function was considered unimportant, as in greenlings (DeMartini, 1976), some synchrony and clumping occurs. Synchrony and clumping in these species may be in response to filial cannibalism.

Because females often prefer as mates males that already have eggs, it would be advantageous in many instances for males to either obtain eggs for their nests or to "appear" to be obtaining eggs. Egg stealing by male sticklebacks may be an example of the former, and courtship by nesting male bluegills of males behaving like females may be an example of the latter. Stickleback males enter the nests of other males, rob them of eggs, and return to their own nests to deposit the eggs (Iersel, 1953). Rohwer (1978) hypothesized that this is a courtship tactic aimed at attracting females whose interest is in reducing filial cannibalism by males. Other male fishes that occupy nests and guard eggs when resident males are removed (e.g., darters: Constanz, 1979; sculpins: Staples, 1980) may similarly be practicing a courtship tactic.

In bluegills, females select males near centers of spawning activity, perhaps to reduce not only egg predation by conspecifics and others but also filial cannibalism and nest abandonment. In this species, nesting males and "female mimics," small sexually mature satellite males, show behavior virtually indistinguishable from that of normal courting heterosexual pairs (Dominey, 1980). Such male–male "courtship" may be attractive to females and conceivably could create spawning centers in the vicinity of the nesting male (Dominey, 1981c). In this case, males may be using the tendency of females to deposit eggs in spawning centers (to avoid filial and heterocannibalism) to their advantage.

Heterocannibalism in Relation to Sexual Selection

Hrdy (1979) limited her discussion of infanticide in relation to sexual selection to cases in which another's offspring were destroyed as the result of competition between members of one sex for the reproductive investment of the other sex or to cases in which the killer increases its chances of mating. As such, heterocannibalism as sexual selection in fishes is probably rare, in part due to the reversal in the caregiving roles. We know of no cases in which females kill or eat a male's offspring to gain access to the male as a spawning partner. Such cases might occur when nesting sites or caregiving males (as in sticklebacks: Kynard, 1978) were limited and in which females could effectively destroy a male's clutch (e.g., in fishes that spawn discrete clumps of demersal eggs, such as sculpins or bullheads). In such cases, pseudocourtship by females might be used to gain access to the eggs. Pseudocourtship as an egg-eating tactic has been observed in greenlings (DeMartini, 1976), longear sunfish (Keenleyside, 1972), and bluegill sunfish (Dominey: personal observation).

Heterocannibalism as Resource Competition

The killing of conspecifics could almost always be interpreted as resource competition, but it is doubtful that heterocannibalism could evolve in fishes in primary response to competition except in unusual cases. The impact that an individual can have on the numerous offspring produced by the population (with which his/her offspring must compete) will usually be slight. Cases of resource competition heterocannibalism may occur, however, when conspecifics are present at low densities and offspring have only limited access to some resource, such as refugia. Hole nesting cichlids (Taborsky and Limberger, 1981) or substrate spawners on patch reefs where young remain on the reef would be likely species to examine for evidence of resource competition heterocannibalism.

Sibling Cannibalism as Resource Competition

Since fishes typically do not feed their offspring, fratricide of the type practiced by birds (see Mock, Chapter 1, this volume) as resource competition is not generally expected. However, internal gestation is sometimes associated with feeding offspring and a kind of "intrauterine" sibling cannibalism occurs in live-bearing poeciliids (Turner, 1947; but see Meffe and Vrijenhoek, 1981). Developing embryos apparently ingest embryos or parts of embryos that have died; whether killing ever occurs in these cases has not been demonstrated. Much better documented is intrauterine sibling cannibalism in sharks (Wourms, 1977) and the strong possibility of such cannibalism in an extinct holocephalan fish (Lund, 1980). Some species of sharks have adopted this tendency as a way of feeding the offspring, with females providing large numbers of trophic eggs that are eaten by developing embryos (Gruber and Campagno, 1981). In other species, [e.g., sand sharks (*Odontaspis tauris*)] living embryos are active sibling cannibals inside the oviduct, even snapping at intruding fingers (Springer, 1948)! Only single embryos survive in each oviduct. Although exploitation is also occurring, intrauterine cannibalism in these sharks is perhaps best categorized as resource competition.

CONCLUSION

Cannibalism, as killing and consumption of young conspecifics, is far more common in fishes than in terrestrial vertebrates. We suggest that high fecundity (small offspring) and the predominance of external fertilization (resulting in the deposition of helpless embryos in a potentially hostile environment) have both contributed to the prevalence of cannibalism. We also suggest that filial cannibalism, in which parents consume offspring, is favored by the frequent occurrence of male parental care in fishes.

Many parallels can be drawn between cannibalism in fishes and infanticide in other animals. Most cannibalism in fishes is simply intraspecific predation, and such heterocannibalism can have far-reaching effects on fish demography and reproductive behavior. This type of cannibalism is best regarded as exploitation. More surprising is filial cannibalism, in which a male caregiver consumes his own offspring. Such cannibalism can be regarded as parental manipulation. Cannibalistic males may increase their ability to care for their remaining offspring or increase their ability to retain tenure at breeding sites and thereby fertilize additional eggs. Cannibalism in response to resource competition and sexual selection is less common in fishes, although sibling cannibalism as resource competition occurs in sharks in the form of intrauterine cannibalism.

Fishes are the most phylogenetically diverse and largest group of vertebrates. Fishes also have an extreme diversity of mating systems and modes of parental care when compared to other vertebrates. The fact that theoretical models of infanticide developed primarily for terrestrial mammals (Hrdy, 1979; Sherman, 1981) would apply also to fishes

indicates the strength of the evolutionary approach toward understanding animal social behavior.

ACKNOWLEDGMENTS

We thank G. W. Barlow, J. R. Baylis, L. Brown, E. E. DeMartini, P. V. Loiselle, S.
Rohwer, and P. W. Sherman for comments on the manuscript.
W. J. Dominey was supported by a NSF Postdoctoral Fellowship and a NIH Individual
Research Service Award.

4

The influence of conspecifics on egg and larval mortality in amphibians

Martin P. Simon

INTRODUCTION

Amphibians in common with most other animals experience their highest mortality during early stages of development (Turner, 1962; Wassersug, 1975; Heyer, 1979). Therefore, knowledge of the major factors affecting the mortality of amphibian eggs and larvae, also referred to as propagules, is essential for understanding the evolution of life-history patterns in amphibians (Wilber and Collins, 1973; Heyer, 1973). In this chapter, those behaviors performed by conspecifics that directly affect the mortality rate of amphibian eggs and larvae are considered. This chapter addresses the following questions: What are the major sources of amphibian propagule mortality? In what ways can parents and other conspecifics affect the mortality rate of propagules? Finally, what is the adaptive significance of the killing of eggs and larvae?

Reproductive Patterns and Mortality Rates in Amphibian Propagules

Table I summarizes the major modes of reproduction of the three orders of amphibians: Anura (frogs and toads), Urodela (salamanders and newts), and Gymnophionia (caecilians). The reproductive modes of amphibians summarized in Table I are based on egg size, clutch size, site of egg and larval development, mode of development, and presence or absence of parental care. Amphibians clearly exhibit a

Table I. Patterns of reproduction in amphibians[a]

Site and mode of development	Egg size[b]	Clutch size[c]	Parental care
Anurans			
Aquatic eggs and larvae			
Large, permanent bodies of water	Small	Large–very large	No
Small, ephemeral bodies of water	Small	Medium–large	No
Constructed basins or nests	Medium	Small–medium	Few
Nonaquatic eggs; aquatic larvae			
Arboreal eggs	Medium–large	Small–medium	Many
Eggs in terrestrial sites	Small–medium	Medium	Some
Eggs on land, larvae carried to water	Medium–large	Small	Yes
Eggs deposited on the back of the female	Large–very large	Small	Yes
Nonaquatic eggs; no aquatic larvae			
Eggs in nests, larvae in nests	Small–medium	Medium–large	No
Eggs and larvae carried inside or on parent until metamorphosis	Large–very large	Small	Yes
Eggs on land, no larval stage	Medium–large	Medium–large	No
Live-bearing[d]	—	Small	Yes

66

Urodeles

Reproductive mode	Egg size[b]	Clutch size[c]	Live-bearing[d]
Aquatic eggs and larvae			
Slow-moving bodies of water	Small	Medium–large	Many
In sites in fast-moving water	Medium–large	Small–medium	Yes
Nonaquatic eggs; aquatic larvae			
Eggs on land near water, larvae in ponds or streams	Medium	Medium	Yes
Eggs develop in oviduct of female, larvae in water	Medium–large	Small	Yes
Nonaquatic eggs; no larval stage			
Subterranean, terrestrial, or arboreal eggs; direct development	Large	Small–medium	Yes
Live-bearing[d]	—	Small	Yes
Gymnophiona			
Nonaquatic eggs; aquatic larvae	Large	Small–medium	Yes
Nonaquatic eggs; no larval stage			
Eggs laid on land; direct development	Small–medium	Small	Yes
Viviparous	Small	Small	Yes

[a] This table is a synthesis of information presented by Salthe (1969), Crump (1974), Duellman (1978), and Wake (1977).

[b] Egg size = diameter of eggs (small = 1–2 mm; medium = 2–5 mm; large = 5–10 mm).

[c] Clutch size = number of eggs or neonates laid or born during a given reproductive period (very small = 1–5; small = 6–40; medium = 41–120; large = 121–2000; very large = 2000–20,000).

[d] Live-bearing = ovoviviparous, viviparous.

tremendous range of variation in virtually all aspects of their reproductive biology, and the potential importance of a particular mortality factor depends to a large extent on the particular reproductive pattern exhibited by a species. Table II provides a list of mortality rates for selected species of amphibians. Despite the lack of data on mortality rates of amphibian species with specialized breeding patterns, certain

Table II. Mortality rates in amphibian eggs and larvae

Species	Reproductive mode[a]	Mortality[b] (%)	Authority
Anurans			
Acris gryllus	A/A	89–99[c]	Blair, 1957
Bombina bombina	A/A	46[c]	Bannikov, 1950
Bufo americanus	A/A	85[c]	Miller, 1909
Centrolenella colym-			
biphillum	T/A	7[d]	McDiarmid, 1978
C. fleischmanni	T/A	29–39[d]	Greer and Wells, 1980
C. valeroi	T/A	23[d]	McDiarmid, 1978
Cophixalus parkeri	DD	<5[c]	Simon, 1980
Eleutherodactylus coqui	DD	23[c]	Townsend: personal communication
Phyllomedusa guttata	T/A	5[d]	Lutz, 1947
Pseudophryne bibroni	T/A	5[d]	Woodruff, 1976
P. dendyi	T/A	6[d]	Woodruff, 1976
P. semimarmorata	T/A	4[d]	Woodruff, 1976
Rana aurora	A/A	95[c]	Calef, 1973
		95–99[c]	Licht, 1974
R. clamitans	A/A	86[c]	Martof, 1956
R. pipiens	A/A	94[c]	Merrell, 1968
R. pretiosa	A/A	97[c]	Turner, 1960
		95–99[c]	Licht, 1974
R. sylvatica	A/A	96[c]	Herreid and Kinney, 1966
R. temporaria	A/A	100[c]	Seale, 1982
Urodeles			
Ranodon sibricus	A/A	75[d]	Bannikov, 1958
Ambystoma jefferson-			
ianum	A/A	75[c]	Piersol, 1910
A. maculatum	A/A	95[c]	Shoop, 1974
A. tigrinum	A/A	97[c]	Anderson *et al.*, 1971
Desmognathus ochro-			
phaeus	DD	47[c]	Forester, 1979
		31[c]	Tilley, 1972

[a] A/A = aquatic eggs and larvae; T/A = terrestrial eggs and aquatic larvae; DD = direct development (no larval stage).

[b] Mortality = percentage of cohort dying within the specified time interval.

[c] From oviposition to postmetamorphic stage.

[d] From oviposition to larval stage.

trends seem evident. As pointed out by several workers (e.g., Lutz, 1947; Salthe and Duellman, 1973; Heyer *et al.*, 1975), species having aquatic eggs and larvae experience more severe propagule mortality than do species with more terrestrial modes of development. Factors other than site of development have also been proposed to be important in determining the rate of propagule mortality, for example, egg size and clutch size (Salthe, 1969; Salthe and Duellman, 1973), mode of development (Salthe and Duellman, 1973), and amount of parental care (Wells, 1981).

Causes of Propagule Mortality in Amphibians

Given that propagule mortality is extremely high in most species of amphibians, what are the important causes of this mortality? In an attempt to answer this question, relevant literature on the causes of propagule mortality in anurans and, to a lesser extent, urodeles and caecilians was surveyed. Information on propagule mortality was available for 121 species in 45 genera and 14 families of frogs (Simon, 1982). Predation by vertebrate and invertebrate predators was reported as being an important source of mortality in 58% of these species, while other biotic factors, for example, fungal infestation, intrinsic genetic defects, competition, disease, and starvation were reported to affect mortality in 22% of all species. Extremes in temperature and desiccation were important sources of mortality in 47% of all species; other abiotic factors such as anoxia, drowning, osmotic shock, mechanical damage, and low pH were also mentioned. It is important to note that the sample of anuran species for which mortality data was available included several biases. Most species (63%) for which data have been published were either from the nearctic (32%) or were neotropical (31%), and most species (80%) had a fully aquatic mode of development. Furthermore, most of the data on mortality were obtained in the course of field observations. Another major source of information was laboratory experiments specifically aimed at determining the tolerance of given species to high and low temperatures. The most notable attempts to systematically analyze mortality factors in anurans include the works on *Bufo americanus* by Miller (1909), *Rana sylvatica* by Herreid and Kinney (1966), *R. aurora* by Calef (1973) and Licht (1974), *R. pretiosa* by Licht (1974), *Pseudophryne bibroni, P. dendyi,* and *P. semimarmorata* by Woodruff (1976, 1977), and *Eleutherodactylus coqui* by Townsend (1983).

In contrast to anurans, the most often cited causes of propagule mortality in salamanders are: fungal attack (Forester, 1979), intraspecific oophagy (Kaplan and Sherman, 1980), predation by other salamander species (Bishop, 1941; Forester, 1979) and arthropods (Kryszik, 1980), desiccation (Bruce, 1975), and freezing (Anderson *et al.*, 1971). Due to a lack of detailed studies, there is a real scarcity of information on mortality rates and the causes of caecilian propagule mortality. However, over 50% of all caecilian species are viviparous and therefore without free-living egg or larval stages. Clearly, egg and larval mortality are obviated by this form of development (M. Wake: personal communication). Nevertheless, Wake (1980) found that female *Dermophis mexicanus*, a viviparous caecilian, contained in their oviducts desiccated, partially developed embryos indicating that some propagule mortality does occur within the body of the female early in the course of development.

INTRASPECIFIC INFLUENCES ON PROPAGULE MORTALITY

The four main categories of intraspecific interactions that affect mortality rates in amphibian propagules (intraspecific competition among larvae, cannibalism, noncannibalistic egg killing, and parental egg desertion) will now be examined in more detail.

Intraspecific Competition among Larvae

It has been known for some time that mortality rates of anuran larvae raised under laboratory conditions are related to larval densities (Yung, 1885; Goetsch, 1924). The effect of crowding was regarded by early workers as an example of a widespread phenomenon observed in many groups of aquatic and marine organisms, whereby growth rates and survivorship are reduced at high densities. More specifically, it has been established, primarily under laboratory conditions, that increased crowding of amphibian larvae can directly result in increased premetamorphic mortality (Brockleman, 1969; Smith-Gill and Gill, 1978). In addition to a direct increase in mortality, other studies have shown that larvae raised under high densities may exhibit a lower average growth rate and/or increased time to metamorphosis (Rose and Rose, 1961; Wilbur and Collins, 1973; Wilbur, 1976; Travis, 1980). These effects can indirectly result in increased mortality by increasing the probability that the slower-developing larvae will succumb to various biotic and abiotic mortality agents (Wilbur, 1980; Smith-Gill and Berven, 1979; Travis, 1981). For example, delay of only a few days in time to metamorphosis, resulting from the effects of intraspecific competition, could be fatal to a population of larvae living in a habitat frequently subject to periodic drying, flooding, freezing, or influxes of tadpole predators.

Although intraspecific competition has been reported to be an important direct or indirect cause of amphibian larval mortality in nature (Brockleman, 1969; Wilbur, 1972, 1980; Steinwascher, 1978), others believe that intraspecific competition may be of only secondary importance compared to the effect of predation or catastrophic, density-independent factors (Calef, 1973; Heyer *et al.,* 1975; Cecil and Just, 1979).

Exploitative competition. Most larval anurans are indiscriminate detritus feeders or planktivores (Jenssen, 1967; Wassersug, 1975) and as such may not be food limited in nature (Calef, 1973; Wassersug, 1975; Cecil and Just, 1979). However, field and laboratory studies by several workers (Brockleman, 1969; Wilbur, 1977; Steinwascher, 1978; and others) have shown that a decrease in the amount of food per individual at high population densities may partially explain the growth-inhibiting effects of crowding in amphibian larvae.

Dickman (1968), for example, demonstrated that phytophagy by *Rana aurora* tadpoles in the wild caused a significant reduction in the standing crop of periphyton algae on which they fed. Wilbur (1977) showed that the growth rate of woodfrog tadpoles (*Rana sylvatica*) reared at high densities responded positively to increases in food levels. Studies dealing specifically with the role of food availability in intraspecific competition among larval salamanders are rare, although there is some evidence that exploitative competition for food may also occur in this group (Bishop, 1941; Wilbur, 1972).

Anoxia resulting from intraspecific competition for oxygen under crowded conditions may also be an important cause of anuran tadpole mortality (Yung, 1885; Licht, 1967). However, Richards (1958) found no differences in tadpole survivorship or growth rate in aerated versus nonaerated aquariums. Occurrences of oxygen deprivation of amphibian larvae in nature are virtually undocumented but may be a factor for species that breed in sites subject to high temperatures or seasonal reduction in water volume (Wassersug and Seibert, 1975; Kluge, 1981).

Interference competition. Numerous authors have proposed that anuran larvae excrete a substance that inhibits the growth of other conspecifics living in the same body of water. This conclusion is based on several studies that have shown that early-staged tadpoles placed in water that was previously occupied by several larger tadpoles of the same species had a lower growth rate than control groups even though a super abundance of food was available to the experimental subjects. The exact nature of this growth-inhibitory factor has been heatedly debated, and suggestions include a general fouling of the environment (West, 1960), tadpole feces (Rose, 1960), algal cells or parasites found in tadpole feces (Richards, 1962; Licht, 1967), and species-specific, soluble, growth-inhibiting substances (Rose and Rose, 1961; Stepanova, 1974; Steinwascher, 1978).

In contrast to mechanisms involving the excretion of growth-inhibiting substances, Biliski (1921) suggested that mechanical agitation caused by increased physical contact of tadpoles under crowded conditions explains the inhibitory crowding effect. Other authors have proposed similar explanations involving increased psychological stress of tadpoles induced by decreased individual space and/or increased contact between individuals (Adolf, 1931; Lynn and Edleman, 1936; John and Fenster, 1975). Pourbagher (1969) suggested that high densities of tadpoles causes a stress-related decrease in resistance to disease that is reflected in increased mortality or decreased growth rates. Finally, Gromko *et al.* (1973) and Steinwascher (1979) proposed that the inhibitory–crowding effect is due in part to increased rate of transmittance of internal parasites.

A common observation concerning amphibian larvae is that their competitive abilities are size related. This may be due to a number of factors such as the greater rate of food intake by larger tadpoles (Steinwascher, 1978; Wilbur, 1977) or the greater sensitivity of small tadpoles to growth-inhibiting substances (Heusser, 1972). Pomeroy (1981) has observed that large *Scaphiopus multiplicatus* tadpoles aggressively displaced smaller tadpoles from the center of shrinking puddles of water in temporary ponds. This behavior increased the probability of survival of the larger tadpoles at the expense of the smaller tadpoles, which were subject to lethal desiccation as the water level decreased. Also, Savage (1952) and Wilbur (1977) have found that larger tadpoles of two species of frog actively interfered with the ability of smaller conspecifics to acquire food resources.

Propagule Cannibalism

Cannibalism is a direct means by which amphibians can directly affect the mortality of conspecific propagules. Intraspecific predation and cannibalism in animal populations have been recently reviewed by Fox (1975a) and Polis (1981); the existing literature on these phenomena in amphibians will now be considered in detail. (See also Crump, 1983 for a review of egg cannibalism in anurans.)

Occurrence of cannibalism. Table III summarizes published accounts of amphibian cannibalism on eggs or larvae. This may not be an exhaustive survey but does include most of the readily accessible information on this subject. Cannibalism of anuran propagules is fairly widespread taxonomically and geographically, occurring in at least 10 of the 20 families of frogs and in all major zoogeographic regions. In urodeles, propagule cannibalism is known to occur in at least 5 of the 8 families, and is found in both Old World and New World species. No published accounts could be found of cannibalism in caecilians. Cannibalism in amphibians can be divided into several forms based on the stage of development (eggs, larvae, adult) of the victim and predator in the interaction.

Adult cannibalism of eggs. Consumption of eggs by adult conspecifics has been reported for a number of amphibian species. In anurans, intraspecific oophagy occurs primarily in species that have a terrestrial

Table III. Egg and larval cannibalism in amphibians

Species	Mode of reproduction[a]	Parental care[b]	Type of study[c]	References
Adults on eggs				
Anurans				
Cophixalus parkeri	DD	+	FO, FE	Simon, 1982
Dendrobates auratus	T/A	+	FO	Wells, 1978
D. pumilio	T/A	+	LE, LO	Weygoldt, 1980
Eleutherodactylus coqui	DD	+	FO, FE	Townsend, 1983
Sphenophryne brevicrus	DD	+	LO	Tyler, 1963
Urodeles				
Ambystoma tigrinum[d]	A/A	−	LO	Hamilton, 1948
Aneides ferreus	DD	+	LO	Storm, 1947
Cryptobranchus alleganiensis[d]	A/A	+	FO	Smith, 1907
Desmognathus fuscus	T/A	+	FO	Wood and Clarke, 1955
D. ochrophaeus	T/A	+	LE, FO, FE	Tilley, 1972; Forester, 1979
Dicamptodon copei[d]	A/A	+	FO	Kaplan and Sherman, 1980
D. ensatus[d]	A/A	+	FO	Kaplan and Sherman, 1980
Ensatina eschscholtzi	DD	+	FO	Stebbins, 1954
Necturus maculosus[d]	A/A	+	FO	Bishop, 1941
Plethodon cinereus	DD	+	LO	Highton and Savage, 1961
Taricha torosa	A/A	+	FO	Kaplan and Sherman, 1980
Adults on larvae				
Anurans				
Ceratophrys sp.	A/A	?	FO	Noble, 1927
Pyxicephalus adsperus	A/A	+/−	FO	Loveridge, 1947
Rana catesbeiana	A/A	−	LO, LE	Cecil and Just, 1979
Xenopus laevis	A/A	−	LE	Savage, 1963

continued

Species	Mode of reproduction[a]	Parental care[b]	Type of study[c]	References
Urodeles				
Desmognathus fuscus	T/A	+	FO	Surface, 1913
D. ochrophaeus	T/A	+	FO	Wood and Wood, 1955
Eurycea bislineata	A/A	+	FO	Surface, 1913
Gyrinophilus porphyriticus	A/A	+	FO	Bruce, 1972
Notophthalmus viridescens	A/A	−	FO	Burton, 1977
Larvae on eggs				
Anurans				
Anotheca coronatum	A/A	−	FO	Duellman, 1970
Dendrobates histrionicus	T/A	+	LO, LE	Zimmermann and Zimmermann, 1981
D. lehmanni	T/A	+	LO, LE	Zimmermann and Zimmermann, 1981
D. pumilio	T/A	+	LO, LE	Weygoldt, 1980
Halophryne sp.	A/A	−	FO	Noble, 1929
Hyla arborea	A/A	−	LE	Heusser, 1971
H. brunnea	A/A	−	FO	Laessle, 1961
H. pseudopuma	A/A	−	FO, FE, LE	Crump, 1983
H. zetecki	A/A	−	FO	Starrett, 1960
Hymenochirus boettgeri	A/A	−	FO	Sokal, 1962
Philautus sp.	A/A	−	FO	Wassersug *et al.*, 1981
Rana esculenta	A/A	−	LE	Heusser, 1971
Scaphiopus multiplicatus	A/A	−	FO	Pomeroy, 1981
Urodeles				
None known				

Larvae on larvae

Anurans

	Mode of reproduction[a]	Parental care[b]	Type of study[c]	Reference
Anotheca spinosa	A/A	–	FO	Duellman, 1970
Bombina variegata	A/A	–	LE	Heusser, 1971
Bufo calamita	A/A	–	LE	Heusser, 1971
Ceratophrys ornata	A/A	+	FO	Noble, 1931
Hyla rosenbergi	A/A	–	FO	Kluge, 1981
Lechriodus fletcheri	A/A	–	FO	Martin, 1968
Megistolotis lignarius	A/A	–	LO	Tyler *et al.*, 1979
Rana sylvatica	A/A	–	LO	Bleakney, 1958
Scaphiopus bombifrons	A/A	–	FO, LE	Bragg, 1964
S. couchi	A/A	–	FO	Bragg, 1962
S. hammondi	A/A	–	FO	Bragg, 1962
S. holbrooki	A/A	–	FO	Ball, 1936
S. multiplicatus	A/A	–	FO, LE	Pomeroy, 1981
Xenopus laevis	A/A	–	FO, LE	Savage, 1963

Urodeles

Ambystoma jeffersonianum	A/A	–	FO	Smith, 1911
A. maculatum	A/A	–	FO	Clarke, 1980
A. talpoideum	A/A	–	FO	Allen, 1932
A. tigrinum	A/A	–	FO	Burgess, 1950
Hemidactylium scutatum	A/A	–	LO	Blanchard, 1934
Salamandra salamandra	A/A	–	FO	Parâtre, 1894

[a] Mode of reproduction: A/A = aquatic eggs and larvae; T/A = terrestrial eggs and aquatic larvae; DD = direct development (no larval stage).
[b] Parental care: + = yes; – = no.
[c] Type of study: FO = field observation; FE = field experimentation; LO = laboratory observation; LE = laboratory experimentation.
[d] Known to retain aquatic larval characteristics at sexual maturity.

egg stage and perform some type of parental care (Wells, 1981). In contrast, adult egg cannibalism occurs in urodeles whose modes of reproduction vary widely. About one-half of the cannibalistic urodele species have a terrestrial egg stage; the others have aquatic eggs, and a little over 80% of these species are known to brood their eggs.

It seems likely that egg cannibalism will only occur if the adults and eggs share the same habitat (aquatic or terrestrial). In 15 of the 16 species listed in Table III (adults on eggs), the adults and eggs either are both aquatic or both terrestrial. If the syntopy of adults and eggs is an important predictor of egg cannibalism in amphibians, then one would expect to find egg cannibalism in aquatic species by aquatic adults (e.g., *Xenopus, Ooeidozyga, Conraua*). In fact, Barbour and Loveridge (1928) reported finding frog eggs in the stomachs of adult *Xenopus muelleri*, but the eggs were not identified. Adults of *X. laevis* commonly eat their own eggs when kept under laboratory conditions (J. Savage: personal communication).

One of the major outcomes of the habitat separation of propagules from adults is the elimination of competition between adults and earlier life stages (Wassersug, 1975; Wilbur, 1980). A different, but not mutually exclusive, result of this habitat separation may be a reduction in the likelihood that the eggs (and larvae) will be cannibalized by the adults. Dominey and Blumer (Chapter 3, this volume) believe that the nearly universal occurrence of egg and larval cannibalism in fishes results from the coexistence of preadult life stages and adults in the same habitat.

Another interesting relationship between reproductive mode and egg cannibalism in amphibians is that a higher than expected proportion of species known to eat conspecific eggs also exhibit some form of parental care. Only 25–40% of all terrestrial breeding amphibian species exhibit parental care, whereas 100% of the species of anurans known to cannibalize eggs also care for their eggs. Of all species of urodele egg cannibals, 82% have parental care compared to 64% overall in this taxon. Two contrasting hypotheses have been put forth to explain the high correlation of egg cannibalism with parental care. One is that parental care is the result of selection to defend against a high level of egg cannibalism (heterocannibalism) already in existence (Salthe and Mecham, 1974). In the second hypothesis, the cause and effect are reversed. Egg cannibalism (filial cannibalism) is selected in species exhibiting parental care as a way of supplementing their energy intake during egg brooding (Rohwer, 1978). Most egg cannibalism in amphibians appears to be heterocannibalism, but available data on filial cannibalism is discussed at the end of this section.

Adult cannibalism of larvae. Consumption of conspecific larvae by adults appears to be somewhat less common than egg cannibalism and occurs mostly in species with aquatic or semiaquatic adults. The low frequency of adult cannibalism of larvae can again be partially explained by differences in habitat of adult amphibians and their larvae.

Cannibalism of eggs by larvae. Predation on eggs by conspecific larvae or paedogenic adults has been reported in at least 10 species of anurans and 2 species of urodeles. The number of potential egg-cannibalizing frog species is probably limited by the fact that in most frog species, tadpoles are primarily herbivores or detritus feeders (Kenny, 1969). The highly predatory and opportunistic feeding habits of most larval salamanders (Bishop, 1941; Goin *et al.*, 1977) suggest higher frequencies of larval cannibalism on eggs than the available literature indicates.

Six of the 10 examples of egg cannibalism by amphibian larvae listed in Table III (Larvae on eggs) occur in species in which eggs and tadpoles develop in temporary or very restricted bodies of water (in the axils of leaves, trunk holes, ephemeral ponds, etc.). Two of the exceptions, *Rana esculenta* and *Hyla arborea,* have been observed to cannibalize eggs only under laboratory conditions. The adaptive significance of this behavior is clearly exploitative (Hrdy, 1979; Dominey and Blumer, Chapter 3 this volume): The larvae gain direct benefit from consuming the eggs. Because of the spatial and temporal restrictions of the oviposition sites or the high density of larvae, food can be extremely limiting, and eggs may be one of the few food sources available to the developing larvae (Wassersug *et al.*, 1981).

Trophic eggs. An interesting case of egg cannibalism by larvae has been reported recently by Weygoldt (1980), who observed the parental care behavior of females of the poison-arrow frog *Dendrobates pumilio* in laboratory terrariums. The females of this species were observed carrying a single, newly hatched tadpole from their terrestrial nest sites to water-filled bromeliad leaf axils. Later, the female provided an unfertilized egg once or twice a week to each tadpole as the primary, if not only, source of food. This behavior has been also observed in *D. histrionicus* and *D. lehmanni,* in which females carry their tadpoles to restricted bodies of water and feed them with unfertilized eggs (Zimmermann and Zimmermann, 1981).

Larval cannibalism of larvae. Intraspecific larval predation is the form of cannibalism most often reported in amphibians and has received the most detailed attention by herpetologists. Bragg and Bragg (1959), Orton (1957), and, recently, Pomeroy (1981) studied the morphology, behavior, and ecology of cannibalistic larvae of several species of spadefoot toads (*Scaphiopus*), a group widely known for this behavior. *Scaphiopus* eggs are laid in temporary pools or other small bodies of water. Development of the embryos and larvae is extremely rapid, and metamorphosis may occur less than 2 weeks after fertilization. During this time, intraspecific competition for food or space may become intense as the pond evaporates. Associated with larval cannibalism in spadefoots is the presence of a well-defined polymorphism. Within one population, there may exist a noncannibalistic omnivorous morph, a cannibalistic carnivorous morph, and an intermediate morph. The cannibalistic and noncannibalistic morphs differ in several aspects of their appearance, behavior, and ecology.

Pomeroy (1981) was able to induce the formation of all three morphs within the same sibling cohort by providing different diets. Ingestion of live prey items (e.g., fairy shrimp, tadpoles) produced the cannibalistic morph, whereas the noncannibalistic morph developed if the tadpoles were fed diets of small, particulate, filterable food. There was some genetic component to the polymorphism as well. Certain breeding lines exhibited a greater tendancy toward the cannibalistic morph regardless of the type of diet ingested.

Larval polymorphism associated with larval/larval cannibalism has also been studied in *Xenopus laevis* (Savage, 1963) and the tiger salamander, *Ambystoma tigrinum* (Powers, 1907; Rose and Armentrout, 1976). In the latter species, not only are breeding sites similar to those of *Scaphiopus,* but the species has evolved a very similar pattern of larval cannibalism. Predaceous, cannibalistic morphs coexist in ephemeral ponds with two noncannibalistic morphs on which they prey. As in certain species of *Scaphiopus,* the cannibalistic forms of *A. tigrinum* are larger, have larger heads, more developed teeth and mouths, and are more aggressive than the smaller, noncannibalistic form. The factors causing polymorphism are not well studied but may have a substantial genetic basis (Pierce *et al.,* 1981). Dietary differences during development have also been implicated (Powers, 1907).

Filial cannibalism. Filial cannibalism, a term denoting the consumption by a parent of its own offspring, was first applied to fish (Rowher, 1978). Filial cannibalism in amphibians has not yet been studied in detail. However, eggs of the salamander, *Cryptobranchus alleganiensis,* have been found in the stomachs of guarding males (King, 1939), and it has been assumed that the consumed eggs are part of the clutch of the guarding male. Guarding males of other species of aquatic breeding cryptobranchid salamanders are said to chase away their mates immediately after oviposition to prevent them from eating their own eggs (Salthe and Mecham, 1974).

In anurans, the author knows of no published account of filial cannibalism occurring in nature. However, Townsend (personal communication) has frequently observed filial cannibalism in the neotropical frog, *Eleutherodactylus coqui,* under field conditions. Guarding males will eat many or all of their eggs but only when the male or their eggs are disturbed by human manipulation or conspecific or invertebrate predators. Tyler (1963) observed a guarding parent of a terrestrial breeding microhylid (*Sphenophryne brevicrus*) consuming its own eggs while confined to a small container. Simon (1982) examined 71 brooding adults of *Cophixalus parkeri*, a terrestrial breeding frog from New Guinea, and found no frog eggs in their stomachs. It is interesting to note that *C. parkeri* would seem to be a prime candidate to have evolved filial cannibalistic behavior (Rohwer, 1978; Dominey and Blumer, Chapter 3 this volume). In this species, care of young is primarily by the male in a territory that he defends for long periods of time. Also in *C. parkeri*, the guarding parent has a greatly reduced food intake during the very long brooding behavior (Simon, 1982), yet filial cannibalism does not occur in this species.

In fact, two features differentiate this and many other anuran systems from the fish-mating systems described by Dominey and Blumer (Chapter 3, this volume). One feature is that the male cares for only one relatively small clutch at a time. One egg, therefore, represents a much greater proportion (5–10%) of the male's total reproductive output than does a single egg eaten by a male fish guarding a nest in which several relatively large clutches have been deposited. Another feature is that the energy required to defend a nest may be much lower in frog species than in comparable fish systems (Wells, 1981), and energy intake, therefore, may not be a factor limiting the ability of the male to care for eggs. *Cophixalus parkeri* has been observed to actively defend nest sites; however, most of the care given to the young is by passively sitting on or near the eggs. This is in marked contrast to the very energetically expensive patrolling and chasing behaviors of stickleback fish. The higher reproductive cost of eating an egg and the lower net contribution of egg eating to offspring defense may explain the lack of filial cannibalism in *C. parkeri* and, perhaps, for the many other frog species that have similar reproductive biologies and parental behaviors. This author predicts that filial cannibalism will most likely be found in species that care for more than one clutch at a time and/ or actively defend nest sites against potential egg predators. Males of *E. coqui*, discussed previously, are known to occasionally care for two or three clutches at a time and aggressively repulse intruding conspecifics from nest sites (Townsend *et al.*, 1984).

Sibling cannibalism. Egg cannibalism by larval siblings occurs in certain tropical frog species that lay their eggs in water-filled leaf axils or treeholes. The relatedness of predator and prey in these larval interactions is strongly inferred from the observation that, usually, all the eggs found at a given site are deposited by a single female (Wassersug *et al.*, 1981). Recent studies have shown that tadpoles of *Rana cascadae* (O'Hara and Blaustein, 1981) and *B. americanus* (Waldman and Adler,

1979) can recognize siblings in a multiclutch school and will preferentially associate with siblings relative to nonsibling conspecifics. Blaustein and O'Hara (1982) proposed that sibling recognition may be an importrant determinate in prey selection and suggested that tadpoles may preferentially avoid eating their own siblings.

Noncannibalistic Egg Killing

In the majority of instances in which amphibian eggs and larvae are killed by conspecific adults, the prey is consumed and used as an energy source. However, recent reports have revealed a few cases in which amphibians are killed but not eaten by conspecifics. Kluge (1981) conducted an exhaustive study of the reproductive biology of *Hyla rosenbergi*, a nest-building gladiator frog from Central America. Eggs are laid in small, water-filled nests that are actively defended by the attending male. Nonguarding, intruding, male *Hyla rosenbergi*, if given access to the nest, agitated the floating egg mass. Although this behavior caused the eggs to sink and ultimately die of oxygen deprivation, it was not known if egg killing was the primary function of egg-mass agitation. In any case, the eggs were not consumed by the intruder.

Scott and Starrett (1974) observed males of the neotropical tree frog, *Agalychnis spurelli*, using their hind legs to scrape fertilized eggs of conspecifics from leaves. The eggs fell into the water below and failed to hatch. Scott and Starrett suggested that most of the egg loss in the high-density population they studied was due to this scraping behavior rather than to predation or other causes.

Wells (1978) and others have observed females of *Dendrobates auratus*, a Central American poison-arrow frog, crushing eggs of conspecifics in the laboratory. Only a few of the eggs were subsequently eaten by the intruding females. This behavior has been observed with sufficient frequency in relatively "natural" terrariums to suggest that the behavior is more than an artifact of laboratory conditions (K. Wells: personal communication).

Parental Desertion of Propagules

In studies of other vertebrates, one of the most often cited forms of infanticide is the desertion of the offspring by the attending parent at an early and highly vulnerable stage of development (Hrdy, 1979; Sherman, 1981). Parental care in amphibians is widespread and occurs in all three orders. In anurans, 10–20% of the species found in 14 of the 20 families exhibit some form of parental care (McDiarmid, 1978; Wells, 1981). Parental care is known to occur in about 65% of the species of salamanders (Salthe and Mecham, 1974; Brame, 1967) and 100% of the caecilians species for which information on the reproductive biology is known (Wake, 1977). Amphibian parental care occurs in species with various reproductive modes but is most common in species that lay a few large eggs in terrestrial or semiterrestrial sites (Table III).

Before discussing the effects of egg abandonment on offspring mortality, it is important to consider the frequency and conditions under which parents desert their offspring. Available information suggests that guarding female salamanders will rarely abandon their eggs before hatching and then only under duress (Highton and Savage, 1961; Juterbock, 1982). Blanchard (1934) demonstrated that the likelihood that a guarding female of the salamander, *Hemidactylum scutatum,* would desert her eggs before hatching depended upon the density and spacing of other brooding conspecifics. If the density was low and the clutches were overdispersed, the female would remain with her eggs until hatching. If, however, there were several clutches clumped together, all but a few females would abandon their eggs.

Wells (1981) suggested that parental attendance in some frogs may be facultative rather than obligate, and that egg abandonment may be related to site- or time-specific environmental conditions such as intensity of mortality agents, population density, likelihood of multiple matings, etc. For example, Kluge (1981) found that *Hyla rosenbergi* males will defend their nests against predators and conspecifics at high adult densities but will abandon their nests at lower densities. On the other hand, other species of frogs are highly tenacious in their guarding behavior and will seldom, if ever, abandon their young until after they hatch. Only 3 of 132 clutches of *Cophixalus parkeri* encountered in the field were without a guarding adult present, and only 5% of parents deserted their clutches after being disturbed repeatedly during a field experiment (Simon, 1980, 1982). Townsend *et al.* (1984) found similar tenacity in egg guarding by male *Eleutherodactylus coqui.*

Several methods have been used to study the effects of parental desertion on the mortality rate of amphibian propagules. One method has been to compare differences in egg and larval mortality rates between two species that are closely related taxonomically and share similar habitat requirements but differ in their propensity to attend eggs or larvae. McDiarmid (1978) examined the differences in hatching success between two congeneric species of frogs that deposit their eggs on the upper surface of overhanging leaves. The two species exhibited many biological similarities but differed in the amount of time they attended their eggs. One species, which continuously guarded its eggs, had an average of 7% prehatching mortality. The other species, which abandoned its eggs during the daylight hours, suffered 23% prehatching mortality.

Another method used to ascertain the effects of parental egg desertion on premetamorphic mortality has been to simply note the condition of eggs found in the field without an attending parent. For example, several workers have reported that the prehatching mortality rates of terrestrial breeding plethodontid salamanders are extremely high (virtually 100%) in egg clutches in which the normally attending parent is absent (Salthe and Mecham, 1974; Forester, 1979). In the terrestrial-breeding, New Guinea microhylid frogs, egg mortality was 100% in those few clutches without a parent in attendance (Simon, 1980, 1982). In contrast, Woodruff (1976, 1977), in his study of three species of Australian myobatrachid frogs, found no difference in egg mortality between egg clutches attended by a parent and those that were abandoned. He concluded that in these three species, egg desertion had no apparent effect on prehatching mortality rate.

A third method for assessing the effects of parental desertion on juvenile mortality consists of removing attending parents from their egg clutches and comparing the survivorship of these experimental clutches to controls in which the parent was allowed to remain with its eggs. Highton and Savage (1961) reported a threefold increase in mortality rate of embryos of the terrestrial breeding salamander, *Plethodon cinereus*, when the attending female was removed from her clutch. Tilley (1972) reported similar increases in mortality of embryos of *Desmognathus ochrophaeus* when the guarding parent was removed and the eggs subsequently reared in the laboratory. Forester (1979), also working with *D. ochrophaeus* females, found that the prehatching mortality of embryos increased from 47% when the female remained with her clutch to 100% when the female was removed.

Removal of the attending parent of *Cophixalus parkeri*, a New Guinea microhylid frog, resulted in 85% prehatching mortality of the developing embryos (Simon, 1980, 1982). When the parent remained with its clutch, only 5% mortality was observed. Taigen *et al.* (1984), working with the neotropical leptodactylid frog, *Eleutherodactylus coqui*, have shown that the removal of the attending male from developing eggs resulted in high mortality due to desiccation.

The observational and experimental data collected so far suggests that offspring desertion in those amphibian species known to care for their offspring is relatively uncommon but often has disastrous consequences for offspring survivorship when it does occur.

ADAPTIVE SIGNIFICANCE OF AMPHIBIAN EGG AND LARVAE KILLING

It should be evident that the degree of amphibian egg and larval mortality can be substantially influenced by the behavior of conspecifics. The occurrence of this intraspecifically induced mortality is now considered within the context of proposed ideas concerning the adaptive significance of infanticide in birds and mammals. Several authors

have recently discussed the idea that, in general, infanticide and cannibalism of young may be adaptive and should not be regarded as merely
aberrant or pathological behavior (Fox, 1975a; Hrdy, 1979; Polis, 1981;
Sherman, 1981). The ecological conditions surrounding the widespread
occurrence of intraspecifically induced propagule mortality in amphibians indicates that in most instances it should also be considered adaptive. There have been a few attempts at classifying the various instances of infanticide into categories based on the presumed adaptive
significance of the behavior to the killer. Hrdy (1979), in particular,
recognized four general categories of infanticide: exploitation, resource
competition, parental manipulation, and sexual selection.

Exploitation

Cannibalism is the most common cause of intraspecifically induced
propagule mortality in amphibians as it is also in invertebrates (Polis,
Chapter 5, this volume) and fish (Dominey and Blumer, Chapter 3, this
volume). Most cases are clear examples of exploitation in which the
killer utilizes the victim as a food source. In fact, many amphibian
species may be highly dependent on cannibalism as a means of obtaining nutrients for normal development and a reasonable chance of surviving to reproduction. Several studies (e.g., Weygoldt, 1980; Pomeroy,
1981) have shown that larval growth is greatly reduced or stopped
altogether if cannibalism is experimentally prevented in normally cannibalistic species. Also, the existence of trophic polymorphism in many
amphibian species indicates that cannibalism may be a highly evolved
trait in this group. This pattern contrasts markedly with that of most
birds and mammals in which cannibalism is primarily a facultative
rather than obligate behavior. The heavy dependence on cannibalism
in many amphibian species reflects the habitat characteristics of the
developing larvae in which high quality food is severely limited. Another difference between the patterns of exploitative cannibalism that
is seen in amphibians and those of other vertebrate groups is that in
amphibians most cannibalistic encounters are usually between individuals at early developmental stages (larvae/larvae, larvae/egg) rather
than between adults and juveniles as is commonly the case in mammals.
This can be explained in part by differences in the habitat of adult
amphibians and their propagules. After oviposition, most adults have
little contact with their eggs or larvae. Also, larvae are often under
severe time constraints to metamorphose quickly if they are to avoid
desiccation or predation. In particular, these time constraints, coupled
with the transient nature of their habitats, may place amphibian larvae
under intense selection to eat the highest quality food available—often
conspecifics.

Resource Competition

Another important adaptive function of intraspecifically induced propagule mortality in amphibians, the reduction of intraspecific competition for resources, is exhibited in a number of different forms. In cannibalistic species, killing and consuming a conspecific may not only reduce competition for resources (space or food) but also provides food to the cannibalizing individual. The dual adaptive significance of cannibalizing potential competitors has been discussed by Fox (1975a), Polis (1981), and others and may be especially applicable to amphibian systems in which required resources become increasingly limited during the developmental period of the larvae (e.g., *Scaphiopus* spp.).

The secretion of growth-inhibiting substances by anuran larvae can also be considered as analogous to resource-competition infanticide. The increased discrepancy between the size of larvae due to these inhibitory substances results in larger individuals obtaining a disproportionately greater share of the available food, a potentially limited resource. Also, if, as has been reported, growth-inhibiting substances can directly cause the death of a segment of a population of anuran larvae, then the surviving individuals would increase their per-individual share of resources, albeit without directly utilizing their conspecific larvae as food.

Finally, two of the known cases of noncannibalistic egg killing (Scott and Starrett, 1974; Kluge, 1981) can be explained almost completely in terms of competition for nest sites. Egg destruction by conspecifics occurred in especially high frequencies in areas where clutches were found at high densities. These examples of egg killing correspond fairly closely to the resource-competition model Hrdy (1979) proposed in which the "death of an infant" (in this case frog eggs) "results in increased access to resources for the killer or ... descendants." Unlike many examples of infanticide in mammals and birds, dominance hierarchies and "xenophobia" have little or no role in the occurrence of noncannibalistic egg killing in amphibians (see Hrdy, 1979).

Parental Manipulation

Egg cannibalism by guarding parents may be a form of parental manipulation of offspring in some amphibian species. There are published reports of guarding parents eating their own diseased or dying eggs to inhibit the spread of fungus or other microorganisms to other propagules (Tilley, 1972; Salthe and Mecham, 1974; Forester, 1979). Forester (1979) demonstrated experimentally that brooding female salamanders (*Desmognathus ochrophaeus*) selectively consumed eggs that were dead or infected with fungus. When females were prevented from consuming infected eggs by having their mouths sewn shut, their clutches succumbed to fungal infections within a short time. These experiments demonstrated that the removal of a few defective propagules improved the chance of survival of the rest of the clutch. This situation may be analogous to infanticide of defective offspring among mammals and birds (Hrdy, 1979). Cannibalism of eggs by a guarding parent after the intrusion of egg predators (Townsend, 1983) represents another example of parental manipulation in which the parent, by eating its eggs during times of suboptimal ecological conditions (heavy predation pressure), defers parental investment. In a sense, the eggs are "reabsorbed" by the guarding parent (in this case the male) when the chances for successful brooding of eggs are slim.

The preceding examples notwithstanding, manipulation of offspring does not appear to play as important a role in the selection of offspring killing by amphibian parents as it does in mammals and birds (Hrdy, 1979; Sherman, 1981). With three exceptions (Weygoldt, 1980; Zimmermann and Zimmermann, 1981), brooding amphibians do not provide any food to their offspring, as do most birds and all mammals. Therefore, the amount of care (primarily in the form of passive egg brooding) given per individual offspring probably does not depend heavily upon the number of offspring in the clutch. Thus, there seems to be little selective advantage (to itself or its offspring) for an amphibian parent to reduce the number of developing embryos it is guarding as would be the case in lactating mammals, for example, in which killing some of her offspring would increase the per-individual amount of milk consumed by the remaining offspring.

Sexual Selection

The possibility exists that some of the observed instances of amphibian egg cannibalism or egg destruction may be the result of intense intrasexual competition for opportunities to reproduce. Unlike mammalian or avian systems, it is quite common for the male parent to provide as much or more parental investment than the female (McDiarmid, 1978; Wells, 1981). Therefore, one would expect to find amphibian species in which females rather than males are the primary agents of egg destruction (see Introduction). Indeed, Wells (1978) considered the egg-crushing behavior of females of *Dendrobates auratus* to be primarily competition between females for access to males. Because of the large amounts of male parental investment in the form of egg brooding and tadpole transport, the number of males available to females may be considerably less than the number of females seeking mates. By destroying another female's eggs, the killer releases the guarding male from his parental care responsibilities and is then able to secure a mating from the now unencumbered male. Sexual selection may also explain adult egg cannibalism in *D. pumilio*, a species closely

related to *D auratus* but having a contrasting form of parental investment. In this species, it is the female, not the male, who provides most
of the parental care in the form of egg transport and production of
trophic eggs, and it is the males who cannibalize the eggs (Weygoldt,
1980). Although the killing of propagules as a result of reproductive
competition appears to be less common than in mammals, it seems
likely that further study of amphibian species which have parental
care will reveal that sexual selection is a strong force in the evolution
of egg cannibalism in this group.

SUMMARY

The mortality rates of egg and larval (propagules) amphibians is
highly variable and ranges from over 95% in many aquatic breeding
species to less than 10% in some terrestrial species. The general causes
of this mortality are reviewed. Special attention is given to those factors
of egg and larval mortality that are influenced by the behavior of conspecifics: exploitation and interference, intraspecific larval competition,
egg and larval cannibalism by adults and larvae, noncannibalistic egg
killing, and parental desertion of propagules. The available information
indicates these factors can have a significant impact on the mortality
rate of premetamorphic amphibians. Egg and larval killing in amphibians is discussed in the context of previously proposed theories concerning the adaptive significance of infanticide in birds and mammals. Most
of the known instances of egg and larval killing in amphibians are
clearly exploitative, however, some can be regarded as examples of
resource competition, parental manipulation of offspring, or sexual selection. Many patterns of intraspecifically induced propagule mortality
in amphibians are closely analogous to types of infanticide known
for birds and mammals, while other aspects of infanticide in these
"higher" vertebrates have no counterpart in amphibians.

ACKNOWLEDGMENTS

Numerous people made constructive comments on the manuscript and provided useful
information on many of the topics presented. For this assistance, I would like to thank:
Kentwood Wells, Mike Ryan, Dan Townsend, Meg Stewart, Marvalee Wake, Larry Pomeroy, Bill Jameson, Bob Drews, and Kathy Ono. I am also grateful for the comments
and suggestions provided by Glenn Hausfater and Sarah Blaffer Hrdy, the editors of
this volume.

5 | Intraspecific predation and "infant killing" among invertebrates

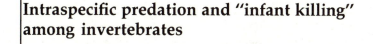

Gary A. Polis

INTRODUCTION

The invertebrates are a tremendously diverse assemblage of animals; they form some 30 phyla and are estimated to represent over 95% of all species and individuals of animals living today. If extinct animals are included, this figure exceeds 99%. Intraspecific killing and cannibalism are widespread. During preparation of this chapter, reports describing intraspecific killing and predation for almost 1000 species distributed among 11 phyla of invertebrate were encountered. A single chapter on this subject, therefore, cannot be comprehensive. Instead, it highlights some phenomena that occur repeatedly among invertebrates and that generally have received little attention in research on infanticide and related phenomena among vertebrates. It is hoped that this approach will stimulate scientists working on infanticide in vertebrates to inspect their particular group for similar phenomena.

There are marked differences not only in the biology of invertebrates compared to vertebrates but also in the basic approach used by researchers to investigate the two groups. For example, it is relatively easy to distinguish particular vertebrate individuals and to analyze specific behaviors. Thus, with the exception of fish, much research on cannibalism and infanticide among vertebrates focuses on the actions and/or disappearance of specific individual subjects. Invertebrates, however, are both much more abundant and difficult to recognize individually. For these reasons, research is often conducted at the level of the population or cohort rather than concentrated on the behavior of individuals. In particular, studies of infanticide and cannibalism among invertebrates often emphasize population-wide phenomena such as cycles, survivorship, and other aspects of demography as well as energetic constraints on reproduction.

A striking difference between invertebrates and vertebrates is the degree that individuals recognize one another. Many vertebrates—primarily birds, mammals, and some reptiles and amphibians—recognize both conspecifics and offspring; some higher vertebrates are also able to identify commonly encountered neighbors. Despite some notable exceptions, there is a general lack of individual recognition among the invertebrates. Even parents may not recognize their own progeny, and many species may not recognize immature conspecifics. Thus, cannibalism and infanticide are more likely to be indiscriminate among the invertebrates than in vertebrates, particularly mammals.

Incidental Cannibalism in Invertebrates

Differences between invertebrates and vertebrates in individual recognition, combined with several modes of feeding unique to invertebrates, often leads to what is called here *incidental cannibalism*. Specifically, in many invertebrate groups, cannibalism of eggs and young occurs as a normal and inevitable by-product of feeding behavior. With the exception of fish (and possibly gerbils, see Elwood and Ostermeyer, Chapter 19, this volume), this phenomenon has no known parallel among vertebrates. Such cannibalism is well illustrated with filter feeders. Most marine and many aquatic invertebrates spend their early existence in the plankton as eggs and larvae. These stages are commonly strained and eaten by conspecific adults during normal filter-feeding behavior. This form of cannibalism has been observed in corals (Glynn, 1973), copepods, and several species of bivalve mollusks (see references in Polis, 1981). Such incidental cannibalism potentially occurs in all filter feeders that undergo a planktonic existence (Woodin, 1976; Polis, 1981) and, in several species, cannibalistic filter feeding is the major source of mortality for eggs and larvae (Polis, 1981). Intraspecific predation of eggs and young also occurs as a by-product of other modes of feeding. Suspension and deposit feeders from several phyla ingest immature conspecifics as they process sediment for organic material that forms the bulk of their diet. This activity is sufficient to clear the area around their burrows of eggs and small larvae—both their own and those of conspecifics—and may even prevent a new generation from being established (Johnson, 1959; Jonasson, 1971; Woodin, 1974, 1976).

Indiscriminate cannibalism likewise occurs among herbivorous invertebrates. Thus, some species of butterfly larvae eat not only leaves but also conspecific eggs and small larvae that are attached to the leaves (Rausher, 1979; Stamp, 1980). Eggs and larvae are similarly eaten when bark beetles enlarge their wooden galleries and when intertidal limpets and aquatic insects graze the substrate for diatoms and algae (see references in Polis, 1981). Finally, many facultative euryphagous predators apparently eat immature conspecifics just as readily as heterospecific prey. This is the case for some protozoa (Giese, 1973), chaetognath arrowworms (Pearre, 1982), carnivorous copepods (McQueen, 1969; Landry 1978a, b; Lonsdale et al., 1979), spiders (Edgar, 1969, 1971; Hallander, 1970; Turner, 1979), scorpions (Polis, 1980), and insect predators (e.g., Fischer, 1960; Fox, 1975b). Indeed for all these animals, young conspecifics are the same size as normal heterospecific prey.

In at least some of the preceding cases, it is possible that these feeding types may actually prefer conspecifics to immature individuals of other species. Analyses of selectivity indexes for at least a few species show that they eat conspecifics in greater proportion than their relative abundance (McQueen, 1969; Kawai, 1978). These species, however, also feed commonly on congenerics and other closely related species. Furthermore, many other species show a negative preference for conspecifics (King and Dawson, 1973; Fox, 1975b; Landry, 1978a; Lonsdale et al., 1979); and some species eat conspecifics in the precise proportion that they are present in the environment (Giese, 1973; Duelli, 1981). However, interpretation of dietary-selection indexes based simply on relative abundance of potential prey is difficult since factors such as hunger, availability, apparency, catchability, and antipredator adaptations also greatly influence diet composition. However, the fact that cannibalism generally increases as the abundance of alternate prey decreases suggests that conspecifics are for most species either a less-preferred or less-available prey type (Polis, 1981).

SOME GENERAL CHARACTERISTICS OF INTRASPECIFIC PREDATION IN INVERTEBRATES

Several other general characteristics emerge from the scattered reports of intraspecific predation among the invertebrates. First, immature animals form the bulk of intraspecific prey, although adults are also occasionally cannibalized (Polis, 1981). In particular, eggs and newborn stages are not only a rich source of energy and nutrients but also relatively defenseless unless guarded by a parent. Many authors report adaptations that reduce cannibalism on eggs and immature animals. Such adaptations include temporal (Edgar, 1971; Polis, 1980) or spatial (Edgar, 1969, 1971; Fox, 1975c; Gallepp, 1974; Hallander, 1970; Murdoch and Sih, 1978; Trpis, 1973; Tschinkel, 1978) separation from adults; behavioral mechanisms (Forster, 1970; Gallepp, 1974; Lonsdale et al., 1979;

Murdoch and Sih, 1978; Tschinkel, 1978); or morphological characteristics (Duelli, 1981; Gallepp, 1974; Gilbert, 1980; Landry, 1978a) that decreases the probability that eggs and young will be cannibalized. The variety of anticannibalism adaptations are illustrated by consideration of backswimmers, *Notonecta hoffmanni* (Fox 1975b, Murdoch and Sih, 1978). Young animals sometimes form 40–50% of the weekly diet of adults and older nymphs, although the average proportion is usually much lower. Such predation explains 50–100% of all mortality experienced by the youngest age group. Most young live in spatial refuges in vegetation at the side of pools. This usually allows young to escape intraspecific predation. However, the number of refuges decreases seasonally when drying causes the pools to shrink. At these times, the population of young animals drastically declines due to cannibalism. Young also change their feeding behavior when in the presence of adults; they become much less active and feed only 10% as much as when adults are absent. Such behavior decreases the chance of detection and predation by older conspecifics.

Second, invertebrate cannibalistic predators may be adults, juveniles, or even newborn animals. However, with the exception of species that practice sibling cannibalism (see last major section), adults and older animals are usually but not always more cannibalistic than younger animals. This is because predation intensity among invertebrates generally increases with predator size due to an increase in attack rate, an increase in feeding capacity, and a decrease in handling time. Further, larger animals are relatively invulnerable to retaliatory attacks by smaller immature animals. The importance of size relationships can be illustrated by considering the desert scorpion, *Paruroctonus mesaensis* (Polis, 1980). In over 150 cases of cannibalism observed in the field, larger scorpions were always the predator. Conspecifics formed 14% of all prey eaten by adults but less than 7% of the diet of the smallest age class; further, only 18% of all intraspecific prey were adults (mostly males eaten after mating), whereas 63% were from the smallest age class.

Third, females are more frequently cannibalistic than males. In general, it is very difficult to determine the sex of immature invertebrates. For this reason, the sexual identity of intraspecific predators and prey are usually not reported. However, in over 87% of those cases that sex differences were reported, females were more cannibalistic on eggs and young as compared to males. (This does not include the cases of female parental cannibalism on their own offspring.) Females are the major intraspecific predator in rotifers (Gilbert, 1980), squid (Kore and Joshi, 1975), several species of arachnids (e.g., Hallander, 1970; Polis, 1980; Turner: personal communication), and several orders of insects (e.g., Duelli, 1981; Gallepp, 1974; King and Dawson, 1973).

Males are the major cannibal in a species of braconid parasitoid wasp and *Tribolium* on pupae (see references in Polis, 1981). Males are the only cannibals in a species of prawn (*Macrobrachium rosenbergii*, Forster, 1970) and several species of autoparasitic wasps in the family Aphelinidae (Askew, 1971). In the case of these wasps (*Encarsia* and *Coccophagus*), females are parasitoids on homopteran scale insects, and males are rare. However, when males are produced, they develop not as parasitoids of scales but as internal hyperparasitoids of larval females of their own species.

Fourth, in many but not all cases, the rate of intraspecific predation increases with hunger and with a decrease in availability of alternate foods (see Fox, 1975a; Polis, 1981, for complete discussion and references). This author found over 35 references reporting this widespread relationship in invertebrates. It occurs in the protozoa, flatworms, gastropods, crustacea, and in several orders of arachnids and insects. In fact, in many groups or invertebrates, periodic scarcity of alternate foods is the major factor promoting cannibalism on newborn and immature animals. As is well known, the environment of many species is characterized either by a marked fluctuation in food availability or a more or less regular seasonal decrease in natural foods. At these times, the rate of cannibalism increases predictably often to very high levels. The scorpion, *P. mesaensis,* will serve as an example. The proportion of intraspecific prey in the diet is an inverse function of prey availability. During midsummer, the desert environment becomes very stressful: temperatures reach an annual maximum (surface temperatures $>50°C$ daily), the abundance of insect prey drops to an annual minimum (an order of magnitude less than spring), and the average growth rate (weight) actually becomes negative for part of this period. Intraspecific predation, especially on newborns, becomes common. Conspecifics may constitute up to 25–50% of the diet ($\bar{X} = 16\%$). During this time, the population of newborn animals decreases by about 60%. In a few unique cases, the presence of high-quality alternate food actually has the opposite effect of promoting, rather than inhibiting, cannibalism through the production of voracious "giant cannibal morphotypes." Such morphs occur in *Amoeba,* flagellates, several genera of ciliates, and *Asplancha* rotifers; vertebrate parallels can be found in at least two genera of amphibians (Polis, 1981).

Another general characteristic of invertebrate cannibalism is that it is often a direct function of density. This author found 50 references on invertebrates that reported increased rates due to overcrowding or high densities (see Fox, 1975a; Polis, 1980, 1981). There are at least two explanations for this relationship. First, as discussed earlier, conspecifics may not be distinguished from other food, and increased rates of cannibalism occur for the same reasons that predators exhibit density-dependent responses to heterospecific prey. Such cannibalism is probably frequent and is best exemplified by species that eat conspecific eggs and young as a by-product of normal feeding activities. Second, individuals of many invertebrate species maintain interindividual space or territory in which they are intolerant to conspecifics. Crowding increases the frequency with which conspecifics violate a critical minimum *Lebensraum* and thus promotes the observed increase in the rate of cannibalism.

POPULATION CONSEQUENCES OF INTRASPECIFIC PREDATION

Demographic consequences of infanticide and intraspecific predation have been the subject of two recent reviews (Fox, 1975a; Polis, 1981). Population-level effects of cannibalism are thus discussed here only briefly to reemphasize that intraspecific predation of eggs and young significantly influences the population structure and dynamics of several species of invertebrates. As mentioned previously, cannibalism is one of the major causes of mortality in many species. A large proportion of the entire population or of specific age-classes may be eaten: for example, 31–50% of copepod eggs and larvae, >80% of all prawn, 94–99% of black widow eggs and nymphs, 30–75% of dragonfly nymphs, 50–100% of first instar backswimmers, 6–50% of water boatman eggs, 0–43% of ladybird beetle eggs, 10–58% of butterfly eggs, and 16% of moth larvae in pine cones (see references in Fox, 1975a; Polis, 1981). In some species, cannibalism may be so intense that a particularly numerous age-class of older conspecifics may eat nearly 100% of the eggs and/or young produced by a population. As may be expected, the decimation or elimination of a cohort often causes violent fluctuations in recruitment and an age/size distribution that is heavily skewed to favor adults. This situation occurs in polychaete and molluskan filter and deposit feeders (reviewed in Polis, 1981), copepods (Landry, 1978b), and at least eight families of insects (e.g., Jonasson, 1971; Mertz, 1969). Cannibalism is so severe in some strains of *Tribolium* beetles that whole populations may become extinct when all recruitment is eaten by a large cohort of old adults that are no longer capable of laying eggs (Mertz, 1969).

Intraspecific predation apparently acts as a density dependent regulator of population size in flatworms, leeches, sea slugs, copepods, crayfish, scorpions, spiders, and many species of insect (Fox, 1975a; Polis, 1981). Further, it has been repeatedly suggested that cannibalism at low food levels may serve as a "lifeboat strategy" to decrease the probability of extinction and to increase the long-term persistence of populations that live in environments characterized by large fluctuations in food reserves (Polis, 1980, 1981). The term *lifeboat strategy* was used by Giese (1973) in describing cannibalistic morphotypes of *Blepharisma* protozoan ciliates. Individuals in a population of cannibals survived periods of food deprivation by eating others, whereas individuals in noncannibalistic populations starved to death. Similar results were obtained for three species of sheep blowfly (Ullyette, 1950) and different strains of mite (Croft and McMurtry, 1972). Under conditions of inadequate per-capita food, the populations of the two cannibalistic blowfly species and the cannibalistic mite strains persisted while the noncannibalistic populations became extinct.

SELECTION AND EVOLUTION OF INTRASPECIFIC PREDATION

Genetic Basis

As discussed below, cannibalism confers many advantages to the individual. However, in order for selection to operate on intraspecific predation, the expression of this trait must be genetically controlled. Unfortunately, there has been little research on the genetic basis of cannibalism in invertebrates, but the few existing studies do suggest that there is a strong genetic component to the behavior. The existence of genetic strains with different cannibalistic tendencies constitutes some of the best evidence on this question. Strain-specific differences occur in flatworms, rotifers, mites, *Tribolium* beetles, and *Heliothis* corn earworms (reviewed in Fox, 1975a and Polis, 1981). Extremely voracious strains of *Heliothis* were over 20 times more cannibalistic than the least cannibalistic strain (Gould *et al.,* 1980). Likewise, different strains of *Tribolium* show marked differences in their propensity to eat conspecific eggs, larvae, or pupae (King and Dawson, 1973; McCauley and Wade, 1980; Mertz, 1969; Wade and McCauley, 1980). In *Tribolium,* the intensity of cannibalism is inversely proportional to population size. Those strains with the smallest equilibrium population of adults are most cannibalistic (up to 95% of all pupae are eaten). This is in contrast to strains exhibiting relatively large populations. In these strains, as few as 15% of all pupae are eaten.

These strain-specific differences in cannibalism show simple patterns of inheritance, a fact that provides additional evidence that cannibalism is genetically controlled. For both *Tribolium* and *Heliothis,* the progeny of reciprocal crosses of strains exhibit an intensity of cannibalism intermediate to those exhibited by parental stocks. The restriction of cannibalism to particular life-story stages and differences in the cannibalistic propensities of closely related species provide further evidence that cannibalism is genetically determined and responsive to selection (Fox, 1975a).

Exploitation of Conspecifics as Resource

There are clear advantages to the cannibalistic predator. Cannibals not only gain substantial nutritional benefits but eliminate potential competitors and, in many cases, potential predators. The nutritional benefits alone may be substantial. To understand the energetic role of cannibalism, one must analyze diet in terms of weight or volume rather than simple frequency. Since conspecifics are often some of the heaviest prey items, they may be an important food source even when their frequency in the diet is not particularly high. In summer, for example, in the scorpion, *P. mesaensis,* and fourth instar *Chaborus* midge larvae, conspecifics form 9% and from 1–5%, respectively, of the diet by frequency (Polis, 1980; Fedorenko, 1975). However, conspecifics form 28% and 15–40% of the diet by weight, respectively.

In addition to supplying energy, conspecifics may be an important source of protein, especially for herbivores and granivores. This may partially explain why cannibalism is so common in these otherwise nonpredaceous groups. It is likely that the extensive cannibalism observed among termites may also be a protein-conservation tactic that supplements their low-protein diet (Wilson, 1971). The nutritional benefits of cannibalism are manifested in invertebrates by higher developmental, growth, and survival rates, increased size, and increased reproduction as compared to conspecifics unable to cannibalize (Fox, 1975a; Polis, 1981). Thus, cannibalism may be, in part, an adaptation for obtaining nutrients to promote higher fitness as compared to less cannibalistic conspecifics.

Decreased Future Predation

Intraspecific killing and predation of younger animals confers one advantage to some invertebrates that has no parallel among vertebrates. By killing conspecifics, individual arthropods are able to decrease future intraspecific killing and predation on themselves. Arthropods are unique in this respect because they must periodically pass through quiescent stages (i.e., molting and, for some insects, pupation). These stages are immobile and thus highly vulnerable to predation by smaller conspecifics (e.g., Corbet and Griffiths, 1963; Forster, 1970; Kaddou, 1960; King and Dawson, 1973; Tschinkel, 1978). For these animals, killing and cannibalism reduces the probability that they themselves will be cannibalized subsequently. This phenomenon occurs in tree hole-dwelling mosquitoes of the genus *Toxorhynchites* (Corbet and Griffiths, 1963; Lounibos, 1979; Trpis, 1973). Usually only one individual is found in each tree hole. Larvae are highly cannibalistic, and it has been reported for laboratory populations that older larvae may embark on a "killing frenzy" in the days immediately before pupation.

However, if even one younger conspecific escapes the killing frenzy by hiding in a refuge, it will attack and eat the pupa. It should be noted that such cannibalistic behavior is not universal among *Toxorhynchites;* some species are only rarely cannibalistic.

Sexual Selection

Individuals also produce an effective increase in their own fitness through intraspecific predation specifically by reducing the fitness of other individuals of the same sex. This may occur by directly cannibalizing or killing sexual competitors or by eating their offspring. Eggs and immature stages of termites and social *Hymenoptera* are commonly killed and eaten along with defeated adults during territorial wars between rival colonies (Brian, 1965; Wilson, 1971). However, during these battles, the killing is not limited to immature stages. In contrast, some social insects cannibalize only the progeny of rival reproductives. This phenomenon occurs frequently among species of *Polistes* paper wasps that associate in communally constructed nests (Brian, 1965; Wilson, 1971; Kasuya *et al.,* 1980). Founding queens each build their own brood cells in which their young develop. In most species studied, queens invade one another's combs and eat larvae and pupae. In some species, a hierarchy is established, and one queen becomes dominant over subordinate nestmates. Dominance is expressed when the alpha female eats most, if not all, of the brood of the other queens.

Similar behaviors are exhibited by some bumblebees (*Bombus*), miner bees (*Dialictus* and *Lasioglossum*), and species of *Lasius* ants (Brian, 1965; Wilson, 1971). When food is scarce, females of the primitively social *Lasioglossum* bees may destroy the eggs of other females and substitute their own in the empty cells. A slightly different situation occurs in the honeybee (*Apis mellifera*). The first queen to mature kills all pupae and larvae that are developing into queens (Brian, 1965; Wilson, 1971). Also, in many species of social *Hymenoptera,* the queen will forage around the colony and eat eggs laid by workers (Brian, 1965; Wilson, 1971); these eggs may develop into males and represent a means for workers to reproduce independently of the queen. However, in other species of social insect, workers routinely lay infertile "trophic eggs" that are eaten by the queen and her brood. In these cases, oophagy has lost its competitive quality and has been transformed into "an important form of food exchange among cooperating members of the same colony" [Wilson, 1971: 281].

All of the preceding forms of killing and cannibalism may occur within the same colony. There is only one report of intercolonial cannibalism on immature stages. Foundress queens in two species of *Polistes* were observed to attack nearby nests (Kasuya *et al.,* 1980). Larvae and pupae were eaten immediately by the invading female; she also carried some prey back to her nest to feed her own larvae. In one case, two queens reciprocally attacked each other's nest. Clubionid (*Clubiona*) and salticid (*Portia*) spiders also raid the nests of conspecifics (Jackson, 1982; Pollard, in press). Normally, mothers guard their nests and attempt to repulse all intruders. *Clubiona* mothers are always successful guards, and eggs are eaten only if the nest is unattended. *Portia* mothers are sometimes driven off. In these cases, the invading female eats the eggs. Nest guarding, a defense against such intraspecific predation, occurs in many spiders and other arachnids as well as in seastars, octopus, and many species of social and nonsocial insects. Likewise, some cricket females guard their nests by killing or eating intruding conspecifics that may themselves cannibalize the female's brood (Choudhuri and Bagh, 1974).

Offspring Survival

In scorpions and probably many other cannibalistic species, mothers also decrease potential predation on their own offspring by eating conspecifics in the territory around their burrows (Polis, 1980, 1981). Such behavior allows young to disperse into an area that is largely absent of older conspecific predators. Thus, in the scorpion, *P. mesaensis,* the tendency for adults to be regularly distributed is largely due to cannibalism among adults. Active discrimination of oviposition sites is another important prepartum behavior that functions to decrease killing and intraspecific predation on eggs and newborn. Females of many species will not deposit eggs in areas already occupied by older conspecifics or previously laid eggs (Salt, 1961; Askew, 1971; Mitchell, 1975; Rausher, 1979; Stamp, 1980). Such discriminatory behavior also occurs among granivorous and herbivorous insects and internal parasitoid wasps. In these species, older larvae kill and/or eat all or most of younger eggs and larvae. Thus, there is a much lower survival rate for the progeny of later ovipositing females as compared to conspecifics that were the first to place eggs on the host organism. For example, in the swallowtail butterfly (*Battus philendor*), only 19% of the second set of eggs laid on a plant survived compared to 49% of the first eggs (Rausher, 1979). Reduced survival was attributed to cannibalism that occurred as a by-product of leaf eating and displacement from the leaves by normal activity of older larvae. Similarly in the bean weevil, *Callosobruchus,* the survival of the second egg laid on a bean is approximately one-half of the first (Mitchell, 1975). Older larvae frequently eat smaller conspecifics in the same bean (Utida, 1942).

Resource Competition

Intraspecific killing and predation sometimes function as a tactic to secure exclusive use of an area. The defended area may correspond to a territory or simply may be a discrete food resource. Such aggressive behavior often results in approximately regular spacing. Cannibalism and killing of immature conspecifics is reported to be the primary mechanism producing overdispersion or territory in marine worms (Johnson, 1959), bivalves (Woodin, 1974), and many species of insects including moth larvae in apples, pine cones, and corn (Andrewartha, 1971; Coyne, 1968; Gould *et al.*, 1980), aquatic dipteran larvae (Jonasson, 1971; Lounibos, 1979; Trpis, 1973), beetle larvae (Tschinkel, 1978), lacewing larvae (Duelli, 1981), larvae of granivorous insects (Crombie, 1944; Mitchell, 1975), and larvae of parasitoid wasps (Askew, 1971; Fisher, 1970).

The parasitic *Hymenoptera* are a particularly good example showing how intraspecific predation and killing function as a tactic to produce regular spacing and gain exclusive use of a territory (Askew, 1971; Finney and Fisher, 1964; Fisher, 1970; Salt, 1961). Females from several families of wasps oviposit within the bodies of other insects. Larvae feed internally on tissue, eventually causing the host's death. In many species, only one adult parasitoid emerges from each host, regardless of the number of eggs laid: supernumerary larvae are destroyed by older larvae of the same or different species. Supernumeraries introduced early in the development of the first parasitoid larvae are killed outright by physical attack. Attacked larvae are either eaten or left to die. For example, as many as 52 dead first instar *Macrocentrus ancyolivorus* were found in a single moth larva in which only one parasitoid developed (Finney and Fisher, 1964). At a later stage in the development of the original parasitoid, newly introduced larvae die when they are physiologically surpressed by chemical secretions from the older larvae.

Other insects that are cannibalistic in defense of resources include *Heliothis* (Gould *et al.*, 1980) and several beetle and moth species that infest grain (e.g., *Callosobruchus, Rhizopertha, Sitotroga* [Utida, 1942; Crombie, 1944; Mitchell, 1975]. The corn earworm, *Heliothis zea*, shows a highly regular distribution. Eggs are laid on the silk, and larvae crawl to the husk to feed. The first larvae to reach the husk eats all subsequent arrivals, although there is sufficient food for many animals to mature. The larvae of granivorous insects develop within the seeds on which they feed. In many species, younger larvae, attempting to use an occupied seed, are eaten by the resident. Cannibalism in these species has probably been subject to selective forces similar to those that act on other forms of interference competition that produce intraspecific spacing. Thus, under these circumstances, cannibalism and killing assure that individuals will have access to sufficient resources. For example, in the bean weevil, *Callosobruchus*, 7–17% of all beans cannot support two larvae (Mitchell, 1975). Individuals effectively increase their average survivorship by this amount when they kill or eat a conspecific.

Nevertheless, the question then arises as to why killing and cannibalism have evolved in animals whose resources are relatively abundant (e.g., parasitoids in a host's body, *Heliothis* on a stalk of corn)? The answer is complex, but aside from nutritional benefits of cannibalism and the elimination of a potential future predator, such behavior may occur because there is a selective advantage to animals that do not tolerate conspecifics. Tolerance may lead to overcrowding and subsequent depletion of resources below a level necessary for normal development. Alternately, the intensity of killing and cannibalism may be regulated by the principle of greatest stringency (Wilson, 1975). The level of interference evolved so that the quantity of resource defended will always be adequate, even in the most unfavorable (stringent) times. Thus, during most periods, it appears that territorial sizes are too big or aggressiveness too intense relative to the existing abundance of resources.

Superterritoriality

It is clear that intraspecific killing and predation produce many benefits that tend to raise the fitness of cannibals (and, for some benefits, killers per se) relative to less cannibalistic conspecifics. Verner (1977) suggested another way by which relative fitness could be increased as a result of interference or aggression. In proposing the "superterritorial hypothesis," he reasoned that since fitness is relative to the rest of the population, it can be raised either by acting to increase one's absolute contribution to the future gene pool or by decreasing the contribution of other individuals in the population. Aggressive behavior should evolve both to increase reproductive capacity by ensuring access to resources and by denying resources to other individuals, thereby decreasing their reproductive capacity. Thus, natural selection should favor aggression including intraspecific predation merely because it excludes less aggressive conspecifics from breeding, hence lowering population size.

However, Rothstein (1979) offered two important criticisms of Verner's hypothesis that aggression can evolve to increase the aggressor's relative fitness by reducing the population of competitors. First, models of frequency-dependent selection show that the frequency of "superaggressors" does not normally increase in the population, especially if there is much cost to such aggression. Second, superaggression is a spiteful rather than selfish behavior both because it may be more costly than normal levels of aggression (as just suggested) and because all individuals in an open population, not just the superaggressor, benefit equally from a general reduction in population size. The superaggressor uses more energy and is thus actually relatively less fit than normal aggressors. Such arguments tend to limit the evolution of aggression for its own sake; Rothstein correctly maintained that aggression that functions solely to reduce the fitness of others is unlikely to evolve under most conditions.

Nevertheless, these objections are not fully applicable to intraspecific predation and killing. Although the arguments based on frequency-dependent selection are generally correct, they are sensitive to the parameter values assigned to the benefits. Cannibalism and killing totally eliminate a competitor, thus producing much greater benefits than those used by Rothstein in his model. Higher benefits may well increase the frequency of genes for these behaviors and thus allow the evolution of "supercannibalism" and "superkilling," even within the constraints of Rothstein's own model. Moreover, the spite argument is correct as applied to killing but not cannibalism. This is so because cannibalism is characterized by a net energy gain from feeding rather than the net energy loss that characterizes killing per se and other forms of superaggression. Supercannibals do not suffer the same relative disadvantage as superkillers because net benefits exceed net cost. Thus, cannibalism may evolve, in part, because cannibals enjoy higher relative fitness by both contributing more genes to the next generation (benefit from received energy) and inhibiting the genetic contribution of others (benefit from competitor removal).

KILLING AND CANNIBALISM AMONG RELATIVES

Three hypotheses may explain the evolution of cannibalism between relatives: individual fitness, inclusive fitness, and parental manipulation (Alexander, 1974; Eickwort, 1973; Fox, 1975a; O'Connor, 1978; Polis, 1980, 1981; Wilson, 1975). In all cases, the cannibal benefits both phenotypically (i.e., personal and nutritional status) and genotypically (i.e., contribution to future gene pools), whereas the victim loses phenotypically due to death. For individual fitness (selfishness), cost is incurred also to the victim's genotype. However, for inclusive fitness (kin selection), there is genotype benefit for the victim: cannibalism increases the proportion of the victim's genes in the next generation via genes shared by relatives who benefit from the victim's death. For parental manipulation, there is cost to the victim's genotype, but both the cannibal and parent benefit. Alexander (1974:337) explained that "parental manipulation of progeny refers to parents adjusting or manipulating their parental investment, particularly by reducing the fitness of certain progeny in the interests of increasing their own inclusive fitness via other offspring." As a caveat, however, one must note that it is operationally difficult to distinguish between the three hypotheses. Further, since the cannibal always benefits, some biologists maintain that it is unnecessary to invoke selection above the level of the individual.

Parental Cannibalism of Young

Parents from many species occasionally kill and eat their own progeny. Although some cases of this cannibalism are undoubtedly abnormal (e.g., Kaston, 1968), in some species it regularly occurs and has obvious selective value. For example, dead, moribund, and diseased eggs and offspring are routinely destroyed by termites, ants, and bees (Brian, 1965; Wilson, 1971). Further, many species of arthropod use progeny as a food source during periods of food scarcity and to sustain parents when they are unable to forage (e.g., claustral periods while guarding nests or eggs) (Brian, 1965; Wilson, 1971). In many social insects, founding queens commonly eat their own eggs or feed them to the first group of larvae (Wilson, 1971). In general, there is a direct relationship between colony hunger and brood cannibalism (Wilson, 1971). The brood is a final food reserve that normally functions under emergency conditions to keep the queen and workers alive. Such cases of parental cannibalism are clear examples of parental manipulation as the parent sacrifices some offspring to increase the fitness of itself and other offspring.

Sibling Cannibalism on Eggs

Some invertebrates cannibalize eggs, embryos, and newborn animals from within their own clutch. For many of these species, the victim essentially functions as a *de facto* "food cache" or temporary store of energy and nutrients for its siblings. The use of siblings as food caches apparently evolved under conditions that disfavor easy conversion of either material tissue or high levels of ambient food directly into offspring tissue. There may be selection to produce well-nourished offspring via sibling cannibalism if females are unable either to supply eggs with enough yolk or to provision offspring as they develop (Alexander, 1974; Polis, 1980, 1981; Wilson, 1971). Such intrabrood cannibalism is characterized by the use of some offspring as extended parental investment sacrificed to profit other offspring: Victims essentially function as packages of live meat for their kin. Alexander (1974) discussed this type of cannibalism under his "ice box hypothesis."

An extreme case of the food cache strategy occurs in animals that normally produce infertile "nurse" or "trophic" eggs that serve as the first food of newborn. There are reports of over 100 species of invertebrates producing nonviable eggs that are regularly eaten by siblings. Such eggs are critical to the biology of many of these species. They often form a large part of the clutch: 95% in black widow spiders (*Latrodectus*) (Kaston, 1968); 8–97% in muricid snails (Lyons and Spight, 1973); 0–53% in the honeybee (Brian, 1965); 40–60% in some crickets (Choudhuri and Bagh, 1974); and 5–40% in coccinellid beetles (Banks, 1956; Kaddou, 1960; Kawai, 1978). In some snails, spiders, and ants, tropic eggs form all or most of the early diet (Lyons and Spight, 1973; Kaston, 1968; Wilson, 1971). Further, egg cannibalism may greatly decrease clutch size: In black widow spiders, two and five spiderlings emerged from clutches of 153 and 124 eggs, respectively (Kaston, 1968); in *Thais emarginata*, a rock snail, an average of 16 young developed from egg capsules of more than 500 eggs (lyons and Spight, 1973). In many of the preceding species, siblings not only eat trophic eggs but also viable ones. For example, siblings eat an average of 27% of all eggs laid by the coccinellid beetle, *Harmonia* (Kawai, 1978). However, an average of only 15% of all eggs are trophic eggs, and the remainder of the cannibalized eggs are fertile embryos.

Sibling Cannibalism on Larvae

Sibling cannibalism on newborn animals is also widespread among the invertebrates. It occurs in marine snails, mites, spiders, scorpions, termites, Hemiptera, ants, bees, wasps, beetles, and butterflies. In these cases, newborn may also serve as food caches if offspring are differentially vulnerable to cannibalism. Variability in size is the paramount factor that predisposes smaller animals to a higher risk of being eaten. Variability may be produced by unequal partitioning of embryonic material, asynchronous production or hatching of young, or differential feeding of young (Alexander, 1974; Polis, 1981, and to follow). Ingestion of eggs and siblings also eases the necessity that young animals immediately find external food sources. Early cannibalistic feeding allows newborn to avoid the high levels of mortality that normally occur during critical early stages. Siblings form a guaranteed food source, thereby decreasing early food requirements, increasing survivorship, and accelerating growth and development (Banks, 1956; Brown, 1972; Duelli, 1981; Eickwort, 1973; Kaddou, 1960; Kaston, 1968; Kawai, 1978; Polis, 1981; Valerio, 1974). In some arthropods, a diet of only eggs allows development to older instars. In fact, while in the egg case, *Latrodectus* can develop to within one or two molts of full maturity solely on sibling eggs and littermates (Kaston, 1968). Increased growth also decreases the probability of starvation and predation. In some cases, there is the further benefit that the next generation of parasites will be reduced when nondeveloping parasitized eggs are eaten along with trophic eggs (Root and Chaplin, 1976).

Overall, the food cache strategy allows parents to provision developing young progressively. Parental tissue may be converted into food for offspring in a manner analogous to parental provisioning in placental mammals and those species of birds and anthropods that feed young regurgitated food (Alexander, 1974; Polis, 1981). The production of expendable offspring to be eaten by siblings could be viewed as an energetic alternative to producing fewer eggs, each containing more nutrients.

Brood Reduction through Sibling Cannibalism

Sibling cannibalism is an integral part of the egg-laying strategy of many species. Several features associated with egg laying appear to be adaptations for the regulation and timing of intrabrood predation. Cannibalism is minimized when all littermates are approximately equal in size and well synchronized in development (Banks, 1956; Kaddou, 1960; Dimetry, 1974; Toot and Chaplin, 1976; Duelli, 1981; Polis, 1981). However, egg laying in many species is characterized by hatching asynchrony and differences in size at birth (runt production). These traits facilitate the consumption of eggs and newborn by older siblings. In coccinellids, there is a direct correlation between the variance in hatching time within a clutch and the proportion of eggs and newborn larvae that are cannibalized (Banks, 1956; Kaddou, 1960). For example, when all eggs of *Hippodamia* hatch at the same time, there is no cannibalism of larvae or viable embryos. If hatching is spread out over as little as 1 hour, 33% of all embryos and larvae are eaten by littermates (Kaddou, 1960). The spatial distribution of eggs also influences the intensity of sibling cannibalism. In all of the preceding examples of sibling cannibalism, eggs are laid in batches. Such aggregations encourage predation among litermates. In some cannibalistic groups of insects, eggs are laid either singly or clumped, e.g., coccinellids (Brown, 1972; Dimetry, 1974), lacewings (Duelli, 1981), butterflies (Stamp, 1980), and mosquitoes (Watts and Smith, 1978), and high cannibalism rates occur only when eggs are clumped.

Other factors also promote sibling cannibalism. In many of these species, young animals undergo a quiescent period of several hours to several days immediately after birth and before dispersal. It has been suggested that the primary function of this stage is to allow feeding on eggs and smaller littermates (Banks, 1956; Dimetry, 1974; Valerio, 1974). For example, many coccinellid larvae stay clumped around their empty eggshells for 12–24 hours (Dimetry, 1974). During this time, larvae feed on all inviable eggs, many fertile embryos, and some smaller larvae that have not yet dispersed. Smaller larvae probably remain in the egg mass because they benefit from eating trophic eggs. In muricid snails, larvae of some species (e.g., *Thais haemastoma*) may either become planktonic or stay in the egg mass (Lyons and Spight, 1973). Planktonic individuals are never cannibalistic, whereas those in the egg mass normally feed on trophic eggs.

In many cases, the food cache strategy and cannibalism by siblings and parents can be analyzed in the context of the well-established theory of brood reduction (Alexander, 1974; Lack, 1968; O'Connor, 1978; Polis, 1981 and inclusive references). Brood reduction involves adjustment of larger clutches to the best smaller size that allows maximum production of young under the current conditions of food availability. Large clutches are a bet hedge: in the event of a good year, all offspring may survive. However, if attempts to raise all young under inadequate food conditions retards development or causes the death of the entire brood, then there is selection to destroy young with a low expectance of survival. There should also be selection to eat "surplus" young and thus recycle rather than waste the energy already invested in them.

There is disagreement whether brood reduction by cannibalism evolved by individual and inclusive fitness of the offspring or by parental manipulation. The fact that parents sometimes eat their own eggs and young, feed them to other offspring, and produce runts and trophic eggs is evidence that certain progeny are sacrificed primarily to increase parental fitness. Alexander (1974) also maintained that sibling cannibalism and consequent brood reduction are cases of parental manipulation. Lack (1968) also viewed brood reduction as a parental adaptation. However, Eickwort (1973) concluded that sibling cannibalism among chrysomelid beetles was favored by kin selection because it allowed the average fitness of the clutch to increase. A model by O'Connor (1978) explained brood reduction in terms of inclusive fitness of the victim and individual fitness of the surviving offspring and not in terms of parental manipulation.

Cannibalism and Kin Selection

Clearly, cannibalism among relatives is a common occurrence and may even be favored by kin selection (see Mock, Chapter 1, this volume). However, it is equally clear that in other cases, kin selection should operate to decrease the intensity of cannibalism among relatives. If cannibals destroy a greater fraction of their own genotype compared with conspecific competitors, then cannibalistic behavior should be selected against. Excess destruction of kin will lower the inclusive fitness of the cannibal. A balance should evolve so that cannibalism among kin will occur when the disadvantage of decreasing the frequency of genes shared with the victim is less severe than the consequences of starvation or reproductive failure due to inadequate nutrition.

Thus, it is interesting to determine if the intensity of cannibalism is an inverse function of the average genetic relationship between intraspecific predator and potential prey. Hamilton (1964a) showed that as the average coefficient of relatedness increased within a population, genes for cannibalism (and other forms of interference) should become more frequent only with increasingly larger benefits to the cannibal. Overall, then, one would predict (1) that under favorable feeding conditions, relatives should be eaten proportionately less often than more distantly related conspecifics; and (2) that the rate of cannibalism should be lower in populations of related animals as compared with populations of individuals that are less closely related. There is some evidence among invertebrates to support both of the predictions.

In some species, maternal behaviors act to decrease the probability that the mother will eat her own young. Postpartum females of some spiders (Edgar, 1971; Hallender, 1970), scorpions (Polis, 1980), and *Tribolium* beetles (King and Dawson, 1973) leave the area into which their young disperse. For example, female *Tribolium* prefer to feed in different microhabitats from those in which they oviposit (King and Dawson, 1973). Such dispersal decreases the probability of cannibalism on close relatives and occurs in those species that are apparently unable to discriminate their own progeny. In some spiders and scorpions, the female's normal feeding behavior is inhibited during the period when she carries young (Hallander, 1970; Vannini *et al.*, 1978). After dispersal, these young are regarded as prey by their mothers. In the spider, *Clubiona* (Pollard, in press), and several species of leeches (Elliott, 1973), mothers will feed both on normal insect prey and on conspecific eggs. However, they do not feed on their own eggs, which they are apparently able to recognize. Finally, in one species of *Asplancha* rotifer, the highly cannibalistic campanulate morphotype rarely attacks either its own young or even other individuals of its same phenotype (Gilbert, 1980).

The best evidence supporting the second prediction comes from a series of laboratory experiments on *Tribolium* by Wade and McCauley. This work showed that when many small populations of *Tribolium castaneum* were founded as random samples from a single-source population, the populations differentiated considerably from one another with respect to their productivity (Wade and McCauley, 1980). Controlled crosses of the most and least productive strains demonstrated that these between-population differences had a genetic basis, and that much of the differences in productivity could be accounted for by differences in the rate that pupae were cannibalized (McCauley and Wade, 1980). In a further study, Wade (1980) manipulated the degree of relatedness among populations of *Tribolium confusum* and found that the rate at which larvae cannibalized eggs that were their full siblings decreased relative to the rate at which they cannibalized eggs that were less closely related to them. Such experiments demonstrated that cannibalism rates can evolve rapidly (i.e., a few generations), and that the rate of change was significantly influenced by the degree of relatedness between cannibal and victim. In summary, these experiments provide definitive evidence that kin selection can reduce as well as increase the rate of cannibalism among relatives.

6 Mammalian reproduction: Constraints on the evolution of infanticide

Virginia D. Hayssen

For the purposes of this chapter, infanticide is defined as the killing of conspecifics during the interval between their conception and weaning. Among mammals, infanticide benefits the perpetrator either by securing increased mating opportunities or by increasing access to resources through elimination of competitors (see Introduction to this volume). This chapter places infanticide in the broader context of mammalian reproduction. In particular, it illustrates how factors that influence the sequence or timing of reproductive events also constrain or facilitate the evolution of infanticide. First, the various events comprising the mammalian reproductive cycle are outlined, and the potential for infanticide at various stages within the cycle is reviewed. Then, intraspecific conflicts (e.g., between sexes or generations) involved in the timing of reproductive events and the duration of reproductive intervals are examined. Finally, this chapter examines specific evolutionary constraints on a facet of the reproductive cycle, the interbirth interval, which is critical to the evolution of infanticide as a male reproductive strategy (Chapman and Hausfater, 1979).

THE MAMMALIAN REPRODUCTIVE PATTERN

The mammalian reproductive cycle can be broken into an irreversible sequence of states or stages, such as gestation or lactation (Fig. 1). The duration of any given state is often characteristic for a species

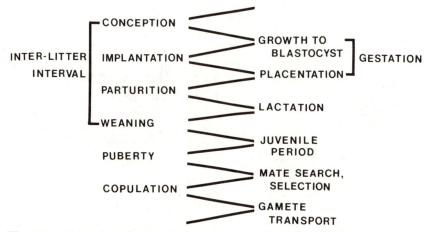

Figure 1. The series of stages (right) and events (left) that comprise the general mammalian reproductive pattern.

and can be the result of allometric relationships, the taxonomic position of the species, or adaptation to a particular niche. Transitions between consecutive states are, by definition, of short duration and may be thought of as events (e.g., conception or birth). Such events are often triggered by specific environmental or physiological stimuli, such as photoperiod or endogenous hormone levels. Species-specific reproductive patterns are thus characterized by differences either in the duration of various states or in the stimuli required to initiate particular events. These patterns may reflect adaptations to temporal variation in food availability, predator density, or disease transmission (Baker, 1938; Sadleir, 1969; Gilmore and Cook, 1981) or may simply be a function of body size or phylogenetic inertia.

In addition to its sequential character, a second aspect of the mammalian reproductive pattern is its inherently social nature, which centers around individual females. Almost every stage requires that a female interact with at least one other conspecific. Conception requires the interaction of females with males, while gestation and lactation require the cooperation of females and their progeny. Even sexual maturation (puberty) can be influenced by conspecifics (*Mus:* Vandenbergh, 1967; *Rattus:* Vandenbergh, 1976; *Sus:* Mavrogenis and Robison, 1976; *Microtus:* Hasler and Nalbandov, 1974; *Dicrostonyx:* Hasler and Banks, 1975). Furthermore, the optimal temporal and energetic investment into each stage may be different for each participant as measured by individual fitness. For example, a female langur monkey may wish to solicit parental care for her unweaned offspring from a new resident male. His intentions may be quite the contrary (i.e., to minimize both his and her investment in an infant sired by his predecessor and competitor) (Hrdy, 1977b).

For reproduction to be successful, the stage(s) of greatest energetic demand must be coincident with a time or season when sufficient energy is available. Thus, the sequential nature of the reproductive process requires that the earliest event be timed appropriately with respect to environmental conditions during later stages. However, the social nature of the pattern engenders conflict regarding this timing, since the stage of greatest energetic demand for one participant may not be coincident with that of its partner.

For most facets of the reproductive cycle, the outcome of social conflict with respect to the timing of reproductive events will be biased in favor of the female. Both components of a female's evolutionary fitness, her survivorship and her reproductive success, depend directly on how she manages the complex temporal, biotic, and energetic demands of her current reproduction. A female that attempts to reproduce in the face of harsh environmental conditions may severely decrease her survivorship as well as limit her ability to reproduce again when conditions improve. If so, her fitness will be significantly reduced compared with that of females that cease reproduction during harsh times. Although male reproductive success is decreased when females terminate reproduction, male survivorship is not impaired. Therefore, a male will usually be able to reinseminate females when conditions improve. In addition, female survivorship benefits males as well, since a male's ultimate reproductive success requires that the females he inseminates be able to survive until his offspring are weaned. Consequently, the interplay between the environment and female survivorship and its subsequent effects on both male and female reproductive success, as well as offspring survivorship, provide the backdrop against which social conflicts regarding the timing and/or duration of reproductive phenomena must be resolved.

Conception

Although, by definition, infanticide cannot occur at this point in the mammalian cycle, the fusion of male and female gametes is a complex event replete with the conflict between male, female, and offspring, which motivates infanticide or siblicide at later reproductive stages. At copulation, a female receives not only sperm but also seminal fluids and an assortment of bacteria and other potential disease agents. As long as a few sperm reach the few eggs that she will ovulate, a female benefits (increases her survivorship) by destroying the mass of excess sperm, ejaculate, and miscellaneous debris, thus preventing the transmission of disease vectors to her peritoneal cavity.

Complex morphological and physiological barriers exist to prevent the invasion and growth of bacteria and other microflora within the female reproductive tract. The vagina, uteri, and oviducts are separated by undulating mucus and/or muscle sphincters both at the cervix and at the uterotubal junction. These barriers regulate the transfer of particulate material and fluids, including sperm and seminal plasma, between the segments (Koester, 1970). Cellular (e.g., leukocytes and macrophages) and chemical (e.g., pH) defenses also exist to dispose of potentially harmful debris. Both sperm and zygotes must protect themselves or be protected against such maternal defense mechanisms. Copious ejaculate, copulatory plugs and locks, as well as the morphology of intromittent organs may be adaptations used by males to overcome these barriers (Hogarth, 1978). The zona pellucida and other mucoid membranes that surround the fused gametes, usually until the zygote implants, function to protect the embyro (McLaren, 1972).

Conception is primarily under control of the female. Mammalian sperm, when deposited within the female tract, are incapable of performing their biological function. They are chemically unable to fuse with female gametes and do not possess the energetic resources to travel under their own power to the site of conception (Austin, 1972). Capacitation of sperm, which involves a chemical alteration of the sperm head, is under the control of the female as it is dependent upon the secretions of epithelial cells that line the uteri and/or oviducts (Bedford, 1970). Transport of sperm from their point of deposition, either the vagina, as in humans, cows, sheep, and rabbits (Bedford, 1970), or the uterus, as in myomorph rodents, pigs, horses, and dogs (Bedford, 1970), to the ovary (tenrecs: Asdell, 1964) or oviduct (most mammals: Nalbandov, 1964) where conception occurs is also under the female's control. Muscular contractions of the tract push sperm toward the site of conception as do beating cilia that line the oviducts. The morphology and fluid dynamics of the female reproductive tract are such that sperm are transported toward the ovary to the site of conception while the freshly ovulated eggs and, subsequently, the newly formed zygote are transported in the reverse direction toward the uterus (Koester, 1970).

In addition to the conflict between males and females regarding the optimal condition of the female reproductive tract, potential conflict exists between males and their progeny. The ejaculate that males deposit within the female tract may alter the biological characteristics of that area with respect to pH, ionic concentrations, etc., such that it is detrimental to the survival of young that must develop there. Mammals with sperm deposition into the vagina avoid extensive contamination of the uterus with cervical barriers. Those mammals with sperm deposition directly into the uterus may force the zygote to develop in the oviduct until the uterine environment can be adjusted and excess debris removed.

Male–offspring conflict is also present in mammals that exhibit post-partum estrus. In this case, the physical and hormonal remnants of the recent pregnancy may create a uterine or vaginal environment dele-terious to sperm (cattle: Casida, 1968). Mammals with two separate reproductive tracts avoid these difficulties by transporting sperm up one tract after giving birth from the other (*Macropus:* Tyndale-Biscoe and Rodger, 1978). For other mammals, the physical and chemical prop-erties of seminal fluids may protect sperm viability. However, the lower fertility of this estrus (horses: Jainudeen and Hafez, 1980; cows: Casida, 1968) suggests these mechanisms may not be wholly effective.

Although conception requires the interaction of both male and female (and involves conflict between them and their progeny), its occurrence is primarily dependent on the female and her physiological condition. Once copulation is completed, the timing and location of conception, as well as its occurrence, are determined by the female.

Gestation

Conception initiates the first stage in the life of a mammal, a period of cellular differentiation and growth that transforms the one-celled, mucin-coated mass into a multistructured individual able to breathe and suckle. In monotremes (the platypus and echidnas), gestation as previously defined begins within the mother, continues through the incubation of an egg, and is terminated by hatching. For the other two groups of mammals, the metatheria (marsupials) and the eutheria (placentals), the entire gestation period occurs within the female repro-ductive tract. During both gestation and the following lactational stage, the primary interactions are between a female and her offspring. Par-ent–offspring conflict appears in many forms (Trivers, 1974).

Gestation can be divided into two component phases. The first is a period of cell division (cleavage), which occurs while the zygote, still enclosed within protective membranes, is transported down the oviduct to the uterus. The second phase is one of placentation, in which foetal and maternal tissues become intricately intertwined.

During the first phase of gestation, the cells that will become either trophoblast or embryo are confined within the zona pellucida, a noncel-lular, shell-like coat of maternal origin that surrounds the developing zygote. This coat and other thicker ones that surround the zygotes of monotremes (Griffiths, 1978), marsupials (Tyndale-Biscoe, 1973), rabbits (Boving, 1972), dogs, and horses (Blandau, 1961) protect the zygote from disintegrating during cell cleavage or as it is buffeted by uterine contrac-tions (McLaren, 1972) but may also prevent the zygote from altering its environment during this early phase. In addition, this maternal coat may retard embryo development if it limits nutrient and gas exchange (Blandau, 1961).

In kangaroos, embryonic development may be arrested completely at this stage by the suckling of an older sibling or by maternal exposure to harsh environmental conditions (Sharman and Berger, 1969). Developmental arrest due to the neurohormonal correlates of suckling is also common in the laboratory rodents, *Mus* and *Rattus* (Gidley-Baird, 1981), and is only a step away from siblicide. In fact, embryo death as a consequence of lactation has been recorded for domestic ungulates (Jainudeen and Hafez, 1980).

The foregoing examples of delays during the first phase of gestation are not obligatory features of the gestation of these mammals but rather are sporatically induced by either conspecifics or environmental conditions. However, an obligatory delay during this phase of gestation is a feature of the reproductive pattern of mustelids (weasels and skunks), seals, some bats, an armadillo, the roe deer, and a marsupial *Setonix* (Renfree and Calaby, 1981; Enders, 1963).

In the peramelid marsupials (the bandicoots) and eutherian (placental) mammals, the loss of the zona pellucida is usually coincident with implantation. The second phase of gestation begins with the invasion of the foetal trophoblast into the endometrial folds of the maternal uterus. The initial choriovitelline placenta is supplemented by a chorioallantoic placenta as gestation progresses (rabbits: Brambell, 1948; bats: Wimsatt and Enders, 1980; bandicoots: Padykula and Taylor, 1976). From this point, the eutherian trophoblast functions as an extensive endocrine system which, in some sense, takes hormonal control over the maternal metabolism, providing the foetus with warmth, food, shelter, and protection. In its most exaggerated form, the female plays host to her parasitic offspring throughout the rest of gestation.

The separation of gestation into two phases is important with respect to determining which conspecific (parent or offspring) has the potential to commit infanticide. During the first phase of gestation, continuation of reproduction is entirely under control of the mother. Physical or biotic stress may induce her to resorb her current litter and resume reproduction when conditions improve (sheep: Ulberg and Sheean, 1973; rats: Sod-Moriah, 1971; rabbits: Shah, 1956). In eutherians, termination of reproductive effort after placentation will be much more difficult due to the size and invasive extent of the trophoblast. Environmental stress during this period may result in the development of smaller or malformed young rather than the termination of pregnancy (Benson and Morris, 1971; Yeates, 1958). It is in the best interests of the foetus to prevent its own termination. Through the trophoblast's control of maternal metabolism and reproduction, the foetus can resist its own resorption. Foetal death after extensive trophoblastic development is perhaps most likely to be caused by sibling competition.

Thus, one would predict that maternally induced preimplantation embryo resorption will be much more frequent than postimplantation abortion. Infanticide that occurs before implantation is difficult to quantify since the remnants of the embryos will be resorbed often before the female is observably pregnant. Brambell (1948) briefly reviewed prenatal mortality in rabbits, squirrels, rats, stoats, swine, and sheep and concluded that most prenatal mortality occurred before, during, or just after implantation. More recent investigations on domestic ungulates (cattle, swine, horses, and sheep) have confirmed that the period of maximal embryonic mortality occurs before or immediately following implantation (McLaren, 1980). For the few rodents that have been studied, the pheromonally induced pregnancy block (Bruce effect) is also more effective before implantation (*Mus:* Bruce, 1959; *Meriones:* Rohrbach, 1982; *Peromyscus:* Bronson and Eleftheriou, 1963; microtine rodents: Richmond and Stehn, 1976), although it may occur after some foetal invasion of maternal tissue has occurred (Schadler, 1981; Stehn and Jannett, 1981). For some other rodents, foetal death after placentation is greater than that before. However, in both cases, suitable implantation sites are limited, and sibling competition for these sites may be the cause of foetal death (*Lagostomus:* Weir, 1971; *Cricetulus:* Droogleever Fortuyn, 1929). Examples of both pre- and postimplantation infanticide can be found for other groups; for example, the extensive preimplantation embryo loss in *Elephantulus,* a macroscledid (van der Horst and Gillman, 1941), and postimplantation loss in some vespertilionid bats (Wimsatt, 1975) and the tenrec, *Hemicentetes* (Bluntschli, 1938). From these limited data, it appears that embryonic loss prior to the point at which extensive trophoblast invasion occurs is more frequent than foetal death after this event.

Birth

Parturition, or birth, terminates gestation and requires the interaction of a female and her offspring. For monotremes as well as birds the timing of hatching would appear to be determined by the foetus, who must break out of its shell. For marsupials, Lillegraven (1975) has suggested that the maternal immune system forces the foetus to crawl out of the uterus. Recent data from Walker and Tyndale-Biscoe (1978) on the gestation lengths of females exposed to paternal antigens before pregnancy refute this hypothesis, leaving open the question of, Who controls parturition in marsupials? Since removal of the pituitary gland from the mother prevents parturition in some kangaroos (Hearn, 1973), the endocrinological basis of birth in marsupials may be maternal.

In eutherians, the most sophisticated analyses on parturition have been performed on sheep and indicate that maturation of the foetal adrenal/pituitary axis is necessary for the induction of labor (Liggins *et al.*, 1973; Thorburn and Challis, 1979). Results from work in primates are similar to those on domestic ruminants and also indicate foetal control of parturition (MacDonald *et al.*, 1978). However, in rabbits and laboratory rodents (reviewed by Nathanielsz, 1978), foetal decapitation does not alter the timing of birth, implying that parturition may be controlled by maternal, not foetal, factors in these animals. In general, the available data suggests that birth will be foetally controlled in mammals with precocial young and maternally controlled in mammals with altricial young. Precocity, then, may require the early maturation of a foetal neuroendocrine control network and be a consequence of strong foetal control during gestation. Under this scheme, precocity is not solely the result of K-selection or predation pressure but is partially due to the self-interest of the foetus who "prefers" the womb to the world. Support for this hypothesis comes from the work of Case (1978), who has shown that gestation length tends to be longer for precocial than for altricial animals even though overall foetal growth rate is the same. Further experiments on the control of parturition in the leporids, a family that contains both precocial (hares) and altricial (rabbits) species, may clarify questions of foetal development and control of parturition since the confounding effects of body size and evolutionary history could be circumvented.

Lactation

Parturition marks not only the end of gestation but also the beginning of lactation. It is during this stage of extrauterine growth that infanticide is most detectable by an observer and least dangerous to a female. For females, lactation is the most energetically costly of all reproductive stages (Fig. 2), since milk must not only maintain her young but also provide energy for their growth and development (marsupials: Fleming *et al.*, 1981; rodents: Millar, 1978; Randolph *et al.*, 1977; McClure and Randolph, 1980; bats: Studier *et al.*, 1973; artiodactyls: Brockway *et al.*, 1963; Campling, 1966; lagomorphs: Pommerenke *et al.*, 1930). During gestation, the female provides nourishment directly to her offspring. During lactation, the food she consumes must be broken down and resynthesized into milk before being transferred to her young, who must then break it down once again. These extra metabolic steps make lactation less energetically efficient than gestation. Also, because a female carries her young within her during gestation, there is little extra cost involved in maintaining the body temperature of her offspring. Thermoregulation of young once they are outside the womb adds substantially to the temporal and energetic demands on a female (McClure and Randolph, 1980). She must either be with her young to

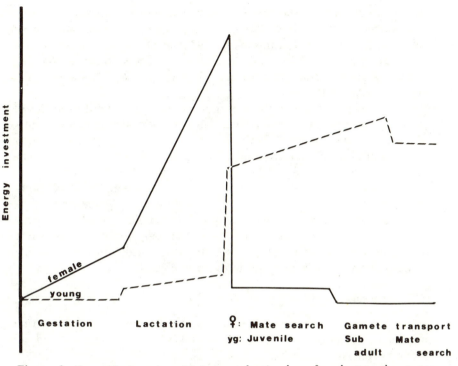

Figure 2. Energetic investment into reproduction by a female over the course of a reproductive bout compared with the energetic investment (i.e., nutrient acquisition) of offspring for their own growth and physiological maintenance over that same period, illustrating the energetic conflict between females and their offspring throughout a reproductive cycle.

keep them warm or provide them with additional food so that they may be able to generate heat themselves.

Throughout gestation and lactation, a female must allocate energy to either foetal nutrition or to maternal body tissue. Factors that affect maternal "decisions" regarding such allocations include the quantity and quality of available food, the endocrinological state of the female (Flatt and Moe, 1971), and, perhaps, the quality of her offspring. During gestation, foetal tissues may alter the hormonal status of the female. During lactation, young can physiologically alter their mother's metabolism only via the stimulus and hormonal correlates of suckling, and this the female can terminate easily.

The end of lactation is marked by weaning, the operational definition of which varies with both author and animal. Den emergence, first solid food, dispersal from the nest, independence, cessation of lactation, and maintenance of weight after isolation from mother have all been used to approximate the point at which a female terminates direct metabolic investment into that litter (e.g., Tomich, 1962; Galef, 1981; Ewer, 1973; Clark, 1977; King *et al.*, 1963). At this point, the female's daily energetic investment into reproduction drops sharply, and the entire energetic burden falls on her offspring (Fig. 2). This shift is the source of weaning conflict.

Weaning is followed by a variable juvenile or subadult period of growth in which both physical tissues and behavioral responses mature. Offspring are no longer directly dependent on their parents for their nourishment but neither are they sexually mature. Their energetic burden rises until they reach adult size, when growth usually ceases.

Puberty terminates the juvenile stage and is followed by the competition or search for a mate, culminating in copulation. After copulation, the male gametes may remain within the female reproductive tract for a few hours (but up to several weeks in vespertilionid bats: Wimsatt, 1942) before they and the female's gametes are transported to the site of conception, thus beginning the cycle again.

SOCIAL CONFLICTS INHERENT IN THE REPRODUCTIVE CYCLE

Conflict between conspecifics during the reproductive cycle can be manifested in many ways: between siblings, between parents, and between parent and offspring.

Sibling Conflict

One of the hallmarks of the mammalian radiation is the extensive provisioning of maternally refined nutrients to immature offspring. These nutrients, however, are not infinite, and nonidentical siblings may be in conflict regarding the allocation of maternal resources. Even if maternal energetic resources were not limiting, nutrient procurement sites may be. Thus, siblings may not have equal access to maternal resources. Siblicide (Mock, Chapter 1, this volume) may allow surviving offspring to receive a larger proportion of available nutrients or even exclusive access to them.

The best documented case of in utero siblicide occurs in the pronghorn, *Antilocapra americana* (O'Gara, 1969). In these animals, the blastocyst implanting first in each horn sends out invasive processes that pierce and devour all other embryos implanting in that horn. Maximum litter size is two, no matter how many eggs are ovulated and fertilized. Sibling competition clearly results in death in these animals.

For many mammals, such as, rats, mice, guinea pigs, rabbits, cats, dogs, cows, and sheep (Wimsatt, 1975), the entire uterus is potentially able to support embryonic and foetal development. However, in some mammals, such as, elephant shrews, tupaiids, glossophagine bats, viscachas, and pangolins (Wimsatt, 1975), only a restricted portion will accept blastocyst implantation and support embryonic and foetal development. If blastocysts outnumber implantation sites, *in utero* sibling competition will occur. An extreme example of this is found in the elephant shrew (*Elephantulus myurus*) in which two embryos are brought to term out of the 100 eggs that may be produced and fertilized. Although some eggs may never fuse with sperm, the presence of only two implantation sites (one in each horn) forces sibling conflict and eventual death (van der Horst and Gillman, 1941; 1942; Tripp, 1971). The plains viscacha (*Lagostomus maximus*) also illustrates competition for implantation sites. In this case, up to seven zygotes implant, but all except the two most distal to the ovaries are resorbed during the first two-thirds of gestation (Weir, 1971).

Not all portions of the uterus will support development equally even in mammals without morphologically distinct implantation sites. For instance, in swine (Perry and Rowell, 1969), rabbits (Rosahn and Greene, 1936), mice (McLaren, 1965), and guinea pigs (Ibsen, 1928), foetal weight is correlated with uterine position; smaller foetuses often occupy the middle segments of the uterine horns. In addition, foetal size decreases as litter size increases (Hagen *et al.*, 1980). Thus, there is the potential for competition between blastocysts before implantation. The excellent work of Boving (1972) on the spacing of blastocysts in the rabbit uterus indicates that zygotes spend about 3 days in the uterus before implanting equidistant from one another. The physical mechanism of spacing has been determined, but the competitive interactions between blastocysts for implantation sites have not yet been examined.

Competition for parental resources also occurs during lactation. The finite number of mammary glands may result in conflict between siblings if litter size exceeds the number of teats. If a phase of permanent teat attachment occurs during lactation, as in *Neotoma* (Hamilton, 1953) and dasyurid and didelphid marsupials (Tyndale-Biscoe, 1973), only the first young to find teats will have a chance for survival. For mammals without permanent teat attachment, sharing of teats is possible. However, milk composition changes during the course of a suckling bout (rabbits, pigs: Cross, 1977), and subsequent young may not obtain equal nourishment. In addition, young that suckle later may not be able to suckle as long, especially if females control bout termination. Aggressive interactions between siblings for teat ownership have been observed in pigs (Fraser and Jones, 1975) and cats (Ewer, 1973) and result in the establishment of a dominance hierarchy among siblings.

Parent–Offspring Conflict

Conflict between parent and offspring can arise concerning the duration of either gestation or lactation. During gestation, a foetus is warm, wet, and protected. It receives nutrients that do not require digestion. All these benefits are lost at birth. Thus, the foetus may benefit by extending gestation whenever it is able to do so. Although gestation is energetically more efficient than lactation, long gestations with continued foetal growth may decrease a female's ability to evade predators quickly and may increase the potential for a hazardous birth once it occurs. Partitioning resources into lactation rather than gestation allows a female to terminate reproduction with less risk. For instance, the marsupial mode of reproduction with extremely short gestations compared to lactation and extremely altricial neonates allows a female to divest herself of a current reproductive attempt during almost the entire reproductive period, with little or no risk to her survival (Parker, 1977). She can cut her losses almost as soon as conditions deteriorate and renew reproduction when conditions improve.

The end of lactation is also a period of conflict between females and their young, for at this point offspring must obtain a large proportion of their energetic requirements for both growth and maintenance. The decrease in growth rate observed in many mammals at weaning is evidence of the difficulty of this transition (golden mouse: Linzey and Linzey, 1967; arctic pika: Puget and Gouarderes, 1974; elephant seals: Bryden, 1969). Many carnivores (Ewer, 1973) provision juveniles after weaning, thus diminishing the potential conflict between parent and offspring at this point. The evolutionary context for parent–offspring conflict has been debated by Trivers (1974), Alexander (1974), and Dawkins and Carlisle (1976).

Parental Conflict

The major energetic demands on a female occur during lactation. Fat storage during gestation can alleviate some of the energetic burden of lactation (Randolph *et al.,* 1977). The total energetic cost of reproduction then rises since energy must be first turned into fat, but the energetic burden is more evenly distributed over time. The major energetic demands on a male occur during the time of mate search and selection. The conflict arising between males and females over the timing of copulation depends on the duration and intensity of the mate-competition period and its timing relative to lactation.

Contingent upon the pattern of female receptivity during the course of a year, the pattern of male energetic investment will vary greatly. In a highly predictable environment, offspring and female survivorship may be strongly correlated with the timing of birth. Natural selection will operate such that females give birth synchronously at that time. Since intraspecific variation in gestation is small (Kiltie, 1982), copulation and conception must occur in all females a set time in advance of birth. In those cases in which females are seasonally receptive, a male must compete with other males for access to as many females as possible over a short period of time (Fig. 3). Thus, male–male competition will be high, and a male's major energetic demand will be concentrated into a short period just prior to gestation. Since a female's receptivity, or lack thereof, is due to environmental cues, not conspecific ones, infanticide, in these cases, will not shorten a male's wait until the next opportunity for insemination and will not increase his reproductive success (Hausfater, Chapter 13, this volume, and references therein).

If females are not seasonal breeders, male investment into mate competition will be more uniform throughout the year (Fig. 3), and there will be relatively less conflict between males and females regarding the timing of copulation. Lack of receptivity in females may be due more to the hormonal correlates of lactation than to environmental factors, and thus infanticide by males may operate to bring females into estrus early (*Presbytis:* Hrdy, 1976) and increase male reproductive success.

If there is a sharp period of seasonal food abundance, it will be of advantage to males to have this period coincide with that of competition

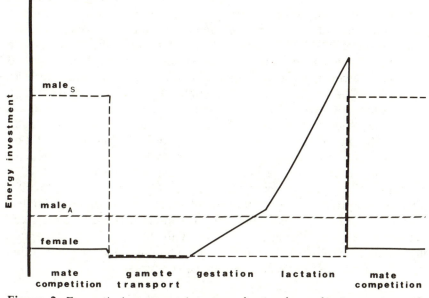

Figure 3. Energetic investment into reproduction by males in species with synchronous female receptivity (male$_S$) or asynchronous female receptivity (male$_A$). Male investment is compressed into one period when females are seasonally receptive (male$_S$) but may be distributed over the entire cycle when females are continuously receptive (male$_A$).

for mates. A female's greatest energetic demand is during lactation, however, and it will be advantageous for her to be lactating when food is most readily available. Since reproductive events occur in series, the timing of one event, such as copulation, will also time the others. Males that provision females during gestation or lactation or protect vulnerable young may lessen the disadvantages females face if lactation or birth occur at unfavorable periods, thus allowing copulation to occur at a period more favorable to males (cf. Kleiman and Eisenberg, 1973). The interdependence of conspecifics for ultimate reproductive success suggests that the exact placement of reproductive events within environmental cycles will be determined by the constraints on each of the participants at each stage of the cycle.

INTERBIRTH INTERVALS: DEFINITION

The term *interbirth* or *interlitter interval* refers to the time between the birth of successive litters. It is the length of gestation plus the time to the next conception, usually the length of lactation. In addition to its importance in the calculation of reproductive effort, reproductive value, and the intrinsic rate of population growth, the interbirth interval is a parameter in the assessment of the reproductive advantage accrued to infanticidal males who shorten a female's return to estrus (Chapman and Hausfater, 1979). Unfortunately, the interval is difficult to measure in the field, as one needs long-term studies of individually marked females. However, as a first approximation, the minimum interbirth interval can be assumed to be the length of gestation plus the length of lactation, with two caveats. First, the presence of a fertile postpartum estrus may shorten the interbirth interval to just the gestation length. Second, the minimum interbirth interval may be longer than gestation plus lactation if animals are constrained to breed once per year or once every other year, as may be the case with many large-bodied mammals living in temperate climates. This constraint may be facultative, as in captivity these animals will often breed year round (primates: Lancaster and Lee, 1965). The interbirth interval realized by a given population will be strongly correlated with the time from conception to weaning but may also be affected by such things as mate availability, environmental factors, and population density.

INTERBIRTH INTERVALS: DESCRIPTION AND CONSTRAINTS

A histogram of time from conception to weaning for 356 species from 15 orders is presented in Fig. 4, using data from 280 primary and secondary sources on mammalian life-history parameters. The data

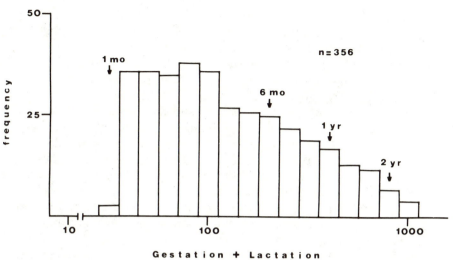

Figure 4. Histogram of the interval between conception and weaning (the minimum interbirth interval) for 356 mammalian species. The major secondary literature sources used were Sacher and Staffeldt (1974); Case (1978); Millar (1977, 1981); Bryden (1972); Mentis (1972); Leitch *et al.* (1959); Western (1979); Kenneth and Ritchie (1953); Asdell (1964); Bekoff *et al.* (1981); Collins (1973); Leutenegger (1973); Banfield (1974); Corbet and Southern (1977); Russell (1982); Weir (1974); Watts and Aslin (1981); Kekagul and McNeely (1977). Primary sources will be available in Hayssen (in preparation).

base is subject to the multitude of caveats associated with such a compilation: variations in sampling methods, sample sizes, and methods of estimation abound. Many parameters were not readily available for every species, so sample sizes for various analyses that follow differ. Some parameters were available from many sources. In these cases, the mean, or weighted mean if sample sizes were given, was calculated after discarding known typographical errors and extreme estimates. The shortest intervals (about 1 month) are found in the small microtine rodents, whereas the longest intervals (2.5–3.0 years) are attained by large aquatic mammals such as ceteceans, eared seals, and walruses. The geometric mean is 125 days, the median 109 days, and the mode 36 days.

Both gestation and lactation are strongly correlated with body size (Kihlstrom, 1972; Zeveloff and Boyce, 1980; Millar, 1981). This author's own data, which include monotremes, marsupials, bats, and aquatic mammals, in addition to the terrestrial eutherians investigated by the authors just cited, indicate that adult body weight accounts for about 60% of the variation in gestation length and 44% of the variation in lactation length. Not surprisingly, the correlation of gestation plus lactation with adult weight shows that 68% of the variation in minimum interbirth intervals among mammalian species can be explained by allometry alone (Fig. 5). The fact that allometric correlations are stronger for the interval between conception and weaning than for either of its components demonstrates that species partition temporal resources differently between gestation and lactation. For example, both the hill kangaroo (*Macropus robustus*) and the Hawaiian monk seal (*Monochus schauinslandi*) have minimum interbirth intervals of approximately 1 year. However, the kangaroo spends 1 month in gestation and lactates for the remainder of the year, while the seal spends 11 months gestating followed by about 1 month in milk production (Ealey, 1963; 1967; Kirkpatrick, 1968; Bryden, 1972).

McNab (1980) has suggested that diet may impose additional constraints on reproductive parameters via a presumed effect on metabolic rate. Perhaps herbivores, whose caloric assimilation is near maximal at most times, will have less energy to devote to the rapid development of young and, therefore, will have longer gestations than have carnivores, which may be able to take advantage of periodically abundant, high-energy prey to produce young more quickly. McNab suggested

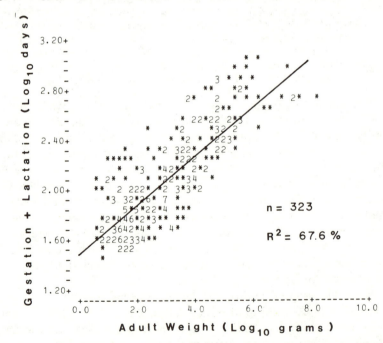

Figure 5. The relationship between minimum interbirth interval (defined as the duration of gestation and the duration of lactation) and adult body weight for 323 mammalian species from 15 orders. Integers represent the number of species superimposed at that point.

that ingestion of food with low "caloric density," such as leaves or social insects, may cause the evolutionary depression of basal metabolic rates, which may in turn slow reproduction and cause longer interbirth intervals.

Habitat may also affect reproduction. Whales, with their giant size and large amounts of subcutaneous fat, may spend less energy on thermoregulation and thus be able to spend more on reproduction (Bartholomew, 1972). This may account for the extremely fast growth observed in whales (Case, 1978). If the energetic cost of locomotion and physiological maintenance is lower in aquatic mammals than in terrestrial mammals, then whales and seals may be expected to have shorter interbirth intervals relative to body size. On the other hand, tiny volant bats, which probably spend large amounts of energy just obtaining enough food to live, may be expected to have longer gestations or lactations.

A third constraint on reproduction may be phylogenetic inertia. Polygenic characters, such as the duration of reproductive stages, might have been canalized millions of years ago, when the ancestors to the extant mammalian orders or families diverged. The variation within taxa available for adaptation to present conditions may thus be limited.

The relative effects of these constraints on the timing of reproductive events can be assessed by multiple analysis of variance models, which partition the variance in gestation and lactation length into components relating to allometry, phylogeny, habitat, and diet. Those factors that explain larger proportions of the variation can be assumed to impose more stringent constraints on reproductive durations. Table I presents the results of such an analysis for the minimum interbirth interval of 340 mammalian species. Body size, phylogeny, habitat, and diet together explain 85% of the variation in the time from conception to weaning among mammals. Habitat and diet have little predictive power, since they account for only 2% of the variation, while allometric relations, as already seen, account for 67% of the variation. Phylogeny (variation among orders and among families within orders), however, explains about one-half of the remaining variation after factoring out body weight. An unknown, and perhaps sizable, portion of the residual variation may be due to the nature of the data base, a compilation of studies using varied definitions and means of measurement. This strongly suggests that phylogenetic factors constrain mammalian interbirth intervals to a greater extent than do ecological ones: 83% of the variation can be explained by variations in body size and distant evolutionary history alone.

Thus, species-specific reproductive characters (gestation and lactation) appear to be conservative in their evolution. Since taxonomic position is a key factor in the evolution of interbirth intervals, analyses

Mammalian Reproduction and Infanticide

Table I. Analysis of the variance in interbirth intervals[a]

Gestation and lactation	F	df	Incremental R-square	Cumulative R-square
Adult weight	1423.94	1	0.67	0.67
Subclass	20.27	2	0.02	0.69
Order (subclass)	25.68	12	0.14	0.83
Habitat	3.28	5	0.01	0.84
Diet	10.22	2	0.01	0.85

[a] Data for mammalian species with respect to allometric, ecological, and phylogenetic factors. The incremental R-square indicates how much additional variation is explained by the inclusion of that variable into the model. "Adult weight" is the common log of the adult weight in grams. "Subclass" refers to the taxonomic separation of mammals into prototheria, metatheria, or eutheria. "Order" is nested within subclass and compares mammals among the 15 phylogenetic orders represented by the dataset. "Habitat" divides mammals into broad categories according to whether they are generally aquatic, semiaquatic, fossorial, semifossorial, terrestrial, semiarboreal, arboreal, or volant. "Diet" is tripartite: herbivorous for those mammals that ingest plant material; carnivorous for those that ingest animal material (including insects); and omnivorous for those that ingest both. Due to the large sample size, all F-statistics are significant at $p < 0.0001$, except that for "Habitat," which is significant at $p < 0.007$.

of reproductive strategies (such as infanticide or developmental precocity) that may depend on the duration of gestation and lactation must be conducted within a given taxonomic level and should not be extrapolated to unstudied taxa. This is the only way to assure that each data point is an independent example of the phenomena in question.

The interval between successive litters is one of three temporal parameters (the other two being ages of first and last reproduction) that determine a female's reproductive output and a population's rate of increase. Mathematical models of infanticide also suggest that the value of the interbirth interval may determine whether or not this reproductive strategy is advantageous to a given male. The results presented here, from 340 species representing 15 orders, indicate that the minimum interbirth interval is tightly constrained by body size and phylogenetic history. Variation between species in the time from conception to weaning is not correlated with the species' ecological niches as reflected by habitats and diets.

CONCLUSIONS

The stages and events of the reproductive cycle provide the context for infanticidal behavior. Reproduction is a complex process that requires, at each stage, the interaction of conspecifics who may be in conflict regarding the exact timing of, or energetic investment into, that stage. Infanticide is only one of many manifestations of that conflict.

The complicated physiological, genetic, and social interactions that regulate the duration of gestation and lactation, as well as other reproductive stages, suggest that reproductive patterns are a characteristic of social groups, not of individuals. The evolution of reproductive patterns requires coordinated changes in several conspecifics and must, at least marginally, improve the fitnesses of each participant at each step. Because of its effect on the population parameter, and the intrinsic rate of increase, changes in the fundamental interbirth interval may have effects on intrademic (or traitgroup) selection (Wilson, 1979; Wade, 1978).

Infanticide can take many forms, may occur at any time during the reproductive cycle, and may be perpetrated by males, females, and offspring. It may provide a mechanism by which individuals can alter reproductive patterns at the expense of other interactants. Infanticide by males may alter the short-term timing of a female's reproductive cycle and increase male reproductive success. Female-induced infanticide may allow apportionment of reproductive effort into future, rather than current, offspring during environmental stress, while siblicide may allow surviving siblings to obtain increased energetic resources. Documented cases of infanticide are generally the more dramatic ones that occur during lactation, yet the evolutionary effect of infanticide at other stages may be as pronounced. Future investigations of the less-observable forms of infanticide may reveal a broader context for, and consequences of, this phenomenon.

ACKNOWLEDGMENTS

This chapter would not have been possible without the assistance of R. Lacy in the interpretation of the statistical analyses as well as in the stimulation of creative thought. I am also greatly indebted to J. Burnham, who made data collection twice as fun and half as time-consuming. In addition, W. Wimsatt and J. Wright made their extensive reprint collections available to me, greatly improving the data base for Chiroptera and Carnivora. Finally, E. Adkins Regan, G. Hausfater, R. Lacy, J. Stelzner, and J. Wright reviewed an earlier draft of this chapter, and their cogent comments much improved the final form.

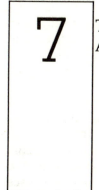

7

The evolutionary ecology of sex allocation: A primer

Eric L. Charnov

INTRODUCTION

Infanticide, the killing of unweaned or parentally dependent infants, is one of a variety of behavioral and physiological mechanisms that animals and humans use to modify the sex ratio of their offspring (Hrdy, 1979; Johansson, Chapter 23, this volume). From both theoretical and empirical perspectives, offspring sex-ratio manipulation is currently a major focus of research by behavioral biologists, evolutionary ecologists, sociobiologists, demographers, and anthropologists. However, parental manipulation of offspring sex-ratio distribution is, in fact, a special case of the more general problem of sex allocation in plants and animals, and it is this latter issue that constitutes the topic of this chapter. As such, the present review is intended as a primer for readers interested in recent theoretical developments concerning the evolution of sex allocation as well as for those interested in the strategy and findings of recent investigations of sex-ratio manipulation in animals. This review begins by discussing, in general terms, the use of natural selection as an explanatory principle. In attempting to understand, for example, the distribution of separate versus combined sexes (i.e., dioecy versus hermaphroditism), theoretical predictions (e.g., When should an organism be a hermaphrodite?) are sought in terms of the reproductive consequences of possible alternative states or the transition between states. In short, it is asked when or under what environmental, social, or life-history conditions natural selection favors one or the other form of sexuality. The theory is tested by arranging experiments, or geographic or taxonomic comparisons, to see if selection acts as one thinks it does or if a particular form of sexuality is matched to predicted environmental conditions. Thus, it is necessary to understand sexuality in terms of the ultimate causes (the *why* questions) rather than the proximate mechanisms (the physiologic *how* questions). Seeking answers to the way in which nature is structured, in terms of *why* questions, is used here as *selection thinking*.

This chapter really has three simple, but important, messages, if one is to understand what evolutionary ecology does and does not do. First, the value of ultimate as opposed to proximate questions is demonstrated and explained. Second, it is shown that selection thinking very often involves not *genetic determinism* in the sense of genes controlling toe number, but rather the evolution of facultative responses. A *facultative response* is a short-term (within-generation) response to altered environmental conditions. Restated, this second message is that genes often "say things like": Look around this breeding season and produce the best number of babies for the prevailing food conditions, where best relates to the reproductive interests of the parents. In particular, selection theory often allows predictions as to what the response will be, that is, to determine just what an organism will do in response to altered conditions (of course, within certain limits). Third, it is necessary to emphasize that the trait selected for in social situations often differs, depending upon whose interests selection is acting on— that is, *conflict of interest* often characterizes problems in the evolution of social behavior (see Hayssen, Chapter 6, this volume).

To illustrate these three notions, Lack's theory of bird clutch size is discussed, and then the chapter continues by considering, in some detail, the evolution of sex ratios and related problems—an area known as the *theory of sex allocation* (Charnov, 1982). In the 1940s, the great British ecologist, David Lack, became interested in the factors affecting clutch size in birds. Why did some species attempt to rear but a single offspring, while some titmice produced a dozen? And why did clutch size within a species alter from year to year or with latitude? His approach to the determinants of clutch size consisted of asking the ultimate question of the consequences on the parents' fitness of them rearing a clutch of a particular size. The fundamental idea was quite simple. Suppose that the survivorship to adulthood of each offspring declined with increasing clutch size (perhaps due to less food available for each child), as shown in Fig. 1. Disregarding clutch size influences on parental survival, this survival decline would mean that some intermediate clutch size would be the value that resulted in the largest number of surviving offspring, a fairly good measure of parental fitness.

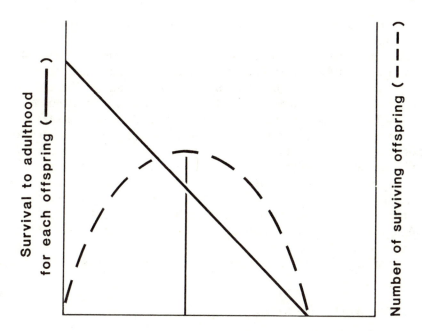

Clutch size

Figure 1. Lack's hypothesis for evolution of clutch size. If the survival of an individual offspring to adulthood declines with increasing clutch size, an intermediate clutch size (shown on the figure) results in the greatest number of surviving offspring—this is a measure of parental fitness. Natural selection is expected to favor parents who produce this clutch.

Reviews of this idea are to be found in most ecology texts and, of course, Lack's own writings (especially 1954, 1966, 1968).

It is not the purpose of the chapter to discuss the many additions and alterations that have been made to this basic framework; needless to say, the idea has generated a tremendous amount of very fruitful research. The importance of the idea lies in its ultimate question form. Between-species variation and within-species variation from year to year (or between habitats) are to be understood in terms of alterations in shape of the survival curve of Fig. 1. The shape of the curve itself is to be understood as a function of environmental variables such as food availability or nest-predation patterns. Nowhere in the conception do the underlying physiological mechanisms play much of a role—that is, to understand clutch size is to first understand the tradeoff curve. For some species (e.g., *Parus major,* the great tit) the year to year variation in clutch size may be twofold; in years of plentiful food, the parents attempt to rear twice as many children (Perrins, 1965). Thus, selection on clutch size often favors temporal plasticity, and in theory this is to be understood as year to year shifts in the tradeoff relations.

In 1974, Robert Trivers noted that virtually all models for the evolution of life-history attributes (such as clutch size) assigned control to the parent. That is, the distribution of resources among offspring had classically been assumed to evolve to increase or maximize the parents' fitness. He pointed out that if the offspring is allowed to control the resources it obtains from the mother, selection operates on it to take more than the amount that the parent is selected to give. Thus, parent and offspring disagree over the quantity of resource to be given to the offspring. This perspective on life-history evolution was unknown prior to 1974 and raises many new questions, particularly for organisms such as birds who receive abundant parental care. Conflict of interest has proved important in understanding many other processes. Examples are male–female relations, animal fighting, and even interactions within an individual (i.e., intragenomic conflict, as discussed later).

SEX ALLOCATION THEORY

The problem of sex allocation (Charnov, 1982) is introduced here through a simple classification of the forms of sexual reproduction and five general questions. While certainly not exhaustive, the scheme used here is sufficient for the purposes of this chapter. Most animal or plant species produce only two types of gametes: large and small. In dioecious (= gonochoric) organisms, males and females are separated throughout their lives (an individual produces only one size of gamete throughout its lifetime). In hermaphroditic organisms, a single individual produces both large and small gametes during its lifetime. Hermaphroditism takes two forms: sequential—an individual functions early in life as one sex and then switches to the other sex for the rest of its life; simultaneous—an individual produces both kinds of gametes in each breeding season (more or less at the same time). Within sequential hermaphroditism, protandry (male first) is distinguished from protogyny (female first).

In relation to the foregoing scheme, the problem of sex allocation may be stated as follows:

1. For a dioecious species, what is the equilibrium sex ratio (proportion males among the offspring) maintained by natural selection?
2. For a sequential hermaphrodite, what is the equilibrium sex order (protandry or protogyny) and time of sex change?
3. For a simultaneous hermaphrodite, what is the equilibrium alloca-

tion of resources to male versus female function in each breeding season?

4. Under what conditions are the various states of hermaphroditism or dioecy evolutionarily stable? For example, when does selection favor genes for protandry over dioecy, or when is a *mixture* of sexual types stable?

5. When does selection favor the ability of an individual to alter its allocation to male versus female function in response to particular environmental or life-history situations?

These problems are very similar to one another in that each involves working out an equilibrium under natural selection, where the possible genotypes have different genetic contributions through male versus female function. Answers to these questions must, of course, consider the biology of the organisms—growth, morphology, mortality, competition (inter- and intraspecific), predation, patchiness in the environment, etc.—as well as possible genetic factors (e.g., inbreeding, autosomal versus cytoplasmic inheritance). Nevertheless, the phrase, "the problems are very similar to one another," is meant to indicate that all five questions are really one question phrased in different forms.

Consider a typical diploid organism. R. A. Fisher (1930) noted the seemingly trivial fact that with respect to autosomal genes, each zygote gets one-half of its genome from its father and one-half from its mother. To put it simply: everyone has exactly one father and one mother. However, far from being trivial, this fact holds the key to understanding sex allocation in diploids (and a similar principle holds for haplodiploids). Regardless of whether the concern is with dioecy, simultaneous hermaphroditism, or sequential hermaphroditism, one-half the autosomal genes come via the male function and one-half via the female. This fact has two important implications. First, an individual's reproductive success through male function (sperm) is to be measured relative to the male function of other individuals and vice versa for the female function. Second, since one-half the zygote genes come via each pathway, male and female function are in a real sense equivalent means to reproductive success. Consider, for example, dioecy and the sex ratio. If many daughters are being produced, then large reproductive gains accrue to the producers of sons that are relatively scarce. Selection then favors more sons, and an equilibrium will be established where reproductive gains through male and female offspring are equalized. Note that the process generates its own natural selection: It is the scarcity of one sex that itself makes increased production of that sex worthwhile. This is a form of frequency-dependent natural selection and is based on the inevitable fact of reproductive biology that everyone has one mother and one father.

Theoretical Analyses of Sex Allocation

The problem of sex allocation may be visualized as in Fig. 2. The axes are fitness through male and female functions. The curve represents the possible tradeoffs, with the endpoints representing all male function and all female function. Consider three cases: (1) In a species that is dioecious, the curve represents sons and daughters, and the concern is about the evolution of the sex ratio; (2) in a species that is a sex reverser, the axes represent reproductive gain while a male versus reproductive gain as a female. The tradeoff curve then represents various proportions of the lifetime spent as a male versus a female; (3) in a species that is a simultaneous hermaphrodite (consider it a plant), the axes represent reproductive gain via seeds versus pollen. Using population genetic arguments (Charnov, 1982), it is possible to show that the equilibrium favored by natural selection is often that value on the tradeoff curve that maximizes the product of the fitness through male function multiplied by the fitness through female function.

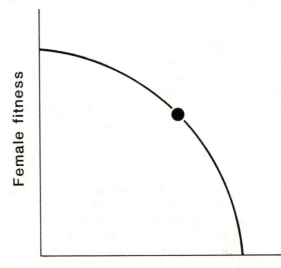

Male fitness

Figure 2. Sex allocation. The figure graphs a hypothetical tradeoff between male fitness and female fitness. The axes may be labeled in any of a number of ways. For example, they may be son production versus daughter production, the problem of interest being selection on the sex ratio. Other interpretations (see text) include reproductive gains for time as a male or female in a sex changer; or reproductive gains for pollen versus seed in a hermaphroditic plant. For all of these seemingly different cases, the equilibrium favored by selection takes the same form shown by the dot on the tradeoff curve. This dot marks the value that maximizes the product of the gain through male fitness multiplied by the gain through female fitness.

By casting the problem of sex allocation in the broad form shown in Fig. 2, a very general natural selection answer is found to the ultimate questions; an answer that is quite independent of any detailed considerations of proximate mechanisms. Indeed, only at this level of analysis do the five questions posed earlier turn into different forms of the same question. While there are several good examples for testing this theory (Charnov, 1982), discussion is restricted here to one particular situation: that of sex-ratio control in spatially highly structured populations of wasps and mites. The appendix to this chapter shows in detail some of the simple calculations that underlie sex-ratio selection in panmictic populations.

Sex-Ratio Control in Wasps and Mites: Local Mate Competition

In 1967, W. D. Hamilton constructed the first sex-ratio theory for spatially structured populations. Here, the sex ratio favored by selection for Hamilton's situation is calculated. He proposed the following population structure (labeled Local Mate Competition and abbreviated LMC): the world consists of a large number of islands which in one generation are colonized by n fertilized females. These females produce sons and daughters, and mating takes place only within each island. The males die and the newly fertilized females (the next generation) then disperse to recolonize islands. Since germinations are discrete, the islands are vacant at the end of each generation. Suppose that into a large population a mutant female is introduced who alters her sex ratio from a proportion r of sons to $\hat{r}$. While rare, this mutant will occur in a group with $n - 1$ normal females. Her fitness will be the number of migrants to which she contributes genes through her production of daughters and through females inseminated by her sons. If each mother produces b offspring, the mutant's fitness (W_t) will be

$$W_t = \text{(her daughters)} + \text{(females fertilized by her sons)}$$

or

$$W_t = b(1 - \hat{r}) + \{\hat{r}b/[b\hat{r} + (n - 1)rb]\}[b(1 - \hat{r}) + (n - 1)(1 - r)b]$$

If $\hat{r} = r$, the mutant's fitness equals the normal female's. The equilibrium, or favored sex ratio is r^* for which the mutant cannot do better by setting $\hat{r} \neq r$. It is required that $\partial W_t/\partial \hat{r} = 0$ when $\hat{r} = r$; if this is a maximum, then W_t will decrease for $\hat{r} \neq r$ (at least near r). Applying this rule to W_t, the value is:

$$r^* = (n - 1)/2n \tag{1}$$

If $n = 1$, strict sibmating and $r^* = 0$ occurs, which in practice means that a female should only produce enough sons to ensure the insemination of her daughters. The result here is that $r^* = 0$ since the model implicitly assumed a very large family size. As n gets large, $r^* \to \frac{1}{2}$, as shown in Fig. 3. This is the result Hamilton (1967) first derived and applied to a diploid population. It is possible to show that this value maximizes the following product relation where $m = $ no. of sons produced and $f = $ no. of daughters produced:

$$f \cdot m^{[(n-1)/(n+1)]}$$

The exponent $(n - 1)/(n + 1)$ shows how sons are devalued as a function of mating group size, relative to daughters.

Many parasitoid wasps (and some mites) meet or at least approximate the breeding structure assumed in this model. It is also interesting that many variations in the detailed assumptions about population structure do not alter the basic prediction of a steady rise in the sex ratio with increasing group size from female biased to an asymptote near ½. Does nature obey these rules? A brief discussion of some of the key LMC data follows (a more complete discussion is in Charnov, 1982).

In his original formulation of the LMC hypothesis, Hamilton (1967) listed 26 insect and mite species that were haplodiploid and typically had sib-mating. All had a strong female bias in the sex ratio. Scolytid bark beetles were of particular interest since they could be divided into two general life histories. In the first, a female and her brood occupied a gallery under bark, and mating took place before dispersal from the larval host. In the second type, mating took place after dispersal upon arrival at the new host. In the first, there is typically sib-

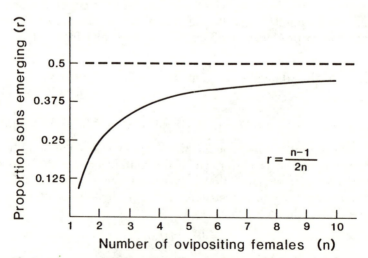

Figure 3. Local mate competition and the sex ratio. As given in Eq. (1), increasing numbers of associated ovipositing females causes the equilibrium sex ratio to go from very female biased to near equality.

mating, the sex ratio is strongly female biased, and males are often flightless (reviewed in Beaver, 1977). In the second, sex ratio at emergence from the larval host is near equality (data in Bartels and Lanier 1974; Bakke 1968).

Parasitoid Wasps

In a later paper on fig wasps, Hamilton (1979) showed a general positive relationship between the presence of winged males (an indicator of how much mating takes place after dispersal from the host fig) and the proportion of males. Waage (1982) studied LMC in the hymenopteran family Scelionidae. The large majority of species parasitize the eggs of *Lepidoptera* and *Hemiptera*. A single wasp egg is laid per host egg, but Waage argued that the degree of LMC was probably related to the dispersion of host eggs. The hosts ranged from those depositing eggs singly to those with masses of up to ~1000 eggs. Wasp species attacking eggs deposited singly should show little LMC, as should those attacking large masses. Here, the mass exceeds the egg-laying capacity of a single female, and the mass would most likely attract several wasp females. Excluding species attacking singly deposited eggs, LMC should generally decline with increasing size of the egg mass attacked. He examined field data (his own and from the literature) and assigned each species to an egg mass of typical size. Data for nearly 30 species showed the expected trend, with the sex ratio increasing from female biased to near equality, as a function of increasing egg mass size.

Probably the strongest evidence for the LMC model comes from wasps and mites in which the degree of LMC varies dramatically through space and time, and where theory predicts a facultative, short-term alteration in the sex ratio. LMC is more likely in a gregarious parasitoid, in which several eggs are laid on a single host, and where most mating takes place among the children emerging from the host. This effectively provided the material for Hamilton's 1967 list. Here, LMC declines if superparasitism occurs because mating then takes place among the broods of two or more females. LMC may occur in solitary parasitoids if the hosts are clumped so that mating mostly takes place among the offspring emerging from a single clump, as just discussed for the Scelionidae (Waage, 1982). LMC declines for both gregarious and solitary species if the hosts are clumped with several mothers ovipositing on a clump. One wasp species (*Nasonia*) has been well studied with respect to these effects.

Nasonia vitripennis

This is a small (1–3 mm) gregarious, parasitoid wasp (family Pteromalidae) that attacks the pupae of cyclorrhaphous flies (blowflies). It has been much studied (particularly its genetics), and the general biology is well known (reviews in Whiting, 1967; Cassidy, 1975). Edwards (1954) and Wylie (1958) described the host-finding and oviposition behavior. *Nasonia* females parasitize pupae from 1 to several days old (Wylie, 1963; Chabora and Pimentel, 1966). Upon locating a host puparium, a female climbs on and searches its surface, tapping rapidly with her antennae. She drills through the puparium wall with her ovipositor, which then is plunged deep within the pupa. At this time, she presumably assessed host suitability for oviposition and also injects a venom that kills and preserves the pupa (Beard, 1964; Wylie, 1958). Eggs are laid in a circle around the sting site in the space between the pupa and the puparium. Following oviposition, females feed on host fluids, which are necessary to mature additional eggs (Edwards, 1954; King and Hopkins, 1963). Multiple attacks are made upon a single host before oviposition is complete (Wylie, 1965). During the interval between attacks, while new eggs are maturing, a female may rest quietly or move about the immediate vicinity of the host, possibly assessing the presence of nearby hosts. After several batches of eggs are laid, a female leaves in search of new hosts. The final clutch size ranges from 10 to 50 eggs. The sex ratio of the primary parasite is 10–15% males. Superparasitism occurs when a female oviposits on a previously parasitized host.

Nasonia was of particular interest to Hamilton (1967) since the superparasite increased the proportion males among her brood, as is predicted by LMC theory (Wylie, 1966; Holes, 1970, 1972; Werren; 1980a; 1983). Males have short wings and cannot fly, so that mating takes place on the host or, if hosts are clumped, in the immediate vicinity. There are several laboratory studies of sex-ratio alteration related to the degree of crowding of females. Wylie (1965, 1966) studied *Nasonia* on a housefly host (*Musca*). (Note, however, that *Musca* is not a natural host for *Nasonia,* and mortality was rather high compared to studies on blowfly hosts.) When he confined increasing numbers of wasps with 10 hosts, the sex ratios clearly increase from female biased to nearly equality. Walker (1967) and Velthuis *et al.* (1965) carried out similar experiments (using blowfly hosts) with similar results. Walker's (1967) data were of particular interest since they showed an asymptote at about 60% males. In addition, data from another of her experiments, which varied both host and parasite number, showed that the proportion of males increases (for a fixed number of wasps) as the number of hosts increased or (for a fixed number of hosts) as the number of wasps increased. This shift is predicted by theory since LMC declines with increased spacing of the broods brought about by either decreasing the number of wasps or increasing the number of hosts.

Werren (1980b, 1983) carried out similar experiments also with blowfly hosts. Again, in Fig. 4, a clear rise in sex ratio to near equality is

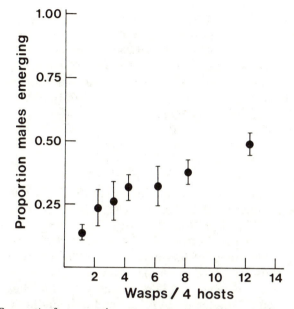

Figure 4. Sex ratio from patches containing 1–12 associated ovipositing females for the wasp *Nasonia* attacking blowfly pupae. Mean values ±2 S.E. are represented (at least 8 replicates per density). The mean values are rather close to those predicted by LMC theory. These experiments eliminated sex-specific mortality as a causal factor. (Redrawn from Werren 1980a,b.)

seen. Werren's work also eliminated differential mortality as a factor (generally unknown in previous work). In all these situations, LMC was altered both because of superparasitism and because the hosts were clumped. In laboratory cultures of *Nasonia,* where several females' broods were reared together (details in Werren 1980b, 1983), the emergent sex ratio was ~50% males.

In nature, *Nasonia* attacks a wide range of blowfly species (Whiting, 1967). Werren (1980b, 1983) has shown that the host situations utilized range from single pupae to thousands of pupae in a patch (i.e., under a large carcass). In general, more females are attracted to larger carcasses. While it is not possible to know the number of females (foundresses) at a given patch, it is possible to estimate the number of wasps emerging from a patch. This should generally be correlated with number of foundresses. Field data (Werren, 1980b, 1983) show a clear rise to a sex ratio near equality. These data also eliminate superparasitism and sex-differential mortality as factors in the sex-ratio shift. Data on many other parasitoids also support the prediction that females kept in groups may shift the sex ratio from female biased toward equality. Some of these are reviewed by Kochetova (1977) and Waage (1982).

For example, *Trissolcus grandis* is a solitary-egg parasite. Viktorov and Kochetova (1973a) showed that females kept alone produced about 13% sons. Females simply kept in tubes that contained traces of other females (previous occupancy) altered their sex ratio to 37% sons. In this same species, females kept in groups also produced more sons (Viktorov, 1968). Viktorov and Kochetova (1973b) showed a similar result for *Dahlbominus fuscipennis,* a gregarious ectoparasite of sawfly pupae. They also eliminated differential mortality as a cause of the sex-ratio shift.

Mites

Spider mites are small, haplodiploid creatures (~0.5 mm length) that suck out the contents of leaf cells. They are of immense economic importance (Welch, 1979; Wrensch, 1979). The general life history (with reference to the genus *Tetranychus*) has been reviewed by Mitchell (1973), from which most of this discussion is drawn. A postdispersal, fertilized, female mite feeds in a restricted area, which she marks out with silk. All of her eggs are laid in this area, and the young feed and develop within the territory. At the end of immature development, the young enter a quiescent deutonymph stage, and most are still in the original territory or very near (McEnroe, 1969). Adult males actively guard female deutonymphs and mate with them upon emergence as adults (Potter *et al.,* 1976a,b). Since sperm competition favors the first male to mate (Helle, 1967), such guarding is of much importance to male reproductive success.

Only at this one stage are females available for mating, and males often much outnumber available females and actively fight for possession of the quiescent deutonymphs, particularly at high population densities (Potter, 1978, 1979). At low population densities, sib-mating is probably the rule (Mitchell, 1973; McEnroe, 1969). However, at high densities, the territories are more closely packed, and much of the mating is among nonrelatives. After mating, on the first day of adult life, females become restless and disperse. This response is strong in crowded conditions but weak when resources are abundant. After dispersal, females settle down to begin a new cycle. Males do not disperse. They are much smaller than females (15–30% a female's weight) and stop growing at maturity. Females continue growing as adults. The sex ratio at maturity is often very female biased (Mitchell, 1972), and McEnroe (1969) suggested that this was due to LMC. If the territory is considered a feeding resource that a mother allocates to sons and daughters (under low population density), a sex ratio of 20% males translates into a resource allocation of 5% into males.

Two published studies have considered the impact of crowding on the sex ratio at maturity (Wrensch and Young, 1978; Zaher *et al.,* 1979).

Both confined various numbers of fertilized females to leaf discs and looked at the sex ratio produced among the progeny. Since leaf areas were very similar in the two studies, Fig. 5 shows a graph of the data as sex ratio versus female-mite density. As theory predicts, the sex ratio increases with density to almost equality.

These wasp and mite data very strongly suggest that the sex ratio is adjusted (often facultatively) to the conditions of the breeding scheme. With mostly sib-mating, mostly daughters are achieved; with more random mating, the ratio rises to near equality.

An Aside to Higher Plants

Most higher plants are hermaphroditic, producing pollen and seeds more or less at the same time. It has been realized for some years (reviewed in Charnov, 1982) that self-fertilization was rather like sib-mating, and it was predicted that highly selfed plants should allocate little resource to pollen. Consider the work of Lloyd (1972a,b) on the genus *Cotula* (Compositae). There are about 80 species with gender expression as follows: dioecy ~10; monoecy ~24; gynomonoecy ~35; perfect flowers ~10. In the species tested, there were no physiological barriers to selfing. In the monoecious species, a floral head has both male and female florets. Floret length was an approximate indicator

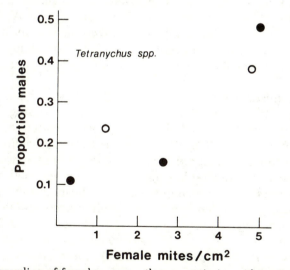

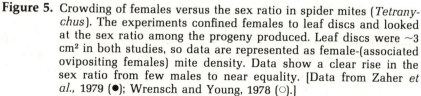

Figure 5. Crowding of females versus the sex ratio in spider mites (*Tetranychus*). The experiments confined females to leaf discs and looked at the sex ratio among the progeny produced. Leaf discs were ~3 cm² in both studies, so data are represented as female-(associated ovipositing females) mite density. Data show a clear rise in the sex ratio from few males to near equality. [Data from Zaher *et al.*, 1979 (●); Wrensch and Young, 1978 (○).]

of the level of selfing—shorter florets meaning more selfing. As first noted by Lloyd (1972b), there is a significant linear average regression (correlation coefficient = 0.61, sample size = 17) of average proportion male florets versus floret length, although visual inspection of the data suggests (with the exception of one point) a relation with an asymptote at about 60% male flowers (Charnov, 1982). Perhaps some of the scatter is related to variation among the species in seed size. This positive relation is predicted by LMC theory.

In sum, these LMC examples drawn from wasps, beetles, mites, and higher plants illustrate well the power of an ultimate-question perspective. Some of the examples are a good demonstration of selection favoring facultative shifting of a major life-history parameter (sex ratio) in response to shifts in a social environment.

SEX ALLOCATION AND INTRAGENOMIC CONFLICT OF INTEREST

The calculation for Figure 3 [Eq. (1)] assumed that the genes controlling the sex ratio are autosomal, nuclear genes. The wasps and mites are haplodiploid, but the autosomal control assumption gives almost the same answer as mother control under haplodiploidy. However, other forms of inheritance are possible; for example, genes located on sex chromosomes or nonnuclear, cytoplasmic DNA. There are a wide array of possibilities. Figure 6 shows the equilibria that would result from various forms of control. XX♀ is haplodiploidy with mother control; note how close this is to the result predicted under autosomal control.

Figure 6 illustrates well the degree of conflict over sex ratio shown by the various "genes" that may be present in a single individual. Many of these control possibilities are indeed known in nature (review in Charnov, 1982; Bull, 1983). Cytoplasmic control of pollen production (allocation to male function) is well known in hermaphroditic plants. In many cases, interaction between the various genetical elements has also been studied. For example, cytoplasmic inheritance of being a female (turning off pollen production) is often accompanied by nuclear genes ("restorer genes") that "combat the cytoplasmic DNA to restore pollen production." Indeed, at least two extrachromosomal factors affecting sex ratio are now known from *Nasonia* (Werren *et al.*, 1981; Skinner, 1982), and their affects are now being studied in the author's laboratory. The autosomal perspective was used for much of the previous data discussion because for most sex-allocation problems, it appears at present to be the most correct one. However, conflict of interest is always potentially part of a sex-allocation pattern in nature.

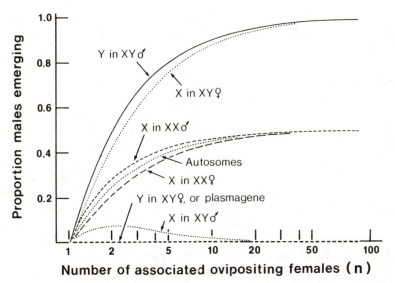

Figure 6. ESS sex ratios under local mate competition (LMC). Assuming Hamilton's (1967) original population structure, the graph shows the sex-ratio equilibrium as a function of the number of associated ovipositing (founding) females (*n*) and the particular part of the genome assumed to control the sex ratio. Note how close the answers are for autosomal and X, in XX♀ (= haploidiploidy), control. Also note the conflict of interest shown by various genomic components. (Graph redrawn from Hamilton, 1979. See this reference for detailed discussion and method of derivation of results.)

CONCLUSION

This chapter discusses three major topics. First is the value of ultimate questions, contrasted to proximate questions. While it is stressed what one gains by casting problems such as sex allocation in the ultimate framework, one must also be aware that the physiological mechanisms are themselves of much interest. However, ultimate questions are often just very different questions from hypotheses concerning physiological mechanisms. There is, however, no reason not to ask natural-selection questions about the proximate mechanisms themselves. Indeed, Bull (1983) has done just this for sex-determining mechanisms under dioecy. The second topic is that natural selection often endows the organism with plastic responses to the environmental change that an individual may see during its lifetime. What can be done here is to calculate what the response ought to be, using fitness enhancement as a guide to the options "chosen." And finally, conflict of fitness interest is an important part of all social interactions. A symposium devoted to infanticide illustrates certain male–female conflicts quite well. Sex allocation provides some of the best examples of intragenomic conflict, where an "individual" is not even an "individual" with respect to fitness interests (Charnov, 1982).

APPENDIX: BASIC SEX-RATIO THEORY

This appendix is a treatment of sex-ratio evolution for diploids taken from an early paper by Shaw and Mohler (1953). While R. A. Fisher (1930) clearly was the path breaker in sex-ratio theory, Shaw and Mohler (1953) provide a very elegant discussion, and to this author's knowledge, the first explicit use of an argument based on the concept of an Evolutionarily Stable Strategy (ESS). The beauty of their argument is its utter simplicity. Consider a population n reproductive females of a dioecious species with discrete generations. Each of these females will produce C eggs, a proportion r of them being sons. Suppose that a proportion S_m of the sons and S_f of the daughters survive to breed. Introduce into this population a single mutant female who alters her sex ratio to $\hat{r}$. The question of interest is: will this female contribute more or fewer genes to the next generation contrasted to a typical female in the population? Suppose that the population of reproductive adults, who are the offspring of our original $n + 1$ females, themselves produce a total of K children (the grandchildren of the original females). One-half of the genes in these grandchildren came via males, one-half via females. This mutant female (here called "mom") will thus contribute genes to the following number of grandchildren through her sons:

($\frac{1}{2}$) (number of grandchildren) (proportion of reproductive males who are mom's sons)

(it is necessary to multiply by $\frac{1}{2}$ since one-half the genes passed by mom's children did not come from her—they came from her mate, the children's father)

To write the foregoing symbolically:

$$= 1/2(K)[(S_m C\hat{r})/(S_m C\hat{r} + nS_m Cr)] \qquad (A1)$$

The same argument obtains through her daughters:

$$1/2(K)\{[S_f C(1 - \hat{r})][S_f C(1 - \hat{r}) + nS_f C(1 - r)]\} \qquad (A2)$$

Finally, adding Eqs. (A1) and (A2) gives the total representation of mom's genes in grandchildren, her total fitness: W_t.

Provided n is large, this sum will be approximated well by

$$W_t = 1/2(K)\{[S_f C(1 - \hat{r})]/[nS_f C(1 - r)] + [(S_m C\hat{r})/nS_m Cr]\} \qquad (A3)$$

Before looking at the implications of Eq. (A3), first the result may be generalized. Define: $\hat{m}$ = surviving sons from mom; m = surviving sons from each additional female; $\hat{f}$ = surviving daughters from mom; $\hat{f}$ = same from other females. With these in mind, W_t may be generally written as

$$W_t = (1/2) \left(\frac{K}{n} \right) (\hat{m}/m + \hat{f}/f) \qquad (A4)$$

or

$$W_t \propto \hat{m}/m + \hat{f}/f \qquad (A5)$$

Eq. (A5) is the general form of the Shaw–Mohler Equation for sex ratio. Shaw and Mohler (1953) worked with Eq. (A3), to which the discussion now returns. The $(1/2)/K/n$ is simply a proportionality factor, and the equation may be written as (canceling S_m, S_f, and C):

$$W_t \propto \hat{r}/r + (1 - \hat{r})/(1 - r) \qquad (A6)$$

But, this is simply a linear equation in $\hat{r}$.

If mom is the same as all other females, $\hat{r} = r$ and Eq. (A6) (where $\propto$ is simply replaced with $=$) is equal to 2. Mom contributes more genes (than the average female) to grandchildren if $W_t > 2$. In Fig. 7, W_t is graphed as a function of $\hat{r}$ for two assumed r values, namely, $r = \frac{1}{4}$, or $\frac{3}{4}$. If $r = \frac{1}{4}$, W_t is a line with positive slope, and all $\hat{r} > \frac{1}{4}$ have $W_t > 2$. That is, selection favors females who produce more sons. If $r = \frac{3}{4}$, the reverse obtains, and females with $\hat{r} < \frac{3}{4}$ are more

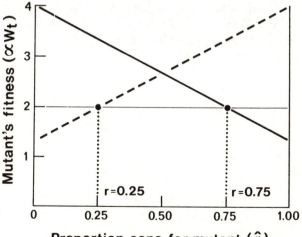

Proportion sons for mutant ($\hat{r}$)

Figure 7. Fitness (W_t, Eq. [A6]) for a mutant female is plotted as a function of her sex ratio ($\hat{r}$) for two population sex ratios ($r = 0.25$, 0.75). She has the same fitness ($W_t = 2$) as a typical female when $\hat{r} = r$. The mutant is favored by selection of $W_t > 2$. For $r < 0.5$, $\hat{r} > r$ is favored (the reverse for $r > 0.5$). The ESS is $r = \frac{1}{2}$.

fit. With reference to Eq. (A6), if $r > \frac{1}{2}$, mothers are favored who produce an $\hat{r}$ smaller than r; for $r < \frac{1}{2}$ mothers are favored who produce an $\hat{r} > r$. In this way, selection moves the sex ratio toward $\frac{1}{2}$. If $r = \frac{1}{2}$, W_t does not change with $\hat{r}$. This is the ESS sex ratio. From this biological argument follows a surprising prediction. Note that r (or $\hat{r}$) is the sex ratio near or at conception, and that the survival rates to adulthood (S_m, S_f) cancel out of the argument. That is, differential survival to adulthood for sons versus daughters does not alter the ESS primary sex ratio away from equality, at least in this simple situation. Nor does the mating system (monogamy versus polygamy) affect the result, since the arguments remain the same under each.

Now, consider a slight alteration in the model. Mom has R units of resource to divide among her children. Let each son survive to adulthood at rate S_m; each daughter at rate S_f, but now allow sons and daughters individually to be of different cost to the parent. Suppose a son costs C_1 units of resource and a daughter C_2. It follows that a female allocating q proportion of the R resource to all her sons will have RqS_1/C_1 breeding sons and $R(1 - q)S_2/C_2$ breeding daughters. Likewise, a mutant female who alters her q to $\hat{q}$ will produce these numbers with q replaced by $\hat{q}$. If the reader will repeat the argument leading to Eq. (A3) with these new values, it should come clear that W_t now reduces to

$$W_t = \hat{q}/q + [(1 - \hat{q})/(1 - q)]$$

This, however, is the same as Eq. (A6) with the rs replaced by the qs. Thus, the ESS q is $\frac{1}{2}$. This is the simplest version of Fisher's hypothesis that in equilibrium, selection favors equal allocation of resources to sons and daughters.

II INFANTICIDE IN NONHUMAN PRIMATES: A TOPIC OF CONTINUING DEBATE

Infanticide in nonhuman primates: An introduction and perspective

Glenn Hausfater

Infanticide in animals and humans is a controversial topic. This is especially so when the discussion turns to nonhuman primates. The chapters in Part II have been selected to provide readers with a representative sample both of the nature of the data concerning infanticide among nonhuman primates and the nature of the debate concerning the interpretation of those data. However, as an unfortunate consequence of the latter consideration, readers who are not familiar with the "infanticide controversy," especially as concerns langur monkeys, may very well be more confused than enlightened by the conflicting views expressed in these chapters. Thus, these brief introductory notes are intended to clarify certain basic issues and positions in the long-standing debate over the frequency and significance of infanticide among nonhuman primates. Although I obviously run the risk of making the situation worse, rather than better, I present here my own personal (and admittedly idiosyncratic) perspective on the infanticide controversy. In particular, I first discuss specific points of disagreement in the infanticide controversy and then consider some deeper issues that I believe to underlie the range of opinions held by primatologists concerning infanticide and its role in the social life of nonhuman primates in the wild.

With respect to specific points of disagreement, I view the infanticide controversy as basically reducing to the dual questions of (1) What level of detail of observation is required for an infant's disappearance to be attributed to infanticide? and (2) What kinds of evidence are required to refute any given hypothesis concerning the events thus observed? Furthermore, I consider the extent of disagreement over the first of these issues to have been amplified by what I see as the use by some reviewers of much more stringent standards of evidence in regard to observations of infanticide than is the case in other realms of behavior, especially predation and feeding behavior. Nevertheless, it is also true that when one distills all reports of infanticide in langurs, as done by Vogel and Loch (Chapter 12, this volume) and by Boggess (Chapter 14, this volume), one finds that in only a handful of cases have fieldworkers actually observed a fatal attack on an infant.

Yet the crux of the issue is how one deals not with the cases in which observations are relatively complete but with those in which observations are incomplete due either to the habits of the monkeys, the habits of the observer, or both. How does one treat cases in which the observational record is truncated due to the fact that the infant and its attacker fell into foliage; or cases in which the wounding of an infant was clearly observed during daylight hours, but the infant's disappearance occurred only on the subsequent night when, for understandable reasons, observations were not in progress; or cases similar to the preceding but in which the infant's disappearance occurred several days after the observed attack? Even among those infant disappearances for which observations are relatively complete, how should one deal with the data in terms of hypothesis testing if, for example, the infant's age was not known with certainty?

Clearly, this is not a realm where evidencial rules will come easily and in many ways is the obverse of the problem as to when life begins, discussed both by proponents of legislative restrictions on abortion and by Scrimshaw (Chapter 22, this volume). Here, of course, the issues become: when did a particular infant's life end, and how does one assign the cause of death? Complications of a severe wound? Infanticide? Or, perhaps the former following the latter? Certainly, we should not dismiss altogether incomplete observations of a given event merely because they are so; afterall, no observational record can in reality be considered unequivocally "complete." However, neither should we accept uncritically, for the sake of expanding our sample of "verified" cases of infanticide, an elaborate set of assumptions about what might have preceded or followed the brief sequence of events that was actually observed. In these regards, I consider the chapters by Crockett and Sekulic (Chapter 9, this volume) and by Leland *et al.* (Chapter 8, this volume) as exemplary both in their conservative treatment of very complex observational datasets and in their use of these data to test the predictions of specific alternative hypotheses.

With respect to such predictions, the two most strongly debated and mutually exclusive explanations of infanticide are the "sexual selection" and "social pathology" hypotheses. As outlined in the volume introduction, the sexual selection hypothesis predicts that infanticide among nonhuman primates should be directed primarily by adult males against unweaned infants sired by their competitors. In contrast, the social pathology hypothesis states that infant killing in primates is an aberrant behavior that is seen only in populations at high densities. Further, such populations are assumed to have reached abnormally high densities as a result, in most cases, of provisioning of food resources by humans or through other forms of human disturbance. Rather than summarize these various hypotheses (and evidence in support of them) any further, I will merely refer the reader to the volume introduction as well as to the position paper and detailed review of data by Boggess (Chapter 14, this volume), an advocate of the social pathology/enforced proximity hypothesis, and to the formal replies to that chapter by Hrdy (Chapter 16, this volume) and by Sugiyama (Chapter 15, this volume), strong proponents of alternative viewpoints (Sugiyama, 1965a; Hrdy, 1977a,b, 1979).

These latter three contributions to this volume, even given the brief nature of the reply chapters, should provide readers with a relatively good sense not only of the conviction with which positions are held in the infanticide debate but of the major points of disagreement concerning the correctness of various predictions drawn from various explanatory models. The magnitude of these disagreements is made even more striking when one realizes that draft copies of these three chapters were circulated among the authors prior to publication, and that ample opportunity was afforded to all concerned for modification and revision of their views in light of each other's criticisms. Clearly, these authors read and interpret the existing literature on langur infanticide very differently, and much more interchange than provided either by the infanticide symposium itself or by the preparation of this volume will be required to produce any higher level of agreement.

The debate over the frequency and function of infanticide in langurs has had the unfortunate side effect of distracting attention from the burgeoning body of data that suggests that infanticide is an important element in the social organization of many nonhuman primate species other than langurs. The various field reports and data summaries included in this section provide readers with access to recent information on infanticide in these species. However, one finds here also, as in the case of langur monkeys, differences of interpretation concerning the data on infanticide. Thus, several chapters in Part II present somewhat different tallies both of the species for which infanticide has been reported and of the number of observed cases of infanticide in each of these species. However, I believe that these latter discrepancies are actually relatively minor, and reflect differences among the authors in access to the primary literature rather than any major disagreements over hypotheses or data. In fact, in my view, these latter chapters actually show quite substantial agreement concerning the kinds of data required to test particular hypotheses and the nature of the hypotheses themselves. More importantly, in several cases, the authors are themselves currently involved in long-term investigations that hold the promise of eventually providing such data.

Apart from considerations of hypothesis testing and data, the controversy over the frequency and significance of infanticide among nonhuman primates is, to my mind, also extremely interesting from the standpoint of the sociology of science. In many ways, the study of primate behavior has been the weak sibling of field zoology. Theoretical issues and concepts have been generated almost exclusively in the latter discipline (based on studies of nonprimate animals) and only subsequently assimilated by students of primate behavior. In the case of infanticide, however, the flow of ideas and issues has been almost precisely the opposite. Largely due to the writings of Hrdy (1974, 1977a) on infant killing in langurs, infanticide emerged from its status as a laboratory artifact to that of a phenomenon considered not only appropriate for study by zoologists (and psychologists, see Part III) but also amenable to evolutionary explanation. Obviously, however, this latter development cannot be considered apart from the widespread acceptance of sociobiology and other evolutionary paradigms in behavioral biology as a whole (Trivers, 1972; Wilson, 1975).

This change of status for infanticide as a research topic is made even more interesting by the fact that within the subdiscipline of primate behavior, the first reports of infant killing in langurs (Sugiyama, 1965a, 1965b) were largely dismissed as having little general significance for our understanding of the social organization of primates in their natural environment. However, again directly attributable to Hrdy's (1974) interpretation of infanticide among the langurs at Mt. Abu as an expression of sexual competition, this phenomenon came to be recognized as more widespread and important, at least among the Colobines, than was previously thought to be the case. Then, as an increasing number of reports of infanticide in other species were published (Struhsaker, 1977; Goodall, 1977; Rudran, 1979; Butynski, 1982) the possibility began to receive open consideration that infanticide may actually be an important phenomenon in the order Primates as a whole. The data-based chapters in Part II give a good indication of just how far this change in attitude toward infanticide as a research topic and as a normative feature of primate social organization has progressed.

However, in an intellectual and sociological process analogous to the second law of thermodynamics, every theoretical advance provides new impetus for the diametrically opposed school of thought and perhaps more strongly in the case of primate behavior than in most other fields. In part, the strength of this opposing reaction to the idea that infanticide might be a normative aspect of social behavior of some primate species was perhaps due to what may be called the "disciplinary schizophrenia" of primatologists themselves. By the latter term, I mean that students of primate behavior have been drawn from several very different intellectual traditions, primarily psychology, anthropology, and zoology. The anthropological tradition in particular has tended to approach the study of primate societies as a branch of ethnography. The focus of these studies has thus been social roles, relations, and norms and, more generally, the significance of social structure for the harmonious and adaptive functioning of societies.

In contrast, the zoological tradition has focused primarily on differences in reproductive success and survival among individuals within societies rather than on differences between societies per se. The distinction may not be so clear-cut as I have drawn it, for zoologists have certainly also attempted to understand within-species variability in social organization, but I believe that it is nonetheless a real and important one. Furthermore I believe that as a result of the peculiarities of their research questions and outlook, primatologists from the zoological tradition have generally been predisposed to accept the idea that a behavior could be good for the individual but detrimental to the group, population, or species as a whole. In contrast, primatologists in the anthropological tradition have been much more hesitant to accept explanations of behavior based on advantage to the individual as opposed to that of the group.

However, it is also the case that many fieldworkers, regardless of their training and tradition, have come to accept the importance of infanticide as a behavioral phenomenon among nonhuman primates based not on theoretical grounds but rather as a result of having actually observed the behavior in the wild themselves. Thus, in reading accounts of infanticide in Kibale Forest primates one cannot help but be struck by how much the acceptance or rejection of various explanations for this behavior seems to depend on the observers' impressions of the specificity with which infants were targeted as victims by incoming males in contrast to the extent of agreement per se between these observations and the predictions of any specific hypothesis (Leland et al., Chapter 8, this volume). Likewise, recent observations of infanticide accompanying adult male replacement at Jodhpur have resulted in a rather substantial change of position by the members of that research team concerning both the nature of the langur mating system and the frequency of infanticide in that species (cf. Vogel, 1979 with Vogel and Loch, Chapter 12, this volume).

On the other hand, such changes of perspective and position can be seen as very encouraging developments for they indicate that the behavior of our study animals in the wild can be at least as important as our particular intellectual tradition in the evaluation of theory and hypotheses, if not more so. Still there remains a distressing tendency for field workers, regardless of tradition, to dismiss events reported at one site if similar events have not been observed at their own site. More generally, we all still far too frequently fail to appreciate how many situations, both ecologically and evolutionarily, can lead to certain behaviors being expressed by a species in one habitat or at one site, but not at others. Yet, despite such problems and biases, participants at the Wenner-Gren Foundation symposium that gave rise to this volume were still able to achieve substantial clarification of various hypotheses and to reach relatively close agreement on data and research strategies required to test those hypotheses.

However, as will also become clear in reading the following chapters, even given the extent of agreement already reached on the kinds of data and observational designs required to test specific hypotheses, we are still lacking sufficiently large and precise datasets to actually carry out a rigorous evaluation of competing alternative hypotheses. And as my own contribution (Hausfater, Chapter 13, this volume) to this part makes clear, use of incomplete, inaccurate, or otherwise discrepant datasets can significantly affect our assessment of the truth or falsity of any specific hypothesis. Thus, it seems likely that primate infanticide will remain controversial until an adequate number of long-term studies of langurs and other primate species are both undertaken and completed.

Regardless of when, or if, the infanticide controversy is resolved, I believe that the controversy itself remains one of the most interesting and productive in behavioral biology today. In particular, the dispute over the frequency and significance of infanticide among nonhuman primates has forced us to question certain fundamental assumptions concerning not only the social behavior of nonhuman primates in their natural environment but also the design and validity of observational studies of such behavior. The infanticide controversy has also provided an important stimulus to new thinking and research on the causation and function of infant killing and related phenomena in animals, both primate and nonprimate species alike, and I believe that this will continue to be the case for some time yet to come. In my opinion, such questioning and research is, after all, what science is all about, and I hope that the following chapters will be viewed by most readers as an important contribution in this regard.

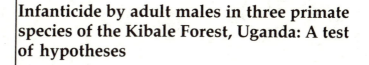

8 | Infanticide by adult males in three primate species of the Kibale Forest, Uganda: A test of hypotheses

Lysa Leland
Thomas T. Struhsaker
Thomas M. Butynski

INTRODUCTION

Infanticide by adult or subadult males has been observed under "natural" and nonmanipulative conditions in the wild for perhaps a dozen species of nonhuman primates and is strongly suspected from circumstantial evidence for several others. These cases have been reviewed by Angst and Thommen (1977) and Hrdy (1979) and are summarized in Table I according to social organization. As can be seen from this table, the majority of these species are found in, or adjacent to, areas of human disturbance. Such disturbance includes food provisioning, agriculture, and extensive and recent habitat destruction which may result in the compression of animals into higher densities. High population density is itself thought by several authors to be a major factor affecting the occurrence and frequency of infanticide (Eisenberg *et al.*, 1972; Rudran, 1973, 1979; Hrdy, 1974, 1977a,b, 1979). Other authors consider human disturbance to be the primary cause of infanticidal behavior (Curtin and Dolhinow, 1978; Boggess, 1979 and Chapter 14, this volume).

Infanticide by adult males has also been observed in three primate species living without human interaction in a relatively undisturbed, mature rain forest. These species are the redtail monkey (*Cercopithecus ascanius schmidti*), blue monkey (*Cercopithecus mitis stuhlmanni*), and red colobus monkey (*Colobus badius tephrosceles*). All three spe-

Table I. Summary of observed and strongly suspected cases of infanticide by male nonhuman primates in the wild

Social organization	Species	Report and/or observers	Evidence[a] OI	OW	SI	Habitat/size	Human influence on group or population
Predominantly one-male groups	Hanuman langur (*Presbytis entellus*)	Sugiyama (1965b) Mohnot (1971a) Hrdy (1974) Makwana (1979) Vogel and Loch (Chapter 12, this volume)	*	*	*	Forest; savanna; croplands; villages	Food provisioning; crop-raiding; habitat destruction; reduction of predators (Bishop *et al.*, 1981)
	Purple-faced langur (*Presbytis senex*)	Rudran (1973)			*	5 km² archeological parkland including secondary forest	Habitat destruction; reduction of predators
	Black and white colobus (*Colobus guereza*)	Oates (1977)			*	560 km² forest reserve; mature rain forest	Minimal
	Redtail monkey (*Cercopithecus ascanius*)	Struhsaker (1977)			*	560 km² forest reserve; mature rain forest	None
	Red colobus (*Colobus badius rufomitratus*)	Marsh (1979)	*			52 km² flood plain; gallery forest	Habitat destruction
	Red howler (*Alouatta seniculus*)	Rudran (1979) Crockett and Sekulic (Chapter 9 this volume)	*	*	*	30 km² cattle ranch llanos; savanna and woodland	Grazing of domestic stock; reduction of predators
	Campbell's monkey (*Cercopithecus campbelli*)	Galat-Luong and Galat (1979)			*	Research campus; relict patch of secondary forest	Habitat destruction; poaching of monkeys; some provisioning (Bourliere, Hunkeler, and Bertrand, 1970)
	Silvered-leaf monkey (*Presbytis cristata*)	Wolf (1980)	*			City park; planted trees	Habitat destruction: reduction of predators; some provisioning (Bernstein, 1968)

Social organization	Species	Reference	OI	OW	SI	Habitat	Observed threats
Multimale, patrilineal groups	Blue monkey (*Cercopithecus mitis*)	Butynski (1982)	*			560 km² forest reserve; mature rain forest	None
	Chimpanzee (*Pan troglodytes*)	Goodall (1977) Goodall *et al.* (1979) Nishida *et al.* (1979)	*		*	83 km² national park; rain forest and woodland Mountain range; rain forest and woodland	Habitat destruction; food provisioning (Wrangham, 1974[a]; Nishida, 1979)
	Gorilla (*Gorilla gorilla*)	Fossey (1979) Fossey (Chapter 11, this volume)	*			375 km² national park; montane	Habitat destruction; poaching of gorilla (Harcourt and Fossey, 1981)
	Red colobus (*Colobus badius tephrosceles*)	Struhsaker and Leland (in preparation)	*			560 km² forest reserve; mature rain forest	Minimal
Multimale, matrilineal groups	Chacma baboon (*Papio ursinus*)	Busse and Hamilton (1981)	*			Savanna and woodland	None
	Olive baboon (*Papio anubis*)	Packer (1980) Collins *et al.* (Chapter 10, this volume)	*			83 km² national park; rain forest, woodland, and beach	Habitat destruction; food provisioning (Wrangham, 1974[a])
	Yellow baboon (*Papio cynocephalus*)	Shopland (1982)	*			300 km² national park; savannah and woodland	None

[a] OI, OW, and SI indicate cases of observed infanticide, observed wounding of infant, and suspected infanticide, respectively.

153

cies have been studied from 5 to 13 years in the Kibale Forest, Uganda, in which time four cases of infanticide have been witnessed and several others are strongly suspected (see following and Tables I and II). Although these cases are few in number, they are important for an understanding of infanticide because they suggest that human interaction and disturbance may not be as critical in influencing infanticide in primates as previously supposed.

This chapter summarizes and compares infanticide in redtail monkeys (Struhsaker, 1977), blue monkeys (Butynski, 1982) and red colobus monkeys (Struhsaker and Leland, in preparation) and reviews prevalent hypotheses concerning the cause and function of infanticide by males. Data from Kibale and elsewhere are presented that support the hypothesis that this behavior is best explained as an adaptive reproductive strategy. Finally, the conditions and variables that may affect the frequency of infanticide in particular social organizations and populations are discussed.

METHODOLOGY

Study Area

The Kibale Forest is a 560 km² reserve located in western Uganda. Of the reserve, 60% is mature evergreen forest with the remainder composed of swamp, grassland, woodland thicket, and colonizing bush. Approximately 14% of the northern sector of the reserve has been selectively felled over the past 30 years (see Kingston, 1967; Wing and Buss, 1970; and Struhsaker, 1975 for details). The Ngogo study site (ca. 600 ha), where the *Cercopithecus* infanticides occurred, lies in the center of the reserve and is largely composed of, and surrounded by, undisturbed mature forest and small patches of colonizing thicket and grassland (Ghiglieri, 1979).

Compartment 30 (ca. 300 ha) of the Kanyawara study site, where the red colobus infanticides occurred, consists of undisturbed mature rain forest lying 10 km northwest of the Ngogo study area and is connected to it by continuous undisturbed forest. Although selectively felled forest, exotic tree plantations, and grassland border parts of this compartment, primate densities in this study area do not appear to have been significantly affected by these factors, especially when viewed in terms of the general stability of these populations over the past 13 years (Struhsaker, 1975; Oates, 1977; Struhsaker and Leland, in preparation).

In addition to the three species discussed in this chapter, five other anthropoid species live sympatrically in both study areas: black and white colobus (*Colobus guereza*), L'hoest's monkey (*Cercopithecus*

Table II. Details of infanticide in Kibale species[a]

Species/male	Date of infanticide[b]	Age/sex of infant	Tenure after infanticide	Copulations with mother after infanticide
Redtail[c] New	(1) 6–35 days after replacement [OI]	Approximately 1 week	12–13 months	Not determined but highly probable
	(2) 41–75 days after replacement [OI]	1 day	11–12 months	Not determined but highly probable
Blue[d] AM2	(1) 4–35 days after replacement [OI]	6-month-old female	4–7 days	Not determined but unlikely
	(2) 4–35 days after replacement [SSI]	3 months	4–7 days	Not determined but unlikely
	(3) 1–35 days after replacement [SI]	5 months	4–42 days	Not determined but unlikely
AM5	(1) 2 days after replacement [SSW]	7 months	4–19 days (infant not killed)	
Red colobus[e] Whitey	(1) 5 days after male's 1st copulation [OI]	1–1.5-month-old male	Still present (>11 months)	11 days later
	(2) 7 days after male's 1st copulation [OSSW]	6.5-month-old male	Still present (infant not killed) (>11 months)	
	(3) 31 days after male's 1st copulation [SSI]	1.5–2 months	Still present (>10 months)	<13 days later
	(4) approximately 5 months after male's 1st copulation [SI]	4 months	Still present (>5 months)	<9 days later

[a] Data from Struhsaker (1977), Butynski (1982), and Struhsaker and Leland (in preparation).

[b] I, infanticide, W, wounding; O, observed; SS, strongly suspected (due to chases, etc.); S, weakly suspected (due to disappearance).

[c] Birth peak: two annual peaks, but births in most months; gestation: 140 days (based on blues); weaning: approximately 1 year; interbirth interval: 1.5–2 years.

[d] Birth peak: one peak but births in all but 2 months; gestation: 140 days (Rowell, 1970b); weaning: approximately 1–1.3 years; interbirth interval: approximately 20 months in captivity (Sieber, 1981).

[e] Birth peak: broad peak, but births in all months; gestation: approximately 200 days (based on *Presbytis entellus*: Hrdy, 1977b); weaning: approximately 1.5 years; interbirth interval: approximately 24–27 months.

155

lhoesti), gray-cheeked mangabeys (*Cercocebus albigena*), olive baboons (*Papio anubis*), and chimpanzees (*Pan troglodytes*). Although
the densities of the three latter species are higher at the Ngogo site,
densities of redtail monkeys, red colobus, and particularly of blue monkeys are higher at Kanyawara (Butynski, 1982; Struhsaker and Butynski:
unpublished data). Both study areas are protected from human exploitation, and there is no food provisioning or any other form of human
interactions with the animals.

Data Collection

Similar methods were used for studying all three species; these methods have previously been described in detail by Struhsaker (1975). A
summary of information on the number of groups consistently monitored and the number of hours of observation of each group in the
course of a long-term research program in the Kibale Forest is provided
in this section.

Redtail monkeys. Systematic monthly samples on infanticidal S
Group at Ngogo were carried out for 540 hr over a 12-month period
in 1975–1976 and have been continued on an opportunistic basis to
the present. In 1973–1975, another group was studied systematically
at Kanyawara for 13 months (552 hr) followed by opportunistic observations for a further 10 months. Several hundred hours of observation
have been made on four other Ngogo groups over the past 8 years.

Blue monkeys. Systematic monthly samples were conducted on infanticidal Group 33 at Ngogo for 1210 hr during 20 months in 1978–
1980. During the same time period, four groups at Kanyawara were
studied systematically for a total of 1514 hr. Rudran (1978) had previously studied two of these Kanyawara groups for 2125 hr during 1973–
1974. Monitoring of these five groups plus three additional groups resumed in 1981 and has continued to the present.

Red colobus. The initial samples on this species totaled 1112 hr
and were obtained over an 18-month period in 1970–1972 on infanticidal
CW Group at Kanyawara (Struhsaker, 1975). Both systematic and opportunistic observations on this group have continued to the present
and total roughly 3000 hr over 13 years. J. Skorupa and L. Isbell studied
two additional groups at Kanyawara for 18 months during 1980–1981,
and two groups have also been studied at Ngogo since 1975.

EVIDENCE OF INFANTICIDE IN KIBALE: A REVIEW

Redtail Monkeys

Redtail monkeys live in one-male "harem" groups averaging about
35 individuals (range: 12–50). Related females apparently remain in
their natal group for life and defend territories against other redtail

groups. Males leave their natal group around puberty and become solitary until they are able to replace a harem male in another social group. This species feeds primarily on fruits and insects at Kibale (Struhsaker, 1980).

Group S at Ngogo was of typical size and contained one adult male and approximately 10 adult females with their offspring. After 4 months of study, the original harem male was replaced by a new adult male, who subsequently killed two newborn infants in the group within 1–2.5 months of his take-over. He was replaced 11–12 months later (see Struhsaker, 1977, and Table II for details).

Blue Monkeys

In the Kibale Forest, blue monkeys have a one-male group organization similar to redtails. Group size averages 17–20 (range: 10–33) (Butynski: unpublished data; Rudran, 1978). Their diet consists primarily of fruit and insects. Group 33 of Ngogo contained 17–20 individuals: one adult male and 10–13 adult females with their offspring. No other blue monkey group bordered its home range, which was 7 times larger than the average range size of four other groups at Kanyawara, 23 times that of blue monkeys in Kenya (DeVos and Omar, 1971), and 35 times that of blue monkeys in the Budongo Forest of Uganda (Aldrich-Blake, 1970). Solitary male blue monkeys were seen relatively frequently at Ngogo but rarely at Kanyawara.

After 8 months of systematic study, the original harem male was replaced by another adult male. The new male (AM2) was observed to kill one infant, and strong circumstantial evidence (aggression, specific vocalizations, and wounding of the female whose infant disappeared) suggested that he killed another infant about 2 hr later. A third infant, who disappeared during AM2's brief tenure, might also have been a victim of infanticide. AM2 was replaced within 4 to 7 days after the observed infanticide.

At least five more adult-male replacements occurred in this group in the next 11 months, but only two of these five subsequent incoming males were observed chasing adult females with clinging infants. One of these (AM5) was involved in 13 aggressive encounters during his residency, and one female and her infant were probably wounded as a result of his aggression. None of the five infants in the group disappeared during AM5's tenure of 5–20 days. The second of these males was involved in only one aggressive encounter, but an infant disappeared during the first month of his tenure. Two other infants disappeared during the first month of tenure of yet a third male, but no aggressive interactions between him and females were witnessed. Except for AM5, neither replacement nor immediate interactions between incoming males and group members were observed (see Butynski, 1982, and Table II for details).

Red Colobus

Red colobus contrast sharply with redtails and blue monkeys in phylogeny, ecology, social organization, and migration patterns (Struhsaker, 1975, 1978a, 1980; Struhsaker and Leland, 1979). In Kibale, red colobus live in large, multimale, patrilineal groups averaging 50 individuals (range: 8–80). Males remain in their natal groups for life or emigrate as old juveniles; they rarely join other social groups. Females transfer to other groups as old juveniles or subadults and infrequently as adults (more rarely still with dependent infants). Red colobus are primarily folivorous, and study groups at both Kanyawara and Ngogo shared their entire home ranges with several other conspecific groups.

The CW Group at Kanyawara numbered 33 individuals prior to the infanticides, including 3 adult males, 1 subadult male, and 14 adult females and their offspring. No males had ever successfully immigrated into this group. Infanticide was committed by the subadult male, Whitey. In the twelfth year of the study of this group, he was observed to kill one infant, is presumed to have wounded another infant in an observed encounter, and is strongly suspected to have killed a third infant which disappeared following a series of intense chases over a 2-week period. A fourth infant also disappeared within 5 months of the initial infanticidal attacks, but no aggression was observed by Whitey against the mother and this infant.

The period of infanticide coincided with the rapid physical and sexual maturation of Whitey from a large juvenile to subadult; he had not been observed to copulate before his infanticidal attempts began. This is the only known case of infanticide involving an adult male killing an infant born in his natal group. Despite extensive study of this and four other groups of red colobus, no other evidence of infanticide has been gathered for this species in Kibale (see Struhsaker and Leland, in preparation, and Table II for details).

THE KIBALE DATA IN RELATION TO HYPOTHESES CONCERNING INFANTICIDE

In this section, six hypotheses concerning the causation and function of infanticide are evaluated, and data from Kibale, which support the hypothesis that infanticide by males is an adaptive reproductive strategy, are presented.

Hypothesis 1: Sexual Selection

This hypothesis predicts that a male will kill infants not directly related to him in order to increase, on average, his own opportunities to breed. The increase in breeding opportunities is typically obtained through the termination of lactation in a female following the death of her unweaned infant, thereby reducing the time until she resumes ovulating (Hrdy, 1974; Sugiyama, 1965b; Chapman and Hausfater, 1979). Correspondingly, young infants who are dependent on their mothers for milk should be more susceptible to infanticide than older infants in the later stages of weaning (Hrdy, 1979). (Weaned "infants" in this chapter are considered juveniles.) The primary cause of infanticide as a reproductive strategy is competition among males for females; the ultimate function is increased reproductive success for the perpetrator.

Relatedness of infants to infanticidal males. In all three Kibale species, it is unlikely that any of the infanticidal males were directly related to the infants they either killed or wounded. In both the redtail and blue monkeys, infanticide occurred less than 2.5 months after the males had first joined the group. These males, therefore, could not have been sires of these infants unless through kleptogamy (that is, copulations by females with males outside their troop), which has been infrequently observed and is considered a rare behavior among these particular Kibale species. In red colobus, the infanticidal male was not seen to copulate with any female prior to his infanticidal attacks, making it highly unlikely that he sired any of the infants in the group. Furthermore, there is strong evidence that this male was conceived outside the group (his mother having immigrated when pregnant), so it is doubtful that he was closely related to any of the males in the group and thus to the infants he might have killed or injured.

Age of infants. All four infants whose deaths were observed were still dependent on their mothers: In redtails, two were less than 1 week old; in red colobus, the infant was 1.5 months old; and in the blue monkeys, the infant was 6 months old (Kibale blue monkeys are not completely weaned until about 1 to 1.3 years of age: Butynski: unpublished data). Other infants suspected to be victims of infanticide were also young enough to have been maintaining lactation and thereby delaying ovulation on the part of their mothers (Table II).

Increased opportunities to breed. Because of the difficulty in identifying a majority of the adult females in the redtail and blue monkey groups, it was usually impossible to ascertain which females lost their infants, which copulated with the infanticidal male, which subsequently gave birth, or the relevant interbirth intervals. Nor are data on the interval between the death of an infant and subsequent ovulation sufficient to determine the minimum amount of time an infanticidal male must remain in the group if he is to successfully inseminate the mother of the victim. However, since females in these two species are not highly seasonal breeders, it is expected that they resume ovulating relatively quickly, although probably not for at least several weeks after the death of their infants. If an infanticidal male extended his tenure at least long enough to breed successfully with the victim's mother, then presumably he would gain a reproductive advantage.

In the redtails, the infanticidal male remained in the group for 11–12 months after the last observed infanticide. Therefore, it is likely that he gained a reproductive advantage by killing the two infants, since it is improbable that their mothers would have resumed ovulating within this time period if their infants had not been killed. This male is presumed to have sired 6 or 7 infants during his tenure.

Because harem male AM2 was replaced 4–7 days after the only observed infanticide in the blue monkey group, it is unlikely that he bred with the victim's mother.

In the red colobus group, all three females whose infants were killed or disappeared solicited copulations with the infanticidal male within 2 weeks of the death of their infants. To date (April 1983, nearly a year since the first infanticidal attempts), only one of the females has given birth. Her infant was born 8 months after the observed killing of her infant, thus reducing the typical interbirth interval of 24–27 months by about two-thirds. However, in red colobus, which live in multimale groups, it is difficult to determine paternity because females are promiscuous. Nonetheless, the infanticidal male definitely increased his opportunities to breed, although it cannot be stated with certainty whether he increased his actual breeding success.

Infanticide, in fact, would reduce a male's opportunity to breed only if he or the mother were inadvertantly killed or reproductively incapacitated in the process. In addition, a direct reproductive advantage would not be gained by an infanticidal male if the mother of the infant victim were a strictly annual and seasonal breeder. Because these situations were not applicable to the Kibale species, it is concluded that all three males who committed infanticide increased their opportunities to breed. Such opportunities, however, may not always be realized. For instance, competition between males for females, a male's sexual competence, or female choice of mate (especially in patrilineal societies where females rather than males move between groups) will influence a male's breeding success. In Kibale, the infanticidal blue monkey, AM2, was unable to take advantage of the opportunity to breed with the mother of his infant victim because of his exceedingly short tenure. Although the red colobus male, Whitey, copulated with all mothers of infants who were either killed or disappeared, actual reproductive success might have been lessened due to competition with other males in the group as well as to Whitey's own sexual inexperience. In general then, it is concluded that, on average, males increase their opportunities to breed through infanticide even though not all males are successful at realizing the resultant opportunity.

Hypothesis 2: Exploitation

This hypothesis predicts a gain in inclusive fitness to the perpetrator of infanticide through the fatal use or consumption of the infant (Hrdy, 1979). While we consider Hrdy's examples of agonistic buffering and the taking of the infant by females other than the mothers (so-called "aunts" or allomothers) to be primarily incidental causes of infanticide on the part of the exploiter (except in some instances of "aunting to death": Hrdy, 1976), we see cannibalism in most instances as a secondary consequence of sexually selected infanticide by adult males. For example, in the two cases of infanticide in Kibale redtails, both of which were accompanied by cannibalism, the male who gained a potential reproductive advantage by killing the two infants is viewed as then having also taken advantage of the protein at hand to improve his fitness.

Hypothesis 3: Social Bonding

In some species, aggression by males against females is thought to establish social bonds between them (Itani, 1954; Kummer, 1968). Infanticide by males is considered another means of forming rapid social bonds with the females whose infants are killed, resulting in quicker integration into the group (Sugiyama, 1965b; Parthasarathy and Rahaman, 1974; Angst and Thommen, 1977). Unfortunately, this hypothesis is difficult to test due to the lack of both operational definitions of such terms as *social bonding* and *integration* and a delineation of their functions. According to Sugiyama (1965b:414), infanticide is a kind of aggressive demonstration that first "cuts off the relationship between the females and infants" in order to "attract their attention more fully to" the infanticidal male. The females then come quickly into estrus resulting in copulation which makes "more firm the ties between male and female" [p. 417]. In other words, a reproductive advantage gained through infanticide is considered a means to social bonding rather than the converse, as one might expect. While infanticide inevitably involves aggression and may simultaneously serve to "bond" the female more closely to the male, we believe that its primary function is to gain a reproductive advantage. Aggression toward the mother after infanticide may further strengthen the social bonds and thus the probability that the female will subsequently copulate with him.

In the red colobus group, preliminary data indicate that the infanticidal male, Whitey, achieved rapid integration into the reproductive sector of the group. He gained a potential reproductive advantage not only with the mothers of his victims but also with other receptive females in the group. His proportion of total group copulations increased from 0 before his infanticidal attempts to more than 50% in the subsequent 6-month period. He copulated with 9 out of 10 receptive females, and no other individual male copulated with any of these females more than Whitey. Perhaps most important was the response of receptive females toward him. Although red colobus males typically initiate copulations, females initiated slightly less than 60% of all copulations with Whitey. In contrast, they initiated from 0 to 39% of copulations with each of the other three males. This unusually high proportion of female solicitations may reflect appeasement or deception as much as preference for Whitey.

Nevertheless, it cannot be concluded with certainty whether infanticide itself contributed to Whitey's rapid sexual access to females in his group or if other factors were involved. Furthermore, young red colobus males may attain rapid sexual integration without either committing infanticide or aggressing against females (Struhsaker, 1975).

Hypothesis 4: Competition for Resources

This hypothesis predicts that the death of an infant will, on average, result in increased access to resources for the killer and his descendants (Rudran, 1973, 1979; and reviewed in Hrdy, 1979). This hypothesis is rejected as the ultimate function of infanticide for the following reasons: First, the hypothesis requires data showing (a) that intragroup competition for food is potentially limiting to the physical and/or genetic fitness of the infanticidal male; and (b) that he does, in fact, gain some ecological or reproductive advantage through infanticide by reducing food competition. In no case of infanticide in nonhuman primates, including the Kibale cases, has adequate data been provided to support either of these two conditions. Furthermore, in one-male groups where a male's tenure is relatively short and groups tend to defend territories, infanticide is unlikely to reduce effective resource competition for the male during his tenure or for any offspring he might have sired in neighboring groups.

Second, an infanticidal male must first reproduce before any competitive advantages can be realized by his direct descendents. Consequently, if infanticide does, in fact, have any effect on resource competition, this effect must be secondary to the ultimate function of reproductive success. Third, the death of any conspecific means that there will be fewer animals to compete for resources. Thus, if this hypothesis were correct, males should select against the most vulnerable individuals in the group (Hrdy, 1979; Introduction, this volume) and those with a greater immediate impact on food resources, such as recently weaned juveniles or semiindependent infants. The latter are not only small and lacking in agility, speed, and strength, but they also are without the constant protection of the mother (at least in arboreal species where infants must be transported as well as fed). In Kibale, all infanticidal males, particularly among the blue monkeys and red colobus, aggressed almost exclusively against adult females and their dependent infants. Other more vulnerable youngsters were not attacked.

Hypothesis 5: Population Density

According to this hypothesis, infanticide functions as a density-dependent mechanism to control growth in size of groups and populations (Sugiyama, 1965b; Eisenberg *et al.,* 1972; Rudran, 1973, 1979; Ripley, 1980; and reviewed in Hrdy, 1979 and Hausfater and Vogel, 1982). However, to invoke this hypothesis as the ultimate causation of infanticide by males relies on the concept of *group selection,* which presently lacks convincing data or compelling arguments (see also Hrdy, 1977b). Furthermore, primate density has rarely been defined in terms of the carrying capacity of the habitat. This hypothesis also does not explain infanticide in areas of extremely low density, such as in the blue monkey group at Ngogo.

Hypothesis 6: Social Pathology

This is the only hypothesis suggesting that infanticide may be an individually maladaptive behavior (Dolhinow, 1977; Curtin and Dolhinow, 1978; Boggess, 1979). Habitat destruction and food provisioning are considered to be the primary causes of infanticide in certain groups and populations because these factors are believed to result in an "abnormal" increase in population density. For three reasons, this hypothesis can be rejected in the cases of infanticide among Kibale Forest primates. First, the two study areas consist of virtually undisturbed mature forest where there is no artificial provisioning or other form of human interaction. Second, all infanticidal males were selective and persistent in directing their attacks only against unrelated dependent infants. Hence, the red colobus male did not attack his mother's infant, any infant of a female he had previously copulated with, nor the more vulnerable semiindependent young in his group. Such findings are predicted by the sexual selection hypothesis but not by the social pathology hypothesis (see Introduction, this volume). Finally, there is strong evidence that females have evolved behaviors that sometimes forestall infanticide, particularly in red colobus (Struhsaker and Leland, in preparation); this would not be expected if infanticide were a pathological or abnormal phenomenon of no evolutionary significance. Overall, then, no conclusive data we can find from Kibale or from other wild primate populations supporting the hypothesis that infanticide by unrelated adult males is a maladaptive behavior.

Summary

In conclusion, the preceding hypotheses, except sexual selection, are rejected as the ultimate causation of infanticide among Kibale primates. Since under most conditions there will be a potential reproductive advantage for males who kill unweaned and unrelated infants, we believe that other hypotheses should be invoked only after the sexual selection hypothesis has been rejected. In nearly all instances of infanticide in primates, sexual selection is the most inclusive, simple, and testable hypothesis as well as the only one dealing with reproductive success, which is the most immediate and direct means of improving genetic fitness.

Moreover, the sexual selection hypothesis encompasses most, if not all other, hypotheses as secondary effects of reproductive competition. For example, after committing infanticide, a male gains in fitness if he cannibalizes his victim. Infanticide and aggression, as noted in the discussion of the social bonding hypothesis, may also integrate the male socially and sexually more quickly into the group, resulting in greater reproductive success even with females who might not have had infants. At the same time, by killing infants sired by other males, an infanticidal male reduces the reproductive success of his competitors and may also increase his own fitness and that of his offspring by reducing competition for resources. While infanticide always reduces population density to some extent, this again would be a secondary effect that may further enhance survival of the infanticidal male's offspring.

CONDITIONS INFLUENCING THE FREQUENCY OF INFANTICIDE

Assuming that infanticide by males is an adaptive reproductive strategy, it is possible to investigate the conditions under which this behavior is most likely to occur. This section deals with variables that may help explain the variability in frequency of infanticide by males in Kibale and elsewhere according to particular social organizations and populations.

Social Organization

Certain social organizations among primates are expected to exhibit a greater frequency of infanticide than others due primarily to factors related to a male's relative (1) competitive pressure to reproduce in terms of his average life tenure in social groups; (2) likelihood of encountering unrelated infants; (3) risk from counterattack; and (4) potential for reproductive success. These variables are discussed according to the three basic social organizations in which infanticide is known to occur: one-male groups and patrilineal and matrilineal multimale groups (Table I). The wide variation found within and between such social systems is not taken into consideration here.

One-male groups. Based on these four variables, species or populations that have predominantly one-male groups are predicted to have a higher frequency of infanticide than those having a multimale group organization. First, in populations of one-male groups, most males presumably spend a large proportion of their reproductive lives outside of social groups, either as solitaries (as in Kibale redtails and blues) or in all-male bands or otherwise nonreproductive groups (as in Hanuman langurs: Sugiyama, 1965b; and red howlers: Rudran 1979). Consequently, when such males gain access to social groups, especially after replacing the harem male, they are under pressure to maximize their reproductive success in a short period of time. Second, after a recent replacement, the incoming male would probably not be related to any infants in the group. Third, an infanticidal male would incur relatively low risk from severe counterattack by adult group members because only related females (not adult males) would be potential defenders of infants. Finally, a harem male usually has almost exclusive access to estrous females, especially when compared with males in multimale groups.

The data from Kibale support this conclusion, not only in redtail monkeys and blue monkeys, but also for the suspected cases of infanticide in black and white colobus (Oates, 1977). The only other one-male species in Kibale is L'hoest's monkey, which has yet to be studied but which we predict will have a relatively high rate of infanticide as well.

The majority of species outside Kibale in which infanticide has been observed or strongly suspected have also had one-male social organizations (Table I). Even in species where both one-male and multimale groups exist within the same population (e.g. Hanuman langurs: Sugiyama, 1965b; Hrdy, 1977b; purple-faced langurs: Rudran, 1973; red howlers: Rudran, 1979), infanticide has been observed predominantly in one-male groups or one-male before infanticidal males immigrated. Further support to the prediction that one-male groups have a higher frequency of infanticide than multimale groups is provided by species that are predominantly multimale but perhaps due to environmental conditions also exhibit one-male social systems. For example, infanticide after adult-male replacement was suspected in a one-male population of red colobus on the Tana River in Kenya after only 5 months of study (Marsh, 1979).

Multimale groups. In contrast, species or populations with multimale group organization are expected to have a lower frequency of infanticide than those with one-male groups. First, males are under less competitive pressure to commit infanticide because they generally spend a larger proportion of their adult lives in social groups with access to females. This is particularly so in the many multimale species in which females tend to be promiscuous (e.g., Kibale red colobus; chimpanzees: Goodall, 1968; baboons: Hausfater, 1975). Second, promiscuity could produce confusion concerning paternity among males who copulated with a particular female. Because of their possible paternity, these males would then be expected to defend, or at least tolerate, her subsequent infant (Hrdy, 1977b, 1979; Hausfater, Chapter 13, this volume). Thus, promiscuity may not only confuse the issue of relatedness of males to infants, but it may also increase the number of potential defenders of infants, thereby elevating the risk of counterattack against infanticidal males. Finally, the probability that an infanticidal male will successfully breed with the victim's mother is reduced in multimale groups due both to competition among males for females within the group and to female promiscuity.

Infanticide in the wild has been witnessed in all three patrilineal multimale species: red colobus, chimpanzees (both found in Kibale), and gorillas (Table I). In such social organizations, some or all males remain in their natal group for life, whereas usually all females tend to emigrate around puberty to join other groups. Rarely do females with infants transfer between groups. Males who remain in their natal group, therefore, are presumably related and are unlikely to encounter unrelated infants of females living in the same group.

Although two cases of infanticide in patrilineal species involved resident males killing infants in the same group, through unusual circumstances the infants were probably not related to these males. In red colobus, Whitey was conceived outside his natal group; and in gorillas, the infanticidal male, Beetsme, is one of the few known cases of a male successfully immigrating into a social group (Fossey, Chapter 11, this volume). There are no known cases of a male conceived and born within a patrilineal social group committing infanticide against any infant conceived and born in the same group.

In contrast to the two preceding cases, the majority of infanticides in patrilineal species involved extragroup animals. In gorillas, extragroup males (usually solitary silverbacks) killed infants of primiparous females in social groups, possibly as a means of attracting them as mates (Fossey, Chapter 11, this volume). In chimpanzees, males killed (or were seen cannibalizing) infants of extragroup females, usually at the interface of two communities (Goodall, 1977; Goodall et al., 1979; Nishida et al., 1979; and reviewed by Fossey, Chapter 11, this volume). Infanticide by males in chimpanzees may be related to the frequency in which adult males of one community are likely to come into contact with females with infants from another community. Human disturbance may increase this frequency by altering ranging patterns and use of particular areas. For instance, suspected infanticide by males in the Mahale Mts. occurred in the vicinity of the food-provisioning ground, which is situated in a large area of overlap between two communities and is frequently used by both (Nishida et al., 1979; Nishida, 1979).

Goodall *et al.* (1979) have suggested that recent habitat destruction outside Gombe Park might have increased intercommunity hostility. Ranging patterns of females with infants might also have been affected.

In Kibale, two primate species, mangabeys and baboons, have a matrilineal multimale social organization: Most females usually remain in their natal group for life, and all males tend to emigrate. Mangabeys have been under observation in Kibale for over 10 years with no indication of infanticide (Waser, 1974; Freeland, 1977; Wallis, 1978; Struhsaker and Leland, 1979; Leland: unpublished data). Despite numerous long-term studies of multimale species outside Kibale, there are few cases of infanticide by males observed under natural, nonmanipulative conditions in the wild (Table I). Recent immigrant males are predicted most likely to be infanticidal due to their presumed unrelatedness to infants in the group. Infanticide by these males, however, is expected to be rare in matrilineal multimale societies primarily because of the potentially strong defense of infants by resident group members (Hrdy, 1979; Packer, 1979a; Busse and Hamilton, 1981), including possible sires (especially if recognition of paternity has been confused by promiscuity) and adult female relatives in the group.

One-Male Groups, Population Density, and Extragroup Males

Several previous studies have attempted to demonstrate a relationship between population density and frequency of infanticide (e.g., Sugiyama, 1967; Yoshiba, 1968; Eisenberg *et al.*, 1972; Rudran, 1973, 1979; Hrdy, 1974, 1977a, 1979; Curtin and Dolhinow, 1978; Boggess, 1979). It is unlikely however, that there will be a simple direct correlation between infanticide and population density (Hrdy, 1979) because of basic differences in carrying capacity among habitats and species (Oppenheimer, 1977). A high density need not be detrimental to either animals or habitats if the carrying capacity is high; but high density may indeed be deleterious if it exceeds the carrying capacity of the environment, such as through population compression due to recent habitat destruction or through population concentration due to irregular food provisioning (Bishop *et al.*, 1981). However, even in these latter cases the real issue is not the factors that have increased a population up to or beyond the carrying capacity of its environment but the factors within such populations that tend to increase the frequency of infanticide.

We suggest that the relative frequency of infanticide in one-male groups will be higher in populations where competition among males for access to females in social groups is particularly intense. Greater competition is expected to result in more frequent replacements and therefore shorter tenures. Infanticide would be expected to increase in two ways: (1) with more take-overs, more males will have the opportunity to commit infanticide; and (2) with shorter tenures, males are under greater pressure to commit infanticide in order to enhance their reproductive opportunities (Hrdy, 1974, 1979). There appear to be two important variables that may influence the degree of competition among males for social groups: density of extragroup males per social group and, secondarily, the degree of resource competition between extragroup males and social groups.

Density of extragroup males and adult sex ratio. We contend that the relative number of extragroup males per one-male social group in a population and/or the adult sex ratio of the total population (including extragroup males) may be more reliable than population density per se in predicting the frequency of infanticide, because these variables tend to reflect more precisely the relative degree of competition among males for females (Butynski, 1982). Thus, we predict that the more extragroup males per social group or the closer the adult sex ratio of males to females in the total population approaches unity (or even exceeds it), the greater the competition between males. By using these two variables, one may be able to predict the frequency of infanticide independently of population density.

Support for this prediction is found in the data on blue monkeys at Ngogo where the subpopulation density was extremely low, but the density of extragroup males per social group was high ($\sim 8 : 1$), and the adult sex ratio approached unity. This group had six replacements in 12 months and at least two harem males committed or attempted infanticide. These figures can be compared to those from the Kanyawara site, where in a 20-month period, no solitary males were seen and no replacements or infanticides occurred in four study groups.

In studies of Hanuman langurs (*Presbytis entellus*), several researchers have suggested that an increase in population density results in a greater number of extragroup males (Sugiyama, 1965b; Hrdy, 1974, 1979; Hausfater and Vogel, 1982). However, while there may be a direct correlation in terms of absolute numbers, these researchers have provided little data to substantiate that extragroup males have a proportionally greater representation in populations of higher rather than lower densities. In predominantly one-male populations, the number of extragroup males would be expected to increase relative to the population as a whole if social group size also increased, but not if average group size remained constant and the number of groups increased. According to data presented by Oppenheimer (1977: Table 6), there seems to be no correlation between high population density and larger social group size. However, Hrdy (1979) and others have suggested that the size of all-male bands may increase at higher densities, and these in turn may be more successful in taking over reproductive groups, resulting in a higher rate of replacements.

Alternatively, a population containing multimale groups at a low density may form one-male groups in the same area at a higher density, perhaps in response to food competition. This would also result in proportionally more extragroup males. Among Hanuman langurs, there does, in fact, appear to be some correlation between low densities and multimale groups and between high densities and predominantly one-male groups (Yoshiba, 1968; Hrdy, 1977a,b; Curtin and Dolhinow, 1978).

Human disturbance is another factor that may affect the relative density of extragroup males and/or the adult sex ratio in some Hanuman langur populations. Under some conditions, extragroup males are thought to use marginal habitat outside the ranges of social groups, especially in areas of food scarcity (Crook, 1972, and see following), and to be more vulnerable to attack by predators, particularly in open habitat (Struhsaker, 1969; Struhsaker and Leland, 1979). However, direct or indirect food provisioning and the elimination of major predators (e.g., leopards) may increase survivorship of extragroup males in a population.

Mohnot *et al.* (1981) have recently provided supportive data for this hypothesis in a high-density population of langurs in Jodhpur, India, in which several cases of infanticide have been reported (Mohnot, 1971a; Makwana, 1979). Over the past 10 years, they found a 44% increase in extragroup males, while the population and average size of bisexual groups remained stable. Mohnot *et al.* (1981) attributed the increase to the expansion of cultivation: The population relies heavily on crops for sustenance, but extragroup males invade these areas more readily than members of bisexual groups, and consequently their survival rate is higher.

Support for the hypothesis in terms of the adult sex ratio in other species comes from a population of red howlers (*Alouatta seniculus*) in Venezuela, which also has a relatively high rate of infanticide (Rudran, 1979; Crockett and Sekulic, Chapter 9, this volume). The adult sex ratio at this site approaches unity (1:1.03), although it remains unclear why there is such a high proportion of adult males in the population. Similarly, the Virunga gorilla population has an adult sex ratio of 1:1.06, including both silverback and blackback (sexually mature) males (Harcourt *et al.*, 1981). Fossey (1979:182) suggested that the most likely reason for the intensity and frequency of aggressive competition for females (resulting in infanticide) is the high proportion of males to females, especially if one considers this species to be effectively living in one-male breeding units (Harcourt *et al.*, 1981; Fossey, Chapter 11, this volume).

Resource competition between extragroup males and social groups. A social group usually has priority of access over extragroup males to food and other resources in its territory, especially when resources are scarce (e.g., Gartlan and Gartlan, 1973; Rudran, 1973). Competition for resources between extragroup males and social groups may be particularly intense if: (1) a population is compressed into a relatively small area due to habitat destruction; (2) it is subject to periodic (seasonal) shortages of food and water; or (3) limited food and water supplies are concentrated in only a few sites. As a result of such competition, extragroup males may be forced to use either inferior habitat in a different area from social groups and/or resources that are of lower quality or quantity but in the same ranges of social groups. It is suggested here that extragroup males in such situations may be under greater pressure to take over social groups (which have access to critical resources) than are extragroup males living in areas where resource competition is not so intense. By taking over a social group, these males gain access not only to females but also to food and other environmental resources, such as water and sleeping sites, which are crucial for their own survival and reproductive success.

Few studies have provided sufficient ecological data to test this hypothesis. The following two examples, however, suggest that food competition between extragroup males and social groups may be particularly intense in some situations. Sugiyama (1965b) suggested that because bisexual groups of a high-density population of Hanuman langurs in Dharwar, India, occupied the more optimal forest habitat, extragroup males were forced to use inferior habitat. This in turn might have caused them to attack bisexual groups "more actively and more frequently than in other districts [p. 408]." The relatively high frequency of infanticide in this area might thus have been due in part to the intense competition between males for access to food resources in territories of social groups, with take-overs as the means of access to both food and mates.

In a large population of purple-faced langurs (*Presbytis senex*) living in a 5 km² archeological park in Polonnarua, Sri Lanka, extragroup males used ecologically inferior habitat (Rudran, 1973). Here take-overs were frequent when compared to a population in the larger, ecologically richer, less densely populated, and relatively undisturbed area of Horton Plains. Thus, in this situation, marginal habitat used by extragroup males might also have influenced the higher rate of take-overs and, consequently, the higher rate of suspected infanticide in Polonnarua.

It is important to emphasize that the conditions relating to the frequency of infanticide described in this chapter are largely speculative and are meant only as preliminary and general guidelines. Clearly, more data are required to test these variables and others that have not been discussed here. For instance, particular social groups within a population may be more vulnerable to male replacement and infanticide than others (e.g., the Ngogo blue group; the Hillside troop of Hanuman langurs: Hrdy, 1977a,b); and an individual male's tendency to commit infanticide in a given situation may be influenced by such factors as age or previous reproductive success (see Angst and Thommen, 1977). The circumstances underlying the occurrence and frequency of infanticide by males are indeed complex and compounded by variables interacting synergistically at different levels. We stress the need for more long-term and comparative studies, especially those dealing with individual-male life histories.

CONCLUSIONS

Consideration of several social and ecological variables suggests that the reproductive success of infanticidal and noninfanticidal males, particularly in populations of one-male groups, is contingent on the same general set of factors: their ability (1) to retain tenure at least long enough to breed; (2) to breed with as many females as possible; and (3) to remain in the group at least until the survival of their offspring is insured against infanticide by other males. However, an infanticidal male will, with a few minor exceptions, gain a reproductive advantage over a noninfanticidal male by bringing more females into estrus within a shorter period of time (Chapman and Hausfater, 1979). Furthermore, infanticidal males may also gain a variety of secondary advantages (as described previously), even though they may not always be able to breed with the mother of every victim.

In Kibale, the redtail and red colobus infanticidal males very likely gained a direct reproductive advantage; the male blue monkey clearly did not. Nevertheless, this latter male suffered no obvious disadvantage by committing infanticide and probably gained as much as a noninfanticidal male would have under the same conditions, if not more, via secondary effects. Infanticide in the Ngogo blue monkeys is important in illustrating that unusually intense competition by males for females may occur not only in areas of low density but also in habitats not influenced by human disturbance. Human disturbance may affect the degree of competition among males for social groups in predominantly one-male populations but not, we believe, the characteristics of one adaptive response to such competition: infanticide. In other words, disturbance such as rapid and extensive habitat destruction in this century has probably expanded and intensified conditions that tend to increase competition among males rather than created those conditions in the first place. The fact that one-male groups, replacements, and infanticide exist even in undisturbed habitats support this view.

ACKNOWLEDGMENTS

The authors acknowledge with gratitude the President's Office, National Research Council, and Forest Department of Uganda for permission to conduct our research in Kibale. Thanks are also extended to the Department of Zoology, Makerere University, for local sponsorship. We are particularly grateful to the New York Zoological Society for financial support. We would also like to thank Glenn Hausfater and Sarah Blaffer Hrdy for their editorial assistance.

9 Infanticide in red howler monkeys (*Alouatta seniculus*)

Carolyn M. Crockett
Ranka Sekulic

Carolyn M. Crockett
Ranka Sekulic

INTRODUCTION

In this chapter, evidence is presented confirming that, while seldom actually observed by researchers, infant killing by adult male red howlers (*Alouatta seniculus*) in Venezuela occurs frequently. In particular, it is believed that infanticide occurs coincident with many changes in adult-male membership as well as with changes in breeding status of coresident males. The data on observed and inferred cases of infanticide permit the examination here of several hypotheses advanced to explain this behavior (see Hrdy, 1979; Sherman, 1981).

STUDY AREA AND METHODS

Data were collected at Hato Masaguaral, a private wildlife reserve and cattle ranch located in the *llanos* (plains) of Guárico State, Venezuela. In the study site, native wildlife species are protected while domestic animals are controlled so as to have a minimal impact on the howlers' habitats and food resources. Red howlers were studied in two habitat types: An open shrub woodland (Mata) located near the ranch houses and a gallery forest (Gallery) located about 4 km east of the open woodland study area and about 1 km west of the Río Guárico (Troth, 1979).

Collection of data on infanticide was incidental to studies focused on other topics. Crockett carried out census work and studies of feeding behavior in October 1978, March 1979–February 1981, and November – December 1981. Sekulic (1982a,b,c,d) studied the howling and ranging patterns of four Mata troops during August 1979–August 1980.

Troops in the census study were contacted approximately monthly in the Mata and less frequently in the Gallery. All adults and many immatures in census troops were identifiable as individuals; the remaining immatures were identified only as to age/sex class. Each of Crockett's two main study troops was contacted 5 or more days per month; Sekulic contacted her study troops nearly daily. All members of the main study troops were individually identifiable.

RESULTS

Male Changes

Twenty-five Mata troops and 18 Gallery troops were monitored for 850 troop-months and 364 troop-months, respectively, where troop-months equal the number of months between the first and last observation, regardless of whether the troop was contacted every intervening month. Table I summarizes 26 male-change situations observed or inferred in the 43 troops during the total of 1214 troop-months. These changes took a variety of forms, representing a range in "success" and "rapidity."

Replacements and incursions. Nine changes were complete replacements of the original adult male(s) by new adult and/or subadult males (Table I, A–I). In eight of these nine changes, two males replaced one or more males. In the ninth change (E), one subadult male replaced an adult male, but a nearly adult natal male remained in the troop (T. Pope: personal communication). Five of these male changes were rapid replacements and occurred within a month or two between census contacts (A–E). In Change F, the new males coresided with the original male for at least 3 months but ousted him before 7 months had elapsed (J. Robinson: personal communication). The remaining replacements occurred during gaps in observation of 5–13 months (G–I).

The success of completely replacing the resident male(s) during the study period was dependent on the number of males entering the troop. Two males were more successful than one (Fisher's exact test, Sokal and Rohlf, 1969; $p = 0.036$; $n = 12$ changes). Three of the four changes in which only one male entered a troop resulted in overlapping incursions in which the new male coresided with the original adult male through the end of the study period (Table I, J–L). In all three cases, a second male joined a single adult male, and the new male eventually became dominant to the original male.

In Table I, Changes M and N are two unsuccessful incursion attempts by solitary males that were associated with infant injury and disappear-

Table I. Troops with known ("male change") or possible ("change?") changes in adult-male membership or status[a]

	Replacement		Incursion		Status change		Associated cases (Tables II
Troop	Rapid	Other	Overlap	Attempt	Known	Possible	and III)
Male change							
M53	A						1, 2, a
M58	B						Long IBI
M76	C						3, 4, 5
M56	D						No young infants
M72	E				O	T	—;[b] 15, 16, 17; 19
G9		F					6, 7, 8
M64		G					Long IBI
G6		H					b
G8		I				U	9; —
G21			J	M			10; 13
M74			K		P		11, 12; —
M71			L			V	c; 20
M63					Q		18
Change?							
M51				N	R		—; 14, d
M62					S		—
M75						W	f
M77						X	g
M78						Y	—
M61						Z	e

[a] Replacement = complete replacement during study period; Overlap = Overlapping incursion; Attempt = unsuccessful incursion attempt; Possible = possible or unsuccessfully attempted status change (see text for more complete definitions); M = Mata troop; G = Gallery troop; IBI = interbirth interval. Upper-case letters indicate male-change events. Numbers in right-hand column correspond to Infanticide Cases in Table II and lower-case letters correspond to Injury Cases in Table III. Semicolons separate cases associated with more than one male change in same troop. Changes A–D and F–I: two males entered; Changes E and J–L: one male entered. Timing and details of Changes A–D, F, K, L, O, and P are the best documented of male-change situations.
[b] —, Indicates no related information in the tables that follow.

ance. In both instances, the troops that they attempted to enter contained a single adult male. It is expected that the frequency of unsuccessful incursions was underestimated since troops were not observed continuously.

Status changes. Twelve situations (Table I) were classified as known (O–S) or possible (T–Z) status changes between coresident males associated with the subsequent emigration or disappearance of one of them.

While determining that troops had experienced replacements and incursions was straightforward, the identification of status-change situations requires some explanation. In red howlers (Sekulic, 1983a) as well as mantled howlers (*Alouatta palliata:* Glander, 1980) one male, designated as the "breeding male," usually does all or most of the mating during a female's period of peak receptivity. For example, only 3 of 26 copulations with troop females involved a male that was not clearly dominant (Sekulic, 1983a); the three exceptions occurred during periods of unstable male relations.

Thus, a status change was operationally defined as a shift between adult males in the frequency of mating with receptive females. However, since mating data or independent assessment of male dominance status was not available for all troops, the criterion was established that to classify a troop as having experienced status change, a male known to have been the previous breeding male subsequently left a troop after coresiding with one or more other adult males. The breeding male was identified by mating data (Changes O, P, and V: Sekulic, 1983a; Changes Q and S: Mack, 1978) or because he was the only adult male present prior to the immigration of a new male (Changes R and V: Rudran, 1979; Table IV, Troops Albizia A and S). Change V posed some problems in that the breeding male was observed to kill an infant; in this case, the two adult males in the troop had severe wounds at the time of the infant's conception, and the occurrence of a temporary status change at that time was hypothesized (see Sekulic, 1983a, for details).

Change V and all other cases in which one adult male emigrated or disappeared were classified as possible status changes or attempted (and unsuccessful) status changes (T–Z), since known status changes were associated with eventual male emigration. For purposes of analysis, 13 troops in Table I having at least one change known to have occurred during the study period were classified as "Male Change," and 6 troops having only known changes that probably occurred prior to the study period (R and S) or possible or unsuccessfully attempted status changes (W–Z) were classified as "Change?" All 24 remaining troops were classified as having known or assumed breeding male stability; these included troops with only one adult male and those that had more than one adult male, but the only males emigrating were immature or approaching adulthood and were presumed to be natal (i.e., were not known to have immigrated).

Infanticide, Suspected Infanticide, and Suspicious Injuries

Rudran (1979) reported one observed and three inferred cases of infanticide associated with the entrance of new adult males into red howler troops. During the study period reported here, Sekulic (1983a) observed one infanticide that occurred after an inferred temporary status change (Change V, Case 20), and 19 infant disappearances were considered as possible cases of infanticide (Table I, right column; Table II). Immatures through 12 months of age are classified as infants. An additional seven infants received severe injuries of a sort suggesting that they had survived infanticide attempts (Table III). In sum, the dataset here is composed of 1 case of observed infanticide and 26 cases of infant disappearance or severe injury without disappearance.

Of the 26 cases, 14 disappearances and 3 injuries were considered to be "very probably" infanticide or attempted infanticide. These cases included 8 disappearances and 2 injuries that occurred after four complete male replacements, 3 disappearances and 1 injury after 3 overlapping incursions, and 3 disappearances after a status change in which the former breeding male was ousted and died of injuries shortly thereafter (Change O); the latter three infants all disappeared after the death of the ousted male.

Another two disappearances and one injury among the 27 cases were considered "probably" infanticide or attempted infanticide. In these cases, the reconstruction of male-change events was less clearcut, and thus the infant disappearance or wound could not be unequivocally tied to the male-change event. One disappearance coincided with an unsuccessful incursion attempt (Change M), and the second was associated with a status change, the exact timing of which was not determined (Change Q). The injury occurred after the temporary emigration and reentry of the subordinate of two adult males (Change Z).

An additional three infant disappearances and three injuries occurred in troops classified as having known or possible male changes, but the relationship between the former and latter events was unknown; thus, the interpretation that these cases resulted from infanticide or attempted infanticide was regarded as "questionable."

While a few infant disappearances (especially the "questionable" category) might have been misinterpreted as infanticides, the intermittent contacts with troops reported here surely underestimated the frequency of infanticide. For example, following two male replacements (B and G), adult females gave birth after unusually long interbirth intervals (more than 24 months, compared to a normal average of 16.6 months). One interpretation is that unrecorded births and infanticides occurred between contacts with these troops.

Comparison of infant mortality in stable troops and troops that experienced male change during the study period indicates a strong relationship between infant disappearance and male change. Table IV presents the number of infants born in the 43 study troops through February 1981 and those that died during the first year of life (infant disappearances are assumed to be deaths). The troops are grouped according

Table II. Infanticide cases

Case no.	(Change)	ID no.	Sex[a]	Age (in months) at		Certainty[c]	Behavior[d]	Could dad kill?[e]	Did mom mate?[f,g]
				Change[b]	Death				
Replacements									
1	(A)	5382	F	7	8	VP		No	(Yes) *
2	(A)	5393	U	−3	0.5	VP		No	(Yes) *
3	(C)	7674	M	2	2.5	VP		No	Yes *
4	(C)	7683	F	1	1.25	VP	[MA, OA]	No	(Yes) *
5	(C)	7682	F	2	3	VP	[MA, OA]	No	Yes *(1)
6	(F)	0982	F	0.25	0.75	VP	S-FG, MA, OA	No	No; Yes?
7	(F)	0981	F	3	3.6	VP	S-FI, OA	No	Yes; No? (2)
8	(F)	0994	U	−1.5	0.6	VP	S-FI, (MA), OA	No	Yes? (2)
9	(I)	0872	M	?	9–24	Q	S-NI, (MA), OA	—	— (2)
Overlapping incursions									
10	(J)	2174	M	?	4–14	VP		No	?
11	(K)	7484	F	1.25	1.25	VP		Yes	Yes *
12	(K)	7493	U	−4	0.33	VP		No	Yes? *?
Attempted incursions									
13	(M)	2185	F	2	2	P	[MA, OA]	—	—
14	(N)	5182	F	4	4	Q		—	—

Status changes

15	(O)	7286	F	2	2.5	VP	(MA)	No	(Yes?) *(1)
16	(O)	7278	M	-0.75	0.6	VP	S-FG, MA, OA	No	Yes *(1)
17	(O)	7273	M	-5	0.5	VP		Yes	(Yes) (3)
18	(Q)	6391	U	?	0.5	P		Yes	? *?

Attempted status changes?

19	(T)	7281	F	?	0.1–5	Q	NI, MA	—	—
20	(V)	7173	M	-6?	0.03	O		Yes	Yes *

[a] F = female; M = male; U = unsexed.

[b] Age at change: minus sign indicates months prior to birth.

[c] O = Observed; VP = very probable; P = probable, Q = questionable.

[d] S = stalking of victim by suspected infanticidal animal observed; FI = presumed father interceded in stalking event; NI = presumed father did not intercede; FG = father gone; MA = mother aggressive toward suspected infanticidal animal; OA = other troop members aggressive toward suspected infanticidal animal; (MA, OA) = aggression observed after infant's death.

[e] "Could dad kill?" = "Yes" indicates that victim's presumed father could have killed his own offspring.

[f] "Did mom mate?" after infant's death with male presumed to have killed her infant: Yes = observed mating; Yes? = apparent consortship but mating not observed; (Yes) = presumed infanticidal male(s) were only adult males present; "." indicates two possible estrous periods seen.

[g] * Next infant born to female was sired by new or newly dominant male; *? = probably sired by new or newly dominant male. (1) Mother gave birth to another (surviving) infant, but an intervening abortion or birth and death are suspected; (2) mother had not given birth to a recorded infant, but a subsequent unrecorded birth and death were possible; (3) mother probably aborted during tagging in January 1981.

Table III. Injury cases attributed to possible infanticide attempts[a]

Case no.	(Change)	ID no.	Sex	Age (in months) at Change	Age (in months) at Injury	Cer-tainty	Injuries; S/MA/OA
Replacements							
a	(A)	5381	F	6	8; 10	VP	Head/eye and base of tail; ear (two separate injuries)
b	(H)	0682.1	F	<3.5	<3.5	VP	Head; avoidance of new males by troop members
Overlapping incursion							
c	(L)	7174	M	2	2.5	VP	Base of tail; (S-FI, MA, OA)
Attempted incursion							
d	(N)	5181	F	3	3	Q	Ear
Attempted status change?							
e	(Z)	6183	F	.75	.75	P	Head; mother injured slightly (MA?)
Possible status changes							
f	(W)	7581	F	?	3	Q	Head
g	(X)	7782	F	?	<4	Q	Ear

[a] All of these infants survived through December 1981. Injuries on two other infants were noted during the study period, but these were not associated with male-change situations. Abbreviations defined as in Table II.

to stability of male membership and status: 24 troops had known or apparent breeding male stability during the entire study period ("Stable"), 13 troops had male replacements, successful incursions, or status changes during the study period ("Male Change," Table I), and 6 troops only had changes that probably occurred prior to the study period or equivocal changes ("Change?," Table I). Tests of independence compared the number of infants that lived versus died for Stable troops and for troops with known or suspected changes (Table IV). At over 31%, infant mortality was significantly higher in troops with Male Change compared to about 9% mortality in Stable troops and troops with suspected changes.

In all cases where the timing of the male change was known, the disappearance of infants occurred within 1 month (and more usually about 2 weeks) after the change or after the infant's own birth after a change (six of the infanticide cases were born after a male change; Table II). Such a coincidence is highly unlikely by chance, suggesting

Table IV. Infant mortality, troop stability, and habitat and statistical tests of independence[a,b]

			Infants			
Stability	Habitat	n of troops	Born (no.)	Lived (no.)	Died (no.)	Died (%)
Stable	Mata	10	46	42	4	8.70
	Gallery	14	32	29	3	9.38
	Total	24	78	71	7	8.97
Change?	Mata (only)	6	26	24	2	7.69
Stable +	Mata	16	72	66	6	8.33
change?	Gallery	14	32	29	3	9.38
	Total	30	104	95	9	8.65
Male change	Mata	9	45	32	13	28.89
	Gallery	4	15	9	6	40.00
	Total	13	60	41	19	31.67
All troops	Mata	25	117	98	19	16.24
	Gallery	18	47	38	9	19.15
	Total	43	164	136	28	17.07

[a] Using Yates' correction (Sokal and Rohlf, 1969).
[b] Tests of independence, where ns = not significant; * = significant at 0.05 level; ** = significant at 0.01 level; *** = significant at 0.001 level.

Chi-square tests (no. lived versus no. died)	χ^2	$d.f.$	Significance
Stable versus Change? versus Male change	13.43	2	***
Stable versus Change?	0.04	1	ns
Stable versus Male change	9.98	1	**
Change? versus Male change	4.42	1	*
(Stable + Change?) versus Male change	12.65	1	***
Stable versus (Change? + Male change)	5.84	1	*
Mata versus Gallery	0.05	1	ns

G-test $(2 \times 2 \times 2)$	G	$d.f.$	Significance
Stability versus Mortality	13.74	1	***
Stability versus Habitat	0.63	1	ns
Habitat versus Mortality	0.002	1	ns
Interaction	0.27	1	ns
Stability versus Mortality versus Habitat	14.64	4	**

a causal relationship between male-change events and infant disappearances. Of 255 troop-months during which eight troops with nine closely monitored changes were studied, 14 infants disappeared in the 9 troop-months representing the 1 month following the change (or birth), and 2 infants disappeared in the 246 remaining troop-months (one-sample $\chi^2 = 309.8$; $df = 1$; $p < 0.001$). The mean age of infanticide cases at the time of a male change was 0.68 months (SD = 3.1; range = -5–7; $n = 15$) and 1.88 months at death (SD = 2.0; range = 0.03–8; $n = 17$).

Furthermore, direct observation of males' behavior strongly suggests their responsibility for infant deaths. Of the 14 very probable infanticide cases, adult males were observed stalking five infants prior to their disappearance; one injury case was also stalked. Given the two infanticide cases attributed to unsuccessful incursion attempts (Cases 13 and 14), it is notable that the invader males in Change F were observed stalking mothers with young infants on the first day of the incursion, when the incursion's eventual outcome was far from resolved. Aggression (e.g., chasing and howling) directed by the victim's mother and/ or other troop members toward the implicated or potentially infanticidal male(s) was observed in 10 of the 27 cases (Tables II and III; see also Sekulic, 1983a,b). The resident males who were the likely fathers actively defended their infants (intervening without physically contacting the stalking male) in three cases but did not defend them in two other cases. In most instances, fathers were already gone at the time of infant disappearance or no pertinent observations were made.

In sum, the observations suggest that most infant disappearances associated with male change events are infanticides, that the killers are new or newly dominant males, that males specifically attack young infants, and that mothers and other troop members attempt to defend the troop against potentially infanticidal males.

Reproductive Cycling of Females Following Infant Loss

Red howler females typically return to a receptive condition 1–2 weeks after losing infants (observed cases: 8, 9, 11, 7–11, 10–13, and 19 days after infant death). Females have not been known to conceive during this first period of receptivity, and documented conceptions occurred about 35, 30–40, 54, and 73–84 days after the previous infant's death (conception dates were estimated by backdating 191 days' gestation; Crockett and Sekulic, 1982). The mean interbirth interval (IBI) between infants that died before the next sibling was conceived and the next sib's birth was 10.5 months (SD = 2.9; range = 7.75–15; $n = 12$). During the same period, the mean IBI after surviving infants was 16.6 months ($n = 42$), significantly longer than if the infant had died (Mann-Whitney U = 45; $n_1 = 12$; $n_2 = 42$; $p < 0.001$, 1-tailed). Shortened interbirth intervals are facilitated because red howlers in the study area give birth throughout the year, although seasonal peaks are evident (Crockett and Rudran, in preparation).

Figure 1 is a plot of age at death for 12 infants against the number of months (IBI) between their birth and that of their subsequent sibling. Based on the regression line, infants that die at age 9.04 months will

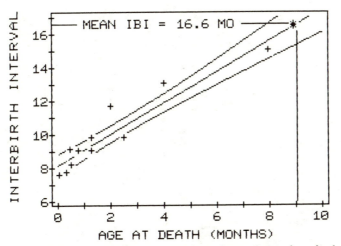

Figure 1. Interbirth interval (IBI; in months) after infants that died plotted
against their age at death. The linear regression is IBI = 0.93 times
Age at death + 8.2 months (95% population mean confidence limits are given; Imhof and Hewett, 1982). Pearson's correlation coefficient = 0.97; + = Infanticide cases 1,2,3,4,6,11,12,13,14,18,20 (Table II); * = Infant death attributed to botfly infestation on throat.
For IBI = 16.6 months (the mean after surviving infants), Age at
death = 9.04 months.

produce an IBI equal to the mean after surviving infants (16.6 months).
Thus, only by killing infants younger than approximately 9 months
of age will a male reduce a female's IBI. In fact, the oldest suspected
infanticide victim was 8 months old, and most were under 4 months
(Table II).

This tendency to kill only younger infants is even more apparent
when corrected for the availability of potential victims of various ages.
For the nine male-change situations in which the timing was precisely
known, the survival of 36 individuals through 23 months of age at the
time of male change was compared to the survival of 73 individuals
who were born in 26 troops that were stable during their gestation
and subsequent life up to 24 months (Fig. 2). Only 25% of 20 infants
under 9 months of age escaped death or injury after male-change situations, while all 16 older individuals survived unharmed; mortality in
stable troops was much lower and unrelated to age (2 × 2 × 2
G-test, Stability versus Fate versus Age; all comparisons $p < 0.002$
except Stability versus Age, $p = .45$, not statistically significant).

Reproductive Success of Infanticidal Males

Males suspected of infanticide usually succeeded in siring infants
in the troops that they entered. In at least 10 cases, the known or
presumed infanticidal male mated with the victim's mother, based on

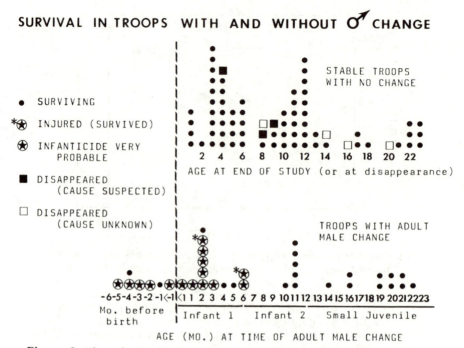

Figure 2. The relationship between age at the time of a male change and subsequent survival of infants and small juveniles. For comparison, the age at the end of the study period (February 1981) or at disappearance for individuals whose gestation and subsequent life up through 23 months were spent under stable conditions are presented (see text).

direct observation in six cases and implied by the presence of only the infanticidal male in the troop in four other cases (Table II). However, Cases 1–8 occurred after more than one male entered a troop, and it is possible that one male killed an infant and another mated with its mother. The next recorded infant born to a female who lost an infant was sired by a new or newly dominant male in nine instances and probably so in two more; in a twelfth instance (after Case 6), the infant might have been sired by the formerly dominant, subsequently ousted male. The two males who failed in their incursion attempts (Changes M and N) presumably failed to sire offspring in the troops they attempted to enter. No subsequent births had been recorded for four cases' mothers by December 1981, and no data implicating paternity were available for the final two of 20 cases.

Infanticide in association with male status changes leaves open the possibility that males may mistakenly kill their own infants. This is so because during transitions of status that coincide with female receptivity, more than one male may succeed in mating with the same female (cf. Struhsaker and Leland, 1979). In four cases, a male could have killed his own infant since he could have mated with the victim's mother at the time of its conception (Table II). In two of these four cases (11 and 17), the implicated infanticidal animal was actually observed to mate with the victim's mother during the estrus of conception. In Case 11, the suspected father was absent during most of the infant's gestation and reentered after its birth; the infant disappeared on the day the male reentered. In Case 17, both the implicated infanticidal male and the subsequently ousted male consorted with the female, although only the former was observed to mount.

Habitat Differences in Population Density, Male Tenure Length, and Infant Mortality

The two habitats studied differed considerably in population density of howlers. The open woodland of the Mata supported more than twice the population density of the gallery forest (February 1981 estimates: 84–112 per km² versus 36 per km²). Despite this twofold difference, the average breeding male tenure was only about 1 year shorter in the Mata than in the Gallery, as estimated by dividing troop-months by the number of times that a breeding male changed. Overall, the breeding male changed a maximum of 20 times and a minimum of 15 times during the study period for an average tenure of 5.06 to 6.74 years. Of these, 11–15 changes occurred in the Mata and 4–5 changes occurred in the Gallery, producing tenure estimates of 4.72 to 6.44 years in the former habitat and 6.07–7.58 years in the latter. Mata tenures of 6 months and 10 months occurred in their entirety during the study period, and tenures of about 1 and 3 years could be inferred from changes that terminated tenures begun during Rudran's (1979) study.

Mortality during the first year of life did not differ significantly between the two habitats (Table IV); 16.24% of Mata infants died versus 19.15% of Gallery infants. Thus, the differences in breeding-male tenure length and infant mortality are much smaller than the difference in population density. However, an effect of population density may eventually be demonstrated. All detected Gallery male changes with associated infanticide events occurred between November 1980 and December 1981 during the latter part of the study, and the population growth rate in the Gallery has been much higher than in the Mata (21% per annum versus 6% per annum during the period 1979–1981; Crockett: unpublished data).

DISCUSSION

Reproductive success for most male red howlers is dependent upon their ability to enter and breed in a troop; forming new troops and breeding in the natal troop are less frequent options. Immigrating males may rapidly replace the breeding male, or they may coreside for months or years before succeeding or failing in their quest. Observations of invaders at the onset of incursion suggest that infanticide is but one aspect of a behavior complex involved in attempts to usurp the role of breeding males. If infant disappearances coinciding with male changes can be accepted as infanticides, the data presented here indicate the occurrence of one infanticide every 5.9 troop-years (17 observed, very probable, and probable in 1214 troop-months), or about one case of infanticide per average male tenure. By killing infants early on, invaders may swing the incursion's outcome in their favor. The return of females to a receptive condition after infant death may provoke status-determining male–male confrontations which could be advantageous to the new males. Furthermore, females who have already lost infants may cease supporting the defending male.

The observations discussed in this chapter provide little evidence that usurping males increase risk to themselves by killing infants. Mothers that attacked known or presumed infanticidal males did little damage, and harrassments and chases by troop members usually only delayed the nearly inevitable infanticide of younger infants. On the other hand, when new males succeeded in siring infants in their new troops, inferred infanticide resulted in these infants being born after shorter than average IBIs, enhancing their fathers' reproductive success.

The Sexual Selection Hypothesis

The sexual selection hypothesis has been advanced to account for the evolution of infanticide in a variety of animals (Hrdy, 1979). The selective advantage rests on whether the infanticidal animals can produce more offspring and/or produce offspring sooner than noninfanticidal animals (Chapman and Hausfater, 1979). The data on red howlers is generally consistent with the sexual selection hypothesis. Red howler males can sire more offspring and do so sooner after infanticide since interbirth intervals are shortened. Infanticide may also increase the likelihood of a male's breeding in the first place by provoking male–male confrontations necessary for the resolution of status.

The success of replacing resident males was enhanced when coalitions of males entered (cf. Bygott et al., 1979), while a single immigrant male rarely achieved quick replacement. Thus, incursions frequently resulted in coresidence of more than one adult male, and status changes among them have been associated with infanticides. Hence, it is possible that fathers may sometimes kill their own infants, and in two cases there was reason to suspect that this actually happened. Any calculation of reproductive success associated with infanticide in red howlers would have to be devalued by the probability of making a mistake (i.e., killing one's own offspring). This complicates mathematical modeling of infanticide (e.g., Chapman and Hausfater, 1979), but surely this is the only way to evaluate reproductive success in social systems where both infanticide and male coalitions exist.

Other Hypotheses

Other hypotheses accounting for infanticide have been proposed, and the data here are pertinent to two of them. Proponents of the social pathology hypothesis (e.g., Curtin and Dolhinow, 1978; Boggess, 1979 and this volume, Chapter 14) suggest that infanticide in langurs (*Presbytis entellus*) does not represent a behavior evolved through a genetic advantage to individuals that practice it. Rather, they interpret infanticide as a nonadaptive side effect of atypically high aggression accompanying a recent, more rapid pattern of male-membership change. This new pattern is suspected to be an artifact of recent environmental pressures, especially high population densities induced by encroachment of human populations.

The social pathology hypothesis is inapplicable to the red howler data. Although some red howler infant disappearances occurred during periods of social stress when male–male aggression was noted, others disappeared during periods of tranquility. For example, three infants disappeared after the previous dominant male was dead and the implicated killer was the only adult male in the troop (Change O). In two other troops (Changes A and K), infants born to females that were pregnant at the time of a male change disappeared shortly after birth but months after the change and when male–male relations were stable. Furthermore, victims were not random, as may be predicted by the social pathology hypothesis, but were infants of an age shown to result in reproductive advantages for males suspected of killing them.

The red howlers in the study reported here live in a relatively undisturbed habitat in somewhat larger troops and at higher densities than this species in Columbia, where it is sympatric with two or three primate species (Defler, 1981). Population densities of the howlers in the area of this study are also within the range of densities of langurs where take-overs are reported (Table 3 in Hrdy, 1979). Considering that red howlers are the only primates in the Mata and are sympatric in the Gallery with only one other primate species (*Cebus nigrivittatus*), the densities recorded simply cannot be viewed as "crowded" compared to densities of other arboreal primate communities (cf. Crockett Wilson and Wilson, 1977; Heltne and Thorington, 1976; Struhsaker and Leland, 1979). The frequency of male change and infant mortality was not related to the more than twofold difference in population density found in the two red howler habitats that were studied.

The resource competition hypothesis has been proposed by Rudran

(1979) who first observed infanticide at the study site discussed in this chapter. The sexual selection and resource competition hypotheses are not mutually exclusive, since any case of infanticide that yields a reproductive advantage will also probably eliminate a food competitor. Rather, the sexual selection hypothesis suggests that individual fitness is improved directly, while the resource competition hypothesis implies inclusive fitness benefits realized through increased survival of one's offspring and other relatives because more food will be available to them.

The sexual selection hypothesis makes specific predictions about the sex of infanticidal animals and the age of their victims that are borne out by the red howler data. The resource competition hypothesis does not make these predictions. First, the sexual selection hypothesis clearly predicts that in polygynous societies, adult males should be the killers because of the greater variation in male reproductive success compared to that of females (Trivers, 1972). The red howler data implicate adult males in all inferred cases, and both observed cases of infanticide (Sekulic, 1983a; Rudran, 1979) were by adult males. Infanticide that implicated adult males has also been reported for *Alouatta palliata* (Clarke, 1981).

The resource competition hypothesis predicts that adult females should be as likely to kill infants as are adult males (Hrdy, 1979), or that adult females should be even more likely to do so than adult males (e.g., see Wasser, 1983a). Wasser's argument derives from the idea that females' behavior should maximize offspring quality (reproductive value), whereas males' behavior should maximize offspring quantity. In the study area here, where starvation appears to be infrequent, differences in food availability to a growing howler probably would have a greater influence on its size and health relative to peers than on probability of survival per se. If so, mothers might kill their offspring's competitors if the increases in offspring quality sufficiently outweighed potential costs such as injuries incurred during the attacks. So far, females in the study area have not been implicated in suspected infanticides.

Another way in which the predictions of these two hypotheses differ is with respect to age of victims (Hrdy, 1979). The sexual selection hypothesis combined with reproductive data from the study population makes a specific prediction that victims should be less than 9 months old, in close agreement with the actual ages of infanticide cases (Figs. 1 and 2; Table II). In contrast, the resource competition hypothesis predicts that any vulnerable nonrelatives should be victims. It could be argued that the upper age limit found for suspected victims is simply an artifact of older infants or juveniles being too risky to kill. However, infants under 5 or 6 months of age usually cling to the mother, especially in threatening situations. Thus, the infanticidal animal attacking a small infant also would be confronting its mother.

Female Counterstrategies

Because adult females clearly experience decrements in reproductive success as a result of their infants' deaths, they should have evolved behaviors to reduce the occurrence or impact of infanticide (Hrdy 1977b, 1979; Chapman and Hausfater, 1979; Hausfater, Chapter 13, this volume). The option of a "pseudoestrus" or soliciting copulations from new males and thereby "deceiving" them about the paternity of unborn infants reported for langurs (Hrdy, 1977b) appears to be unavailable to red howlers. A female copulating when she was pregnant (as determined retrospectively from the birth of her infant) was never observed. Infants born after a male change and sired by the previous male were usually infanticide victims (Table II; Fig. 2). However, Glander (1980) observed one postconception copulation in *A. palliata,* raising the possibility that under some circumstances, a false estrus may be possible for red howlers.

Pregnancy blocking or abortion may reduce maternal investment in offspring that are potentially susceptible to infanticide (Labov, 1981a). However, given the number of pregnancies brought to term after male change, there is as yet little evidence that this phenomenon occurs in red howlers.

Attempts at defense of infants by mothers and other troop members may forestall infanticide but are rarely successful; a similar lack of success is reported for langurs (Hrdy, 1977b). A few infants might have escaped for this reason, however (e.g., Case c). If a red howler female's infant is very young when a male change occurs, it may not be advantageous for her to defend it indefinitely (see also Sekulic, 1982d). If the infant's death were inevitable, abandonment or absence of defense should occur as soon as "futility" was determined, in order to reduce maternal investment. The fairly consistent 2-week delay between male change and infant disappearance may reflect a lowering of matenal defenses after a period of "assessment."

Female red howlers reduce the deleterious effects of infanticide by quickly returning to a receptive condition and usually conceive 1–3 months after infant loss. However, when a take-over or status change proves to be only temporary or if the invasion is by more than one male, impregnation by the "wrong" male could result in another infanticide, thus further reducing the female's reproductive success. A female who delayed pregnancy until the outcome of male–male competition was decided may be at an advantage. In none of four documented cases did females conceive during their first estrus after infant loss, but preliminary data suggest that red howler females typically cycle more than once prior to conception (Crockett and Sekulic, 1982). Nevertheless, a rapid return to a receptive (but infertile) condition would be advantageous to females when sexual solicitations precipitated male fighting, speeding the resolution of male-status relationships. That such a female strategy exists is suggested by observations during Change F in which solicitation by one female of one of two invaders coincided with fresh injuries on the two males.

Observations on the number of cycles prior to conception as a function of stability of male relationships (or number of adult males) are necessary before it can be concluded that female red howlers do have a sort of false estrus. However, similar adaptations have been proposed for lions (*Panthera leo;* Packer and Pusey, 1983b).

Infant Counterstrategies

Infants themselves have little defense when new males enter a troop. However, infants that are born into troops prior to a status change and that have associated with a male that is not their father prior to his rise to rank of breeding male may reduce their chances of being killed. One of the survivors (Fig. 2) falls in this category. This infant was 5.5 months old when her presumed father was ousted (Change O), and she was observed to approach and interact with the newly dominant male on numerous occasions. One interpretation is that the infant was "demonstrating" her maternal independence to the male. This seems a plausible ruse since males may very well use "independence" as a cue to "assess" infant age and thus whether infanticide would be adaptive. Females and infants generally avoid new males, and this potential infant counterstrategy may only be possible with familiar males and by infants that are old enough to travel independently of the mother.

CONCLUSION

Cases of infanticide and suspected infanticide in red howler monkeys are sufficiently common that it has been possible to examine several hypotheses proposed to account for infanticidal behavior. The social pathology hypothesis is inconsistent with the red howler data. The resource competition hypothesis is difficult to reject outright, but it fails to predict the age/sex specificity of attackers and victims. The sexual selection hypothesis, whereby males increase their reproductive success through infanticide, is supported by observations, and the evolution of infanticide through natural selection is the most likely explanation of this phenomenon in red howlers.

Infanticidal behavior appears to be widespread in this red howler study population, but its reproductive benefits for individual males depends upon their success in attaining breeding status. Variation in male reproductive success appears to be influenced primarily by the ability of males to enter troops and to become the breeding male in them. The risk of death or failure has been demonstrated by case histories of troops (Rudran, 1979; Changes D and O, this study, resulted in deaths of adult males). Furthermore, males' reproductive success may be related to their ability to form coalitions with other males (who are not necessarily close relatives: Wasser, 1982; Sekulic, 1983a; Packer and Pusey, 1982), since associations of more than one male are more successful than singletons at entering troops and replacing resident males and probably at repelling invasions.

ACKNOWLEDGMENTS

This research was funded by a Smithsonian Institution International Environmental Science Program Grant to J. F. Eisenberg and by Smithsonian and Friends of the National Zoo Fellowships to the senior author. We thank D. Mack, T. Pope, J. Robinson, and R. Rudran for information on troop histories prior and subsequent to our own observations. We thank G. Hausfater, S. Blaffer Hrdy, C. Janson, J. Robinson, R. Rudran, S. Stringham, and S. Wasser for helpful comments on various versions of this chapter. R. Brooks, J. F. Eisenberg, and M. Reaka made contributions to many aspects of this research. We are most grateful to Tomas and Cecila Blohm for their hospitality and permission to conduct our research at Hato Masaguaral. Special thanks to the organizers of the Wenner-Gren Symposium for stimulating the completion of this chapter and to the Wenner-Gren Foundation for sponsoring the symposium.

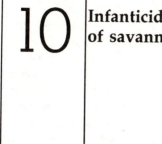

10 Infanticide in two populations of savanna baboons

D. Anthony Collins
Curt D. Busse
Jane Goodall

INTRODUCTION

Infant killing among primates has been reported most often in species that form groups that have only one breeding male, such as langurs, redtail monkeys, blue monkeys, and gorillas (reviewed by Hrdy, 1981; Butynski, 1982). One interpretation, derived from Sugiyama's description (1965b) of infanticide in langurs (*Presbytis entellus*), is that infant killing is a reproductive strategy of advantage to males when they migrate into a new group, and that it has been favored by sexual selection (Hrdy, 1974). In some species, females will resume menstrual cycles soon after their infants die and suckling ceases, and male newcomers then gain a correspondingly earlier opportunity to sire the females' next infants (e.g., Sugiyama, 1965b). Infant killing, therefore, would be particularly advantageous to males whose reproductive tenure is brief (Hrdy, 1974; Chapman and Hausfater, 1979). The major alternative explanation states that such killings result from social disturbance arising at high population density, ultimately caused by human alteration of the habitat (e.g., Curtin and Dolhinow, 1978). An evaluation of these and other hypotheses to explain infant killing in langurs is given by Hausfater and Vogel (1982).

Infant killing has been reported least often in species that form large groups that have multiple breeding males, such as rhesus macaques, Japanese macaques, and baboons (Angst and Thommen, 1977). Among

193

the savanna baboons—olive (*Papio anubis*), yellow (*P. cynocephalus*), and chacma (*P. ursinus*) baboons—males almost invariably leave the troop in which they were born and breed in one or more subsequent troops. A newcomer cannot be the father of any infants present in the troop for the first several months after he immigrates and may gain a reproductive advantage by killing them. However, should he kill any such infant and should the mother conceive soon thereafter, the male still would not be guaranteed to impregnate her because other males in the troop would also attempt to do so. Also, should a newcomer try to kill an infant, other males who are possible fathers of the infant may defend it from attack. On both counts, therefore, there is less likelihood of infant killing in multimale than in one-male groups.

Despite these reasons for expecting infant killing to be rare in multimale groups, evidence that infant killing does occasionally occur among savanna baboons is accumulating as more studies focus on the behavior of immigrant males. The present chapter describes evidence of infant killing in two widely separated populations of savanna baboons and summarizes its contexts and apparent causes. First, however, evidence of infant killing among other populations of savanna baboons is briefly summarized.

Published Evidence of Infant Killing in Baboons

For chacma baboons, J. Vincent described an adult male killing two young males on the periphery of a troop, and the South African Parks Board described an adult male seizing an infant from its mother, running off with it, and beginning to eat it (both cited by Saayman, 1971). W. H. Buskirk (personal communication) observed an adult male attack an infant (about 5 months old), dragging it along the ground as a second male gave chase. The infant died 2 days later. Other apparent cases of infant killing in chacma baboons (Busse and Hamilton, 1981) are included in the data presented here.

For yellow baboons at Mikumi, Rhine *et al.* (1980) reported that a subadult male attacked a 9-month-old male, though not fatally, and also that a 4-month-old female died with wounds on the back of her neck which could have been inflicted by adult males. At Amboseli, Altmann (1980) described a male (probably natal) running off with a 2-year-old female in his mouth, inflicting fatal wounds. Also, Shopland (1982) reported that a young infant received fatal wounds and its mother received severe injuries during an encounter between two troops, while Pereira (1983) reported three abortions and an infant death following the immigration of a male into a troop. These observations of abortion are particularly striking because only three other abortions had been detected during 10 years of research at Amboseli. It has been suggested that abortion in the presence of immigrant males could be a female reproductive tactic of foregoing further investment in an offspring that is likely to be killed following parturition (Hrdy, 1979; Pereira, 1983).

For olive baboons at Gilgil, Smuts (1982) provided evidence that a 4-month-old female was killed by an adult male (or males) after becoming separated from her mother. Other likely cases of infant killing in olive baboons (Packer, 1980, and personal communication) are included in the data presented here.

In contrast to savanna baboons, the closely related hamadryas baboons (*P. hamadryas*) live in one-male groups, and infant killing, at least in captivity, is more often reported in this species (Zuckerman, 1932; Angst and Thommen, 1977; Rijksen, 1981). For free-ranging hamadryas baboons, Kummer *et al.* (1974) described how, when two breeding males were artificially removed from their groups, the arrival of replacement males was soon followed by an infant death in each group. The one infant examined had suffered deep puncture wounds that could have been inflicted by male canine teeth.

INFANT WOUNDING AND MORTALITY AMONG CHACMA BABOONS AT MOREMI, BOTSWANA

Methods and Background

This section summarizes information on infant wounding and mortality among chacma baboons (*Papio ursinus*) at the Moremi Wildlife Reserve, Botswana, from August 1977, to June 1980. The habitat has been described by Tinley (1973) and Hamilton *et al.* (1976); study conditions have been described by Busse (1984). Two habituated troops, C and W, were the focus of study. Each troop averaged 69 members, including 6–12 adult males and 19–25 adult females. Patterns of male migration between troops were typical of those for savanna baboons as described by Packer (1979a): males emigrated from their natal troop before reaching adulthood and sometimes migrated repeatedly thereafter. The median tenure of males at alpha rank was 5 months (range = 1.5–12+ months; $n = 11$ alpha males; Busse, 1984), which is shorter than that reported for any other savanna baboon population (cf. Hausfater, 1975).

Births occurred throughout the year, and females resumed menstrual cycles an average of 11.5 months ($\bar{X} \pm$ SE $= 356 \pm 18$ days, $n = 21$ females) after the birth of a surviving infant. Conception occurred another 6 months later, 17.5 months (532 ± 6 days, $n = 13$ females) after the previous birth. By contrast, when an infant died the mother resumed menstrual cycles 1 month later (36 ± 6 days, $n = 8$) and conceived 4.5 months (134 ± 7 days, $n = 8$) after the death. As a consequence, interbirth intervals were significantly shorter when infants died ($\bar{X} = 13.5$ months, $n = 8$) than when they survived to weaning ($\bar{X} = 23.5$

months, $n = 13$) (Mann Whitney $U = 0$, $p < 0.01$), and this was true whether death was from injury by other baboons or from other causes.

Mortality

During the study, 56 infants were born: 29 survived to 1 year of age, and 17 died or disappeared and were presumed to have died. Another 10 were less than 1 year of age at the end of the study. Depending on survival outcomes of these 10, infant survivorship to 1 year of age was between 52 and 70%.

Causes of mortality were known or suspected for 12 of the 17 deaths. One infant was seen dead the morning of birth and was probably stillborn. Another infant appeared to have been born blind; it died when it was 74 days old. Three infants disappeared with their mothers, and an orphan disappeared with its subadult male caregiver (Hamilton *et al.*, 1982). These four disappearances might have all resulted from predation (Busse, 1980). Another orphan received little care and disappeared 75 days after its mother had disappeared. The infant, 10.5 months old, was in poor health when it disappeared.

Two infants died after sustaining wounds of unknown origin but which could have been inflicted by males (Table I). One of these, an 11-month-old female (SA), received lacerations on her head and lower back and lost the use of one leg. Four weeks later, it lost the use of its other leg after receiving another laceration. The infant disappeared 3 days later. The second infant (TX) that died from wounds was a newborn that received multiple lacerations and punctures. The mother had deep lacerations in one leg and was seen carrying the dead infant 30 minutes after both had been seen healthy (M. P. Rowe: personal communication; Table I). This was the only adult female ever observed with any wound other than a tear in a perineal swelling. Attack by lion or leopard was unlikely in this case, because observers had been with the troop continuously that day. At different times, four other infants received lacerations of unknown origin but which could have been inflicted by males. These infants recovered from their wounds.

Two other infants were killed by adult males, and another infant died after it was carried persistently by an adult female. These incidents are described subsequently in detail along with observations of two nonfatal attacks that are relevant to the discussion of infanticide. The two killings and two nonfatal attacks were mentioned briefly by Busse and Hamilton (1981).

Observed Cases of Injury or Mishandling

Kidnapping. One infant (MZ) in W Troop died after being taken from its mother, the lowest-ranking female, by another low-ranking female, PG, who was 4 months pregnant. When first seen on the day

Table I. Infant deaths following maltreatment from other baboons at Moremi

Infant	Troop	Date	Age	Gender	Circumstances
Circumstantial observations					
SA	W	16 Feb 1979	10.8 mo	F	Infant received lacerations on its head and lower back, losing the use of one leg. Four weeks later, the infant appeared to receive a second wound on its back, and it lost the use of its other leg. It disappeared 3 days later (C. Busse and K. S. Smith).
TX	C	29 Jun 1980	1 day	M	Mother was seen carrying a dead newborn, which had multiple lacerations and punctures. The mother had deep lacerations on one leg. Both had been seen healthy 30 min earlier. When the mother abandoned the carcass, it was partially eaten by a high-ranking female (M. Rowe, N. Rowe, and K. S. Smith).
Direct observations					
MK	C	1 Sep 1979	4 days	Unknown	Adult male BB seen eating infant after mother had been tranquilized (C. Busse, W. J. Hamilton, D. Melton, and K. S. Smith).
RF	C	8 Sep 1979	8.1 mo	M	Adult male seen biting an infant in the head at dusk. The next morning, an infant was found dead with canine puncture wounds in its skull (W. J. Hamilton and K. S. Smith).
MZ	W	6 Feb 1980	2 days	Unknown	Newborn infant was taken somehow from its mother by a pregnant female. The infant died within 2 days. The mother was the lowest-ranking female in the group (C. Busse and K. S. Smith).

of birth, the infant was already in possession of PG; thus, circumstances surrounding the change of possession of the infant were not known. When next seen 2 days later, the infant had died, presumably from inanition. Nevertheless, PG continued to carry the infant for another day, as mothers sometimes do after their own infants die.

Attacks on infants. The first observed attack occurred in C Troop on 1 September 1979, while a female was being captured to obtain a blood sample and morphometric measurements. The female, carrying her 4-day-old infant (MK), was tranquilized using a blow-dart, a procedure that had been used successfully with mothers and infants previously. After being hit, the female ran into dense vegetation before the drug took effect. Observers found her 9 minutes later, immediately after hearing the sounds of two males fighting. She was lying tranquilized and uninjured while the alpha male, BB, was 10 m away, biting into her infant, who was already dead. (Females with infants were no longer darted after this incident.) The second ranking male, JT, was sitting 5 m from BB and was holding a 3-month-old infant, DN, whom he carried regularly (Busse, 1984). The male biting the infant had immigrated 76 days earlier, well after the victim had been conceived. He partially consumed the carcass then abandoned it after most troop members had left the vicinity; a low-ranking immigrant male, BF, then consumed the remains.

The mother's next conception was 6 months after this attack, during her third menstrual cycle. By this time, BB had dropped to rank number three. BB consorted with her for 5 days of her second cycle, but he was not observed consorting with her during the first and third (conception) cycles. The mother was seen on 3 days during the conception cycle, and each time she was being consorted by a low-ranking male (RK). The timing of deturgescence of her perineal swelling was not precisely known, however.

The second attack occurred in C Troop on September 8, 1979, 1 week after the first. An observer, who was unfamiliar with this troop, saw an adult male bite an infant at dusk (W. J. Hamilton III: personal communication). The next morning, a mother was carrying a dead infant (RF). Observers retrieved the body, that of an unweaned 8-month-old male, after the mother abandoned it that afternoon. Necropsy revealed several head wounds, including a skull puncture below the ear.

The third attack occurred in C Troop on September 23, 1979. A low-ranking immigrant male, BF, who had partially cannibalized the first victim, was observed biting an unweaned 11-month-old female behind the ear (K. S. Smith: personal communication). Several days later, the infant exhibited severe incoordination that persisted for several weeks before the infant recovered. The male had joined the troop 98 days before this attack.

The fourth attack, which was not directly observed, occurred in W Troop on October 28, 1979. Following an outburst of screaming by numerous troop members, a weaned 14-month-old male, seen healthy moments earlier, was bleeding steadily from a 3-cm long scalp laceration. The screaming was directed toward an adult male, of unknown origin, who had just arrived and was chasing troop members near the injured individual. During 10 minutes of chasing, the male hit, but did not wound, a 6-year-old subadult male that had just picked up a 12-month-old infant who was separated from its mother. As he hit the subadult, the outsider was mobbed by several adult and subadult males, who charged and screamed at him.

INFANT WOUNDING AND MORTALITY AMONG OLIVE BABOONS AT GOMBE, TANZANIA

Methods and Background

This section summarizes information on infant wounding and mortality among olive baboons (*Papio anubis*) at Gombe National Park, Tanzania, for a 10-year period beginning May 1972. The habitat and study conditions at Gombe have been described by Goodall (1968) and Clutton-Brock and Gillett (1979). Daily observations on identifiable individuals have been made by Tanzanian observers over the full 10 years, while European and American observers also contributed records through 1974. Initially, there were three habituated troops: A, B, and C; but when B Troop split in 1978, the resultant D Troop was also added to the observation schedule. The four troops varied in size between 20 and 60 animals, containing 6–12 adult females and 2–12 adult males. All but one of the males that matured to adulthood during this study left their natal troop and joined another. Male tenure at alpha rank averaged 3.75 years ($n = 4$ males; Packer, 1979a,b), which is considerably longer than that reported at Moremi.

Preliminary analysis of data from 33 females since 1975, combined with a previous analysis by Packer (1979a), allows female reproductive patterns to be compared with those from Moremi. At Gombe, females resumed menstrual cycles an average of 10 months after the birth of a surviving infant (range 3.5–24.1 months, $n = 25$ females; Packer, 1979a). Conception occurred about 8.5 months later, averaging 19 months (range 11–37 months, $n = 24$ females) after the previous birth. In contrast, when an infant died, the mother resumed menstrual cycles 1 month later (median 29 days, range 7–199 days, $n = 13$ females; Packer, 1979a) and conceived a median of 5 months after the death (range 1–26 months, $n = 20$ females). As a result, interbirth intervals were significantly shorter when infants died (median 12.8 months, range 9–35 months, $n = 20$ females) than when they survived to weaning (median 25 months, range 17–43 months, $n = 23$ females) (Wilcoxon $T = 5$, $n = 11$ females, two-tailed test, $p < 0.01$).

Assignment of the likely paternity of the infants was based on daily recordings of sexual consortships, in combination with Hendrickx and Kraemer's (1969) finding that copulations during the week preceding deturgescence of the female's perineal swelling are most likely to result in conception, with highest probability 3 days before rapid deturgescence. With deturgescence starting on day (D), this fertile period is annotated from D-7 to D-1, following Hausfater (1975). Males who consorted on D-3 in a conception cycle were considered most likely fathers, others as possible fathers, while those absent from the troop were designated nonfathers.

Mortality

Table II lists the available data on causes of mortality up to the age of 2 years, not including 9 full-term stillbirths and 12 aborted pregnancies, based on 186 conceptions recorded over 10 years. Of 165 infants born alive, 58 had died or disappeared before reaching 2 years of age. Those who disappeared are presumed dead, since the chances of survival outside the mother's troop at that age are minimal. With 22 of the 107 survivors still below that age in April 1982, survivorship lies between 51 and 65% over the first 2 years.

The circumstances of 26 of the 58 infant losses (45%) are unknown. For 2 infants, there are no records at all; another 14 infants, reportedly healthy beforehand, disappeared and their bodies were not found. A further 10 infants were seen dead but with neither evidence of disease beforehand nor external injury.

Table II. Source of mortality in 58 cases of infant death at Gombe during the 10-year period beginning May 1972[a]

Source of mortality	Number of infants	Percentage of total
No data	2	3.4
Disappeared	14	24.1
Died without obvious cause	10	17.2
Neonatal deaths (within 3 days of birth)	7	12.1
Died after obvious illness	3	5.2
Died after insufficient mothering	3	5.2
Killed by chimpanzees	1	1.7
Died with wounds	12	20.7
Died after maltreatment from other baboons	6	10.3
	58	

[a] Table includes only live-born infants less than 2 years of age.

More evidence is available for the remaining 32 cases of infant death or disappearance. Seven infants died within 3 days of birth. Since three of these were noticeably weak from birth and two were unable to suckle properly, these are classified as neonatal deaths which implies inviability, although illness and injury cannot be ruled out. Another three infants succumbed following apparent illness when older (at 26, 125, and 169 days), while three more died apparently because their mothers could not provide adequate care—the mothers of two infants had limb injuries and the third infant was the weaker of twins. One infant was a victim of predation by chimpanzees; similar cases of predation by chimpanzees, outside of the present sample, have been described by Wrangham (1974b) and Packer (1980).

In 12 cases, infant death was associated with wounding: Four infants died after being seen with wounds, and eight were found dead but with wounds on their bodies. Further details about these 12 cases are given in Table III. Some of the wounds might have occurred through accident; they might also have been inflicted by predators, although observations of chimpanzees over this period suggest that their attempts at predation upon baboons were not frequent. Other potential predators are uncommon at Gombe, and it seems likely that if they had been close enough to inflict injuries on an infant, they then would have been successful also in eating the infant rather than merely leaving a wounded victim. The descriptions of these infant deaths, which are summarized in Table III, suggest that in at least five cases the wounds had been inflicted by other baboons. Bilberry (BB) and Moss (MO) might have been injured during fighting within the troop; while Mint (MI) and Rice (RC) sustained fatal wounds during intertroop encounters, in both of which one troop withdrew from the other, although it is unclear whether members of their own or the other troop would have been most likely to have caused the wounds. Deep puncture wounds on some infants (e.g., Almond [AM]) suggest that their aggressors might have been adult male baboons with large canines, although there are some records of adult females inflicting severe wounds on infants, albeit not fatal ones.

Finally, six deaths can be directly attributed to injury or mishandling from other baboons (Table IV). Since these amount to 10% of all deaths in the sample, or 19% of those deaths to which causes have been attributed previously, their circumstances are described subsequently more fully. Three of the six infants died from fatal wounds, which means that when combined with the 12 deaths with wounds from Table III, 26% of the 58 infant losses in the four troops were associated with wounding. Table IV also includes a seventh case involving an infant in an unhabituated troop outside the main study population, but which is discussed shortly because it was so clearly observed.

Table III. Twelve baboons who died with wounds before 2 years of age—Gombe 1972–1982

Infant	Troop	Date	Age	Gender	Circumstances and details of wounds, where known
Algiers (AG)	A	13 Feb 1974	1.5 mo	Unknown	Found dead. Small wound on anus, head misshapen (J. Kikwale).
Dodoma (DM)	A	ca. 21 Jun 1976	19 days	M	Found dead with cuts on its muzzle, shoulder, left ribs, right thigh (A. Sindimwo and M. Hamisi).
Yaida (YI)	A	7 Mar 1979	17.8 mo	F	Healthy on March 6. Found dead with a large cut on right leg, other small wounds on arms and over left ribs. Had been healthy the previous day (K. Kuwe).
Almond (AM)	B	3 May 1973	4.9 mo	F	Found dead with 12 wounds distributed on left forelimb (1), both hind-limbs (1 left, 2 right), over ribs (4), left scapula (1), left lumbar region (1) right flank (1), and lower abdomen (1). Eight of these were described as puncture wounds, 25–75 mm diameter (N. Nicolson et al.).
Mint (MI)	B	12 May 1973	2.0 mo	M	Died with wound on right of lower back during a break in observation when B Troop was displaced by another troop. The mother ate the body (C. De Sieyes).
Moss (MO)	B	21 May 1973	8.5 mo	M	Found dying where 2 min earlier had been heard loud vocalizations of males. Observer (A. Sindimwo) suspected he had been killed by other adult males. The mother apparently did not know whereabouts of infant's body. An adult male (immigrant 10 months earlier) bit and pulled at the body with his teeth 25 min after death (A. Collins).

Wheat (WH)	B	5 Nov 1975	3.0 mo	M	Found dead with wound on right arm. Had been healthy the previous day (A. Sindimwo).
Agaric (AI)	B	2 Sep 1979	3.8 mo	F	Seen at midday 1 September with large laceration on left arm and other small wounds on that arm and left side of head. Dead by next morning (K. Kuwe).
Bilberry (BB)	B	19 Jan 1980	14 days	F	Found dead with six small wounds on head. Possibly killed during a major fight heard the previous evening (A. Sindimwo).
Rice (RC)	B	2 Jan 1981	16.2 mo	M	Wounded during aggressive intertroop interaction between B and D Troops on December 25. Four wounds including one behind right armpit, another penetrating the body wall. Thereafter walked tripedal, could not stand for long or climb trees. Condition severe by January 1, dead on 2 January (A. Sindimwo).
Rhubarb (RU)	B	23 Jul 1981	ca. 8.3 mo	M	Observers attracted by commotion found infant severely wounded while adult male chased nearby baboons very aggressively. Infant died within minutes. Wounds not described (C. Athumani and A. Sindimwo).
Macbeni (ME)	C	3 Nov 1975	14 days	F	Found dead with wound on right buttock (P. Nyabenda and M. Katota).

Table IV. Observations of infant death following maltreatment from other baboons at Gombe[a]

Infant	Troop	Date	Age	Gender	Circumstances and details of death
Dar (DR)	A	7 Aug 1976	2 days	M	Weakened after prolonged kidnapping by female SB on second day of life. Dead on third day (A. Sindimwo and M. Hamisi).
Unguja (UN)	A	20 Jul 1979	6.4 mo	F	Adult male BR attacked mother and infant on July 9. Infant had five wounds on chest and neck and impaired use of right arm. Wounds became infected; infant died 11 days after the attack (K. Kuwe).
Denmark (DN)	A	30 Jul 1979	7.2 mo	F	Infant attacked by adult male AC. Bitten on head, lower abdomen, and later stomach and ribs before infant died (K. Kuwe).
Blossom (BS)	B	10 May 1976	1.5 mo	F	Repeatedly carried by brother BR, with mishandling and prevention of suckling, during preceding fortnight. Died while in possession of BR (A. Sindimwo).
Mangold (MA)	B	25 Apr 1981	8.4 mo	F	Killed by adult male SG during aggression also involving adult females and immatures. Two wounds, in chest and back (A. Sindimwo).
Gulliver (GU)	C	8 Sep 1975	8 days	M	Repeated kidnappings during first week of life by adult male LEO. Progressively weakened and died (A. Sindimwo, M. Trudeau, and C. Hunter).
L Troop Infant (LI)	L	8 Sep 1979	ca. 8.5 mo	F	Adult male FA attacked mother with infant during peaceful intertroop encounter between L and A Troops. Both mother and infant injured, the latter fatally on left cheek, by right ear, and on left shoulder (K. Kuwe).

[a] Includes all six cases in Table II; the seventh case was observed in an unhabituated troop.

Observed Cases of Fatal Injury or Mishandling

Kidnapping. Three infants died after being kidnapped, that is, when another baboon gained possession of the infant and prevented the mother from retrieving it, usually by threat or avoidance. Such instances can be compared with the more numerous cases of kidnapping that were not fatal.

In the first case, an adult female took the infant Dar (DR) on his second day of life and carried him ventral despite his evident distress, while the mother followed closely behind. By the time the mother had retrieved Dar, nearly 4 hr later, the infant could hardly cling and could not suckle, and next day he was dead. The long-term records at Gombe contain only one other case of persistent carrying by an adult (multiparous) female; she carried one particular infant seven times in its first 8 weeks for periods of up to 2 hr. Both of these carriers had in common that they were in the last 2 months of pregnancy, that their previous pregnancies had been unsuccessful, and that they were higher ranking than the mothers of the infants concerned. There are more numerous reports of kidnapping by nulliparous females between 3 and 6 years old, most of whom were undergoing adolescent cycles; the longest kidnapping was for 1.5 hr, and none of them proved fatal.

The second fatal kidnapping was by an adolescent male, the brother of the infant concerned. Male Blackberry (BR), aged 5 years 7 months, showed repeated interest in his infant sister, grooming her when she was on the mother and carrying her when she was not, but he handled her badly and sometimes dragged her along the ground. When she was 34 days old, he took her for 77 min, during which he handled her roughly, despite her cries of distress, and threatened the mother away. Eventually, he and the infant became involved in an exchange of aggression with other troop members, in which another male juvenile (aged 4.5 years) took the infant for 20 min and a 2-year-old male also tried unsuccessfully to do so. On the 45th day, the infant died while again in BR's possession. Although these kidnappings appeared to have caused her death, it may be relevant that she had been weak since birth, and that her mother was old; she died 3 months later. The male might well have had easy access to the infant precisely because he was her brother.

Reports of males aged between 4.5 and 7.5 years carrying infants are not infrequent at Gombe, usually involving infants up to 50 days in age being carried at most 1 hr. These males are sometimes, but not usually, close kin to the infants. One 7-year-old male who appropriated a 3-day-old infant for over 20 min was, however, known to have mated with the mother during the cycle of the infant's conception and so was a possible father of the infant; despite this, he handled the infant roughly.

The third fatal case involved an adult male, Leo (LEO), who took infant Gulliver (GU) on at least 3 of its first 7 days of life for periods of 50 min, 1 hr, and 2 hr, and implicitly at other times as well since observation was not continuous. Leo handled the infant carelessly but not aggressively, and by threatening away the mother he also prevented suckling. The infant progressively weakened, its skin became pallid, and small abrasions appeared on its face; it died 9 days after birth. Leo had been in the troop at least 4 years, and having consorted with the mother when this infant was conceived (on D-7, at the beginning of the period of maximum fertility), he was a possible father. It is not known whether he consorted with the mother when she next conceived. Although there are numerous other records of adult males at Gombe carrying infants in a variety of circumstances, which may include denying the mother access to her infant, the carrying of this particular infant was unusually persistent.

Fatal attacks on infants. The observations most relevant to theories of infanticide are those in which baboons delivered fatal attacks upon infants. Four cases were observed in sufficient detail to describe here; two of them were attacks upon the mother and infant together.

The first incident (observer: K. Kuwe) occurred in A Troop on 20 July 1979. Adult male Blackberry (BR) attacked female Utah (UT) and her infant Unguja (UN); the mother with her infant then fled into the lake, a common tactic during fights on the beach at Gombe. Other baboons ran toward the altercation, at which time BR fled and UT left the water still carrying UN. However, BR resumed his attacks on the mother, and she again ran into the water, sometimes submerged up to her neck, while BR waited for her at the water's edge. Despite her calls, no one aided her, and she was able to leave the water only after BR left the beach. The mother was not visibly injured, but the infant had five wounds on her chest and neck and could not properly use her right arm. Subsequently, these wounds became infected, and UN died 11 days later. The male, BR, was 8 years 10 months old and had immigrated from his natal troop 9.5 months before; since UN was already 6 months old at this time, he could not have been her father. He was neither alpha male at the time of the incident nor when the mother next conceived, although he did consort with her on that cycle (on day D-1, near the end of the fertile period) and could have fathered her next infant, although another immigrant male was more likely to have done so.

The second such incident (observer: K. Kuwe) was observed in unhabituated L Troop when members of A Troop were close by on September 8, 1979. The aggressor male, Fargo (FA), had transferred into L Troop from A Troop 2 months previously. Three males of A Troop were as close as 10 m from L Troop baboons, watching them, when FA attacked an L Troop female with her infant ventral, threw them

Figure 1. Adult male LEO holds a newborn infant (GU) that he kidnapped from its mother. The infant died as a direct result of LEO's intervention (photo by J. Goodall).

down, and bit her. He was chased off by an estimated 25 L Troop and the 3 A Troop baboons, but he returned and attacked the female again. As she fled, the infant fell to the ground, but FA continued in pursuit of the mother. The infant was dead. After 20 min, the mother and another adult male returned to sit close to the infant. FA also returned and twice resumed his attacks on the mother, apparently to prevent her from retrieving the infant.

The mother was cut near the right ear and above the eyes, the infant was cut on the left shoulder, the left cheek, and near the right ear. Male FA was just over 9 years old and had transferred in from his natal troop 69 days before; because the infant was aged 8–9 months, he could not have been its father. Nothing is known of his dominance rank, his social position, or of his mating partnerships after this incident.

Both of the preceding attacks involved considerable aggression toward the mothers, but the other two attacks observed were directly upon the infants themselves. One attack (observer: K. Kuwe) occurred in A Troop on July 30, 1979. Infant Denmark (DN) went to adult male Acacia (AC) and presented. AC threatened her, at which DN vocalized with hair erected and tail raised. AC chased DN, knocked her down, then dragged and threw her about 2 m. Baboons nearby vocalized, AC became more aggressive and chased them before returning to the infant and biting her in the head, the groin, and below the navel. A number of baboons, including the infant's mother and grandmother, began threatening AC. The grandmother harassed AC with particular persistence, and he attacked her, inflicting a deep cut on the crown of her head. Despite this, she continued to harass him. AC was chased off a short distance, but then he returned, chased other baboons from the infant, and dragged her another 10 m. Four minutes later, he bit her stomach and ribs, at which she emitted a weak cry of distress. After 9 minutes, he dragged her again, bit her, and then began to groom her. Twenty-two minutes after the initial attack, DN stopped breathing. During the next hour, AC remained near DN's body and once chased three adolescent males away. He repeatedly touched, sniffed, and licked the corpse (including blood). He threw it (once), groomed it (four times, amounting to over 20 min of grooming), made as though to mount it (once), and bit the ribs on the left side.

The infant's wounds included canine puncture wounds on the crown of the head and on the right cheek; an abdominal bite had exposed the gut. This male had transferred in from his natal troop 8 months earlier when he was 7 years old. Because the infant was 7 months old at death, AC could not have been its father. AC was neither alpha male at this time nor when the mother next conceived, and he was not seen to consort with her at that time.

The fourth attack (observer: A. Sindimwo) was in B Troop on April 25, 1981. Observers were attracted to the vocalizations of a number of baboons and arrived to see male, Sage (SG), chasing females and juveniles. SG then climbed rapidly up a nearby tree and attacked infant Mangold (MA), bit her, and descended with the screaming infant in his mouth. SG walked to the beach, shaking his head as though to kill her; MA was still screaming, but other baboons were some distance away. SG then dropped the body and left it, already dead. Within 15 min, the mother arrived with an adult male (the probable father of this infant) and retrieved the body. The infant had two main wounds, in the chest and on the back. Male SG was 7 years 11 months old, and was alpha male in this, his natal troop: his mother and most of his siblings had left when the troop divided 16 months previously. The infant was not from SG's immediate matriline, and although he had been in the troop when the infant was conceived, he had not been seen to consort with the mother. Despite his alpha rank, he was not seen consorting with her when she next conceived.

Other Evidence of Fatal Attacks

In light of these observations, several other infant deaths will be mentioned. First, male SG might have inflicted fatal wounds also on infant Rhubarb (RU). Observers arrived to find this male acting aggressively, chasing baboons (notably the infant's mother), and threatening the observers while the infant lay bleeding from two wounds. No other large males were close, but a natal male (7 years old) threatened from a distance. The infant died shortly afterward. The male's relationship to this infant was the same as in the previous example: the mother had been in his natal troop but was not of his immediate matriline, and he had been present when the infant was conceived but was not seen to consort with the mother. He did consort on D-1, however, at her next conception.

Second, three B Troop infants died of wounds during a 3-week period in 1973 (Almond [AM]; Mint [MI]; and Moss [MO]; all mentioned in Packer, 1980). While it is not clear how they had been wounded, it is interesting that an adult male approached one of them about 25 min after its death and bit it (Table III); he did so furtively and alone. Other males had paid little attention to the body shortly before. This male was about 8 years old and had immigrated after this infant (and one of the other two) had been conceived.

Third, one infant, Mango (MN)—not part of the sample in Tables II and III—was probably wounded while being carried ventral by male, Ebony (EBN), during a fight with male, Grinner (HUH), (observer: C. Packer; cited by Packer, 1980). Carrying the infant, EBN began to harass HUH, who retaliated aggressively. There was a long fight during which the infant remained ventral on EBN. HUH then chased EBN away; the next day, the infant was found so badly wounded (both legs were paralyzed, apparently as a result of a bite at the base of the spine) that it eventually fell victim to predation by chimpanzees.

Finally, in 1968 two infants were killed and another was attacked unsuccessfully by chimpanzees while the infants were in the company of adult male baboons (Ransom, 1981: 287). During these incidents, the male baboons were with the infants for other reasons than to protect them from chimpanzees. One of the infants was actually clinging to the chest of a male baboon when a chimpanzee seized it (Ransom, 1981).

DISCUSSION

Although these results provide new evidence of infant killing in savanna baboons, much of this evidence is circumstantial, and few of the deaths were well observed. Therefore, no attempt can be made to refute either of the major hypotheses—sexual selection or social disturbance—advanced to explain this behavior among primates. The sexual selection hypothesis, however, does generate specific, testable predictions as to which males are most likely to kill which infants. In contrast, the hypothesis that infant killings result from social disturbance makes no such specific predictions. In the following discussion, the data are examined to see how well they accord with predictions of the first hypothesis. Then, an examination of the proximate causes of the incidents provides an opportunity to evaluate the role of social disturbance. Kidnappings are considered first; male attacks on infants are considered second.

Kidnapping

At Gombe, it is not unusual for infants to be carried even for long periods by baboons other than their mothers, but this carrying does not usually prove fatal to the infants. The chief risks appear to be the possibility of injury during careless handling and in the postponement of suckling for long periods (Packer, 1980). The long-term data feature several kidnappings by the same individuals, suggesting individual differences in motivation or opportunity; and it is also clear that particular infants tended to be kidnapped on repeated occasions, which may reflect differences in maternal restrictiveness or negligence. The four infants that died in this way were younger than the majority that sustained wounds. There is considerable qualitative difference between fatal kidnapping and aggressive wounding, so that the two prevailing hypotheses concerning infant killing (see above) may not be applicable to kidnappings at all.

The two fatal kidnappings by adult females, one from each study-site, accord remarkably in that both were by females in late pregnancy who were dominant to the mothers of the infants. Altmann (1980: 206) described a similar kidnapping that, although not fatal, was also by a female who was dominant to the mother; while Strum (1975: 679) described a fatal incident involving a pregnant female. Although such behavior may represent reproductive competition among females, its accordance with general differences between high- and low-ranking mothers (Altmann, 1980) and with the reproductive state of the kidnappers suggest equally that the behavior could be social accident.

The possibility that kidnapping by males represents reproductive competition within that sex, in accordance with the sexual selection hypothesis of infanticide, is not supported by the two cases observed. This is primarily because of the relatedness of the kidnappers to the infants; one kidnapper was the brother, the other possibly the father. The adolescent male did not thereby gain mating access to his mother (who died shortly afterward); and there is no evidence that the adult male consorted with the mother of his victim when she next conceived, although she did conceive as early as 4 months after the infant's death. The proximate reasons for kidnapping by males are not always obvious but may be related to the short-term advantages of infant carrying that occur in several contexts (Ransom and Ransom, 1971; Altmann, 1980; Packer, 1980; Busse and Hamilton, 1981; Stein, 1981; Smuts, 1982).

Sexual Selection Hypothesis

The cases of male attacks upon infants, with or without their mothers, are now examined, first in terms of the identity of the males, then of that of the infants, and finally in terms of the likelihood of subsequent matings between the males and the infants' mothers. The sexual selection hypothesis predicts that males who kill infants will be recent immigrants who could not have fathered the infants. Of the two males who killed infants at Moremi, one (BB) had immigrated 2.5 months beforehand; the other was not identified. Two nonfatal attacks were by males (BF and an outsider) who could not have fathered the infants. Of the four fatal attacks at Gombe, males FA, AC, and BR had transferred in 2.5, 8.25, and 9.5 months before, respectively; male SG had remained in his natal troop. Thus, the majority of attackers were immigrant males in accordance with the prediction. The four Gombe males were young adults between 7.5 and 9 years of age; three of them were in their first troop of residence after emigration from their natal troop.

The sexual selection hypothesis predicts not only that infanticidal males are likely to be immigrants, but specifically that the infants they attack are those conceived before their arrival who could not be their offspring. Since the gestation period of baboons is 6 months, any infant born less than 6 months after a male's arrival would be at risk of attack. Of the five fatal attacks in which the males' identities were known, two involved infants born before the males arrived (males BB and FA) and two involved infants born shortly afterward (for AC, 1 month; for BR, 4 months); thus, for four of these five attacks, the males could not have fathered the infants. In the fifth attack, the male SG had been in the troop at the infant's conception but was unlikely to have fathered the infant, judging from mating records.

Conversely, older infants whose mothers have already resumed menstrual cycles should be at less risk because their mothers will not conceive any earlier should they die. At Gombe and Moremi, females resume menstrual cycles an average of 10 and 11.5 months after the birth of an infant that survives, and they conceive an average of 19 and 17.5 months after the birth. Of the six infants (including RF at Moremi) killed by males, five were between 6 and 9 months old. The sixth (MK) was only 4 days old, although the opportunity for this attack was inadvertently created when observers tranquilized the mother. Nevertheless, all six deaths support the prediction.

The sexual selection hypothesis depends in part on the assumption that because infant killing leads to earlier conception by the mother, the male attacker thereby gains an earlier opportunity of impregnating her. Although the reproductive cycle data from Gombe and Moremi support the first part of this assumption (also see Altmann et al., 1978), there are scant data to examine the second. The Moremi female whose 4-day-old infant was killed conceived again 6 months later (i.e., earlier than average), but observations were only sufficient to show that the male mated in her second cycle and probably not in her conception cycle. Three Gombe females all resumed cycling within 1 month of infant death and conceived earlier than the norm (i.e., 12, 14, and 16 months postpartum, and this despite the fact they had cycled as much as 6–8 months before conceiving). Only one of these females was seen to consort with the attacking male in her next conception cycle.

The sexual selection hypothesis also predicts that attacks should be directed at the infants rather than at their mothers. Two fatal attacks at Gombe were directed at infants (DN and MA) apart from their mothers, confirming that attacks can focus specifically on infants. In one case at Moremi, however, mother and infant (TX) were wounded at about the same time; and two attacks at Gombe were on mothers with infants ventral (UN and LI). It is not possible to say whether these two attacks at Gombe were directed more at the mother or the infant: once, only the infant was injured, and once, the male continued to harass the mother even after the infant was dead.

In summary, the fatal attacks upon infants at Gombe and Moremi have several features in accordance with predictions based upon sexual selection as the ultimate cause of this behavior. First, all but one of the observed attacks were by newcomer males who had immigrated after their victims were conceived and who could not have been their fathers. The exception involved a resident male who was unlikely to have been the father. Second, the victims were young enough that their deaths advanced the subsequent conceptions of their mothers. In contrast, there was only limited evidence that any of the attackers sired the next infants. The sample size was small, however, and the data were insufficient to assess what might have happened had they not killed the infants.

Social Disturbance Hypothesis

The discussion that follows examines the proximate causes of some of these incidents to evaluate the role of social disturbance in producing infant deaths. Social disturbance, characterized by high frequencies of fighting and by unstable dominance relationships, can originate from several sources, of which three are described here. Any of these sources may result in accidental injuries to infants, as these are the individuals least capable of defending themselves.

One source of social disturbance is from encounters between troops. Aggression during intertroop encounters is not limited to fighting between members of different troops, but more often involves males chasing females and young of their own troop away from members of other troops (Buskirk et al., 1974; Cheney and Seyfarth, 1977; Packer, 1979a). These encounters between troops provided the context for four attacks on infants (as also at Amboseli; see Shopland, 1982). In the present samples, one infant (BG) was wounded by a male from a different troop; another infant (in L Troop) was killed by a male member of the same troop, while the troop from which he had recently emigrated was nearby. Two other infants (MI and RC) received fatal wounds during approach–withdrawal encounters between two troops, but the attacks were not observed.

A second source of social disturbance is from the arrival of immigrant males, who sometimes are unusually aggressive for several months after their entry (Ransom, 1981: 259ff). This aggression can include persistent chasing of females (Pereira, 1983; D. A. Collins, unpublished). Immigrant male AC was frequently involved in aggressive interactions with other troop members during the period in which he killed infant DN. The fact that four of the five identified attackers had recently immigrated supports such disturbance as a proximate cause of infant killing, but at the same time it is consistent with sexual selection as an ultimate cause.

A third source of social disturbance is from changes in agonistic relationships among males within a troop. Natal male SG's rise to alpha rank in Gombe B Troop in late 1980 was followed by a 7-month period of considerable social disturbance, when SG was frequently involved in aggressive interactions with natal and resident males. Four infants died during this period. SG was seen to kill one of the infants (MA) and was strongly suspected of killing a second (RU). Causes of death for the other two infants were unknown. It is likely that the unusual degree of social tension was implicated in the deaths that occurred during this period.

Periods of social disturbance are sometimes characterized by relatively high frequencies of triadic interactions, in which one male carries an infant during a confrontation with another male, sometimes referred to as "agonistic buffering" (Deag and Crook, 1971). These interactions occasionally escalate to fights, during which infants may be injured. For example, following one triadic interaction observed at Gombe, an infant (MN) was found badly wounded and later was killed by chimpanzees (Packer, 1980). During the period of disturbance when four infants died following SG's rise to alpha rank, three adult males (two natal, one a long-term resident) carried infants with unusual frequency during interactions with SG. In all, five of the infants in Tables III and IV had been carried frequently by males in the months before death (MI, RC, RU, ME, and MA, excluding those mishandled in kidnapping) as had two in the larger sample (Table II). Thus, the carrying of infants by males during aggressive interactions may be implicated in some of these deaths in addition to the death of MN.

Events that immediately preceded the attacks were observed in only two cases. In one, an infant (DN) exhibited "ambivalence" behavior (Packer, 1979a) as it approached an immigrant male (AC). The male attacked the infant but was mobbed by other troop members defending it—only after chasing them did he inflict the fatal bites. In another attack, the male (SG) was first observed to be chasing females and young before he ran to the infant (MA) and bit it. There are two points of interest here. First, young baboons may show ambivalence to immigrant males (Packer, 1979a) both when alone and when in close vicinity of their male carriers (Ransom and Ransom, 1971); but in both contexts, ambivalence may be sufficient to elicit threats as in the case of DN. Second, both these fatal attacks occurred immediately after the male had been chasing other troop members, suggesting that a high level of aggressiveness might have promoted these killings.

The sources of disturbance previously identified—intertroop encounters, male transfer between troops, and changes of agonistic relationships within troops—are expected to be most prevalent at high population densities. Infant killing among langurs has been attributed to high population density (Curtin and Dolhinow, 1978), which might underlie some of the fatalities reported here, especially at Gombe, where the density of baboons is relatively high (Ransom, 1981). The necessary comparative data on population density in baboons and its relation to rates of intertroop encounters, male migration, and fighting within troops are not yet available, however.

CONCLUSION

Adult male savanna baboons at two African field sites have been observed fatally biting five infants (MK, UN, DN, MA, LI) and are suspected of killing at least eight others. These results add to the evidence of infant killing among primates living in multimale groups. Several features of these killings support the hypothesis that this behavior is a reproductive tactic of advantage to immigrant males, even though this hypothesis was originally formulated for primates living in one-male groups. However, the proximate causes of these killings remain elusive. Their circumstances suggest the importance of social disturbance, occurring during intertroop encounters, following the entry of immigrant males or arising from intense agonistic relationships between males in which infants are sometimes involved. Injuries occurring in any of these contexts are likely to take their heaviest toll upon infants. Further study of the relationships between adult male and infant baboons and of the causes and consequences of infant deaths will be required to definitively test these hypotheses. Regardless of the causes of infant killing, however, results of this and other studies (Packer, 1979a; Smuts, 1982, and in Hrdy, 1979; Busse and Hamilton, 1981; Stein, 1981) suggest that the combined protectiveness of most troop members toward infants limits the likelihood of infants being killed and contributes to the rarity with which infant killing is observed in multimale troops.

ACKNOWLEDGMENTS

The authors thank Glenn Hausfater, Sarah Blaffer Hrdy, Craig Packer, and Michael E. Pereira for valuable comments on drafts of this chapter. D. A. Collins and Jane Goodall would like to thank the Director and staff of Tanzania National Parks, the staff of the Gombe Stream Wildlife Research Institute, and especially Apollynaire Sindimwo for his contributions to the long-term study. D. A. Collins also thanks the Jane Goodall Institute for support and the Zoology Department of Edinburgh University for their hospitality. Curt D. Busse would like to thank Mr. K. T. Ngwamotsoko and the Office of the President, Botswana, for permission to conduct studies in the Moremi Wildlife Reserve. He also thanks William J. Hamilton III, Matthew P. Rowe, and Kenneth S. Smith for contributing observations. Research at Moremi was funded by NIH grant 5 R01 RR01078 (W. J. Hamilton III, P.I.). Chapter preparation was supported in part by NIH grant RR 00165 and NIMH grant 1 T32 MH 16543 to Emory University.

11

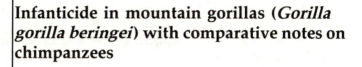

Infanticide in mountain gorillas (*Gorilla gorilla beringei*) with comparative notes on chimpanzees

Dian Fossey

Among the great apes, infanticide (the killing of maternally dependent offspring by conspecifics) has been reported among both common chimpanzees (*Pan troglodytes schweinfurthii*) and mountain gorillas (*Gorilla gorilla beringei*). Thus far, there is no indication that infanticide occurs among either of the other two great ape species, pygmy chimpanzees (*Pan paniscus*) or orangutans (*Pongo pygmaeus*), although Galdikas (1980) did report that two young rehabilitant orangutan females might have been killed by a young male rehabilitant. With respect to common chimpanzees, detailed descriptions of infanticidal episodes have been published by Goodall (1977) and Kawanaka (1981), respectively, for populations in the Gombe National Park and the Mahali Mountains of Tanzania, as well as by Suzuki (1971) for the Budongo Forest population of Uganda. In contrast, no comparable report concerning infanticide among mountain gorillas has yet been published, although brief descriptions of two infanticidal episodes were given by Fossey (1979, 1981). This chapter presents new and detailed information on the nature and frequency of infanticide among mountain gorillas and suggests that this behavior may occur with some regularity in at least one population of this species.

Over the last 15 years at the Karisoke Research Centre in Rwanda, researchers have directly observed, or have inferred from strong circumstantial evidence, nine episodes of infanticide among mountain gorillas as well as one case of attempted infant killing under the unusual circumstances of returning a captive infant to the wild. Most of these incidents took place during violent intergroup interactions that occurred when one silverback adult male challenged another for possession of females. In particular, infanticidal males were often relatively young silverbacks who were in the process of forming their own reproductive units.

Infanticide among mountain gorillas has also often had the effect of precipitating the emigration of the victim's mother to another social unit, and in three cases, the unit to which the mother transferred was in fact that of the infanticidal male. Thus, as in many other primate species, infanticide among gorillas appears to be primarily a reproductive tactic by which an adult male enhances his chances of gaining breeding females and thereby of siring additional offspring. However, in contrast to most other primate species where adult females gain little or nothing from the death of their offspring (Hrdy, 1979), infanticidal episodes among mountain gorillas result in the mother of the victim gaining an opportunity for rank advancement through becoming one of the initial females to bond with the infanticidal male. This is so because the dominance status of adult females in gorilla groups parallels the females' order of acquisition by the silverback.

By way of comparison, researchers at the three chimpanzee study sites just mentioned have recorded 12 cases of infanticide during 12 years of concurrent monitoring. All of these occurred during violent intra- or intercommunity conflicts, but in only one instance did the victim's mother transfer into the community of the known infanticidal male (Kawanaka, 1981). The selective advantage obtained by infanticidal individuals among chimpanzees is far less apparent than for gorillas. In part, this may reflect the fact that due to the nature of the chimpanzee mating system, the paternity of victims cannot be inferred with any certainty. In this regard, chimpanzees contrast sharply with mountain gorillas, which have the more restricted access to females expected in a mating system based on harem units. Also, infanticide among chimpanzees frequently is accompanied by cannibalism, a rare occurrence in gorillas.

This chapter presents a detailed summary of long-term data on infanticidal episodes in gorillas and then compares these observations to reports of infant killing and cannibalism in chimpanzees. Since the aggregate number of infanticidal episodes for gorillas is actually quite small, each case is described individually. Consistency has been lent to these descriptions by organizing the material under a series of subheadings that highlight specific data relevant to testing prevailing hypotheses concerning infanticide in primates (see Introduction, this volume). This review has not been presented to test those hypotheses per se but rather to point out the kinds of data that are presently available, and which yet need to be collected, so as to carry out the kind of rigorous testing that these hypotheses deserve. Furthermore, this review serves to underscore the fact that while infanticide among the great apes, especially gorillas, shows many similarities to infanticide in Old and New World monkeys (see other chapters, Part II, this volume), it is equally true that infanticidal episodes in both chimpanzees and gorillas show many features that are unique to this family, possibly reflecting their exceptional cognitive and social development.

BACKGROUND INFORMATION

Study Site and Demography

The infanticidal episodes described in this chapter occurred in the 375 km² conservation area surrounding the six extinct volcanoes of the Virunga mountain chain. Although some 240 mountain gorillas live in the Virungas today, the main study population consists of three groups totaling 37 individuals and 1 lone silverback male. The ratio of adult males to adult females is 1:1.7, and the mature to immature ratio is 1:1. The behavior and ecology of these study groups have been monitored since 1967 by the author and other investigators working from the Karisoke Research Centre of Rwanda within an area of approximately 25 km² surrounding the field station. Over the past 15 years, the mean number of individuals under consistent observation from the Centre has averaged 36 (range: 29–48), and in census and behavioral work from the Centre the animals have been classified into six age–sex categories. These same categories are used throughout this chapter and are defined as follows: (1) sexually mature males (silverbacks), 13–15 years or older; (2) sexually immature males (blackbacks), ages 8–13 years; (3) adult females, over 8 years; (4) young adults of both sexes, ages 6–8 years; (5) juveniles of both sexes, ages 3–6 years; and (6) infants of both sexes, 0–3 years.

Female gorillas are considered adolescents as of the time of their first observed sexual swelling that occurs, on the average, during the seventh year of life ($n = 13$; range: 6.4–8.6 years) (Fossey, 1982). Gorilla female adolescents do not undergo sexual cycles every month, but when they do enter estrus, their period of receptivity lasts from 3 to 5 days. The period of adolescent sterility averages 16 months ($n = 10$; range, 10.4–20.5 months). The period of receptivity for fully adult females is shorter than that for young adult females and lasts from 1 to 3 days per month. The median cycle length for 7 fully adult females was 26 days ($n = 24$; range: 25–40 days). The mean age at first parturition was 10 years ($n = 10$; range: 8.7–12 years); gestation averaged 260 days. The mean interbirth interval for 13 females was 39 months ($n = 26$; range: 14–59 months). When only viable births (those in which consecutive infants survived up to or beyond weaning) were considered, the mean interbirth interval for 10 females was 47.1 months ($n = 18$; range: 36–59 months). Among 7 females who had nonviable births (i.e., abortions or stillbirths) or whose dependent infants died or disappeared, the mean interbirth interval was 22.8 months ($n = 9$; range: 14–40 months. Thus, a substantial shortening of the interbirth interval results from the premature death of an infant, whether from infanticide or other natural causes.

In captivity, male gorillas may reach sexual maturity as early as 8 years of age (Schaller, 1963), but free-living male gorillas become sexually mature much later, between 13 and 15 years of age. This difference is probably due to the fact that, in the wild, males need to gain experience in interactions before they can acquire and retain females.

Gorilla Social Organization

Mountain gorillas live in relatively stable, cohesive, familial units termed *groups* that range in size from 2 to 20 individuals with a median size of 10 (Fossey, 1974). Each established group, as opposed to a newly forming group, contains at least 1 silverback male, usually 1 or 2 black-back males, 3 to 6 adult females, and 4 to 6 immatures. No gorilla group, either established or newly forming, can exist without a silverback leader. The leader is dominant over all group members and has almost complete exclusivity of breeding access to the females he has acquired from other groups during the group-formation process. The tenure of a silverback is typically terminated by death. Over a 15-year period, 2 aged silverback leaders (ca. 50 years old) died of natural causes, and 2 others were killed by poachers while in their prime (ca. 35 years). One aged silverback's group remained intact following his death because his sexually mature son "inherited" the group, but in the second case, the aged silverback's small group disintegrated under the inexperienced leadership of his sexually immature son. In the two cases in which prime silverbacks were slain, the groups were absorbed into other units because of the absence of sexually mature male residents at the time of the killings (Fossey, 1981; A. H. Harcourt and K. Stewart: personal communication).

The tight bonding of females to their harem leader and the small number of males within any one unit means that the paternity of offspring can be inferred with nearly complete certainty among gorillas. Paternity is unquestionable when there is only one sexually mature silverback within a gorilla group. Extraneous or nonresident silverbacks do not have breeding access to a group's resident females. Whenever two sexually mature males reside within a single group, strong inferences of paternity can be drawn from observations of courtship behavior and copulations. Dominant silverbacks usually express sexual interest only in those females they acquired from other groups. Thus, a group's younger females are generally bred by males who have matured to silverback status within their natal groups. These females have been sired either by the dominant silverback or his predecessor and thus may be related to the sexually maturing male with whom they mate. Over a 15-year period, 3 such males sired 12 offspring within their natal groups; 1 of these offspring was born to the sire's full sister and 3 to half-sisters; the relationship between the parents of the remaining 8 infants was not known.

Migration of Maturing Males and Females

Upon approaching sexual maturity, males will usually leave their natal groups if no potential breeding opportunities are available or if a second male resident is more closely related to the dominant silverback. The emigrant male travels for about 1 year peripheral to his natal group (i.e., within 300 m of them) before spending several additional years of more distant travel completely away from the group. During this time, males gain familiarity with other geographic areas and obtain experience in interactions with other silverbacks and the females contained in their groups. It is only through encounters with these harem units, which may last from several hours to 2 days, that silverbacks acquire females and form or enlarge their own groups. These encounters are usually marked by a high degree of physical aggression and display. Thus far, during the course of the Karisoke study, 10 males have reached sexual maturity. Two were successfully breeding within their natal groups until killed by poachers, and one is currently doing so. One other male successfully established a newly forming group outside of Karisoke's main study area, 1 is currently traveling alone but with an increasing frequency of interactions; and 1 has been assimilated into an unusual all-male group. For the remaining 4 males, data are incomplete.

Like males, females approaching sexual maturity also usually leave their natal groups if no potential breeding opportunities are available. Unlike males, however, females rarely travel alone. They transfer directly to a lone silverback or to another group. Characteristic among gorilla females is a linear dominance hierarchy in which rank order basically depends upon order of entry into the group. For this reason, it is advantageous for an emigrating female to avoid transferring to a large, well-established group of several matrilines but rather to select a lone silverback or smaller unit where she and her offspring will enjoy a high-rank position.

Over the past 15 years, 18 females are known to have transferred between social units 32 times. Ten of these females emigrated from a common natal group either simultaneously or within a few months' time of one another. The impression here is that females transferring as such a pair are far more likely to successfully integrate themselves into an existing dominance hierarchy than are individual females. As well, these female pairs generally achieve higher reproductive success than singletons because of diminished tendencies toward further movements and thus a reduced exposure to infanticide. Of the 10 females who transferred as pairs, data are incomplete for 2 who, after their first transfer together, left the study group. The remaining 8, over a period of 102 months (June 1974–December 1982) carried out a total of only 14 transfers (two pairs transferred twice after brief stays in two groups) and gave birth to 13 offspring, none of whom were subjected to infanticide.

In contrast, 8 females emigrated singly from their natal groups or from the group in which they were first contacted in 1967. Of these 8 females, data are incomplete for 5, but it is known that 3 of these 5 females gave birth at least once, and that all 3 infants were subsequently lost (1 to infanticide, 2 to unknown causes). A sixth single-transfer female and her juvenile were killed by poachers, and among the remaining 2 singleton females, only 1 infant was born over a 53-month period (July 1978–December 1982).

Over this same 15-year period, 8 adult females have remained within their natal group or within the group in which they were first contacted in 1967. Four of these 8 females are now deceased, but during the observational period, these "nontransfer" females bore 13 offspring, only 1 of which was a victim of intragroup infanticide. Despite the increasing amount of data on female transfers, it still is not known whether female transfers primarily reflect the reproductive interests of the females themselves or that of the silverbacks by whom they are eventually acquired.

The female-transfer process between established groups or from a group to a lone silverback almost always involved overt aggression between the leader of the female's current group and the competing silverback. No adults were known to have been directly killed during these intergroup interactions, though bite wounds inflicted in such encounters resulted in the eventual death of one female and systemic pathologies in three silverbacks. Additionally, 38% ($n = 13$) of all infant deaths over 15 years of study were directly attributable to infanticide. Another 23% were strongly suspected to have been infanticide. Given the long period of dependency of the gorilla infant upon its mother and the violent means by which silverbacks acquire their harems, it seems likely that all sexually mature males at some time in their lives carry out infanticide, and that most females probably have at least one infant that falls victim to the attack of a silverback.

INFANTICIDAL EPISODES

Nine cases of gorilla infanticide and one attempted infant killing are described here. The victims of the lethal attacks ranged in age from newborn to 11 months; the victim of the attempted killing was an estimated 30–33 months of age. The infanticidal episodes are presented in order of decreasing observational detail, thus increasing extent of inference.

Case 1

Victim. Thor, an 11-month-old female, was born in June 1973 to primiparous female, Macho, in Group 8. At the time of her death, Thor appeared in good health and weighed 4.6 kg. When killed, Thor had one paternal half-sibling in the group, a blackback male named Peanuts, and was estimated as about 12 years of age. Thor's mother, Macho, had transferred from her natal group, Group 4, to Group 8 when about 10 years of age. Thor was sired by the aged silverback leader of Group 8, Rafiki, who died of pneumonia 28 days prior to Thor's death by infanticide.

Infanticidal episode. Thor's death was observed by A. H. Harcourt and an autopsy was conducted by the author in conjunction with staff members at the University of Butare (Rwanda). On May 19, 1974, Group 4 (then consisting of 10 members) and the 3 members of Group 8 approached each other, seemingly without aggressive tendencies, near the periphery of their respective ranges. The following day, a violent physical interaction occurred between Uncle Bert, the silverback leader of Group 4, and Macho, Thor's mother. At this time, Thor was bitten several times by Uncle Bert. The fatal wound was believed to have been a 5-cm bite wound into the infant's skull. A second wound of 12 cm was found in the victim's lower ventral abdominal wall exposing the colon, cecum, appendix, and breaking the pubic symphysis. That same night Macho left Thor's body some 10 m away from the site of her night nest.

Five months following Thor's death, Macho transferred back to her natal Group 4 during an unobserved interaction between Group 4 and blackback male Peanuts, the only remaining adult male from Group 8. Trail signs (blood deposits, silverback hair tufts, large areas of trampled vegetation) indicated that the interaction had been violent in nature. Fourteen months after Thor's death, Macho gave birth to her second infant, a male named Kweli. Since her time with Group 4 substantially exceeded the gestation period for gorillas, it is safe to presume that Kweli was sired by the leader of Group 4, Uncle Bert, the same male who had killed Thor.

Key elements and overall impressions. The infant death followed the loss of the silverback leader of the infant's group and preceded the mother's transfer to the group of the infanticidal male. The resultant interbirth interval was less than that for the population as a whole, 25 months compared to 39 months. Thus, the male who committed the infanticide: (1) eliminated an unrelated offspring sired by one of his competitors; (2) added a female to his own group; and (3) shortened his waiting time to insemination of that female.

Case 2

Victim. Frito, a 3-month-old female, was born on June 22, 1978 to multiparous female, Flossie, in Group 4. At the time of her death, Frito appeared in good health and weighed 2.3 kg. She had two full siblings in Group 4: a 7-year-old sister (Cleo) and a 4-year-old brother (Titus), as well as two half-siblings, an 8-year-old sister (Augustus) and a 3-year-old brother (Kweli). Frito's mother, Flossie, had been in Group 4 for at least 11 years prior to Frito's birth. She occupied the highest rank and was strongly bonded to the silverback leader, Uncle Bert, the presumed sire. Uncle Bert was killed by poachers 21 days prior to the infanticide. Following Uncle Bert's death, the remaining adult males in the group were a sexually immature silverback (Beetsme), an immigrant to Group 4, and a natal blackback male (Tiger).

Infanticidal episode. Frito's death was observed by D. Watts and an autopsy was conducted by the author. The death occurred on August 14, 1978 during a violent intragroup interaction between the sexually immature silverback, Beetsme, and Flossie despite the protective efforts of the blackback, Tiger. The fatal wound, inflicted by Beetsme, was believed to have been a 3-cm bite in Frito's brachial plexus that splintered the humerus and severed the right brachial artery and vein. Flossie carried Frito's body for 2 days. During this time, she was repeatedly attacked by Beetsme, and Tiger consistently came to her aide. During the seventh attack, Flossie dropped Frito's body and did not attempt to retrieve it, possibly because she was still being pursued by Beetsme. She did, however, look back to where the body lay for a full minute following the attack. Later the same day, Beetsme strutted and directed running attacks toward Flossie an additional four times.

Three days following the infanticide, Flossie presented and copulated with Beetsme twice. Between the two copulations, Beetsme directed 13 separate incidents of aggression toward Flossie in the form of chasing, strutting, and hitting. Following the second copulation, he aggressively displayed 18 times toward Flossie. Seven days following Frito's death, Flossie transferred to Group N and remained in that group of eight members (including four adult females), a total of 18 days before next transferring to Group S, composed of four members, including one nulliparous female. In both transfers, she was accompanied by her 7-year-old daughter; however, her 4-year-old son remained in Group 4. Approximately 11 months following Flossie's transfer to Group S, she gave birth to her sixth infant (Anjin). Since Flossie's time in Group S was greater than gestation, it may be assumed that this infant was sired by the Group S dominant silverback (J.P.).

Key element and overall impressions. The infant death followed the loss of the silverback leader of the infant's group, and the unrelated infanticidal male had come from another group 31 months previously. The infant's killing preceded the transfer of the mother to another group. The resultant interbirth interval was less than that for the population as a whole, 14 months compared to 39 months. However, the silverback male in whose group the female eventually settled, rather than the infanticidal male, obtained the reproductive advantage resulting from the shortened waiting time to insemination of this female.

Case 3

Victim. Mwelu, an 8-month-old female, was born around April 6, 1978 to primiparous female, Simba, in Group 4. Mwelu had shown normal physical and social development, appeared in good health, and weighed 3.87 kg at the time of her death. She had no siblings in Group 4 and possibly for this reason maintained unusually close physical contact with Simba, her mother. Simba was herself born into Group 4 and as an orphan had been closely protected throughout her juvenile stage (3–6 years) by Group 4's silverback leader, Uncle Bert. Perhaps due to Uncle Bert's protection, Simba was seldom involved in intragroup disputes and was well accepted by other group members. Although Uncle Bert showed no sexual interest in Simba, a young natal silverback, Digit, did do so and was most likely the sire of Mwelu. Both Digit and Uncle Bert were eventually killed by poachers, but Simba and Mwelu remained with younger Group 4 males for 5 months thereafter.

Infanticidal episode. Events surrounding Mwelu's death were inferred by tracking and later observations made by I. Redmond who also did the autopsy. On December 5, 1978, Group 4, led by the victim's mother, Simba, made an approach toward Group N. On the basis of spoor evidence, it is strongly suspected that the infant was killed by Nunkie, the dominant silverback male of Group N, on the morning of December 6, 1978. Mwelu's body was found 14 m from the night nests of Nunkie and Simba and 27 m from the nests of the remaining members of Group 4. Rigor mortis had not yet set in. The presumed fatal bite was to the skull; another deep wound was evident in the groin region. A third wound was found on the inner surface of the left thigh, and the rib cage had been crushed. Simba transferred to Group N the same day that Mwelu was killed, and she began to solicit copulations with the silverback male of that group 55 days later. Few data are available on Simba after this time, although it is known that she gave birth to an infant 32 months after joining Group N.

Key elements and overall impressions. As in the previous case, the infant's death followed the loss of the silverback leader of its group. A lack of breeding opportunities for the mother of the infant, coupled with her vulnerability in a leaderless group, seemed to promote this female's search for another social unit. Her resultant encounter with another group coincided with her infant's death due to bite wounds most likely inflicted by the silverback of that group. Following the infant's death, the mother transferred to the presumed killer's group and bred with him.

Case 4

Victim. Curry, a 9-month-old male, was born in August 1972 to a primiparous female, Bravado, from Group 5. Curry's physical and social development appeared normal at the time of his death; he had no siblings in the group. Bravado, when first observed in September 1967, was estimated at nearly 6 years old and was associated closely with the then current silverback leader. In January 1971, at the estimated age of about 9 years, Bravado transferred to Group 5 from her presumed natal group, Group 4. Group 5's leader and dominant male was Beethoven, estimated as more than 40 years of age, and he was the only sexually mature male in the group at the time of Curry's conception.

Infanticidal episode. The infanticide was inferred from tracking observations made by A. H. Harcourt, the author, and local staff. Curry's autopsy was conducted at the Ruhengeri Hospital with the assistance of R. Elliott. Curry was killed on April 14, 1974 following 2 days of interactions between Group 5 and an unidentified silverback. The silverback's trail merged with that of Group 5 to form a large area of flattened vegetation; broken branches, loose dung deposits, and some blood droppings were found in this area. Subsequently, individual trails of Group 5 members scattered in all directions, indicative of the animals' extreme fear, before merging together to form a single, rapid flight trail. Curry's body lay on this trail some 500 m from the interaction site. The fatal wound was thought to be a 7.5-cm-long bite in the lower groin which fractured the femur. Additionally, there was a 3.5-cm clavicular bite, a 3 cm-long cranial bite, and seven lesser wounds. Group 5 rapidly traveled another 1.5 km from the interaction site before building their night nests. The group's travel was unusually rapid the next day, and they covered 2 km. Two months after Curry's death, Bravado transferred to a small, lesser-known group, and no further observations are available on her.

Key elements and overall impressions. The infant death occurred during an encounter of the infant's group with a lone silverback who can safely be assumed to have been unrelated to either the victim or its mother. After a few months delay, the infant's mother transferred from her group to join another silverback and his small group. It was not known whether or not this was the infanticidal male, nor is it known how shortly thereafter she again reproduced.

Case 5

Victim. Banjo, a 5-month-old infant of undetermined sex was born the first week of October 1975 to a primiparous female, Pantsy, in Group 5. Banjo's physical development seemed normal at the time of death. Banjo's relatives within the group included a grandmother, uncle, half-brothers, and half-sisters. Banjo's mother, Pantsy, was estimated as about 17 months old in September 1967 when first seen in her natal group, Group 5. The single sexually mature male in this group, Beethoven, was probably the sire of Banjo.

Infanticidal episode. The infanticide was inferred from tracking and dung examination by the author and local staff. Banjo disappeared in the twenty-sixth week of life during a series of intense intragroup aggressive interactions in March 1976. The infant's body was never found despite intensive searching. However, 133 fragments of bone, teeth, and the hair of an infant gorilla were found in the dung of two other group members, the dominant female (Effie) and her young adult daughter (Puck). Although meat eating of any kind is extremely rare among mountain gorillas, cannibalism seems likely. A 16-month study involving extensive examinations of gorilla dung revealed no similar bone or teeth fragments. Within 2 months following Banjo's death, Pantsy was observed copulating with her paternal half-brother, Icarus. Eleven months following Banjo's death, Pantsy gave birth to a female, Muraha, presumably sired by this male.

Key elements and overall impressions. In this case, the infant death was not preceded by the loss of the group's silverback leader nor the infant's presumed sire. The infanticide also did not result in the transfer of the mother to another group. It did result, however, in a change of mating partners for the mother and a very short interbirth interval of 16 months.

Case 6

Victim. Phocas, a 1-day-old male was born February 24, 1967 to female, No Name, of Kabara Group 2. The first morning of life, the infant appeared healthy and was seen clinging independently to its mother's abdomen as she chestbeat at the author. Paddy, the dominant and only silverback in Kabara Group 2, was estimated as 25–30 years of age and was the presumed sire of Phocas.

Infanticidal episode. Phocas' death was observed by the author and local staff, and an autopsy was later performed by the author. On the night of February 23, 1967, a lone silverback took an adult female from Kabara Group 2 and night nested with her 60 m below the nest site of the group. Throughout the night and the early morning of 24 February 1967, visual and auditory observations confirmed that the lone silverback copulated with the unidentified female at least five times. During this time, there were also numerous vocal exchanges between the silverback of Kabara Group 2 and the lone silverback. Early on the morning of the 24 February, the female returned to Kabara Group 2 despite the efforts of the lone silverback to herd her away. Displays by both silverbacks continued throughout the day as the lone male followed roughly ½ km behind the group. About 9 hours later, the lone male charged directly into the group, and No Name ran toward him as if to impede his charge. She stood bipedally to chestbeat within arm's length of the silverback, who struck at her ventral surface. Immediately after the blow, a soft wail was heard from the infant, who had been clinging to his mother's ventrum throughout this interaction, and the wail was followed by an outbreak of intense screaming from Kabara Group 2. The lone silverback then chased the group out of the author's sight.

The following day, the infant's body was observed being dragged by his mother who, at that time, was seen to have received serious head wounds. No Name dragged and carried Phocas' body for 3 days before finally leaving the highly decomposed corpse in a day nest. Autopsy results revealed that the infant's rib cage and midsection had been crushed and the neck broken. About an 8-cm portion of the umbilical cord was still attached. By March 1, 1967, the mother's own physical condition had greatly deteriorated, and when the group was contacted on March 4, 1967, No Name was not with them and was presumed dead.

Key elements and overall impressions. The infant death in this case was not preceded by the loss of the silverback leader of the infant's group but did occur during the intrusion into the infant's group of a silverback male attempting to obtain an adult female from that group. Clearly, this case of infanticide had the effect of eliminating the offspring of a rival silverback, but the infanticidal male did not directly gain additional reproductive success from the infant's death.

Cases 7, 8, and 9

Victims. Three male infants' bodies were recovered from various census groups outside the main study area. One infant was a newborn, another estimated as 4 months old, and the third an estimated 9 months old; mothers and sires were unknown.

Infanticidal episodes. In the cases of both the 9-month-old and the 4-month-old victims, adult male vocal displays had been heard from the areas where the bodies were eventually found. Specifically, the 4-month-old infant was found in an adult's nest near an interaction site but had no external wounds; the 9-month-old infant had groin and head wounds, apparently inflicted by the bite of a silverback. The newborn had a fractured skull also seemingly the result of a bite wound from a silverback.

Key elements and overall impressions. Wound morphology and auditory clues were suggestive of infanticide; however, no direct observations were available, and thus infanticide remains only an inference.

Case 10: Attempted Infanticide

Victim. Bonne Année was, at the time, a 30–33-month-old wild-caught female of unknown parentage. This infant female was recovered from poachers after 2–3 weeks in captivity and was brought to the Karisoke Research Centre on 1 January 1980. After a 2-month recovery period, she was presented successively to two groups (Group 5 and Group 4) for the purpose of reintroduction to the wild. Bonne Année's site of origin was not precisely known, but she was almost certainly alien to both of the groups to which she was introduced.

Attempted infanticide episode. Bonne Année was released to Group 5 by the author and J. Fowler on March 1, 1980. The group consisted of the aged dominant silverback (Beethoven), his sexually mature silverback son (Icarus), four adult females, and their respective offspring. The dominant female, Effie, was in her sixth month of pregnancy; her matriline consisted of three daughters and one grandson. The matriline of a second adult female, Marchessa, consisted of a daughter, two sons, and one granddaughter. Effie and her young adult daughter, Tuck, were the first members of Group 5 to approach Bonne Année and immediately began biting, throwing, dragging, and hitting her. The author recovered the infant from the two females, but after 10 minutes, Bonne Année voluntarily returned to them. Effie and Tuck immediately resumed their harassment of the infant but were stopped twice by Beethoven. However, upon the elderly silverback's departure, his son, Icarus, joined Effie and Tuck for more vicious attacks on Bonne Année until Beethoven interrupted them again. When he left this second time, Icarus and Tuck immediately resumed their abuse of the infant until the author again intervened for fear of the infant's life.

Twenty days later, on March 20, 1980, Bonne Année was released to Group 4, an unusual all-male group composed of three silverbacks, three blackbacks, and one immature male. None of the individuals in this heterogeneous assemblage of males were closely related to each other as they had come from at least three different natal groups. Bonne

Année was instantly accepted by the males and remained an integral member of Group 4 until succumbing to pneumonia 14 months later. *Key elements and overall impressions.* The infant was attacked only when released into a stable group bonded with strong inter- and intra-generational kinship ties. It is particularly noteworthy that adult females were active in the attacks of this infant, an occurrence inferred in Case 5 and also reported among chimpanzees (see below). In contrast, the infant was readily accepted in a group of more heterogeneous composition and structure that had neither a strong female dominance hierarchy nor strong kinship ties.

COMPARISON WITH INFANTICIDE AMONG CHIMPANZEES

Salient features of the preceding nine episodes of gorilla infanticide are summarized in Table I, while comparable information from the literature on chimpanzees in given in Table II. Available data on infant mortality in chimpanzees at Gombe show that between 1965 and 1976, 8 of 29 live-born infants died during the first year of life, and that at least one-half of these deaths can be attributed to infanticide (Goodall, 1977). At Mahali Mountains, infanticide was known to account for 22% (n = 18) of all infant deaths in a sample of 33 live-born infants between 1965 and 1979 (Kawanaka, 1981). No comparative data are available for the third chimpanzee study site, Budongo. Chimpanzees, unlike gorillas, live in large multimale, multifemale aggregations known as "communities" (Goodall, 1977). In a process analogous to group changing by maturing gorilla females, adolescent female chimpanzees frequently transfer between communities (Pusey, 1980). In 11 cases where data were available from Gombe and Mahali, the mothers of 5 of the victims were from a community other than that of the attacker, and their infants had been sired outside of the attacker's community. The other 6 mothers of infanticide victims had been born in the attacker's community or had immigrated into it before their offspring were conceived. Since these 6 infants were presumably sired within the same community in which they were killed, the possibility exists that they were killed by male relatives.

With respect to the identity of the infanticidal individual, Table II shows three kinds of infanticidal episodes among chimpanzees: (1) adult males killing and cannibalizing infants of females from neighboring communities; (2) adult males killing and partially consuming infants from their own communities; and (3) adult females killing and cannibalizing infants from their own communities. Both intra- and intercommunity infanticide by males has been reported from the Mahali Mountains field site, while only intercommunity infanticide by males has been observed at Gombe. Likewise, chimpanzee infanticide by females has

Table I. Gorilla infanticide episodes, Karisoke Research Centre[a]

Date	Infant (mother)	Occasion	Aggressors	Animals present	Observers	Comments
1. May 1974	Thor: 11-mo female [Macho's]	Intergroup interaction Groups 4, 8	Uncle Bert (Group 4)	3 adult males, 5 adult females, 5 immatures	Harcourt	Macho emigrates to Group 4; interbirth interval 25 mo
2. Aug 1978	Frito: 3-mo female [Flossie's]	Intragroup interaction Group 4	Beetsme (Group 4)	2 adult males, 3 adult females, 3 immatures	Watts	Flossie emigrates to Group S; interbirth interval 14 mo
3. Dec 1978	Mwelu: 8-mo female [Simba's]	Intergroup interaction Groups 4, N	Nunkie (Group N)	3 adult males, 6 adult females, 5 immatures	None	Simba emigrates to Group N; interbirth interval 40 mo (not consecutively followed)
4. Apr 1973	Curry: 9-mo male [Bravado's]	Intergroup/silverback interaction Group 5, lone silverback	Lone silverback (?)	3 adult males, 5 adult females, 7 immatures	None	Bravado emigrates to lesser known group; interbirth interval not known
5. Mar 1976	Banjo: 5-mo sex? [Pantsy's]	Intragroup interaction Group 5	Effie (?) Puck (?) (Group 5)	2 adult males, 4 adult females, 5 immatures	None	Pantsy remains in Group 5; interbirth interval 14 mo; cannibalistic inference
6. Feb 1967	Phocas: newborn male [No Name's]	Intergroup/silverback interaction Group 2, lone silverback	Lone silverback	3 adult males, 5 adult females, 2 immatures	Fossey Sankwekwe	No Name severely wounded, disappeared, and assumed dead
7. ? 1971	9-mo ? male	?	?	?	None	Bodies recovered from lesser census groups
8. ? 1973	4-mo ? male	?	?	?	None	
9. ? 1973	Newborn male	?	?	?	Fossey	
10. Mar 1980	Bonne Année: 30-33-mo female (captive)	Attempted reintroduction to wild via Group 5	Attempted infanticide by Icarus, Effie, Tuck (Group 5)	3 adult males, 4 adult females, 6 immatures	Fowler	Bonne Année retrieved from Group 5 and later successfully reintroduced to wild via Group 4

[a] Gorilla infanticide episodes listed in order of decreasing observational detail. See text for further information.

Table II. Chimpanzee infanticide episodes[a]

Date (site)	Infant (mother)	Occasion	Aggressor(s)	Present	Cannibal(s)	Observer(s)	Comments
1. Nov 1967 (Budongo)	Newborn sex? (unknown)	?	Adult male(s)?	5 adult males, 1 female, 1 infant	Adult males	Suzuki	Killed by eating; umbilical cord seen; intermittent feeding; bizarre behavior
2. Sept 1971 (Gombe)	1.5–2-year sex? (stranger's)	Intercommunity	Adult males	5 adult males, 2 females, 2 immatures	3 adult males	Bygott Plooij	Severe attack on mother; killed by eating; intermittent feeding; bizarre behavior
3. Aug 1975 (Gombe)	3-week female (Gilka's)	Intracommunity	Adult female	2 adult females, 2 immatures	1 adult female and all offspring (3)	Do Fisoo Matama	Killed by biting into frontal bones; continuous feeding for 5 hr
4. Oct 1975 (Gombe)	1.5–2-year male (stranger's)	Intercommunity	Adult male(s)?	4 adult males, 1 adult female	3 adult males	Bambanganya	Ad. males found with carcass; bizarre behavior; large portion abandoned
5. Nov 1975 (Gombe)	1.5–2-year female (stranger's)	Intercommunity	Adult males	5 adult males, 2 adult females, 4 immatures	None	Mpongo Sulemani	Severe attack on mother; infant seized; bizarre behavior; abandoned; died of injuries
6. Jan 1976 (Gombe)	1-week male (Melissa's)	Intracommunity	Adult female(s) (inferred)	?	None	Mpongo	Mother found in large group carrying her dead, bleeding infant

No. Date (Location)	Victim	Type	Killer(s)	Witnesses	Consumers	Observers	Comments
7. Oct 1976 (Gombe)	3-week male (Gilka's)	Intracommunity	Adult females	2 adult females, 2 immatures	1 adult female and all offspring (3)	Mpongo Kipuyo Do Fisoo	Severe attack on mother; infant killed by biting into forehead; continuous feeding for 5 hr
8. Nov 1976 (Gombe)	3-week female (Melissa's)	Intracommunity	Adult females	2 adult females, 1 immature, victim's mother, and 1 immature offspring	1 adult female and 1 offspring	Lukemai Bambanganya	Severe attack on mother; victim's mother and 1 immature offspring stay to watch continuous feeding for 2 hrs+
9. Apr 1974 (Mahali)	3-year male (Wamkime's)	Intercommunity	Adult male	?	Adult males	Field staff	Most of carcass consumed
10. Jan 1976 (Mahali)	1.5-year male (Wantendele's)	Intercommunity	Adult male(s)?	?	?	Field staff	Severe attack on mother
11. Jan 1977 (Malahi)	2-mo male (Ndilo's)	Intracommunity	Adult male(s)?	Adult males	Adult males	Norikoshi	Intermittent feeding for 8 hrs+
12. Jun 1979 (Mahali)	1.5-mo male (Wakasunga's)	Intracommunity	Adult male	Adult males, females, immatures totalling 14 individuals	2 adult males, 1 adult female	Seifu Kanawaka	Most of carcass consumed after continuous feeding for 3 hr

[a] From Suzuki (1971), Goodall (1977), Kawanaka (1981). Chimpanzee infanticide episodes reported from the Budongo, Gombe and Mahali Mountains study areas.

been reported only from Gombe, and the same mother–daughter pair was involved in all events.

Several other differences in infanticide also exist between these two chimpanzee study sites. At Mahali, corpses of infanticide victims were nearly entirely consumed, either through intermittent or continuous feeding by adult males. In contrast, at Gombe only the one infanticidal mother–daughter pair were observed to completely cannibalize their victims, while infanticidal males consumed very little of their victims or none at all. Similarly, "bizarre" behavior directed at the victim's corpse—pounding, poking, playing with, or flailing the body—was not observed at the Mahali Mountains site. Such behavior has been frequently reported at Gombe but was shown only by infanticidal adult males and not by the infanticidal female pair. Other than these few differences and similarities between study sites, the data on infanticide in chimpanzees do not easily lend themselves to drawing conclusions or generalizations concerning the phenomenon of infant killing and cannibalism.

CONCLUSIONS

Observations of infanticide among gorillas and chimpanzees are surprisingly common when the small base of reliable data for these two species is taken into account. Although data on this subject are rapidly increasing, the formulation of any single comprehensive and clear-cut explanation of infanticide among the great apes remains elusive. At present, cases of infants killed by adult male gorillas are virtually always associated with the formation of new breeding bonds by females and seem best explained by the sexual selection hypothesis. However, that fact that among chimpanzees, and possibly also among gorillas, both sexes have been implicated in killing infants leaves open the possibility that this behavior may also stem from competition for resources or paternal investment in offspring. Such ambiguity of explanation is not lessened by knowing that killers sometimes consume all or part of the corpses of their victims, an event most parsimoniously explained as direct exploitation of the infant as a food source (Hrdy, 1979). Finally, the involvement of one particular mother–daughter pair in all of the known cases of female infanticide among chimpanzees— as well as the association of bizarre behavior with infanticide in this species—raises the possibility that some of the cases reviewed may indeed reflect idiosyncratic or pathological behavior of little evolutionary significance. As for most primate species, the precise causes and consequences of infanticide among the great apes are yet to be determined. Nevertheless, it does seem safe to assume that infanticide will eventually prove to be of importance for understanding both the struc-

ture of individual life histories among the great apes and the dynamics
of their groups, communities, and populations.

ACKNOWLEDGMENTS

The author remains deeply indebted to the National Geographic Society for their
long-term support to the Karisoke Research Centre and to the students and assistants
who have contributed toward the research results of the Centre, particularly during
my absences. I should also like to express my appreciation to Glenn Hausfater for
organizing the Wenner-Gren Symposium No. 88, and to both Glenn Hausfater and Sarah
Blaffer Hrdy for many hours devoted to editing this chapter.

12 Reproductive parameters, adult-male replacements, and infanticide among free-ranging langurs (*Presbytis entellus*) at Jodhpur (Rajasthan), India

Christian Vogel
Hartmut Loch

INTRODUCTION

Since the first report of infant killing in Hanuman langurs (*Presbytis entellus*) by Sugiyama (1965b), numerous hypotheses regarding the biological function and/or causation of infanticide in langurs have been developed (reviewed in Hausfater and Vogel, 1982). Most discussion, however, has concentrated on the sexual selection hypothesis (Hrdy, 1974). The aim of this chapter is to test this hypothesis as well as its basic assumptions against field data from our long-term study (1977–1982) of langurs at Jodhpur (Rajasthan), India.

Evidence of Infanticide in Relation to Hypothesis Testing

Evidence of infanticide in *Presbytis entellus*, usually in connection with or following adult-male replacements in bisexual troops, has been published in detail for three study sites in India: Dharwar (Sugiyama, 1965a,b, 1966), Jodhpur (Mohnot, 1971a; Makwana, 1979), and Mt. Abu (Hrdy, 1974, 1977b) (Fig. 1). Further reports of infant killing—not yet published in detail—come from Harihar (Parthasarathy and Rahaman, 1974), from Polonnaruwa, Sri Lanka (Dittus and Ripley: personal communication), and, more recently, from Jodhpur (Sommer, in press). At several other places where extensive field studies have been carried out (e.g., Kaukori and Simla in India, Melemchi and Junbesi in Nepal; Fig. 1), infanticide has not been observed (Boggess, Chapter 14, this volume).

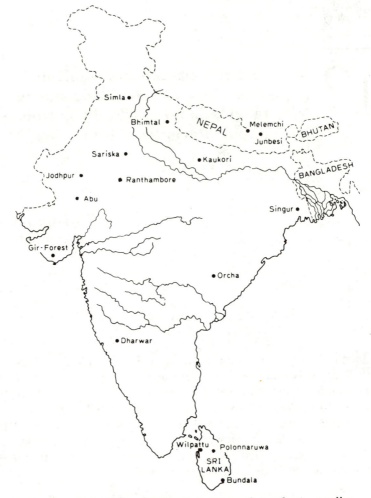

Figure 1. Location of main study sites of *Presbytis entellus.*

In total, the death or disappearance of about 50 infants has been attributed to infanticide (Table I; cf. Boggess, Chapter 14, this volume). It should, however, be emphasized that in only three or four of these cases has infanticide actually been witnessed and described by a scientific observer. All the other instances are suspected cases of infanticide that have been inferred (1) from observed male attacks on infants; (2) from attacks on mothers carrying unweaned infants that resulted in injuries to the infants; (3) from observations of freshly wounded infants; (4) from examination of dead infants that had obviously been killed by biting; (5) from disappearances of infants around the time of male replacements; or (6) from reports by local informants (Table

Table I. Presumptive evidence of infant killing in *Presbytis entellus*[a]

Reference	Troop	Infanticide	Biting of infants	Living infants with injuries	Dead infants with injuries	Infant's disappearance attributed to infant killing	Infanticide observed by others and reported to the author	Page numbers of references
				Dharwar				
SUGIYAMA (1965b)	30			AI (♂/9.8 mo)[b]		Bi(♀/10.7 mo), AI (♂/10.0 mo)[b], FI (♂/7.1–8.1 mo), CI (♂/6.5–7.5 mo), Ii (♀/11.7 mo)[b], Ej (♀/1–2 years)		pp. 391,392; pp. 391,392,394; pp. 395,397; pp. 395,397; pp. 397–398; pp. 395–397
SUGIYAMA (1965a, 1966)	2		Ii (♀/11.6 mo)[b]	Ii (♀/11.6 mo)[b], KI (♂/7.0 mo)[b], RI (♂/7.0 mo)[b]		Ui (♀/6.2 mo), KI (♂/7.0 mo)[b], SI (♀/6.6 mo), RI (♂/7.0 mo)[b]		p. 49; pp. 49–51; p. 51; pp. 51–53
				Jodhpur				
MOHNOT (1971a)	Bijolai (B26)	(♂/3.3 mo)[b], (♂/3.4 mo)[b], (♀/3.1 mo)	(♂/3.3 mo)[b], (♂/3.4 mo)[b]			(♀/4.0 mo), (?/1 week)[c]		pp. 188–190,193; pp. 191–192, 193–194
MAKWANA (1979)	Kaga A			(♂/1 year), (♂/4 mo), (♂/1 year), (♂/1 year), (♂/5 mo)		3 inf. (?/1–2 mo)		pp. 297–298; p. 298; p. 298; p. 298; p. 298

continued

239

Table I. (*Continued*)

Observations by the author

Reference	Troop	Infanticide	Biting of infants	Living infants with injuries	Dead infants with injuries	Infant's disappearance attributed to infant killing	Infanticide observed by others and reported to the author	Page numbers of references
				Mount Abu				
HRDY (1977b)	Hillside 1971					4 inf. (?/?)	2 inf. (?/?)	pp. 243,247,267
	Bazaar 1972					(?/8–9 mo)	2 inf. (?/8–9 mo)	pp. 37,249–250,267
	Hillside 1972		Scratch (♂/5–6 mo)^b	Scratch (♂/5–6 mo)^b		Scratch (♂/9–11 mo)^b	Mira (♀/5.5 mo)	pp. 242,255–258, 260–261
	Hillside 1973		Pawla (♀/3–4 mo)^b	Pawla (♀/3–4 mo)^b		Virginia (♀/13–15 mo)		pp. 262,263
	Bazaar 1975				(?/newborn)^b	[Pawla (♀/5–14 mo)^b]^d (?/newborn)	(?/newborn)^b,e	pp. 40,265
	Hillside 1975					[(♀/?)]^f		pp. 69,267
	Toad Rock 1975		N.M. (♀/12–13 mo)^b	N.M. (♀/12–13 mo)^b		[(♀/1.7–5.6 mo)]^g		pp. 268,278

^a Additional reports on infant killing without giving details are cited in: Sugiyama (1967) for Dharwar: 4–5 infants of Troop 1; Mohnot (1974) for Jodhpur: 6 infants (black-coated) of Mandore (B7), 3 infants (black-coated) of Kaga South (B16), unknown number of Old Residency (B21); Parthasarathy and Rahaman (1974) for Harihar: 3 infants (babies).
^b Identical individuals.
^c 6.5 months after observed copulation with the new alpha male.
^d Attribution uncertain.
^e Infant of Short.
^f Reported missing by another observer.
^g Daughter of Harietta, reported missing by another observer.

I). Thus, the empirical base is actually much weaker than is usually recognized by authors who refer to these cases as constituting the best-documented evidence of infanticide in any primate species (cf. Boggess, Chapter 14, this volume).

Ecology, Demography, and Reproduction

In the absence of more detailed information on the events surrounding presumed cases of infanticide in langurs, it is of course difficult to effectively address issues of proximate and ultimate causation. These difficulties are compounded by the absence of systematic, long-term data on basic aspects of langur biology. Langur ecology at various sites has been treated by several authors (Yoshiba, 1967; Hladik and Hladik, 1972; Ripley, 1970; Winkler, 1981), but available data are nevertheless inadequate to compare resource availability between sites. Further, the carrying capacity of various langur study sites cannot yet be evaluated, a problem made worse by the use of noncomparable measures of population density at these sites.

Although information on demographic parameters such as male tenure, troop size and composition, and proportion of extratroop males in population, etc., are critical for testing several mathematical models of infanticide (Chapman and Hausfater, 1979; Hausfater *et al.*, 1982b), precise estimation of these parameters requires longitudinal data of the sort as yet obtained only from the site at Jodhpur. For example, from numerous field reports, it was generally known that langurs could be found living either in one-male or in multimale troops, and this characteristic of troops was often used as a means of comparing both populations and habitats (Oppenheimer, 1977; Vogel, 1977). However, from the longitudinal study at Jodhpur, it is now known that bisexual troops alternate periods of one-male composition with periods of multimale structure and, furthermore, these transitions between one-male and multimale phases are critical with respect to the occurrence of infanticide (see following). Unfortunately, there is a lack of longitudinal data on extratroop males—particularly on kinship relations, composition, stability, and ranging behavior of all-male bands—which would allow us to fully understand the causative factors in changes in the adult-male composition of bisexual troops of langurs.

Yet the most essential body of data for testing the sexual selection hypothesis for langur infanticide concerns reproductive parameters (Chapman and Hausfater, 1979; Hausfater, Chapter 13, this volume). The longitudinal data from Jodhpur on interbirth intervals and on the length of component parts of this interval differ substantially from previous estimates based on cross-sectional population surveys or on discontinuous observations of particular females in the field (compare Tables II and III). It is important to point out that an error of only 1 or 2

Table II. Data published between 1963 and 1977 on the reproductive parameters of female langurs

Parameter	Value	Reference
Length of ovulatory cycles	19–68 days[a] (average 21–26 days)	David and Ramaswami (1969); Ramaswami (1975)
	24–34 days[b] (average 26–28 days)	Hrdy (1977b)
Gestation period	172 days[a]	Ramaswami (1975)
	6–7 months[b]	Sugiyama (1967)
	200 ± 10 days (6.5 months)[a]	Hrdy (1974)
Interbirth interval (without premature loss of the preceding infant)	20–24 months[b]	Jay (1963); Sugiyama (1967)
	15–30 months[b] (mostly 19–24 months)	Hrdy (1977b)
Lactational amenorrhea[c] (birth to termination of weaning)	13–20 months[b]	Hrdy (1977b)
First postpartum estrus to subsequent conception	average about 2 months[b]	Hrdy (1977b)
Observed intervals between losses of unweaned infants and next estrus	1–33 days[b]	Data from Sugiyama (1965b, 1966), Mohnot (1971a), cited in Hrdy (1974)
	within 1 month[b]	Hrdy (1977b)
Observed intervals between losses of unweaned infants and subsequent births	5.5–27 months[b]	Sugiyama (1965b, 1966), Mohnot (1971a), Hrdy (1974, 1977b)

[a] Data from captive colony.
[b] Field data.
[c] It has been assumed that the first postpartum estrus starts after weaning process of the preceding infant has been finished (Hrdy, 1977b). See also Chapman and Hausfater (1979).

months in these estimates can have major consequences in calculation of the reproductive advantage potentially obtainable by infanticidal males (Hausfater and Vogel, 1982; Hausfater, Chapter 13, this volume). Thus, it cannot be emphasized too strongly that only longitudinal data from uninterrupted observations will provide reliable information to perform such calculations.

In the sections that follow, recent demographic, reproductive, and behavioral data obtained from the study at Jodhpur are reviewed in more detail as pertinent to understanding the nature and frequency of infanticide in this and other populations of langurs.

THE LANGURS OF JODHPUR

Jodhpur is located on the eastern fringe of the Great Indian Desert (Fig. 1). This arid region is characterized by extremely hot summers (maximum temperature up to 50°C) and moderate winters. Most of the rainfall is during the monsoon (July–September) but averages only about 360 mm per year. The langurs at Jodhpur breed year round. Vegetation at the site is characterized by open thorn scrub and small trees (e.g., *Acacia, Prosopis, Euphorbia*); the ecology of Jodhpur has been described in detail by Winkler (1981). The langurs are well habituated to the local human population, who consider the monkeys sacred and regularly provide them with food. Hence, Jodhpur langurs are not shy and are easily observable in an open habitat; observations are further enhanced by the fact that the monkeys remain primarily at ground level. Apart from feral dogs, Jodhpur langurs do not have natural predators.

The langur population at Jodhpur is geographically and genetically isolated; there are no other monkey populations sufficiently close that migration may occur into or out of the Jodhpur area. Nevertheless, the langur population has been fairly stable during the last decade, averaging around 1000 animals, perhaps with a slight increase between 1977 and 1980. The population consists of about 30 bisexual troops, regularly organized as one-male troops, and an unknown, probably fluctuating number of all-male bands. The size of bisexual troops ranges from 8 to about 80 animals, each troop occupying its own home range. All-male bands appear to be less stable in size as well as in individual composition. There are indications that all-male bands may split into subgroups, which then rejoin periodically. They are rather "nomadic," their traveling routes often covering the home ranges of several bisexual troops.

The main observation area was located about 7 km west of the city of Jodhpur and was less densely populated by langurs and less disturbed by man than many localities closer to the city. There were five bisexual troops, and two of them, B and KI, were the main focus of the study. All members of these two troops were individually recognizable. The goal of the long-term project was to describe the ontogeny of behavior. It was planned to follow as closely as possible selected focal animals from birth to adulthood in Troops B and KI. Unfortunately, the project, which began in January 1977, was terminated prematurely by the Indian government in December 1980, although a single student (V. Sommer) was permitted to continue observations at Jodhpur from October 1981 through December 1982.

Female Reproductive Characteristics

Female langurs reach sexual maturity at around 3 years of age. In the best-documented case, a young female of Troop B showed her first behavioral estrus when she was exactly 35 months of age, 15 days after her first observed menstruation. She conceived at approximately 40 months of age and gave birth to a male infant which survived for at least 6 months.

There is general agreement on menstrual cycle and gestation length from both free-ranging populations and laboratory colonies (compare Tables II and III). However, the estimates of interbirth interval and of duration of lactational amenorrhea based on longitudinal records from Jodhpur (Table III) are significantly shorter than those recorded for other free-ranging populations (Table II). Interestingly, the interbirth intervals of the longitudinal sample at Jodhpur are nearly identical to those reported for the captive colony of langurs at Berkeley, Califor-

Table III. Female reproductive parameters for the Jodhpur population, longitudinal data

	Range	Mean	n
Length of ovulatory cycles	19–29 days	24 days	45
Gestation	196–202 days	6.6 mo	3
Interbirth interval of 10 females (without premature loss of the preceding infant)	11.2–20.2 mo	14.9 mo	17
Interbirth interval of 14 females (including loss of the preceding infant)	8.2–20.2 mo	13.9 mo	21
Interval between delivery and first postpartum estrus (without loss of the preceding infant)	80–141 days	3.5 mo	5
Interval between delivery and next conception (without loss of the preceding infant)	4.6–13.4 mo	8.3 mo	17

nia (J. Laws: personal communication; D. Harley, in preparation). Differences in reproductive parameter estimates have important ramifications for particular predictions derived from the sexual selection hypothesis and therefore need special attention. There are at least three possible explanations for differences in estimates of interbirth intervals.

1. Whereas the langur population of Jodhpur, like Abu, has nonseasonal breeding, Sugiyama's data from Dharwar indicate a seasonally breeding population. In the latter case, a given female who failed to become pregnant by the end of one breeding season may have to wait several months until the breeding season of the subsequent year before resumption of mating. Hence, an irregular sequence of intervals of either 12 months or 24 months throughout a female's reproductive lifetime would be expected. On the basis of reproductive data from Jodhpur, 2-year intervals would be expected more frequently than 1-year intervals in a comparably structured but seasonally breeding population. Hence, the calculation of the mean interbirth interval for a seasonally breeding population could easily result in a figure between 20 and 24 months, Sugiyama's widely cited estimate from Dharwar (Table II). Thus, the difference between Jodhpur and Dharwar could simply be explained by seasonality of breeding, but of course the question remains: Why are some langur populations seasonal breeders whereas others are nonseasonal breeders?

2. Differences in interbirth interval estimates between various nonseasonally breeding populations (like Jodhpur and Abu), however, may well be due to differences in methodology (i.e., cross-sectional versus longitudinal data collection procedures) (Vogel, 1979). This can be aptly demonstrated by the data from Jodhpur. Whereas the uninterrupted longitudinal observations yielded an average interbirth interval of 14.9 months (Table III), the cross-sectional census data from the same population and during the same period of time indicated average interbirth intervals of around 18 to 20 months, figures close to Hrdy's (1977b) estimates for the langurs at Abu.

Estimates based on cross-sectional surveys or on discontinuous observation periods (such as Hrdy's data) necessarily will be biased toward higher figures, because abortions, stillbirths, and births with subsequent early death of infants will inevitably escape the observer's attention, especially during the gaps between periods of data collection. The longer these gaps, the larger the resultant error and consequently the higher the calculated value of the average interbirth interval. Thus, it is as yet undecided whether interbirth intervals or the duration of lactational amenorrhea differ significantly between Jodhpur and Abu. Rather, it is believed that uninterrupted longitudinal observation of known individuals at Abu would result in interbirth interval estimates comparable to the data from Jodhpur, estimates that are in concordance with those of the langur colony at Berkeley, California, and seem to be valid for nonseasonally breeding langur populations in general.

3. The idea may also arise that the short interbirth intervals at Jodhpur could be a result of artificial food provisioning on an ad lib. basis (Hausfater, Chapter 13, this volume). This assumption, however, cannot be supported by field data from Jodhpur. Despite the fact that the proportion of a troop's food obtained from humans varied markedly depending on home range location (Winkler, 1981), the cross-sectional data (collected over 4 years) do not reveal significant differences in interbirth intervals between heavily and lightly provisioned langur troops. Moreover, this argument in any case would not be able to explain the reported differences in reproductive parameters between Jodhpur and Abu, since the langur population of Abu is provisioned, in general, to the same degree by local people as that at Jodhpur.

With respect to various components of the overall interbirth interval, the data indicate that the mother of a surviving infant can resume regular estrous cycles as early as 80 days after delivery. In one of the best-documented cases, the interval between first observed postpartum estrus and subsequent conception was 1.5 months (i.e., two cycling periods). In four females of Troop KI, the mean interval between first postpartum estrus and conception was 134 days (about 4.5 months). From these data, it is inferred that at least the first two postpartum periods of estrus are anovulatory as previously suggested by Hrdy (1977b).

The shortest interval between delivery and next conception (without loss of preceding infant) at Jodhpur was 4.6 months, with the average value being 8.3 months (Table III). This indicates that at Jodhpur the loss of an infant greater than 4.6 months of age would not necessarily accelerate subsequent conception by the mother and hence benefit an infanticidal male. Estimates of interbirth interval length in many previous studies have implicitly assumed that mothers resume cycling only after having weaned their previous infant. However, at Jodhpur most females actually resumed cycling (and several had even conceived) before they had even started to wean the preceding infant.

The observed minimum interbirth interval without loss of the previous infant has been 11.2 months (Table III). The comparable figures for females who lost one infant before conception of the next were: (a) for a female who had a premature stillbirth: 8.2 months; (b) for a female whose infant drowned at 11 days of age: 9.1 months; (c) for a female whose infant disappeared at age 82 days: 10.5 months; (d) for a female who lost her infant at approximately 4 months of age: 11.6 months, which apparently is not less than the observed minimum interval without premature loss of an infant.

The data indicate that if a mother loses her infant before it has reached about 8 months of age, the interval between delivery of that infant and subsequent conception as well as the overall interbirth interval may be shortened (cf. Boggess, Chapter 14, this volume). But on the basis of these data, such a reduction in time to next conception can be verified only up to an age of around 4 months. Further, it may well be virtually impossible to obtain appropriate field data on the magnitude and frequency of such reductions if the age of infants lost or killed exceeds the critical value of about 4 months. In any case, the earlier the loss, the more considerable the reduction in interbirth interval.

Male Reproductive Characteristics

Although it has not been possible to continuously follow the life history of a male beyond 3 years of age, there is strong evidence that males reach full sexual maturity at least 2 years later than females (i.e., about 5 years of age at the earliest). Furthermore, observations of male replacements (see following) suggest that immature males older than 1–1.5 years of age will be forced to leave their natal troop since following adult-male replacement in the troop, the new resident male will not tolerate their presence.

Information on tenure length for breeding males in bisexual troops is crucial for evaluating hypotheses concerning infanticide in langurs. Specifically, a male's tenure determines the number of offspring he will sire as well as his ability to protect his own offspring from an infanticidal successor (Chapman and Hausfater, 1979). Fairly accurate longitudinal data exist for five tenure lengths from Troops B, KI, and KII at Jodhpur; a sixth tenure length can be roughly calculated using data reported by Makwana and Advani (1981). In order of increasing length, these tenures lasted about 3 months, 7.5 months, 32 ± 6 months, 39 ± 2 months, 41 ± 4 months, and 43 months. However, the extremely short tenure of 3 months, of course, should rather be considered as a period of interim leadership within an extremely prolonged process of adult-male replacement (see following). It is thus assumed that normal tenures at Jodhpur last on average for 3 years, a value that draws substantial support from the cross-sectional census data for the entire population.

Although it would always be to the advantage of a resident male to extend his tenure, thereby increasing the number and the chances of survival of his own offspring, there is chronic pressure from all-male bands to replace the resident male of a bisexual troop (see Sugiyama, Chapter 15, this volume) and there may also be internal factors constraining male tenures. For example, the eldest daughter of a resident male will reach full reproductive maturity at 45–50 months after her father's take-over. Hence, in the case of very long tenures, father–

daughter incest becomes likely. However, in the authors' opinion, pressure from all-male bands is more important than intragroup factors in determining the timing of adult-male replacements and thus tenure lengths.

PROCESS OF MALE REPLACEMENT AT JODHPUR

Infanticide by langur males has virtually always been observed and described in connection with replacement of the resident male in a bisexual troop, although obviously not all replacements are infanticidal. In so far as the wounding or killing of infants has been witnessed, the offender has always been a recent adult-male immigrant to the group and, hence, obviously was neither the father nor a close genetic relative of the victim (cf. one inferred case of a male killing his own offspring in Mohnot [1971a] as reviewed by Boggess, Chapter 14, and by Hrdy, (Chapter 16, this volume).

Over the past 5 years, limited information has been obtained for seven adult-male replacements in several bisexual troops at Jodhpur other than those that were focal units in the longitudinal study. There is sufficient data on these replacements, however, to substantiate that they were not rapid; some lasted a few weeks, others several months. In all cases, more than one male was involved in the initial take-over of the troop, and the final winner in the competition for residency in the troop was not readily predictable from the behavior of males during the course of the replacement. There were no indications of infanticide during these seven replacements.

However, four other adult male replacements occurred in the main study troops, B and KI, and these events were observed in detail. In Troop B, the adult male replacement process lasted from September to November 1980 and in Troop KI from October through November 1981. Both of these replacements apparently were not infanticidal. However, adult-male replacements with infanticide did recently occur in Troop KI during June 1982 and again from September through December 1982 (Sommer, in press).

Adult Male Replacement in Troop B

Troop B was composed of 1 adult male, 8 adult females, 9 juveniles and subadults of both sexes, 3 older infants (all females, aged 6.5–8.5 months), and 4 young infants (2 males and 2 females, 2–5.5 months of age). The resident male had been with the troop from at least February 1977 (Makwana and Advani, 1981) to September 1980, (i.e., 43 months). However, in the second week of September 1980, he left the troop, apparently without outside pressure since no extratroop males were in proximity to the troop at this time. A few days after his disappearance, several males could be seen at some distance from the troop, and on September 16, a 9-week period of intense competition began among extratroop males.

In total, there were at least 40 males involved in competition for leadership of the troop, ranging in age from juvenile to adult; 31 of these males could be individually identified. The males probably belonged to 3 or 4 all-male bands or subgroups, and during the competition there were numerous fights among these males. Three different males (Males 6, 22, and 27; Fig. 2) followed one another for varying lengths of interim leadership, which lasted from 10 to 24 days, before the second of these individuals (Male 22) finally established himself as the new resident male of Troop B in November. None of these males, including the new resident male, were immediately accepted by the adult females of Troop B, all of whom behaved very cautiously toward the males.

During the 2 months of intense male–male competition, all adult females in the troop showed estrous behavior. There were marked individual differences in the frequency and duration of estrus as well as in copulatory activities among the females. However, most females had contact with more than one male, and most copulations were carried out with males other than the successive interim males, who were kept busy by their multiple competitors. Two females showed extremely prolonged estrus: One of whom was accompanied by a 9-month-old infant, while the other one was the eldest surviving daughter of the former resident male, 2.9 years of age, who started cycling just after her father had left the troop. Unfortunately, no observations of Troop B were allowed by the Indian government during 1981. However, in February 1982, when the troop was revisited, no infants of an age such that they could have been sired during the period of intense competition were found.

All juvenile males of Troop B left their natal troop around the beginning of the competition. Furthermore, during this highly disruptive period, three older infants (two females, 6 and 9 months old, and one male, 6 months old) disappeared from the troop. Two other infants (7.5-month-old female and 6.5-month-old male) and a 12-month-old juvenile female were injured, although the wounding itself was not observed. The female infant was wounded during the time of intense male competition, while the two others received their injuries 1–4 weeks after Male 22 had finally established himself as the new troop leader. Although it cannot definitely be excluded that one or the other of these incidents could have resulted from infanticidal activities or intentions, there was no observed indication that infanticide actually had occurred or been attempted. Neither infant was endangered by its injury (on the back and hind limb, respectively), and the wounds healed within a few days. The juvenile female had a deep wound in the tail, which paralyzed tail movements.

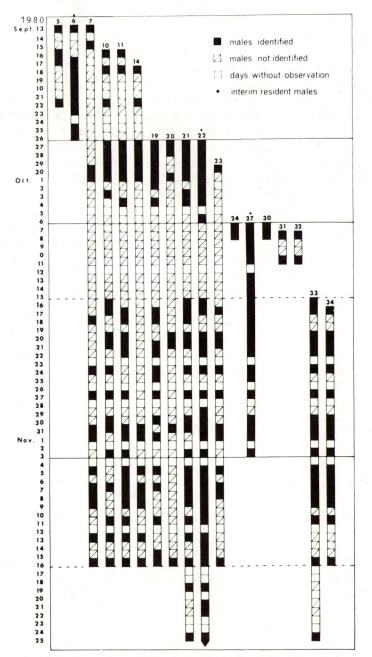

Figure 2. Observation dates, identity, and number of males present in troop and tenure lengths of interim resident males during replacement process in Troop B. See text for further details.

In contrast to the preceding individuals, the youngest black infant, just 2 months old and theoretically the infant in greatest jeopardy, was neither injured nor did it disappear at the time of intense male–male competition. Furthermore, none of the adult males, including the three interim leaders, were ever observed to attack infants. The same is true with respect to the male who finally settled as the new troop leader. When infants were attacked, the aggressors were exclusively subadult and older juvenile extratroop males, individuals who clearly did not have much chance of becoming the new resident male of the troop. The most dangerous instances for infants were mass chases involving males, or males and females, which appeared to result from the extreme build-up of tension in the group. Nevertheless, adult females reacted to the extratroop and interim males with great caution and in cases of "perceived" danger protected their infants by vehemently attacking the males either alone or in coalitions.

Adult Male Replacements and Infanticide in Troop KI

The first continuously documented replacement of a resident male of Troop KI occurred in October–November 1981. This replacement was apparently not accompanied by infanticide and in general was similar to the replacement in Troop B. The new resident male remained in the troop until June 1982, when he was himself replaced and this time by a male who did commit infanticide.

At the end of May 1982, Troop KI consisted of 23 animals: 1 adult male, 11 adult females, 8 juvenile males and females, and 3 infants all still in their black natal coat. The infanticidal take-over actually occurred in June 1982, when no observer was with the troop. However, by early July, when field observations were resumed by V. Sommer, the new resident male had already established his position. At that time, two juvenile males had left their natal troop. This new resident male (Rip) was observed to attack all three infants in the troop, all of whom were under 4 months of age. The first infant (a 1-month-old male) was severely wounded on July 9 and died the following day. The second infant (a 3.6-month-old male) was badly injured in the face on July 13. He seemed to recover but due to the wound had difficulties suckling and disappeared 7 days later. The third infant (a 3-month-old female) was also threatened by the new male, but the mother (sometimes with the help of other females) was successful in protecting her infant, who in fact survived.

The mother of the first infant showed estrous behavior 13 days after the death of her infant (about 6 weeks after its birth). Several copulations between the mother and the infanticidal male were observed. The mother of the second infant resumed estrus 16 days after its disappearance, that is, about 4 months after the infant's birth. This female, too, mated with the infanticidal male. The mother of the third infant (who survived the attacks) also exhibited estrous behaviour and subsequently mated with the new resident male. In fact, 10 of 11 adult females in Troop KI solicited the new resident male during the first month of his residency. In addition, one female in the troop gave birth to a healthy female infant on July 30. No attack was observed by the new male upon that infant, although clearly he was not the sire. The mother (a primiparous female), however, kept apart from the male.

In mid-September 1982, this male was himself wounded and subsequently disappeared. Intense competition among extratroop males began again and was not definitely terminated by late December 1982, when observations were interrupted. However, during this period at least 42 males (belonging to three all-male bands or subgroups) were involved. As was the case in Troop B, three interim leaders were successively able to dominate all other competitors for some period of time but were not able to establish themselves as the new resident male of the troop.

Interestingly, one of the interim leaders was the former resident male of Troop KI (Zipfel), who was the probable progenitor of one of the two surviving infants in the troop. This male, however, was subsequently driven from the troop by the all-male bands, and on the same day his daughter (then 3.2 months old) also disappeared. It is suspected that this infant was killed during the aggressive encounters on that day. The mother resumed estrus 13 days later (thus, about 3.5 months after the infant's birth) and was observed mating with several males on this and the following day. In the midst of this period of intense social disruption, another female gave birth (on October 11) to a healthy male infant.

From late November onward, another male (Fleck) was able to establish himself as the sole resident male of Troop KI. During the limited observations, he consistently kept all other males away from the troop, so he seemed assured of being the final winner of the prolonged competition for troop leadership. In any event, from the first day that Fleck started to establish his leadership, he also began to chase and repeatedly attack the two infants still with the troop. On November 25, the only day of his leadership when he was undisturbed by the presence of competitors, he succeeded in wounding the younger infant (1.5 months of age) so seriously that it died the following day. The older infant (the same female that had barely escaped the attacks of Rip 4 months before) was about 7.5 months of age and rather independent, but she too was injured by this male. Nevertheless, she once again managed to survive despite Fleck's repeated attempts to catch her. Interestingly, this infant's mother had already returned to estrus and solicited Fleck several times.

In sum, within a period of 6 months, Troop KI was invaded by two different infanticidal males who made repeated attacks on all five infants in the troop. Three of the infants died from injuries inflicted by the males, and one disappeared from unknown causes. One infant did survive, but it also was repeatedly attacked by both males and injured twice. With one exception, the mothers of infants that disappeared or were killed exhibited behavioral estrus within the 16 days of their infant's death or disappearance.

DISCUSSION

How well do the preceding observations accord with the sexual selection hypothesis of infanticide? The following predictions derived from that hypothesis should be verified by the observations if infanticide is, indeed, an evolved reproductive strategy among adult male langurs at Jodhpur.

1. The new resident male should exclusively kill unrelated infants. Hence, he should cease killing by one gestation period after takeover.
2. The new resident male should only kill infants still young enough to prevent their mothers from resuming sexual cycles due to lactational amenorrhea.
3. A lactating female whose infant is killed should resume sexual cycles earlier than if her infant had survived.
4. The subsequent interbirth interval for such females should be considerably abbreviated, and in fact the extent of this shortening should be inversely correlated with the age of the infant.
5. The infanticidal male should be in a position to control the subsequent sexual activities of the victim's mother. This means that in general he should kill infants only after the male–male competition for troop leadership has been decided in his favor.
6. In addition to killing infants born before his entry into the troop, it would also be advantageous for a new male to kill infants sired by the preceding male but born after completion of the takeover.

The data from Jodhpur are in accordance with predictions (1), (3), and (5): both infanticidal males killed only unrelated offspring (1), and both attacked infants only after they had established themselves as sole resident males of Troop KI (5). The victims' mothers showed estrous behavior significantly earlier than mothers of surviving infants (3). The data accord reasonably well with prediction (2). Under undisturbed reproductive conditions at Jodhpur, the critical age up to which an infant is likely to prevent its mother from conception is around 4 months. In Troop KI, only infants younger than 4 months of age were killed. Except for one older infant, all infants attacked by the two infanticidal males were less than 4 months of age, and certainly none of the infants in that age group were spared such assaults. Nevertheless, one infanticidal male repeatedly attacked and twice injured a 7.5-month-old infant that did, however, manage to escape. This latter case is not in accordance with prediction (2), since the mother of that infant had resumed sexual cycling months before and (despite being pregnant again) persistently solicited the male. Hence, a successful infanticide would not have resulted in any reproductive advantage for the male.

At present, it is not known, whether the observed early return to sexual cycling in these mothers actually resulted in a shortened inter-birth interval (prediction [4]). This leaves open the question as to whether they just displayed a "pseudoestrus" (Hrdy, 1977b). At least two of the mothers did show menstruation before and after their estrus, and this may be an indication that they were undergoing physiologically normal cycles. Another female showed an early estrus without observable preceding menstruation, but this was then followed by menstruation and subsequent estrus within reasonable intervals. Two other mothers might have displayed a "pseudoestrus": One female whose infant disappeared showed a 4-day behavioral estrus only once, 13 days after that event, accompanied by mating but without observed menstruation either before or after. Another female, the mother of the surviving (7.5-month-old) infant, obviously already was pregnant during the 5 days that she exhibited extensive estrous behavior (V. Sommer: personal communication).

According to prediction (6), a new resident male should also kill those infants that are born within one gestation length (6.5 months) after his take-over. However, there is no indication that this occurred in Troop KI. The first infanticidal male in this troop was never observed to attack the infant that was born about 1 month after his take-over, although he definitely was not its father. In general, no attacks on infants, whether born before or after either adult-male replacement, were observed in Troop KI at any time later than 1 month after the establishment of the respective male.

The question of why infanticidal-male replacements appear to occur at such a relatively low frequency at Jodhpur may tentatively be answered by pointing to recent mathematical analyses of langur infanticide by Hausfater (this volume, Chapter 13; Hausfater et al., 1982b). These models demonstrate that in a population characterized by male tenure and female reproductive parameters similar to those at Jodhpur, one would expect only one in four adult-male replacements to be accompanied by infanticide, and this is true whether infanticidal tendencies in males are genetic or facultative.

CONCLUSIONS

In sum, the sexual selection hypothesis appears to draw substantial support from the Jodhpur data, although clearly there still remain some inconsistencies and open questions. These remaining concerns can only be resolved by empirical studies on the following topics:

1. It has become obvious that not all infants that disappear or are injured during adult-male replacement are in fact victims of infanticidal males. The wounding and/or disappearance of so many older infants around the time of take-over is as yet unexplained, particularly the disappearance of juvenile and older-infant females.

2. So far, there is no reliable data concerning the reproductive advantage, if any, obtained by infanticidal males over their lifetime in comparison with noninfanticidal males.

3. There is a general lack of reliable information on kinship relations between the adult females within bisexual troops as well as between cooperating males residing in all-male bands.

Clearly, these gaps in the knowledge of the behavioral ecology of langurs can only be filled by long-term field studies focusing on individual life histories as well as on the genetic structure of langur populations.

ACKNOWLEDGMENTS

The authors wish to thank Volker Sommer for providing as yet unpublished material and Paul Winkler for critical support through all stages of preparing this chapter. Our project was supported financially by the "Deutsche Forschungsgemeinschaft" (DFG), Grant Nos. Vo 124/11 to 13–5, and by the "Deutscher Akademischer Austauschdienst" (DAAD). We are indebted to all those Indian and German institutions that facilitated our field work and stay at Jodhpur.

13 | Infanticide in langurs: Strategies, counterstrategies, and parameter values

Glenn Hausfater

INTRODUCTION

In several primate species, adult males have been observed to inflict fatal wounds upon unweaned or otherwise maternally dependent infants, a behavior commonly referred to as *infanticide* (Hrdy, 1979). The infanticidal male in most of these instances had only recently joined the group or had recently become the dominant male after previously occupying a more subordinate position (Leland *et al.*, Chapter 8, this volume). In other cases, infanticide has been inferred when a healthy infant disappeared from the group following a series of attacks on the infant and its mother by a recent adult-male migrant to the group (Crockett and Sekulic, Chapter 9, this volume). Whether inferred or directly observed, infanticide in primate groups has been most frequently and, in my opinion, most convincingly explained as a reproductive strategy whereby the migrant or newly dominant male increases his own reproductive success at the expense of adult females, their infants, and the former dominant male of the group.

Briefly, the suckling primate infant produces in its mother a prolonged period of lactational amenorrhea (Altmann *et al.*, 1978). Amenorrhea ends spontaneously when the infant is weaned by its mother. However, amenorrhea will also be terminated if the infant dies prior to weaning, for example, due to disease or fatal wounds inflicted by a predator or conspecific. Under the latter circumstances, the female rapidly re-

257

turns to breeding condition, usually within 1 month of the death of her infant. Thus, when an adult male kills an infant that is both unweaned and unrelated to himself, he effectively speeds the mother's return to estrus and does so at little cost to himself. Furthermore, infanticide as previously described eliminates offspring sired by competing males and also reduces the number of immature animals that will be in competition with the new male's own progeny for food, maternal care, and, eventually, mates (Hrdy, 1979; Introduction, this volume).

Infanticide is obviously costly to females in terms of offspring numbers and presumably lifetime fitness. Yet females carrying unweaned infants generally respond passively, albeit warily, to the presence of a new and potentially infanticidal male in their group (Mohnot, 1971a; Busse and Hamilton, 1981). Reports of active defense of infants from adult-male attackers indicate that postreproductive females, or coalitions of individuals of all ages and sexes, rather than specifically mothers themselves, were the most vigorous defenders (Hrdy and Hrdy, 1976; Butynski, 1982). However, despite such resistance at least some infants within these groups were eventually killed by the migrant male. Although it may at first seem curious that females do not make a more concerted and effective effort to repel infanticidal males, it is important to recall that many Old World monkey and ape species are quite dimorphic. Adult males weigh up to twice as much as adult females and have substantially longer canine teeth (Napier and Napier, 1967). Females in these species are thus at a strong disadvantage in fighting with an adult male and by doing so probably would put both themselves and their infants in jeopardy of serious wounding.

Females not only are exposed to greater costs than males in defending an infant from attack but may actually have less to gain from successful defense of their infant than an infanticidal male stands to gain from the infant's death. Thus, according to the calculations of Chapman and Hausfater (1979), an infanticidal male langur can increase his lifetime reproductive success over twofold by committing infanticide, compared to not doing so, and in many cases a migrant male who failed to eliminate unweaned infants would have little opportunity to breed before he was himself replaced by yet another incoming male. By contrast, for an adult female to suffer a commensurately large reduction in her own lifetime reproductive success would require that she lose approximately 40% of all offspring to infanticide, a figure that seems unrealistically high given available data on the frequency of infanticide in most primate species.

Nevertheless, it is also the case that any female who prevented the killing of her infant by an infanticidal male would be at a considerable reproductive advantage compared to females who did not do so. Thus, while individual males may have more to gain from killing infants than individual females do from preventing infant deaths, one would still expect there to be strong selection in favor of females who prevented infanticide. The latter would be especially true if effective counterstrategies involved relatively little cost to females in terms of increased probability of death or wounding. In fact, it would generally be to a female's advantage to engage in such low-cost counterstrategies even if not 100% effective in preventing infant deaths.

Clearly, the validity of arguments and models such as those just presented, as well as the ability to test predictions drawn from them, depends, to a large extent on understanding the factors that determine the reproductive success of adults of both sexes and, more specifically, of infanticidal and noninfanticidal males. Variables generally believed to be of greatest importance in this latter regard are the average length of residency of adult males in groups (referred to as male *tenure*), the interval between successive births or conceptions for females, and the proportion of that interval spent in lactational amenorrhea (Chapman and Hausfater, 1979; Hausfater and Vogel, 1982). As several chapters in this volume demonstrate, our knowledge of these reproductive and demographic parameters is as yet incomplete, even for such well-studied species as langurs. The task of selecting appropriate parameter values for use in model building and hypothesis testing is made even more difficult by considerable intra- and interpopulational variability within species in these same demographic and reproductive characteristics. As a result, nearly all previous models of infanticide, both literal and quantitative, have made implicit or explicit assumptions concerning the value of various parameters. Obviously, the predictions of these models are likely to hold true for any given population only in so far as the actual parameter values for that population correspond at least roughly to those assumed in the model.

In one of the first quantitative analyses of the reproductive consequences of infanticide, Chapman and Hausfater (1979) provided an algebraic method for computing the expected reproductive success of infanticidal and noninfanticidal males after any given tenure in a group of langur monkeys or other suitable species. This model was subsequently modified and expanded in order to obtain precise predictions concerning both the reproductive advantage of infanticide for males in specific langur populations and the proportion of infanticidal and noninfanticidal males expected in those populations at equilibrium (Hausfater and Vogel, 1982; Hausfater et al., 1982b). However, as noted previously, the validity of these predictions depends largely on the accuracy of the parameter values used in formulating the model. Thus, it is of more than passing interest that recent data from a longitudinal study of langurs at Jodhpur, India, suggest that the interbirth interval for this species under some ecological conditions may be substantially shorter than previously suspected (Chapter 12, this volume). At present, it remains an open question as to whether the Jodhpur estimates are in any sense more representative of langurs as a species than earlier estimates based on cross-sectional data from several other study sites, but it is clear that a reassessment of the reproductive consequences of infanticide in light of these new data is warranted.

This chapter reevaluates the conclusions of the Chapman–Hausfater model concerning the reproductive advantage obtained by adult male langurs through infanticide. Specifically, the same basic formulation as that of Chapman and Hausfater (1979) is used to calculate the expected reproductive success of infanticidal and noninfanticidal male langurs under a variety of conditions but with parameter values for the model estimated exclusively from the Jodhpur data rather than from pooled data from several widely scattered study sites, as was previously the case. Results of this analysis thus provide alternative estimates both of the reproductive advantage potentially obtainable by males through infanticide and of the range of tenure values across which infanticide would be selectively advantageous for males. In addition, comparison of the model in its original form to that based on the Jodhpur data provides an effective means of quantitatively assessing the sensitivity of conclusions of the model to changes in specific parameter values.

The second focus of this chapter is female counterstrategies to infanticide. Although this latter topic may at first glance seem quite unrelated to the preceding sensitivity analysis of the Chapman–Hausfater model, the reproductive consequences of various hypothesized counterstrategies to infanticide can in fact be evaluated quite precisely using essentially the same methodology. This is so because most proposed counterstrategies to infanticide hinge upon behavioral or physiological mechanisms which result in either an increase in the length of the interbirth interval overall or an increase in the proportion of that interval spent undergoing sexual cycles by females. Thus, just as new data on langur reproductive parameters from Jodhpur were used to produce alternative estimates of the reproductive advantage obtained by males through infanticide, so too were various hypothetical modifications of these parameters incorporated into the Chapman–Hausfater model as a means of obtaining estimates of the effects on adult-male reproductive success of specific female counterstrategies to infanticide. Of course, the precise parameter values used in these alternative formulations of the model were not estimated from actual field data representative of any given natural population of langurs but from logical consideration of the mechanisms and functioning of particular counterstrategies of interest. Therefore, in addition to the preceding reevaluation of the Chapman–Hausfater model based on recent data from Jodhpur, the

present chapter also includes a quantitative analysis of the consequences for male and female reproductive success of two general forms
of female counterstrategy to infanticide. In sum, this chapter explores
the robustness and generality of the conclusions of the Chapman–Hausfater model across a range of reproductive parameter values that are
believed on empirical or theoretical grounds to be of significance in
understanding the frequency and occurrence of infanticide among langurs and other primate species.

Briefly, the Chapman–Hausfater (1979) model uses a series of conditional equations to determine the number of offspring produced per
female by an infanticidal male after any given tenure in a group of
langur monkeys or other appropriate species. In addition to male tenure,
other important variables in the model are the length of the interval
between successive conceptions for individual females in the group,
called the *interconception interval,* as well as the proportion of this
interval during which females undergo sexual cycles, pregnancy, or
lactational amenorrhea. An example of the way in which these demographic and reproductive parameters are related to each other in the
conditional equations and in determining offspring production is as
follows:

Imagine an infanticidal male who enters a group, kills the unweaned
infant of a particular female, and then remains with the group for T
months before he is himself replaced by a noninfanticidal successor.
With respect to that particular female, the infanticidal male will produce exactly one offspring if his tenure, T, fulfills the condition (Eq.
1):

$$I_1 - (G_1 + A_1) \leq T < I_1 - (G_1 + A_1) + I_2 \qquad (1)$$

where I_1 and I_2 are the length of successive interconception intervals
for the female during the infanticidal male's tenure and G_1 and A_1,
respectively, are the number of months spent by the female in pregnancy and amenorrhea during interval I_1.

In contrast, a noninfanticidal male will produce one infant by this
female after the same tenure as in the preceding equation only if T
fulfills the condition (Eq. 2):

$$I_1 - (m - \tfrac{1}{2}) \leq T < I_1 - (m - \tfrac{1}{2}) + I_2 \qquad (2)$$

where m is the month of entry of the male with respect to the onset
of the female's current interconception interval (i.e., Month 1 of the
interval, Month 2 of the interval, or so on). For most primate species,
$I_1 - (G_1 + A_1)$ will, on average, be less than $I_1 - (m - \tfrac{1}{2})$, so an

infanticidal male will generally produce one offspring by the female after a shorter waiting time, and thus shorter tenure, than his noninfanticidal counterpart. In similar fashion, a series of conditional equations were formulated by Chapman and Hausfater (1979) that allow comparison of offspring production by infanticidal and noninfanticidal males after any given tenure and under either replacement condition (i.e., infanticidal or noninfanticidal successor male).

Assumptions of the Model

Although the foregoing example concerned offspring production by a single male and female after specific tenure and interconception interval lengths, iterative computational procedures can be used to calculate the expected reproductive success of infanticidal and noninfanticidal males after any given tenure and with female interconception interval lengths free to vary over any specified range (Chapman and Hausfater, 1979). Calculation of expected reproductive success for infanticidal and noninfanticidal males by this method requires several assumptions, however. First, the model assumes that the time elapsed between the death or weaning of an infant and the resumption of sexual cycles by its mother is negligible. Second, the infanticidal male is assumed to engage in this behavior only within the first month following his entry into the group. Infants born, for example, 2 months after the take-over of a group are thus not considered in jeopardy of infanticide. Both of these assumptions are reasonably consistent with available data on langur infanticide but are nonetheless the subject of considerable debate (Vogel, 1979; Boggess, 1979 and Chapter 14, this volume).

It is further assumed that groups taken over by infanticidal and noninfanticidal males do not differ as to number of adult females or female reproductive characteristics. In particular, the number of menstrual cycles experienced by females prior to conception is assumed to follow a geometric distribution, and the menstrual cycle itself is assumed to be precisely 1 month in duration. The timing of entry of males into groups is assumed to be independent of the reproductive states of females in those groups. Also, the groups obtained by infanticidal and noninfanticidal males are assumed to be similar with respect to rates of miscarriage, spontaneous abortion, and sources of adult and infant mortality other than infanticide. Finally, male offspring are assumed to follow the same reproductive strategy as their fathers: sons sired by infanticidal males are assumed to become infanticidal themselves as adults; likewise, sons of noninfanticidal males are assumed to pursue a noninfanticidal reproductive strategy. However, it is important to note that such father–son similarity in reproductive strategy can arise through genetical or nongenetical mechanisms with only minor consequences for the conclusions of the model (Hausfater *et al.,* 1982b).

Langur Reproductive Parameters

Few longitudinal data on reproductive parameters of langur monkeys were available when the Chapman–Hausfater (1979) model was first formulated. Thus, parameter values for the model were estimated based on cross-sectional data published by several different observers from several different study sites. Both gestation and amenorrhea were considered constants in the original formulation and were set at 7 and 13 months duration, respectively. The former value was consistent with data published by Hrdy (1977b) and by Roonwal and Mohnot (1977); the latter value was consistent with estimates of average amenorrhea length under natural conditions as published by Hrdy (1977b) and Jay (1963). The number of month-long menstrual cycles a female experiences prior to conception is dependent upon the probability of conception on any given cycle. In the original model, a conception probability of $\frac{1}{3}$ was used and was consistent with information then available for several primate species (Czaja et al., 1975; Hendrickx and Kraemer, 1969), albeit not specifically langurs. Together with the preceding assumptions, these particular parameter values resulted in an average interconception interval of 23 months, a figure that was itself in agreement with estimates published by Jay (1963).

Long-term observations on langur monkeys near Jodhpur were first begun by Mohnot (1971a), and over the past few years have been extended by Vogel (1976; 1979) and his students. In particular, the latter work has produced a small but very precise sample of reproductive histories for identifiable females in two study groups (Vogel and Loch, Chapter 12, this volume). These longitudinal records indicate that females at Jodhpur have an average interconception interval length of just under 15 months, fully one-third shorter than the value of 23 months originally used in the model. Gestation in this population, measured as the time from last signs of behavioral estrus to the birth of an infant, averages approximately 6.5 months. Further, the mean interval from birth of an infant to the first signs of behavioral estrus (i.e., solicitation of males and/or mating) by its mother is only 3–4 months, although infants are not fully weaned until at least 6 months of age.

One clear implication of the Jodhpur data is that the death of an infant greater than 4 months of age will generally have little effect on an infanticidal male's reproductive success: In most instances, its mother would have already returned to breeding condition (Vogel and Loch, Chapter 12, this volume). However, the Jodhpur longitudinal data also show that once females resume sexual cycles, they typically require 5 month-long menstrual cycles to again become pregnant. Thus, the appropriate conception probability (per estrus) for females in this particular langur population appears to be $\frac{1}{5}$ rather than $\frac{1}{3}$ as used in the original formulation of the Chapman–Hausfater model.

Table I summarizes the original and alternative parameter values

Table I. Reproductive parameter values used in the original formulation and in the present reevaluation of the Chapman–Hausfater (1979) model of langur infanticide.[a]

Values	Gestation (months)	Amenorrhea (months)	Menstrual cycle length (months)	Conception probability (per cycle)	Average interconception interval (months)
Original	7	13	1	1/3	23
Alternative	6.5	3.5	1	1/5	15

[a] Parameter values for the model as originally published were estimated from cross-sectional data obtained at several different study sites (see text for details). Parameter values used in the present reanalysis of the model were estimated from longitudinal data obtained by Vogel and co-workers in the course of their long-term study of langurs at Jodhpur, India (Vogel, 1979; Vogel and Loch, Chapter 12, this volume).

used in evaluating the Chapman–Hausfater model as applied to langurs. It is important to note, however, that although the Jodhpur data were obtained through more systematic sampling procedures than was the case in earlier studies, it is also true that certain groups within this population supplement their natural diet with a variety of foods of human origin received as religious offerings from local townspeople. (Langurs are believed to be the incarnation of the god Hanuman and are thus considered sacred animals in India.) This is an important consideration since studies of several nonhuman primates species have shown that provisioned or laboratory-reared animals have substantially shorter interbirth intervals than do individuals of the same species under more natural conditions (Dittus, 1975; Altmann *et al.*, 1977; Mori, 1979). In fact, the average interbirth interval at Jodhpur is in close agreement with that from the captive langur colony at Berkeley, California, a colony in which the animals are fed a highly nutritious diet on an ad lib basis (Dolhinow and DeMay, 1982; Harley, in preparation). Thus, while the value of 23 months used in the original formulation of the model may well be an overestimate of interbirth interval length for langurs under natural conditions, a value of 15 months seems quite likely to err in the opposite direction (i.e., to be an underestimate). Nevertheless, comparison of the results of the model using these two alternative sets of reproductive parameter estimates serves both to establish biologically meaningful upper and lower bounds for the reproductive advantage obtained by langur males through infanticide as well as to indicate how robust the predictions of the model are across this relatively wide range of parameter values.

ALTERNATIVE CALCULATIONS OF THE REPRODUCTIVE CONSEQUENCES OF INFANTICIDE

Figure 1 shows the expected reproductive success of infanticidal and noninfanticidal males under conditions of subsequent replacement by a male of either type as calculated in the original formulation of the Chapman–Hausfater model. The characteristics of the successor male are an important consideration in determining expected reproductive success for males of either type since an infanticidal successor male places in jeopardy the most recent cohort of offspring sired by the original male, regardless of the characteristics of that male. Results of analysis of the model for the noninfanticidal replacement condition (i.e., when a male of either type will be replaced by a noninfanticidal successor), serve to elucidate the consequences of infanticide for adult-male reproductive success at the time of origin of the behavior in a population. In other words, if one imagines infanticide as being intro-

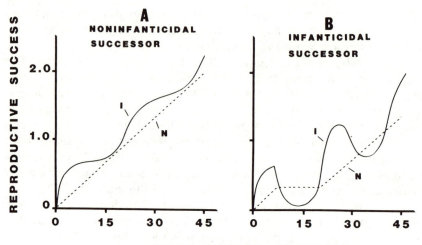

MALE TENURE (MONTHS)

Figure 1. Expected reproductive success of infanticidal (solid line) and noninfanticidal (broken line) males under conditions of subsequent replacement by a noninfanticidal (A) or infanticidal (B) successor
male. These curves were calculated from the Chapman–Hausfater
(1979) model using pooled data from several different study sites
to obtain composite estimates of the reproductive parameters of
langurs. See Table I and text for further explanation.

duced into a population by a single migrant male, that individual is
certain to have a noninfanticidal successor, and this will in fact be
the case for most infanticidal males until this reproductive strategy
has been adopted by a majority of males in the population.

In the original model, infanticidal males replaced by noninfanticidal
successors had a reproductive advantage compared to their noninfanticidal counterparts at all tenures from 1 to 80 months (Fig. 1A) (Chapman
and Hausfater, 1979). Although at several specific tenures (e.g., 20
months, 35 months) this advantage was actually quite small, in most
cases infanticide conferred a substantial reproductive advantage on
adult males. For example, an infanticidal male replaced by a noninfanticidal successor after a tenure of 25 months would be expected to produce one-third more offspring than a noninfanticidal counterpart replaced under the same conditions. Based on equilibrium models of
infanticide (Hausfater et al., 1982b) as well as on population genetics
theory (Hartl, 1980), infanticide as a reproductive strategy would be
expected to spread in any population characterized by the demographic
and reproductive parameters used in original formulation of the Chapman–Hausfater model.

Figure 2A summarizes the expected reproductive success of infanticidal and noninfanticidal males under similar replacement conditions

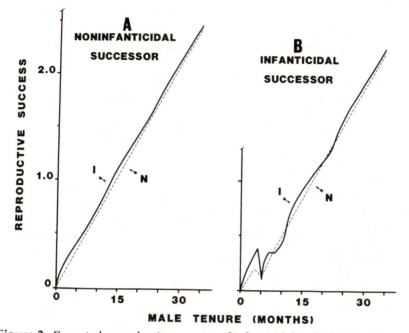

Figure 2. Expected reproductive success of infanticidal (solid line) and noninfanticidal (broken line) males under both replacement conditions as calculated from the Chapman–Hausfater model using reproductive parameter estimates based on longitudinal data from the langur population at Jodhpur, India. See Vogel and Loch (Chapter 12, this volume) for a complete discussion of the characteristics of this population and a description of the dataset from which these estimates were obtained.

(i.e., noninfanticidal successors) but calculated using the alternative reproductive parameter values based on data from Jodhpur. Although these alternative parameter values produced a rather substantial reduction compared to Fig. 1A in the reproductive advantage obtained by adult males through infanticide, at no tenure shown in Fig. 2A, nor at tenures from 46 to 80 months inclusive, were infanticidal males actually predicted to produce fewer offspring than their noninfanticidal counterparts. As was the case in the model as originally formulated (Fig. 1A), infanticide in this alternative formulation proved most advantageous for males at very short tenures (e.g., 2 months, 13 months), and in fact for tenures exceeding 30 months the expected reproductive success of infanticidal and noninfanticidal males differed only very slightly, in the hundredths place.

Despite the fact that use of the Jodhpur parameter values made infanticide much less advantageous for males than was the case in the original model, it is important to emphasize that infanticidal males in the Jodhpur-based model nevertheless exhibited higher reproductive

success at all tenures than did their noninfanticidal counterparts. Furthermore, even though the reproductive success of infanticidal males
replaced noninfanticidally differed only slightly from that of their noninfanticidal counterparts at most tenures, the small reproductive advantage obtained by adult males through infanticide, as calculated using
the Jodhpur parameter values, would still be sufficient to assure the
spread of this behavior in the population, albeit at a much slower
rate than produced by the original parameter values (Hausfater *et al.,*
1982b). Thus, this reanalysis of the Chapman–Hausfater model based
on the Jodhpur data did not result in any substantive modification of
at least one major conclusion of the model as originally formulated:
that infanticide once introduced into a population would be expected
to increase in frequency among the adult males in that population.
Nevertheless, a small reproductive advantage, such as that obtained
by infanticidal males in the Jodhpur-based model, would be highly
susceptible to elimination by a variety of stochastic and deterministic
processes, including, for example, female counterstrategies to infanticide as discussed below.

Expected Reproductive Success under Conditions of Subsequent
Replacement by an Infanticidal Male

Figure 1B shows results from the original version of the model concerning the reproductive advantage obtained by adult males through
infanticide once a population has come close to fixation for this trait.
More specifically, this figure compares the reproductive success of infanticidal and noninfanticidal males following their replacement at any
given tenure by a male who is himself infanticidal. Under this replacement condition, infanticide was generally advantageous for males, but
at tenures around 15, 35, 55, and 80 months, infanticidal males were
actually expected to produce fewer offspring than their noninfanticidal
counterparts. Although it may at first seem counterintuitive that infanticidal males would ever produce fewer offspring than noninfanticidal
males, these particular tenures represent times when an infanticidal
male's most recent cohort of offspring is unweaned and thus subject
to infanticide by his successor. In contrast, a noninfanticidal male's
most recent cohort of offspring is still being carried *in utero* by adult
females in the group and will be born only after the successor male
has ceased killing infants. In this regard, it is important to recall that
infanticidal males are assumed in the model to engage in infant killing
only in the first month following their take-over of a group.

On the other hand, the reproductive disadvantage of infanticide at
the preceding tenure times is more than offset by the substantial advantage obtained by adult males through infanticide at most other tenures.
In particular, at tenures around 25, 45, and 65 months, an infanticidal

male would be expected to produce from 1.5 to 2.5 times as many offspring as would a noninfanticidal counterpart replaced under the same conditions. Thus, at least using the original composite parameter values, when infanticide is disadvantageous, it is only slightly so. In contrast, when infanticide is advantageous, it is generally greatly so.

Although it may be difficult to discern without viewing a graph of output from the model over a wider range of tenures, the wave-like oscillations of the solid line in Fig. 1B are increasingly dampened with increasing tenure time. Examination of Fig. 2B shows that use of the Jodhpur reproductive parameters in the Chapman–Hausfater model resulted in a substantially less peaked waveform and in more rapid dampening of these oscillations. In other words, both the maximum reproductive advantage obtained by infanticidal males and the range of tenures values characterized by peak or near-peak advantage levels were greatly reduced by use of the alternative parameter values. As a result, at all tenures beyond 20 months infanticidal males in the Jodhpur model produced no more than 1.02 offspring for each 1 offspring sired by a noninfanticidal male replaced under the same conditions (Fig. 2B). Nevertheless, at certain relatively short tenures (e.g., around 2 months and 13 months), infanticide conferred a rather substantial advantage upon adult male reproductive success, and an infanticidal individual could potentially produce as many as 1.8 offspring for each offspring sired by a noninfanticidal counterpart.

In sum, replacement of the parameter values originally used in the Chapman–Hausfater model with alternative values based on data from Jodhpur produced a marked reduction at all tenures in the reproductive advantage obtained by males through infanticide when they themselves were replaced by an infanticidal male. One may best summarize the present analysis as suggesting that when infanticide is disadvantageous for males, it is only marginally so; and, when advantageous for males, it is again only marginally so. Nevertheless, it is also important to emphasize that use of the Jodhpur parameter values produced some advantage, however small, for infanticidal males across a very much wider range of tenure values than was the case using the original parameter values. This latter point is especially significant since the proportion of infanticidal males expected in a population at equilibrium depends both on the magnitude of the advantage obtained by males through infanticide and on the range of tenure values over which they obtain any advantage whatsoever (Hausfater *et al.*, 1982b).

Equilibrium Proportion of Infanticidal Males

Although both Figs. 1 and 2 show infanticide to be generally advantageous for adult males, this does not imply that the trait will necessarily reach fixation in populations characterized by either the original or alternative set of parameter values. In fact, so long as any sizeable proportion of males are replaced at tenures disadvantageous for infanticide, such populations will not become fixed for this trait, but rather a stable equilibrium will develop between infanticidal and noninfanticidal males. Table II compares the exact range of tenure values at which infanticide is disadvantageous for males in the Chapman–Hausfater model as calculated using the original (Fig. 1) and alternative (Fig. 2) estimates of langur reproductive parameters. Also shown in this table is the expected range of equilibrium proportions in these populations were all males replaced only at certain specific minimally or maximally disadvantageous tenures. In essence, these equilibrium values provide upper and lower bounds for the proportion of infanticidal males expected in populations characterized by either the original or alternative reproductive parameter values.

Briefly, use of the original cross-sectional estimates of langur reproductive parameters yielded stable equilibrium proportions of infanticidal males as low as 3%. The more recent longitudinal estimates from Jodhpur, in contrast, yielded stable equilibria no lower than 23%. In other words, one may expect approximately one-quarter of the adult male replacements in a population such as that at Jodhpur to be accompanied by infanticide. More realistically, the proportion of infanticidal males in Jodhpur-like populations would generally be expected to exceed even this latter figure since it seems unlikely that all infanticidal males would be replaced only at specifically disadvantageous tenures. Thus, even though infanticide proved far less advantageous using reproductive parameter values from Jodhpur compared to the original composite values, the precise proportion of males expected to commit infanticide was much greater in the former case than in the latter.

Table II. Tenure values[a]

Model	Disadvantageous tenures (months)	Equilibrium proportions of infanticidal males
With original parameter values	8–19	0.03–0.90
	32–40	0.11–0.85
	54–61	0.22–0.94
	77–80	0.38–0.75
With alternative (Jodhpur) parameter values	5	0.96
	8–10	0.23–0.55
	21–22	0.80–0.89

[a] Values are presented at which infanticide is reproductively disadvantageous for infanticidal males who are themselves replaced infanticidally in the original and in the Jodhpur-based versions of the Chapman–Hausfater model. Also given is the minimum and maximum proportion of infanticidal males expected at equilibrium in populations characterized by average tenures within the specified ranges. See text for further explanation.

Although populations characterized by Jodhpur-like reproductive parameters would be expected to have a relatively large proportion of infanticidal males at equilibrium, these populations would also be expected to reach that equilibrium only very slowly. This is so because the first infanticidal male will, on average, produce only marginally more offspring than his noninfanticidal counterparts (Fig. 2A), and it is the extent of differential reproduction between infanticidal and noninfanticidal males that ultimately controls the rate of spread of infanticide in such populations. In fact, Jodhpur-like populations would be expected to reach their equilibrium proportion of infanticidal males only after a minimum of 600 generations compared to roughly one-half as many generations, on average, for populations like those at Mount Abu and Dharwar (Hausfater *et al.*, 1982b).

One important consequence of the predicted very slow spread of infanticide in Jodhpur-like populations is that demographic and environmental stochasticity would heavily influence the fate of infanticidal males. In particular, there would be an extremely long period of time during which infanticidal males were present only at very low numbers in these populations. These initial infanticidal males may thus be entirely eliminated from the population merely by the chance action of disease, predation, imbalanced sex ratio of offspring, and so on. Thus, independent of considerations of selective advantage, female counterstrategies, etc., infanticide may be absent from populations like that at Jodhpur merely due to the action of stochastic population processes alone. Nevertheless, the small sample of empiricial data on adult male replacements at Jodhpur presently in the literature suggests that very close to one-fourth of all group take-overs have been accompanied by infanticide (Mohnot, 1971a; Vogel and Loch, Chapter 12, this volume), precisely the proportion predicted by the revised version of the Chapman–Hausfater model.

Violation of Assumptions of the Model

Perhaps even more critical than stochastic population processes for testing either version of the Chapman–Hausfater model would be evidence that one or more of the model's basic assumptions were incorrect. Thus, if groups obtained by infanticidal males had slightly fewer or less fecund females than those obtained by noninfanticidal males, the reproductive advantage gained by the former could be substantially reduced. Although no evidence of such a differential exists in the literature on langurs (in fact, the contrary may be more likely: Hrdy, 1977b), the model can be easily modified to take this factor into account. One would merely need to carry out a linear transformation of the expected reproductive success curve for infanticidal males using a proportionality constant based on, for example, the average number of females in groups obtained by infanticidal males compared to the average number in groups obtained by noninfanticidal males. However, unless such a differential were quite sizeable, the conclusions of the present analysis—both as to the reproductive advantage and as to the equilibrium frequency of infanticidal males—would most likely be changed only very slightly.

More problematic than the foregoing consideration is the possibility that females may modify their aggressive and reproductive behavior specifically in response to the entry of an unfamiliar and thus potentially infanticidal male into their group. In fact, either the presence of an infanticidal male per se or the social disturbance accompanying adult-male replacement (see Vogel and Loch, Chapter 12, this volume) could readily serve as a cue for initiating a series of facultative physiological and behavioral changes by females. Under many circumstances, such modifications of behavior and (reproductive) physiology in response to infanticidal males may prove selectively advantageous for females and could thus potentially serve as the basis for a counterstrategy to infanticide.

THE REPRODUCTIVE CONSEQUENCES OF FEMALE COUNTERSTRATEGIES TO INFANTICIDE

Tactics, Strategies, and Counterstrategies

Females who lose unweaned offspring to infanticidal males will on average produce their own next infanticidal son sooner than females who successfully prevent the killing of their present infant. However, it seems unlikely that the indirect reproductive advantage obtained by the former females through their more rapid production of infanticidal sons (who have increased fitness due to this behavior) will ever outweigh the direct reproductive advantage obtained by the latter females through prevention of the death of their most recent infant in the first place. Furthermore, for most primate species, including langurs, the killing of unweaned infants following take-over of a group is certainly not a foregone conclusion, thus it will almost always be to a female's advantage to continue the investment in, and protection of, her most recent offspring (but cf. Hrdy, 1977b). In this regard, the evolution of female counterstrategies to infanticide in langurs and other primate species appears to differ quite substantially from the model outlined by several authors (Schwagmeyer, 1979; Labov, 1981a; Huck, Chapter 18, this volume) to account for the evolution of "pregnancy block" in rodents.

In the literature on langurs, the tactics most frequently mentioned as a means of preventing infanticide are active defense of infants, emigration of mothers and infants, premature weaning of infants, manipulation by females of the timing of male replacement, increased solicitation of and mating with infanticidal males (i.e., pseudoestrous behavior), and, conversely, refraining from mating with such males (Hrdy, 1977b, 1979). At a theoretical level, however, these and other plausible tactics give rise to only two different forms of counterstrategy to infanticide, referred to, respectively, as the *defensive* and *penalty* counterstrategies.

A defensive counterstrategy, as the name implies, is based on some form of active or passive defense of the infant by its mother, father, or some other group member. By contrast, a penalty counterstrategy does not involve any attempt to forestall infanticidal males but rather depends only on tactics that penalize infanticidal males for their behavior after the fact. Obviously, these two forms of counterstrategy are not mutually exclusive, and female langurs may actually utilize a mixture of both defensive and penalizing tactics when confronted by an infanticidal male. Nevertheless, defensive and penalty counterstrategies are conceptually quite distinct and in particular differ markedly from each other in their potential effects on the reproductive success of infanticidal adult males.

More specifically, a defensive counterstrategy can, at best, reduce the reproductive success of infanticidal males to the same level as that of noninfanticidal males (i.e., make the behavior selectively neutral). A penalty counterstrategy, on the other hand, can actually result in infanticidal males consistently producing fewer offspring than their noninfanticidal counterparts. From an evolutionary perspective, only a penalty counterstrategy has the potential to eliminate infanticide from a population completely (i.e., to make the behavior selectively disadvantageous for males). In the next sections, the consequences of these two forms of counterstrategy for the reproductive success of infanticidal males are considered in more detail using the Chapman–Hausfater model (Figs. 1 and 2) as a means of organizing the discussion.

Reproductive Consequences of Defensive Counterstrategies

When a defensive counterstrategy is successful in preventing the death of an infant, the infanticidal male gains nothing from his efforts but neither does he lose much at attempting infanticide in the first place. When a defensive counterstrategy is ineffective in preventing infant deaths, the male will generally gain increased reproductive success from his efforts and again incurs very little cost in doing so. In fact, as noted by Leland *et al.* (Chapter 8, this volume), possibly the only way in which a male can lose fitness through attempts at infanticide is if he is himself seriously injured by the infant's defenders or if he accidentally also kills the mother of the infant. In terms of the Chapman–Hausfater model, a defensive counterstrategy has the effect of reducing the difference between the solid and broken lines in Figs.

1 and 2 by some fixed proportion, and the magnitude of this reduction is essentially determined by the effectiveness of the counterstrategy in deterring infanticidal males. However, under no circumstances would a defensive counterstrategy result in infanticidal males (solid line) having lower reproductive success than noninfanticidal males (broken line) where they do not already do so in these figures.

The reproductive consequences of a defensive counterstrategy can be visualized somewhat more precisely by considering the effects, in terms of Figs. 1 and 2, of a defense that is completely effective versus one that is to some extent, however small, less than 100% effective. In the former case, an infanticidal male would do no worse nor better than a noninfanticidal male in terms of reproductive success (i.e., the solid and broken lines in Figs. 1 and 2 would converge). In contrast, were a defensive counterstrategy only partially effective, there would still be some residual advantage obtained by infanticidal males (i.e., the solid line would remain above the broken line across some range of tenure values in the figures). Furthermore, given the marked variability of behavior characteristic of most primate species, it is quite unlikely that any defensive counterstrategy would ever be totally effective. Thus, populations in which females pursue a purely defensive counterstrategy will almost certainly offer infanticidal males at least some slight reproductive advantage and as a result would be expected to retain a non-negligible proportion of such individuals (see also Hausfater et al., 1982b).

The Cost of Various Defensive Tactics

Aside from considerations of reproductive success, one would expect the particular tactics used in any counterstrategy to depend heavily on their ecological and fitness costs to females. In particular, active defense of offspring most likely carries with it a relatively high energetic cost for females. Furthermore, this tactic probably also results in a significant increase in the probability that a female will be severely wounded and thus may be quite costly in fitness terms as well. Although several other tactics mentioned previously are essentially variants of active defense of infants, at least a few of these latter alternatives seem potentially much less costly for females than directly confronting an infanticidal male.

For example, in species characterized by a multimale group structure, it has been speculated that polyandrous mating patterns by females confuse adult males as to the paternity of infants born into the group (Altmann et al., 1978). As a result, so long as one or more of a female's mating partners remain in the group, these males constitute potential defenders of her offspring (Busse and Hamilton, 1981; Collins et al., Chapter 10, this volume). Paternity confusion can thus be viewed as a tactic that transfers all or part of the cost of defense of infants from their mothers to their actual or potential fathers. Obviously, however, this tactic is not available to females in one-male groups such as those of many colobines and some cercopithecine monkeys.

Emigration of a mother and her infant from their group following its take-over by an infanticidal male is another plausible defensive tactic as is premature weaning of the infant by its mother. However, even given the incomplete data presently available, there is strong reason to believe that either of these tactics may prove more costly to females than does active defense of young. Specifically, data presented by Crockett (1984) indicate that among red howler monkeys, for example, emigration by females is associated with increased mortality just as it is known to be among males in many other primate species (Dittus, 1977; Jones, 1980). Likewise, except under laboratory conditions of ad lib feeding, the premature removal of an infant from its mother generally has dire consequences for the survival of that infant (Rhine et al., 1980).

Rather than defend their infants per se, females in a one-male group may selectively defend their current resident male so as to influence the timing of his replacement. Specifically, were the resident male replaced only when all infants in the group were already weaned and independent, no infants would be vulnerable to attack by an infanticidal successor male regardless of the number of such individuals in the population as a whole. However, a counterstrategy based on female control of male replacement time would require a degree of reproductive synchrony unlikely to be found in most primate populations as well as a social structure in which concerted aggression by females actually had the potential to prevent one male from ousting another.

Within the realm of defensive tactics, perhaps the one least costly to females is "pseudoestrous" behavior. Briefly, Sugiyama (1965b), Hrdy (1977b), and Vogel and Loch (Chapter 12, this volume) have all remarked on the fact that female langurs quite frequently respond to the presence of a new and potentially infanticidal male in their group with repeated sexual solicitation of the male. Although the evidence is far from compelling, there is reason to believe that in at least a few cases, the soliciting females were in fact pregnant, and thus their behavior has been labeled "pseudoestrous" to distinguish it from true estrous behavior (i.e., sexual receptivity accompanying ovulation). Furthermore, Hrdy (1977b, 1979) speculated that such pseudoestrous behavior by pregnant females inhibited new males from killing infants born to these females shortly after take-over of their group. Pseudoestrous behavior as the basis of a counterstrategy to infanticide has subsequently received widespread attention in review articles and secondary sources even though the infanticide-inhibiting effects of this behavior have yet to be confirmed with systematically collected data on langurs or any other primate species.

Nevertheless, it is interesting to note that laboratory research on rodents has shown that a male's familiarity with a given female is a key factor in inhibiting infanticidal behavior by that male toward her most recent litter (Labov, 1980), and it is certainly plausible that a similar mechanism may be at work in primates. Alternatively, pseudoestrous behavior may produce confusion on the part of males regarding the paternity of newborn infants and thereby inhibit infanticide in the same way that such confusion engenders male defense of infants in multimale social groups. Regardless of the precise mechanism, it seems likely that pseudoestrous behavior carries with it substantially less cost to females than does any defensive tactic involving aggression toward the male.

The Reproductive Consequences of Penalty Counterstrategies

In contrast to defensive counterstrategies, a penalty counterstrategy has the potential to make infanticidal behavior disadvantageous for males both over the short-term and over evolutionary time. The most simple tactic in this regard would be for a female to refrain from mating with any male who killed, or attempted to kill, her unweaned infant. But, if the male did not attempt infanticide, or if her most recent offspring were already weaned, the female would respond to the infanticidal male in the same manner that she would to a noninfanticidal male. For convenience, this type of penalty counterstrategy is referred to as *individually imposed,* meaning that each female as an individual either mates with the new male or refrains from doing so, depending only on his behavior toward her and her infant. However, the preceding should not be taken to mean that a female refrains from mating with an infanticidal male indefinitely, merely that she does so for some specified period of time. Thus, the penalty is not a complete loss of reproductive access by infanticidal males to the mothers of their victims but rather a female-imposed delay in that access.

In the version of the Chapman–Hausfater model based on Jodhpur parameter values (Fig. 2), adult males obtained a reproductive advantage only by killing infants roughly 4 months in age or younger. On average, then, an infanticidal male would obtain a 2-month reduction in waiting time to insemination of the mothers of those infants. Hence, the minimum penalty required to make infanticide selectively disadvantageous for adult males would be on the order of 3 months, while a penalty of only 1 month's duration would be expected to have little consequence for the reproductive success of infanticidal males. Figure 3 shows the result of modifying the Jodhpur-based model (Fig. 2) to

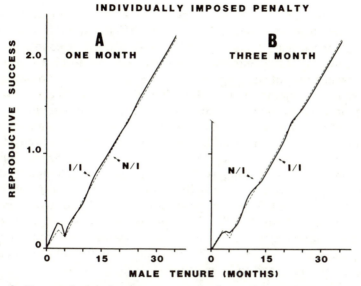

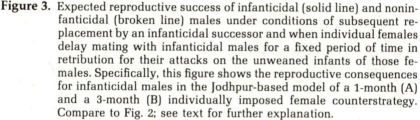

Figure 3. Expected reproductive success of infanticidal (solid line) and noninfanticidal (broken line) males under conditions of subsequent replacement by an infanticidal successor and when individual females delay mating with infanticidal males for a fixed period of time in retribution for their attacks on the unweaned infants of those females. Specifically, this figure shows the reproductive consequences for infanticidal males in the Jodhpur-based model of a 1-month (A) and a 3-month (B) individually imposed female counterstrategy. Compare to Fig. 2; see text for further explanation.

take into account an individually imposed female counterstrategy. As expected, a 1-month penalty (Fig. 3A) produced only a very slight change in the reproductive advantage obtained by infanticidal males. In contrast, a 3-month individually imposed penalty proved effective in almost completely eliminating any advantage gained by males through infanticide. In this latter case, infanticidal males had an expected reproductive success that was actually lower than that of noninfanticidal males at all tenures with the exception of 2–4 months, 7–8 months, and 14–16 months. Obviously, an even longer penalty delay, for example, 4–6 months in duration, would eliminate even these last vestiges of reproductive advantage for infanticidal males and thereby make the behavior unequivocally disadvantageous for males in terms of natural selection.

Of course, delay of reproduction as a counterstrategy to infanticide not only imposes a penalty on infanticidal males but also on the individual females themselves. Thus, one may ask, why this fitness cost should be borne only by females who have lost offspring to infanticidal males

when in the long run all females will benefit from the elimination of
these males from their population. In fact, one could imagine a species
in which the fitness costs associated with a penalty counterstrategy
were shared equitably among all females in a group, and Fig. 4 examines
the consequences of such a *group-imposed* penalty on the reproductive
success of infanticidal males. More specifically, this figure shows the
effects on the reproductive success of an infanticidal male in the Jodhpur-based model when all females in his group delay mating with him
for 1 month longer than usual and do so whether or not he specifically
kills any of their own offspring. Under these conditions, the reproductive
advantage obtained by males through infanticide is eliminated just
as completely as by a 3-month individually imposed penalty. Of course,
in the long run, either type of penalty counterstrategy will entail the
same fitness costs for females, but clearly the group- and individually
imposed counterstrategies necessitate, as a precondition for their evolution, populations with very different demographic and genetic structures, a point returned to later (see Discussion).

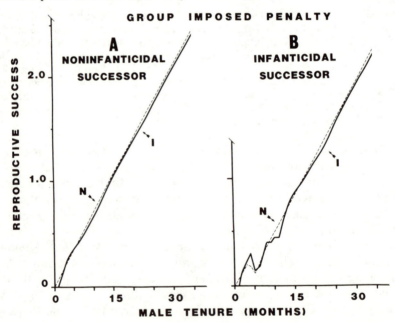

Figure 4. Reproductive consequences of a group-imposed penalty against infanticidal males in the Jodhpur-based model. In the particular version of this counterstrategy shown here, all females in the group
are assumed to delay mating with the infanticidal male during the
first month following his arrival in the group. The effect of this
counterstrategy is to make infanticide selectively disadvantageous
for adult males at nearly all tenures. Compare to Fig. 2; see text
for further explanation.

Proximate Mechanisms Potentially Underlying Penalty Counterstrategies

Many primate species show relatively well-defined mating and birth seasons (Lancaster and Lee, 1965). Were an infanticidal male to take over a group in such a species and then to kill unweaned infants, he would most likely not obtain any reproductive advantage at all through his actions. This is so because seasonality of breeding will generally result in a delay in resumption of breeding activity by the mothers of the infants, although presumably this "penalty" would reflect ecological necessity rather than an evolved counterstrategy per se. Nevertheless, one would not expect infanticide to be prevalent in primate species that are highly seasonal in their mating behavior and births, and this does indeed seem to be the case (Hrdy, 1979).

In addition to the preceding ecological mechanism, a penalty counterstrategy would be relatively easy to evolve in many primate species in terms of basic physiological mechanisms. For example, there is good evidence that the onset or resumption of sexual cycles by primate females can be affected by the level of social stress in their group as well as by the amount of aggression directed by group-mates toward them and their offspring (Rowell, 1970a). Thus, aggression accompanying the take-over of a group by a new and potentially infanticidal male may, in and of itself, produce a temporary cessation of reproductive cycles by females in the group and thereby result in the imposition of a penalty on such a male. In sum, at the level of physiological mechanisms, many primate species seem ideally preadapted for the evolution by females of a penalty counterstrategy to infanticide.

DISCUSSION

Further Evolutionary Considerations

Unfortunately, it is much easier to evolve a penalty counterstrategy to infanticide in terms of physiological mechanisms than in terms of genetic mechanisms acting at the level of individuals or populations. The basic consideration in this regard is as follows: What happens if one female in a group or population does not respond to the presence of an infanticidal male by delaying reproduction? Answer: That female will in the long run produce more offspring than will her counterparts who individually or collectively penalize the infanticidal male for his behavior. In other words, evolution of a penalty counterstrategy to infanticide requires a strong component of altruism on the part of adult females, and thus the evolution of such a counterstrategy is subject to the same constraints and problems that form the basis of so much discussion and theory in contemporary sociobiology (Hamilton, 1964a; Wilson, 1975).

Rather than repeat all of the various arguments and models concerning the evolution of altruistic behavior, it is sufficient to say that at present a model for evolving a penalty-based female counterstrategy to infanticide cannot be constructed without invoking: (1) a high degree of relatedness (≥ 0.5) among females in each group; (2) an extremely low rate (or total absence) of migration of females between groups; and (3) a high degree of reciprocity of behavior by females both within and between groups. Although one or the other of these characteristics may be present in some primate populations, in no single instance does it seem likely that all of the necessary demographic preconditions exist for the evolution of a penalty-based female counterstrategy to infanticide. Thus, it is my conclusion that we are unlikely to find a penalty counterstrategy to infanticide in any primate species, although on theoretical and empirical grounds there is reason to believe that such a counterstrategy may be found among lions (Packer and Pusey, 1983b).

On the other hand, these genetic and demographic considerations do not constrain the evolution of a defensive counterstrategy by females. Obviously, in those species characterized by only a small degree of size dimorphism, females may be able to readily defend themselves against the attack of an infanticidal male. Likewise, in species characterized by not only a high degree of dimorphism but also a multimale social organization, one may expect the joint defense of infants by their mothers and potential fathers to be effective in preventing infanticide. Empirical evidence suggests that this may indeed be the case in blue monkeys (Butynski, 1982), a species that is not extremely dimorphic in either size or weight, and in baboons (Collins et al., Chapter 10, this volume), a multimale species.

However, by far the least costly defensive tactic is pseudoestrous behavior, and this tactic could be readily evolved from the same physiological underpinnings discussed previously with respect to penalty counterstrategies. Nevertheless, the effectiveness of pseudoestrus as a defensive tactic essentially relies on deception, and were this tactic ever highly successful in preventing infanticide, one would then expect there to be strong selection on males in turn to evolve a mechanism for detecting such deception. Indeed, laboratory and field data from several different primate species suggest that adult males can use olfactory and visual cues to determine a female's reproductive state quite precisely, including possibly even the day of ovulation (Michael and Keverne, 1968; Hausfater, 1975). Thus, in so far as male langurs, or males of any other primate species, have the potential to evolve sensory mechanisms for assaying the ovarian state of females in their group, the spread and effectiveness of pseudoestrous behavior will be severely constrained as part of a defensive counterstrategy to infanticide.

In sum, primate infanticide epitomizes the paradox of competition between and within the sexes. All members of a population suffer reduced reproductive success as the result of the presence of even a single infanticidal male in their population. But, once such a male is introduced into the population, the most advantageous reproductive strategy for other males is to also engage in infanticide. The present analysis has shown that females can, in theory, prevent the spread of infanticidal behavior among males by cooperatively or individually penalizing infanticidal individuals. However, any female who did not participate in this counterstrategy would, in the long run, have higher reproductive success than participatory females. In contrast, the counterstrategy that is most likely to be favored by individual selection (i.e., a defensive counterstrategy based on pseudoestrous behavior) is also one that is highly likely to be severely constrained in both its spread and effectiveness by various basic aspects of the biology of primates. Thus, infanticide is an excellent example of a behavioral strategy that produces a short-term increase in reproductive success for some individuals of one sex but that thereby also locks adults of both sexes into patterns of behavior that ultimately result in a decreased rate of reproduction for themselves and for their population as a whole. As with so many other examples in modern behavioral ecology, the present analysis of langur infanticide supports the prevailing notion that evolution does not favor behavior that is "good for the species," but rather behavior that is good for the individual and, moreover, "good" only in the short-run.

ACKNOWLEDGMENTS

Unpublished data from the langur population at Jodhpur was graciously provided to me by Drs. Christian Vogel and Hartmut Loch, thereby making possible work on the analyses described in this paper. These efforts also benefited greatly from extended discussions with Drs. Vogel and Loch.

Dr. Sarah B. Hrdy provided a detailed and helpful critique of an earlier version of this paper. Furthermore, discussions of the topic of female counterstrategies to infanticide with Dr. Hrdy were influential both in my initially choosing to work on this topic and in shaping my thinking on the topic overall.

This manuscript also benefited from a careful reading by C. Saunders, J. Stelzner, S. Cairns, and S. Kirmeyer, all of whom are gratefully acknowledged as is support for this work from the National Science Foundation and the National Institutes of Health.

14 Infant killing and male reproductive strategies in langurs (*Presbytis entellus*)

Jane Boggess

INTRODUCTION

Although published reports of infant killing in the common langur (*Presbytis entellus*) appeared as early as the mid-1960s, it was not until 1974 when Hrdy proposed the sexual selection hypothesis that this phenomenon gained widespread attention. Earlier reports by Sugiyama (1965b, 1966) and Mohnot (1971a) were primarily of concern to the relatively small community of people studying langurs, and while these accounts were received with interest, the significance of infant killing was generally viewed as limited and only relevant to special conditions.

With the publication of Hrdy's (1974) sexual selection hypothesis, these formerly isolated events were taken as evidence of a widespread and adaptive strategy. This publication had considerable impact on primate research, and by the end of the 1970s, it had spawned a major controversy within the field of primate biology. Based largely on the strength of Hrdy's review of three sites where infant killing had been reported, a model for male reproductive success was accepted by many as typical for langurs and by some as a basis for interpreting the existence of a similar strategy in other species of monkey. Within a fairly short period of time, a number of reports appeared of suspected infant killing in various primate species, including both cercopithecines (Struhsaker, 1977, 1978b) and other colobines (Wolf and Fleagle, 1977; Oates,

1977). The majority of these accounts were actually reports of infant disappearances during periods of male take-over, and, in some instances, the data presented were not new, but the investigator had, in light of the sexual selection hypothesis, reevaluated older field data and concluded that infants that disappeared during periods of male membership change were in fact victims of infanticide (cf. Leland *et al.*, Chapter 8, this volume).

The field data for langurs (*Presbytis entellus*) have had a key role in the development and acceptance of the sexual selection hypothesis. While reports of infant killing in most other primate species have been fragmentary, the data for langurs appear to many to be strong and incontrovertible, demonstrating the existence of an evolved male reproductive strategy within the species. However, previous reviews and discussions of the sexual selection hypothesis (Hrdy, 1974, 1977a,b, 1979; Ripley, 1980; Hausfater and Vogel, 1982), for the most part, have not been coupled with a strict review of the data, many of which are difficult to access and exist in numerous different sources. Thus, this chapter takes a close look at these field data in light of both the sexual selection and other hypotheses that have been put forward to explain infant killing in langurs (*Presbytis entellus*).

In particular, Dharwar, Jodhpur, and Abu, the major sites where infant killing has been reported, are reviewed in detail. In addition, data are summarized from two strikingly different populations of langurs—Rajaji and Junbesi-Ringmo—which do not show male take-over or infant killing. On the basis of these five datasets, the major hypotheses concerning infant killing in langurs are evaluated.

HYPOTHESES

Proximate Explanations of Infant Killing

In the mid-1960s, Sugiyama (1965b,1966) reported infant killing in association with troop-male membership change at Dharwar. His conclusions regarding the significance of these events were based largely on the correspondence of increased female sexual activity immediately following adult male replacement in bisexual troops, and he noted that the loss of an infant had the effect of stimulating estrus in the mother. Observations of bisexual troops indicated that a number of factors, "such as severe fighting among males, change in troop leader, or a severe attack with killing of infants [could] activate sexual activity of females [Sugiyama, 1967:233]."

Sexual competition for females was assumed to be the cause of male membership change in troops (generally in the form of adult male replacement), with copulations between the new resident troop male and estrus females functioning to promote social bonds between the new male and troop females (Sugiyama, 1965b:413). At Dharwar, large numbers of males lived outside of bisexual troops that were closed breeding units. Adult male replacement was stated to occur as the result of attacks on bisexual troops by all-male bands (Sugiyama, 1965b, 1966). Increased population density was cited as the most likely factor influencing Dharwar population dynamics, particularly the large numbers of males outside of bisexual troops and the high frequency of turnover of adult male residents in the one-male bisexual troops (Sugiyama, 1965b:407–408).

Sugiyama's conclusions are noteworthy, not only for the information they contain about Dharwar but because of the foundation they have given to subsequent (and conflicting) hypotheses about infant killing. Specifically, as relevant to the sexual selection hypothesis, Sugiyama's reports (1) correlated infant loss with the onset of estrus; (2) suggested that adult males may have the capability to discern their own offspring from those sired by other males; and (3) indicated that male tenure within any given bisexual troop was short. However, the same body of data provided correlations (4) between take-overs and infant killing and (5) between very high population density and infant killing—factors that underlay many of the alternate explanations of infant killing such as those proposed by Curtin (1977), Curtin and Dolhinow (1978), and Boggess (1979, 1980).

Mohnot was the second field investigator to report infant killing in langurs (*Presbytis entellus*), in this case again in conjunction with a series of all-male band attacks on a bisexual troop. Mohnot (1971a) also concluded that the all-male band attacks on the troop were related to male competition for females. However, his conclusions differed from those of Sugiyama concerning the significance of infant killing. While infant killing at Jodhpur did hasten the onset of estrus, most of the infant-deprived females copulated with males other than the infanticidal male, thereby making it difficult to argue that these behaviors functioned to promote sociosexual bonds between the new male and troop females. Thus, Mohnot (1971a) hypothesized that infant killing resulted from redirected aggression exhibited by the new male in an intense conflict situation. Infants were killed both during and in anticipation of all-male band attacks on the troop. As Mohnot wrote: "It appears that the simultaneous sexual excitement and enragement made the new leader very aggressive, and this might have been the stimulus behind infant killing. His post-killing behavior supports this presumption. Each time after the killing the leader looked relaxed and mild [Mohnot, 1971a:196–197]."

The Sexual Selection Hypothesis

Clearly, both Sugiyama and Mohnot attempted to explain infant killing only at the level of "proximate" mechanisms. In contrast, Hrdy (1974) stressed ultimate (i.e., evolutionary) factors and developed a model that explained infant killing in association with adult male replacement in terms of sexual selection as discussed by Trivers (1972). According to this model, infant killing is a reproductive strategy "whereby an invading male increased his own reproductive success at the expense of the former leader or dominant male (who would typically be the father of the infant killed), the mother, and of course the infant [Hrdy, 1979:22]." Because of characteristics intrinsic to langurs, this species was assumed to be predisposed to take-overs as a form of troop male membership change, and infant killing was viewed as an evolutionary adaptation to conditions in which males are frequently displaced from breeding groups.

Hrdy proposed that in one-male breeding units, where adult male replacement occurs frequently, infant killing permits a new resident adult male to efficiently use his short tenure in the troop. By killing infants fathered by the previous (rival) male resident, the new male induces sexual receptivity in the mothers, and they thus more quickly bear his own offspring. The following assumptions are critical to Hrdy's hypothesis: (1) infant killing is an evolved behavior (i.e., that a high rate of adult male replacement in bisexual troops and attendant infant killing are not recent or atypical phenomena for *Presbytis entellus*); (2) bisexual troops are closed breeding systems (i.e., that a male's take-over of a troop assures his exclusive reproductive access to troop females); (3) attacks on infants only occur when a nontroop male enters a new troop and are made with some assessment of paternity (i.e., that a male does not kill his own offspring).

In early publications, Hrdy (1974) suggested that infant killing was species-typical for langurs (*Presbytis entellus*). This position has been modified in recent years as a result of the attention given to new published data from sites where neither infant killing nor take-overs have been reported. Now recognizing the pronounced intraspecific variability in langurs with regard to the occurrence of these behaviors, Hrdy (1979) and others (e.g. Hausfater *et al.*, 1982b) have suggested that infant killing as a behavior may be facultative and thus occur on a behavioral scale as a function of specific environmental or (more probably) demographic conditions. Take-overs and infant killing are still assumed to be routine occurrences at some sites, specifically Dharwar, Jodhpur, and Abu and, in conformance with Hrdy's initial hypothesis, are believed to be the result of sexual selection and thus adaptive for the individual infanticidal male (Hrdy, 1979).

Criticisms of the Sexual Selection Hypothesis

The sexual selection hypothesis has been contested by a number of investigators who have observed free-ranging langurs in the wild (see Curtin, 1977; Curtin and Dolhinow, 1978; Vogel, 1979; Boggess,

1979, 1980). Attempts to disprove Hrdy's model largely have rested on an evaluation of the available reproductive data for troops in which infant killing has occurred. In addition, Vogel (1979) and co-workers have denied that either rapid ("smooth") adult male replacement or infant killing is typical of adult male membership change in bisexual troops at Jodhpur (but see Vogel and Loch, Chapter 12, this volume, for a recent modification of this conclusion).

Through a general review of (1) bisexual troop adult male composition and their patterns of change in studied langur populations and (2) demographic and environmental characteristics associated with these study sites, Curtin and Dolhinow (1978) and Boggess (1979, 1980) have described a different pattern of adult male competition in langurs from that proposed by Hrdy (1974). In these review articles, the adult male social dynamics that prevail at Dharwar, Jodhpur, and Abu have been identified as atypical for the species. Further, these reviews argue that specific environmental and demographic factors clearly separate the populations at Dharwar, Jodhpur, and Abu from most other langur populations. Take-over and infant killing have then been explained as a response to these environmental/demographic conditions rather than as evolved reproductive strategies.

Specifically, Curtin and Dolhinow (1978) have both argued that the pattern of male take-over accompanied by infant killing has only been found under crowded conditions or where langurs have extensive contact with humans. They point out that at the time of the Dharwar study, the area had just been subjected to extensive recent deforestation and that the predator population had been greatly diminished (for a recent comment on this view, see Sugiyama, Chapter 15, this volume). Langurs at Jodhpur and Abu live in habitats drastically altered by man and are extensively provisioned by humans. These conditions, which have occurred in recent historical time, have resulted in social crowding for the langur populations that live there. Curtin and Dolhinow (1978) argue that because these conditions are very recent (especially within the framework of evolutionary time), the behavioral traits of infant killing and rapid take-over cannot represent linked strategies that have evolved in response to them. They point to the origin of the male take-over pattern in the powerful male rivalries that are species-typical for langurs but which at other sites are balanced by processes that allow gradual adult male replacement in multimale bisexual troops. Social crowding and increased levels of human harassment are seen as removing two important requisites—space and time—for the more species-typical pattern of gradual resolution of male–male conflict. As a consequence, the typical pattern of adult male competition cannot occur at these stressed sites, and rapid turnover of males accompanied by infant killing is seen instead.

Boggess (1979), in addition to reviewing other data for Dharwar, Jodhpur, and Abu, has analyzed the proximate factors that contribute to infant mortality in association with troop membership change. This review has suggested that the level of both intra- and intersexual aggression among adults may be critical in determining the occurrence of aggressive behaviors toward infants, and that infant killing results from varied circumstances and can involve different sets of factors. While recognizing that this type of evidence has no direct bearing on the proof of infanticide as a male reproductive strategy, it has challenged that aspect of Hrdy's hypothesis that presents infant killing as the result of organized and goal-oriented male behaviors. Boggess (1979) also pointed out that these data concerning proximate causation gain special significance if Hrdy's central hypothesis about sexual selection and infanticide is not supported by available reproductive data.

Infant Killings as Population Regulation and Maintenance of Genetic Variability

Ripley (1980), in her recent review of langur socioecology, has stressed the role of yet another set of evolutionary factors in producing male take-over and infant killing. Her observations of langurs at Polonnaruwa indicated that infant killing occurs there, however, with one important difference from infant killing reported at other sites: Bisexual troops in which infant killing occurred were multimale. With these data in hand, Ripley proposed that male take-over and infant killing in langurs functioned to ensure genetic polymorphism and to control population growth.

With respect to infant killing in relation to genetic polymorphism, Ripley pointed out that behavioral variability is central to the adaptive strategy of this successful and widespread species. Further, she argued that infant killing following adult male replacement, however costly and indirect, is one means of preserving a polymorphic potential within a highly subdivided population. Through these behavioral traits, close inbreeding and genetic homogeneity are avoided in one-male (and many multimale) bisexual langur groups.

The basis for Ripley's hypothesis stating infant killing in langurs functions as a population control mechanism is as follows: Langurs, unlike most colobines, are foraging generalists.

> In order to exploit the sort of fluctuating resources in the environment in which behavioral generalists are successful, a high reproductive rate seems essential as a means of rapid recovery from population downturn resulting from a run of particularly unfavorable seasons. With sufficient mortality from these causes, infanticide is rare. During favorable times some sort of countervailing controls must be applied to prevent intolerable local density accumulation, and if dispersal is blocked, infanticide is more common [Ripley, 1980:380].

Dharwar

This langur study site in Mysore State, India, was the first location where infant killing was reported. During a 22-month study between June 1961 and April 1963, a team of investigators, including Sugiyama, Yoshiba, Kawamura, Parthasarathy, and Miyadi, collected data on approximately 44 langur troops. The study included an initial 3-month roadside survey in which 44 troops were censused and an intensive study of 9 langur troops (Sugiyama, 1964, 1965a,b, 1967; Sugiyama *et al.,* 1965; Sugiyama and Parthasarathy, 1969; Yoshiba, 1967, 1968).

Reports from Dharwar described a process of troop membership change that occurred rapidly and frequently resulted in the complete replacement of resident troop males by nontroop male(s) concomitant with a marked increase in sexual activity. These changes generally resulted from all-male band attacks on bisexual troops, with the majority of these attacks occurring during the first half of the mating peak between May and August (Sugiyama, 1967). In "successful" attacks, adult males from the all-male band either drove out resident adult, subadult, and, in many cases, juvenile males or took females and immatures from the bisexual troop.

Case histories. During the 22-month study, investigators directly observed six cases of major troop membership changes: four of these changes occurred naturally, and two were the result of the experimental removal of one troop's only adult male (Sugiyama, 1965b, 1966, 1967). On the basis of census data from 1961 and 1962, investigators hypothesized that at least four other instances of major troop membership changes occurred (Yoshiba, 1967:236).

Of the 10 major changes in troop composition, infant mortality was associated with 3 of them. These deaths involve a total of 13 or 14 infants and 1 juvenile. In all cases, the new resident male in the troop was assumed to have killed the infants (Sugiyama, 1965b, 1966, 1967). Data supporting the manner of death, however, are largely based on circumstantial evidence. In the case of Troop 1, a two-male take-over was reported in March 1963. When this troop was again observed 1 month later, 4 or 5 infants were missing (Sugiyama, 1965b, 1967).

In the case of Troop 2, four infants disappeared over a period of 4 days; the disappearances occurred about 1 week after the investigators had removed the troop's only adult male. During the interval in which the infants disappeared, two adult males from adjacent Troops 3 and 4 associated with females and immatures in Troop 2. These males engaged in agonistic interactions with each other, and one of them (the male from Troop 4) directed aggressive behaviors toward the females of Troop 2. These aggressive behaviors toward the females continued, even after all of the infants had disappeared (Sugiyama, 1966). There were no direct observations of adult males attacking infants, although wounds were observed on two of the infants before they disappeared, and on one occasion the adult male from Troop 4 was observed grabbing at, but not touching, one of the infants.

In the case of Troop 30, five infants and one juvenile disappeared over a 2-month period. Three of these infants and the juvenile disappeared after adult male replacement occurred within Troop 30. Two of the infants disappeared while this change was occurring. The mortal injuring of one infant was observed, and this infant was bitten by the new adult male resident. The new male was also observed attacking troop females that had lost infants; these observed attacks constituted a primary source of evidence that, in fact, it was the new adult male that had killed the infants in the troop (Sugiyama, 1965b:392, 397).

Adult male assaults on infants that did not result in mortality also were observed in association with troop male membership changes. Three males took over Troop 7 in October 1962. These males evicted the resident male and themselves stayed with the troop for 1 month, whereupon one of these three males drove out the other two. The new resident male made assaults on all of the troop's six infants, but these attacks did not result in any deaths (Sugiyama, 1965b).

Adult male replacements. The patterns of adult male residence in troops affected by membership change varied both before and after these changes occurred. Before the preceding events, Troop 1 had three adult males; afterward, when membership had stabilized, this troop had two adult male residents. Troop 2 initially had one adult male. After this male was experimentally removed, Troop 2 continued for several months without a full-time adult male resident. For the first few months, the adult male in adjacent Troop 4 moved back and forth between his troop and Troop 2. This pattern was then repeated by the adult male in Troop 3 for a period of time until a successful merger occurred between Troops 2 and 3. Troop 30 had one resident adult male before and after the take-over.

Interbirth intervals. Data on length of birth intervals (i.e., the length of time between the death of one infant and birth of the subsequent infant) are available for 8 of the 14 or 15 females who lost infants (Table I). For these females, the average interval between births of killed infants and births of subsequent offspring is approximately 16 months. This compares to the normal-birth interval reported for Dharwar of 20–24 months (Sugiyama et al., 1965). While data from Troops 2 and 30 show a definite correlation between shortened birth intervals and take-over and infant killing, it is not clear which (or both) of the variables are responsible for the shortened interval. For example, when male membership change occurred in Troop 7, there were six unweaned infants in the troop. Infant killing did not occur in Troop 7, but nevertheless, shortly after the take-over the new male copulated with most, if not all, of the troop's females (Sugiyama et al., 1965; see also Vogel

Table I. Interbirth intervals for infant-deprived females

Site/troop	Average interval for females	Number of females where interval unknown
Dharwar/Troops 1, 2, 30 (Sugiyama, 1965b, 1966, 1967; Sugiyama *et al.,* 1965)	16 months ($n = 8$)	6–7
Jodhpur/Troop B26 (Mohnot, 1971a; Hrdy, 1974:49)	21 months ($n = 4$)	1
Jodhpur/Troop Kaga A (Makwana, 1979)		3
Abu/Troop B6: 1971 (Hrdy, 1974:28)	"Normal" intervals	3
Abu/Troop B3: 1971–1972 (Hrdy, 1977b:38–40)		3
Abu/Troop B6: 1972–1973 (Hrdy, 1977b:73)	24 months ($n = 4$)	
Abu/Troop B3: 1975) Hrdy, 1977a)		2
Abu/Troop B6: 1975 (Hrdy, 1977a)		2

and Loch, Chapter 12, this volume). The study ended 4 months after these copulations occurred, so it is not known whether these were fertile matings actually resulting in shortened interbirth intervals.

Paternity. Only minimal data are available from Dharwar concerning the paternity of infants killed (Table II). In the case of Troop 1, paternity of infants killed can probably be assigned to males other than those that invaded the troop, thus precluding the possibility that males were killing their own offspring. No paternity data exist for infants killed in Troops 2 and 30 because these infants were conceived before troop compositions were established and reproductive data were collected.

Reproductive data demonstrating paternity of subsequent offspring born to infant-deprived females at Dharwar are weak (see Table III). For about five infants, observation of sexual activity or circumstantial evidence suggest that they might have been conceived by a male reported to have engaged in infant killing. For the subsequent offspring born to the remaining 9 or 10 infant-deprived females, paternity data are lacking either because the times of their conception are unknown or because more then one adult male associated with their mothers during the interval in which they were conceived.

Jodhpur

The second langur (*Presbytis entellus*) study site where infant killing was reported was Jodhpur in western India. Beginning in 1967, Mohnot

Table II. Genetic relationship between killed infants and infanticidal male

Site/troop	Paternity known		Paternity unknown	Comments
	Killed infants sired by male(s) other than infanticidal male	Killed infants sired by infanticidal male		
Dharwar/Troop 1 (Sugiyama, 1967; Sugiyama et al., 1965)	4–5			On the basis of troop composition data, it can be assumed that the infants killed were sired by male(s) other than the infanticidal male(s)
Dharwar/Troop 2 (Sugiyama, 1965b, 1966; Sugiyama et al., 1965)			4	Infants conceived before the study began or during the summer roadside survey before the composition of Troop 2 was established
Dharwar/Troop 30 (Sugiyama, 1965a; Sugiyama et al., 1965)			6	Infants conceived before study began in mid-June 1961
Jodhpur/Troop B26 (Mohnot, 1971a)		1	4	There are no published data on paternity of the four infants killed immediately following take-over; the fifth infant killed in Troop B26 is reported to have been sired by the new (infanticidal) male resident
Jodhpur/Troop Kaga A (Makwana, 1979)			3	Infants conceived in 13-month gap in observations
Abu/Troop B6 for 1971 (Hrdy, 1974:27.)			6	Infants conceived before study began

				Comments
Abu/Troop B3 for 1971–1972 (Hrdy, 1974:30)			3	Infants conceived before study began
Abu/Troop B6 for 1972–1973 (Hrdy, 1974)	2?	2?		Paternity of these infants is uncertain although data suggest that two of the offspring were conceived by one male and two of the off-spring were conceived by another male. The genetic relationship between these infants and the infanticidal male is equivocal because none of the killings were witnessed, and several males associated with the troop. However, one male was most visibly associated with the disappearances of the infants and is the male Hrdy (1974) associated with at least some of the infant deaths
				It is important to note three of these four infants killed are the reported offspring of the previous infanticidal male resident. That is, the females, Itch, Bilgay, and Oedipa are reported to have lost two successive crops of offspring to infanticidal males
Abu/Troop B3 for 1975 (Hrdy, 1977b)	2			Infants conceived in a 15-month gap in observations during which troop-adult-male membership changes occurred
Abu/Troop B6 for 1975 (Hrdy, 1977b)	2			Infants conceived in gaps in observations during which troop adult male membership changes occurred
Total	6–7	3	30	

Table III. Genetic relationship between subsequent offspring born to infant-deprived females and infanticidal male

Site/troop	Paternity known		Paternity unknown		Comments
	Offspring sired by infanticidal male	Offspring sired by noninfanticidal male	Infant-deprived females associate with multiple adult males	No data	
Dharwar/ Troop 1 (Sugiyama, 1967; Sugiyama et al., 1965)			4–5		Two adult males associated with infant-deprived females in Troop 1. Identity of infanticidal male(s) unknown. Study ended before females delivered.
Dharwar/Troop 2 (Sugiyama, 1966:49–54; Sugiyama et al., 1965:86)	2		1	1	Female K disappeared about 7 months after infant loss without having delivered. The other three females conceived in or near July 1962 when males from Troops 1, 4, and 5 associated with females in Troop 2. The presumed infanticidal male was observed copulating with only two of the three infant-deprived females.
Dharwar/Troop 30 (Sugiyama, 1965a:223, 1965b:397, 399)	3		2	1	Female A had not delivered 10 months after infant loss when study ended. Females F and I appeared to have conceived during the tenure of the new infanticidal male. The remaining 2 females possibly conceived during the first half of June when Troop 30 came into contact with the previous male resident, the new adult male resident, and an all-male band. It should be noted that one female (E) conceived before infant loss.

294

Jodhpur/Troop B26 (Mohnot, 1981a)	5			Following take-over, all infant-deprived females copulated with members of the all-male band. Only one infant-deprived female copulated with the infanticidal male. Conceptions did not occur until about 1 year after take-over on the average.
Jodhpur/Troop Kaga A (Makwana, 1979)		3		Infant-deprived females copulated with males in neighboring troops as well as the new male in Kaga A.
Abu/Troop B6: 1971 (Hrdy, 1974:28)	2	2	1	One female disappeared after take-over and there are no reproductive data for her. Oedipa and Harrietta gave birth about 4 months after take-over and infant killing occurred, and therefore conceived before these events during the tenure of the previous male resident.
Abu/Troop B3: 1971–1972 (Hrdy, 1977b:38–40)	2	3	3	Infant-deprived female, Quebrado, did not deliver during the next 4 years of study. The other two females were not individually identified. The reproductive history for all troop females is as follows: one female delivered 3 years after take-over; one female other than Quebrado had not delivered after 4 years when the study ended; five females delivered 1 year after take-over during the tenure of the new male.

Continued

295

Table III. Genetic relationship between subsequent offspring born to infant-deprived females and infanticidal male—*Continued*

| Site/troop | Paternity known | | Paternity unknown | | Comments |
	Offspring sired by infanticidal male	Offspring sired by noninfanticidal male	Infant-deprived females associate with multiple adult males	No data	
Abu/Troop B6: 1972–1973 (Hrdy, 1977b:253, 261–264)			4		Bilgay conceived in the early fall of 1972 when both Shifty and Mug were assumed to associate with the troop. Itch conceived in the fall of 1973 when Mug and possibly Shifty and an all-male band associated with Troop B6. Oedipa and Pawless conceived in 1974 when Mug or Righty were associating with Troop B6.
Abu/Troop B3: 1975 (Hrdy, 1977a)				2	Females lost infants during last study; no subsequent data on their reproductive histories.
Abu/Troop B6: 1975 (Hrdy, 1977a)					Killings and take-over occurred after Hrdy's last study at Abu.
Total	7̄	2̄	19–20	2̄ / 10	The total number here is one less than for Table I because two of the infants killed were twins.

296

(1971a,b, 1974) collected data over 5-year period on the ecology and behavior of langur troops living in this vicinity; several cases of infant killing in association with one instance of membership change were reported.

Mohnot's (1971a) account of infant killing at Jodhpur is an important one because he was able to observe directly the manner of death and the events leading up to them for three of the killed infants. With the exception of Sugiyama (1965b), who witnessed the mortal injuring of one infant at Dharwar, most field investigators reporting infant killing have not observed the actual social interactions resulting in infant mortality but have had to base their reports on circumstantial evidence or on the observations of local informants.

Case histories. Mohnot's (1971a) published account of infant killing in association with troop membership change involved a troop that had just suffered mass mortality from unknown causes. Within a short period of time, Troop B26 was reduced from 82 members to only 7 adult females and 4 infants. Approximately 9 days after this reduction, an all-male band began a series of attacks, which occurred on 10 separate occasions over a period of about 1 month, on Troop B26. After the second attack, one of the males from the 22-member all-male band remained with the troop.

In subsequent attacks, fighting (with injuries) occurred between the new adult male resident in Troop B26 and members of the all-male band and also between members of the all-male band themselves. During the attacks, members of the all-male band remained with Troop B26 for amounts of time ranging from less than 2 hours to about 4 days, and at these times males from the all-male band were observed copulating with six of the troop's seven females (Mohnot, 1971a).

Four of the infants in Troop B26 were killed during the 1-month-long interval in which the all-male band made repeated attacks on the troop; a fifth infant, 1 week old, was reported killed approximately 6 months later (Mohnot, 1971a). In three of the cases, Mohnot (1971a) directly observed the new adult male resident in Troop B26 kill the infant. In the other two cases, the infants disappeared from the troop and were assumed to have been killed by the new male (Mohnot, 1971a). All of the infants were 3 months of age or younger at the time of death. Two of the killings occurred when the new male in Troop B26 was in a state of great agitation (e.g., he was intensely vigilant and engaged in tooth grinding and other vocal displays) as a result of anticipated attacks from the all-male band (Mohnot, 1971a). The other two killings are reported to have occurred after the all-male band had attacked Troop B26 and was associating with it (Mohnot, 1971a:191,193). Unlike Dharwar, where adult males were observed attacking females even after their infants had been killed, neither the adult male resident in Troop B26 nor members of the all-male band were observed to attack females (Mohnot, 1971a: p. 197).

Interbirth intervals and paternity. There are several aspects of the reproductive data collected from Troop B26 after the infant killings that are noteworthy: (1) While the four females who initially lost infants came into estrus shortly thereafter, males belonging to the all-male band copulated with all of them, but the new (infant-killing) adult male resident in the troop only was observed copulating with one of them (Mohnot, 1971a: Table III). (2) The remaining three females in Troop B26 that had no infants also came into estrus; two of these females came into estrus during the interval when the all-male band made repeated attacks on Troop B26, and they were only observed copulating with members of the all-male band. (3) The only female who conceived during or immediately after the take-over apparently was impregnated by the new male resident; shortly after this female delivered, this adult male is reported to have killed the infant, his own offspring (Mohnot, 1971a; Table III). Finally, (4) the time interval between births of infants killed and births of subsequent offspring for the four infant-deprived females was approximately 21 months (Table I). This compares to the average "normal" interbirth interval reported for Jodhpur of 15.5 months (see Vogel and Loch, Chapter 12, this volume). On the average, then, infant-deprived females in Troop B26 must not have conceived until 1 year after the troop membership change had occurred.

Subsequent studies at Jodhpur. Makwana (1979) has also reported on infant mortality in association with troop membership change at Jodhpur. During his 11 months of study (two periods in 1975 and 1977), two adjacent one-male bisexual troops each experienced adult male replacement on several occasions as the result of attacks on them by all-male bands. One of these changes in the Kaga A Troop was associated with the mortality of three young infants and one adult female. The killings were not observed, although the new male resident was observed assaulting an infant on the day following these deaths, and wounds on infants and one adult female were observed for about 1 month after adult male replacement occurred. The deaths and some of the woundings are known to have occurred during intervals when the all-male band either attacked or approached the troop.

Published reproductive data are not available for infant-deprived females in the Kaga A Troop with the exception of the following set of observations: following adult male replacement and infant killing in the Kaga A Troop, females presented on an almost daily basis. However, few (only five) copulations were observed. Three of these occurred during a 4.5-week interval following infant killing, and they were with the male resident of a neighboring bisexual troop (Table III). Only two copulations were observed with the infanticidal male, and these occurred more than 2 months after infant killing. Also of note is the fact that the first three copulations apparently occurred within the proximity of the infanticidal male in Kaga A but without his directing aggressive behaviors toward the copulating pair (Makwana, 1979).

Adult-male replacements. In addition to Mohnot and Makwana, other investigators, including Vogel (1979), have collected data on langurs at Jodhpur. On the basis of data published by these investigators, a composite picture of Jodhpur has emerged that tends to suggest that one-male troops are not closed breeding systems and that infant killing is not typically associated with troop membership change at this site.

During Vogel's 4-year study at Jodhpur, seven cases of major troop membership change were observed. The type of troop membership change described by Vogel is similar to the change reported for Troop 7 at Dharwar. Take-overs of one-male bisexual troops at Jodhpur normally include a transition period, which in six cases out of seven lasted for at least 2 months. During these periods, a number of males alternately associated with the troop and copulated with females in estrus. Although troops in all cases eventually reverted to a one-male composition, it was apparently difficult to predict *a priori* the new male who subsequently took up residence in the troop (Vogel, 1979). During the initial 4-year study period, infant mortality was associated with only one instance of troop male membership change. In this case, three infants disappeared during the prolonged replacement process that Troop B experienced in the fall of 1980. Although the cause of mortality was unknown, adult males are not thought to have injured these infants (but see Vogel and Loch, Chapter 12, this volume, for an additional report of a very recent case of take-over and infant killing in Troop B at Jodhpur).

Qualitative data provided by Mohnot (1971b) and Makwana (1979) also provide evidence that one-male bisexual troops at Jodhpur are not necessarily closed breeding systems. Mohnot (1971b) states that during the mating season, all-male bands were frequently in close proximity to one-male bisexual troops. Male residents of the all-male bands were often able to associate closely with estrous females during these months and occasionally remain with them for a full day. Contact between bisexual troops and all-male bands, which typically occurred during the context of crop raiding, was more frequent during the mating season than other periods of the year. Similarly, Makwana observed females from one troop present to and copulate with the adult-male residents of the adjacent bisexual troop (Makwana, 1979).

Mount Abu

Hrdy (1974, 1977a,b, 1979) studied langur troops living in and around the town of Abu, Rajasthan, in India in five discrete periods between 1971 and 1975. Study periods were from 1.5 to 3 months in length and were separated by gaps of 6–15 months. During the study periods, seven bisexual troops were monitored for membership changes, three of these intensively (Hrdy, 1977b). Most bisexual troops at Abu are one-male; adult males occur as isolates, in pairs, or in all-male bands. Frequency and type of membership change varied from troop to troop.

Case histories. Nine take-overs were recorded, seven of which occurred in two troops. The adult male composition in these two troops varied, both before and after take-over. In three take-overs, males entered troops that had no permanent adult male resident. In three other take-overs, the male entered troops that had one adult male resident, and in one case, a male entered a troop that had three adult male residents. After take-over had occurred in two of these cases, the troops had part-time adult male residents. When these males were away, the troops ranged without any adult male resident (Hrdy, 1977a).

Specifically, Troops B3 and B6 experienced the most frequent take-overs. Between 1971 and 1975, three adult males (Shifty, Mug, and Righty) independently moved between Troops B3 and B6, and these changes resulted in six separate take-overs (Hrdy, 1974, 1977a,b). A seventh take-over apparently occurred in the summer or fall of 1975, when a fourth male (Slash-Neck) took over Troop B6 (Hrdy, 1977a,b). At least six of the seven instances of male membership change in Troops B3 and B6 were not directly observed by the investigator.

Furthermore, data presented by Hrdy (1974, 1977a,b) suggested that all three take-overs of Troop B3 occurred when the single adult male resident in Troop B6 left that troop and entered Troop B3. Take-overs of Troop B6 between 1972 and 1975 appeared to be the result of absence of permanent male residents in that troop (i.e., on three separate occasions, males entered Troop B6 after the troop's only adult male resident left the troop). Hrdy (1977a:45) associated the disappearance of about 17 infants with male membership changes in Troops B3 and B6 between 1971 and 1975. Infant deaths were reported to have occurred after take-overs, and the new male residents were believed to have killed most, if not all, of the infants (Hrdy, 1974, 1977a).

Five infant deaths are associated with two cases of male membership change in Troop B3, and 12 infant deaths are associated with three or four cases of male membership change in Troop B6. Nine of the 17 infants disappeared while the investigator was away from the study site. In 2 or 3 of these infant deaths, local informants supplied the investigator with information regarding the manner in which the infant died (Hrdy, 1974:30, 39; 1977a:43). The other 8 of the 17 infants reported missing disappeared from the troop while the investigator was at the study site. However, observations of the troop were not made on the days when the infants actually disappeared. Again, local informants witnessed 3 of the 8 infant deaths and gave the investigator an account of the manner of death (Hrdy, 1974).

As most of the Abu data about infant killings depend on temporal correlations between male membership and disappearance of infants rather than direct observations, the precise relationship between the two events is difficult to establish. Data for the first take-over of Troop B6, which show that within 1 month adult-male replacement occurred and all of the troop's six infants disappeared, strongly support Hrdy's conclusion that infant deaths occurred as a result of take-over (Hrdy, 1974:27–30). Similar evidence supports the relationship between take-over of Troop B3 in April 1975 and the one infant death that occurred shortly thereafter. However, in other cases, the temporal relationship is much weaker. In Troop B6, for example, several infant deaths are linked to the adult male Mug's entry into that troop in the spring of 1972, although: (1) Mug was only a "part-time" resident of that troop for at least the first year; (2) infants disappeared during two 6- to 8-month gaps in observations; (3) infants are believed to have been killed from between 4 months up to perhaps 1 year after Mug entered the troop; and (4) A five-member all-male band might have been associating with the troop when the infants disappeared.

Although the figure of 17 infants reported missing after male membership change occurred may, in fact, represent some infants that died from causes other than intratroop aggression, Hrdy (1974, 1977a) did observe assaults by adult males on mother–infant pairs. Two infants were injured as a result of these assaults, but both recovered, and none of the observed assaults resulted in the infants' death.

Paternity. Very few data are available from Abu that document paternity of killed infants or paternity of subsequent offspring born to infant-deprived females (see Table II). Approximately 10 of the 17 infants reported killed were conceived before Hrdy's first study began (Table I). For the other 7 infants, no observations were carried out either at the times of their conceptions or births (Table I). Likewise, in only a few (four) cases at Abu can the paternity of subsequent offspring born to infant-deprived females be assigned to specific males (Table III). In these cases, one-half of the infants appeared to have been sired by the presumed infanticidal male and one-half were not.

Interbirth intervals. Data that show length of birth intervals between infants that disappeared and subsequent offspring born to infant-deprived females are not available in 10 of the 17 cases (Table I). In 6 of the 7 cases where data are available, they indicate average or longer than average birth intervals. In only 1 case are data presented that show a curtailed birth interval.

Rajaji

The langur population at Rajaji was studied by Julia Vonder Haar Laws and Jack Laws (1983) for 11 months in 1977. The density of langurs at Rajaji is relatively high (ca. 80 km²) with about 75% of the adult males living outside of bisexual troops. Troop size compared with many langur sites tends to be large (25–80 members per group), and of the four troops studied only one, the smallest, was a single-male troop. Home ranges overlap extensively, with the best-studied troop having a home range of 1.5 km. The habitat of Rajaji is relatively undisturbed: The site occurs within the Rajaji Wildlife Sanctuary and is largely covered by mixed deciduous subtropical forest. The troops are thus protected, and their limited contact with humans occurs during a few weeks out of the year when a couple of small clearings are grazed with cattle. The population exhibits well-defined birth and mating seasons.

Quantitative records of interactions among males showed that relations between the all-male band and the bisexual troops were relatively unaggressive, with overt fighting (as opposed to threats or displacement) a rare occurrence. The main study troop was observed for 1108 hr, and during this period 57 agonistic interactions were observed between males in the all-male band and males in the main study troop. Most of these interactions were threats and displacements, and only two instances of biting were observed, and these occurred during the nonmating season.

The all-male band temporarily associated with the main study troop on a number of occasions during the nonmating season, and during the mating season associated with it for a prolonged period of time. In addition, on a number of occasions individual adult males entered into or departed from the main study troop. Males associated with the all-male band were sexually active with females from the bisexual group, and these males obtained almost as many copulations (about 45%) as the resident troop males. Female sexual presentation to males followed a similar pattern with about 42% of them occurring toward members of the all-male band and the rest toward resident troop males. For 41% of the total number of copulations and sexual presentations ($n = 149$), the adult male could not be individually identified. Because nontroop males were considerably less well habituated, it should be noted that the actual as opposed to observed distribution of these sexual behaviors may be somewhat higher for nontroop males than the figures presented here indicate.

Junbesi-Ringmo

Boggess (1979, 1980, 1982) and Curtin (1982) studied langur troops in the Solu region of Nepal for 32 months over three periods (1972–1974, 1976, 1978). Multimale troops constituted an average of 65% of the troops in this area, and the few (ca. 25%) adult males living outside of bisexual troops were isolates or in pairs. Six troops were studied at Junbesi-Ringmo, and five of these changed in composition between one-male and multimale over a 6-year period. Troops became multimale only through the addition of new adult males and not through the recruitment of their own immatures.

Adult male replacement. Adult male replacement occurred at this site, but very gradually, with the process taking several years. Data from the main Junbesi study troop, in which adult males were recognized individually during all three study periods, showed that complete adult male replacement occurred within a 3.5-year period. Gradually new adult males entered bisexual troops at this site; over a period of months, agonistic interactions changed between immigrant males and established adult male residents, and eventually the new males were able to exclude other longer term male residents from the troop. Most of the observed exclusions occurred during the mating season and were related to male sexual competition for females.

The intermale behavioral interactions producing these changes were aggressive, sometimes resulting in wounds. Social interactions among adult males were characterized by a virtual absence of affiliative behaviors. Data suggest that within multimale troops, the dominant male does most of the breeding. However, through a process of gradual adult-male replacement and eviction of subadult males from their natal troops, close inbreeding is avoided.

Langur troops at this study site live in a habitat that is marginal, although relatively uninfluenced by man. Troop home-range size is large (avg. 6.5 km²), and population densities correspondingly low (ca. 2/km²). In view of these demographic features, the large number of troop-male membership changes observed at this site are significant and support the hypothesis that intense male sexual competition for females occurs independent of population density and may be species specific for *Presbytis entellus.*

DISCUSSION

As should be apparent from the preceding case histories, the systematic testing of hypotheses concerning infant killing in langurs is difficult, if not presently impossible. Most generally, the problem is lack of suitable data to test alternative hypotheses, but in a few cases hypotheses are framed in such a way as to deny disproof. Of the hypotheses put forward to explain male take-over and infant killing, sexual selection is probably the least difficult to test, in that many of the kinds of data required are straightforward (Chapman and Hausfater, 1979). Basically, to substantiate the sexual selection hypothesis one would have to establish a lack of genetic relationship between infanticidal males and the infants killed and establish that the infanticidal males did, in fact, father offspring subsequently born to infant-deprived females. One must also show a significant decrease, relative to other langur females, in the amount of time between the birth of infants killed and births of the subsequent offspring to infant-deprived females. Finally, one must demonstrate that infant killing is correlated with differential reproductive success, and that males that practice it leave a disproportionate number of surviving offspring. Other factors, such as the degree of relatedness among males, are also important, although their bearing on the general acceptance of the sexual selection hypothesis is not so significant.

Testing the Sexual Selection Hypothesis

In terms of paternity and birth-interval data in langurs (*Presbytis entellus*), the following conclusions can be drawn relevant to the sexual selection hypothesis.

Paternity of infants killed. In the majority of cases (approximately 75%) the killed infants were conceived either before the study began or during observation gaps of 1 year or more in which troop male membership changed (Table II). In these cases, it is impossible to assign paternity to specific males with any reliability. Paternity can be tentatively assigned to the remaining sample of infants (9 or 10 cases) on the basis of known troop composition or observed sexual activity during the periods of conception (Table II). Data indicate that the four or five infants in Troop 1 at Dharwar and two infants in Troop B6 at Abu were sired by males other than the presumed infanticidal male. However, in the remaining 3 cases (1 at Jodhpur and 2 at Abu), troop composition or observed sexual activity data show that males might have killed their own offspring.

In summary, in about two-thirds of the cases where paternity can be assigned, males are assumed not to have killed their own offspring, and in one-third of the cases the presumed infanticidal male might have killed his own offspring. Nevertheless, it is important to note that in only about one-fourth of all cases can any paternity inferences be made at all.

Paternity of subsequent offspring. As with infants killed, it is impossible to reliably determine the paternity of most (75%) of the subsequent offspring born to infant-deprived females (Table III). Of the sample of infants where paternity can be assigned to specific males, there are seven cases where the infanticidal male and two cases where a noninfanticidal male is the most likely sire of the subsequent offspring. In a large number of cases (65%) where paternity cannot be assigned, it is because more than one adult male was associating with the troop during intervals when infants were conceived. In most of the remaining cases, there are no paternity data because observations stopped before the female gave birth or because the female left the troop and therefore was not observed. These facts are extremely important because they introduce the probability that a significant number (i.e., more than one-half) of the infant-deprived females were inseminated by a male other than the presumed infanticidal one (Table III).

   Birth intervals. Out of the total sample of 38–39 infant-deprived females, there are birth-interval data for 18 of them (Table I). These data show an average birth interval of approximately 20 months as opposed to the 2-year interbirth interval that earlier had been considered normal for the species (Jay, 1965; Sugiyama, 1967). This calculation does not include the sample of females that had not delivered when the study ended (in one case, about 4.5 years later) or when they disappeared from the troop (Table I). These figures vary somewhat from other published reports of birth intervals (see Hrdy, 1979:18), probably as a function of the respective methods of analysis. Whether this average figure of 20 months is reproductively significant or not remains to be seen. New published data on the distribution of interbirth intervals for populations in specific ecological settings indicate significant intraspecific variation. While some populations, such at Dharwar or Junbesi-Ringmo, may average 20–24 months, other populations show interbirth intervals of only 15.5 months (see Vogel and Loch, Chapter 12, this volume). If these data on females are broken down by site, the results are very equivocal, and only at Dharwar is any reduction apparent at all: Eight females showed an average interbirth interval of 16 months. At Jodhpur, four females averaged 21 months (as opposed to the 15.5-month interbirth interval considered normal for this site), and at Abu six females had an average interbirth interval of 24 months (Table I).

   Overall male reproductive success. In terms of the fourth dataset—evidence that infanticidal males have greater reproductive success than noninfanticidal males—nothing definitive can be stated at this time. The problems in measuring differential reproductive success are enormous, as measurement requires lifetime reproductive histories that show not only that infanticidal males leave more offspring but that these offspring survive and are not in turn eliminated by incoming infanticidal males (cf. Chapman and Hausfater, 1979). With respect to the data from Dharwar, Jodhpur, or Abu, none of these precise measures exists.

   Despite this, there are several lines of evidence one can offer that argue against the likelihood that infant killing is correlated with differential reproductive success. The strongest evidence that such is not the case has already been presented: Analysis of paternity of subsequent offspring born to infant-deprived females does not, in fact, demonstrate that on the average infanticidal males inseminate those females whose infants they have just killed. The data from Jodhpur in particular argue against the sexual selection hypothesis. At this site, the characteristic male take-over pattern includes a fairly long transition where a number of males associate with the bisexual troop and copulate with females. At this site, intergroup copulations occur as well, both between two bisexual groups and between all-male bands and bisexual groups. Published data from Abu are less clear on this point than data from Jodhpur, but they also suggest that take-over does not always assure reproductive access to females. As discussed earlier, more than one-fourth of observed take-overs of Troops B3 and B6 resulted in situations where the troop did not have a full-time resident and/or the troop associated with members of an all-male band for a prolonged period of time.

In both published reports of infant killing at Jodhpur involving Troops B26 and Kaga A, the investigators' observations of sexual activity showed that most of the copulations occurred between noninfanticidal males and infant-deprived females. Data from Jodhpur as well as Abu also indicate that in some instances, males appear to be killing their own offspring. Furthermore, in the only study that recorded infant killing among successive crops of infants, three of the infant-deprived females lost consecutive offspring, both times as a result of infant killing (Table II). These data are important because they underscore two arguments that seriously weaken the sexual selection hypothesis: (1) Male take-over does not necessarily assure reproductive access to troop females; and (2) infant killing, as a behavior, does not appear to be a more effective strategy for male reproductive success than other patterns of male–male competition even within those populations where it occurs.

Maintenance of Genetic Variability and Population Regulation Hypotheses

Ripley's (1980) hypothesis that infant killing is a mechanism to ensure genetic polymorphism is based on the following assumption: Within some populations of langurs, infant killing by sexually competing males is required to counteract the inbreeding that results from the characteristic langur breeding structure of one-male groups or multimale troops where only one male does the breeding or from multimale troops that grow by interval recruitment (Ripley, 1980). Review of available data, however, simply does not bear out this assumption. Outbreeding occurs at all of the sites reviewed, and thus infant killing is in no way required to prevent inbreeding. At Dharwar, for example, bisexual troops are characterized by frequent changes in male membership, and immature males are routinely excluded from their natal groups (Sugiyama, 1965b, 1967). Immature males are also excluded from their natal groups at Jodhpur (Mohnot, 1978), and further, troops at this site do not appear to be closed breeding units in the first place. Little is known about the relations between immature males and adult males at Abu, but, again, adult-male replacement appears to occur frequently.

In the two populations—Rajaji and Junbesi-Ringmo—which do not exhibit take-over or infant killing, male competition for females takes two very different patterns, both of which result in females within their reproductive lifetimes being inseminated by a number of different males. At Junbesi-Ringmo, adult male replacement occurs gradually, and troops have closed breeding systems where one male does most of the breeding. However, because of the dynamics of intermale dominance, males frequently transfer between troops and actively breed in any one troop for only several years. Subadult males at this site are also evicted from their natal group before becoming sexually active. At Rajaji, most of the adult males live outside of bisexual troops, but during the mating season females within any one troop copulate with a number of males, including males in all-male bands.

Ripley (1980) and a number of other investigators (e.g., Curtin and Dolhinow, 1978; Boggess, 1979) have linked the occurrence of infant killing to environmental factors. All of these explanations share a common trait: Given the nature and extent of data available, they are currently untestable. Ripley's (1980) second hypothesis, which states that infant killing functions to limit populations in times of abundance, requires very refined ecological data having to do with diet and resource distribution and availability. These are data that simply do not exist for any population of *Presbytis entellus*.

Enforced Proximity Hypothesis

Most of the other environment-related arguments center on the controversy of whether or not human intervention at Dharwar, Jodhpur, and Abu results in the occurrence of infant killing. Curtin and Dolhinow (1978) and Boggess (1979) suggested that because of human intervention, populations at these three sites showed increased levels of aggression between males outside of bisexual groups and those living in such groups, and that the infant mortality associated with these sites is incidental to this aggression and without evolutionary significance. They argued that through logging or urbanization of habitat, enforced proximity or "crowding" has occurred, and that this has affected the frequency and patterning of agonistic interactions among langurs. However, human intervention is not viewed as the only variable affecting the linked occurrence of male take-over and infant killing. They also acknowledged various demographic factors, such as the relative and absolute number of males outside of bisexual groups, the population size, etc., which have contributed to the conditions producing infant killing at these sites. However, in contrast to Hrdy's (1979) proposal, these demographic variables alone are not thought to produce infant killing. In support of this conclusion, Rajaji is introduced: an undisturbed site showing a high population density with a high proportion (ca. 75%) of adult males outside of bisexual groups but not exhibiting male take-over or infant killing.

It is known that troops at Abu and Jodhpur (including the Kaga A Troop) are provisioned and have extensive contact with humans in these urban and semiurban sites. Data from Abu also suggest an interesting intrasite correlation between frequency of male take-over and infant killing and level of troop contact with humans. Troop B3, for example, which experienced about one-half of the take-overs with infant killing at Abu "moved within the confines of the main part of town [Hrdy, 1977b:57]"; the Toad Rock IPS, and School Troops had fewer contacts with humans and experienced either one or no take-overs and no infant killing. When the Dharwar population was studied in the early 1960s, part of the site had been logged (Yoshiba, 1968:240). Both Yoshiba (1968) and Sugiyama (1965b) pointed out the decrease in predation at Dharwar and the extremely high concentration of langurs in the remaining forested areas. In addition, Sugiyama (1965b:407–408) suggested that when the population was studied, it had exceeded the site's ecological support capacity. A subsequent survey of Dharwar tends to confirm this assumption. By the mid-1970s, the population had declined by more than 50%, but the site showed no appreciable reduction in forest over nonforested habitat (Sugiyama and Parthasarathy, 1979:866–867).

This evidence notwithstanding, it is clear that there are a number of problems attendant to the demonstration and acceptance of the hypothesis that enforced proximity results in infant killing. Enforced proximity (or "crowding") has no precise definition. It is a relative term that depends on a number of spatial variables that control nonsocial and social activities. The broad indices used in primate studies to measure a population's use of the environment (population density, home-range size, ranging patterns) are meaningless when applied here and cannot be used to measure social crowding. Such ecological parameters as the distribution and availability of resources or the extent to which substrate utilization affects interindividual visibility have enormous impact on the patterning and frequency of social interactions. It should also be noted that with respect to the environment of urban-dwelling groups, these parameters are technically even more difficult to quantify, partly because of the vast array of confounding variables.

Human disturbance to the habitat has been used by Hrdy (1979) as a proxy for measuring social crowding, with the implied assumption that those sites that are most disturbed will also be those sites most affected by social crowding. Human disturbance to the habitat affects almost all langur populations. The lack of data regarding this issue has been recognized by a number of investigators, and Bishop *et al.* (1981) have made preliminary attempts to qualitatively describe human disturbances to different langur habitats. This attempt is an important one, but in no way can it be used as a proxy for determining social crowding. As an example of the kinds of problems that arise, one can examine the scores given to Dharwar and Junbesi-Ringmo. They are approximately equal (2.0 to 2.25, respectively, out of a value range of 1–4); however, the populations at these two sites have responded very differently to these pressures as can be seen in the striking contrast in demographic data between these two sites. Population density at Junbesi-Ringmo is about 2 langurs per km² and 85–135 langurs per km² for forested areas at Dharwar; home-range size for Junbesi-Ringmo averages 6.6 km² and in forested areas of Dharwar averages 0.49 km² (Sugiyama, 1964).

Resolution of this general controversy is not likely to happen quickly. Adequate ecological data are absent from most langur (*Presbytis entellus*) studies, as almost without exception they have focused on social behavior. In addition, these data tend to be somewhat "political." A significantly disturbed site adds a major confounding variable to the interpretation of behavior, and when given the choice, few, if any, investigators would prefer to see their data interpreted as the result of human intervention in population ecology and social behavior.

Proximate Explanations

In contrast to the amount of attention given to the possible ultimate causes of infant killing, little has been said about the more proximate factors eliciting this behavior. Data presented by Mohnot (1971a) showed a strong sequential correlation between the new male's very visible agitation in anticipating attack from the all-male band and his sudden biting of the infants. Mohnot's explanation that in these intense conflict situations, infant killing was the result of adult male-redirected aggression seems plausible. However, on the basis of other published data, it is difficult to interpret all cases of infant mortality in terms of redirected aggression. At Dharwar, for example, several of the infants were killed after troop-adult male membership had stabilized, and in these cases intermale aggression seems an improbable factor in eliciting infant killing.

There is evidence suggesting that in some cases intersexual aggression might have triggered infant killing. Both Sugiyama (1965b) and Hrdy (1974, 1977a) observed adult males directing aggression toward mother–infant pairs. At Dharwar, many of these assaults on mother–infant pairs did not cease after the infant disappeared, but the male continued to make assaults on the mother alone. In these situations, it is difficult to avoid the conclusion that the target of the assaults was the mother and not the infant. The cause of this intersexual aggression has not been demonstrated, but it may lie in the fact that females with dependent infants tend to avoid new males, and the repeated assaults on these females result from the persistence of some new males in attempting to interact with all troop females in order to make genital inspections, to mount them, and so forth (Boggess, 1979).

CONCLUSION

A case-by-case review of the data surrounding infant killing in langurs (*Presbytis entellus*) fails to support any major hypothesis that assigns ultimate (i.e., evolutionary) value to this behavior. The assumption that males practicing infant killing gain increased reproductive opportunities has yet to be demonstrated from field data on *Presbytis entellus*. Examination of the data from Dharwar, Jodhpur, and Abu show a substantially less regular pattern of behavior than that predicted by the sexual selection hypothesis, with many of the reproductive data for infant-deprived females in conflict with expectations were infanticide an evolved reproductive strategy within the species. Similarly, the proposal that infant killing functions as a mechanism to defeat inbreeding is not consistent with what is known about male sexual competition in langurs. In sum, available data are inadequate to demonstrate that infant killing in *Presbytis entellus* has evolutionary significance.

With regard to alternative hypotheses, those explanations that present infant killing as incidental to male take-over remain largely supported by qualitative site and population descriptions, and unlike the sexual selection hypothesis, they lack precise measures for testing. What is apparent is that among langurs as a species, male sexual competition for females assumes a number of different social patterns, including adult male replacement. However, it is not at all clear what many of the determining factors are and how they operate to cause this variability. It is suggested that with respect to this issue, the sexual selection model has served an extremely important function. It has acted as a catalyst in directing attention toward "organismic" problems and in the process has undoubtedly prompted a more considered assessment of how various environment and species characteristics interact to determine langur reproductive strategies.

15 Proximate factors of infanticide among langurs at Dharwar: A reply to Boggess

Yukimaru Sugiyama

THE ENVIRONMENT OF DHARWAR FOREST

The first scientific observations of infanticide in any animal species in its natural habitat resulted from field studies of Hanuman langurs (*Presbytis entellus*) at Dharwar, south India (Sugiyama, 1965b). Curtin and Dolhinow (1978:471) have stated that the environment of langurs at Dharwar was "greatly disturbed by human activities" at the time of this author's original and follow-up studies. Also, Boggess (Chapter 14, this volume) as well as Curtin and Dolhinow, have asserted that langur population densities of Dharwar were either absolutely or effectively extremely high [Chapter 14, this volume, p. 308] because "the forest near Dharwar had recently been cleared and the langurs concentrated in what little remained" [Curtin and Dolhinow, 1978:471]. More generally, cases of infanticide among langurs at Dharwar and elsewhere have been dismissed as "maladaptive behaviors occurring in isolated and rare situations [Boggess, 1979:104]." In fact, especially during 1961–1963 when infanticide was first recorded at Dharwar, the forest had not been strongly affected by human activities. The forest had been left for natural growth and could best be described as mixed secondary growth dominated by teak trees (*Tectona grandis*). Although patchy cuttings of about 0.5–1.0 ha each were done every 60 years under Forest Department policy, there was little uncontrolled cutting. Predators were reduced in numbers, but there was at least one tiger and many jackals and domestic dogs in the main research area. Certainly, the local people never gave food to langurs.

Furthermore, langurs were not in any way confined to only a restricted small area of forest. The forest was continuous for more than 100 km in each direction, except east, though it was studded with villages and cultivated fields. Population density of langurs in Dharwar forest in 1961 and 1976, respectively, was 85.3 and 52.1 animals/km² (Sugiyama, 1964; Sugiyama and Parthasarathy, 1979). Similarly, population density in 1962 in Sagar forest, an undisturbed area about 140 km south of Dharwar, was about the same as that at Dharwar forest (Sugiyama: unpublished data). Langurs in Dharwar forest did not appear subject to nutritional stress or did the forest appear to lack sufficient natural food sources to accommodate the observed density of langurs. Evidence of the good nutritional condition of langurs at Dharwar was revealed by the annual birth rate. In Troops 1–8 (except 5) of the main research area at Dharwar between October 1961 and September 1962, a total of 62 females gave birth to 29 infants. These data yield a rate of 0.47 birth/female/year and give an interbirth interval of 24 months (Sugiyama et al., 1965). In fact, this rate is far higher than that of Japanese macaques (Macaca fuscata) in their natural condition (0.30–0.35) (Sugiyama and Ohsawa, 1982).

Although infanticide among langurs at Dharwar was initially viewed by many authors with skepticism, the large number of primate and nonprimate species for which infanticide has recently been reported suggests that the observations at Dharwar should not be considered mere artifacts of unusual local conditions. Confirmed cases of infanticide have now been reported not only for Hanuman langurs but also for an array of other mammalian species: lions (Panthera leo) (Bertram, 1975b; Packer and Pusey, Chapter 2, this volume), Belding's squirrels (Spermophilus beldingi) (Sherman, 1981), red howler monkeys (Alouatta seniculus) (Crockett and Sekulic, Chapter 9, this volume), and several others in their natural habitat. It seems more fruitful not to dismiss all of these cases as "social pathologies" but rather to systematically investigate how and why males kill conspecific infants and to do so in terms of the adaptive significance of this behavior.

MALE–MALE RELATIONS AND INFANTICIDE

As a result of the high carrying capacity of the Dharwar forest and the resultant high population density of langurs, the troops in the forest strongly defended their territories. In the most dense area of occupancy (more than 100 animals/km²), these territories were about 9 ha on average. It was thus difficult for surplus males (from all-male parties) to steal into the troop's territory; the open understory of the forest made it easy for the troop male to detect the nearby males. Thus, all-male parties could not intrude into a troop's territory without receiving strong resistance from the troop's resident male. Surplus males at Dharwar, therefore, could not get sufficient food, refuge from predators, or opportunities to approach females unless they took over a troop through severe fighting. In these particular geographic and social features, Dharwar contrasts markedly with the Himalayan hill range (Sugiyama, 1976a). Surplus males of the Himalayan range are able not only to steal into the home range of a troop but also to approach troop females without being detected or attacked by the troop's resident males as home-range size is large and the terrain effectively conceals the movements of surplus males. Thus, take-overs at Dharwar result in a sudden and precipitous removal of barriers to surplus males consorting with troop females, and this is one of the important proximate factors contributing to the occurrence of infanticide at this site, a factor also emphasized by Boggess (1979).

However, even at Dharwar, take-overs were not always accompanied by intense aggression and infanticide, and a second important proximate factor is the season of year. Take-overs that occurred during or a little before the mating season were almost always characterized by strong aggression, and this in turn was directed primarily at anestrous females carrying unweaned infants. In most cases, the death of an infant was immediately followed by a high level of sexual activity between the usurper and the mother of the victim. It was clear that infanticide had the effect of immediately arousing sexual activity in the victim's mother (Sugiyama, 1965b, 1966), whether or not the male might have anticipated this effect before killing infants. In contrast, nonmating season take-overs did not always result in infanticide. For example, Troop 2 (after the usurper left) was integrated into Troop 3 in February 1963 during the birth season, and Troop 7 was taken over in October 1962 after the mating season was over. In neither troop was infanticide observed, although infants sired by the former male were still present in the troop. Some sexual activity between the usurper and females without infants was observed in the latter case; however, this activity lasted only 10 days. There was only one case of usurpation in which infants were killed by the usurper when the take-over occurred well prior to the onset of the mating season.

In regard to other proximate factors in infant killing, it is instructive to compare Japanese macaques to langurs. Many solitary and party males of Japanese macaques approach troop females a few months before and during the mating season. The dominant troop male usually tries to chase them off and to interrupt their copulation attempts, but he eventually gives up after the intruding males succeed in establishing close relationships with the more peripheral female members of the troop. Some of these intruding males stay in the troop even after the mating season ends and become troop members (Sugiyama, 1976b). In Japanese macaques, neither troop usurpation nor infanticide has been seen. Although it has not been studied in detail, a similar process of male integration into troops is suggested by observations on langurs in the Himalayan range (Sugiyama, 1976a; Boggess, 1980). Thus, infanticide in langurs, in accordance with Boggess' view (Chapter 14, this volume) must be studied in the broader context of factors that influence the nature of male take-overs and male–male aggression.

Nevertheless, a general theory of infanticide and male–male aggression must take into account that it is mating-season sexual excitement of the part of the usurper that manifests itself as the severe aggression leading to infanticide. Second, the strong aggression is against infants of anestrous females and results in the mothers' rapid return to breeding condition. Third, there is no evidence that infants are attacked specifically because they are the offspring of the attacker's competitor. Rather, infants seem to be attacked because they themselves are an obstacle to activation of the mothers' sexual receptivity. Fourth, in geographic and demographic settings where surplus males are able to have frequent and gradual interactions with troop females, these males establish social relationships with the females that eventually lead to mating. It is important to recognize that these latter matings occur without the kind of explosive aggression seen in populations characterized by more strict exclusion of surplus males from bisexual troops (e.g., Dharwar).

Finally, the ultimate acceptance or rejection of any hypothesis concerning the adaptive nature of infanticide—for individuals (e.g., sexual selection) or for groups (e.g., population control)—will depend on determining the proximate factors as well as demographic and ecological conditions underlying infanticide. These factors constitute as important an answer to the question of why males kill infants as does an answer framed in terms of the genetic contribution of infanticidal males to subsequent generations.

ACKNOWLEDGMENT

The author wishes to thank Dr. Glenn Hausfater, the organizer of the Wenner-Gren symposium on "Infanticide in Animals and Man," for his critical reading and revisions of a preliminary draft. I wish to extend my thanks to members of Ecology Seminar of the Primate Research Institute, Kyoto University, for their critical discussions.

16 Assumptions and evidence regarding the sexual selection hypothesis: A reply to Boggess

Sarah Blaffer Hrdy

Jane Boggess' doctoral dissertation (1976) and subsequent articles on troop male membership changes among langur monkeys at the Junbesi-Ringmo site in Nepal (1979, 1980) contain the most carefully documented and well-reasoned of the various critiques of the view that infanticide is an evolved reproductive strategy among langurs. Along with the writings of Vogel (1979), Schubert (1982), and a series of publications by Dolhinow (1977), Curtin (1977), and Curtin and Dolhinow (1978, 1979), Boggess' criticisms have served the important function of warning against uncritical acceptance of the sexual selection hypothesis to explain infant killing by males among langurs and other species.

Such skepticism is especially timely in the current climate of enthusiastic and occasionally overly credulous acceptance of any theory with a logical evolutionary ring to it. Hence, cases of infant killing that range from isolated instances among captive animals to contemporary child abuse are being attributed, uncritically, to the killer's quest for reproductive advantage. Whether or not these proposed explanations are valid remains to be demonstrated. At present, the sexual selection hypothesis remains just that, a hypothesis (see Alcock 1979:12–14, for admirable treatment of this point).

Data on lifetime reproductive success of males who commit infanticide and males who do not have never been collected. Boggess stresses how few cases of infanticide among langurs have actually been witnessed, and she is right. On points such as these, Boggess and I are

315

in complete agreement. Where we differ is in our assessment of what evidence is relevant for testing the sexual selection and other hypotheses concerning infanticide, and on how this evidence should be evaluated. Boggess stresses the poor quality of the data, I stress the consistency of patterns in the limited data that we do have both for langurs and for other species. Furthermore, although we agree on what the basic outlines of a sexual selection model should look like, we disagree on the basic assumptions of the model and on the predictions that it generates. Because our differences reflect two fairly widespread schools of thought among biological anthropologists, I will discuss them here in some detail.

PREDICTIONS OF THE MODEL

A major difference between Boggess and myself is our attitude toward natural variation. In my view, the sexual selection model assumes that infanticidal behavior is heritable. It predicts that a male will typically not be the father of the infants he kills, and that on average, the infanticidal male will mate sooner than if those infants had lived. The key phrase here is "on average." I know of no grounds for expecting that take-overs must invariably be accompanied by infanticide, or for assuming that all males who attempt infanticide will necessarily succeed, or even for supposing that those males who do succeed will always gain from it. Even in a population where the infanticidal trait is present, only a portion of males may possess it, and/or the trait may be facultatively expressed, occurring only in certain social situations (e.g., confrontation between the male and unfamiliar mothers) or environments (e.g., where breeding is not confined to a fixed season). Hence, the finding at Jodhpur that roughly one take-over out of four is accompanied by infanticide (Vogel and Loch, Chapter 12, this volume) is not only consistent with the sexual selection model, but it is a direct prediction of at least one mathematical formulation of that hypothesis (Hausfater, Chapter 13, this volume).

The sexual selection model can not be invalidated merely by noting that some males who killed infants failed to benefit or in some situations even decreased their fitness by doing so. What would invalidate the model, however, would be if males routinely killed their own offspring, or if on average, males failed to benefit reproductively from infanticide. Instead, we find a remarkably consistent pattern in that males who have been members of a troop and who have probably sired offspring therein do not suddenly go berserk and attack their own infants. Rather, among a number of different primate species and with very few exceptions, infanticide is only reported when males enter a troop or a breeding system from outside of it.

In fact, Boggess' treatment of those few cases that do appear to contradict the sexual selection model raises an interesting issue. It has struck me more than once that critics of the sexual selection model sometimes apply a double standard: The criteria for accepting negative evidence appear to be far less stringent than the criteria applied to data that support the sexual selection model. Hence, her Table I includes—without so much as a query—the case of an infanticidal male at Jodhpur who "killed" his own offspring 6 months after entering the troop. Clearly, such an incident fails to conform to the pattern I have just outlined. Yet, it is worth noting that (as usual) evidence for paternity is less than conclusive; even more important, there is no evidence at all to suggest that the infant that disappeared was killed by another langur. No hostile act by the male toward this infant was ever observed nor was there evidence of wounding (Mohnot 1972a; Table 4 and pp. 193–194). While Boggess accepts this case of infanticide without question, she rejects, or includes with a question mark, other cases conforming to the sexual selection model even where there is far stronger circumstantial evidence. My own writing errs in the opposite direction (Hrdy, 1977b), a consequence of the evolutionary bias of my own world view.

Theoretically, there can be little doubt that a usurping male who eliminates unweaned infants thereby gains more breeding opportunities than if those same infants had continued to suckle. However, it is not essential that infanticidal males necessarily have "exclusive reproductive access to troop females" in order to benefit. Here again, Boggess and I disagree, for she assumes that a closed breeding system is a critical assumption of the sexual selection model. Langur troops are subject to both temporary and long-term incursions by outside males. Furthermore, female langurs sometimes leave their natal troops temporarily and travel for periods of time with all-male bands (Hrdy, 1977b; Moore, 1983). It would be unrealistic to assume that the alpha male is the father of 100% of offspring sired in the troop. In fact, as I have recently argued, there has probably been strong selection upon female langurs and other monkeys to spread the possibility of paternity among several males (Hrdy, 1981). A degree of female "promiscuity" is not inconsistent with the model as I understand it so long as the decrease in a male's reproductive success due to inseminations lost to outsiders does not exceed the gain to him from infanticide. What would, however, jeopardize the model would be if (1) outside males had the same likelihood of siring offspring as troop leaders or if (2) males who had mated with particular females turned out to be as likely to kill their infants as males who had not mated with them.

COMPARATIVE EVIDENCE

Unquestionably, the major difference between Boggess and myself is the importance we attach to evidence from other species. While

Boggess tends to discount the importance of reports of infant killing in other species, the existence of this comparative evidence has been central to the development of my ideas on the evolution of infanticide. This difference in emphasis when it comes to comparative evidence arises because although Boggess and I are reading the same field studies, we construe these reports very differently. The main disagreement concerns "suspected killings," and because these cases have become so controversial, it is worth reviewing exactly what the fieldworkers said they saw. In the report on redtail monkeys (*Cercopithecus ascanius*) cited by Boggess, Struhsaker (1977:78) described events that occurred shortly after New Male took over one of the study troops:

> No aggression was shown by New Male toward the [newborn] infant until 1640 hours . . . when he suddenly attacked and killed this infant. Initially I saw a ball of screaming monkeys tumbling down a liana thicket to the ground. New Male then ran off along the ground with the newborn infant in his mouth while being chased by an adult female and several others. . . . The chase terminated within a few seconds and New Male climbed into a tree and began feeding on the dead infant.

In the case of the second infant, Struhsaker did not see what happened until the chase had already begun: An adult female was pursuing New Male, who carried a dead infant in his mouth; the male's muzzle was covered with blood. Struhsaker "surmised" that the male had killed the infant; as in some of the langur cases, Struhsaker extrapolates from fairly complete observations of infant killing in order to interpret a partially observed sequence. Similarly, in an address delivered in 1980, Kathy Wolf of Yale described the killing of an infant silvered leaf monkey (*Presbytis cristata*). The attack took place shortly after a rank reversal when one male precipitously rose above an injured rival:

> Bozo [the new alpha male] calmly approached the adult female and took the infant from her. It looked just like a normal infant transfer until the mother and Max [the former leader] attacked Bozo. He turned and dropped the infant and when the mother retrieved it I could see that Bozo had slashed open the abdomen and [the intestines] were hanging out.

Comparable observations have been reported for South American howler monkeys (see Crockett and Sekulic, Chapter 9, this volume).

Of all the recent field accounts, one might expect Boggess to pay closest attention to the recent study of blue monkeys (*Cercopithecus mitis*) in the Kibale forest (Butynski, 1982). This study is highly relevant to the whole question of "enforced proximity" or crowding. Not only is the Kibale the least-disturbed habitat where primates have ever been studied long term (a point stressed by Leland *et al.*, Chapter 8, this volume), but the blue monkey troop in question has the largest home range (350 ha) ever reported for a harem-dwelling primate; these animals can not be considered abnormally crowded.

During his study, Butynski (1982) reported six harem-male replacements in one of five troops that he monitored. In one such case, the male repeatedly stalked and charged a mother with a new infant. As the male contacted the mother, the two adults "grappled for about two seconds and then [the male] ran from the mother with the head of [the infant] in his mouth and the rest of [its] body dangling" (p. 20). After running for 7 m with the mother in pursuit, the male dropped the infant. The infant caught in the trees for a time and then subsequently fell to the ground: "Blood was clotting a puncture in each temple and brain tissue was protruding from the right puncture. . . ." When the mother did not retrieve the mortally wounded infant, Butynski placed the baby in his knapsack, where it died 6 hours later (p. 21).

Obviously, one cannot deny the factual accuracy of Boggess' contention that even in such cases—which are among the best-documented instances of infanticide—the actual killing of an infant was not witnessed, although I must confess, it would not have occurred to me a few years ago to make the distinction that Boggess does between killing an infant and inflicting life-threatening wounds. In sum, what is a clear instance of infanticide to one researcher (e.g., Struhsaker, 1977) becomes merely fragmentary or "suspected" when viewed by another (Boggess, Chapter 14, this volume).

When researchers notable for integrity differ so profoundly not only over interpretation of the evidence but even on the point of what is admissable as evidence, we must look for underlying causes. Inevitably, what researchers see is affected by their expectations about the natural world and the way that biological and social systems "ought" to work; the resulting disagreement will not be easily resolved. Often frustrating, invariably time-consuming and inefficient, such debates remain, nevertheless, the best antidote we possess against the biases implicit in every researcher's world view.

ACKNOWLEDGMENTS

I thank G. Hausfater for valuable advice.

III

INFANTICIDE IN RODENTS: QUESTIONS OF PROXIMATE AND ULTIMATE CAUSATION

Infanticidal behavior in male and female rodents: Sectional introduction and directions for future research

Jay B. Labov

The difficulties of studying infanticide among wild primates are very apparent, as was detailed in Part II. The evidence for infanticide remains circumstantial in many primate species, and it is conceivable that primate studies may never yield the data necessary to test conclusively hypotheses proposed to explain infanticide.

In many respects, rodents provide vastly superior research subjects for the study of infanticide, particularly as concerns proximate mechanisms. The five chapters that comprise Part III illustrate clearly how research on rodents has been central to a dynamic new effort to systematically study the causes and functions of infanticide in both field and laboratory environments, especially the latter.

THE ADVANTAGES OF RODENTS AS RESEARCH SUBJECTS

Laboratory rodents have several important advantages over primates for testing both proximate and ultimate causes for infanticide. First, most rodents are small enough to be caged and managed easily in a laboratory environment. Many species can be bred readily in the laboratory in large numbers, thereby permitting investigators to accumulate data with sample sizes and replicates that are statistically meaningful and reliable.

Second, the ontogeny and life history of each subject animal can be continuously monitored and easily manipulated. Test animals may be introduced to neonates, either individually or in entire litters, with the mother present or absent, or to the mother alone at any time before, during, or after her pregnancy. Individuals may be retested at various times throughout their lives to ascertain the effects of biological maturation and experience on infanticidal behavior. Hormones and other suspected triggers of infanticidal behavior may be removed or supplied in excess during prenatal, postparturitional, prepubertal, or adult life and their effects carefully monitored. Three chapters in Part III (those by Elwood and Ostermeyer, Svare *et al.*, and vom Saal, Chapters 19, 20, and 21, respectively) review the extensive research effort in progress that has attempted to assess proximate causes of pup-killing behavior.

Third, the idea that infanticide is adaptive and is subject to evolution (Hrdy, 1977b, 1979) implies that this trait is heritable and thus must have some genetic basis. Comparative studies with inbred strains of mice are yielding important information regarding the role of genes and environment on infanticidal behavior. Because many inbred strains are virtually isogenic, behavioral variability within strains must be attributed to differences in environment or ontogeny. However, when different isogenic strains are raised in identical environmental conditions, genetic dissimilarities between strains become apparent. Because mice have been inbred for so long, they are especially useful models for investigating genetic bases for infanticidal behavior.

Svare and colleagues (Chapter 20, this volume) and other workers (e.g., Jakubowski and Terkel, 1982) report different levels of infanticide among wild and highly inbred strains of mice. Surprisingly, these differences are not influenced appreciably by factors such as maternal environment or circulating hormone titers at various developmental stages. However, prenatal interactions of genes and hormones do appear to account for some of the strain differences that have been reported (Chapter 21 by vom Saal and Chapter 20 by Svare *et al.*).

Finally, because of the high intelligence and emotional resemblance of nonhuman primates to humans, researchers are hesitant to carry out the experimental manipulations necessary to systematically study infanticide in primates. Additional constraints on such experimental work exist because some monkeys, such as langurs, are considered sacred and others, such as gorillas, are an endangered species. Laboratory-reared rodents do not present these problems to the same extent. Nevertheless, as noted by Elwood and Ostermeyer (this volume), both laboratory and field workers have become increasingly sensitive to animal welfare and conservation issues and this is true regardless of study species.

INFANTICIDE AND RODENT MATING SYSTEMS

Much recent work dealing with infanticide as an adaptive strategy has focused on reproductive advantages gained by males who kill unrelated offspring (Hrdy, 1979; Introduction, this volume). Research with rodents has also addressed this question. For example, vom Saal and Howard (1982) have demonstrated that male infanticidal behavior significantly reduces gestation of subsequent litters for female mice whose newborn offspring have been the victims of infanticide. Thus, one prediction of the sexual selection hypothesis (that by killing unrelated offspring, males gain an opportunity to mate significantly sooner than would otherwise be the case) has been fulfilled for at least one strain of mice.

Some rodent mating systems are in many ways quite similar to those of larger mammals in which infanticidal behavior has been reported by unfamiliar males under natural conditions (e.g., primates, lions). For example, house mice (*Mus musculus*) sometimes form demes consisting of a dominant adult male, several breeding females and their offspring, and a number of ostensibly nonreproductive subordinate males (Lacy, 1978; Bronson, 1979, 1983; vom Saal, Chapter 21, this volume). The dominant male's position may be usurped from outside the deme so that pregnant and recently parturient females could contact unfamiliar, potentially infanticidal males. These conditions parallel those reported for Hanuman langurs (Hrdy, 1974) and other monkeys (Leland *et al.*, Chapter 8, Crockett and Sekulic, Chapter 9, this volume) and for lions (Packer and Pusey, Chapter 2, this volume) in which infanticidal behavior by immigrant unfamiliar males has been observed or inferred.

Infanticidal behavior by wild rodents has also been reported. Adult male ground squirrels (genus *Spermophilus*) roam ephemerally among spatially and temporally stable matrilineal populations of adult females and their offspring. Sherman (1981) and McLean (1982, 1983) have reported that infanticidal behavior by intruding males and females from neighboring demes account for a small but significant proportion of infant mortality in these diurnal rodents. Other similarities between primate and rodent infanticidal behavior in the wild have also been noted. For example, Hrdy (1977b) reported that female Hanuman langurs, including those with near-term pregnancies, copulated with an intruding unfamiliar male. Hrdy speculated that by permitting the new male to mate, female langurs may confuse paternity and somehow inhibit the male's infanticidal potential. In both inbred and wild strains of house mice, males are also less likely to kill the offspring of a female with whom they have copulated or whose odors they have detected while copulating (e.g., Labov, 1980; Huck *et al.*, 1982; vom Saal, Chapter 21, this volume). To date, this has been one of the areas where experimentation with rodents has been most useful in testing hypotheses generated from field studies of larger mammals.

Although copulation and cohabitation may reduce male infanticidal tendencies, pregnant female rodents apparently do not copulate with males (Dewsbury: personal communication). Thus, females may still suffer loss of reproductive success due to male infanticide. Recently, other female counterstrategies have been proposed that may minimize a female's loss of fitness. Pregnancy blocking (or Bruce effect), where female mice terminate their pregnancies in response to contact with pheromones from unfamiliar males, has been reinterpreted as such a strategy (Labov, 1981a,b; Huck, 1982). While some authors (e.g., Bronson, 1979; Bronson and Coquelin, 1980; Brooks, Chapter 17, this volume) have discounted the Bruce effect as little more than a laboratory artifact, this dismissal may be premature. Huck (Chapter 18, this volume) reviews these conflicting perspectives and expands the model presented here with data suggesting that the Bruce effect might have evolved as a countermeasure to the probability of infanticide by any conspecific, male or female. His data show clearly that pregnant female Syrian hamsters (*Mesocricetus auratus*) terminate their pregnancies when exposed to unfamiliar dominant females (who are infanticidal in the laboratory) but not when exposed to strange males (who do not kill offspring).

Other evidence from field populations suggests that the Bruce effect may be more than a laboratory curiosity. Massey and Vandenbergh (1980) found that urine collected from feral female house mice delayed the onset of puberty in young female conspecifics in the laboratory. Massey and Vandenbergh (1981) also demonstrated that a pheromone in the urine of feral male house mice was able to accelerate the onset of puberty in laboratory-reared juvenile females. While these pheromones may not be identical to the substance(s) that induce pregnancy termination, the fact that they are produced in wild animals indicates that further investigation may reveal the presence of the Bruce-effect pheromone in nature. Furthermore, a phenomenon similar to the Bruce effect has recently been reported in wild horses (Berger, 1983) and savanna baboons (Pereira, 1983), suggesting that this particular reproductive mechanism may be more widespread among mammals than has been suspected previously. At the very least, these recent data from studies of rodents and other species will force the refinement and reevaluation of existing arguments concerning the causes, functions, and adaptive significance of the Bruce effect and other forms of pregnancy termination in mammals.

METHODOLOGICAL PROBLEMS IN STUDYING INFANTICIDE AMONG RODENTS

Although rodents offer unusual opportunities and advantages for understanding infanticide, there are a number of theoretical and practical limitations. There has been considerable controversy over the ontogeny, motivational bases, and adaptiveness of this behavior. While specific details of these problems are addressed by the chapters in Part III, the reader should approach this material with a general understanding of the debate that has emerged among researchers in this field. Some of these questions and problems constituting this debate are outlined here.

Although infanticide has been documented and analyzed extensively in laboratory studies, there is currently little evidence that the behavior is significant either for increasing individual fitness or for secondarily acting as a means of regulating populations in the field. Sherman (1981) observed infanticide in field studies of ground squirrels but reported that only about 8% of infant mortality could be attributed directly to infanticide. In more than 1300 hr of observation, McLean (1983) found only 10 cases in which mortality of young Arctic ground squirrels (*Spermophilus parryii*) could be attributed to infanticide by strange males; of these 10 cases, only 6 were based on actual observation of the killing.

The problem becomes more complex when studying other rodent species. The nocturnal activity patterns and secretive habits of most rodents make it difficult to ascertain how often infanticide occurs. Webster *et al.* (1981) postulated that infanticide by strange males may play a significant role in the population dynamics of meadow voles (*Microtus pennsylvanicus*). In contrast, Boonstra (1980) concluded that infanticide by males was not important for population regulation in this species, although he did suspect that infanticide was occurring in his population at an appreciable frequency. Brooks (Chapter 17, this volume) discusses in detail the problems associated with studying infanticide and related phenomena in natural populations of small rodents.

A second major obstacle when studying infanticide in natural populations is that so little is known about which animals may actually kill young. Is it possible that females are playing a greater role than previously recognized? The sexual selection model (Introduction, this volume) suggests that males that kill genetically unrelated offspring may increase individual reproductive success, and this is supported by laboratory studies of rodents. However, females may also benefit from eliminating unrelated young (see discussion by Brooks, Chapter 17, this volume). Several laboratory studies with gerbils (*Meriones unguiculatus*) (Elwood, 1977; Elwood and Ostermeyer, Chapter 19, this volume), collared lemmings (*Dicrostonyx groenlandicus*) (Mallory and Brooks, 1980), Syrian hamsters (Huck, Chapter 18, this volume), and wild house mice (Jakubowski and Terkel, 1982) have demonstrated that females kill infants, although they obviously may be doing so for different reasons from males. Brooks (Chapter 17, this volume) elucidates proximate motivational factors that may control this behavior in females and suggests that in natural populations female infanticide

may be substantially more important for population dynamics and social interactions than is infanticide by males.

Even if infanticide were to be demonstrated unambiguously in field
populations of rodents, not enough is known yet about rodent social
systems to evaluate objectively whether the behavior may be adaptive.
Since females of some species mate with more than one male, infanticide could actually reduce a male's fitness since he may be killing
offspring that he had sired in such a polygynous or promiscuous mating
system. Furthermore, vom Saal and Howard (1982) showed that subordinate males are less infanticidal than their dominant counterparts
but kill offspring upon becoming dominant. Thus, even in a closed
breeding system in which resident males are probably related (as suggested for wild house mice), a subordinate male who becomes dominant
may kill offspring originally sired by relatives (see vom Saal, Chapter
21, this volume, for a discussion of this point from a different perspective).

Although it is not yet possible to resolve such questions, new field
techniques may soon provide important information about the relatedness of individuals in a deme. Tamarian et al. (1983) reported that
unique combinations of very low levels of radionuclides can be safely
injected into individual females. These isotopes may then be recognized
by whole body counting of emitted gamma radiation. Most importantly,
these isotopes are passed through the placenta and milk to offspring
so that matrilineal relationship may be determined unequivocally. If
further research reveals these radionuclides are also excreted in detectable amounts in the urine, it may be possible to inoculate males and
determine their presence at nests by sampling soil or bedding from
the vicinity of those nests.

While several laboratory investigators provide support for the sexual
selection hypothesis in rodents, it is by no means clear that all cases
of infanticide can be attributed to sexual competition. Some researchers
have reported that cannibalism is common following the killing of pups
(Huck, Elwood and Ostermeyer, and Svare et al., Chapters 18, 19, and
20, respectively, this volume). In other circumstances, dead pups are
largely ignored by infanticidal adults (Mallory and Brooks, 1978; Labov,
1980; McLean, 1983). Hence, under some conditions, pups may be
treated as an exploitable food resource (Hrdy, 1979).

The use of different experimental methods might have contributed
to differences between studies in the occurrence and frequency of cannibalism. Where cannibalism has been reported, the experimental
method involved placing one or two pups into the cage of an adult
who had been physically isolated for some period of time. In contrast,
those studies in which pups were not eaten involved the converse
design of placing the male into the cage of a pregnant or recently

parturient female and her offspring. More research must be undertaken to assess the extent that infanticidal behavior is influenced and altered by this seemingly minor difference in experimental technique.

More must also be learned about how intensive inbreeding may influence the types of infanticidal behavior reported in different laboratories. While there is now substantial evidence to suggest that infanticide is influenced by genotype (Svare et al., Chapter 20, this volume), it is not known whether the behaviors are influenced by the same sets of genes in different strains. Possibly some mice kill and consume pups while others kill but do not consume because of differences in the extent of genetic expression of infanticide. The problem is further exacerbated when the exact genetic background of subjects is uncertain. For example, Svare and Mann (1981) found that C57BL/6J male mice were highly infanticidal as adults. In contrast, Jakubowski and Terkel (1982) also employed C57BL mice in their studies but reported them as virtually noninfanticidal. Where C57BL/6J adult males exhibit greater frequency of infanticide toward single test pups than do females, the opposite appears true in at least one wild strain of house mouse (Jakubowski and Terkel, 1982). Vom Saal and Howard (1982) reported that CF-1 males were inhibited from killing any offspring 3 weeks after copulating, but Huck et al. (1982) found that male Rockland–Swiss albino males killed pups 3 weeks after mating when the latter were in the nest of an unfamiliar female. Care must be exercised when analyzing and interpreting data from different strains of laboratory animals. Generalizations based on the behavior of animals from only one or a few strains is presently unwarranted. This caveat becomes especially important when data are considered within an evolutionary framework.

Clearly, many basic and important questions concerning both short- and long-term aspects of infanticidal behavior, particularly in wild populations, remain unanswered. However, research with rodents over the past 5 years encourages a prediction that some answers will become available shortly. The authors of Chapters in Part III provide a strong foundation for interpreting infanticide as a potentially adaptive behavior. Their continuing research will contribute significantly to the understanding of this complex phenomenon.

17 | Causes and consequences of infanticide in populations of rodents

Ronald J. Brooks

INTRODUCTION

A Historical Overview

Systematic investigation of infanticide in rodents, or for that matter in any group of animals, is a very recent phenomenon. Nevertheless, searching through some of the earlier, popular works of natural history, it soon became apparent that at least as far back as the previous century, naturalists have known or believed that intraspecific killing of young commonly occurred among a wide range of species. Most of these older references tended to be anecdotal, and explanations of infanticide were at the population or species level. Depending on the writer's point of view, infanticide was either beneficial and functioned as a mechanism of population control or was detrimental and a manifestation of aberrant behavior of no benefit to the perpetrator or to the population.

A marvelous example of the former interpretation was Calvert's (1913) attempt to show that Darwin's theory of natural selection was fallacious as well as pernicious. In essence, he argued that natural selection was a cruel mechanism by which nature would curb the increase of populations. "It is to prevent such a struggle for existence and to preserve her offspring from such a fate that she painlessly eliminates them in the earliest stage of existence [Calvert, 1913:33–34]." Nature, Calvert stated, produced unnecessary offspring to compensate

331

for unexpected calamity, hence to ensure continuity of the species. This important excess of progeny was then removed by the "cannibal habit of the male." Therefore, one role of males in population dynamics was to assess population numbers, then to trim the excess by removing progeny, usually their own.

Calvert provided anecdotal illustrations from many species, including man, rabbit, and lion, to verify that infanticide was indeed widespread and usually carried out by the male, but also by the female when she realized that the male had found her doomed neonates. Perhaps one of his examples is worth recounting here. Darwin (1859) used the elephant as an example to show that even the slowest reproducing species would eventually overrun its habitat unless population growth was checked in some way. However, as Calvert pointed out, Darwin did not specify any direct causal agent to slow this growth. "Did he [Darwin] suppose that 'natural selection' was all-potent to arrest its increase without material means being employed? [Calvert, 1913:36]." Calvert then stated that predation, notwithstanding Darwin's statement to the contrary, did remove some elephants, but that this was to no avail in limiting the numbers of this species. "It is therefore impossible to come to any other conclusion than that the young are destroyed in their immaturity (by adult elephants), and a uniform ratio survive to continue the species [p. 36]."

Calvert's claim that infanticide was the means by which a beneficent nature maintained populations at their correct levels not only rendered natural selection irrelevant, it elevated infanticide to a position of considerable importance in population dynamics. The broader notion that infanticide, or any aggression directed toward young conspecifics, functions for the benefit of the species still recurs in the modern literature on rodent behavior and ecology. Some examples follow. Svare and Mann (1981) implied that infanticide would be selected for at high densities and selected against at low densities as a mechanism "whereby rodent populations can control their numbers. . . . [p. 926]." Similarly, Koshkina and Korotkov (1975) concluded that in the red vole (*Clethrionomys rutilus*), young animals were killed or driven away by adults in a perfect example of a harmonious adaptation for population regulation. This group-selectionist logic has also been applied to other forms of juvenile mortality and "excess" reproduction: "Dispersal [translated as juvenile mortality] may act as a safety valve for the population [Krebs and Myers, 1974:312]." "We view high reproductive effort . . . as an adaptation which counters high juvenile mortality and in turn ensures the success of the species [Gaines *et al.,* 1977:1593]." Bujalska (1973:473) regarded excess young as cohorts produced as a population "reserve." Finally, Werner (1978) linked overproduction, infanticide, and cannibalism, stating that young individuals may serve as a "food reserve" for adults and that "cannibalism also may be a means of maximizing the food resources by the different diet of the age classes [pp. 378–379]."

These rather exalted assessments of the biological role of infanticide contrast markedly with the opinion that this behavior is pathological (Calhoun, 1962; Ardrey, 1970; Curtin and Dolhinow, 1978) or that it is a by-product of stress and of density-dependent responses to overcrowding (Christian, 1956; Dickeman, 1975). In this view, infanticide is not adaptive for the population or for the individual who does the killing.

Unfortunately, there is a large subjective element in judgments of whether an intraspecific interaction is beneficial or pathological. Two examples will suffice to illustrate this problem. In a study of population regulation in *Rattus norvegicus*, Calhoun (1962) observed high rates of mortality and cannibalism of young rats when enclosed populations reached high densities. Calhoun defined the killing of young as "pathological" and linked this behavior with a syndrome of "behavior disturbances" that ranged from "sexual deviation to cannibalism" to "pathological withdrawal [p. 139]." He described the behavioral sink in which, as he put it, rats assembled in large numbers just to interact and hence showed "pathological togetherness." In these sink areas, normal social patterns were most disrupted, and infant mortality approached 96%. On the other hand, Calhoun suggested that the aggressive, dominant males were the most "normal" males and noted that they seldom attacked females and juveniles. Other male "types" were apparently on a linear scale of declining normality, going from "homosexuals" (pansexuals) to sleek sleepers to "probers." The latter group committed infanticide, rape, and homosexual acts. (One cannot help but suspect that behavior in this study termed deviant and "pathological" corresponded directly with the author's own view of what constituted abnormal activities in human society.)

As a second example, consider territorial behavior. One often reads that territoriality is beneficial because it regulates populations (Bujalska, 1970, 1973), and certainly there is never any suggestion that territoriality is "aberrant" or "pathological." Yet territorial behavior may reduce relative fitness and survival of conspecifics just as surely as infanticide does. A quote from Lewontin (1974:29) seems appropriate here. "The more important the issue and the more ambiguous the evidence, the more important are the prejudices, and the greater the likelihood that two diametrically opposed and irreconcilable schools will appear." This scenario is even more probable when terminology laden with value judgments is applied to the issue.

Definitions

Most papers specifically dealing with infanticide provide either no definition or simply say it is the killing of young by conspecifics (Hrdy,

1979; Mallory and Brooks, 1978, 1980; Boonstra, 1980; Sherman, 1981; Svare and Mann, 1981). One probably should revel in this rare unanimity, especially when the definition is so simple, but it is important to consider what is meant by "young" and "killing." Viewing this definition broadly, "young" are considered here as individuals between birth and sexual maturity. Young still in the nest are referred to as "nestlings" or "neonates," and postweaned young are referred to as "juveniles."

One could also consider socially induced prenatal mortality (e.g., Bruce effect) as a form of infanticide, although in some cases infanticide is seen as an ultimate cause of the Bruce effect (Labov, 1981a; Huck, Chapter 18, this volume). Loss of unborn young because of social or other disturbance of the pregnant female is well established in laboratory situations (Schwagmeyer, 1979; Mallory and Brooks, 1980; Labov, 1981a). However, pregnancy block by strange males may be an artifact of the laboratory situation (Bronson, 1979), and in some species the Bruce effect probably does not occur (Norris and Adams, 1979). Regardless, there is little evidence that the Bruce effect occurs in natural populations of rodents (Mallory and Clulow, 1977) or that prenatal mortality in general is important in rodent population dynamics (Krebs and Myers, 1974). Therefore, this phenomenon is not considered further.

All studies of infanticide in rodents have assumed that this behavior is a fairly stereotyped pattern of attack that usually results in the immediate death of the young victim. However, in many rodent and lagomorph populations, adults cause increased mortality, but these deaths are not necessarily the direct results of wounding or physical injury (Mykytowycz, 1960; Myers and Poole, 1961; Krebs and Myers, 1974). Clearly, if mortality rates of young animals "drive" population fluctuations or improve relative fitness of the causal individuals, it is not terribly important whether these deaths were brought about by a ritualized bite or by more indirect means. Therefore, should these indirect means of killing or of increasing probability of death in nestlings and juveniles be included as infanticide? Inasmuch as the source of most infant mortality in wild populations of rodents is unknown, the problem is not critical now, but it will be when more precise data become available.

THE DILEMMA

Does Infanticide Occur in Rodent Populations?

Virtually all direct observations of infanticide among wild rodents have come from studies on ground squirrels and marmots (family Sciuridae) (Armitage et al., 1979; Sherman, 1981; McLean, 1982; Michener, 1982a; D. Balfour: personal communication; Brooks: personal observation). Sherman (1981) estimated that infanticide caused the loss of at least 8% of infants in Belding's ground squirrel (*Spermophilus beldingi*) and suggested that infanticide had been recorded in at least seven other species of *Spermophilus* (cf. Michener, 1982a). These studies make clear the importance of long-term observations on known individuals and of establishing genetic relationships among these individuals. Such data are far more difficult to obtain from mouse-sized mammals than from ground squirrels, but unless accomplished, the understanding of social structure of the smaller rodents will remain at its present primitive level, far behind the recent work on sciurids (Michener, 1982b).

Although dozens of field studies of population dynamics of microtine, murid, and cricetid rodents discuss the significance of juvenile mortality, often attributing this mortality to intraspecific aggression by adults, this author is not aware of any published reports of direct observations of killing of nestlings by conspecifics in these animals. References to infanticide in wild rodent populations are few and almost all have appeared within the last 4 years (Lidicker, 1979; Semb-Johansson *et al.*, 1979; Boonstra, 1980; Webster and Brooks, 1981). In fact, the literature gives the impression that the possible occurrence of neonate infanticide has not been considered seriously by most fieldworkers. For example, Myllymäki (1977) postulated that early juvenile mortality in *Microtus agrestis*, the field vole, might be due to predation. However, he rejected this possibility because, "we must assume that a very specialized and effective predator exists, which concentrates on vole nests [p. 476]." He apparently did not consider that other voles may be the "specialized predators." None of the foregoing should be surprising, because virtually all field studies of these rodents use traps to assess population processes, and since nestlings are not trappable, their survival is not monitored directly. Similarly, there are few observations of adults killing juveniles of trappable age, because hardly anyone actually watches behavior in the field. Therefore, the present lack of direct observations of infanticide in these rodents is not critical evidence that it does not occur in the wild.

In marked contrast to the field situation, there is a rapidly growing literature from laboratory studies of rodent infanticide (Elwood, 1977; Mallory and Brooks, 1978, 1980; Labov, 1980; Svare and Mann, 1981; Webster *et al.*, 1981; vom Saal and Howard, 1982). In fact, more is probably known about infanticide in cricetid and murid rodents than in any other group of animals. Unfortunately, those studying rodent infanticide have the same problem as those working on pregnancy block (Bronson, 1979), namely: Do these laboratory data have any relevance to real populations, especially when there is little direct evidence that infanticide occurs in the wild? Even if infanticide does occur in nature, care must be taken in generalizing from laboratory data to wild populations, especially when these laboratory data are derived from inbred strains (Baker, 1981; Jakubowski and Terkel, 1982; Brooks and Schwarzkopf, 1983).

The Dilemma and an Approach to Its Resolution

Given the constraints and difficulties previously outlined, the question arises: how can the significance of infanticide in rodent populations be assessed? The remainder of this chapter provides some guidelines toward solving this dilemma, and the discussion is organized around a series of questions. These are outlined in the next paragraph.

1. What is the effect of infant mortality on rodent population dynamics? Given that, at present, there is limited direct evidence of infanticide, it is important to establish that there is evidence that it may occur in field populations and to determine how it may influence population numbers and social structure.

2. What proportion of infant mortality may be attributed to infanticide? The answer often depends on what is considered as necessary and sufficient evidence of infanticide. Are direct observations required or can infanticide be inferred from analysis of descriptive data on population changes or from the effects of experimental manipulation of populations (e.g., removal experiments)?

3. What is the relationship between social structure and incidence of infanticide? This question is answered largely in the context of Question 2. The animals most likely to commit infanticide and the potential effects of infanticide on social structure are examined.

4. In the context of intraspecific social interactions, could infanticide be an adaptation selected for and maintained even if it rarely occurred and seldom played a direct role in changing population numbers and structure? In other words, is there stronger selection to prevent infanticide than to perform it?

WHAT IS THE EFFECT OF INFANT MORTALITY ON POPULATION DYNAMICS?

What "Regulates" Rodent Populations?

Over the past five decades, hundreds of studies have been directed toward determination of what drives population fluctuations in rodents. In a comprehensive review, Krebs and Myers (1974) claimed that these fluctuations still could not be explained or predicted, and that this fact represented one of the great unsolved problems of animal ecology. Certainly one of the significant difficulties here is that many forces operate on population growth, and it is difficult to disentangle their interactions and their relative importance (Brooks, 1978). In any case, there is no a priori reason to expect that all populations would be regulated in the same way. In addition, it is assumed here that intrinsic population "regulators" did not evolve to serve this function. Instead, such mechanisms were selected for their advantages to individuals, and their effects on population numbers are incidental.

In terms of infant mortality, the concern here is with whether a change in mortality rate is one of the factors that stops populations from increasing indefinitely and/or causes populations to decline to numbers far below peak numbers. Intrinsic factors generally acknowledged to regulate populations in this way are: length of the breeding season, age at sexual maturity, adult female mortality (Krebs and Myers, 1974), dispersal (emigration) (Krebs et al., 1969; Lidicker, 1979; Abramsky and Tracy, 1979), and nestling and/or juvenile mortality (Godfrey, 1955; Chitty and Phipps, 1966; Healey, 1967; Flowerdew, 1974; Krebs and Myers, 1974; Gaines et al., 1977; and many others).

Techniques to Estimate Infant Mortality

Methods used to estimate population numbers in small mammals have severe limitations for measuring infant mortality. First, standard live-trapping techniques usually do not distinguish losses due to emigration from losses due to mortality. Second, they fail to provide direct estimates of numbers of nestlings, and they estimate juvenile numbers poorly. Attempts to circumvent these drawbacks are far from satisfactory. For example, Krebs (1966) and Krebs et al. (1969) estimated mortality from birth to trappable age by the following index:

$$\frac{\text{number of young in traps at time } t}{\text{number of females lactating at } (t - 4) \text{ weeks}}$$

The number of females lactating was determined from how many were trapped at $t - 4$ weeks who seemed to have "active" teats. Litter size at birth could be estimated by calculating mean number of embryos in pregnant females at $t - 4$ or $t - 6$ weeks using a sample of autopsied females from a nearby area of similar habitat to the study area. Given that the assumptions are valid, errors could still arise owing to juvenile immigration or emigration, nonrandom sampling, and female mortality prior to weaning. Direct examination of nests located by radiotracking females is possible (Madison, 1980a,b; Webster and Brooks, 1981), but it is disruptive and would underestimate losses of entire litters. Not surprisingly, few studies of unenclosed populations bother to measure survival of nestlings at all.

Myllymäki (1977) measured nestling mortality in *Microtus agrestis* by combining information from field and enclosed populations. In the field, he estimated time of parturition by palpation and mean litter size by embryo counts in females trapped off the study grid. Then he compared the number of new, trapped recruits with that expected from these embryo counts. In enclosed populations, he marked nestlings

and estimated mortality from the numbers trapped 4 weeks after weaning. "Mortality" was much higher in the unenclosed populations. This
background should make it clear that the actual causes of nestling
mortality are usually unknown or only crudely estimated. For postweaned juveniles, estimates of mortality rates are more precise, but
the causes are nearly as mysterious.

Evidence of Importance of Infant Mortality in Populations

As noted previously and despite the methodological problems cited,
infant mortality is widely accepted as a significant cause of population
changes in numbers, particularly of declines in numbers. This viewpoint
is summarized emphatically by Sadleir (1965). In *Peromyscus maniculatus,* "the most important factor determining the numbers of animals,
and the direction and rate at which they change during the breeding
season, is the extremely low number of juveniles actually recruited
into the population compared with the numbers carried by the pregnant
females [p. 350]." This conclusion at least makes it possible that infanticide could play a major role in population change.

Estimates of mortality between birth and trappable age often exceed
85%. In microtines, Krebs' (1966) study of *M. californicus* indicated
that early juvenile (preweaning) survival was lower in the highest year
than in the lowest year of the population cycle. This improved survival
by itself accounted for the increase following the low (Krebs, 1966),
but Krebs did not conclude conversely that low survival in the peak
year accounted for the subsequent decline. Similarly, Whitney (1976)
found nestling survival in *C. rutilus* and *M. oeconomus* was poorest
during the increase and peak phases of their respective population
cycles. In *Synaptomys cooperi* (the bog lemming), nestling and juvenile
survival was the best predictor of population growth (Gaines *et al.,*
1977), and low juvenile survival could prevent a population from cycling.

In *M. montanus* and *M. californicus,* Hoffmann (1958) concluded
that high nestling and juvenile mortality (over 35%) was correlated
with declines in overall numbers. In particular, he observed that declines occurred when recruitment into the breeding age classes was
reduced owing to low survival in the nestlings and juveniles. Mallory
and Brooks (1978) and Martin (1956) used similar logic to argue that
infanticide or infant mortality could lead to declines in rodent numbers.
In contrast to this view, Krebs (1966) has concluded that population
declines in *M. californicus* were independent of nestling mortality because declining populations sometimes had high rates of nestling survival. These ideas need to be tested with quantitative models.

Mortality rates of young in nonmicrotine rodents are also high. In
wild rats (*Rattus norvegicus*) in enclosures, high infant mortality, not

adult mortality, stopped population increase (Calhoun, 1962). In field studies of *Mus*, DeLong (1967) concluded that declines were largely the result of increased neonatal mortality. Nestling mortality peaked during the decline in population size, and emigration peaked during the increase resulting in an overall increase in mean age of the population, as predicted by Hoffmann (1958). DeLong (1978) counted nestlings in enclosed populations and found nestling mortality varied from 11 to 46%. Lidicker (1965) compared four species of rodents in population cages and concluded that in three of these species, *Peromyscus maniculatus, P. truei,* and *Oryzomys palustris,* nestling mortality was the most important factor regulating numbers, whereas in *Mus,* regulation was by inhibition of reproduction in females. However, studies of *Mus* in enclosures have produced contradictory results (e.g., Brown, 1953; Crowcroft and Rowe, 1957).

Therefore, it appears that neonatal and juvenile mortality are significant to populations. However, in addition to the reservations and constraints referred to earlier, it should be remembered that these conclusions usually rested upon correlations (not necessarily statistical) and were not derived from experiments designed to test hypotheses. This helps to explain that juvenile mortality often was not considered significant even when it reached high levels. For example, Krebs *et al.* (1969) and Lidicker (1979) found mortality of young to be 60–80% in various species of *Microtus* but concluded that because this high mortality also occurred in penned animals and because no declines occurred in these pens, then juvenile mortality was not important in population changes.

Finally, it should be recognized that many workers do not believe that infant mortality "regulates" populations (i.e., stops population growth), but only that it leads to declines (e.g., Krebs and Myers, 1974; Boonstra, 1977, 1978). These authors and others (Abramsky and Tracy, 1979) have concluded that emigration (dispersal) is primarily responsible for stopping population increase.

WHAT PROPORTION OF INFANT MORTALITY IN RODENTS IS CAUSED BY INFANTICIDE?

Causes of Infant Mortality

As noted earlier, the significance of infanticide to total infant mortality is difficult to judge at present. Many studies that report substantial infant mortality, including some that consider it the most important predictor of population changes, do not speculate on its sources (Godfrey, 1955; Lidicker, 1965; Terman, 1965; Krebs *et al.,* 1969; Whitney, 1976; Gaines *et al.,* 1977; Harland *et al.,* 1979; Gipps *et al.,* 1981). Here, evidence that suggests infanticide is a potential source of this mortality is reviewed and further considered in the context of social structure and sex. As is shown in the next section, there is considerable experimental evidence that a substantial fraction of total infant mortality is inflicted through intraspecific attacks. Obviously, other factors also play a role, but at this point, the evidence of infanticide is considered in conjunction with evidence regarding the identity and social circumstances of animals that commit infanticide.

How Are Social Structure and Infanticide Related?

Relationship of aggression, consanguinity, and infant mortality. Several studies of the dynamics of enclosed populations of *Mus* reported substantial infant mortality and attributed this to aggressive behavior of adults (Brown, 1953; Southwick, 1955a,b; Christian, 1956; DeLong, 1967, 1978; Lidicker, 1976), whereas other studies reported much lower levels of infant mortality and found no relationship between adult aggression and neonatal mortality (Crowcroft and Rowe, 1957; Lloyd and Christian, 1967). Lidicker (1976) has suggested that these differences may be related to both size of the enclosure and size of the study population itself. Populations may in fact be regulated by inhibition of reproduction when caged in small groups and by infant mortality when caged in larger groups.

There is another important difference among the preceding studies that would produce such variable results: the degree of inbreeding. For example, Brown (1953) reported contrasting results in two enclosure experiments. In one experiment, he founded each population from small groups of unrelated pairs, whereas in the second, he started with only a single pair. Populations in the second experiment grew larger than those in the first experiment and showed less aggression, greater social stability, and more successful reproduction. Lactating females often attacked males in the first experiment but not in the second. In both experiments, infanticide was the most important factor stopping population growth. However when the population founders were unrelated (Experiment One), virtually all neonates were killed, whereas in the second experiment, litters were not killed until the population reached relatively high densities. Similarly, Lloyd and Christian (1967) and Crowcroft and Rowe (1957) founded their experimental colonies from small numbers of inbred siblings. Most infant deaths reported in Lloyd and Christian (1967) occurred from starvation, not from aggression.

In another experiment relevant to understanding the effects of inbreeding, Lidicker (1976) stocked large enclosures with 15 pairs of unrelated mice and found widespread loss of 1–3-day-old neonates from cannibalism, lactational failure, and abandonment. Mice formed territories (demes) with a dominant male and several females and subordinates. Weanlings that left natal demes and moved into others were usually attacked and killed, and few broke into new groups. In the Norwegian lemming (*Lemmus lemmus*), when colonies were started with one pair, very little aggression occurred, even at extreme densities of 25/m² (DeKock and Rohn, 1972), whereas when colonies were founded from several unrelated pairs, aggression developed rapidly, the populations went through phases of typical fluctuations, and infanticide occurred (Semb-Johansson et al., 1979). From these observations, it is concluded here that the foregoing differences among studies have resulted from differences in the size of groups used in each study and from differences in the degree of genetic relatedness within these groups. Unfortunately, most workers have disregarded kinship as a factor in population dynamics, and only in the past few years has this view begun to change (Mallory and Brooks, 1978; Charnov and Finerty, 1980; Holmes and Sherman, 1983).

Male aggression and infant mortality. In the 1960s, there was great interest in territoriality, especially in the notion of the territorial, dominant male (Ardrey, 1970). Therefore, it comes as no surprise to discover that 1960s descriptive field studies of rodent populations readily attributed juvenile mortality to aggression by adult, territorial males (Frank, 1957; Sadleir, 1965; Chitty and Phipps, 1966; Healey, 1967; Krebs, 1970; Spitz, 1974). Workers assumed that male aggression was an important population process (Krebs, 1970; Turner and Iverson, 1973; Krebs and Myers, 1974), and female aggression was nonexistent or restricted to the period of lactation (Rowley and Christian, 1976). Similar conclusions were drawn from correlations of changes in male numbers and frequency of wounding and juvenile survival (e.g., Chitty and Phipps, 1966).

These speculations fostered a rash of experiments to test the effect of adult males on survival of other adults and juveniles and on changes in numbers. For example, removal of adult males was expected to lead to an increase in juvenile survival, and in fact removal of adult male wood mice (*Apodemus sylvaticus*) did lead to higher juvenile survival and immigration and an increase in population size (Flowerdew, 1974). DeLong (1966) reported that populations of wild *Mus musculus* declined when *Microtus pennsylvanicus* were present. In laboratory tests, he found that male *Microtus* killed *Mus* nestlings in six of eight trials. In contrast, there was no measurable effect on any population parameters when males were removed from wild populations of *C. gapperi* (Watts, 1970) or *M. townsendii* (Boonstra, 1978). Redfield et al. (1978) manipulated adult sex ratio in field populations of *M. townsendii* so that adult males outnumbered females 4:1. Again, there was no effect on survival, reproduction, or growth of juveniles or other classes. Similarly, Krebs (1966) and Smyth (1968) found no clear effects on juvenile survival when adults were removed from microtine popula-

tions. Smyth (1968) concluded that social interactions were not important in microtine population cycles, but the studies of both Krebs (1966)
and Smyth (1968) were confounded by high rates of immigration into
their removal plots. Gipps et al. (1981) tried to relate the spring decline
of M. townsendii to levels of male aggression mediated by testosterone.
He implanted testosterone in young males and an anti-testosterone
(scopolamine-HBr) in large males in another population. In the latter
group, declines in male numbers were smaller than in the control population, and more females bred. However, recruitment remained constant, and on the "testosterone grid" no effect was observed. They
concluded that male spacing behavior alone did not control population
fluctuations.

Males might have influenced infant survival in a study of C. glareolus
(bank voles) in large (550 m²) enclosures (Gipps and Jewell, 1979). In
one enclosure, most males were castrated, and in the other, all were
left intact. Aggression and wounding of males were reduced in the
castrated population, and this population increased significantly faster
than did the intact population. The differences were attributed entirely
to higher mortality of young animals in the intact population. In both
enclosures, numbers eventually greatly exceeded peak field densities.

This experiment, therefore, appeared to provide strong support for
the hypothesis that adult males increase juvenile mortality in rodents.
However, Gipps and Jewell (1979) were not themselves entirely con-
vinced of this interpretation and noted that females were very aggressive and might have caused most of the wounds suffered by males.
Gipps and Jewell further stated that "the possibility that it was aggression by pregnant females that was the cause [of high juvenile mortality]
cannot be ruled out" [p. 551]." More generally, male rodents are often
not territorial (Madison, 1980b; Webster and Brooks, 1981), and although they may cause a high incidence of wounding, it appears that
males and their supposed aggression have little effect on population
processes.

Female aggression and infant mortality. In their major review, Krebs
and Myers (1974) devoted only two sentences to female aggression,
but recent work suggests that females may have a great influence on
juvenile survival. Boonstra (1978) introduced juvenile *Microtus townsendii* into three field populations: an unmanipulated control, one from
which adult males were removed, and one from which all adults were
removed. Survival of juveniles was three to sixfold higher when all
adults were removed than when only males were removed or when
no adults were removed. Boonstra (1978) concluded that density of
adult males had no effect on juvenile survival or recruitment, but that
the presence of adult females increased juvenile mortality. He did not
speculate on the mechanism by which females reduced juvenile survival

except for a brief reference to infanticide in a later paper (Boonstra, 1980). Because removal of males did not reduce pregnancy rate, males must normally compete for mating opportunities (Boonstra, 1977; Gipps and Jewell, 1979; Madison, 1980a,b; Webster and Brooks, 1981). On the other hand, removal of adjacent females improved survival of the progeny of a given female, and Boonstra (1977) concluded that females competed primarily with other females, probably for nest sites, and that juvenile mortality was related to this competition. Similar arguments were made by Sherman (1981) to explain infanticide by female Belding's ground squirrels. Redfield *et al.* (1978) found that juvenile survival and immigration in *M. townsendii* correlated negatively with female density and concluded that females controlled recruitment by reducing survival of juveniles in some unspecified manner.

In other species of rodents, females control population numbers, either by influencing juvenile mortality or by limiting breeding through territorial aggression. A few examples follow: Peak numbers of *C. glareolus* were limited by numbers of breeding females and by juvenile survival, although Bujalska (1970, 1973) still attributed high juvenile mortality to aggression from adult males. In lemmings, females were more likely to kill unrelated neonates than were males (Arvola *et al.,* 1962; Semb-Johansson *et al.,* 1979; Mallory and Brooks, 1980), and in *Lemmus lemmus* (Semb-Johansson *et al.,* 1979) and *Mus* (DeLong, 1978), enclosed populations declined largely from female cannibalism and attacks on infants. In wood rats (*Neotoma flavescens*), females attacked all foreign conspecifics of any age. Most pups were killed by lactating female intruders (Fleming, 1979), again indicating female–female competition. In golden hamsters (*Mesocricetus auratus*), virgin females readily killed strange neonates (Richards, 1966b), and female Mongolian gerbils (*Meriones unguiculatus*) were more prone than were males to cannibalize strange neonates (Elwood, 1977). Finally, in *Peromyscus* spp., most recent work has shown that females (1) were more aggressive than males toward conspecifics (Rowley and Christian, 1976; Ayer and Whitsett, 1980); (2) were territorial (Harland *et al.,* 1979); (3) were restricting recruitment by inducing high nestling and juvenile mortality (Harland *et al.,* 1979; Ayer and Whitsett, 1980); and (4) were significantly more likely to kill pups of unrelated than of related (sibling) females (P. Gleason: personal communication).

Female aggression toward conspecific intruders peaked during lactation in several rodent species (Savidge, 1974; Rowley and Christian, 1976; Svare and Gandelman, 1976; Fleming, 1979). In Belding's ground squirrel (*Spermophilus beldingi*), adult, unrelated females were the age–sex class most likely to kill or attack juveniles or infants (Sherman, 1981). In terms of their proportion in the population (7%), nonresident adult females committed a large proportion (42%) of all observed infanticide. The next most common source of infanticide was 1-year-old males who constituted 11% of the population and yet committed 31% of the observed cases of infanticide. In contrast, adult males represented 14% of the population and were the source of only 4% of all instances of infanticide. Confirmed cases of infanticide in *S. columbianus* (D. Balfour: Personal communication) and *S. armatus* (Burns, 1968, cited in Michener, 1982a) were also committed by females. However, in *S. parryii,* infanticide was committed by adult males (McLean, 1982). It is interesting to consider how this difference between *S. parryii* and those species in which females commit infanticide may be related to broader differences in social organization (Michener, 1982b).

Long-term studies of social mechanisms of population control in rabbits (*Oryctolagus cuniculus*) in Australia provide an important comparison to investigations of rodents. As rabbit numbers increased in both enclosed and free-living populations, infant and juvenile mortality increased. This increased mortality of infants was attributed largely to failure of maternal care (reduced lactation and nest defense) and to disturbances by strange (unrelated) females (Mykytowycz and Hesterman, 1975). Dispersing juveniles were treated amicably by strange males but were attacked and often severely wounded by dominant, strange females and their older female progeny (Mykytowycz, 1960; Myers and Poole, 1961). As in rodents described previously, female rabbits competed violently for nest sites, and these conflicts frequently led to abortion and infanticide (Myers and Poole, 1961).

Male aggression and infanticide: a rejoinder. In reviewing the foregoing material, it becomes evident that although male rodents will kill strange infants under specific conditions (Mallory and Brooks, 1978; Svare and Mann, 1981; vom Saal and Howard, 1982), it was not at all clear that infanticide by adult males occurred at any appreciable frequency in wild rodent populations, despite earlier assertions that male aggression was a major source of infant and juvenile mortality. Experimental studies and direct observations indicated that when intraspecific killing of neonates and/or juveniles did take place, it was more likely to be perpetrated by adult females than by adult males. These latter findings make sense in the context of infanticide as an adaptive behavior that has been selected for at the level of the individual (Mallory and Brooks, 1980). Females are better able to discriminate their own young than are males, and on these grounds alone, females would be expected to be more likely than males to kill strange pups (Mallory and Brooks, 1980; Webster *et al.,* 1981). Further, if females compete for nest sites (Mykytowycz, 1960; Boonstra, 1978; Fleming, 1979; Sherman, 1981), the advantages of winning such competitions seem much greater than the advantages males gain from infanticide (e.g., in microtines, these advantages are elimination of a competitor's litter and slightly larger litters born a few days earlier: Mallory and Brooks, 1978). Females without proper nest sites either fail to breed at all or produce inferior young that are readily outcompeted or killed by more successful individuals.

In contrast to the foregoing view, which is based on studies of wild populations, females of laboratory strains (e.g., *Mus, Rattus, Oryctolagus*) do not attack unfamiliar neonates readily (Calhoun, 1962; Mykytowycz and Hesterman, 1975; Baker, 1981; Brooks and Schwarzkopf, 1983). This difference between wild and laboratory-reared females may be related to selection for high reproductive output and low aggression in the captive environment, but whatever the cause, this difference again underscores the danger of using behavior of laboratory strains to make inferences about the frequency and nature of infanticide in wild populations.

COULD INFANTICIDE BE SIGNIFICANT IN POPULATIONS YET OCCUR ONLY RARELY?

With respect to their value in assessing the role of infanticide, or indeed any social behavior in population processes, most field investigations of small rodents are seriously deficient in two aspects. First, because of an excessive reliance on trapping, these studies usually do not observe social behavior directly, and second, these studies rarely provide any information on genetic relationships among individuals. As noted earlier, there is a desperate need to obtain direct observations of social behavior and to use radiotelemetry, enclosures, electrophoretic techniques, and other methods to advance beyond the limited knowledge afforded by "black-box" trapping methods. Given the current paucity of solid field data, one could justifiably argue that infanticide appears to occur only infrequently simply because there has not been the opportunity or inclination to observe it. However, a good case can be made for the view that infanticide should be a rare event that only occurs under specific circumstances. Further speculation on this possibility in the context of social structure is in the following section.

The Role of Social Structure

Social structure obviously varies among and within different groups of rodents (e.g. Michener, 1982b). The picture that is emerging of social structure in microtine rodents is summarized below. Females tend to have nonoverlapping ranges with other adult females during the breeding season and especially during lactation (Frank, 1957; Kalela, 1957; Bujalska, 1970, 1973; Viitala, 1977; Madison, 1980a; Webster and Brooks, 1981). In all these instances, female territoriality appears to regulate

reproduction, limit numbers of breeding females, and perhaps ultimately limit populations. Radiotelemetric studies indicate that males
often are not territorial and have home ranges that overlap with those
of breeding adults of both sexes (Brooks and Banks, 1971; Madison,
1980a,b; Webster and Brooks, 1981). When these data are combined
with observations on wounding (cited earlier), with direct observations
of male–male aggression over estrous females (Madison, 1980b; Webster and Brooks, 1981), and with evidence of density-independent numbers of breeding females, it is apparent that males compete for females,
whereas females compete for "space" (e.g., territories, nest sites).

Earlier, it was suggested that female rodents are aggressive and
may be more likely to kill infants than are males. Yet data from field
studies invariably indicate that males are far more likely to be wounded
in intraspecific fights. Possibly males are wounded by females (Gipps
and Jewell, 1979), but why are females rarely wounded if they are so
aggressive? It is reasonable to suggest that they settle territorial disputes by "convention" as has been observed in innumerable other territorial species. That is, the female is dominant in her territory, and
intruders quickly retreat without serious fighting. In addition, these
territorial disputes may be mild in intensity when they involve established, recognized neighbors rather than strangers, and this may be a
general rule in territorial behavior.

The Role of Female Territoriality

Females are especially aggressive to strange conspecifics during lactation, but few workers have tried to relate this to function or ecological
context (Fleming, 1979). Obviously, this aggression must be to protect
neonates, but as Fleming asked, "protect them from what?" In the face
of the evidence and knowledge of Darwinian selection, it is hard to
avoid answering: "Infanticide." Why then does infanticide appear to
be relatively infrequent (e.g., Curtin and Dolhinow, 1978; Hrdy, 1979;
Boonstra, 1980)? It is likely that selection for mechanisms to prevent
infanticide (such as territoriality) will be more intense than selection
to commit infanticide since the losses to the victim and its mother
(one only has to consider lactation costs in rodents) are direct and
devastating, whereas the gains to the infanticidal animal are less direct
and less certain. Some recent literature has underestimated the significance of the losses to the female in relation to the gains, especially
to gains for infanticidal males. If this idea is correct, infanticide should
only occur in circumstances when the female's defenses fail. These
failures should be relatively infrequent, and in the context of population
dynamics are most likely to occur when dispersal and/or increasing
numbers leads to mixing of unrelated genotypes.

The Role of Dispersal

Aggression, strife, or "social breakdown" increase when strange individuals enter established social groups. Most studies of the role of behavior on population fluctuations have emphasized the effects of increased crowding (density) on stress and aggression. However, in mice, social disruption can occur without a decrease in space or food or an increase in numbers (Bailey, 1969). Simply increasing the number of social contacts, especially contacts with unfamiliar conspecifics, can cause disrupted social behavior and potentially inhibited reproduction (Bailey, 1969). Dispersal of unrelated individuals into a previously isolated population (deme) should thus produce an increase in aggression (Mallory and Brooks, 1978; Charnov and Finerty, 1980). This view is supported by several studies that show that rodents are, like most other vertebrates, capable of individual recognition, and especially of recognition of kin (Fleming, 1979; Holmes and Sherman, 1983).

In vole population cycles, dispersal is at a maximum during the increase phase. Most workers have regarded dispersal only as a source of mortality or recruitment in their study population. Further, they have implicitly assumed that all individuals in the population were genetically identical or, conversely, that dispersers were somehow a unique genotype from nondispersers (Krebs and Myers, 1974). However, Abramsky and Tracy (1979) found that while populations stopped growing because of emigration, the subsequent decline was related to effects of immigrants. Garten (1976) came to similar conclusions and associated dispersal with increased genetic heterozygosity and behavioral aggression in *P. polionotus*.

In *Microtus* populations, Nygren (1980) inferred from gene frequencies that in low populations, these voles lived in relatively isolated demes with high frequencies of homozygotes and relative low frequencies of heterozygotes (i.e., Wahlund effect). However, as numbers increased, the proportion of heterozygotes increased significantly. These findings support the proposals of Mallory and Brooks (1978) and Charnov and Finerty (1980) that dispersal would lead to increased interaction between unrelated genotypes, and that this interaction would engender increased aggression.

Aggression by resident animals obviously protects the resources, including juveniles and neonates, of the resident social group. Dispersing individuals, especially females, may be expected to attempt infanticide. These attempts would only be made at minimal risk to the perpetrators, therefore leading to infanticidal behavior that is both quick and cryptic. Infanticidal behavior in this context would simply be an adaptive response expected from an animal seeking to establish itself in a new habitat. As such, the behavior is neither pathological nor characteristic of a special disperser genotype, rather, it is an adaptive expression of the competition between unique genotypes.

As noted earlier, these views are essentially speculative because direct evidence of infanticide and social and genetic structure in wild rodents is lacking. Given that infanticide is likely to occur infrequently and cryptically, it is perhaps unrealistic to try to study it directly at this time in free-living populations of mouse-sized rodents. In enclosures, population growth of mice and voles appears to cease when infant mortality rises because of breakdown of nest defense and other aspects of maternal care. A fruitful area for future study would be the investigation of factors that cause females to abort, abandon, or cannibalize litters or to cease to attack conspecific intruders. Similarly, it would be enlightening to learn more of time budgets of males and females to understand the role of territoriality and nest defense and of the tactics of infanticidal individuals. However, the greatest need at present is to integrate the laboratory and field approach to a much greater extent. There is an enormous gap between the field ecologists and those studying behavior of *Mus* in the laboratory. If they could develop a more unified, more Darwinian approach to the problem of infanticide, an understanding of this behavior in rodents would be approached much more rapidly.

ACKNOWLEDGMENTS

The author is grateful to E. G. Nancekivell, J. R. Malcolm, L. Schwarzkopf, and G. L. Stephenson for their valuable comments and assistance during preparation of the chapter.

18 Infanticide and the evolution of pregnancy block in rodents

U. William Huck

INTRODUCTION

Pregnancy block was first observed by Bruce (1959, 1960) in laboratory mice. She noted that exposure to a strange male (or to his odor) prevented implantation in recently inseminated females and caused a return to estrus 4–5 days later. Investigations of the generality of male-induced pregnancy block (Bruce effect) indicate that it is exhibited under laboratory conditions in numerous species of rodents and may occur in natural populations as well (see following).

Several hypotheses for the functional significance of pregnancy block based on individual selection have been advanced. Trivers (1972) and Wilson (1975) suggested that pregnancy block is the product of male–male competition. For a strange male, the adaptive advantages are apparent: he reduces the reproductive fitness of the original male relative to his own and causes the female to return to estrus relatively quickly, thus increasing the likelihood that he will mate with her (Mallory and Clulow, 1977; Mallory and Brooks, 1980). However, as Schwagmeyer (1979) pointed out, pregnancy block involves a physiological response on the part of the female and, thus, could evolve as a trait exclusively advantageous to males only if females were somehow incapable of preventing its occurrence. She further suggested that pregnancy block would be limited to circumstances in which the benefits for the female from mating with the new male outweighed the costs of the delay in reproduction and energetic investment already committed.

An adaptive significance of pregnancy block for females has been difficult to identify. Bruce and Parrott (1960) suggested that pregnancy block functions to promote exogamy. They reported limited evidence that indicates that pregnancy block is more frequent if the two males involved are genetically dissimilar (although how this was measured is not clear). However, this hypothesis appears untenable since in some cases the original male may be superior in promoting exogamy (Schwagmeyer, 1979).

According to Dawkins (1976), pregnancy block may be mutually advantageous not only to a female that has been deserted by her male but also to her new mate. Although she forfeits her initial investment, the female benefits from remating quickly with a male that will provide parental care. Thus, by inducing pregnancy block, the new male avoids parental investment in another male's offspring and gains a mating. This hypothesis cannot account for the evolution of pregnancy block in rodents, however, since male care of young is absent or reduced in most species (Schwagmeyer, 1979; Hartung and Dewsbury, 1979; Labov, 1981a).

Schwagmeyer (1979) suggested that pregnancy block may play a role in mate selection by females. According to this hypothesis, pregnancy block evolved as a strategy by females to increase the likelihood that their offspring will be sired by dominant males. However, while females readily discriminate between dominant and subordinate males (e.g., Huck et al., 1981; Huck and Banks, 1982), there has been little evidence to date to indicate that the incidence of pregnancy block is related to the relative quality of the second male as compared to the original mate (Labov, 1981b; see below).

In the absence of any convincing adaptive function of pregnancy block for females, it has been suggested that this phenomenon is a laboratory artifact (e.g., Bronson, 1979; Bronson and Coquelin, 1980). According to this view, pregnancy block is merely a manifestation of a more general response by females to estrus-inducing pheromone produced by males and, thus, need not be thought of as a physiological entity in its own right.

Recently, several workers have proposed that male infanticide has served as a primary selective pressure for the evolution of pregnancy block as a female reproductive strategy (Bertram, 1975a; Hrdy, 1979; Mallory and Brooks, 1980; Labov, 1980, 1981a). According to this hypothesis, if the potential for male infanticide is high, pregnancy block may be advantageous for a female because the loss of a fertilized egg or newly implanted embryo would reduce her overall reproductive fitness less than would the loss of a newborn litter.

The purpose of this chapter is to review social factors that influence the occurrence of male-induced pregnancy block and infanticide in rodents and to discuss experimental data that suggest that the incidence of pregnancy block is positively correlated with increased risk of infanticide. The chapter concludes with a review of some of the ecological conditions under which these phenomena are likely to have evolved.

PREGNANCY BLOCK IN RODENTS

Characteristics of Pregnancy Block in Laboratory Mice

Pregnancy block has been extensively investigated in laboratory mice. Contact is not necessary for pregnancy block to occur in mice since the effect can be achieved by housing newly mated females in cages recently soiled by strange males (Bruce, 1960; Parkes and Bruce, 1962; see also Bellringer et al., 1980). Subsequent studies showed that the effect is mediated by pheromones associated with urinary proteins (Dominic, 1966; Marchlewska-Koj, 1977, 1980). The finding that anosmic females did not respond to strange males (Bruce and Parrott, 1960; Dominic, 1965) confirmed the role of olfactory cues.

The pheromone(s) that induce this effect are androgen-dependent (Bronson and Whitten, 1968; Bloch and Wyss, 1973) and are not present in castrated mice (Bruce, 1965). Furthermore, androgen treatment of males of a strain that was normally ineffective in inducing pregnancy block caused them to become effective (Hoppe, 1975). An ability in females to block pregnancy can also be induced by androgen treatment (Dominic, 1965).

Pregnancy block depends on the ability of the newly mated female to perceive a difference between the strange male and the stud. The blocking effect of the new male is greater if this male is of a different strain from that of the stud and is reduced by preexposing the female to a number of males or by allowing the stud male to be present when the strange male is introduced (Parkes and Bruce, 1961). Bruce (1961b) reported that the proportion of newly mated females returning to estrus was positively correlated with the length of exposure to a strange male. However, Chipman et al. (1966) showed that three daily 15-min exposures to a strange male terminated pregnancies almost as effectively as continuous contact. The latter finding suggested that pregnancy block is not just a laboratory artifact since levels of contact that are not unrealistic in field situations can produce this effect.

Although mice can discriminate individuals by their odors (Bowers and Alexander, 1967), individual discrimination may not be necessary for pregnancy block to occur. The discovery that male laboratory mice exhibit elevated plasma testosterone levels 30–60 min following exposure to a strange female (Macrides et al., 1975) suggests that the ability of odors from strange males to block pregnancy may be due to the higher concentrations of the testosterone-dependent pheromone in their urine rather than individual discrimination per se. Furthermore, since isolated males have higher baseline testosterone levels than grouped or paired males, exposing females to cages previously inhabited by a single male could have a similar effect. These findings should stimulate further investigations of the effects of mutual interactions on short-term endocrine function.

The physiological and hormonal bases of pregnancy block have been studied extensively since the phenomenon was first reported and have been the subject of several recent reviews (Dominic, 1976, 1978; Aron, 1979; Milligan, 1980). Apparently, pregnancy block and the induction of ovulation in unmated females are encompassed by the same system (Whitten, 1966; Bronson, 1979); both phenomena are caused by an olfactory-induced stimulation of gonadotropin secretion that leads to a subsequent reduction in prolactin secretion.

Generality of Pregnancy Block

Investigations of the generality of male-induced pregnancy block indicated that it is exhibited under laboratory conditions in several species of rodents. Preimplantation pregnancy block has been reported in wild strain house mice, *Mus musculus* (Chipman and Fox, 1966), deer mice, *Peromyscus maniculatus* (Bronson and Eleftheriou, 1963; Terman, 1969), collared lemmings, *Dicrostonyx groenlandicus* (Mallory and Brooks, 1978, 1980), and several species of voles: *Clethrionomys glareolus* (Clarke *et al.,* 1970), *Microtus agrestis* (Clulow and Clarke, 1968; Milligan, 1976, 1979), *M. pennsylvanicus* (Clulow and Langford, 1971), and *M. ochrogaster* (Stehn and Richmond, 1975).

Postimplantation pregnancy block (abortion) has also been reported in several species of voles and deer mice. In prairie voles (*M. ochrogaster*), exposure to strange males caused an interruption of pregnancy as late as day 17 of a 21- to 23-day pregnancy (Stehn and Richmond, 1975; Kenney *et al.,* 1977; Stehn and Jannett, 1981). Midgestational pregnancy block has been reported in *P. maniculatus* (Kenney *et al.,* 1977), *P. pinetorum* (Schadler, 1981; Stehn and Jannett, 1981), and *M. montanus* (Stehn and Jannett, 1981).

Although pre- and postimplantation pregnancy block seem to occur most frequently in various genera of cricetine and microtine rodents, it may be simply because these species are most available for laboratory study. However, male-induced pregnancy block apparently does not occur in several common laboratory species including rats, *Rattus norvegicus* (Bruce, 1967), Mongolian gerbils, *Meriones unguiculatus* (Norris and Adams, 1979), golden (Syrian) hamsters, *Mesocricetus auratus* (see below), and certain strains of inbred mice (Marsden and Bronson, 1965).

With respect to the inbred strains of mice, several hypotheses for the failure of strange males to induce pregnancy block have been suggested. As a result of inbreeding, males of these strains may have more similar body odors and, thus, are less discriminated by the females (Bruce, 1967). Inbreeding might also have affected the ability of males to undergo changes in testosterone levels after brief exposure to the females (Macrides *et al.,* 1975) and/or might have so reduced androgen levels that the urine of these males does not contain sufficient amounts of blocking pheromone (Hoppe, 1975). Direct effects of inbreeding on females (e.g., reduced susceptibility threshold) can also be postulated. A possible limitation to the occurrence of postimplantation pregnancy block in large mammals may relate to the energetic costs involved with aborting offspring as they approach term.

While laboratory studies abound, the existence of male-induced pregnancy block under natural conditions has not been directly established. Mallory and Clulow (1977) inferred the occurrence of preimplantation pregnancy block from the ovarian histology of field-caught meadow voles (*M. pennsylvanicus*) and suggested that pregnancy block was more frequent at higher population densities. However, Stehn and Jannett (1981) have pointed out that similar effects could have resulted from other breeding situations as well.

Perhaps the best evidence for male-induced pregnancy block in free-living mammals comes from Bertram's (1975a) long-term records of the reproductive history of lions in the Serengeti National Park. In the two prides he studied, the arrival of new males in a pride was followed by a period of several months during which almost no litters were born (see also Packer and Pusey, Chapter 2, this volume).

INFANTICIDE IN RODENTS

Although infanticide has been documented in a number of mammalian orders (Spencer-Booth, 1971; Hrdy, 1979), it has received little systematic attention until recently. In part, this was due to the earlier widespread interest in the effects of experimental overcrowding on the social behavior of rodents. The results of those studies led to the hypothesis that infanticide was a pathological, nonadaptive response to extreme or artificial conditions (e.g., Calhoun, 1962). However, the results of several recent laboratory studies and field investigations of infanticide suggest that this behavior evolved in response to positive selection pressure and is predictable and adaptive.

The Sexual Selection Model of Male Infanticide

Infanticide has been considered as a form of postmating competition among males resulting from sexual selection (Trivers, 1972; Wilson, 1975; Hrdy, 1979). Most evidence for this hypothesis comes from the primate literature (e.g., Angst and Thommen, 1977; Chapman and Hausfater, 1979; Hrdy, 1979; Hausfater *et al.,* 1982b). In Hanuman langurs, for example, strange males periodically replace the resident male of a multifemale reproductive troop. Following such take-overs, the new male occasionally kills some or all of the unweaned young (Hrdy, 1974, 1977a). Given the short duration of male tenure in this species, infanticidal males benefit by inseminating females sooner because the loss of their offspring brings lactating females into estrus within 8 days. This avoids the normal 15–24-month period of lactational amenorrhea and allows the new male's young to be weaned before he is replaced by another infanticidal male. Infanticide in lions, whose social structure parallels that of langurs, occurs under similar circumstances (Schaller, 1972; Bertram, 1975a, 1976).

Several conditions postulated as the selective bases for the evolution of male infanticide in langurs and lions also apply in rodents. Male competition for mates is common among rodents (see below), and several laboratory studies have shown that males that kill a female's nursing young can produce their own offspring sooner than do noninfanticidal males (Mallory and Brooks, 1978; Webster *et al.,* 1981; vom Saal and Howard, 1982). In *Mus,* lactation inhibits ovulation, delays implantation, and increases the length of gestation several days (Asdell, 1964; Rugh, 1968; Mallory, 1979). Lengthened gestation due to lactation has also been reported in several species of microtines (Hamilton, 1962; Breed, 1969; Coutts and Rowlands, 1969; Mallory and Brooks, 1978; Webster *et al.,* 1981).

Recent laboratory studies have tested several predictions of the sexual selection hypothesis. For example, the hypothesis predicts that males would kill only unrelated young since infanticide would not increase the male's reproductive success if practiced indiscriminately. As predicted, in several species, males introduced into the nest area of an unfamiliar female and her litter significantly reduced weaning success, whereas sires similarly introduced did not (*D. groenlandicus:* Mallory and Brooks, 1978; *M. pennsylvanicus:* Webster *et al.,* 1981; wild-strain *Mus:* Labov, 1980; and laboratory *Mus:* Huck *et al.,* 1982). In the study by Huck *et al.,* (1982), 19 of 40 strange males but only 2 of 30 sires killed young. In all cases where pup killing was observed, the entire litter was killed within 30 min. Eight of the 19 strange males that killed pups cannibalized some, but only after killing all of them. None of the females were observed killing young, but some licked bleeding pups and ate dead ones.

Apparently, male discrimination of their own versus unrelated young is based on past association with the mother rather than on recognition of the pups themselves. Huck *et al.* (1982) found that male laboratory mice killed their own offspring when these young were in the nest of a strange female, whereas most males did not kill unrelated young in the nest of a familiar female (i.e., a prior mate). Furthermore, prior contact with a female's urine reduces a male's propensity for subsequently killing her young (Huck *et al.,* 1982). Labov's (1980) finding that the pup's genotype did not significantly influence the likelihood of infanticide in wild-strain house mice is consistent with the hypothesis that male discrimination of related versus unrelated young is not based on cues from the pups.

Male Social Status and Infanticide

The tendency for male laboratory mice to kill pups placed into their cages is androgen dependent. Castration of adult males reduces pup killing, while administration of testosterone propionate restores it (Gandelman and vom Saal, 1975; Svare and Mann, 1981). Svare (1979) demonstrated a positive dose response relationship between exogenous testosterone and infanticidal behavior. Similarly, in deer mice, aggression directed by adult males toward juvenile conspecifics is reduced by castration and restored by testosterone administration (Whitsett *et al.,* 1979).

Insofar as social subordination suppresses gonadal function in male rodents (Bronson, 1973; Bronson *et al.,* 1973; McKinney and Desjardins, 1973b; Buhl *et al.,* 1978), it is likely that a male's social status would also affect his tendency to engage in infanticide. This hypothesis was tested independently in two recent studies (vom Saal and Howard, 1982; Huck *et al.,* 1982). In the latter study, social rank was established in male laboratory mice by pairing the same two mice in a neutral arena for 10 min on each of 10–15 consecutive days. A dominant or subordinate male was then placed into the home cage of a female and her litter on Day 1 postpartum. Interactions were observed for the first 30 min, and at the end of 24 hr, the males were removed and surviving pups counted. The presence of a dominant male in the female's cage significantly reduced pup survival, whereas a subordinate did not (Table I). Twelve of 15 dominant males and none of the 15 subordinates engaged in infanticide during the first 30 min. In all cases where pup killing by dominant males was observed, the entire litter was killed. Interestingly, all of the dominant males but only three of the subordinates copulated with the female during the initial 30-min observation period.

Vom Saal and Howard (1982) found that pup killing by male laboratory mice was influenced both by social dominance and sexual experience. In their study, two unrelated newborn pups were placed into the home cage of a dominant or subordinate male for 30 min. Most dominant males without recent copulatory experience killed the pups, whereas dominants that had copulated recently and subordinates, regardless of their prior sexual experience, tended to behave paternally.

Table I. Infanticide in Swiss–Webster mice as a function of male social status[a]

	Number of young (litters)	Number (%) of young not surviving	Number (%) of young not surviving observed killed by male
Control (no male)	228 (21)	10 (4.0)	0 (0.0)
Subordinate male	158 (15)	5 (3.2)	0 (0.0)
Dominant male	145 (15)	119 (82.1)	114 (95.8)

[a] A strange dominant or subordinate male was placed into the cage of a female and her litter on Day 1 postpartum for 24 hr. Control females were left undisturbed. Social interactions were observed for the first 30 min of each replicate. Dominant males significantly reduced the number of surviving young, whereas subordinate males did not. (From Huck et al., 1982.)

Infanticide by Females

Although maternal cannibalism has received considerable attention in recent years (see Fox, 1975a; Hrdy, 1979), the factors regulating female killing of unrelated young have not been well documented. In laboratory mice, the killing of unrelated pups appears to be sexually dimorphic: males tend to kill pups placed into their home cages, whereas most females do not (Svare and Mann, 1981). This difference between the sexes is modulated by concurrent and perinatal androgen levels (Gandelman and vom Saal, 1977; Svare, 1979; Svare and Mann, 1981).

In other species, however, females are more likely to kill strange pups than are males. For example, male golden hamsters rarely attack females or their young and tend to retrieve, rather than kill, strange pups (Dieterlen, 1959; Marques and Valenstein, 1977). When strange pups were placed into their home cages, only 3 of 8 males killed them, whereas all 20 females engaged in infanticide (Rowell, 1961b). Similarly, in tests conducted in a neutral arena, none of 14 males injured pups, whereas 7 of 13 females killed them (Marques and Valenstein, 1976). Female Mongolian gerbils are also more likely than males to kill and cannibalize strange neonates placed into their home cages (Elwood, 1977, 1980). Interestingly, in the latter species, infanticide appears to be inhibited totally in pair-bonded males but in females only when they are in late pregnancy (Elwood, 1980, 1981; Elwood and Ostermeyer, Chapter 19, this volume). Last, nonpregnant collared lemmings also readily engage in infanticide when placed into the home cage of a maternal female (Mallory and Brooks, 1980). In view of the potential importance of female infanticide in natural populations (see below), further comparative investigations of the developmental and hormonal bases of female infanticide are clearly warranted.

Infanticide in Natural Populations

Although anecdotes abound, few systematic investigations of infanticidal behavior in natural populations of rodents have been undertaken.
A noteworthy exception is Sherman's (1981) study of infanticide in
Belding's ground squirrels (*Spermophilus beldingi*). Sherman's data
suggest that infanticide is a regular occurrence in his study population
and constitutes a major source of infant mortality. The most frequent
killers were adult females and subadult males. Since the loss of a
litter generally results in abandonment of the burrow by the mother,
Sherman hypothesized that killer females are able to open up nest
sites for themselves through infanticide. In contrast, the only advantage
hypothesized for infanticidal males is acquisition of a nutritious meal.
Interestingly, infanticidal individuals never killed young of close relatives nor was the frequency of infanticide related to population density.

Earlier reports suggested that infanticide is widespread in this genus,
having been observed in 8 of 11 species (reviewed by Sherman, 1981).
In *Spermophilus columbianus* and *S. undulatus,* several females and
young live in groups dominated by a single, territorial male. Occasionally, unrelated males from nearby territories enter another group and
attack juveniles (Steiner, 1972). In contrast, aggression toward young
by males has not been reported in *S. richardsonii,* a species in which
males are subordinate to females (Quanstrom, 1968).

Aggression by adult males has been found to cause poor juvenile
survival in deer mice (Sadleir, 1965; Healey, 1967) and wood mice,
Apodemus sylvaticus (Flowerdew, 1974). However, in other microtines,
aggression by adult females appears to have the greater effect (Bujalska,
1973; Boonstra, 1978).

RELATIONSHIP BETWEEN THE RISK OF INFANTICIDE AND THE INCIDENCE OF PREGNANCY BLOCK

Earlier it was argued that since pregnancy block involves a physiological response on the part of the female, it should be limited to circumstances in which the benefits for the female from remating outweigh
the cost of losing the first pregnancy. It was further postulated that
where the risk of infanticide by a strange male is high, an early termination of investment in doomed offspring would be selectively advantageous. However, since pregnancy block represents a relatively small
but nonetheless significant loss of a female's reproductive fitness and
since not all males engage in infanticide, it would be selectively advantageous for females to discriminate between potential infanticidal and
noninfanticidal males. Thus, if pregnancy block evolved as a female
strategy to minimize parental investment in offspring that are susceptible to subsequent infanticide, it would be predicted that the incidence

of pregnancy block would be highest in situations where females run a greater risk of male infanticide. This prediction was tested in several experiments detailed in the next section.

Male Social Status and Pregnancy Block in Laboratory Mice

Since the tendency to engage in infanticide is reduced in subordinate male mice, these males should also be less likely to induce pregnancy block. This prediction was tested in two independent studies with laboratory mice (Labov, 1981b; Huck, 1982). In Huck's study, randomly bred Swiss–Webster females were assigned to one of eight experimental groups (see Fig. 1). Females in four of the groups were inseminated by dominant males, and females in the other four groups were mated to subordinates. One day after the original mating, either the original stud, a strange dominant, or a strange subordinate male was placed

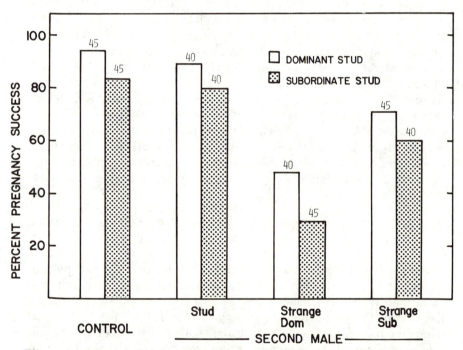

Figure 1. Pregnancy block in Swiss–Webster mice as a function of male social status. Females mated to dominant or subordinate males were subsequently exposed to a strange dominant (DOM), a strange subordinate (SUB), or the original stud male. Control females remained undisturbed after mating. Numbers of females tested is indicated above bars. Pregnancy success was greater for females exposed to subordinate rather than dominant strangers and for females mated with dominant as opposed to subordinate studs. (From Huck, 1982.)

into the female's cage, but separated from her by a wire-mesh partition, for 48 hr. Following these treatments, the females were left undisturbed and any litters recorded. This experimental design allowed tests for (1) the relative efficacy of dominant and subordinate males in inducing pregnancy block, and (2) the possibility that pregnancy block would be less likely to occur in females impregnated by dominant males than in those impregnated by subordinates.

The results of this experiment (Fig. 1) indicated that while exposure to strange males of both social ranks reduced pregnancy success when compared with exposure to stud males, dominant males were significantly more effective. Furthermore, females impregnated by subordinate males tended to run a higher risk of pregnancy block when exposed to strange males than did females impregnated by dominants.

A mechanism for these effects is not difficult to postulate. Since the pregnancy-blocking pheromone is androgen dependent (see above) and since social subordination suppresses gonadal function in male rodents, subordinates may fail to terminate a pregnancy simply because their urine does not contain a sufficient amount of pheromone. It is also possible that the elevated plasma testosterone levels observed in male mice following exposure to unfamiliar females (Macrides *et al.*, 1982) occurs to a lesser degree (or not at all) in subordinate males. In any event, insofar as the tendency to engage in infanticide is also androgen dependent, it would be selectively advantageous for a newly impregnated female to respond differentially to the concentration of testosterone metabolites present in the strange male's urine.

The differential blocking observed in this experiment is also consistent with the hypothesis that pregnancy block evolved as a strategy by females to increase the likelihood that their offspring will be sired by dominant males. However, of the two hypotheses considered—mate selection and avoidance of male infanticide—the latter is more compelling for two reasons. First, the potential loss of an entire litter represents a greater selective pressure than the potential benefits of bearing the young of a dominant male. Second, the mate selection hypothesis does not account for the finding that nearly one-half of the females originally mated to dominant males lost their initial pregnancies when subsequently exposed to another dominant male (Fig. 1). Of course, these hypotheses are not mutually exclusive, and both selective forces could be operating simultaneously.

Labov (1981b) also investigated the relationship between male social status and ability to block pregnancy in laboratory mice. However, in his study, dominant and subordinate males were equally effective in inducing pregnancy block in newly mated females. A possible explanation for this discrepancy in results is that whereas all of Huck's mice were from the same outbred strain (Swiss–Webster), in Labov's study females and strange males were Swiss albinos, but stud males were taken from a randomly bred wild strain. The strain differences between stud and strange males might have overshadowed any effects of the strange male's social status in the latter study.

Infanticide and Pregnancy Block in the Golden Hamster

In contrast with *Mus,* the female hamster is heavier and more aggressive than the male and is usually dominant in social situations (Dieterlen, 1959; Lawlor, 1963; Swanson, 1967; Payne and Swanson, 1970). Females become particularly aggressive with the approach of parturition and in the presence of their pups (Dieterlen, 1959; Wise, 1974). Also, whereas males are unlikely to kill neonates, most females readily kill unrelated pups placed into their home cage or in a neutral arena (see above). In hamsters then, the presence of a strange female poses a greater potential risk of infanticide than does a male. If risk of infanticide is the selective force behind pregnancy block, it would be predicted that, if it occurs at all in this species, pregnancy block would be induced by another female and not by a strange male. This hypothesis is currently being tested, and although preliminary, the data tend to support it.

In the first experiment, the ability of male hamsters to induce pregnancy block in recently mated females was tested. On the day after mating, either the original stud ($n = 40$) or a strange male ($n = 40$) was placed into the female's enclosure for 48 hr. One-half of these pairs were separated by a wire-mesh partition, and one-half were allowed to achieve physical contact. The females were then transferred to individual breeding cages, where they remained undisturbed until parturition. Control females ($n = 20$) were placed into individual enclosures, handled briefly 48 hr later, and transferred to breeding cages. All of the females subsequently delivered litters, thus indicating an absence of male-induced pregnancy block in this species.

Next, the hypothesis that pregnancy block in the golden hamster could be induced by another female was tested. Since hamsters become particularly aggressive during the latter stages of pregnancy (Dieterlen, 1959), recently mated females were paired with another female in the twelfth day of her 16-day pregnancy. Plexiglas partitions were used to limit contact between members of each pair to three, 10-min periods on each of 3 consecutive days. An animal was classified as dominant if its chase–attack score was significantly higher than that of the other member of the pair. Plexiglas partitions were similarly used to limit the access of control females to the empty half of their enclosure. After the last encounter, each female was placed into an individual breeding cage, where it remained undisturbed until parturition.

The results of this experiment are summarized in Table II. Twelve-

Table II. Pregnancy success of recently mated and 12-day-pregnant golden hamsters[a]

Condition	Number of females	Number (%) delivering
Recently mated females		
Control	25	25 (100.0)
Dominant	11	11 (100.0)
Subordinate	17	9 (52.9)
12-day-pregnant females		
Control	25	25 (100.0)
Dominant	17	17 (100.0)
Subordinate	11	9 (81.8)

[a] Hamsters were exposed to each other for three 10-min encounters on each of 2 consecutive days. Dominance was based on relative chase–attack scores. Controls were given brief access to an empty enclosure. Pregnancy success was significantly reduced only in the recently mated subordinate females.

day-pregnant females were dominant to recently mated females in 17 of the 28 pairs tested. All of the control and dominant females and most of the subordinate 12-day-pregnant animals delivered litters. In contrast, pregnancy success was reduced by 47% among the recently mated subordinate females. While preliminary, these data indicate that female-induced pregnancy block can occur in the golden hamster under laboratory conditions. Furthermore, the use of relatively short exposure periods suggests that this effect may also occur in the wild.

SOME BEHAVIORAL AND ECOLOGICAL CONSIDERATIONS

Insofar as a species' social structure produces the selection pressure thought to be responsible for the evolution of infanticide and pregnancy block, an increased understanding of social structure is essential for the ability to formulate relevant hypotheses for laboratory and field investigation. Therefore, it seems appropriate at this point to examine the social milieu in which these phenomena have been proposed to occur. Much of this discussion focuses on *Mus* since it has been the subject of much laboratory and field investigation.

Where they live commensally with man, wild house mice form small, isolated, reproductive units (demes) in which immigration and emigration are restricted (Anderson, 1964; Reimer and Petras, 1968; Lacy, 1978). Demes consist of a single, dominant, territorial male, several breeding females, some of their offspring, and a few subordinate males. In free-living populations, dominant males probably do not retain their status for very long (Southwick, 1955b; Berry and Jakobson, 1974), especially at high population densities (Poole and Morgan, 1973). Thus, in several respects, the social structure of house mice is similar to that of langurs and lions. Therefore, it is possible that similar selection pressures might have operated in all three groups.

The results of a recent study of captive wild house mice indicate that male take-overs in *Mus* may be analogous to those observed in langurs and lions. Baker (1981) placed two males and three female mice into one-half of a population cage. A barrier separated these mice from a similarly constituted group in the other half of the enclosure. In five of six replicates, mice from both sides of the enclosures formed a single social group when the barrier was removed 1 month later. Males were more active in defending their half of the enclosure from intruders than were females. In three replicates, the males of one group were killed. Earlier studies also suggested that males defended their territories more actively than did females (Brown, 1953; Crowcroft and Rowe, 1963). Also, when single strange males or females were placed into established demes, the females frequently survive, whereas the males are killed (Reimer and Petras, 1968).

In *Mus,* if territorial males are periodically replaced by strange males from outside the deme, it may be advantageous for the new male to destroy newly born litters to avoid lactational delay of gestation. This may be particularly important at high population densities where male tenure is short (Poole and Morgan, 1972). Of course, if territorial males are replaced by former subordinates from within the group (Lidicker, 1976), the benefits of infanticide would be reduced since the new male may be genetically related to his predecessor. Thus, in mice as in langurs and lions, the periodic replacement of reproductive males by males from outside the breeding unit may be a necessary condition for the evolution of infanticide via sexual selection.

The spatial and temporal stability of demes increases the likelihood that, if a male has bred, any young he encounters will be his own. Natural selection, then, would favor males that, having mated, do not engage in infanticide. The reduced propensity of recently mated male rodents to kill neonates has been demonstrated in *Mus* and several other species (vom Saal and Howard, 1982; Huck *et al.,* 1982). Furthermore, Hrdy's (1979) suggestion that male recognition of offspring is based on past association with the mother has been verified since laboratory mice killed their own offspring when those young were in the nest of a strange female, whereas males did not kill unrelated young in the nest of a prior mate (Huck *et al.,* 1982).

The breeding units of most microtines are probably small but not as rigidly structured as they are in *Mus* (Eisenberg, 1968; Rogers and Beauchamp, 1976; Kleiman, 1977; Getz, 1978). Aggressive competition for estrous females apparently occurs in some species (e.g., *M. pennsylvanicus:* Madison, 1980a; Webster *et al.,* 1981) and may result in a decrease in the number of males that breed at any given time. Infanticide may be an adaptive strategy for a male who has not bred for two reasons: (1) there is no chance that he will encounter his own young, and (2) if he subsequently mates with the victimized female, his offspring will be born sooner than those of a noninfanticidal male due to the avoidance of lactational delay of gestation. Field studies are required to determine whether levels of male–male competition are correlated with the incidence of male infanticide in rodents.

Once male infanticide is established in a population, selection could operate on females to reduce their investment in susceptible offspring. As previously suggested, then, pregnancy block can be viewed as a female strategy to minimize time and energy investments in young that are likely to be killed. Since pregnancy block is not without cost to a female's reproductive fitness, selection would favor females who recognized differences between potentially infanticidal and noninfanticidal males.

Since male infanticide is androgen dependent, the concentration of testosterone metabolites (TMs) in the male's urine would allow the female to assess the potential danger to her young. From this premise, three predictions follow. First, long-term exposure to urine with low concentrations of TMs should not lead to pregnancy block since this urine is characteristic of subordinate (i.e., noninfanticidal) males. The finding that in laboratory *Mus*, long-term (48-hr) exposure to a strange subordinate male resulted in a lower incidence of pregnancy block than did a similar exposure to a strange dominant (Huck, 1982) is consistent with this prediction. So is the earlier finding that castrated males are ineffective in blocking pregnancies in *Mus* (Bruce, 1965) and *M. agrestis* (Milligan, 1976). Second, exposure to urine with high concentrations of TMs should be effective only if it is prolonged or repeated since a single, brief exposure is likely to result from a transient male that will not remain in the area long enough to jeopardize the survival of a female's litter. Bruce's (1961b) observation that the incidence of pregnancy block in *Mus* is increased if exposure to the strange male is lengthy (48–72 hr) is consistent with this prediction. So is the finding that short-term (15-min) exposures to a strange male are only effective if they are repeated (Chipman *et al.*, 1966). Third, long-term exposure to urine with a high concentration of TMs should not induce pregnancy block if the original stud male is present since the stud's presence indicates that he has not been defeated. The observation that pregnancy block in *Mus* (Parkes and Bruce, 1961) and *P. maniculatus* (Terman, 1969) is greatly reduced if the original male is present during the exposure to a strange male is consistent with this prediction.

Although there have been no systematic investigations of the behavior of the golden hamster in the wild, it is generally believed to be solitary as are other members of its genus (Murphy, 1971, 1976, 1977). Conditions of "irregular rainfall and food supply" (Richards, 1966a: 308) characterize much of the golden hamster's natural habitat, and it is known to hoard grain in underground burrows (Murphy, 1971). Goldman and Swanson (1975) suggested that strange pups are treated as potential food. This view is consistent with the observation that nonlactating females frequently picked up neonates introduced into their cages and placed them on their food pile before eating them. Female hamsters could benefit in two ways from killing and eating another female's young. First, they may benefit directly from the consumption of their victims. The exploitation of infants as a food resource (cannibalism) is a widely spread phenomenon in natural populations (Hrdy, 1979). Second, the death of unrelated infants may reduce competition for an area's food resources by (*a*) reducing the energy requirements of the females whose young are killed and by (*b*) decreasing the number of potential competitors (Hrdy, 1979). Competition for food resources may be especially intense among females with young since energetic demands are particularly high during gestation and lactation (e.g., Kaczmarski, 1966; Migula, 1969).

Although speculative, it is possible to view increased postpartum aggression in hamsters as a female counterstrategy to reduce the vulnerability of newborn young to infanticide. In females that are unable to defeat competitors, natural selection would then favor the evolution of pregnancy block. Females in an advanced stage of pregnancy have invested more parental effort in their offspring and, thus, should be more aggressive and less susceptible to pregnancy block than females in an earlier stage of pregnancy. Although the data support this interpretation, further experimentation is required to accept or reject it.

SUMMARY AND CONCLUSIONS

It has been difficult to postulate an adaptive function of male-induced pregnancy block for female rodents because it involves a physiological response on the part of the female and a consequent loss of reproductive effort. This and the absence of field corroboration has led to the suggestion that pregnancy block is a laboratory artifact. However, recognition of infanticide as an adaptive and predictable behavior has led to the suggestion that it has served as a primary selective pressure for the evolution of pregnancy block essentially as a female counterstrategy to infanticide. In *Mus,* the demic structure of commensal populations, short male tenure, and lactational delay of gestation appear to have been important factors in the evolution of male infanticide via sexual selection. In contrast, female dominance and a solitary social organization have apparently precluded the evolution of male infanticide in the golden hamster. However, in the latter species, exploitation of unrelated infants as a food resource and their elimination as potential competitors might have provided the selective bases for the evolution of female infanticide. Several experiments indicate that recently mated female mice and hamsters discriminate between potentially infanticidal and noninfanticidal conspecific individuals since only the former induce pregnancy block. These results support the hypothesis that pregnancy block evolved as a female counterstrategy to minimize time and energy investment in young that are subject to a high risk of infanticide, whether that risk is posed by males or females.

Although it is known that infanticide and pregnancy block occur in the laboratory and something is understood about their frequency and proximate causation in a limited number of species, very little is known about their occurrence or significance in natural populations. Field studies involving radiotelemetry to monitor movements and paternity exclusion studies (based on allozymes) are necessary to further the understanding of both infanticide and pregnancy block. Judging from recent developments, many exciting discoveries await those interested in the reproductive ecology of rodents.

ACKNOWLEDGMENTS

Thanks are due to K. Wynne-Edwards and L. Conant Huck for their helpful criticism of the chapter and to A. C. Bracken for her help collecting hamster data.

19 Infanticide by male and female mongolian gerbils: Ontogeny, causation, and function

Robert W. Elwood
Malcolm C. Ostermeyer

INTRODUCTION

Gerbils (*Meriones unguiculatus*) are commonly maintained in the laboratory as monogamous pairs occupying single cages which usually results in peaceful cohabitation and a good breeding performance (Thiessen, 1968; Elwood, 1975a). Field observations of family groups inhabiting a single burrow confirm that these animals are naturally social (Tanimoto, 1943). Each group appears to consist of an adult pair and their offspring, which remain with the parents for the first winter (Leontjev, 1964). Thus, the field data suggest that these animals show monogamy on the measures of peaceful coexistence of the sexes within a limited area and late social weaning of the young (Kleiman, 1981).

Many factors influence whether a male remains with the female after mating, but if he should remain, the only way in which he can improve his inclusive fitness is by further investment in the offspring (i.e., paternal care) (Elwood, 1983). On the day of parturition, the male may be ousted from the nest by the female, but thereafter he spends at least as much time with the infants as does the female (Elwood, 1975a). The presence of the male is beneficial to the young (Elwood and Broom, 1978). He helps in cleaning the infants, in nest building, and in keeping the pups warm. Infants reared by both parents show earlier eye opening and more advanced behavioral development than do those reared by the mother alone. Similar to maternal behavior,

367

paternal behavior is influenced by the number of pups in the litter and probably occurs in response to the same external stimuli (Elwood and Broom, 1978). Correlational analyses have indicated a degree of cooperation in the adults' behavior enabling one parent to be with the young when the other is out of the nest (Elwood, 1979).

Juveniles may remain with the parents during the rearing of subsequent litters (McLoughlin, 1980; Payman and Swanson, 1980; Ostermeyer and Elwood, in press). The juveniles may show "parental" activities such as cleaning the pups, nest building, and keeping the pups warm. The sexual maturation of the juveniles, however, is delayed if they are maintained with the parents and subsequent litter (Ågren, 1980; Payman and Swanson, 1980), so that the final social structure appears to be a monogamous breeding pair and the nonbreeding young. This conclusion is congruent with data from field and seminatural studies (Leonjtev, 1964; Ågren, 1976) and unpublished data from this laboratory.

The fact that this species forms harmonious social groups with all members of the group being solicitous of infants made it somewhat surprising when killing of test pups was first observed (Elwood, 1975b). Further investigations have demonstrated that juveniles and adults of both sexes may kill and cannibalize newborn test pups, but that this behavior is inhibited under certain conditions, particularly when there is a high probability that the infants are related to members of a social group (Elwood, 1977, 1980, 1981). As a result, parental care is directed toward closely related infants, while nonrelated infants are utilized as food. It is the aim of this chapter: (1) to review the situations in which pup killing occurs; (2) to determine the causal factors in its inhibition; and (3) to assess the functional significance of these observations. Before embarking on these discussions, however, two points concerning methodology should be made.

In all the experiments discussed herein, a standard test procedure was employed. This procedure was designed to be in accordance with animal welfare laws of the United Kingdom and with the guidelines suggested by the ethical committee of the Association for the Study of Animal Behaviour. All animals not to be tested were removed from the cage, leaving the subject alone. A single infant, less than 36 hr old and born to another family, was placed in the center of the subject's cage. If no harm was done to the pup, the observations continued for 5 or 6 min, (standard within an experiment) and the pup was returned to its parents. If, on the other hand, the subject harmed the pup, the observations were immediately terminated, and the pup was removed and killed. Previous unanticipated observations had shown that once a pup was bitten, it was consumed (Elwood, 1975b). This has been confirmed on a number of occasions by returning a pup to the subject after the pup had been killed by the experimenter, whereupon the subject invariably cannibalized the infant. Thus, in all experiments, the subjects were classified as either those that did no harm or those that attempted to cannibalize the pup.

Each subject was only tested once and with a single pup only. This not only minimized the number of pups exposed to possible stress, but it also ensured that only one datum point was obtained per subject. Methods employed in some other studies have involved placing several pups into the subject's cage (Richards, 1966a; Jakubowski and Terkel, 1982) or placing the subject into another cage containing a full litter (Mallory and Brooks, 1978; Labov, 1980), in which case each dead pup has been counted as an independent datum point. It is strongly advocated that these procedures should not be employed in future on the grounds both of animal welfare and of statistical validity.

CAUSAL FACTORS IN PUP KILLING

Juveniles

The ontogeny of pup cannibalism in the gerbil has been examined using juveniles of both sexes at ages 1, 1.5, 2, 2.5, 3.5, and 6 months (Elwood, 1980). All animals were removed from their parents at 30 days of age, housed in mixed-sex groups until 60 days, and then subsequently maintained in single-sexed groups (or tested at some stage of this procedure). They were housed individually for 2–7 days before being offered a single newborn pup. The results (Fig. 1) indicated that there was a significant increase in pup cannibalism with increasing age of the juveniles. Mature females (6 months) were more likely to kill infants than were similar age males, but at younger ages, there were no significant differences between the sexes.

About one-third of the animals tested at 1.5–2.5 months attempted to cannibalize the test pup. This is in contrast with many observations of juveniles of similar ages that remained with their parents during the birth and rearing of the subsequent litter (McLoughlin, 1980; Payman and Swanson, 1980; Ostermeyer and Elwood, in press). There are no reports of these latter juveniles harming the newborn litter; to the contrary, the juveniles behave in a "parental" manner toward these related offspring.

Causal factors. These observations suggest that two factors may influence the development of pup cannibalism. First, increasing age results in an increasing probability of infanticide. This is in agreement with observations on mice (Gandelman, 1973) and is probably influenced by the onset of sexual maturity (2–2.5 months for onset of sexual activity in gerbils). Sexual maturity is mediated by steroid production, and male mice that have been gonadectomized do not show pup killing

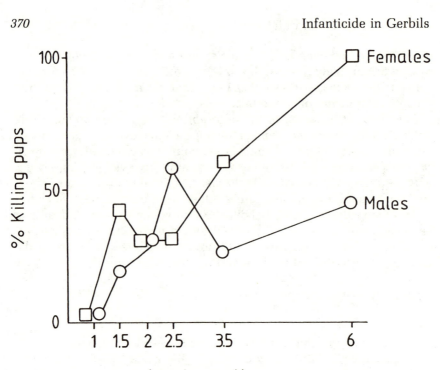

Figure 1. The percentage of animals of different ages that attempted to cannibalize newborn test pups is shown. (From Elwood, 1980, with permission from Bailliere Tindall.)

unless treated with testosterone shortly before testing (Gandelman and
vom Saal, 1975). Testosterone has also been shown to mediate pup
killing in male rats (Rosenberg and Sherman, 1975), but whether estrogens have a similar effect on females has yet to be determined. The
second factor is the presence or absence of the juveniles' parents. However, the continued presence of the parents not only inhibits pup cannibalism, but also suppresses sexual maturity in the juveniles (Ågren,
1980; Payman and Swanson, 1980). It is possible that the suppression
of sexual maturity inhibits steroid production, and that this is the ultimate causal factor for the suppression of cannibalism.

The preweaning social environment may also influence pup cannibalism. This suggestion has been examined by rearing male gerbils in
one of three conditions: (*a*) by a nonpregnant mother without the father;
(*b*) by both parents, but subject removed prior to the birth of the next
litter; or (*c*) by both parents, but subject removed approximately 12
hr after the birth of the next litter (Elwood, 1980). These males were
maintained as described in the previous experiment until 6 months
of age. They were then isolated for 2–7 days prior to being offered a
single test pup. No significant differences, however, were noted in pup

cannibalism between these three groups (38, 46, and 37%, respectively; attempted to harm the test pup).

Adult Females

It is apparent from the previous section that female gerbils are prone to cannibalize newborn pups if given the opportunity. It is rare, however, for females to harm their own pups at parturition. Thus, either females can discriminate between their own and alien pups or they are brought into a maternal state prior to parturition or both. The following section describes experiments designed to test if there are differences in maternal responsiveness toward unrelated test pups during the reproductive cycle.

Naïve female gerbils (i.e., females never having seen newborn pups) were paired with naïve males when both sexes were about 3.5–4.5 months of age (Elwood, 1977). Some 3–6 weeks later, the males were removed; and the females tested. The reproductive status of each female was calculated retrospectively from the time of their parturition (25-day gestation period). Similar tests were also conducted with experienced females (i.e., those having reared at least one previous litter). The results showed that nonpregnant naïve females invariably killed test pups as did the majority of early and midpregnant females (Fig. 2). One-half of the late-pregnant (i.e., within 6 days of parturition), naïve females, however, did not harm the pup. These results resemble those obtained for the experienced females. In both cases, the only group to differ significantly from the nonpregnant females was the late-pregnant group (Fig. 2).

Causal factors. The changes in the responses to test pups of female gerbils during pregnancy are similar to those shown by golden hamsters (Richards, 1966a) and by some mice (Gandelman and Davis, 1973). These changes may be likened to the increasing maternal responsiveness of many female rodents during pregnancy and are probably mediated by the rapid changes in plasma hormone levels at the approach of parturition (reviewed by Rosenblatt and Siegel, 1983). Newly parturient female gerbils accept foster young and do not obviously discriminate between their own and alien young under these conditions.

The suppression of pup cannibalism is thus correlated with the onset of maternal behavior normally seen at the time of parturition. Indeed, late-pregnant females that did not harm the pup often initially showed a startle response followed by a range of activities normally seen during parturition. These included an alternation of licking the pup and licking their own anogenital region in a typical "head between the heels" posture, retrieving the pup to the nest, nest building, and assumption of the lactation posture.

Causal factors in reinstatement of cannibalism. At comparable re-

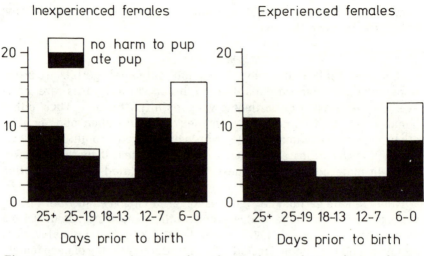

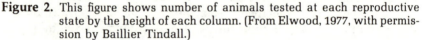

Figure 2. This figure shows number of animals tested at each reproductive state by the height of each column. (From Elwood, 1977, with permission by Baillier Tindall.)

productive states, naïve and experienced females responded to the test pups in a similar fashion. This indicates that the inhibition of pup cannibalism toward the end of pregnancy is not a permanent change in female behavior. Some time after parturition, pup cannibalism is reinstated. Studies have been conducted on the timing of this reestablishment of infanticide after parturition and the role of the female's own young in the maintenance of its suppression (Elwood, 1981). For example, in one experiment, three groups of females were compared: The first group (A) had all their pups removed within 12 hr of parturition; the second group (B) had their litters reduced to three pups on the day of parturition (Day 0); and the third group (C) had their litters reduced to three pups on Day 0 but then replaced with three newborn foster pups between Days 6 and 10.

The results for Group A (Fig. 3) indicated that removal of all offspring shortly after parturition resulted in a rapid reestablishment of infanticide. Of those animals tested between Days 1–5 and between days 6–10, 40 and 72%, respectively, attempted to cannibalize the test pup. In contrast, no female in Group B, which retained a litter of three pups, harmed the test pup when tested between Days 1–10 postpartum. A small number (29%) attempted to cannibalize the test pup on Days 11–15, 50% did so on Days 16–20, and 100% did so on Days 21–25. Thus, the reestablishment of pup cannibalism was delayed by approximately 10 days if the mother retained her natural litter. Females with replacement litters (Group C) did not harm the test pups when tested on Days 16–18. These females appeared to be responding in a manner

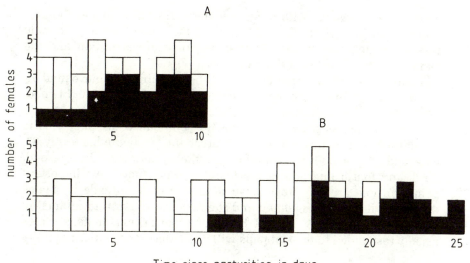

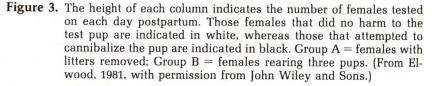

Time since parturition in days

Figure 3. The height of each column indicates the number of females tested on each day postpartum. Those females that did no harm to the test pup are indicated in white, whereas those that attempted to cannibalize the pup are indicated in black. Group A = females with litters removed; Group B = females rearing three pups. (From Elwood, 1981, with permission from John Wiley and Sons.)

more appropriate to the age of the replacement litters than to the time since parturition.

It thus appears that the timing of the reestablishment of pup cannibalism is influenced both by the continued presence of pups after parturition and by the age of those pups. In these respects, these data are similar to general changes in maternal responsiveness toward infants seen in several rodent species. For example, a sharp decline in the maternal responsiveness of female rats occurs if their pups are removed at parturition (Bridges, 1975), whereas female rats may be maintained in a maternal state by repeatedly replacing litters with younger foster pups (Wiesner and Sheard, 1933). In the rat, however, the nonmaternal response is one of avoidance of the pups, not cannibalism.

Adult Males

Unmated juvenile and mature males may cannibalize newborn test pups (Fig. 1). No male, however, has been observed to harm his own pups while a member of an established pair. Thus, as with females, either the male can distinguish between his own and alien pups, or he is somehow brought into a paternal state prior to the birth of offspring to his mate. The procedure to test these possibilities was the same as that used for females and described previously. Naïve males were housed for 3–6 weeks with a naïve female prior to testing each male. The reproductive state of each female at the time of testing the male was calculated retrospectively from the time of parturition and the male allocated to an experimental group (Fig. 4).

The results show a marked change in the probability of pup cannibalism by males according to the reproductive state of the female (Elwood, 1977, 1980, and unpublished data) (Fig. 4). Of those males housed with nonpregnant females, 63% attempted to cannibalize the pup. This is in contrast with males housed with pregnant females where only 33, 8, 14, and 0%, respectively, cannibalized infants during the first, second, third, and fourth quarters of the females' pregnancy. Two important points to note are the progressive reduction of infanticide by males during the females' pregnancy and the absence of harm to infants by males tested ʋithin 6 days of his mate's parturition. In fact, males usually responded to the test pups with the paternal activities normally

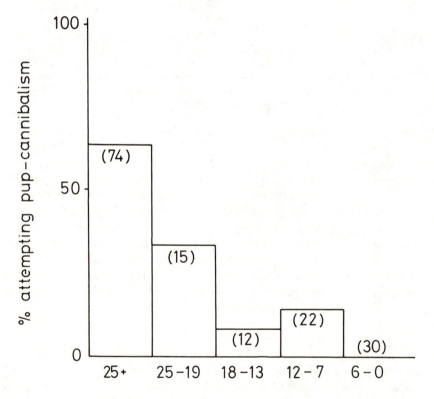

Figure 4. Responses of naïve males toward test pups at different stages in their mate's pregnancy (25+ = nonpregnant). Numbers in parentheses indicate sample size for each group.

exhibited toward their own pups (Elwood 1975a; 1977). Males are thus brought into a paternal state prior to the birth of their offspring. Males do not appear to discriminate between their own offspring or same-age conspecific infants when these are fostered into the nest.

Experienced males have been tested in a similar fashion to that for the naïve males (Elwood, 1977). In contrast to both naïve males and experienced females, no experienced male harmed the test pup, regardless of the reproductive state of his mate. The inhibition of pup cannibalism in experienced males may either be merely a prolongation of the prepartum inhibition documented for naïve males (Fig. 4) or may result from the experience of rearing pups per se (Elwood, 1977). These hypotheses were tested as follows: Naïve males, whose mates were within 6 days of parturition, had their mates removed 1 min, 6 hr, 1–3 days, or 24–28 days prior to being tested (n = 19, 14, 14 and 15, respectively). Experienced males were also tested. Ten experienced males were tested 1–3 days after the removal of their nonpregnant mates, while a further 12 experienced males were tested 1–3 days after the removal of their pregnant mates (within 6 days of parturition).

Results of the preceding experiments indicated that the inhibition of pup cannibalism seen in naïve males was temporary (Fig. 5). Removal of the pregnant female resulted in a reestablishment of infanticide. The longer the time since the removal, the greater was the probability of infanticide. Of those males tested 1–3 days after the removal of the female, 50% attempted to cannibalize the test pup. This finding contrasts with the data for the two groups of experienced males tested 1–3 days after the removal of their females, in which none harmed the pup. It thus seems that experience gained during the rearing of a litter, not the mate's reproductive condition, is responsible for the relatively permanent inhibition of infanticide seen in experienced males.

The finding that the inhibition of pup cannibalism by naïve males is temporary and dependent upon the continued presence of the female indicates that some factor (or factors) initiates the inhibition, and that presumably the same factor (or factors) maintains the inhibition until parturition by the female. At this time, other factors, probably associated with the offspring themselves, result in a permanent inhibition of pup cannibalism in males. The following section describes a series of previously unpublished experiments designed to elucidate the factors involved in the initiation and/or the maintenance of the temporary inhibition of infanticide in naïve males.

CAUSAL FACTORS IN THE INHIBITION OF PUP CANNIBALISM BY MALES

Several hypotheses concerning the causal mechanism for the inhibition of infanticide by males during the females' pregnancy have been

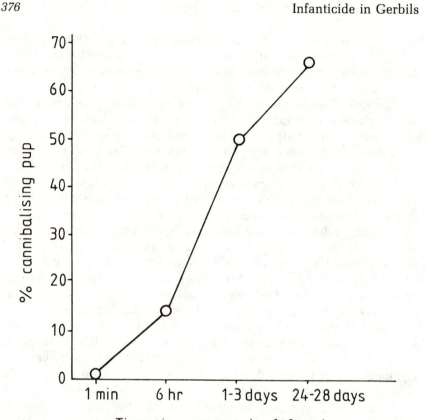

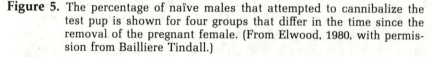

Time since removal of female

Figure 5. The percentage of naïve males that attempted to cannibalize the
test pup is shown for four groups that differ in the time since the
removal of the pregnant female. (From Elwood, 1980, with permission from Bailliere Tindall.)

proposed. First, it is known that gerbils have a sebaceous midventral
gland that in the female increases in size during pregnancy (Wallace,
Owen, and Thiessen, 1973). It is possible that the increased size and
presumably increased secretion of the gland is connected to inhibition
of pup cannibalism by males. More specifically, the midventral gland
of the female may produce a specific inhibitory olfactory substance
only during pregnancy (Elwood, 1977). A related possibility is that substances in the urine of pregnant females may be smelled or ingested
by the male. For example, it is known that levels of progesterone rise
during pregnancy, and thus progesterone or one of its metabolites in
the urine may be the casual factor in inhibition of pup cannibalism
(Elwood, 1977). Finally, the act of copulation per se may have an inhibitory effect on pup cannibalism (Elwood, 1977).

The Midventral Gland

Stated in its simplest form, the first hypothesis is that the development by a female of a large midventral gland and/or secretions therefrom inhibit pup killing in the male. The gland becomes particularly large during pregnancy, but in fact there is considerable natural variation of gland size in nonpregnant females that may explain why approximately 40% of males housed with nonpregnant females fail to harm the test pup (Fig. 4). Perhaps these males were housed with females with particularly large glands. This hypothesis was tested by examining the variation in gland size of nonpregnant females and attempting to relate gland size to the response of cohabiting males toward the test pups.

Animals between 3 and 4 months of age were paired, one male and one female per cage. Four to 6 weeks later, the male of each pair was tested with a single newborn pup. The female of each pair was subsequently killed and examined internally for indications of pregnancy; if these were found, then that pair was discarded from the analysis. The midventral glands of nonpregnant females were examined visually, and their levels of activity assessed (i.e., the characteristic yellow secretion, present or not). Each gland was then excised and examined histologically. In this manner, 26 females were examined and their glandular states related to the responses of their mates toward the test pups.

Of the 26 females, 13 had a visibly active gland and 13 did not. Nine out of the 13 males housed with females with visible glands attempted to cannibalize the test pup compared with 8 out of 13 males housed with females without visible glands. There is no significant difference between these groups (Fisher exact probability test, $p >$ 0.05). For the histological assessment of the female glands, the number of sebaceous gland units (based around a single hair follicle) was counted in three transverse sections. The mean of these three counts was used as the measure of gland size for each female. Glands of females that had been housed with males that attempted to cannibalize the test pup had an average of 4.9 units compared with 4.6 units for those of females with males that did no harm (t-test was not statistically significant).

These results do not support the hypothesis that increased size of the female's gland per se inhibits infanticide in the male. It seems likely that some feature of a pregnant female inhibits pup cannibalism in the male, although the possibility has not been ruled out that some specific olfactory substance, produced by the midventral gland of females only during pregnancy, is the causal factor. This possibility was tested in later experiments described in the next section.

Progesterone Levels in Females and Males

Pup killing in male and female mice and in male rats has been shown to be enhanced by testosterone treatment (Gandelman, 1972, 1973; Rosenberg and Sherman, 1975), but pregnancy in female mice inhibits this effect (Gandelman and Davis, 1973). Pregnancy is marked by an increase in progesterone, which may act antagonistically with testosterone (Erpino, 1975). Increased progesterone during pregnancy may result in high levels of progesterone or its metabolites appearing in the urine of female gerbils, and these may be ingested by the male during allogrooming. It has previously been suggested that this may be the causal mechanism by which cannibalism is inhibited in male gerbils (Elwood, 1977).

In a test of this hypothesis, 12 naïve females, approximately 3 months in age, were housed individually and given subcutaneous injection of 500 μg progesterone (Sigma Chemicals) in 0.5 ml oil. Eleven similar females received the oil only. Each female received four injections at weekly intervals. Three days after the third injection, the females were paired in a novel cage with a naïve male of a similar age. Eight days after pairing, the female was removed and the male immediately offered a newborn pup and his responses noted.

Six out of 12 males housed with progesterone-treated females attempted to cannibalize the pup compared with 5 out of 11 housed with control females (Fisher exact probability test was not significant). Thus, high progesterone levels in the females did not appear to suppress cannibalism in the males. In a variant of this experiment, 12 males directly treated with progesterone were as likely to harm the test pup as were control males. Thus, high progesterone levels in the male or the female do not appear to influence pup cannibalism. Thus, the data do not support the hypothesis that progesterone or its metabolites in the urine of pregnant gerbils are related to suppression of pup cannibalism in males.

Effects of Urine

If not progesterone secretion, then perhaps some other substance in the urine of pregnant females influences cannibalism by males. To test this possibility, 25 mated pairs of gerbils were established. Pairs were maintained as described previously (Elwood, 1980) until each female was within 6 days of parturition, whereupon each female was removed from the cage. In the "urine group" ($n = 12$), the female was placed in a metabolism cage arranged so that her urine ran directly into the nest area of the male. It was unlikely that the male received any visual or olfactory stimuli, other than the urine, from the female. In the "no-urine group" ($n = 13$), the female was placed in a nearby cage so that no urine was available for the male. In both groups, the female was out of the cage for 24 hr prior to testing the male. As removal of the female had previously been shown to result in the reestablishment of pup cannibalism in the male (Fig. 5), the rationale of this experiment was to test if the urine from the pregnant female alone could maintain the inhibition of cannibalism. In fact, 5 out of 12 males in the urine group attempted to harm the test pup compared with 3 out of 13 in the no-urine group (Fisher test was not significant). Thus, it was concluded that the urine of pregnant females was not a sufficient stimulus to inhibit pup cannibalism by males; exposure to female urine did not even produce a slight decrease in male cannibalism.

Other Pheromonal Substances

The midventral gland is used to scent mark the substrate, and females are frequently observed rubbing this gland on various parts of the cage, particularly around the edge of the nest. Whether this has an effect on the maintenance of the inhibition in males may be tested by removing the female and leaving the male in the cage with the old bedding (and scent marks) or with clean bedding. Further, this procedure would indicate if any olfactory substance deposited by the female is a causal factor in the inhibition of male cannibalism. In an experiment on this topic, 54 naïve males, the mates of which were within 6 days of parturition, were the subjects. The female from each cage was removed, and the male either left with the soiled bedding (at least 2 weeks old) or placed on clean bedding. The males were tested either 24 or 48 hr after the removal of the females.

There was no significant difference (Fisher tests) in pup killing between males on old or clean bedding when the female had been removed for 24 hr (13% $n = 15$ and 23% $n = 13$, respectively) or for those separated for 48 hr (38% $n = 13$ and 46% $n = 13$, respectively). There was, however, an overall significant increase in infanticide with increased time since removal of the female (24 hr = 18% and 48 hr = 42%, $p = 0.035$). These results confirm and refine the data given previously (Fig. 5) but clearly do not provide evidence that olfactory stimuli play a role in the suppression of infanticide in the male gerbil. The findings of this experiment were surprising both in view of the great importance of olfaction in rodent reproductive processes (see Bronson, 1968 for review) and in view of previous suggestions of the likely involvement of a pheromone in this phenomenon (Elwood, 1977, 1980).

Other Sensory Cues

Once again, the rationale of this experiment rests on the fact that removal of the female results in a reestablishment of infanticide in the male. Separation of the sexes behind barriers that allow certain stimuli to pass from one to the other should distinguish which stimuli maintain the inhibition. Naïve males, the mates of which were within 6 days of parturition, were the subjects. Pairs were allocated to one of four experimental groups: In Group 1 ($n = 30$), the female remained in the cage until a few seconds before the male was offered a single newborn pup. In Group 2 ($n = 35$), the male and female were separated by a double layer of wire mesh for 24–48 hr prior to testing the male. In Group 3 ($n = 38$) and Group 4 ($n = 36$), the pairs were separated as in Group 2 but with clear plastic and opaque plastic partitions, respectively. Thus, in Group 1, the males continued to have full contact with the female. In Group 2, the males had visual, olfactory, and auditory stimuli, Group 3 had visual and auditory stimuli, but olfaction was reduced, whereas Group 4 did not have visual stimuli.

The percentage of males that attempted to kill the test pup in Groups 1–4 was 0, 11.4, 13.2, and 25%, respectively. Fisher exact probability tests on the original data indicate significant differences between Groups 1 and 3 ($p = 0.048$) and between Groups 1 and 4 ($p = 0.0025$). The difference between Groups 1 and 2 approached significance ($p = 0.077$). These data indicate that males that remained in physical contact with the mate (Group 1) were the only ones to show a total inhibition of pup cannibalism. All other groups exhibited some pup cannibalism which suggests that whatever other factors maintain the inhibition, close physical contact between the sexes is a necessary component. The similarity in infanticide within Groups 2 and 3 again fails to support the hypothesis that olfaction is involved. As the group that showed the highest level of pup cannibalism (Group 4) was the one lacking visual stimuli, it is interesting to speculate whether some visual feature of the female may play a role in the inhibition.

Recency of Copulation

Elwood (1977) considered copulation as a mechanism for the inhibition of pup cannibalism but pointed out that it seemed unlikely that copulation could have an increasing effect with increasing time from the act (Fig. 4). Furthermore, copulation could only play a part in the initiation of the inhibition, not in the maintenance as removal of the pregnant female results in reestablishment of infanticide. More recently, however, this hypothesis has received some support (Labov, 1980; vom Saal and Howard, 1982; Webster, Gartshore and Brooks, 1981). In particular, studies by vom Saal (Chapter 21, this volume) have indicated that infanticide is initially facilitated and then inhibited in male mice after copulation, although this finding has proved difficult to replicate (Svare: personal communication; Elwood and Ostermeyer, 1984).

However, in most of these studies, copulation and postcopulatory contact are not completely separated. For example, Webster, Gartshore, and Brooks (1981) housed male *Microtus pennsylvanicus* with females for 7 days during which copulation probably occurred. vom Saal and Howard (1982) allowed their sexually experienced mice each to mate with two females but did not indicate when they were removed, whereas Labov (1980) removed the males "when vaginal plugs were found in the females." In all cases, the male presumably remained with the female for at least several hours so that it is inappropriate to suggest that copulation per se is the major factor in the inhibition of infanticide. Data on gerbils show an increasing inhibition with increasing cohabitation, and this effect is also reported for mice (Labov, 1980). Thus, it appears that the postcopulatory period may be the important factor in the initiation of the inhibition and not exclusively the act of copulation per se (at least in gerbils). It is possible, however, that copulation facilitates certain interactions between the sexes that may result in the inhibition.

The importance of postcopulatory social interactions is exemplified by a recent report by vom Saal and Howard (1982). Mice that had mated (twice) were placed with another male and allowed to fight. Those that achieved dominance showed a long-term increase in infanticide. Furthermore, sexually naïve dominant males were more likely to kill pups than were sexually naïve subordinate males. Thus, it appears that dominant/subordinate relationships and/or recent aggressive behavior influence the occurrence of infanticide. This suggestion received support from the observations of Mallory and Brooks (1978), who noted that when a strange male *Dicrostonyx groenlandicus* was placed with a female and her newborn litter, the male was usually attacked. Whether he subsequently killed the pups depended upon the severity and duration of the attack, since if he was subdued by the female, he did not kill her infants.

It is proposed that a change in aggressive behavior of the female occurs after copulation (Huck, Carter, and Banks, 1979) and that this is the onset of maternal aggression seen during pregnancy (see Ostermeyer, 1983 for review). In the gerbil, the female becomes increasingly aggressive toward the male during pregnancy, although this falls short of overt fighting. It appears, however, that in late pregnancy, the female is dominant over the male, and he is ousted from the nest prior to parturition. It thus appears possible that subordination of the male is an important causal factor in the inhibition of pup cannibalism.

How may social subordination inhibit pup killing? Reduced testosterone levels may be involved as castrated male rats and mice do not kill infants unless given testosterone (Rosenberg and Sherman, 1975; Gandelman and vom Saal, 1975). Shifts in dominance relationships may also result in shifts in testosterone; testosterone titers fall within hours after the loss of dominance (Buhl, Hasler, Tyler, Goldberg, and Banks, 1978). Females may be able to detect some correlate of high testosterone in males and respond accordingly. Pregnant female mice, for example, attack intact males more than they attack gonadectomized males (Rosenson and Asheroff, 1975). Changes in dominance may influence preputial glands in mice and the amount of scent marking, and this appears to be mediated by testosterone (Mugford and Nowell, 1970; Bronson and Marsden, 1973). As dominant males with high testosterone levels are those most likely to kill infants, maternal aggression may be viewed as a functional response to the threat a male poses (Huck, Banks, and Wang, 1981; Ostermeyer, 1983). Thus, it is speculated that one of the functions of maternal aggression may be to reduce the infanticidal tendencies of their mates by subordinating them.

FUNCTIONS OF PUP CANNIBALISM

The laboratory observations cited previously indicate that gerbils of both sexes start to cannibalize infants when they reach sexual maturity and leave the parental burrow. Thus, juveniles avoid killing their parent's subsequent offspring to which they react in a "parental" fashion (Ostermeyer and Elwood, in press). Presumably juveniles have to search for a suitable living area after leaving the parental burrow, and presumably old abandoned burrows may frequently be utilized by these juveniles. Thus, it is expected that young adults may investigate unknown burrow systems and in so doing may encounter unguarded infants. It appears that it is these infants that are killed. These suggestions for the gerbil fit well with field observations on Belding's ground squirrel (Sherman, 1981) which indicate that 1-year-old males and nonresident females are the most frequent killers of infants.

Clearly, there is no benefit to the parents from the demise of their young, and they could be expected to resist the entry of strange animals into their burrows. The numerous reports of the territorial nature of the Mongolian gerbil would support this point (e.g., Ågren, 1976; Thiessen, 1968). A similar situation appears to occur in Belding's ground squirrel, since intruders only enter burrows when the resident is off the territory (Sherman, 1981). The benefit in killing, therefore, must be to the perpetrator, and this benefit may accrue in a number of ways that have been reviewed recently by Sherman (1981) and Hrdy (1979). With respect to gerbils, the benefits may be as follows:

Infants Used as Food

That gerbils invariably eat test pups after attacking them and that they are often reluctant to give them up when the experimenter attempts to intervene indicates that the pups are an attractive food source to these animals. Gerbils are not strictly herbivorous but take a wide variety of small animals as food (Prakash, 1962). Presumably conspecific infants fit into the category of suitable animal material. This appears to be the case for a variety of rodents which will cannibalize pups when the opportunity arises. These include mice (Jakubowski and Terkel, 1982; Labov, 1980), although there may be strain differences in laboratory mice (vom Saal: personal communication), rats (Rosenberg and Sherman, 1975), golden hamsters (Rowell, 1961a), Belding's ground squirrels (Sherman, 1981), as well as gerbils. Feeding, thus, may be a major benefit obtained from infanticide by rodents. In this respect, observations that food deprivation produces increased likelihood of infanticide in mice (Svare and Bartke, 1978), rats (Paul and Kupferschmidt, 1975), and gerbils (unpublished data) are instructive.

Removal of Competition

The killing of unrelated infants would reduce future competition for resources which may be sought either by the killer or by his or her infants. Alternatively, the killing may be part of a female–female competition for burrows. Sherman (1981) noted that when a female Belding's ground squirrel lost her litter, she was likely to vacate the burrow. Whether this final point may apply to gerbils is not known, but undoubtedly future competition is reduced by infanticide.

Increased Future Reproduction for Males

Increased future reproduction has frequently been cited as the prime reason for infanticide by males of a variety of animals, including rodents (Labov, 1980; Mallory and Brooks, 1978; Webster, Gartshore, and Brooks, 1981). Stated simply, it is suggested that by killing the offspring of another male, the female may come into estrus earlier (Hrdy, 1974; Bertram, 1975a) or may produce the young of the next litter earlier due to a shorter gestation period (Mallory and Brooks, 1978). If the killer is the father of the future infants, he will benefit from advancing the date of birth of his offspring and may in the long term produce extra offspring (Chapman and Hausfater, 1979). There is a postpartum estrus in most rodents, including the gerbil, but the implantation of the blastocysts may be delayed by the presence of infants. For the gerbil, the length of the gestation period is directly proportional to the number of pups being suckled (Norris and Adams, 1971; Elwood, 1975b). Thus, even if a male kills only a portion of a litter and then mates with the female, he can advance the birth date of his own offspring (vom Saal and Howard, 1982). Furthermore, increased numbers of pups being suckled results in fewer pups being produced in the next litter (Norris and Adams, 1971; Elwood, 1975b). Thus, by killing some of the pups of another male, a new male may not only advance the birth date but also increase the number of his offspring. Whether this frequently occurs in natural populations of gerbils, however, is not known.

It is usually stated that killing of infants followed by copulation with the female is effective in increasing the male's reproductive success (Labov, 1980; Mallory and Brooks, 1978). It is equally possible, however, that copulation at the postpartum estrus, followed by infanticide of all or part of the existing litter, could be effective. Indeed, as only 6–10 hr elapse between parturition and estrus, the male would have more opportunities for infanticide after copulation than before. This is a good functional reason not to have copulation as an effective immediate means of inhibiting infanticide. The observation that copulation may in fact have short-term facilitating effects on infanticide is interesting in this respect (vom Saal, Chapter 21, this volume).

As the gerbil is monogamous and as the juveniles are smaller than adults, it is doubtful that male take-overs usually involve fighting. It must frequently be the situation, however, that a male dies sometime during his mate's pregnancy, thus giving a young male from another family the opportunity to take over the burrow and female. It is these males that would be able to benefit from infanticide by advancing their own reproductive success.

Avoidance of Misdirected Parental Care

It would usually be disadvantageous to an animal to direct parental care toward unrelated young, and a variety of mechanisms have evolved to reduce this risk. Thus, in rodents, females are brought into a parental state just prior to parturition by the rapidly changing hormonal state at that time (Rosenblatt and Siegel, 1983). Male gerbils are also brought into a parental state prior to the birth of their first litter. Thus, for both sexes, there appears to be an effective barrier against misdirected parental care, and other infants are cannibalized instead. It seems doubtful, however, that this is the prime reason for infanticide as many species of rodent avoid misdirected parental care by avoiding pups rather than killing them.

Sherman (1981) also considers "spite" and "accidents" as functional explanations for infanticide. As yet, however, there is no evidence to suggest that this behavior may be spiteful in the gerbil, and the fact that changes in the probability of infanticide are so well regulated indicates that these deaths are not accidental. It thus appears that the female gerbil gains two main benefits from infanticide: food and reduced competition. The male will accrue these benefits as well as possibly enhancing his future reproductive success via male–male competition.

DISCUSSION

If the male may apparently gain more from pup cannibalism than can the female, then a number of questions arise from these observations: First, why do fewer unmated males cannibalize than do unmated females? This is possibly an artifact of the rearing conditions and may have no functional basis. It is probable that in the single-sexed groups used to maintain the animals prior to mating, dominance/subordinance relationships are established. These may have long inhibitory effects in subordinate males (vom Saal and Howard, 1982), and this is probably the normal mechanism for the inhibition in males seen during the pregnancy of the female. Thus, some unmated males (but, nevertheless, socially subordinate) may not kill. Females do not rely on this means of inhibition of cannibalism; rather, they depend on precise physiological changes just prior to parturition. Thus, unmated females invariably cannibalize infants if the female is living away from her parents. In natural situations, however, the sexes may show more equal levels of infanticide (but see Brooks, Chapter 17, this volume).

Second, why do males show an earlier inhibition after mating than do females? This is most probably explained by contrasting the certainty the two sexes have about the timing of the birth of their offspring. The female has precise information concerning the date of birth and has an inhibitory mechanism based on fairly precise hormonal changes. The male would have to time 24–25 days from copulation to make full use of his opportunities to cannibalize unrelated infants but to avoid harming his own. Presumably the cost of a mistake is high, and it is beneficial to err on the side of safety. Also, as the causal mechanism for the inhibition of infanticide in the male seems to depend on social interactions, it is possible that in the confined laboratory conditions, he is inhibited somewhat earlier than in natural populations.

Third, why do experienced males cease infanticide when experienced females continue? Again, this appears to be due to the accuracy of information. The female has good information about the time of her next parturition and is not likely to make a mistake and kill her own infants. The male has the problem, however, that the timing of the birth of his next litter is dependent upon the number of pups being reared in the present litter. The gestation period may be 25–43 days (Norris and Adams, 1971). For the first part of this period, the male should be inhibited in pup cannibalism to prevent harm to his litter. Only later may he switch to killing again, but when to switch back? Given the uncertainty for the male, it is presumably more beneficial to have a relatively permanent inhibition than to risk error.

Thus, in the Mongolian gerbil, there is a system that allows both sexes to kill infants for food and possibly other benefits and yet ensures that closely related infants are not harmed. At times when younger siblings may be born or when their own offspring are born, infanticide is inhibited. Thus, a balance is achieved between maximizing reproduction for individuals within family groups and gaining the benefits of infanticide.

ACKNOWLEDGMENTS

The authors would like to express gratitude to the Science and Engineering Research Council of the United Kingdom for their support of this research. Thanks are also due to Frank McKinney and Dick Phillips for their comments on earlier versions of this chapter. Ron Brooks, Bill Huck, Frederick vom Saal, and Glenn Hausfater provided helpful critiques for which we are grateful.

20 | Psychobiological determinants underlying infanticide in mice

**Bruce Svare
John Broida
Craig Kinsley
Martha Mann**

INTRODUCTION

Detailed descriptions of infanticide are being published by ethologists with increasing frequency, yet relatively little is known about infanticide compared to other types of aggressive behavior (e.g., intermale, interfemale, and maternal aggression). Infanticide in laboratory mice is a testosterone-dependent sexually dimorphic behavior. Males tend to exhibit killing of newborns at relatively high levels, whereas virgin females only occasionally kill young. Moreover, genetic constitution is a significant determinant of this behavior in laboratory mice with some strains displaying high cannibalistic tendencies, whereas other strains exhibit little or no pup-killing behavior. This chapter reviews recent data on genetic and hormonal influences on infanticide in two laboratory strains of mice. Its goal is to provide a model for the way in which genes and hormones interact to modulate the killing of young.

HORMONAL INFLUENCES ON INFANTICIDE

Hormonal Influences on Sexual Differentiation

A large literature exists on the influence of gonadal hormones on masculine and feminine behavior patterns (for recent reviews see Leshner, 1978; Adler, 1981; Baum, 1979; Austin and Edwards, 1981). Rather than provide a comprehensive review of these findings, a brief summary is provided for the role of gonadal hormones in producing sexually dimorphic patterns of copulatory and aggressive behavior. In most rodent species, males are more aggressive than virgin females, and males exhibit mounting and ejaculatory behavior while females exhibit lordosis. This behavioral dimorphism is due to differences between the sexes in both perinatal (i.e., organizational) and adult (i.e., activational) gonadal hormones. In the absence of androgen stimulation during early life, brain mechanisms that modulate feminine behavior develop in both sexes. Thus, both females and neonatally castrated males usually exhibit little aggressive behavior when confronted with a strange male intruder. Females and neonatally castrated males will actively solicit copulation and display lordosis when exposed to the ovarian hormones estrogen and progesterone during adult life.

In contrast, exposure of the developing rodent brain to testicular androgens results in defeminization of neural tissues. Therefore, normal males and neonatally androgenized females are relatively refractory to the lordosis-promoting qualities of ovarian hormones. Furthermore, exposure to androgens during early life also results in masculinization of neural tissues leading to the expression of male copulatory and aggressive behavior. It is thought that masculinization and defeminization are independently regulated with the former occurring primarily during prenatal life and the latter during both pre- and neonatal life.

In rodents, testosterone is not the only androgen produced. In peripheral target tissues as well as the brain, testosterone is accumulated and metabolized to form estrogen as well as several other androgens (Jaffe, 1969; Sholiton and Work, 1969). Although the idea that testosterone is the major hormone responsible for masculinizing neural tissue is still frequently debated, it is now generally accepted that the aromatization or conversion of testosterone to estrogen is an obligatory step for both the organization and activation of some masculine behaviors.

Hormones and Infanticide in Outbred Mice

Infanticide in mice is also sexually dimorphic. In outbred Rockland–Swiss (R–S) Albino mice, the subjects of much of these authors' earlier work, approximately 35–50% of adult males but less than 5% of adult females spontaneously kill conspecific young (Gandelman, 1972). Infanticidal behavior in mice has not been extensively studied but generally consists of a relatively short (less than 2 min) latency to the initial attack followed by repeated bites to the head, neck, flanks, and abdomen. The pup is frequently consumed after the initial attack. Noninfanticidal males typically ignore or retrieve pups, while females invariably exhibit parental behavior.

This sex difference in infanticide is modulated by both adult and perinatal androgens. Pup-killing behavior begins to emerge in male

R–S mice at about 35 days of age (Gandelman, 1973), approximately the same time at which pubertal androgens begin to surge (Svare, Bartke, and Macrides, 1978). Castration of adult males reduces infanticide while testosterone propionate restores it, with high doses more effective than low doses (Gandelman and vom Saal, 1975). Nevertheless, individual differences in testosterone levels are not necessarily linearly related to individual differences in infanticidal behavior by adult males (Svare, Bartke, and Gandelman, 1977). Interestingly, depending upon the dose and duration of steroid exposure, 35–100% of female mice can be induced to kill pups by the administration of testosterone propionate in adulthood (Davis and Gandelman, 1972; Svare, 1979). Both aromatization of testosterone to estrogen and reduction of this steroid to other androgens may be important for the activation of pup-killing behavior in R–S mice (Svare, 1979).

Perinatal androgen levels also influence infanticidal behavior in R–S mice. Recall that roughly 50–60% of adult R–S males do not kill pups. The long-term administration of testosterone to nonkiller adult males does not induce infanticide (Gandelman and vom Saal, 1975). However, 100% of adult R–S females will kill pups following chronic testosterone exposure (Svare, 1979). Males have been exposed to gonadal hormones perinatally, whereas females have not, and several recent studies (Gandelman and vom Saal, 1977; Samuels, Jason, Mann, and Svare, 1981) indicate that perinatal hormone exposure has a suppressive effect upon pup-killing behavior in adults. Once again, the aromatization early in life of testosterone to estrogen, rather than reduction of testosterone, appears to be responsible for the observed attenuation of infanticide in males (Samuels *et al.,* 1981).

It is important to note that the hormone–behavior relationships for infanticide depart significantly from those found for intermale aggression and copulatory behavior. In contrast to its suppressive affect on infanticidal behavior, early testosterone exposure is known to facilitate both copulatory and aggressive behavior.

How steroids act to promote infanticide is a question that remains unanswered at present. Mice are olfactory-guided mammals (e.g., Doty, 1976) with both maternal and aggressive behavior critically dependent upon perception of airborne cues (e.g., Gandelman, Zarrow, Denenberg, and Myers, 1971; Mugford and Nowell, 1970). Steroids can alter the electrical activity of the olfactory bulb (Pfaff and Pfaffman, 1969) and may thus produce pup-killing behavior by altering the motivational impact of olfactory cues from young.

STRAIN DIFFERENCES IN INFANTICIDE

Individual differences in genotype account in part for variation in many behavioral traits observed in rodent populations (Fuller and

Thompson, 1978). Animals within any given inbred mouse strain are virtually isogenic (i.e., genetically identical). Recently strain differences have been explored in the infanticidal behavior of C57BL/6J and DBA/2J mice. These animals were born and reared in same-sex groups in the vivarium at SUNY-Albany and were descendents of stock originally purchased from the Jackson Laboratory, Bar Harbor, Maine. These two strains are the oldest inbred lines of mice available to biomedical researchers (Green, 1975). As such, they have been well characterized by investigators from many different disciplines so that behavioral changes can be related to physiology and biochemistry.

Infanticide by Males

C57BL males are androgen deficient as compared to DBA males. C57BL males have smaller testes than DBA males and also show lower adult circulating testosterone levels, decreased spermatogenesis with age, higher testicular content of esterified cholesterol, and lower levels of intermale aggression. C57BL males also do not elicit pregnancy block in recently inseminated females, a phenomenon mediated by androgen-dependent pheromones (e.g., Chapman and Bronson, 1968; Bartke and Shire, 1972; Selmanoff, Goldman, Maxson, and Ginsburg, 1977b). Comparison of C57BL and DBA mice, therefore, provides a unique means for examining the genetic control of testicular function in relation to infanticide.

Our assay for infanticidal behavior has been to place a single 1- to 3-day-old R–S pup into the cage of an experimental animal that has been housed in isolation for 24 hr. R–S pups are used in the test situation in order to standardize the stimulus qualities of the pups, an important methodological feature in behavior–genetic work (Simon, 1979). The pup is left in the cage for a period of 15 min, and the adult's behavior is classified into one of the following categories: (1) retrieve—pup carried to the nest site; (2) kill—pup killed and/or cannibalized; (3) ignore—pup neither killed nor retrieved.

The initial hypothesis was that the higher pubertal and adult androgen levels of DBA compared to C57BL males would result in higher levels of infanticide in the former. To the contrary, C57BL animals exhibited an earlier onset and higher frequency of infanticide than did DBA males (Svare and Mann, 1981). Specifically, significantly more 70- to 90-day-old C57BL mice exhibited pup killing than did similarly aged DBA males (80 versus 30%, respectively). Further, when tested for infanticide at 25, 35, 45, 55, or 65 days of age (Fig. 1), significantly more C57BL males killed young compared to DBA males from age 35 days onward. C57BL males exhibited adult levels of infanticide by 45 days of age as compared to 65 days for DBA males.

In view of the preceding findings, an examination of the source of

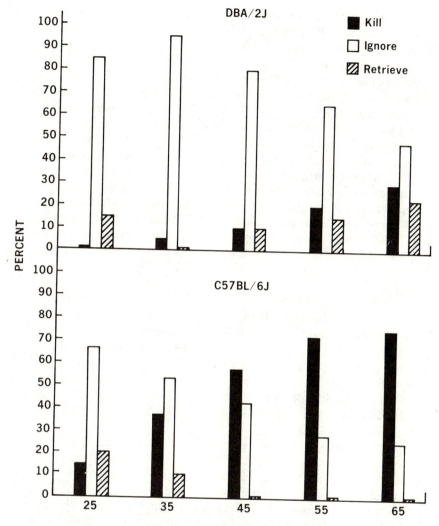

Figure 1. The percentage of 25-, 35-, 45-, 55-, and 65-day-old male C57BL/6J and DBA/2J mice that killed, ignored, or retrieved a single, newborn (1–3-day-old), Rockland–Swiss Albino mouse pup during a 15 min test. Following 24 hr of isolation, separate groups of animals from each age and strain were tested for their reaction toward the newborn. (Adapted from Svare and Mann, 1981.)

the observed strain differences in infanticidal behavior was sought. In a series of experiments in which reciprocally crossed and cross fostered animals were employed (Svare and Broida, 1982), it was possible to rule out the prenatal and postnatal maternal environment as well as the postweaning social environment as factors producing the observed strain differences in infanticidal behavior (Svare, Kinsley, Mann and Broida, in press). Likewise, it was possible to show that no simple experiential factors accounted for these strain differences in infanticide (Svare and Broida, 1982). Thus, regardless of the length of exposure to young (0.25–4 hr), or the sex, age (1–3, 5–7, or 10–12 days), or strain (R–S, DBA, or C57BL) of the stimulus pups, DBA males exhibited lower levels of infanticide than did C57BL males.

In yet another series of experiments, differences between these two strains in adult and pubertal testosterone levels as factors producing strain differences in infanticide were ruled out. Thus, administration of supplemental testosterone, estrogen, and other hormones to DBA males between Postnatal Days 21–50 was not successful in increasing their infanticidal behavior to C57BL levels (Svare et al., in press). Moreover, DBA males made androgen deficient by adult castration also failed to exhibit high levels of the behavior (Svare et al., in press).

Perinatal Androgen Exposure

Next perinatal androgen exposure was examined as a factor accounting for the observed strain difference in infanticide. It was reasoned that C57BL male mice probably are androgen deficient during early life and, hence, highly responsive to their own pubertal and adult androgens with respect to the activation of infanticide. Conversely, it was assumed that DBA males had a greater exposure to testosterone perinatally and were thus less sensitive to the pup-killing stimulus of their high adult testosterone levels.

To examine the foregoing hypothesis, C57BL animals (presumed to be androgen deficient) were supplemented with testosterone during foetal life. Specifically, pregnant C57BL females were treated with 100 μg/day of testosterone propionate on Gestation Days 12–16, a time of rapid sexual differentiation of the brain (vom Saal, 1979; Block, Lew, and Klein, 1971). Pregnant DBA and C57BL animals treated with sesame oil vehicle on the same days served as controls. Males were castrated at birth and, to ensure stable maternal care, were given to nontreated lactating foster mothers from the same strain. The animals were weaned at 25 days of age, and at 60 days of age were isolated for 24 hr and then screened for spontaneous infanticidal behavior. Those animals that did not kill pups were placed on testosterone propionate therapy (500 μg/day) for 35 days and tested for the behavior every 5 days for a total of seven tests.

The results clearly showed that prenatally treated C57BL males continued to exhibit significantly higher levels of both spontaneous and testosterone-aroused infanticide than DBA males. Of both prenatal oil and testosterone-propionate-treated C57BL animals, 40–50% exhibited infanticide on the screening test; 90–100% of the nonkiller animals in these groups exhibited this behavior following testosterone treatment in adulthood. In contrast, prenatal oil-treated DBA animals never exhibited spontaneous infanticide, and only 50% killed pups following testosterone exposure as adults. Examination of anogenital distances at birth, a bioassay for prenatal androgen levels, showed that the prenatally treated C57BL female mice exhibited substantial virilization of external morphology relative to controls, thus confirming the masculinizing effects of the prenatally administered hormone.

Similarly, neonatal castration had little influence on infanticidal behavior in either strain (Svare *et al.,* in press). Neonatally castrated C57BL animals exhibited high levels of both spontaneous (50% killed young on the screening test) and testosterone-aroused killing (70% were infanticidal). Neonatally castrated DBA males never killed young on the screening test, and only 30% became infanticidal after androgen exposure. Supplemental testosterone propionate given to neonatal C57BL males also failed to suppress pup-killing behavior. Following supplementation, C57BL males continued to exhibit significantly higher levels of both spontaneous and testosterone-aroused infanticide than did DBA males (Svare *et al.,* in press). The same result was obtained when supplementation took place both pre- and postnatally.

The above findings are puzzling in several respects. They do not support the thesis that prenatal and/or postnatal androgen deficiencies in C57BL animals account for strain differences in infanticidal behavior. However, the findings may be consistent with recent findings concerning the interaction of estradiol and testosterone during foetal sexual differentiation. These findings are elucidated in a latter section.

Infanticide by Females

There is also a marked difference in infanticide by female C57BL and DBA mice (Mann, Kinsley, Broida, and Svare, 1983). The direction of this difference is the same as that found for males of the two strains. Thus, although they exhibit significantly lower levels of infanticide than their male counterparts, C57BL females exhibit significantly higher levels of pup killing than do DBA females, at least between Days 25 and 45 of life (Fig. 2).

Roughly 30–40% of C57BL females exhibited infanticide prior to 45 days of age compared to 0% of DBA females. Beyond 45 days of age, few, if any, females of either strain killed pups. Similarly, in a recent study of spontaneous and testosterone-aroused pup killing in neonatally ovariectomized females of each strain, 40% of the ovariectomized C57BL female mice exhibited spontaneous pup killing at 60 days of age compared to 0% of DBA females (Mann *et al.,* 1983) (Fig. 3). When nonkiller

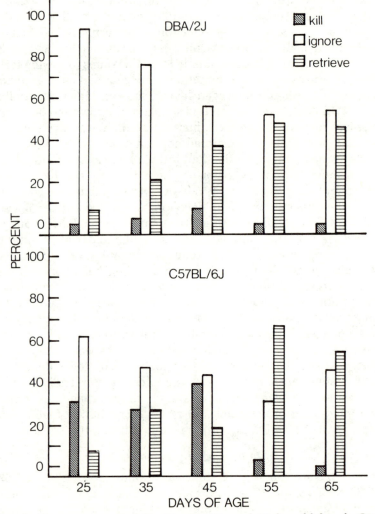

Figure 2. The percentage of 25-, 35-, 45-, 55-, and 65-day-old female C57BL/
6J and DBA/2J mice that killed, ignored, or retrieved a single, newborn (1–3-day-old), Rockland–Swiss Albino mouse pup. Following
24 hr of isolation, separate groups of animals from each age and
strain were tested for their reaction toward the newborn. (Adapted
from Mann, Kinsley, Broida, and Svare, 1983.)

animals were placed on testosterone treatments, significantly more
C57BL females became infanticidal after 35 injections than did DBA
females (80 versus 50%, respectively). Thus, C57BL females exhibit
higher levels of spontaneous infanticide and are more responsive to
the pup killing-provoking property of testosterone treatments than DBA

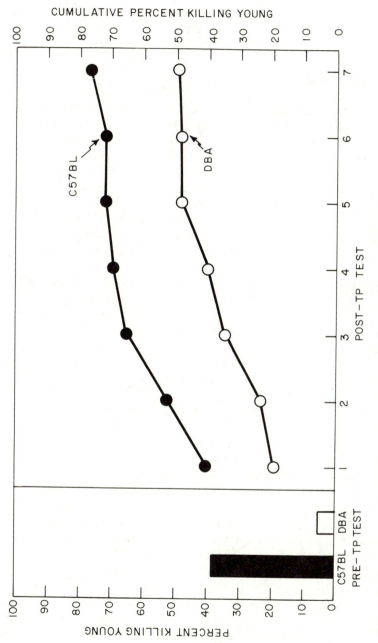

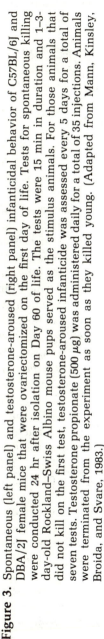

Figure 3. Spontaneous (left panel) and testosterone-aroused (right panel) infanticidal behavior of C57BL/6J and DBA/2J female mice that were ovariectomized on the first day of life. Tests for spontaneous killing were conducted 24 hr after isolation on Day 60 of life. The tests were 15 min in duration and 1–3-day-old Rockland–Swiss Albino mouse pups served as the stimulus animals. For those animals that did not kill on the first test, testosterone-aroused infanticide was assessed every 5 days for a total of seven tests. Testosterone propionate (500 μg) was administered daily for a total of 35 injections. Animals were terminated from the experiment as soon as they killed young. (Adapted from Mann, Kinsley, Broida, and Svare, 1983.)

395

females. To summarize, among both males and females of these two strains, research has failed to elucidate in terms of simple hormonal mechanisms either the between-or within-strain differences in infanticidal behavior.

GENES, HORMONES, AND INFANTICIDE

Clearly, then, the question still remains: Why are strain differences in infanticidal behavior observed among both males and females of these two strains? Also, why is there such large variability in the pup-killing behavior found in both males and females of these two virtually isogenic strains of mice? Perhaps some insight into the answers to these questions can be obtained from recent research on the modulatory impact of the intrauterine environment on sexual differentiation. This research has shown that during foetal life in polytocous (multiple birth) species, male and female foetuses develop adjacent to, and are influenced by, the hormonal secretions of foetuses of the same and opposite sex (vom Saal, Chapter 21, this volume).

The "intrauterine position phenomenon" (IUP) has been extensively studied in mice (vom Saal and Bronson, 1978; vom Saal, 1981), and it has been shown that during the period of sexual differentiation, males secrete higher titers of testosterone than do females (vom Saal and Bronson, 1980a). As a result, female mouse foetuses positioned between two male foetuses ("2M females") have higher amniotic fluid and blood titers of testosterone than do female foetuses not positioned next to male foetuses ("0M females"). Female foetuses positioned adjacent to both a male and female foetus ("1M females") are intermediate in these parameters. It is important to note that intrauterine position by sex is a random event with 0M, 1M, and 2M individuals representing 25, 50, and 25%, respectively, of all foetuses (vom Saal, 1981).

These differences in intrauterine environment are correlated with a variety of sexually differentiated characteristics. In comparison to 0M female mice, 2M females exhibit larger anogenital spacing, are more spontaneously aggressive in direct competition, and during the postpartum period, exhibit lower levels of infanticide and urine mark their environments at high frequencies. Moreover, 2M females are highly sensitive to the intermale-aggression-promoting properties of adult testosterone treatment but less sensitive than 0M animals to the infanticide-promoting properties of the steroid. In comparison to 2M females, 0M females are more sexually attractive to males, exhibit higher levels of spontaneous infanticide, and are more sensitive to the infanticide-promoting qualities of adult testosterone. 1M females generally are intermediate in these characteristics. Thus, by virtue of their greater exposure to the prenatal testosterone of their brothers,

2M females appear to be masculinized morphologically and behaviorally relative to 0M females.

Recent research shows that the sexual characteristics of male mice also are dramatically influenced by intrauterine position (vom Saal, 1983a,c,e, and Chapter 21, this volume). However, IUP effects on males appear to be modulated by foetal estrogen levels from adjacent females and not by testosterone. On Day 17 of foetal life, female mouse foetuses have higher amniotic fluid titers of estradiol than do male foetuses, and males positioned between two females foetuses (0M males) have higher amniotic fluid titers of estradiol than do their 2M counterparts (vom Saal, Chapter 21, this volume). No differences with respect to amniotic or circulating levels of testosterone or anogenital spacing have been observed in 0M and 2M males. In comparison to 2M males, 0M males more frequently mount and obtain intromission with sexually receptive females and also exhibit higher levels of infanticide and lower levels of intermale aggression.

Although the exact mechanism responsible for IUP effects has not been definitively elucidated, the leakage of steroid hormones via the amniotic fluid from contiguous animals is probably of primary importance in the phenomenon in mice (vom Saal, 1981). Regardless of the mechanism, it is clear that variation in phenotype due to IUP in random-bred male and female mice should be predictable and, among other factors, highly correlated with foetal and amniotic levels of steroid hormones. It is also clear that circulating estrogens from foetuses may directly influence male sexual differentiation (vom Saal, 1938a,e, Chapter 21, this volume) as strongly as estrogens derived indirectly via aromatization of the male's own testosterone. Specifically, vom Saal (1983a,c,e, Chapter 21, this volume) has postulated that estrogen may interfere with androgen in the case of some traits (infanticide and intermale aggression) and synergize with testosterone in the case of other traits (copulatory behavior).

Due to IUP effects, variation in behavior among individuals of a given strain may be as great, if not greater, than variation between strains due to their inherent genetic differences. Furthermore, low prenatal testosterone levels in male C57BL mice and concomitantly high prenatal estrogen levels in female C57BL females should "mimic" many of the effects due to IUP in random-bred mice. In essence, it is proposed that C57BL/6J males and females can be considered essentially "0M-biased" animals, while DBA/2J males and females are essentially "2M-biased" animals. It is important to note that by 0M- or 2M-biased actual statistical deviations from the 25/50/25 distribution of IUPs are not implied, but rather that strain peculiarities in hormone levels interact with IUP to produce strain-specific patterns of variation in infanticide and other behaviors. If this model is correct, a number of easily testable predictions can be made with respect to the prenatal hormone environment and infanticidal behavior (see Fig. 4 for a summary of predictions).

First, with respect to the prenatal steroid environment, foetal C57BL males should be androgen deficient relative to their DBA male counterparts, and foetal C57BL females should be estradiol replete when compared to DBA females (Fig. 4). Taking into consideration the effects of contiguous males and females, then foetal C57BL males should be characterized by low blood and amniotic levels of testosterone and high estradiol concentrations in these fluids. Conversely, foetal DBA males should be characterized by high blood and amniotic levels of testosterone and low estradiol concentrations. In a similar fashion, foetal C57BL females would be expected to have low blood and amniotic levels of testosterone but high concentrations of estradiol; DBA females would be expected to show the opposite pattern. Furthermore, males of each strain would be expected to have higher levels of testosterone than females and females higher levels of estrogen than males.

A critical corollary of these predictions is that 0M and 2M males

♂

	OM		IM		2M	
	C57BL	DBA	C57BL	DBA	C57BL	DBA
INFANTICIDE	↑	↑	↑	↓	↓	↓
FETAL T	↓	↑	↓	↑	→	↑
FETAL E	↑	→	↑	↓	↓	↓

♀

	OM		IM		2M	
	C57BL	DBA	C57BL	DBA	C57BL	DBA
INFANTICIDE	↑	↓	↓	↓	↓	↓
FETAL T	↓	↓	↓	↑	→	↑
FETAL E	↑	↓	↑	↓	↑	↓

KEY

OM (SURROUNDED BY 2♀♀s) ↑ HIGH

1M (SURROUNDED BY 1♂ AND 1♀) → MEDIUM

2M (SURROUNDED BY 2♂♂s) ↓ LOW

Figure 4. Predicted results for infanticidal behavior and foetal hormone levels of male and female C57BL/6J and DBA/2J inbred mice arising from different intrauterine positions.

and females within each strain should exhibit foetal steroid profiles at the extremes for their respective strains. Importantly, 1M males and females, a group that normally comprises 50% of the population, is the pivotal condition within each strain from the standpoint of testing this model. Specifically, 1M male and female C57BL mice would be expected to show significantly higher estrogen and lower testosterone than 1M male and female DBAs. These predictions currently are being tested in the laboratory by exploring foetal and amniotic steroid hormone profiles in C57BL and DBA mice from different intrauterine positions.

Second, several predictions concerning infanticide can be drawn from the postulated prenatal steroid hormone environments of the two strains. Recall that intrauterine position by sex is a random event with 0M, 1M, and 2M individuals representing 25, 50, and 25%, respectively, of all the foetuses produced (vom Saal, 1981). It would thus be expected that roughly 75% of C57BL males (equivalent to males in the 0M and 1M conditions) should exhibit infanticide while only 25% of DBA males (equivalent to the 0M condition only) should exhibit this behavior (Fig. 4). The findings deviate only slightly from these expected percentages. In nonmanipulated (i.e., experimentally naïve) adult animals, it has repeatedly been found that 75–80% of C57BL males exhibit pup killing, while 25–30% of DBA males display the behavior (Svare and Mann, 1981; Svare and Broida, 1982). Similarly, the model predicts that roughly 25% of C57BL females (equivalent to the proportion of 2M females) should exhibit infanticide while few, if any, DBA females (0M condition only) should exhibit the behavior (Fig. 4). In fact, recent findings from the laboratory showed that 35% of ovariectomized C57BL females kill young, while 0% of ovariectomized DBA females exhibit the behavior (Mann *et al.,* 1983). Also, as may be expected, C57BL females were significantly more responsive to the infanticide-promoting properties of adult testosterone exposure than were DBA females (Mann *et al.,* 1983).

With respect to postpartum aggression, the model predicts that roughly 75% of DBA females should exhibit this behavior in comparison to only 25% of C57BL females who would be expected to display maternal defense. Indeed, the findings show that 70% of DBA females, roughly equivalent to the proportion of 1M and 2M females, exhibit maternal defense compared to only 20% of postpartum C57BL females (equivalent to the 2M group) (Broida and Svare, 1982). Thus, these findings provide relatively strong, albeit indirect, confirmation of the preceding model of hormone–IUP interaction. While strain differences have not yet been tested with respect to other androgen-dependent behaviors, reports from several laboratories generally support this model. For example, C57BL males which were situated *in utero* between two females exhibit

high levels of copulatory behavior and low levels of intermale aggression, while DBA males (which were situated between males *in utero*)
exhibit the reverse pattern (Selmanoff *et al.,* 1977a, 1977b; Batty, 1978).
In the laboratory, infanticidal behavior as well as other hormone-depen-
dent behaviors (sex and aggression) in C57BL and DBA male and female
mice derived from different intrauterine positions are presently being
explored.

Finally, some of the recent data concerning prenatal testosterone
supplements in C57BL males would initially appear to be inconsistent
with the model developed previously. Testosterone supplementation
either pre- or postnatally did not reduce the infanticidal behavior of
C57BL animals as may be predicted initially. However, if foetal C57BL
males are not just androgen deficient but also estrogen dominated,
as the model predicts, then the failure of prenatal androgen supplements
to suppress infanticide may be explainable on the basis of competition
by estradiol. This theory, although highly speculative at the present
time, receives some support from the recent work of vom Saal (1983a,
c,e, and Chapter 21, this volume).

SIGNIFICANCE AND CONCLUSIONS

Models of the psychobiological mechanisms underlying infanticide
must also take into account genetic variation in this behavior. An essential element of the sexual competition hypothesis is that infanticide
is dependent, at least in part, on genotype and is thus heritable. Unfortunately, most conclusions concerning this topic are based on genetic
correlations that do not provide prima facie evidence for heritability.
Classical Mendellian analysis of the strains employed in this chapter
should ultimately provide answers to the important question of the
heretability of infanticide. Until then, all we can say with certainty
is that genetically distinctive strains of mice differ in their tendency
to kill newborn offspring, and that these differences appear to depend
on the interaction of genotypic features such as species-specific hormone titers as well as on extraorganismic factors such as intrauterine
position.

ACKNOWLEDGMENTS

Preparation of this chapter was supported in part by a research grant from the Harry
Frank Guggenheim Foundation, by Grant BNS80-08546 from National Science Foundation,
and by Grant AGO1319 from National Institute of Aging. The authors gratefully acknowledge the comments of Joseph DeBold, Robert Elwood, Thomas Fox, Sarah Blaffer Hrdy,
Glenn Hausfater, William Huck, Jay Labov, and Fred vom Saal.

21

Proximate and ultimate causes of infanticide and parental behavior in male house mice

Frederick S. vom Saal

INTRODUCTION

The hypothesis that infanticide (i.e., the killing of conspecific young) is adaptive in some situations remains controversial. More generally accepted is the proposition that the killing of a member of one's own species is maladaptive. Infanticide has therefore been regarded as a pathological behavior that only occurs in response to a breakdown in social structure (Calhoun, 1962; Curtin and Dolhinow, 1978). Although a breakdown in social behaviors and an increase in both infanticide and aggression between adults certainly occurs during times of social stress (Lloyd and Christian, 1969; Christian, 1971), this does not rule out the possibility that in other circumstances, infanticide may be adaptive. Hrdy (1979) has proposed four sets of circumstances under which infanticide would be adaptive. Her classification is based upon the nature of the benefit (mates, food resources, etc.) to the infanticidal animal (see Introduction, this volume). In this chapter, only one category of infanticide is discussed: that relating to sexual competition between males, which is referred to as "sexually selected" infanticide. Traits that enhance the ability of individuals to compete with members of the same sex for the chance to reproduce are thought to be subjected to sexual selection, which Darwin distinguished from natural selection (cf. Trivers, 1972).

Three predictions generated from the hypothesis that infanticide evolved through sexual selection (Hrdy, 1979; vom Saal and Howard, 1982) are that: (1) There must exist mechanisms to inhibit males from killing their own offspring; (2) the killing of a female's young must result in her ovulating and mating with the infanticidal male sooner than she could have had her young not been killed (ovulation is inhibited in lactating female mice); and (3) infanticide must be mediated, at least in part, genetically and thus be heritable.

This chapter describes laboratory experiments with house mice (*Mus musculus*) designed to test the first two predictions of the sexual selection hypothesis. The third prediction, that concerning the relationship between genotype and the tendency for male mice to commit infanticide, is addressed by another chapter in this volume (see Chapter 20 by Svare *et al.*), although the present work clearly demonstrates that within a given strain of mice, sex hormones regulate both the prenatal development and adult expression of infanticide. Thus, the problems associated with examining the genetic basis of a behavior that is modulated both by hormones and by experience are also mentioned in this chapter.

METHODS

The test procedure utilized in most of the experiments consisted of placing two 1-day-old mice into the cage of a male and then examining the pups 30 min later. One of three possible behavioral responses was recorded at this time: (1) infanticide—one or both pups were dead; (2) parental behavior—one or both pups were in a nest with the male hovering over them, and the pups were warm; or (3) ignore—neither pup was in the nest or wounded, and both pups were cold (newborn mice cannot thermoregulate). The length of time that the young are left with the male does not appear to be important (15 min to 4 hr; Svare and Broida, 1982; F. vom Saal: unpublished observation). Either infanticide or parental behavior occur almost immediately after young are introduced into a male's cage. Neither the age (newborn, 7 days old, 10 days old) nor the sex of the young influences the tendency of males to exhibit infanticide or parental behavior (Svare and Broida, 1982; vom Saal and Howard, 1982; F. vom Saal: unpublished observation).

Other testing procedures have also been utilized. For example, in some experiments, males were allowed to enter chambers containing females and their nursing young. But, moving males from one cage to another is stressful, and this could potentially interact with other variables in influencing the behavior of male mice toward young. The procedure of placing the young into a male's cage was thus utilized in most experiments so that the greatest number of variables were controlled.

This procedure not only involves the least amount of disturbance to the male but results in a minimal loss of life of young relative to procedures involving the placement of a male with a female and her entire litter.

All males utilized in these experiments were housed individually when 35 days old. Between Day 35 and 40 after birth, blood concentrations of testosterone begin to increase dramatically in male mice, and if males remain housed in groups after this age, they begin to fight (McKinney and Desjardins, 1973a). As will become clear, control of fighting experience is necessary in studies of infanticide in mice.

Unless otherwise indicated, testing for infanticide occurred in early adulthood between 75 and 90 days of age. The tendency of male mice to commit infanticide changes during adolescence, and the ontogeny of infanticide varies in different strains of mice. For example, fewer CF-1 male mice committed infanticide when tested between 55 and 60 days of age ($n = 204$; infanticide = 29%, parental = 55%, ignore = 16%) than when tested again at 90 days of age ($n = 204$; infanticide = 49%, parental = 46%, ignore = 5%; F. vom Saal, in press). In C57BL/6J mice, no change in the frequency of infanticide is observed after males reach 55 days of age (70% commit infanticide), while in DBA/2J male mice, a dramatic increase in the frequency of infanticide occurs between 65 days of age (20% commit infanticide) and 135 days of age (65% commit infanticide; Svare and Mann, 1981).

Statistical Analyses

An important issue in studies of infanticide is the unit of analysis that should be used. In the studies discussed here, individual males serve as the units of analysis, since it is the behavior of particular individuals that is being examined. While this convention may seem obvious, previous studies (cf. Mallory and Brooks, 1978; Labov, 1980; Huck, Soltis, and Coopersmith, 1982) have utilized individual young within a litter as the unit of analysis. Quite often, these previous studies have provided no information concerning how many male mice actually committed infanticide in any experimental condition, but instead have just reported the aggregate number of young killed by all males tested in that condition. This methodological problem has been compounded by statistical testing of such pup mortality data using Chi-square analysis. The use of the Chi-square test on pup mortality data violates a basic assumption of this analytical method, namely, that the data points be statistically independent of each other. Since this latter requirement is fulfilled only when males, not pups, are used as the unit of analysis, the conclusions of many previous studies of rodent infanticide are considered open to question.

MATING-INDUCED, TIME-DEPENDENT FACILITATION AND INHIBITION OF INFANTICIDE

The experiments described in this section were undertaken following the observation that male mice used as colony studs were significantly less likely to commit infanticide than were sexually naïve males. This prompted the question whether mating experience had influenced infanticide in male mice. The data presented in Table I reveal the remarkable effect that mating experience has on the tendency of male CF-1 mice to either commit infanticide or behave parentally toward young. In this experiment, 240 male CF-1 mice were paired with females for 3 hr, after which time the females were examined for vaginal plugs and removed from the male's cage (Day 0 = the day of mating). The males were then randomly assigned to groups to be tested for infanticide at different intervals after mating (30/group). The behavior of these groups of males toward young was compared with the behavior of a group of 30 sexually naïve males (about 45 to 50% of naïve, adult CF-1 male mice commit infanticide). Four days after mating, there was a significant increase in the proportion of males committing infanticide (83%) compared to the naïve controls (50%). However, 12 days after mating, just the opposite was the case: There was a significant decrease in the proportion of males that committed infanticide (10%) compared to controls and an increase in the proportion of males that behaved parentally (83%) compared to controls (23%). This inhibition of infanticide was also observed in males tested at 20, 35, 42, and 50 days after mating. Between 50 and 60 days after mating, however, there was again a facilitation of infanticide and inhibition of parental behavior similar to that observed 4 days after mating. Males tested at both

Table I. Effect of mating on infanticide[a]

Behavior	Pre-mat-ing	Days after mating							
		4	12	20	35	42	50	60	90
Infanticide	50	83	10	10	17	30	23	77	73
Parental	23	17	83	80	63	63	57	17	23
Ignore	27	0	7	10	20	7	20	6	4
χ^2 versus premat-ing group:		10.8	21.3	19.6	10.8	10.6	7.4	5.6	6.8
Significance level (p):		<0.005	<0.001	<0.001	<0.005	<0.005	<0.05	<0.05	<0.05

[a] The percentage of different groups of male mice (30 males/group) that committed infanticide, behaved parentally toward, or ignored two newborn mice that were placed into a male's cage for 30 min. The males were tested at different times after mating with a female.

60 and 90 days after mating were significantly more likely to commit infanticide than were controls (F. vom Saal, in press).

Another 90 males were tested for infanticide, allowed to mate with a female, and then retested for their behavior toward young 1, 8, or 20 days after mating (30/group). The results presented in Table II reveal that infanticide is enhanced relative to premating levels by 1 day after mating. However, males tested 8 days after mating behaved as if they had not mated at all: Only 1 out of 30 males did not exhibit the same behavior on both the pre- and postmating tests. Finally, most of the males tested 20 days after mating behaved parentally. Chi-square analysis performed on the postmating data confirmed that there was a significant effect of length of time since mating on the behavior of males toward young.

The males that were tested with newborn young 20 days after mating (see Table I) were also tested with 10-day-old young 35 days after mating. The objective was to determine whether the behavior of males would be different toward newborn young and toward young that were near the actual age that the male's most recent mating would have produced (parturition is 19 days after mating.) When tested with 10-

Table II. Effect of mating pretest/retest
on infanticide[a]

Behavior	Pretest	Retest after mating
One day		
Infanticide	47	83
Parental	33	13
Ignore	20	4
8 days		
Infanticide	47	50
Parental	43	43
Ignore	10	7
20 days		
Infanticide	43	23
Parental	43	77
Ignore	14	0

[a] Percentage of males that committed infanticide, were parental toward, or ignored two newborn mice that were placed into the male's cage for 30 min. All males were administered a pretest and then allowed to mate with a female 1 week later. The males were then randomly assigned to three groups (30 males/group) and retested at different intervals after mating. 1 versus 8 versus 20 days after mating: $X^2(4) = 25.9$, $p < 0.001$.

day-old mice, only one of the males did not exhibit the same behavior shown on Day 20. Thus, male mice do not behave differently toward newborn and 10-day-old young when tested on Day 35 after mating.

Mice that are between 14 and 20 days old are very active; the eyes open at 13 days of age, and they have a coat of fur by this time. When tested with juvenile mice that were between 14 and 20 days old, most males that had mated between 3 and 6 weeks prior to testing still behaved parentally. It appears, however, that some degree of conflict is engendered in the males by 14–20-day-old young, since many males appeared highly agitated and often roughly groomed the young (F. vom Saal, in press).

As a control for the possibility that males may not reliably exhibit the same behavior toward young on repeated tests, 150 sexually naïve males were tested for infanticide and then retested at 4, 8, 14, 35, or 60 days after the first test (30/group). With few exceptions, males that committed infanticide on the first test committed infanticide on the second test (F. vom Saal, in press).

Pregnancy in house mice lasts about 3 weeks (19–21 days). Young are typically weaned about 4 weeks after birth and, depending on population density, disperse from the natal territory at puberty about 4 weeks after birth (Lidicker, 1975; Bronson, 1979). A male mouse would thus typically be in contact with its own preweanling young between 3 and 7 weeks after mating. The finding that between 2 and 7 weeks after mating there is a significant inhibition of infanticide in male mice is thus striking. In essence, males tend not to be infanticidal at those times that they would be likely to come in contact with preweanling young that they had sired. Within less than 4 days or beyond more than 60 days postmating, there is actually a facilitation of infanticide in previously mated male mice compared to sexually naïve males. Taken together, these findings certainly appear consistent with the hypothesis that selection has operated to inhibit infanticide during the time that a male mouse might kill its own offspring. In addition, infanticide is facilitated at times when a male would encounter the nursing young of another male.

Effects of Mating Experience on Parental Behavior

Mating not only influences infanticide in male mice but also parental behavior. Between 2 and 7 weeks after mating, most male mice build a maternal-like nest, retrieve the young, stimulate micturition in the young by licking the genitals periodically, and hover over the young to maintain their body temperature. These observations suggest that selection has operated not only to reduce infanticide but also to increase parenting behaviors, again, specifically during those times that male mice would be in contact with their own preweanling young. It is difficult to imagine that the facilitation of parental behavior in male mice between 2 and 7 weeks after mating could be so precisely coupled with the length of pregnancy (19 days) and lactation (25–30 days) in female mice unless parenting behaviors in males were also acted on by natural selection (i.e., were adaptive). It could be argued that perhaps these individual parenting behaviors are merely on the opposite end of a behavioral continuum from infanticide such that as the incidence of infanticide decreases, the incidence of this complex of parenting behaviors automatically increases. However, additional evidence (see following) suggests that infanticide and parental behavior are, in fact, independent processes.

Evidence that the characteristics of the young influence the maintenance of parental behavior once it is initiated in male mice was obtained by repeatedly exposing the same 30 males that had been tested for infanticide 4 days after mating (see Table I, Day 4 Group) to newborn young 12, 20, 35, 50, 60, 70, 80, and 90 days after mating. The results of this longitudinal design are presented in Table III and reveal that between the fourth and twelfth day following mating, there was a complete reversal of behavior. Infanticide was facilitated and parental behavior was inhibited on Day 4, while on Day 12 infanticide was inhibited and parental behavior was facilitated. The repeated exposure to young served to maintain parental behavior 90 days after mating (73% of the males behaved parentally; see Table III, Day 90), while most of the males tested for the first time 90 days after mating committed infanticide (73% of these males committed infanticide; see Table I, Day 90 Group). This difference is statistically significant ($\chi^2(2) = 22.5$, $p < 0.001$; F. vom Saal, in press). When the litters of postpartum female rats (Bruce, 1961a; Rosenblatt, Siegel, and Mayer, 1979) or mice (Svare, 1981) are replaced daily with newborn young, behavior characteristic of a female that has just delivered a litter is maintained for extended periods of time (several months). Thus, the young serve as stimuli for eliciting parental behavior in adult females, and as the characteristics of the young change, the behavior of the adult also changes.

Effects of Repeated Mating

Consider the situation in which a male mated with one female and then between 2 and 3 weeks later mated with a second female. It would clearly not be advantageous for the second mating to facilitate infanticidal behavior, since the male may well come into contact with young produced by his first mating. To examine this situation, 14 naïve males were tested for their behavior toward young (43% committed infanticide, 50% behaved parentally, and 7% ignored the young). These

Table III. Effect of repeated exposure to young on infanticidal behavior[a]

	Days after mating								
Behavior	4	12	20	35	50	60	70	80	90
Infanticide	83	10	0	13	13	17	20	20	24
Parental	17	87	93	77	80	73	77	77	73
Ignore	0	3	7	10	7	10	3	3	3

[a] The percentage of a single group of 30 mice that committed infanticide, behaved parentally toward, or ignored two newborn mice that were placed into a male's cage for 30 min. These males were first tested 4 days after mating with a female (see Table I, Day 4 Group) and then were retested at 8–15-day intervals.

males were then mated with first one female (Day 0) and then with a second female 15 days later. Four days after the second mating (19 days after the first mating), infanticide proved to be inhibited and parental behavior facilitated (14% of the males committed infanticide, and 86% behaved parentally; F. vom Saal, in press). Thus, the increase in the incidence of infanticide observed in sexually naïve male mice 4 days after mating was not observed in males that had first mated 19 days and then again 4 days prior to coming in contact with young. Apparently, the facilitation of infanticide within 4 days of mating only operates in sexually naïve males.

There is little precedent in the literature for the time-dependent changes that occur following mating in the behavior of male mice toward young. Particularly unusual is the cyclical facilitation, inhibition, and then facilitation of a behavior as a function of time. However, once male mice become parental, the repeated opportunity to behave parentally can serve to disrupt this temporal sequence and to sustain an inhibition of infanticidal behavior.

Mechanism of Facilitation and Inhibition

At this time, three experiments that were designed to investigate the particular aspect of mating that produces the observed changes in male behavior have been completed. First, a group of 30 male mice were placed with 2 diestrous, nonreceptive females for 24 hr. The absence of mating was verified by repeated examination of the females. Three weeks later, the males were tested with 2 newborn young, and 53% of the males committed infanticide, 27% behaved parentally, and 20% ignored the young. Cohabiting with a female but not mating thus has no effect on either infanticide or parental behavior in male mice. Second, 30 males were pretested for their behavior toward young (56% committed infanticide, and 44% behaved parentally). Two weeks later, the males were allowed to mount (at least 20 times with intromissions) a sexually receptive female, but the females were removed before the males ejaculated. The males were retested 1 day and 20 days later for their behavior toward young. Virtually no change in behavior relative to the pretest occurred in these males at either 1 day (56% were infanticidal) or 20 days (40% were infanticidal). Third, 30 males were pretested for their behavior toward young (43% were infanticidal). Two weeks later, the males were allowed to ejaculate when paired with a sexually receptive female. As soon as the males ejaculated, they were housed individually in a clean cage, thus preventing any post-ejaculatory contact with the female. One day after ejaculating, 83% of these males committed infanticide, while 20 days after ejaculating, 3% committed infanticide (F. vom Saal, in press).

In sum, males that mount and intromit, but do not ejaculate, when paired with a female do not change their behavior toward young, while males that ejaculate but have no postejaculatory contact with a female do change their behavior toward young. It is thus proposed that some aspect of ejaculating with a female (such as vaginal stimulation of the engorged penile cup that forms during ejaculation: McGill and Coughlin, 1970) may serve as the "trigger" for the facilitation and then inhibition of infanticide following mating in male mice. It is interesting that penile engorgement at ejaculation has a significant effect on sperm motility within the uterus and on the establishment and maintenance of pregnancy (McGill, 1970; McGill and Coughlin, 1970; Adler, 1983; Adler, Allen, and Toner, 1982). Male mice have spontaneous ejaculations almost every night (Huber and Bronson, 1980), but these ejaculations (which may be physiologically different from ejaculations during coitus) obviously do not lead to the changes in behavior toward young that occur after ejaculating during coitus in male mice.

INFANTICIDE IN F_1 WILD MALE AND FEMALE MICE

In laboratory mice, there is a pronounced sex difference in the incidence of infanticide, with less than 10% of females typically committing infanticide (Svare et al., Chapter 20, this volume). But, in one recent study using a testing procedure very similar to that described previously, nearly all mice, both male and female, committed infanticide in the F_1–F_4 generation descended from wild house mice trapped in Israel (Jakubowski and Terkel, 1982). In contrast, the F_1 generation descended from wild house mice trapped in a field near Columbia, Missouri did exhibit a sex difference in infanticide. Specifically, 60 males and 82 females were tested for their behavior toward young at 75 days of age. The animals were housed between 2 and 4 per cage from weaning until 5 days before behavior testing, at which time all animals were individually housed. Males and females differed significantly in their behavior toward one newborn wild-mouse pup that was placed into a corner of the cage. Of the males, 87% were infanticidal compared to 61% of the females.

Sexually naive wild male mice were also placed into cages containing a wild female mouse and her 2-day-old young, and 15 of 16 males committed infanticide. Other wild males were paired with wild females for 14 days, and then both the male and the female were rehoused individually in clean cages. Two days after the prior female partner had delivered, the males were placed: (1) with their prior partners ($n = 10$; 0% were infanticidal) or (2) with a novel female that had also delivered 2 days previously ($n = 20$; 5% were infanticidal). All animals were observed for 30 min after pairing and then examined daily. The same experiment was conducted with CF-1 mice (11 males/group), and none of the males committed infanticide. Infanticide is thus also inhibited in wild mice 3 weeks after mating, and recognition of the prior female partner is not a factor in this inhibition in either wild or CF-1 mice (M. McCarthy and F. vom Saal, unpublished observation).

F_1 female wild mice have also been examined for their behavior toward young during pregnancy. Females that had committed infanticide prior to becoming pregnant are still infanticidal 2–12 hr prior to delivery. In addition, many females that had previously ignored or parented young prior to mating committed infanticide when tested just prior to parturition. When 22 virgin females were tested prior to mating, 63% committed infanticide, while 91% of these same females committed infanticide just prior to parturition. But, when these females subsequently delivered their own young, they all behaved parentally, suggesting that some variable associated with parturition (such as vaginal–cervical stimulation) served to inhibit infanticide and induce the onset of parental behavior (M. McCarthy and F. vom Saal: unpublished observation). Vaginal–cervical stimulation has been reported to influence the onset of parental behavior in sheep (Keverne et al., 1983).

INTERACTION OF DOMINANCE STATUS AND PRIOR MATING EXPERIENCE

Where stable territories are observed in populations of house mice, a deme (breeding group) generally consists of between 2 and 4 males and 6 and 8 females (Bronson, 1979). An interesting feature of mouse demes is a nonlinear dominance hierarchy among males and possibly also among females (Lloyd and Christian, 1969; Christian, 1971; vom Saal, 1981). Thus, there is only one dominant male within a deme, and all other males are subordinate. How likely these subordinate males are to mate and produce young is a matter of considerable debate (cf. Oakeshott, 1974), but there is general agreement that dominance status does influence reproductive success in male and female mice (cf. Lloyd and Christian, 1969). For example, in one study utilizing genetic markers, over 90% of offspring were reported to be produced by the one dominant male in a breeding group (DeFries and McLearn, 1972). Given that excess subordinate males remain within a mouse deme and that most wild male mice are infanticidal, the obvious question arises as to whether subordinate males might kill the offspring of the dominant male.

The influence of dominance status on infanticide was examined in adult male CF-1 mice. Males were paired for 1 hr each day for 7 days, and dominance status was assessed by observations of fighting and rates of urine marking. Males of known dominance status were then tested for their behavior toward newborn young. Table IV shows that relative to males that had neither mated nor fought (see Table I, premating group), the achievement of dominance-enhanced infanticide in males that had never mated (Table IV, C). Conversely, defeat in fighting and subordinate status resulted in an inhibition of infanticide (Table IV, A). This same experiment was next repeated with males that had mated 2 weeks prior to their fighting experience; testing for infanticide thus occurred a total of 22 days after mating. Prior mating experience eliminated the facilitation of infanticide associated with achieving dom-

Table IV. Influence of dominance status on infanticidal behavior[a,b]

	Subordinate		Dominant		Retest of Group D: 90 days after mating
Behavior	(A) Sexually naïve ($n = 22$)	(B) 22 Days after mating ($n = 25$)	(C) Sexually naïve ($n = 34$)	(D) 22 Days after mating ($n = 33$)	($n = 33$)
Infanticide	23	28	82	15	88
Parental	41	60	12	76	12
Ignore	36	12	6	9	0

[a] Percentage of adult male mice that either killed, were parental toward, or ignored two newborn mice that were placed into the male's cage for 30 min. A group of males were allowed to mate with two females while another group of males remained sexually naïve. Fourteen days later, males within each of these groups were paired for 7 days (1 hr per day) and categorized as being dominant or subordinate. All dominant and subordinate males that were sexually naïve as well as dominant and subordinate males that had previously mated were then tested for their behavior toward young. The dominant males that had previously mated (Group D) were retested 10 weeks later (90 days after having mated) (vom Saal and Howard, 1982).

[b] Group A versus C: $\chi^2(2) = 19.9$, $p < 0.001$. Group C versus D: $\chi^2(2) = 31.4$, $p < 0.001$. Group A versus B: not significant. Group B versus D: not significant.

inance in male mice: Parental behavior was facilitated and infanticide inhibited in dominant males 22 days after mating, similar to the effect of mating on the behavior of males that had not previously fought with another adult male (see Table I, Day 20 Group). In contrast to the foregoing result, prior mating experience did not have a significant effect on infanticide in subordinate males (Table IV, B), although there was a tendency for more of the previously mated subordinate males to exhibit parental behavior than was the case for the sexually naïve subordinate males (vom Saal and Howard, 1982).

Dominant males that were tested for infanticide 22 days after they had mated (see foregoing) were retested for infanticide 90 days after they had mated (10 weeks after the first test). At this time, 88% of the males committed infanticide compared to 15% during the previous test 22 days after mating (see Table IV; vom Saal and Howard, 1982). This finding again confirms the previous observation (Table I, Day 90 Group) that 90 days after mating most males commit infanticide.

The results of the previous experiments demonstrate that the tendency of a male mouse to commit infanticide is strongly affected by dominance status. It has been proposed (vom Saal and Howard, 1982) that as a result of continuous defeat, subordinate males within a deme are inhibited from committing infanticide. But, if the dominant male within a deme dies, the subordinate males will fight, and one of them will become the dominant male (cf. Reimer and Petras, 1967; Lidicker, 1976). Since achievement of dominance appears to facilitate infanticide in male mice that have not previously mated, it was proposed that a new dominant male would most likely kill the offspring of his predecessor (an assumption of this hypothesis is that subordinate males do not mate). Although this action at first glance would appear to clearly be advantageous for the new dominant male, it is important to point out that subordinate males in mouse demes are most likely brothers, half-brothers, or offspring of the dominant male. The new dominant male may thus be related by a factor of from 12.5 to 25% on average to the dominant male's offspring that it was killing.

INFANTICIDE AND REPRODUCTIVE SUCCESS IN MALE MICE

The previous experiments reveal that newly dominant male mice kill the young of other males. Infanticide in such a situation is proposed to be adaptive. The potential increase in fitness associated with infanticide by a newly dominant male depends on the relatedness of the male to the victims of the attacks and on whether committing infanticide increases the rate of production of young by an infanticidal male. To examine this latter question, 40 sexually naïve male mice were each placed into one side of a chamber divided by a wooden partition; the other side of each chamber was occupied by a female that had delivered a litter (culled to 8 young) within the previous 15 hr. After 30 min, the partition was removed and the males allowed to cohabit with the females. Upon removal of the partition, 22 of the males immediately killed all of the young, while in 10 cases all of the young survived to weaning. In 8 cases, up to 3 of the 8 young survived to weaning. As predicted by the sexual selection hypothesis, the number of days to the delivery of the subsequent litter (sired by the introduced male) was found to vary significantly as a function of whether or not the introduced male committed infanticide. For females paired with an infanticidal male, the mean ($\pm$SE) interval was 22.1 $\pm$ 0.9 days compared to 29.8 $\pm$ 1.9 days for females paired with a noninfanticidal male (*t*-test, $p < 0.001$). The reason why only a few young survived in 8 of the litters is unknown, but the mean length of time for the next litter to be born under these conditions was 25.5 $\pm$ 2.8 days. None of the 40 males killed any of the young in the litter that they had sired (vom Saal and Howard, 1982).

The timing of male introduction in relation to parturition is an important feature of the preceding experiment. The first night after a litter is born, female mice go through a period of postpartum estrus. Implantation of the embryos is delayed in female mice that mate at postpartum estrus and subsequently lactate. The length of the delay varies in different mouse strains and also depends on the number of nursing young: the larger the litter, the longer the delay (Mantelenakis and Ketchell, 1966). In lactating CF-1 mice, the delay in implantation following insemination at postpartum estrus is 1 week (F. vom Saal: unpublished observation), which is exactly the difference in the length of time to produce the next litter observed in the previous experiment for the infanticidal and noninfanticidal males. This finding suggests that the difference between infanticidal and noninfanticidal males in the length of time to produce young is due to the fact that implantation was delayed in the females that continued to nurse young after insemination during postpartum estrus. Thus, males were placed with females prior to postpartum estrus to provide the strongest test of the hypothesis that committing infanticide would significantly shorten the interval males must wait prior to the production of their own offspring. If males had been placed with lactating females on the day after postpartum estrus, noninfanticidal individuals inevitably would have experienced a delay of at least 1 month before the original litter was weaned and the female ovulated again.

The same experiment was repeated with 20 males that had mated with another female 3 weeks prior to being placed into boxes containing a lactating female (the females had each been inseminated by another male). Upon removal of the partition, the males were observed with the female and her litter for 30 min, and during this time none of the males was observed killing young. The males again remained with the females until 5 days after their own offspring were born. Under these circumstances, the interval to the birth of the subsequent litter that was sired by these males was 28.3 ± 2.0 days. Of the 160 young that were alive at the start of this experiment (8 young/female), only a total of 6 young did not survive to weaning at 23 days old, and no more than 2 young died in any litter. This percentage of young is lost even when males are not present, suggesting that these few deaths were attributable to natural causes and not infanticide (vom Saal and Howard, 1982).

Not only do these studies show that infanticide can be reproductively advantageous for male mice in some circumstances, but they also confirm, using a different testing procedure, that prior mating experience completely inhibits infanticide in male mice 3 weeks after mating. In CF-1 male mice, (as well as wild males), recognition of either the individual female with which a male mated or of genetically related young does not appear to play any critical role in modulating infanticide and parental behavior. In contrast, there is a recent report that in Swiss Webster mice, recognition by males of the females with which they have mated plays a role in the inhibition of infanticide (Huck *et al.,* 1982).

FEMALE COUNTERSTRATEGIES TO INFANTICIDE

Female mice do not exhibit intense aggression toward intruders into the nest area until after postpartum estrus (Svare, 1981). Perhaps this is an unavoidable consequence of the fact that a female mouse cannot simultaneously mate with and attack a potentially infanticidal male during postpartum estrus. Nevertheless, during the first 2 days after birth, newborn mice may be particularly vulnerable to infanticide by a new dominant male in a deme. One possible female counterstrategy to infanticide in this situation may involve communal nesting. Females with different aged young may share and jointly defend a common nest area. Since female mice in a deme are probably related, protection of another female's young should result in an increase in inclusive fitness. Precisely this sort of communal nesting in a freely growing population of CF-1 mice has been observed (F. vom Saal: unpublished observation). Investigators working with other laboratory and wild strains of mice (Saylor and Salmon, 1971; Lloyd, 1975) have made similar observations. These observations are far from conclusive, and it is clear that the issue of possible female counterstrategies to infanticide (such as communal nesting) needs to be examined in a study of wild mice in a natural or seminatural environment (see Schwagmeyer, 1979, and Huck, Chapter 18, this volume, for a more detailed discussion of this issue).

Of the three predictions of the sexual selection hypothesis cited at the beginning of this chapter, only one remains to be substantiated, namely, that the tendency of males to commit infanticide (and also to behave parentally) is at least partially genetically determined and thus heritable. Presumably, once the complex of genes involved in regulating infanticide appears in a population of mice, there would rapidly be an increase in the frequency of this complex in the population (Hausfater *et al.*, 1982b), and this would probably be true even in situations in which the selection coefficient was low (Wills, 1981). However, the fact that infanticide is modulated (along with aggression, sex behavior, urine marking, and other behaviors; see reviews by Beatty, 1979; Gorski, 1979; vom Saal, 1983b) by hormones during both perinatal and adult life in mice makes the study of the genetic basis of infanticide quite complicated. Traits that are modulated hormonally, and which are also influenced by experience, are thought to be polygenic, and it has proved extremely difficult to develop either mathematical models or analytical techniques for determining with any precision the genetic contribution to such behaviors (cf. Lande, 1980).

A random developmental event in polytocous (multiple-birth) species, including mice, is the position that a foetus occupies in the uterus relative to foetuses of the opposite sex. The intrauterine position phenomenon (IUP) refers to the fact that foetuses can develop next to, and possibly be influenced by the hormonal secretions of, foetuses of the same or opposite sex (Fig. 1; vom Saal, 1983d; vom Saal and Bronson, 1980a; vom Saal, Grant, McMullen and Laves, 1983). Since intrauterine position is a random event, male foetuses that develop next to female foetuses do not differ systematically in genotype from male foetuses that develop next to other male foetuses (vom Saal, 1981). This phenomenon is thus of particular relevance to the problem of determining what component of the variance in the tendency of male mice to commit infanticide is mediated genetically (vom Saal, 1983a). To obtain offspring from known intrauterine positions, female mice are time-mated, and the young are delivered by Cesarean section and raised by foster mothers (vom Saal, 1981).

Hormonal Consequences of IUP

During the period of sexual differentiation (in mice between about Day 14 of gestation through the first week of postnatal life), males secrete higher titers of testosterone than do females (vom Saal and

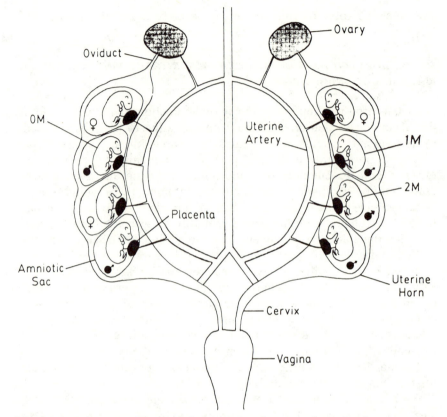

Figure 1. Schematic diagram of the uterine horns and uterine loop arteries of a pregnant mouse at term. The intrauterine position of foetuses is determined at Cesarean delivery. The labels 0M, 1M, and 2M refer to the number of male foetuses that an individual is contiguous to (2M = between 2 males, 1M = next to 1 male, and 0M = between 2 females). This scheme is used to identify both male and female foetuses, but only males are labeled in this figure.

Bronson, 1980a; Weisz and Ward, 1980). During prenatal but not postnatal life, female mouse foetuses that are located between two male foetuses (2M females) have higher amniotic fluid and blood titers of testosterone than do female foetuses that do not develop next to a male foetus (0M females; vom Saal and Bronson, 1980a), and intrauterine position thereby influences morphology, physiology, and behavior in female mice (vom Saal and Bronson, 1978; 1980b; vom Saal, Pryor and Bronson, 1981). These findings led to the prediction that male mice that developed between two male foetuses (2M males) may also differ in prenatal hormone titers and in adult behavior from males that developed in utero between two female foetuses (0M males). Contrary to this expectation, 0M and 2M male mouse foetuses were not found to differ in their blood or amniotic fluid titers of testosterone. But, female mouse foetuses were found to have significantly higher amniotic fluid titers of estradiol than male foetuses, and 0M male foetuses had significantly higher amniotic fluid titers of estradiol than did 2M male foetuses (vom Saal et al., 1983). Estradiol in the amniotic fluid is presumed to be in equilibrium with estradiol in the foetal bloodstream (Belisle and Tulchinsky, 1980).

IUP and the Activational Effects of Testosterone

Prior research had revealed that infanticidal tendencies in mice were influenced by hormones during both prenatal and early postnatal life (Gandelman and vom Saal, 1977; Svare et al., Chapter 20 this volume). 0M and 2M male mice, as well as 1M males (those that developed between a male and a female foetus in utero), were therefore compared for their behavior toward two newborn mice that were placed into the home cage of each male as described previously. The results presented in Table V reveal that intrauterine position strongly influenced the behavior of male mice toward young. Most 0M males committed infanticide and most 2M males behaved parentally; 1M males were equally likely to kill or behave parentally toward young (vom Saal, 1983c).

There is evidence that indicates that parenting behaviors and infanticide are not influenced by hormones in the same way during perinatal life in male mice. Parenting behaviors and infanticide thus appear to be independent and not simply responses to young that represent oppo-

Table V. Effect of intrauterine position on infanticide[a]

| Behavior | Intrauterine position of male[b] | | | Total |
	2M	1M	0M	
Infanticide	23	40	63	42
Parental	67	37	27	43
Ignore	10	23	10	15

[a] The percentage of gonadally intact, 75-day-old 0M, 1M, and 2M male mice (30/group) that committed infanticide, were parental toward, or ignored two newborn mice that were placed into a male's cage for 30 min (vom Saal, 1983c).

[b] $\chi^2(4) = 14.2$ $p < 0.01$. 2M = between two male foetuses; 1M = between a male and female foetus; 0M = between two female foetuses.

site ends of a behavioral continuum. The evidence supporting this hypothesis was obtained in a study utilizing 0M and 2M male mice that had been castrated at birth or at 28 days of age (about 1 week prior to puberty). These males were tested for their behavior toward young when they were 75 days old without being treated with exogenous hormones. The results presented in Table VI reveal that most of the 0M males and the 2M males that had been castrated at birth behaved parentally or ignored the young. In contrast, significantly more 2M males than 0M males behaved parentally when castrated at 28 days of age. Thus, more 2M males behaved parentally toward young regardless of whether castration had occurred at 28 days of age (Table VI[B]) or whether they were gonadally intact (Table V).

A possible explanation for these findings is that at birth, most males (regardless of prior intrauterine position) have the potential to behave parentally, but the tendency to behave parentally is suppressed some time between birth and 28 days of age in gonadally intact 0M but not 2M males. In other words, it is suggested that males that developed in utero between male foetuses are influenced by the hormonal secretions of their testes after birth in a different way from those males that developed in utero between female foetuses. Since the difference between 0M and 2M males in the tendency to commit infanticide required the presence of testes or exogenous testosterone to be observed, while the difference between 0M and 2M males in the tendency to behave parentally toward young did not require that the animals be gonadally intact or treated with testosterone, it is concluded that the method by which infanticide and parental behavior are mediated by hormones is quite different.

Table VI. Effect of pre- and postnatal hormones on infanticide[a]

Behavior	(A) Castrated at birth[b]		(B) Castrated when 28 days old[c]	
	2M (n = 20)	0M (n = 20)	2M (n = 18)	0M (n = 14)
Infanticide	15	10	0	14
Parental	60	50	61	14
Ignore	35	40	39	72

[a] The percentage of adult 0M and 2M male mice that had been castrated at Cesarean delivery or when 28 days old that committed infanticide, were parental toward, or ignored two newborn mice that were placed into the male's cage for 30 min. The males were tested without being treated with testosterone when they were 75 days old (vom Saal, 1983c).
[b] Not significant.
[c] Parental versus nonparental: $\chi^2(1) = 5.4$, $p < 0.05$.

These findings are particularly intriguing since the influence of peri-natal testosterone exposure on infanticide is opposite to that for aggres-sion between adult males (vom Saal, 1983b). Exposure of mice to ele-vated titers of testosterone during early life results in an increase in sensitivity to the activational effects of testosterone on intermale ag-gression in adulthood (vom Saal, 1979). In contrast, for infanticide, a mouse that is exposed to elevated titers of testosterone around the time of birth is less sensitive to the activational effects of testosterone on infanticide in adulthood (i.e., less likely to commit infanticide) than is a mouse that is exposed to low titers of testosterone during early life (Gandelman and vom Saal, 1977; Samuels *et al.*, 1981). Thus, both intermale aggression and infanticide are behaviors that are modulated by testosterone during early life and then activated by testosterone in adulthood, but during perinatal life testosterone appears to have a sensitizing effect on the neural areas mediating intermale aggression and a desensitizing effect on the neural areas mediating infanticide in terms of the capacity of these neural areas to respond to testosterone in adulthood. It may seem contradictory that circulating testosterone should be necessary for both intermale aggression and infanticide to be exhibited by naïve, adult, male mice, while the same hormone could have such different effects on these behaviors during an earlier period in life. During development, however, enzyme systems as well as hor-mone receptors, which allow tissues to respond to hormones, are known to change in some tissues. Thus, for the neural tissues mediating infanti-cide, testosterone appears to be inhibitory during early life and then, at some point prior to adulthood, there is a transition, and testosterone activates these same neural areas. It is also interesting that intermale aggression is activated by testosterone during the early pubertal period (around 35 to 40 days of age), while a dramatic increase in the propor-tion of CF-1 male mice that commit infanticide is observed after 60 days of age (see foregoing). Taken together, the findings lead to the prediction that male mice that were the most sensitive to the activa-tional effects of testosterone on intermale aggressive would be the least likely to commit infanticide.

To examine the hypothesis that adult 0M and 2M males would differ in their sensitivity to both the infanticide- and aggression-inducing ac-tion of testosterone, different groups of 0M and 2M male mice were castrated at Cesarean delivery and then in adulthood were adminis-tered testosterone contained in a silastic capsule. These males were subsequently tested either for aggression against another adult male or for their behavior toward two newborn mice. In the aggression expe-riment (see Table VII[B]), more 2M than 0M males exhibited a 5-sec sustained attack toward a male opponent within the 16-day test period (vom Saal *et al.*, 1983). In the infanticide study, more 0M than 2M

Table VII. Effect of testosterone treatment on aggressive behavior

Behavior	(A) Behavior toward young[a]	
	2M	0M
Infanticide	50	78
Parental	39	15
Ignore	11	7

Behavior	(B) Intermale aggression[b]	
	2M	0M
Percentage attacking within 16 days	70	40

[a] The percentage of 100-day-old 0M and 2M male mice (28/group) that committed infanticide, behaved parentally toward, or ignored two newborn mice that were placed into a male's cage for 30 min. The males were castrated at birth and, in adulthood, administered testosterone (contained in a silastic capsule) for 25 days (vom Saal, 1983c). $\chi^2(2) = 3.4$; $p = 0.18$.

[b] The percentage of 0M and 2M male mice (20/group) that attacked a male intruder. The males were castrated at birth. When the males were 75 days old, 10-minute tests for aggression were administered every other day for 16 days after the males were implanted subcutaneously with a silastic capsule containing testosterone (vom Saal et al., 1983). $\chi^2(1) = 3.6$; $p < 0.05$.

males committed infanticide, while more 2M than 0M males behaved parentally after 25 days of testosterone treatment, although this difference was not statistically significant (Table VII[A]; vom Saal, 1983c). Thus, as predicted, one consequence for male mouse foetuses of developing between two female foetuses is an enhanced sensitivity to the activational effects of testosterone on infanticide and decreased sensitivity to the activational effects of testosterone on aggressiveness toward other males.

The Hormonal Basis of Differences in Behavior due to Intrauterine Position

The data indicate that 0M male mice do not differ from 2M males in their blood testosterone levels during foetal life, but 0M males do have higher titers of estradiol. This finding led to the hypothesis that during foetal life, circulating estradiol attenuates the organizational effects of testosterone on the neural tissues mediating intermale aggression and infanticide (vom Saal, 1983d; vom Saal *et al.,* 1983). 0M male foetuses are exposed to the highest titers of estradiol with the result that they behave as if they had been exposed to much lower titers of testosterone during foetal life than 2M males. Specifically, 0M males are less likely to exhibit aggression and more likely to commit infanticide when treated with testosterone in adulthood than are 2M males. In contrast to the antagonistic effect of estrogen on the action of testosterone in the neural areas mediating infanticide and intermale aggression, estrogens appear to facilitate the effects of testosterone in the neural areas mediating male sexual behavior (mounting, intromitting, and ejaculating). Thus, in adulthood, 0M males are more sexually active than are 2M males in both mice and rats (vom Saal *et al.,* 1983). In summary, during foetal life, the interaction of circulating estrogens and androgens in different neural areas is quite complex. Such differences may be determined by the type of steroid receptors present in particular neural areas during foetal life.

In humans, female foetuses also have higher titers of estrogens than do male foetuses, and this difference is due to sex differences in the secretion of adrenal androgens, which are converted to estrogens in the placenta (Belisle and Tulchinsky, 1980; Winter, Fujieda, Faiman, Reyes, and Thliveris, 1980). The source of estradiol in both the foetal and maternal circulation during pregnancy in mice is unknown. But, the available evidence suggests that it is also of foetal/placental origin, since female mouse foetuses have over twice the circulating titers of estradiol as do their mothers 2 days prior to parturition (vom Saal and Bronson, 1980a). In mice, both sex differences in behavior and variation among males and among females due to intrauterine position may thus result from an interaction of circulating estrogens (possibly derived from adrenal secretions) and androgens.

Intrauterine Position in Relation to the Effect of Mating on Infanticide

Intrauterine position influences the behavior of male mice toward young, and it is obviously of interest to determine whether there is an interaction between IUP and the inhibition of infanticide that occurs between 12 and 50 days after mating in male mice. For example, after mating, not all males behave parentally, and these males may be 0M males, which have a tendency toward committing infanticide. Similarly, after achieving dominance, not all males commit infanticide, and these males may be 2M males. Such a finding would suggest that exposure to different concentrations of hormones during foetal life due to IUP results in an animal being biased toward a particular behavior pattern that cannot be easily altered by postnatal experiences. For example, it is interesting that in an experiment in which colony males were pretested for their behavior toward young and then retested at either 1 or 20 days after mating (see Table II), all of the males that did not commit infanticide 1 day after mating (17% parented or ignored the young) had not committed infanticide on the pretest. Similarly, all of the males that did not behave parentally 20 days after mating (23% committed infanticide) had also committed infanticide on the pretest. Since 0M and 2M males each represent about 20–25% of a population of males (50% of a population of males are 1M males; vom Saal, 1981), a group of 30 males chosen at random with respect to IUP would contain about 7 0M males (23%) and 7 2M males, figures that are very close to those obtained previously. These observations provide indirect evidence that IUP may render male mice differentially sensitive to the short-term facilitating and inhibiting effects of mating on infanticide and parental behavior. In contrast, this author has previously tended to view IUP effects on behavior as biases that could be overridden by postnatal experiences.

ECOLOGICAL CONSIDERATIONS

It is an open question as to what significance findings from studies in the laboratory have for the understanding of the reproductive ecology of wild animals. But, it is not unreasonable to speculate concerning the possible significance of some of the findings described in this chapter in terms of individual reproductive success and population dynamics in wild mice. For example, from an evolutionary perspective, it is quite interesting that foetal hormones act in opposite ways on infanticide and intermale aggressive behavior. Intuitively, these behaviors would seem likely to be positively rather than negatively correlated.

Mice have a period of postpartum estrus and thus have the capacity to produce litters every 3 weeks. If many young survive, a mouse plague can occur. When population density begins increasing and competition for space within the natal territory becomes intense, the aggressive animals within a deme are believed to drive the less aggressive animals away (Lidicker, 1975). When the one dominant male within a deme dies, the subordinate mice will fight until one male becomes dominant. Previously discussed was the likelihood that subordinate males within a deme will be brothers, half-brothers, or offspring of the dominant male, since immigration of males into a deme has been reported to be uncommon (Reimer and Petras, 1967; Lidicker, 1976). The subordinate males will also be related to many females within a deme. It is proposed that there may be a strong selective advantage for males that have the highest sensitivity to the activational effects of testosterone on intermale aggression (i.e., the 2M males) to also have the lowest tendency toward infanticide, since these same males may very well be the most likely to become the dominant male in their natal territory and thus come in contact with genetically related young prior to, themselves, mating. Since there is an increase in the tendency of sexually naïve male mice to commit infanticide after fighting and achieving dominance (see Table IV), a corollary of this hypothesis is that after fighting and achieving dominance, 2M males will still be less likely to commit infanticide than will 0M males (see foregoing).

The finding that 2M males are more aggressive than 0M males after treatment with testosterone suggests that in an environment in which 0M and 2M males were in direct competition, the 0M males should have a greater likelihood of being driven out of the natal environment than the 2M males. The dispersing 0M males that survive (*Mus* are highly successful colonizers) and come in contact with a female with newborn young may be more likely than would 2M males to kill the female's litter and then mate with her. It would be unlikely that the dispersing 0M males would be related genetically to females or young encountered outside of the male's natal territory, and committing infanticide in this situation should result in an increase in the male's fitness. It must be emphasized that the preceding discussion is simply an attempt to provide a plausible hypothesis concerning the observed inverse relationship between intermale aggressiveness and infanticide in 0M and 2M male mice (Table VII).

SUMMARY

The studies described here provide support for two predictions of the sexual selection hypothesis, namely, that there has to be a method for the inhibition of infanticide in situations where a male may possibly kill his own offspring, and that males must potentially obtain an increase in reproductive success as a result of committing infanticide. These experiments have not directly addressed the third prediction that some component of the variance in the tendency of male mice to commit infanticide or behave parentally should be mediated genetically. But, a significant component of the variance in the tendency of male mice to commit infanticide can be accounted for based on intrauterine position, adult dominance status, and prior mating experience. An important aspect of the finding that behaviors such as aggression and infanticide are modulated by prenatal hormone levels in mice is that regardless of the amount of genetic variation within a population, animals in the population will be guaranteed to vary in terms of these behaviors due to the intrauterine position phenomenon.

The overwhelming complexity of the regulation of infanticide by prenatal hormones and then by adult experience is such that the process by which selection could have operated to produce such a system is difficult to imagine. However, it is quite likely that a system that is this complex is mediated by a large array of genes. In the process of attempting to develop infanticidal and noninfanticidal mouse strains through selective breeding, shifts in the frequencies of genes involved in regulating many other traits, in addition to infanticide, will thus likely occur. While the issue of the heritability of infanticide needs to be examined using the techniques of behavior genetics, this will undoubtedly be a difficult task (see Svare *et al.,* Chapter 20, this volume).

In summary, the hypothesis that infanticide is a pathological behavior only observed during times of social stress appears to be untenable, although it is recognized that social stress can result in an increase in infanticide in mouse populations (Christian, 1971) and may be a factor in influencing infanticide in other species as well (Hrdy, 1979). In species that occupy different ecological niches and that have different social structures from mice, other variables will certainly be found to influence infanticide. However, as has proved to be the case with mice, information concerning the reproductive physiology and socioecology of a particular species is essential for understanding which variables play a role in regulating infanticide. The relative lack of such information for most mammals in comparison to what is known about the genetics, physiology, and ecology of house mice will make examining the proximate causes of infanticide in other species as well as speculating about ultimate causation far more difficult than has been the case with mice.

IV

INFANTICIDE IN HUMANS: ETHNOGRAPHY, DEMOGRAPHY, SOCIOBIOLOGY, AND HISTORY

Concepts and classification in the study of human infanticide: Sectional introduction and some cautionary notes

Mildred Dickemann

When I was born, and my mother was still in the birth hut, my father came and hung over the fence, and called out, asking what it was, a boy or a girl. My mother replied, "A girl." And my father said, "Break it and throw it away." But my mother refused, deciding to keep me against his wishes, even though I was a girl. And so I was given my formal name, Letahulozo, Break It and Throw It Away (Account of Kilino Aino, Aiposi, Eastern Highlands, Papua New Guinea, 1958).

At eight o'clock in the evening we were summoned to the headquarters of the community. The Gestapo told us that a convoy of orphans was to leave, and that since the necessary quota would not be supplied by the children's homes, we had to find orphans living with private families and bring them to the transit camp. We young Jewish girls were to go out and look for Jewish children. Even today I do not understand how I found the courage and strength to do it. I was twenty at the time. (Jewish social worker in Berlin quoted in Poliakov [1979.])

Former E.P.A. Administrator Anne Burford insisted last summer that relaxing the lead standard would not harm children. Burford made her statement despite an internal report by Joel Schwartz of the E.P.A.'s energy economics branch, which found that doubling the permissible level of lead emissions in the atmosphere per year would increase the incidence of lead poisoning among black 2- to 4-year-olds in inner city areas by an average of 2 to 4 percent. Schwartz estimated that in Chicago, cases of lead poisoning among 6- and 7-year-olds would rise by 9 percent; in New York City, by 14 percent; and in Louisville, Kentucky, by 44 percent (Freedman and Weir, 1983).

In addressing a behavioral domain newly under investigation, such as infanticide, problems of definition and terminology are acute. Nor are these concerns trivial; they affect not only our ability to communicate hypotheses and ideas to others but also the scope and direction of our research efforts. In concordance with the other authors in this volume, I will use Hrdy's (1979; see also this volume, Introduction) classification of infanticide based on the hypothesized adaptive significance of the behavior in various situations. The application of this taxonomy to particular species and to specific cases serves to highlight the classificatory and theoretical problems that we must address in future analyses of infanticidal behavior. My discussion of these problems will refer primarily to the human species, but it should be clear that my remarks, *mutatis mutandis,* will also apply to any other species under investigation.

We should begin by addressing the delimitation of the phenomenon itself. If the subject of the action is an "infant," What is an infant? Is our real concern with the destruction of young individuals per se or of offspring regardless of age? For at least two of the categories employed here (i.e., resource competition and exploitation), the distinction between young and adult may be quite irrelevant in some species, though not in others (cf. Mock, Chapter 1, and Dominey and Blumer, Chapter 3, this volume, on food particle size and egg/young vulnerability). Even within the category "young," morphologically discriminable stages in development (egg, larva, embryo, foetus, nestling, infant, weanling) may or may not be relevant to the infanticidal behavior of adults. Our initial taxonomy and terminology, like so much else in biology, derive inevitably from lay categories of Western thought (cf. "territory"), in this case from the rather limited behavior of human parental destruction of own young at birth. We should not expect this initial conceptual category to retain its heuristic value much longer as investigation in this area proceeds. In the interim, I would argue that "pedicide," referring to destruction of the offspring (not necessarily young) of self or others, may be a more biologically meaningful and broadly useful term, as I will indicate more fully below.

In humans, the occurrence of all four of the hypothesized functional forms of infanticide identified by Hrdy (1979) is striking. But often, the behavior in question is multifunctional, as so much else human. *Exploitation* of the infant as a food resource (by parent and others) has been reported among Australian aborigines killing offspring primarily for birth spacing (Krzywicki, 1934:121–23, 140–41). Outright infant cannibalism for food alone has probably occurred widely in starvation situations, though no one has attempted to survey the practice. In any case, there is no clear line between conserving energy by birth spacing and by consumption of young: Both can be seen as attempts by the parent to maximize reproduction, but involving differing degrees of wastage. At least among some Eskimos, the value of preserving adults of reproductive age at the expense of the young and the elderly in famine situations was communally understood (Freuchen, ed., 1961:303–402; Weyer, 1932). But the question of the frequency of consumption of own as opposed to others' offspring has never been addressed, nor is it known how regularly infants were consumed in societies practicing customary endocannibalism (Dornstreich and Morren, 1974). The Aztec case involves an even more complex interplay of functions: Sacrifice certainly occurred; humans were certainly consumed, including infants. But the intensity of the practice, its nutritional significance, and its sociopolitical functions are all still matters of dispute (Cook 1946; de Montellano, 1978; Harner, 1977; Padden, 1967). Whatever the resolution of these questions, there is no justification for creating a separate category of "ritual infanticide" unless we have first demonstrated that these behaviors cannot be explained as resource exploitation, resource competition, or in other biologically functional terms.

Resource competition is surely represented in humans by the removal of infants of subordinate groups through the actions of dominant groups and individuals, though the nature of the human maternal-infant bond often dictates that mothers are removed along with them. That human societies clothe these actions in religious or racial ideologies should not mislead a biologist. We do not know, however, why and when children are preferentially selected for destruction, primarily because we have rarely asked the question; Bugos and McCarthy (Chapter 25, this volume) constitute a rare exception. The potential labor value of adults and the sexual and reproductive value of women are likely to be significant variables. Under the Nazi terror, numerous special deportations of children occurred, and children were immediately exterminated upon arrival at the death camps. These eliminations of children of "undesirables" are best understood in the same terms as the destruction of the aged, chronically ill, and other defectives by state euthanasia programs (cf. Poliakov, 1979:183–191, 274–277). On occasion, the motive for such exterminations is overtly stated: A Wehrmacht memorandum of June 1944 states the purpose of a plan to remove 40–50,000 Russian children from controlled areas: "The operation is planned not only to reduce the direct growth of enemy strength, but also to impair its biological strength in the distant future [quoted in Poliakov, 1979:275]." Biblical quotes aside, a survey of the human history of child extermination remains to be done.

On a smaller scale, resource competition occurs among human individuals and families competing for other scarce valuables besides land, industrial resources, and geopolitical power. Human history is full of cases of competition for access to office (read: economic and reproductive dominance), most especially among royalty. We should expect that the greater the value of the office, the greater the benefit of assassination of potential competitors, offsetting the degree of relatedness, but we must also recognize that the skews of historical records might have impeded identification of these competitive acts at lower levels of society. But again, no review of this topic has, to my knowledge, been undertaken.

Reproductive competition (or "sexual selection") may be, theoretically, a subset of resource competition, since the parental effort of the partner is the object of the competition. Lethal child abuse, so far as it conforms to this model (Daly and Wilson, 1981, and Chapter 24, this volume) is such a phenomenon; however we need both data on and analyses of these behaviors in societies other than modern Western ones. Nor should we allow the basic model of reproductive strategies in sexually reproducing organisms to prevent us from searching for cases in which *female* competition for access to males and their parental effort is expressed in pedicidal behaviors. The five cases of communal nesters reviewed by Mock (Chapter 1, this volume) provide evidence for female–female competition in birds; in one of these, there is now further evidence that the competing females are sisters (Mumme *et al.*, 1983). This should lead us to look closely at human females in harem and polygynous breeding contexts, including sororal polygyny, and the consequences of their competition for infant mortality.

It is striking, from the perspective of data on other animals, including nonhuman primates, how small a role extrafamilial homicide of the young appears to play in humans, except in those cases of intrusive acts of powerful states referred to above. This suggests the importance of the human family as a protective system not only against predation but against competitive pedicide by conspecifics. It is perhaps significant that regicide-pedicides and harem infanticides are generally intrafamilial: Access to the young is much easier in multiple breeding units and by relatives. One consequence of this protective role of the family would seem to be the far greater frequency of intrafamilial actions by parents and close kin, which we and members of other societies normally think of when referring to "infanticide," and the greater attention to them in the literature than to any other functional category. The term *parental manipulation* has been suggested for this category (Hrdy 1979), but "reproductive management" or "management of parental effort" perhaps focuses attention more clearly on the assessment of the reproductive value of an offspring as part of an overall reproductive strategy, and less on matters of parent-offspring conflict.

Once again, there are taxonomic problems. Reproductive strategies may properly be said to begin with courtship, insofar as that involves any investment of energy or any decision making that has consequences for reproductive success. The individual's (or its kin group's) reproductive management then extends from a precopulatory phase of courtship and mating (as in human groups practicing child betrothal or even preconception betrothal) throughout the period during which the parent has any capacity for further investment of effort in the offspring or any power to dictate its choices, insofar as such investment or such control has any impact on the reproductive success of the offspring and consequently on that of the parent. It should be noted how greatly this enlarged definition contrasts, for example, with the more limited one of Mock (Chapter 1, this volume). Yet the recognition that we are dealing with a continuum of reproductive management has important consequences, not only requiring us to clarify our classification of the segments within it, but also forcing us to address what lies behind the quite different preferences of various species for management at some points on the continuum rather than others. (This great variation in preferences is dramatically demonstrated by the chapters in this volume.) In sum, we need continually to remind ourselves to look for management strategies along the whole of the continuum of reproductive effort, whatever the species of interest.

When we do indeed look at species other than humans, we find a wide variety of physiological mechanisms employed in reproductive management especially in insects (Polis, Chapter 5, this volume) and rodents (chapters in Part III), and Charnov (Chapter 7, this volume) reminds us that similar mechanisms are operative in plants. Postcopulatory plugs, sperm competition, inducement of ovulation, delayed implantation, pre- and postovulatory pregnancy block (Huck, Chapter 18, this volume), resorption of gametes, and spontaneous abortion are all means of managing both the individual's own energetic investment and the investment of energies of the partner. Clearly the choice of means must to some degree be phylogenetic, that is, a product of the specifics of the reproductive and general physiology, morphology, and development of the species (Hayssen, Chapter 6 this volume), but this is scarcely a sufficient explanation. We will need to specify which attributes of the organism are constraining, whether they be long-term or short-term parental effort, helplessness of the young, speed and timing of insemination, gestation and ovulation, or proportion of previous to anticipated investment at various stages of dependency. In addition, such strategic choices will depend on the sex of the actor, which limits his or her access to the offspring at various stages from conception onward, and also on the degree to which that actor is able to exert control over the actions and physiology of the mate. The history of our understanding of the Bruce effect (pregnancy block), as well as the current dialogue regarding male infanticide in langurs and other monkey species (chapters in Part II, this volume), underlines the importance of calculating the costs and benefits of such actions for *both* sexes, especially in mammals. Several authors in this volume have made suggestions regarding the organismic and environmental correlates of specific forms of pedicide (Introduction, Huck, Chapter 18; Mock, Chapter 1; Dominey and Blumer, Chapter 13; Hausfater, Chapter 13; and Bugos and McCarthy, Chapter 25): I will not review them here.

What I do draw from this perspective is a need to look more closely at human management in the early stages of parental effort. We already have good evidence for some physiological skew in the secondary sex ratio in humans, dependent upon socioeconomic status (Teitelbaum, 1970), although whether it is sufficient to provide reproductive advantage is at present a matter of dispute. Menstrual synchrony occurs in humans, but its function is still unclear (McClintock, 1981; Buckley, 1982). Recently, evidence has been presented that human females with multiple conceptions experience high rates of blighted ova (measured by failure to develop normal foetal heartbeat) and of subsequent spontaneous abortion of one or both conceptuses (Varma, 1979). It would be useful to know the health and socioeconomic status of mothers bringing twins and triplets to term, as opposed to those aborting, as well as the sex ratios of surviving livebirths versus rejected ova.

Most of our data, anecdotal, ethnographic, historical, medical, and demographic, refer to the perinatal management of reproduction. Elsewhere (Dickeman, 1975) I have remarked on the noncomparability of terminologies in this area, a methodological difficulty for workers using any of these classes of data that Scrimshaw (Chapter 22, this volume) also addresses. Only recently have both anthropologists and demographers begun to confront the question of deferred or delayed infanticide, discussed by all of the chapters in this section and the subject of a symposium at the 1982 meeting of the American Anthropological Association (forthcoming in *Medical Anthropology;* see also McKee, 1982). In dealing with these perinatal manifestations and their extension past infancy, we confront a taxonomic and theoretical decision about the far end of the continuum of reproductive management. If the actions of parents, siblings, grandparents, and other kin reduce survivorship of some offspring relative to other offspring or to other kin through differential investment of parental and kin effort, and if those actions can be understood as components of a strategy for a maximizing reproductive success of the actors, what is the difference between these actions and outright infanticide at birth, except in terms of the appropriateness of one strategy over another given the attributes and context of the organism? McKee (personal communication) reports that in a Latin American community with sex-differential mortality in childhood, smaller sized food bowls are regularly used for female children. We know that small inheritances in peasant communities correlate with lower survival rates of family lines (Smith, 1977). Are these not parallel actions but timed at different points in the life history of the individual and indeed of the genetic line? The truth may be that human reproductive management of offspring is, wherever possible, interminable, continuing with less and less impact over several generations, as it is more and more overridden by stochastic and other effects. It is this distinctive attribute of *Homo sapiens* as contrasted with other mammals (although there is certainly inheritance of territory and of status in other mammalian species: see Hausfater *et al.,* 1982a) that allies us so closely with the eusocial insects (Wilson, 1971). Further work in the area of delayed infanticide will eventually lead to some very difficult, but long overdue, theoretical considerations regarding the measurement of reproductive success and the computation of the consequences of various reproductive and life-history strategies over two, three, and more generations in our species.

The chapters that follow certainly represent some of the leading edges of our investigations of human pedicide. Rather than summarizing them, I would like to call attention to certain aspects of the existing literature on humans that I believe have plagued many of our efforts and need to be borne in mind if we are ever to make meaningful biological statements about human behavior in this area. Much effort has been expended, since my early review of this subject in humans (Dickeman, 1975), on attempts to determine the frequency of the practice, relying on previously selected samples of societies and sometimes on previous codings. Scrimshaw (Chapter 22, this volume) reviews some of these; another recent effort is that of Minturn and Shastak (1983). However, it is not at all clear to me whether these efforts have any value. We have known from the outset that none of these practices occurs with the same intensity in all human societies. Whether 10 or 60% of human societies "practice infanticide" is a meaningless statistic, unless it says something about the reasons for the practice. Further, most such cross-cultural studies are of little value in discriminating the incidence of the practice within a society, as the coded data are not sufficiently quantitative. Finally, everything I have said above should induce skepticism regarding the coding and analysis of "infanticide" as a unitary perinatal or postnatal phenomenon. Note here the efforts of Minturn and Shastak (1983) to segregate immediate postnatal from deferred infanticide, something that previous cross-cultural studies have not attempted.

It seems to me that what we need, rather, are competent reassessments of the existing literature on specific cases, as Cowlishaw (1978, 1981) has begun for Australian aborigines, or Schrire and Steiger (1974, 1981) and Chapman (1980) have attempted for Inuit (Eskimo), or as is contained in Howell's impressive !Kung demography (Howell, 1979). Where still possible, we need the kind of ethnographic reconstruction presented by Bugos and McCarthy (Chapter 25 this volume). We also need much more of the kind of quantitative analysis that demographers can contribute, along with their sophistication and scepticism about sources. And we need far more analysis, historical, demographic, and anthropological, of stratified societies, as presented by Johansson (Chapter 23, this volume) and my own comparative efforts (Dickemann 1979a, 1979b, 1981). Until we have done this, we will be hard put to make meaningful statements about the functions and consequences of various forms of the practice in differing ecological contexts.

In so doing, we will have to attend more closely to our definitions of the *environment*. Anthropologists, by and large, heavily indoctrinated into the study of small-scale, classless societies, easily forget that individuals living at different levels and in different subgroups within the same stratified society (i.e., members of different castes, classes, ethnic groups, occupational groups, regional subcultures) live in *utterly different* social environments. The consequence is that total-society generalizations about frequencies and functions, however quantitative, while dangerous for small societies (in which we know there can be marked differences in reproductive strategy and outcome by individual status) are totally nonsensical for stratified societies. For example, no total-society statistics or generalizations about sex ratio will tell us anything at all about human ability to vary the secondary sex ratio, whether through physiological or cultural means, if socioeconomic status plays any role as a relevant variable in adaptive strategies, and it does. I believe sociologists would not be so prone to this error. This same question of social status also impacts markedly our understanding of the controversy regarding group selection in humans, as I will indicate below.

If social variation needs attention, a corollary is that we will have to make a distinction not only between decision maker and perpetrator (cf. Scrimshaw, Chapter 22, this volume), but also between social norms and social acts. The power of human individuals to compel others is a significant species attribute, of which the familial compulsion and the state compulsion mentioned above are subsets. In consequence, studying perpetrators alone will be inadequate for an assessment of reproductive strategies, costs, and benefits, whether within the family, where a female may be constrained to act in a way that compromises her own reproductive success in the interests of mate and kin, or beyond the family, where the interests and policies of elites and power blocs may have profound affect, both direct and indirect, on the reproduction of individuals. Likewise, the matter of norms is a good deal more complex than some have made it seem. There are probably levels of normative behavior in all societies. Public "society-at-large" norms are not coterminous with those of regions, subgroups, or families, nor with those of individuals. Norms are contextual, voiced affirmatively in one context and denied in another. The Japanese data of Bowles (1953) are especially instructive here. It should be recalled that most cross-cultural codings and much other analysis assume a single dichotomy between "customary" or "sanctioned" infanticide and irregular or pathological practices, as though all human behavior were either and only publically condoned or publically condemned. Such oversimplicity will not take us very far. Nor are we in a position to address effectively the questions of consciousness of intent and awareness of consequences. Humans do not function in either conscious or unconscious modes: rather, they manifest degrees of awareness of both motives and consequences, again contextually. And the multifunctional nature of human acts provides numerous "true" rationales for acts that may also have other, more painful, aspects. We are not, I think, at the point in our understanding of the psychosocial dimensions of human behavior that we can make very intelligent statements about how this proximate level of human decision-making and action-taking operates.

This brings me to the related matter of *pathology,* a notion that seems to entangle many who attempt to apply behavioral ecology to humans. If "pathology" means anything biological, it must mean maladaptive behavior, as measured by its consequences for reproductive success. There can be no advantage in importing a redundant and value-laden term into our discussion. On the other hand, "pathology" does have a clear social meaning: pathological behavior in this sense is that which is defined as such by members of the society under study. Such labeling is, for social biologists, a datum about the society itself, not a part of the observer's description or analysis, just as would be "justifiable homicide." These labels, and their consequences, are part of the social milieu in which perpetrators and decision makers act. Some authors confuse "pathological" with nonnormative in the statistical sense, which is equally incorrect. Acts of statistically low frequency may be so merely because the conditions that evoke them are infrequent; this says nothing of their adaptiveness. Thus, for example, a decline in rates of illegitimacy or an increased tolerance for female sexual promiscuity may result in a decline in both infanticides and abortions of such illegitimates. This does not mean that such acts are any less adaptive for an unmarried woman in specific circumstances in twentieth-century United States than they were in nineteenth-century England. It is certainly true that behaviors that reach high frequency tend to be recognized and tolerated by the society in question as customary, but they may not necessarily be approved. Investigators of behavioral phenomena strongly regulated by social codes (and most reproductive behaviors are so regulated) should be advised not to conflate the reproductive consequences of behaviors, their incidence, and the social labels attached to them by the societies in which they occur. The three are entirely separate. The same applies a fortiori to the automatic labeling of responses to high levels of social or environmental stress as "pathological," in whatever species. (The quotations that head this introduction have as one of their functions the elaboration of these points.)

In conclusion, I turn to the long-standing dialogue in anthropology concerning the demographic consequences of infanticide–pedicide. In general, anthropologists have been less willing than biologists to abandon or revise drastically early group selectionist explanations for acts of reproductive limitation (see also Bugos and McCarthy, Chapter 25, this volume). This is in part due to our training in the analysis of behavioral phenomena at the group level and in part due to our lack of familiarity with biological theory. One low-level confusion on the part of some social scientists is that between birth rate or completed fertility, reproductive success, and population growth. An act of reproductive management that increases total survivorship of offspring and hence probably reproductive success does not necessarily reduce total population at all: similarly, high birth rates have no necessary connection with population growth. On the contrary, management strategies may increase population relative to the level maintained without management, in which scarce resources are uniformly but inadequately distributed to all; likewise, high birth rates may be functioning to offset high mortalities in a stable, or even declining, population. That individual acts of family limitation may result, cumulatively, in a low-growth, low natural-mortality population, if all families practice such management, is a group consequence of individual and kin-selected behaviors, not a group means nor a group function. It may also be an evolutionary unstable situation. Biologically fit members of such populations should, the minute resources permit, abandon such strategies, shifting their interfamilial competition from resource maximization and high per-offspring effort to high reproductive rates and low per-offspring effort. Said another way, the only infanticides that have negative demographic consequences are those above and beyond the natural mortality that would have occurred without human intervention. The function of child spacing is to increase reproductive success, not to reduce it, as is the early termination of support for defectives, twins, and excess females insofar as we understand these phenomena. Like other acts of reproductive management, infanticide–pedicide seems to be best understood at present, in all species, as one parameter of interindividual and interfamilial competition for the proportional increase of genes in the next generation, not their delimitation.

Part of the difficulty in dealing with this matter is semantic: "population regulation" may or may not refer to regulatory mechanisms, designed or selected for that purpose, operating at the level of the group (population). It may merely refer to the population consequences of individual acts selected and maintained at the level of the individual or family (for reviews of this question from several perspectives, see Bates and Lees, 1979; Cohen *et al.*, 1980; Dickemann, 1984). I raise this matter because infanticide has played a major role in discussions of population regulation, that is, the existence of Wynne–Edwardian internal self-regulation as opposed to Malthusian external regulation, in human societies. Although my own early review of the literature on human infanticide (Dickeman, 1975) had a strong group-selectionist orientation, I no longer find this position tenable and have not argued for it in subsequent publications. Rather, it is my current view (*pace* Scrimshaw, Chapter 22, this volume) that we are still looking for reproductively altruistic acts in humans, whether involving infanticide or anything else, that reach levels sufficient to have demographic and therefore genetic significance. I do not deny that such acts may exist, but do emphasize that they have yet to be identified and studied, rather than merely talked about.

If nothing else, these cautionary notes will testify to the importance of continuing the dialogue between disciplines, especially between biology and the social sciences, which is represented by this volume. If biologists have something to learn from the human species as a peculiar phenomenon that tests the adequacy of their formulations, social scientists have much to learn from biologists in the use of explanatory frameworks, in taxonomic precision, in the kinds of data and data manipulations necessary for the falsification of hypotheses, and perhaps most importantly, in my view at least, in the very theoretical framework itself.

22 Infanticide in human populations: Societal and individual concerns

Susan C. M. Scrimshaw

When his child was but three days old, Laius bound its feet together and had it thrown by sure hands upon a trackless mountain. . . . (Sophocles, *King Oedipus*, as translated by Yeats)

INTRODUCTION

Infanticide has been practiced over a wide span of time and in many different cultures, possibly even dating back to the upper Paleolithic (Carr-Saunders, 1922). The attempt to kill the infant Oedipus is one of the more notorious historical instances of infanticide, although Romulus and Remus were reportedly cast into the River Tiber in 753 B.C. (Morse, 1963). Another famous survivor, Moses, was saved from a mass infanticide when his mother set him afloat in a basket on the Nile.

The ancient Greeks destroyed weak, deformed, or unwanted children; the Chinese wanted many sons and few daughters and did not let some infants, particularly daughters, survive. Japanese farmers spoke of infanticide as "thinning out," as they did with their rice fields (Langer, 1974). In India, many daughters were not allowed to live (Williamson, 1978). Eskimos left babies out in the snow, while in the Brazilian jungle, undesired infants were left under the trees (Balikci, 1967; Krzywicki, 1934; Wagley, 1969). In London in the 1860s, dead infants were a common sight in parks and ditches. In nineteenth-century Florence, children were abandoned or sent to wet nurses who neglected

439

them, while during the same period in France, thousands of infants were sent to wet nurses in the countryside, never to return (Trexler, 1973a; Kellum, 1974; Shorter, 1977; Langer, 1974).

In one of the more complete and most recent reviews of infanticide among humans, Dickeman (1975) found that the practice was used in hunter–gatherer, horticulturalist, and stratified agrarian societies for purposes ranging from population control to maintenance of the social structure. The practice has been so common that one anthropologist has even called infanticide "the most widely used method of population control during much of human history [Harris, 1977]." However, just as the occurrence of infanticide has varied over time and across cultures, so have the stated and inferred reasons for the practice. Modern demographers and anthropologists have included infanticide in the continuum of behaviors that affect fertility and help to control family size. These behaviors range from the avoidance of conception to the killing of an infant or young child (Davis and Blake, 1956; Polgar and Marshall, 1976). But infanticide can occur for other reasons such as deformity or even ritual sacrifice. This chapter catalogues infanticidal behaviors among humans and the stated proximate reasons for such behaviors. The problem of documenting the incidence of human infanticide is also discussed. Finally, some speculations are made on possible ultimate functions of this behavior.

DEFINITIONS AND FORMS OF INFANTICIDE

As Dickeman (1975) has pointed out, a precise definition of infanticide in human populations is not arrived at easily. Langer (1974; p 353) described it as "the willful destruction of newborn babies through exposure, starvation, strangulation, smothering, poisoning or through the use of some lethal weapon." Similarly, it has been defined as killing of "a child within the first year of life [Kluge, 1978:33]" or simply "child killing" (Trexler, 1973a:98) without reference to age. However, Dickemann (this volume, Introduction, Part IV) suggests a broader definition of infanticide and has used the phrase "foeticide–infanticide–pedicide" to underscore the wide age range during which destruction or termination of parental investment can occur.

In most societies where infanticide occurs, the event takes place very early in life, before the infant or very young child has the status of a real person in the society. The problem of defining infanticide is similar to the problem of defining the beginning of life in induced abortion. When a society has the technology to intervene *in utero* to save a life, the failure to intervene could be attacked as infanticide, just as induced abortion has been called infanticide by some groups in the United States (Scrimshaw, 1983). As Williamson (1978:62) pointed out, "the line between abortion and infanticide is not always clear." She mentioned that both the Kamchadal of Siberia and the Yanomamo of Venezuela kill the foetus through the wall of the abdomen at some point during the last few months of pregnancy.

In fact, the definition of when a life is taken is usually dependent on a cultural definition of when a life begins, which may take days, weeks, or even years (Ford, 1964). In modern United States society, this is often when a foetus can survive outside the mother's uterus, although technological developments are constantly lowering the foetal age at which that is possible. Among the Machigenga, a newborn is not accepted until its mother has nursed it, often a day after birth (Johnson, 1981). Among Andean Indian groups, a child may not be acknowledged as a permanent family member until it has survived its first year (Whitehead, 1968). The Peruvian Amahuaca do not consider children fully human until they are 3 years old (Williamson, 1978). Naming, another criterion of humanity, was delayed until the seventh day after birth among the Japanese in earlier times (Bacon, 1891).

Another question is that of deliberate killing as opposed to behavior that ultimately leads to the death of an infant or child. Mock (Chapter 1, 1, this volume) defines infanticide as "behavior that makes a direct and significant contribution to the immediate death of an embryo or newly hatched (or born) member of the performer's own species." In human populations, behaviors other than deliberate killing ultimately lead to death in many instances. Dickemann (this volume, Introduction, Part IV) states that it is necessary to view foeticide–infanticide–pedicide in the context of a broad range of reproductive manipulations in order to make statements about the selection of this behavior in meaningful cost–benefit terms. Behaviors such as "agressive neglect" (Dickeman, 1975), and underinvestment (Scrimshaw, 1978; Ware, 1977, 1981) add to the complexity of understanding and measuring infanticide because in some situations child neglect is not the result of a conscious decision. As discussed by Neel (1970), Chandrasekhar (1959), Harris (1977), Ware (1977, 1981), and Scrimshaw (1978), parents may simply favor some children over others. Because resources are scarce, the results are sometimes fatal for the neglected child (see Johannson, Chapter 23, this volume). In other instances, parents may decide a child is "not for this world" and refuse to seek medical treatment or invest resources in the child (Gutierrez de Pineda, 1955:19). Underinvestment, ranging from conscious to unconscious, is currently more prevalent than the deliberate killing of a child (Dickeman, 1975).

Such underinvestment, or passive infanticide, can be defined as "any combination of medical, nutritional, physical or emotional neglect of an infant or young child in comparison to other children in the family or to children of families in similar socioeconomic and educational circumstances [Scrimshaw 1983:716]." In some instances, this neglect will lead to death, but there will also be many survivors, who may be physically and/or emotionally compromised due to the neglect they experienced. "It is important to note that underinvestment is defined in *relative* terms in that the best an impoverished family can provide would frequently be considered inappropriately poor diet and health care by modern medical and nutritional standards. Neglect occurs when an infant or child receives *less* than the family might be able to provide, and less than family members know should be provided [Scrimshaw, 1983:722]." As illustrated by several chapters in this volume, underinvestment may take place in animal populations as well as in human populations.

Despite the complexities of definitions, the term *infanticide* is used throughout this chapter to mean behavior ranging from deliberate to unconscious which is likely to lead to the death of a dependent, young member of the species. In humans, these behaviors (past and/or present) include the following, which are not necessarily mutually exclusive: deliberate killing, placing in a dangerous situation, abandonment where survival is possible, "accidents," excessive physical punishment, lowered biological support, and lowered emotional support (Scrimshaw, 1983). A distinction is made between placing a child in a dangerous situation and abandonment, because a dangerous situation such as a raging river leaves little chance for survival, whereas a doorstep or even a back alley offers some hope. "Accidents" are used here to refer to incidents where children are severely burned or battered in situations that parents claim are "accidental" but that might, in fact, have been induced by parents. In some societies, deliberate killing, placing the child in a dangerous situation, and abandonment are culturally sanctioned under specific circumstances. This is discussed in more detail along with reasons for infanticide.

Deliberate Killing

Deliberate killing is documented in the past for cultures such as the Eskimo (Balikci, 1967), the Japanese and Chinese (Langer 1974), and the Tapirape (Wagley, 1969). In India, sometimes the mother would smear opium or another poison on her nipples, or the baby would be drowned in a jar of milk (Chandrasekhar, 1959). More commonly in many cultures, a midwife or either parent would smother the child (Langer, 1974). In the latter half of the twentieth century, such reports are rare, in part because overt killing appears to have been replaced by neglect (Dickeman, 1975) and, in part, because it is no longer sanctioned and is concealed when it does occur. Methods such as smothering are reported for both the !Kung (Howell, 1979) and the Tikopia (Firth, 1957). In some parts of Africa and New Guinea, an infant is buried with its mother if the mother dies in childbirth or soon after (B. Gray: personal communication). During 1 year (parts of 1980 and 1981) of collecting newspaper stories on infanticide in Los Angeles, deliberate methods such as stabbing, smothering, and throwing a newborn out of a fourth-storey window were reported.

Placing the Child in A Dangerous Situation

Placing the child in a dangerous situation such as the jungle or the Arctic tundra appears to be the most widely practiced method of deliberate infanticide. While this would appear little different from outright killing, the difference is that the individual does not actually take the child's life, does not "shed blood." Apparently, the even slight distance from killing created by this difference is important, since so many societies and individuals choose this form. In addition, several researchers speak of the reluctance with which this abandonment is done and the need to rationalize it. B. Gray (personal communication) said that the Yaudapu Enga of New Guinea tell stories of supernatural beings who take abandoned children and rear them to live privileged lives.

Abandonment

In other cases, children are abandoned where there is more hope of their survival. Langer (1974) mentions that in 1833, 164,319 babies were left with foundling hospitals in France; few survived. Babies are still being left at hospitals and churches in both the developing and the developed countries today.

"Accidental" Death

"Accidents" that seem suspicious have occurred both historically and recently. A common form in nineteenth-century Europe was "overlying," where a baby in bed with its parents would be found smothered to death in the morning. It is clear from the literature that this was often a covert form of infanticide (Langer, 1974; Shorter, 1977). Other types of "accidents" that are sometimes not accidental include burns, which are frequently reported in contemporary literature on child abuse as well as in the past (Gil, 1970; Kellum, 1974).

Excessive Physical Punishment

Excessive physical punishment can range from what is now called "the battered-child syndrome" where children are beaten (sometimes lethally) to situations in the past where conditions such as epilepsy were attributed to demoniacal possession, and "the sufferer was thrashed soundly to expel the demon" (Radbill, 1974:3). In child abuse today, the excuse of "beating the devil" out of a child is still sometimes heard. Gil (1970) comments that one common "cause" of contemporary child abuse in the United States is an unreasonable level of expectation for children's behavior. As is discussed later, children who are perceived as unattractive or difficult may be at higher risk of excessive physical punishment and even mortality.

Lowered Biological Support

A child who is allotted a disproportionately small amount of family resources in the form of food and medical attention experiences reduced biological support. Lack of necessary provisions due to poverty or scarcity (as in the case of famine) represents a fact of life, not a parental decision concerning allotment of resources and should not be defined as unconscious infanticide. It is when one or more family members receive resources at the expense of a particular infant or child that parental involvement in infant death may be invoked. This lack of support occurs in contemporary societies and has probably replaced conscious, overt infanticide in many cases. Differential infant mortality, particularly where female children are concerned, often reflects differential care (see, e.g., Singh, Gordon, and Wyon, 1965). As is discussed later in greater detail, not only female children but also closely spaced children, high birth-order children, children from large families, and children who are perceived as "difficult" have been identified as having a greater likelihood of experiencing such selective neglect (Scrimshaw, 1978). Emotional support may be generally withdrawn under similar circumstances and for similar reasons as physical support.

OVERT REASONS AND RESPONSIBILITY FOR INFANTICIDE

Hrdy (1979) classified infanticide among animals into five categories: exploitation (e.g., cannibalism), resource competition, parental manipulation, sexual selection, and social pathology. Table I records behaviors under three of these same categories—parental manipulation, competition for resources, and pathological behavior—as well as under the uniquely human category of "ritual and dynastic politics." Where appropriate, the likely "decision maker" in most societies is also indicated. Sexually selected infanticide, defined by Hrdy as gaining reproductive advantage by destroying another's offspring in order to produce one's own, is only anecdotally recorded for human populations. Nor has the consistent exploitation of other people's children as a food resource (e.g., cannibalism) been described for humans. Furthermore, while individual cases of stepparents mistreating stepchildren and favoring their own are contained both in folklore and in individual cases (see Daly and Wilson, Chapter 24, this volume), such behavior is best explained by the fact that the child is a poor vehicle for parental investment

Table I. Decision maker and proximate reasons for infanticide

	Decision maker			
	Society[a]	Birth atten- dant	Family	Mother or father
Parental manipulation				
Twins	X		X	X
Deformed, physical birth defects	X	X	X	X
Mental defects of infant	X	X	X	X
Mother dies			X	
Father dies			X	X
Bad omens at birth (zodiac, caul, year, etc.)	X			
Wrong sex (usually a girl)			X	X
Infant unattractive, disliked[b]				X
Mother labeled "defective" (e.g., retarded or epileptic)	X	X	X	
Avoid postpartum sex taboo (mother afraid will lose husband)				X
Did not want children				X
Hatred of spouse				X
Illegitimacy			X	X
Child not own (stepparent)				X
Competition for resources				
Overpopulation	X			
Famine or other disaster	X		X	X
Too large a family			X	X
Too close spacing			X	X
Ritual and dynastic politics				
Power (e.g., Herod, Richard III)	X			
Ritual sacrifice (Isaac)	X			X
Pathological behavior				X[c]

[a] By "society," a politically powerful figure in the society, unrelated to the infant, is indicated.
[b] This can occur with older infants and young children as well.
[c] While any member of society can exhibit such behavior, it is most frequently parents who hurt children due to pathological behavior.

by the stepparent rather than by competition for mating opportunities. There is no direct reproductive advantage to mistreatment of stepchildren because their elimination does not usually mean that the stepparent will then produce more offspring with the biological parent of the stepchildren.

Parental manipulation appears to be one of the most common reasons for infanticide in human populations. As defined by Hrdy (1979:16), this occurs when the death of an infant "will improve the chances for survival of either the mother or existing offspring, or otherwise lead to greater net reproduction fitness of either the mother or the father." In human infanticide, parental manipulation includes both overt and passive infanticide with children who are not likely to prosper. In many cultures, people feel they have no choice but to destroy an infant either for its sake or for that of other children in the family. For example, whereas in a few cases both twins are destroyed, in most cases, one, the male twin or else the stronger twin, is allowed to live. The feeling is that the mother cannot successfully nurse both twins, and that if she tried, both would die. Through infanticide, at least one twin has a chance (Lorimer, 1954; Howell, 1979).

In an analysis of 70 societies described in the Human Relations Area Files (HRAF) a unique anthropological resource that contains data for over 300 cultures organized by topic, Granzberg (1973) wrote that 18 societies did not permit one or both twins to live. He found this occurred predominantly in societies where it would have been difficult, if not impossible, to successfully rear both twins due to economic, technological, and ecological factors. Some peoples have similar feelings when the mother dies. In nomadic or peasant societies where the alternatives to breast milk are not a viable option, few babies survive if their mother dies in the intrapartum period or during the first few months postpartum. People feel it is better to get it over with and bury the baby with its mother.

Both physical and mental deformities are common reasons for infanticide (Ford, 1964; Montag and Montag, 1979). In many parts of the world, such children would have trouble surviving even if attempts were made to keep them alive, but in any case choices are often made to rear only children who are strong to begin with. As mentioned earlier, modern medicine has intensified the dilemma surrounding children with mental or physical defects since so many more can now be kept alive, but not without economic and emotional costs. In some instances, even if there is no apparent problem with the child, it is condemned because a parent (usually the mother) has an affliction such as mental retardation or epilepsy. For example, Wagley (1977:251) reports that the Tapirape did not allow the children of epileptic women to live, and they "were buried immediately after birth."

The quality of the parents' relationship may also influence the extent to which a child is perceived as a good investment. A mother who fears that she will lose her husband during several years of culturally mandated abstinence from sexual relations while nursing a child may prefer to lose one child in order to maintain the integrity of the family unit (e.g., the !Kung: see Howell, 1979). This may also increase survival chances for her other children. Illegitimate children, who will not have a father or appropriate support system, are also poor investments, as are children of parents who are at odds ("hatred of spouse," Table I) and who will presumably invest less in them.

Female infanticide is common to many societies (Carr-Saunders, 1922; Krzywicki, 1934; Dickeman, 1975). In such cultures, males are considered stronger and more valuable than females. Placing a higher value on male work, assigning important rituals to men only (as in India where a man must have a son to officiate at his funeral), giving most or all the political power to men, and having customs that dictate that men inherit to the detriment or exclusion of female heirs, all encourage the preservation of male infants and the devaluation of female infants. When the cost of rearing daughters is high, either due to lower prestige, the need to accumulate a dowry, or time lost suckling a daughter when it could be spent getting pregnant with a more desirable male child, parents and family members are less likely to keep a female child alive.

In sum, it could be argued that parentally manipulated infanticide in humans maximizes reproductive success by improving the quality of those children who do survive to reproduce and by directing parental investment to one's own children and children produced in a viable relationship. This idea is explored in more detail later in this chapter.

Competition for resources is interpreted narrowly by Hrdy (1979) to mean killing of an individual whose food (or other resources such as territory) could be utilized by another individual or family. In human populations, such infanticide may sometimes occur (an extreme example would be the Ik: Turnbull, 1972), but more often, decisions are made at the level of the society. Furthermore, the individual who benefits the most may not be the one who commits the infanticide. For example, the Tapirape only allow three children per family; all others must be exposed in the jungle. This policy is explicitly linked to scarce resources for the entire community (Wagley, 1977). Children of high birth order may be explicitly neglected in order to better provide for their older siblings (Scrimshaw, 1978). No clear line separates infanticide due to competition for resources from that due to parental manipulation, and there is considerable overlap between these two categories. (Note that this difficulty is not unique to human infanticide: Hrdy, 1979; Mock, Chapter 1, this volume.)

Infanticide in the context of ritual and purposes related to the maintenance of political power also occurs in human populations. The acquisition and maintenance of power can motivate infanticide on both large and small scales. In an example of the former, King Herod ordered the killing of all males under 2 years in Bethlehem shortly after the birth of Christ. He allegedly did this in order to preserve his throne,

since he had been told that a child had been born who would be
"King of the Jews" (Matt. 1:16). On a smaller scale, Richard III, an
English king of the fifteenth century, is said to have murdered his two
young nephews in the Tower of London in order to keep the throne
for himself. Ritual sacrifice, although rare in past times and virtually
nonexistent in the present, may similarly be interpreted as quest for
power. The prime motivation for infant sacrifice was the protection
of society at large. Hence, an infant might be sacrificed at planting
time in order to ensure a good harvest. Infant killing as a result of
individual pathological behavior occurs in most societies, although it
is very unevenly documented (see Daly and Wilson, Chapter 24, this
volume).

In general, Table I indicates that the decision maker in infanticide
is most often the infant's mother or father, although other family members may be involved. The family or individual is involved when the
reasons for the infanticide are both at the individual level and at the
societal level. The society tends to mandate infanticide in areas affecting the entire society in either ecological (overpopulation) or social
(illegitimacy) domains. It should be noted, however, that individual
reasons are not always acceptable to society, nor are social reasons
always acceptable to individuals. For example, some Eskimo women
apparently want daughters (Freeman, 1971).

Table I also includes reasons underlying unconscious decisions contributing to the death of a child. Individual and societal pressures operate in the same way as in the case of overt infanticide. When boys
are valued by societies and individuals, fewer resources are invested
in girls. This was dramatically illustrated by the Khanna study in India
which found that boys receive more food and medical care than girls,
and that the death rate in the first 5 years of life was considerably
higher for girls than for boys (Singh et al., 1965; Wyon and Gordon,
1971). It must be noted that although the "reasons" for unconscious
infanticide are sometimes explicitly voiced by parents as they discuss
their ill or deceased children, more often they represent interpretation
or even guesswork by the researcher who is observing and analyzing
a set of behaviors and their consequences, (e.g., Chandrasekhar,
1959:124–125).

IMPLEMENTATION OF INFANTICIDE

In general, the more overt and direct methods of infanticide are
more likely to be performed at nonfamily levels, by nonrelatives. The
mother is less likely to destroy her infant by violent means, but she
is also the one who most frequently implements the infanticide decision,
at least on the basis of reports in the available literature, although
her behavior may be very discreet, leaving few clues for researchers.

It is perhaps not that uncommon for a mother (and her midwife) to leave a "quiet" newborn female infant alone, but to stimulate and resuscitate a desired male baby. Implementation of infanticide by the mother is most common because she has the most opportunity (she can conceal infanticide by saying it was a stillbirth) and because in the case of birth defects or a female birth she may be "blamed" for the problem.

Lower biological and emotional support, both of which often correspond to the unconscious behavior that may lead to infant or child death, are almost always the result of maternal behavior. This is largely because in most societies; the mother is the prime controller and distributor of resources such as food and home medical care, is the most likely to seek health care outside the family, and is a major source of emotional support to her children.

Another important distinction between overt, deliberate infanticide and passive infanticide is that overt infanticide almost always occurs at birth or very shortly thereafter. In many cultures, such an infant is still not considered a legitimate member of society (see earlier). Howell (1979) specifically noted for the !Kung that infanticide is not considered murder. Life begins not at birth, but when the baby is acknowledged by the society through naming. It is far more difficult to deliberately kill a child who has been around for several years. Unconscious or passive infanticide, on the other hand, tends to occur after some time has elapsed, but even so it is most common within the first 2 years of life. The demise of an infant through neglect is usually due to a combination of nutritional, medical, and emotional deprivation. This can take agonizingly long.

INCIDENCE OF INFANTICIDE

Accurate data on actual frequencies of infanticide are virtually nonexistent. A great deal of ethnographic material is summarized in the HRAF. Because of the nature of anthropological research, these data derive from small societies, although the files themselves include representatives of fairly large populations, such as the Ibo of Nigeria, the Eskimo of Alaska and Canada, and the Aymara of Bolivia and Peru. The data were collected from the eighteenth century on, but the majority of reports are from twentieth-century populations.

Divale and Harris (1976) reported on a search of the HRAF files for populations having data on age–sex structure and where the presence or recent presence of warfare could be detected. Their analysis of 112 cultures (561 populations) that met these criteria also included a discussion on infanticide. While their sample was not random, they felt it was generally representative of the universe of preindustrial societies both because of its large size and because the universe of HRAF societies is reasonably representative of the world's major geographical regions (Divale and Harris, 1976). Table II is derived from their list of societies. Although the authors did not specify what they meant by words such as "common" and "occasional," a rough estimate of the incidence of infanticide may be obtained. Whereas all of the Asian societies listed practiced infanticide "commonly," and 58% of the African societies do so, few societies in Oceania were reported as societies "commonly" practicing infanticide. It should be noted, however, that there are no data on infanticide for 58% of those Oceanic societies. On the basis of the general ethnographic literature for the region, it is probably more frequent than indicated.

On a global basis, 36% of the preindustrial cultures in the sample of Divale and Harris practiced infanticide commonly, and 13% practiced it occasionally. It was clearly identified as not practiced in only 9% of the 112 cultures (Scrimshaw, 1983). These figures are in accordance with the historical and archeological literature cited at the beginning of this chapter, which suggests that human societies have practiced infanticide for a long time.

If data on overt infanticide are rare, evidence of differential care or passive infanticide is even more elusive. At best, indirect evidence may be sought for infanticide that emerges from the examination of sex differentials in mortality and morbidity (see also Johansson, Chapter 23, this volume). On a strictly biological basis, slightly more males than females are born, and slightly more males die at all ages. If sex differentials in mortality exist, males, not females, would be expected to die at higher rates (Stolnitz, 1956). Yet, in India, the opposite is the case. The Khanna study indicates that boys receive more food and medical care than girls (Singh et al., 1965) and that in the first 5 years of life, the female death rate was 74/1000/year compared to 50/1000/year for males (Wyon and Gordon, 1971).

Welch (1974) reported similar data from Bangladesh, where a girl is more likely to survive in a family with more boys than girls. Similarly, D'Souza and Chen (1980:258) found for Bangladesh "pronounced excess female mortality over male mortality." The postneonatal mortality rate for males in 1974 was 98.4/1000 live births while the female rate was 126.3. In all, the mortality rates for females were "significantly higher" through age four and then were normal through age 14 (D'Souza and Chen, 1980:260).

These are not isolated patterns. Ware (1981) noted that Asia, Jordan, Pakistan, and Sabah show greater infant mortality for female babies, while female mortality exceeds male mortality at ages 1–4 years in nine populations: Burma, India, Jordan, Pakistan, Sabah, Sarawak, Sri Lanka, Thailand, as well as Bangladesh. In Japan, recent evidence of

Table II. Frequency of infanticide in 112 societies: World area[a]

Frequency of infanticide	Asia		Africa		North America		Oceania		South America		Totals	
	n	%	n	%	n	%	n	%	n	%	n	%
Common	6	100	7	58	11	48	12	22	4	25	40	36
Occasional	0	—	0	0	3	13	4	7	7	44	14	12
Not common	0	—	0	—	1	4	1	2	0	—	2	2
Not practiced	0	—	0	—	3	13	6	11	1	6	10	9
No information	0	—	5	42	5	22	32	58	4	25	46	41
	6	100	12	100	23	100	55	100	16	100	112	100

[a] Table constructed from Human Relations Area Files data compiled by Divale and Harris (1976:533–535).

"passive" female infanticide is provided by work showing a significant rise in female mortality in 1966 due to accidents and violence (Kaku, 1975). The rate fell again the next year, while the rates for males remained unchanged for the period from 1961 through 1967. Kaku (1975) speculated that the 1-year rise in mortality was due to differential care because of the belief that girls born in that year, the year of the Fire-horse, were particularly ill fated.

According to reports from China, female babies are still sometimes drowned, and mothers of daughters are sometimes beaten and ill treated. In some rural areas, boys are said to outnumber girls 5:1 (Parks, 1983). In the Middle East, data from Jordan, Lebanon, Syria, and Palestinian Arabs document poorer nutritional status and higher mortality rates for girls than for boys from ages 1–5 (Cook, 1964; Kimmance, 1972). With the exception of some Latin American Indian groups (Scrimshaw, 1978; Chagnon 1968), there tends to be less evidence of higher female infant and young child mortality for Africa or for Latin America.

Based on such surveys, it appears that both lowered biological support as well as lowered emotional support are more common today than the more overt killing and exposure of infants that occurred in the past in societies ranging from hunter–gatherer to industrial (Dickeman, 1975).

CONVENIENCE OR ADAPTATION? BEYOND THE OVERT REASONS FOR INFANTICIDE AND RELATED BEHAVIORS

As Hrdy (1979) noted, since offspring are essential to the survival of any species, it is surprising at first to find behavior that contributes to the death of offspring; still stranger to imagine that there may be selection for such behavior. Up to this point, the reasons for infanticide or neglect discussed here have been those given by the members of societies that practice overt infanticide or give evidence of passive infanticide. The following discussion concentrates on the outsider's interpretation of possible underlying reasons for the practice. Anthropological, biological, and demographic perspectives are considered.

Population Control and Adaptation to the Environment

Historically, infanticide has been directly linked to fertility regulation. It is important to note that both from the perspective of the culture (emic perspective) and from the outsider's viewpoint (etic perspective), infanticide for the purposes of fertility regulation occurs both to regulate fertility within families and for the society as a whole. In some instances, the adaptive value of these practices may be quite distinct; that is, parental considerations and societal considerations may be separate. It must be noted, however, that sometimes parental behaviors follow social norms which may have developed as part of an overall societal adaptive strategy (either conscious or unconscious). Wrigley (1978) used the phrase "unconscious rationality" to refer to patterns of behavior in animals that benefit the species, even if individual members of the population are unaware of the consequences. Wrigley (1978) and others (Alland, 1970; Freeman, 1971) considered that something similar occurs in human behavior and may develop as a result of a trial and error process, comparable to the economic concept of "the invisible hand of the marketplace."

In fact, regulation of either familial or societal fertility is one of the most common reasons cited for overt infanticide (Abernathy, 1979; Dickeman, 1975; Carr-Saunders 1922). This is often expressed in terms of limiting the population in order to avoid food shortages. Firth (1961:202) wrote that the Tikopia practiced infanticide in proportion to available food. The midwife turns the baby face down at birth at a word from the father. This is done unwillingly, "with limited resources in mind," and only after the family already has at least one child of each sex. Elsewhere, societies limit population in relation to the scarcity of goods associated with prestige. "Competition for essential resources is replaced by competition for socially valued goods [Wilkenson, 1973:48]." Thus, the money that must be set aside for a dowry can make a female child less attractive to her parents (Scrimshaw, 1983).

The societies that explicitly state that they practice infanticide in order to limit population include such ancient cultures as the Greeks (Langer, 1974), large societies in the recent past such as Japan and China (Lorimer, 1954; Langer, 1974), and recent preindustrial cultures such as the Eskimo (Freeman, 1971), Mckenzie Dene (Helm, 1980), Australian aborigines (Howitt, 1904; Goodale, 1971), and the Jakun and Sakai of Malaya (Skeet and Blagden, 1906). Others, such as the Yaudapu Enga of New Guinea (B. Gray: personal communication) and the !Kung Bushmen (Howell, 1979; Lorimer, 1954) practice infanticide in order to increase spacing, but this also has the effect of reducing completed fertility rates.

When infanticide is consciously related to the need to regulate population size in relation to scarce resources, it is easy to see the link between behavior and adaptation to a specific environment (Dickeman, 1975). What is happening when the overt reason for infanticide is that females are of little value, especially in a society where they may do a great deal of the gathering or agricultural labor? What is the link when the overt reason is that the mother fears a long postpartum sex taboo will drive her husband away? Why were females declared less valuable? Why does the postpartum sex taboo exist? Anthropologists, ethologists, and biologists have discussed these questions in terms of adaptation in the biological sense.

Anthropological ecologists theorize that "beliefs and behaviors that affect fertility, death and disease rates are major factors in the adaptations of human societies. Over time, every society develops behavioral strategies which maximize gains and minimize losses in its population size relative to particular environments [Alland, 1970:203]." "Good" mini–max strategies improve these relations in terms of the numbers of individuals particular environments can support and are, therefore, adaptive in strictly biological terms. For any given biocultural adaptation, there is a maximum population level beyond which energy extraction may create irreversible environmental changes inimical to the survival of the group. This level has been called *carrying capacity*. When a population approaches carrying capacity, Malthusian checks on size may begin to operate, and the group may or may not become stabilized and avert environmental degradation by the evolution of more "successful" strategies (Alland, 1970:203). These theories help explain why behavior that is detrimental to individual survival (such as infanticide) may be practiced since the possibility of survival or the quality of life of the entire group may be enhanced if fewer individuals are present (Scrimshaw, 1978).

For example, female infanticide can be seen either as an intermediate mechanism for population control or as an end in itself. If infant mortality is viewed as a means of population control, it is of course more efficient to eliminate females; a few males could keep a population of females reproducing, but there is a limit to the number of offspring a woman can have during her reproductive span. Also, reducing the female population before their reproductive years will have a greater effect on population size than killing males at any age. Divale and Harris (1976) have taken the argument a step further by saying that female infanticide is indeed a form of population control, but that the rules and norms devaluing women arise from warfare, which places a premium on men as fighters. They argued that warfare and male-dominated social structures provide the motive for female infanticide, which is the real population regulation mechanism.

Critics of Divale and Harris (Hirshfeld *et al.*, 1978; Lancaster and Lancaster, 1978; Fjellman, 1979) have questioned both their data and their interpretation of the value of women. Divale and Harris (1976) admitted that the link with warfare appears weak, and that female infanticide can occur in the absence of warfare. Another problem is that it is not clear that either sex ratios or rates of infanticide are precisely reported for many of the societies they examined.

Other discussions of female infanticide acknowledge that the ultimate function may be the reduction of rates of population growth, but that the proximate utility may be maintenance of the social structure. The most detailed discussion of this idea is provided by Dickemann (1979a). In some cases, female infanticide served to offset heavy male mortality rates from hunting and warfare, but in other instances, it could be attributed to "asymmetrical marriage alliances." In societies such as India, China, and Europe, the preferential marriage was hypergamy, with women marrying men of higher castes or classes. Large dowries were necessary for a woman to do this. This created an excess of women at the top, and preferential female infanticide would then emerge. Thus, Dickemann argued that female infanticide is the consequence of male competition rather than the cause. However, in Europe, female celibacy was also a mechanism for dealing with the problem of excess women (Dickemann, 1979a; Trexler, 1973b). While an excess of women could constitute a societal problem, particularly where monogamy was the norm, the high cost of providing a dowry for a woman produced by the competition for good husbands would be enough to precipitate differential treatment of male and female infants.

Whether infanticide is practiced explicitly for population control or for other stated reasons, it must be recognized that it is more adaptive than one other common mechanism for fertility and population control: induced abortion. Under poor medical conditions, induced abortion carries with it higher risks than pregnancy and childbirth of maternal mortality and subsequent infertility due to infections. Thus, while infanticide carries a higher risk for the mother than if she had prevented a pregnancy and not gone through pregnancy and birth with their attendant risks, it is still safer than inducing an abortion under poor conditions (Tietze *et al.*, 1976). Abstinence, of course, is safer than either abortion or infanticide, and has also been used by many cultures, particularly to prolong intervals between births.

Maximizing Reproductive Success

The preceding section discusses infanticide and behavior leading to differential infant mortality as a mechanism for societal adaptation to a given environment, a means of preventing population growth beyond that which could be managed with existing resources. A completely different argument can be made along the lines that infanticide is a means whereby individuals maximize their own reproductive success. In the strictest sense, the biological concept of adaptation revolves around an individual's success in passing on his or her genes to subsequent generations.

Scientists studying nonhuman primates argue that in several species, males kill infants when they become the dominant male of a breeding unit (Hrdy, 1979; and chapters in Part II, this volume). The mothers of these infants go into estrus soon after their offspring's death and copulate with the new dominant males. If their infants had remained alive, it might have been several months to several years before the females were again ready to reproduce. By killing the offspring of the previous male, the new dominant male avoids protecting the previous male's offspring and at the same time increases his own chances of having offspring. Pregnant females have been suspected to "fake" estrus when a new male takes over their troop (Hrdy, 1977b). Hrdy pointed out that something similar occurs in human groups such as the Yanomamo, where a woman whose child is about to be killed by an invading male reminds the infanticidal male that he once coupled with her (Biocca, cited in Hrdy, 1977b). However, she stressed that at present, there is no evidence of a genetic basis for such behavior in humans or that males thereby gain increased reproductive success.

Direct extrapolations from nonhuman primates to human are not justified on the basis of current knowledge. While there is no clear evidence of a genetic imperative for human infanticide, there is evidence of social support for behavior that does, in fact, maximize reproductive success. For example, Trivers and Willard (1973) wrote that variations in sex ratios can be explained in terms of the potential reproductive values of the offspring of each sex. Parents can maximize their reproductive success by raising more children of the sex that is most likely to succeed reproductively. Thus, Dickemann's (1979a:323) discussion of female infanticide and social stratification elaborated the Trivers and Willard model with examples of stratified societies where "male reproductive success shows extreme variance, men of high rank acquire access to a disproportion of females." With the intense competition among women for high-status mates, a high-status family is better off producing fewer female offspring, in order to concentrate its resources on fewer dowries, and more male offspring who will stand a better chance of reproducing than will the females.

Some anthropologists have challenged this reproductive success model by arguing that it is incompatible with the ecological model of adaptation in terms of matching population size to environmental carrying capacity. Bates and Lees (1979), for example, believed that behaviors such as infanticide, which regulate population growth, can all be explained in terms of either biological advantage or social convenience. The problem is one of definition of proximate and ultimate explanations. The ultimate effect of behaviors such as infanticide is to reduce growth rates, which may, in fact, alleviate more immediate problems such as crowding and limited food supply.

Another biological argument concerning infanticide comes from the work of Blurton-Jones and Sibly (1978), who argued that !Kung women are probably maximizing their reproductive success by wide birth spacing, achieved in part with the aid of infanticide. After a careful analysis of environmental, nutritional, social, and individual factors, they suggested that without spacing, women would bear more children but may actually raise fewer to adulthood due to the problems of feeding self and children, physical costs of additional births, and similar factors. Thus, paradoxically, having fewer births may allow Bushmen women to actually raise more children to adulthood, thus passing on replicates of their genes to future generations (Blurton-Jones and Sibly, 1978).

Social Stability

As has already been discussed, one effect of preferential infanticide has been support of existing social structures such as hypergamy (Dickemann 1979a). In addition, societies with heavy male mortality can "avoid" the problem of "excess" females by eliminating them through preferential female infanticide. In societies such as the Tiwi, where females are highly valued and successful males have over 20 wives, excess males can be dealt with the same way and, in fact, are (Goodale, 1971). Another social explanation for female infanticide is described by Freeman (1971:1015) in an analysis of reasons for female infanticide among the Eskimo. He said that the decision is made by the baby's father, and that it is an "explicit demonstration of male dominance." Freeman suggested this demonstration functions to reduce household tension. While it is possible that reduction of tension is one outcome of female infanticide among the Eskimo, it is doubtful that this effect alone is sufficient justification for infanticide. Certainly the harsh environment that men more readily exploit under the adaptation system developed by the Eskimo as well as the higher mortality of males compared to females provide other reasons for the development of the practice. In a detailed examination of four Eskimo tribes, Riches (1974) showed a relationship between the harshness of the environment and female infanticide, where the tribes under the greatest pressure also had the highest sex ratio. However, most existing social structures are one or more levels "removed" from the basic problems of adaptation to the environment, and social structures that encourage differential infanticide (either legitimately or covertly) can still be considered as regulating population growth through this mechanism.

Family and Individual Concerns

Family and individual concerns often interact with social concerns as, for example, when infants of "unwed" mothers are at higher risk. However, the family or individual concerns come in to full play when infanticide is not mandated at the societal level, even though social pressures may influence the immediate behavior of the individual or family toward a specific child. Because of this, family and individual levels permit behavior that results in increased likelihood of infant and child mortality, albeit in many cases not explicitly infanticide.

Such behaviors include failure to nurse newborns in situations where substitutes are unavailable or dangerous, failure to care properly for physical and emotional needs of infants and children, failure to feed children properly, and failure to seek timely and appropriate medical attention. For these behaviors, distinctions need to be made between lack of knowledge of proper procedures (such as how to identify severe illness in a child) and failure to act when the parent knows what ought to be done. It is here that differential care becomes a useful concept. When one observes different children in the same family being treated differently, as in the case of the Khanna study (Wyon and Gordon, 1971) in India or Wray and Aguirre's (1969) work in Colombia, then behavior is occurring that may lead to otherwise avoidable infant mortality. Often, the parent or parents do not engage in this differential treatment of infants and children on a conscious level but unconsciously favor some children.

These behaviors are extremely difficult to document, even in more overt instances such as child abuse and child abandonment. The best evidence comes from differential mortality rates, where mortality is higher than expected for given categories of infants and children (such as females or closely spaced children). In Latin America, Puffer and Serrano (1973:248–249) reported that infant deaths increase with ascending birth order. In Recife, Brazil, 13.7% and 13.9% of first- and second-born children, respectively, died in infancy, whereas 50.7% of fifth- or later-born children did so. In Monterrey, Mexico, the figures are 15% and 14.2% for first- and second-born, and 48.6% for fifth or higher births. In both Greater Santiago, Chile, and in Monterrey, the infant mortality rates were 40/1000 live births for first-born children and 90/1000 for fifth or higher birth orders.

Parity above five has been associated with higher infant mortality in many studies (Wyon and Gordon, 1971; Radovic, 1966; Roberts and Tanner, 1963). It is difficult to sort out behavioral and biological factors for this category of high mortality since high-birth order children are born to older women who also might have been physically depleted by earlier pregnancies. Some studies have separated the effects of age from parity and found that high parity does have an effect on infant mortality (Oxhorn, 1955; Omran, 1971; Wolfers and Scrimshaw, 1975). In an analysis of data from British Columbia, Newcombe (1965) found that the increased risk of infant death at higher birth order was independent of the mother's age at birth. In discussing differences between the mothers of normal and of malnourished children in India, Graves (1977) noted that mothers of malnourished children felt significantly more negative about the pregnancy that produced the malnourished child. The index and control children were of similar age, but the index children were of higher parity than the control children. Aguirre (1966) went a little further in describing infants and young children being "allowed to die" when attacked by disease, calling this "masked infanticide."

Another susceptible group of children appears to be members of closely spaced pairs. Kwashiorkor, the synergistic effect of malnutrition and infection, has long been described as the disease that affects the elder of two children when it is replaced at the breast by a younger sibling. The Khana study reported that birth interval is the greatest influence on mortality in the first year of life. In that population, both infant mortality and second-year mortality decline as the birth interval lengthens (Wyon and Gordon, 1971).

An analysis of urban Ecuadorian data showed that the second child of a closely spaced pair was more likely to die (Wolfers and Scrimshaw, 1975). The analysis of the fertility histories of roughly 2000 women who had two or more pregnancies controlled for many obvious factors such as economic status of the family, mother's age at the child's birth, birth order, and sex. Nonetheless, postneonatal and infant mortality was strongly influenced by the interval between the conception of one child and the birth of another. While the survival chances of the first child of a pair were somewhat influenced by birth interval, the second child was particularly susceptible if the interval was short and the first child was alive at the time the second was conceived. Thus, a family with a closely spaced pair of children appeared to "invest" more (financially and emotionally) in the care of the first child, who had already survived the critical first year of life (Scrimshaw, 1978).

There are many other discussions of differential care in the literature. In a discussion of differential mortality in India, Simmons *et al.* (1980:14), stated that "other things being equal, a child's survival will be determined by how much it is wanted," usually along the two dimensions of desired number of children and desired sex composition. In an analysis of sex differentials for infectious causes of death in Bangladesh, D'Souza and Chen (1980) stated that the reason for these differentials is probably neglect, especially in terms of feeding, which then renders an infant more susceptible to infection. In Korea, one study showed that for 100 male children under the age of 5, there were 85 visits to the health center in a year but only 50 visits a year for 100 female children (Ware, 1981).

In sum, the methods for passive infanticide include outright abandonment as well as neglect in the areas of feeding (breast feeding and supplementation as well as nonbreast feeding), sanitation, medical care, supervision, and attention. The undesirability of a particular child is sometimes explicitly voiced by parents as they discuss their ill or deceased children, but more often the occurrence of passive infanticide is a matter of judgment by the researcher, either by means of direct observation of parental behaviors or of inference.

The field of child abuse has documented another level of individual and family behaviors that sometimes lead to infant mortality. This is discussed by Daly and Wilson (Chapter 24, this volume) as is the larger issue of differential treatment of children within the same family. In the case of both differential treatment and in many instances of child abuse, it must be pointed out that the expressed responsibility for the death shifts from the parent to other factors, which have labels like "illness," or "he was so bad I had to hit him." The parent no longer feels directly responsible but lets fate or other forces take over.

It is important to point out, however, that many contemporary behaviors that lead to such "unnecessary" infant mortality are not adaptive since the death of the abused child does not increase the reproductive success of its parents and, in fact, probably has just the opposite effect. In contrast, in developing countries, children who receive better food and care at the expense of others are indeed more likely to survive than if all children in the family had received equal resources.

To summarize, family and individual concerns that motivate either overt or passive infanticide can probably be attributed to several underlying functions. These functions do appear to go beyond mere convenience for family members and include maximization of biological (i.e., reproductive) fitness in some instances and family-size control in others, particularly when fertility control has failed or has not been among the options culturally available. Family-size regulation on this "micro" level may be carried out independent of (and even in contradiction with) the cultural population policy, or it may be facilitated by culturally permitted behaviors.

CONCLUSIONS

Infanticide in humans has occurred throughout history. It has taken and continues to take many forms, and it occurs not only with newborns but with older infants and occasionally in young children. Practiced overtly and decisively (usually at birth or shortly thereafter) in the past, in present times it is forbidden in most settings, and so unwanted children experience neglect and abandonment instead. On the surface, such destructive behavior seems unreasonable. Analysis of infanticide at several levels, however, has revealed valid reasons for this behavior, reasons that may be expressed overtly in some cases and otherwise remain unconscious. In human populations, infanticide functions as a means of fertility control at both population and family levels. The practice of infanticide for this reason is made culturally and personally acceptable in many societies by a definition of life that requires a "waiting" period after birth before full membership in society is bestowed on an infant. Such practices and definitions have been particularly common in societies where the prevention of pregnancy was ineffective, unknown, or culturally unacceptable, and this is still the case today in many developing nations. Induced abortion, a poor substitute method of fertility control with a higher cost in maternal lives and impaired fertility, accompanied infanticide throughout most of human history. Along with population and family-size regulation, infanticide frequently serves as a means of maximizing the resultant output (in terms of number and quality of offspring reaching adulthood) of parental investment by allowing parents to select the healthiest, most desirable children to rear. More generally, then, infanticide has served a second purpose: that of maximizing individual reproductive success. In most societies, the rationale for infanticide represents a intertwining of societal (i.e., social structural) and familial goals and probably serves multiple purposes. Thus, it is often difficult to assign a single ultimate utility to this behavior.

A question can be raised about parallels between human infanticide and that in nonhuman primates or even that in other mammals. To date, there is no evidence for any heritable component or genetic basis for human infanticide, and the question itself may even be slightly absurd. There is already conjecture, but still inconclusive evidence, however, of a biologically programmed period during which the critical emotional attachment of mother and infant takes place. If such an attachment period can be substantiated in humans, one would predict that cultural and personal interventions to destroy or abandon an infant would occur before this period of attachment is reached. In the case of deferred infanticide or passive infanticide, an attachment may never be formed with an unwanted child or one not eligible for rearing. Clearly, careful research is needed to address questions concerning the time course of infanticide, neglect, and abuse vis-à-vis the period of most intense formation of the mother–child bond.

Some reasons for infanticide will be slow to disappear. For example, the treatment of deformed children is a complex issue. Modern technology, which can produce a good quality of life for many such children, is still unavailable or unaffordable for many, and even with it, such children are very costly to rear. Some parents do not want to make the attempt, even with the technology and financial resources at hand, because the "quality" of their offspring is still an issue. The complexities of infanticide or even differential care, when infants are physically or mentally compromised, will continue to be debated for a long time. Likewise, social pathologies are unlikely to disappear. People will still occasionally kill or neglect children for individual gain or for less rational motives. Perhaps the greatest tragedy of all in today's world is that modern contraceptives and even induced abortion have not sufficiently replaced infanticide as a means of fertility control. Further, infanticide has been superceded in many societies by abandonment, neglect, and differential care rather than methods of fertility control less costly in terms of lives and resources. The pressures on scarce family resources and various social pressures instead have mandated what Neel (1970) called a "far crueler" process of neglect and abuse. Ironically, the decline of infanticide may result in more suffering for older infants and children, and even adults, than when an infant's fate, be it life or death, was determined swiftly, early, and irrevocably (Dickeman, 1975).

ACKNOWLEDGMENTS

I am greatly indebted to Mildred Dickemann for her valuable comments on earlier versions of this chapter and to Sarah Blaffer Hrdy and Glenn Hausfater for their superb editing. Glenn, Sarah, Mildred, and our colleagues who participated in the Conference on Infanticide in Animals and Man in the summer of 1982 also helped shape the theoretical considerations in this chapter and added greatly to my understanding of infanticide in nonhuman populations. I would also like to thank Susan Holtby for her assistance with the bibliography.

23 Deferred infanticide: Excess female mortality during childhood

Sheila Ryan Johansson

INTRODUCTION

In all human cultures, some infants are either murdered or neglected in a manner almost certain to induce premature death (Dickeman, 1975). As a systematic practice, however, infanticide seems to be more pervasive and intense among those cultures that have not yet urbanized and industrialized. Not all premodern or "primitive" cultures practice institutionalized infanticide, but among those that do, the anthropological evidence seems to indicate that female babies are more likely to be eliminated than male babies (Harris, 1975). Technically, of course, infanticide refers only to the deliberate elimination of human infants under 1 year of age, but here are considered a set of related phenomena extending well beyond infancy, since the specific forces that lead adults to devalue female newborns are diverse and do not necessarily cease to operate once the first year of life has passed.

In this chapter, it is argued that in European and European-settled countries, unwanted female children were covertly eliminated after infancy during childhood and adolescence. By this it is meant that from the ages of 1–3 years (sometimes later) through 19 years (an age at which most European females were still unmarried and free from childbearing), girls died at higher rates than boys. This excess female mortality in youth was most widespread and most pronounced during the nineteenth century, in the early and middle phases of European economic development. As European societies became industrially mature and heavily urbanized, excess female mortality disappeared. This has led some researchers to blame excess female mortality in the pre-childbearing years on the rise of capitalism, a claim that is misleading if by "capitalism" is meant the process of industrialization itself (Tabutin, 1978). The fact that most countries exhibiting excess female mortality (hereafter EFM) were still preponderantly agricultural during the process of economic modernization has led others to blame the timeless stresses of agrarian life on the female constitution (Shorter, 1982). In general, all of the newer research on EFM in both Europe and the currently developing world has emphasized the determining role of socioeconomic forces to the exclusion of biological or sociobiological explanations. This chapter continues to do so, while giving greater consideration to the interaction between specific disease climates and the monetization of agricultural production, in the context of social and economic forces that shape short-term parental strategies involving investment in children.

It is argued here that the rigors of traditional agrarian life were not innately hard on European females vis à vis males. Wherever women and girls were active and important in traditional agriculture, they were not subject to systematic EFM. Since the roles of women in premodern agriculture varied from time to time and place to place in traditional Europe, there were no clear patterns of EFM much before the nineteenth century. As economic modernization spread, however, particularly in agriculture, it gave specific cash values to various forms of farm production. Since wives and daughters were disproportionately involved in production for household consumption (which continued to remain outside the cash economy) while men and boys were disproportionately involved in production for the market, the labor contributions of women and girls were perceived as less and less valuable to the family economy relative to those of men and boys. Household resources available for investment in children were concentrated more and more on sons. This created a demographic pattern in which agricultural development was accompanied by declining child mortality for both sexes, but death rates for boys fell faster than those for girls until EFM emerged as a result of differential rates of decline. By the late nineteenth century, agrarian Europe was generally characterized by EFM before childbearing although rarely, if ever, by female infanticide. (Infanticide, in all probability, was minimized early on by the interaction between religious norms that forbade it—while saying nothing about the necessity for equal treatment after infancy—and the determination of civil magistrates to both detect and punish the deliberate elimination of young infants).

In the meantime, wherever development led to modern forms of industrialization and urbanization, it generally created a relative abundance of paying jobs for young girls. In the cities and regions where young women found remunerative employment, their continued value to the family economy eliminated youthful EFM and gave females the usual mortality advantages over males. Once most urban women were married and subject to the rigors of childbearing as well as the other stresses and deprivations of the married state, however, EFM often persisted.

Meanwhile, the fact that EFM at the national level often peaked in late adolescence and the early twenties was a reflection of the strength of tuberculosis in the overall cause of death pattern. In fact, the particular age-specific incidence of EFM in Europe reflected the age-specific problems of tuberculosis itself more than any other single factor.

By way of reviewing the evidence for the foregoing hypotheses, it is necessary to first consider (1) the nature of traditional misconceptions about male/female mortality differentials; (2) the apparent relationship between life expectancy at birth and the level of EFM in modern demographic data; and (3) scattered demographic data from pre-nineteenth-century populations. Subsequently, this chapter reviews the history of Swedish data on age–sex mortality differentials in the context of its experience with agricultural modernization and the spread of tuberculosis in order to analyze the postulated interactions in greater detail.

MALE/FEMALE MORTALITY DIFFERENTIALS

Traditional Misconceptions

In his study of global mortality trends in the century prior to 1950, George Stolnitz (1956) noted that the history of mortality differentials between the sexes had never received much scholarly attention. As a result, several misconceptions had received an undeserved currency: (1) regardless of time, place and life expectancy at birth, females have a natural survival advantage over males; and (2) females die at a higher rate than males only in the reproductive years as a result of the biological risks inherent in pregnancy and childbirth (Stolnitz, 1956:32). Having reviewed the available historical data, Stolnitz argued that before the 1920s, it was typical to find that females died at higher rates than males from childhood through mid-life. Moreover, wherever EFM existed, male/female differentials were generally most pronounced in adolescence, not during the childbearing years. Stolnitz had no definitive explanation for his unexpected findings and, thus, they seemed to pass unnoticed by most demographers, even historical demographers.

In the early 1960s, the United Nations did a survey of world mortality patterns (using exclusively twentieth-century data) slightly more extensive than the one carried out by Stolnitz (1956). Essentially, one result of the United Nations' survey was a graph of age-specific death rates for males and females determined for populations characterized by three different values of e_0, the demographic variable denotating expected longevity at birth. The value of e_0 is used here to represent the number of years to be lived, on average, by the members of a cohort (or group of people born in the same time period) subject to a given set of age-specific probabilities of dying. It is important to point out, however, that since the expectation of life at birth (e_0) is heavily influenced by infant mortality, this measure does not provide a good estimate of the subsequent years remaining to an individual who has already matured.

The results of the United Nations' study are shown in Fig. 1 and indicate that when life expectancy at birth (e_0) is under 30, EFM begins on average at the age of 5 and persists markedly until women reach their forties. When e_0 is as high as 50, EFM is greatly diminished and confined almost entirely to childhood and adolescence. As e_0 rises to modern levels, exceeding 60 or more, EFM disappears. Males die at higher rates than females at every age, a pattern that has been called biologically "natural" whenever degenerative diseases dominate cause of death patterns (Madigan, 1957).

The United Nations' synthesis of national mortality patterns clearly implies that there is a regular inverse association between EFM and e_0, an association so regular that it could be suspected that biological factors were at work. But Stolnitz himself suggested that it would never prove easy to explain EFM, because genetically influenced mortality propensities (if they existed) are rarely expressed independently of a specific environmental context. Nevertheless, the question remains, do females have some biologically derived propensity to die at higher rates than males during childhood and adolescence when life is hard and life expectancy low? It is possible also to ask whether or not it is biologically inevitable that mature females (those in their childbearing years) die at higher rates than males when fertility is high and overall life expectancy low? While the former is open to doubt, almost all authorities have agreed that it was natural and expected to find EFM in the childbearing years, irrespective of the social and economic conditions females might have found themselves in. In other words, all things being equal between males and females, the latter would have died at higher rates than males solely because of the risks associated with pregnancy and birth.

But this is not what modern data show: To date, the most detailed examination of EFM in both childhood and adulthood has been done by Samuel Preston (1976). His cross-national comparisons of *Mortality Patterns in National Populations* (based on data from 140 national

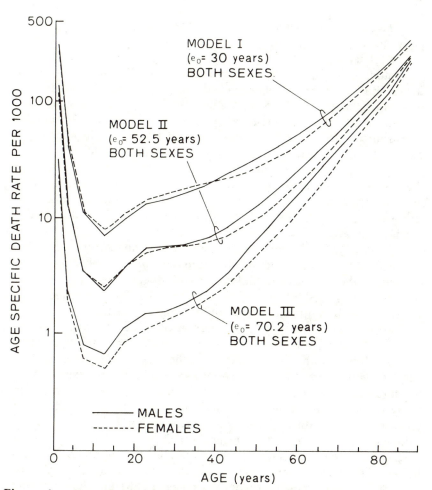

Figure 1. Age- and sex-specific death rates as a function of the expectation of life at birth. (From United Nations, 1962.)

populations, some of which involve the same country at different time periods) argued that EFM in both childhood and adulthood is the result of social and economic discrimination against young girls, the effects of which are carried over into adulthood. When e_0 is low and most childhood death is caused by infectious and parasitic diseases, girls die of these causes at higher rates than boys because they are relatively less well fed and cared for than their male counterparts. Even those females who survive into adulthood are in a relatively debilitated state, making it harder than necessary for them to survive infections. Since differentials for particular causes of death covaried positively from population to population, Preston could not find a basis for arguing that EFM at any age was due to biological factors that impinged uniquely on a particular disease (1976:132) or even a particular stress like childbearing.

Preston explained his findings by arguing that EFM was most severe at low life expectancies because low life expectancy societies were agrarian in character. It was in agriculture that females were most devalued, particularly as girls, and hence least well treated. As societies industrialized and urbanized, their overall levels of life expectancy rose while sex discrimination declined and, with it, EFM.

It is also of interest to note that Preston's findings with respect to EFM and e_0 differ from those of the United Nations. Whereas the latter had found EFM only in childhood and adolescence at moderate levels of life expectancy at birth, Preston found EFM only in adulthood at comparable levels of e_0.

Since Preston wrote, anthropologists and demographers have contributed further evidence to substantiate the social and economic perspective on the causes of EFM. In modern India and Bangladesh where EFM in infancy, childhood, and adulthood is still quite marked in national-level data, anthropologists and demographers have observed in rural areas the types of parental behavior that, they believe, produces EFM through most of life. Starting in infancy, girls are stinted nutritionally, emotionaly, and with respect to medical care (D'Souza and Chen, 1980:257–258). In addition, in some villages that are relatively well disposed to girls, the type of aggressive childhood grabbing that increases a boy's share of his household's food supply is discouraged in girls because it is uncouth and immodest. (The author is indebted to J. C. Caldwell of Australia for this observation.)

Thus far, twentieth-century, national-level, demographic data and the qualitative observations derived from current field research have created a rather simple picture of the causes of EFM. Low life expectancies at birth characterize agrarian societies, agrarian societies devalue females, particularly young ones, and this devaluation is translated into forms of material discrimination/deprivation that artificially raise the death rates of young girls and those of adult females. As the traditional agrarian sector is diminished by modernization, e_0 rises, discrimination against girls is reduced, and EFM disappears: first in childhood, then in adulthood (as shown by Preston), or the reverse if the United Nations is used. There seems to be little room for either biology or sociobiology in this story.

Were a sociobiological theory of EFM in childhood and adolescence to be proposed, it would presumably focus on the supposedly superior reproductive advantages sons would confer over daughters (i.e., more grandchildren would be produced by the former than the latter). But I do not know of any empirical evidence that has, in fact, demonstrated that a European son was more likely to have a larger number of surviving children than a daughter, although in fact such calculations could be made using family reconstitution data. There is no sociobiological formulation of EFM in childhood, although Dickemann (1979a) has formulated one that covers infanticide.

But matters are not that simple. Socioeconomic theories about the causes of EFM are based on quantitative data that come from late nineteenth- and early twentieth-century Europe, combined with qualitative/quantitative observations that come from present-day India, Bangladesh, and other developing countries. Late nineteenth-century European agriculture was far from traditional, and the sex differentials characterizing the national aggregates reflect the complex distortions imposed on earlier patterns by the very process of agricultural modernization, not traditional agriculture itself. The agrarian sector of most developing countries is also in the middle of modernization and commercialization. Thus, current mortality differentials may not be representative of the "traditional" agrarian past.

In addition, parental strategies used in currently developing countries to eliminate unwanted daughters may have little in common with those once used in Europe. European data do not suggest any marked resort to female infanticide. As indicated in Fig. 2, European data (line B) seem to indicate that girls were most harshly treated from the age of 5 or so to mid-adolescence, whereas in the Indian subcontinent, the force of parental displeasure is felt less keenly after the first year of life until childbearing begins (Fig. 2, line C). It is not at all unlikely that in the European case, a different cause of death patterns based partly on nonvolitional factors is involved.

For example, the Coale and Demeny, *Regional Model Life Tables* (1966) (which are based almost exclusively on historical data from European countries), show that within Europe, EFM mortality in childhood began at quite different ages from those in the Third World and ended at different ages as well, even when overall level of life expectancy at birth is controlled. In the model life tables based on the historical experience of Southern European countries (the "South" family), when $e_0 = 20$ (level 1), EFM begins at age 1 and persists through advanced middle age; the differentials exhibited are quite large. In the set of tables based on the historical experience of Scandinavia (the "North" family), when e_0 is also 20, sex differentials are much less marked and involve a narrower range of ages. When e_0 rises to 55 (mortality level 15), EFM has disappeared entirely from both North and South, whereas it is still evident in a mild form in both the "East" and "West" family of tables, based, respectively, on the historical experience of Eastern Europe and Western Europe (the latter with some overseas European and non-European datasets included). In the middle

MALE/FEMALE DEATHS

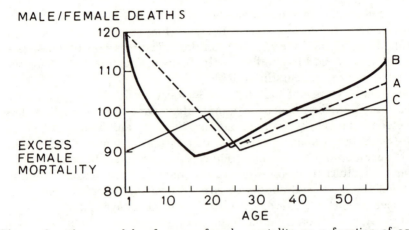

Figure 2. Three models of excess female mortality as a function of age. Models A, B, and C are loosely based on the actual experience of three different areas. Model A approximates many present-day African countries where excess female mortality is absent in infancy and childhood but present in the childbearing years. Model B represents the historical experience of nineteen-century Europe. Model C represents present patterns in the Indian subcontinent. There, excess female mortality is most severe in infancy and diminishes (temporarily) through childhood. In Europe, there is no infanticide. Excess female mortality appears in late childhood, reaches a peak in adolescence, and diminishes thereafter.

ranges of e_0, regional experience is even more diverse. The differences are significant but not necessarily indicative of finely tuned differences in parental behavior.

The Coale and Demeny "regions" are aggregations of national-level data. At the national level itself, variation is even more pronounced. As discussed in the section on Sweden, subnational variation shows even more pronounced contrasts. It is this variation that gives a more fruitful approach for teasing apart biological from socioeconomic pressures before and during the modernization process, as these impinged upon EFM.

THE HISTORICAL EXPERIENCE OF EUROPE

Excess mortality in infancy and childhood may well antedate the evolution of human cultures, since it has been detected in some primate groups (Dittus, 1979). In addition, some paleodemographers working with prehistoric skeletons have speculated that the apparent preponderance of male skeletons in adulthood (especially among those who seem to have attained the age of 40 or more) also indicates EFM among early hunting–gathering populations (Hadingham, 1979:140). Almost invariably, the supposed excess of males is attributed to the rigors of childbearing (Akekseev, 1973–1974:76), although infanticide is sometimes suggested as well. (Since it is difficult to age and sex prehistoric skeletons, others have discounted these apparent indications of the early appearance of EFM.) From the ancient world to the early modern period, scattered reference to female infanticide exists, and some medieval census-type documents have been interpreted as evidence for large-scale female infanticide (Coleman, 1976). Until the sixteenth century, demographic documentation is so uneven and its interpretation so fraught with problems that the existence of female infanticide in Europe remains doubtful. (A possible exception may be Renaissance Florence. See Trexler, 1973a.)

From the seventeenth century onward, however, the spread of parish registration (whereby local religious authorities registered baptisms, burials, and marriages) had become sufficiently widespread and reliable in Western Europe that some tentative conclusions can be drawn (see especially Wrigley and Schofield [1981:249–251; Tables 7.19 and 7.22]). There is little, if any, evidence for the systematic, stable, widespread elimination of females at or near the time of birth. Certain parishes at certain time periods seem to have a suspiciously high ratio of male baptisms, but variation at the parish level is of a very high order (Wall, 1981). Generalizations based on the experience of a parish or two over a brief span of time are inherently risky.

However, there are some seventeenth-century localities that display EFM in childhood and many that do so during the childbearing years. Again, variation is the only consistent rule, since at one time one group of parishes will show EFM in childhood whereas a neighboring group will not. Over time, they may exchange patterns. Some will show EFM in adulthood for one cohort and not the next. Amidst all the variation, it is hard to see any consistent pattern from place to place or even class to class. Moreover, sex-linked mortality differentials were neither large nor consistent. Very possibly, the narrowness of the differentials and their instability in time and space indicate the predominance of biological and ecological factors in the underlying patterns of causation.

For example, if a group of peasants whose diets were marginal were examined, any shortage of essential vitamins and minerals, especially iron, would be more harmful to females than males. Iron plays a key role in immunological mechanisms. Yet females, especially those menstruating or pregnant, need larger amounts of it than males. If both sexes were equally badly nourished, females would be disproportionately harmed by the resulting deficiency of iron, irrespective of other social and economic conditions (Weinberg, 1978). No doubt many other possible biologically linked factors were also at work.

But by the nineteenth century, the picture is quite different. Almost

every European country for which there is reliable data on age and
sex mortality differentials shows a pattern of marked EFM in childhood
and adolescence (Tabutin, 1978), which means that this pattern pre-
dominated consistently at the local levels as well. In between, the
transition is complex and the role of random variation less likely.

One of the first countries to show marked, widespread, EFM in childhood and adulthood was colonial America. The differentials calculated
by Fogel and his group based on geneological records from the seventeenth and eighteenth centuries show very heavy EFM in childhood;
death rates for young females aged 1–9 were sometimes more than
twice as high as those for males (R. Fogel: personal communication,
based on data compiled by the History of Human Mortality Project).
Females were at a disadvantage in both Northern and Southern colonies
but especially in the latter, possibly because of a susceptibility to malaria (see Demos, 1965:54; Rutman and Rutman in Vinovskis, 1972:305).
Colonial America was a relatively wealthy place; food supplies were
abundant. But it was a colonial outpost where much agricultural production was already market-oriented. Certainly the sex-specific demand
for child labor, as measured by the sex-ratios of white indentured servants imported from England, was heavily male. For every one female
imported to do mostly domestic work on the farm, 8–10 males were
indentured and transported (Wells, 1975). The relative undesirability
of female indentured servants might have had something to do with
the fact that from the seventeenth century onward, the English-speaking
people were developing a prejudice against heavy field work for girls
and women. Some women continued to do it, but the reluctance to
use daughters in the field might have made them seem increasingly
burdensome to support in an essentially rural economy.

Throughout the nineteenth century, EFM remained a fact of American
mortality (Condran and Crimmon, 1979:12), but it diminished with the
rise of industrialization and urbanization. In Massachusetts in the early
nineteenth century it was already absent in Boston although present
in small towns and most rural communities (Vinovskis, 1972:211).

Although EFM was never so pronounced in England as it was in
America, the first national-level data, covering the late 1830s, show a
clear if muted pattern of EFM (Table I). It must be remembered, however, that by 1830, England had been industrializing and urbanizing
for 50 years. As shown in Table II, EFM was not found among 5–15
year olds in any of the industrialized counties of England and Wales,
whereas it remained very marked in the predominantly rural counties.

The same pattern can be found on a smaller scale at the subcounty
level. Cornwall, a moderately industrial county in the late 1830s, exhibited moderate EFM, much like England as a whole. But within the
county, its mining districts (which provided a relatively abundant sup-

Table I. Age- and sex-specific
death rates in England
and Wales (1838–44)[a]

Age	Males	Females
0–1	205.1	154.4
0–4	70.7	60.4
5–9	9.3	9.0
10–14	5.0	5.5*
15–24	8.0	8.3*
25–34	9.6	10.1*
35–44	12.5	12.4
45–54	17.8	15.5
55–64	31.4	27.8
65–74	66.1	58.8
75–84	144.9	132.0
85–94	296.5	275.5

[a] Age groups in which females died
at higher rates than males are starred.
From Ninth Report of the Registrar-
General, England and Wales, 1845 (p.
177).

ply of employment opportunities for young girls) were not characterized
by EFM in childhood, whereas the predominantly agrarian districts,
in which girls could find employment only as servants, were invariably
those in which girls died at higher rates than boys (Johansson, 1977).

The European country that was characterized by EFM for the longest
time period was Ireland. It was not until the middle of the twentieth
century that modern female-favoring mortality differentials established
themselves. In his study of Irish demography, Kennedy (1972) argued
that the "gross subordination" of women among Irish farm families
was responsible for the persistence of high levels of EFM. Irish farm
wives and daughters worked very hard. But they worked for the family,
not for a wage or the cash sale of a crop. Males who did so were
invariably regarded as more productive and more deserving of whatever resources a family had. As a result, Irish females were overworked
and underfed and more likely than males to die of the prevailing infectious diseases.

The interesting feature of EFM in Ireland is that mortality differentials favoring males became more marked through the nineteenth and
early twentieth century. Kennedy does not comment on this trend, but
it is consistent with the observation that traditional agrarian life tends
to minimize differential investment in sons and daughters, whereas
agricultural commercialization tends to temporarily maximize it, and
with it EFM in childhood.

Table II. Age-specific death rates, males and females, England, 1837[a]

County	Proportion in agriculture	Age-specific death rates (5–15)/10,000		Excess female mortality	
		Male	Female	Yes	No
Very rural					
Bedford	62	58	65	X	
Huntingdon	62	57	63	X	
Hereford	62	46	51	X	
Cambridge	61	71	71	X	
Rutland	61	44	55	X	
England and Wales	34	61	60		X
Very industrial					
Cornwall	38	50	52	X	
Northumberland	27	59	54		X
Stafford	27	68	62		X
Durham	21	84	72		X
West York	20	62	56		X
Surrey	17	71	69		X
Lancaster	11	71	65		X
Middlesex (London)	4	84	78		X

[a] From W. Farr (1974:570). *Mortality in Mid 19th Century Britain* (Vital Statistics or the statistics of health, sickness, diseases and death, 1837a). Reprinted in the *Pioneers of Demography* series, Gregg International, 1974:570.

In Fig. 3, a simplified model of EFM in childhood in Europe is presented. The traditional agrarian era is characterized by minimal (or variable) sex-linked mortality differentials in childhood. As agricultural modernization begins and spreads, EFM mortality in childhood becomes the rule. Its appearance is generally a result of the fact that while childhood mortality declined for both sexes, it fell faster for males than females. This, in turn, is related to the fact that the commercialization of agriculture tends to enhance the real or perceived value of male labor relative to that of both wives and daughters. Ultimately, industrialization and urbanization redresses this balance by first providing more employment opportunities for girls and ultimately by raising living standards to such a degree that differential investment ceases or continues without involving marked material deprivation. Child mortality continues to fall, but it generally falls faster for females than for males.

Meanwhile, it is generally in the middle or late stages of agricultural commercialization that most European nations began recording and

MALE/FEMALE MORTALITY
DIFFERENTIALS (AGE 5-25)

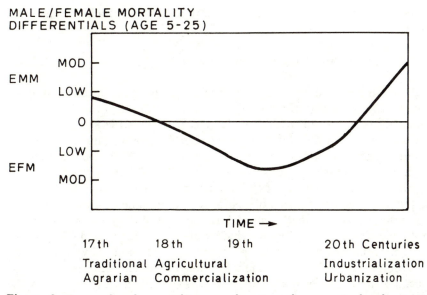

Figure 3. Excess female mortality as a function of economic development over time in Europe.

publishing data on age- and sex-specific mortality rates; these rates were used in the creation of model life-table systems like those of Coale and Demeny, and it is these rates that create the impression that EFM in childhood is invariably a function of low levels of life expectancy.

In one sense, this historical process is being reenacted in India at the present time. India has been in the throes of agricultural commercialization for many decades now, and her national aggregates are still dominated by this slowly modernizing agrarian sector. Thus, in the course of the twentieth century, mortality differentials for the two sexes in India have shown a slow increase in the male advantage over time, a phenomenon that has puzzled Indian demographers since the relative disadvantage of young girls has increased in a time of generally falling child death rates (Jain, 1975). In the meantime, there are areas in India that are free of EFM in childhood: some large cities, of course, but also rural areas of India in which female agricultural labor remains valuable and perceived as such (Miller, 1981).

There are few European countries, however, in which all the stages of EFM in childhood can be observed over the whole course of development using high quality data. The major exception is Sweden, hence its relevance for the historical study of EFM, despite the fact that EFM was never very pronounced there. In the following concluding section, Swedish national aggregates and provincial data are used in order to trace the emergence of EFM in childhood to the principal stages of economic modernization.

EXCESS FEMALE MORTALITY IN SWEDEN

Sweden's government began publishing national-level data on age–sex-specific mortality rates from the middle of the eighteenth century. Not only is it the oldest such series but it was and is still one of the highest quality data series produced in Europe (Kalvemark, 1977). From its inception, the parish-level data from which it was compiled could be used without major adjustments for underregistration or substantial age mid-reporting (Hofsten and Lundstrom, 1976). Its major shortcoming is the assignment of cause of death. In the eighteenth and nineteenth centuries, cause of death was determined by local pastors who were not necessarily medically knowledgeable (Widen, 1975:93). It was not until 1910 that Swedish death certificates were filled out by physicians.

When the Swedish government first began published mortality statistics, less than 10% of the population was urbanized, and only a small fraction of the population was involved in nonagricultural production. The agrarian sector was dominated by family farms that relied as much on the work of women and children as of men. Swedish peasant women were very hard working. One measure of their value to their husbands was that peasant brides did not generally bring their husbands a cash dowry. Swedish girls were used in a wide variety of tasks, including those that involved heavy field work and other forms of outdoor labor. It is not necessarily the case that males and females were equally valued, but girls were not necessarily more expensive to raise and endow than boys, and the labor services of adult women were essential to the successful operation of a fairly self-contained family farm.

From the middle of the eighteenth century, however, Sweden's population began to grow. This growth disrupted traditional agrarian life in several ways. The reluctance to subdivide family farms led to the increasing proletarianization of the rural population (Winberg, 1975). As more families came to be composed of wage-earning fathers (and to a lesser degree, sons) and females who, albeit hard-working, were unwaged, the perceived importance of male labor must have been enhanced.

But the pace of agricultural transformation was relatively slow until the 1870s, after which both mechanization and commercialization proceeded at a rapid pace. Both developments could be expected to affect the evaluation of female labor inputs in ways previously discussed. In addition, there was some rural industrialization based on forest-related industries and mining. Neither form of rural development provided ancillary occupations for Swedish women. (However, the rise of commercially oriented dairy farming did not necessarily diminish the labor value of women.)

Countering these developments was the increase in urbanization and the rise of mechanized manufacturing which also began in the 1870s. Historically, this type of development tends to offset and eventually overcome the economic devaluation of females at the household level. The fact that in Sweden industrialization and urbanization began at approximately the same time as intensive agricultural commercialization would lead to the expectation that EFM itself might have appeared in a muted form and lasted for a relatively brief period of time compared to other European countries.

This is, in fact, what is observed in Sweden. Absolute EFM (when female death rates at certain ages are absolutely higher than those for males) only occur from the late nineteenth century to the early twentieth century. It is most marked in the groups aged 5–9 and 10–14, the historical experience of which is graphed in Fig. 4. There it is evident that for the 5- to 9-year-old group, EFM emerges after 1880 as a result of the fact that childhood death rates fell faster for boys than girls until the early twentieth century, when differential rates of decline were reversed. For the 10- to 14-year-old group, the story is similar.

However, trends are more complicated than absolute mortality differentials seem to indicate. When the history of relative differentials (which do not necessarily include absolute EFM) is examined, it is possible to see that the eighteenth-century mortality advantage of Swedish females was slowly eroding for many age groups, before any absolute disadvantage appeared. From 1750 to 1800 in Sweden, there were no age groups in which females, on average, had higher death rates than males, including the childbearing years (Sundbärg reprinted in *Urval,* 1970). It is argued here, therefore, that the mortality experience of the last half of the eighteenth century can be used as a standard against which to assess relative mortality advantages of females and males in the nineteenth century. This is done in Fig. 5. Here the ratio of male/female death rates (for specific age groups) in 1750–1800 is treated as a given (whatever its value) standard against which nineteenth-century deviations are measured. When a bar rises above the line, females have increased their percentage advantage. When a bar falls below the line, females have lost ground compared to the 1750–1800 standard. The picture across age groups is not homogeneous. Female infants seemed to have gained an increasing mortality advantage across the nineteenth century, a development that could indicate that there was, in fact, some female infanticide in the eighteenth century. Young females (aged 1–3) first gained ground and then lost it over time. The mortality advantage of the 10–19 year olds started to deteriorate in the early nineteenth century. They, as always in the European

Deaths/1000

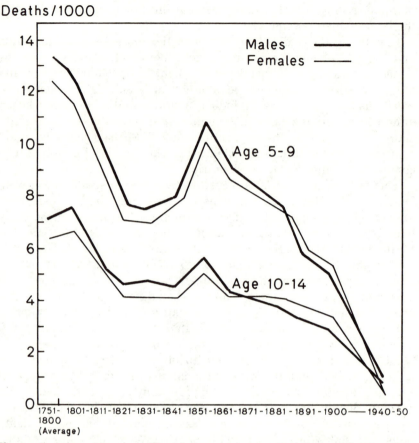

Figure 4. Age and sex–specific death rates (ages 5–9 and 10–14) for Sweden, 1751–1951.

experience, are hardest hit by EFM. The experience of childbearing women is quite erratic, especially in the 20- to 29-year-old group. But a relative deterioration can be detected from about 1830–1840 onward. This deterioration is particularly marked and regular in the 30- to 34-year-old group. By 1890–1900, all age groups from 5 to 34 have experienced a marked deterioration in their former mortality advantage.

Why? Can it not be argued that the loss of a former female mortality advantage is due to the rise of industrialization and urbanization? Probably not, since in the urban sector, there was little or no EFM, and it was the most rural and agrarian counties in which EFM was most marked.

As late as 1910, after four decades of economic development, Sweden was still a predominantly rural–agrarian country. Less than 25% of

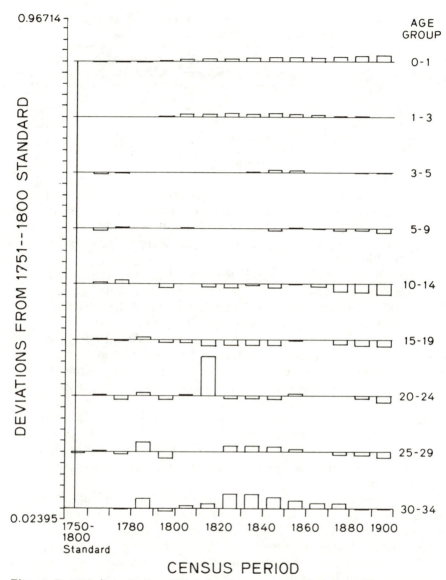

Figure 5. Male/female Swedish mortality rates by census and age group: Nineteenth-century changes compared to a 1750–1800 standard.

its population lived in towns of 2500 or more and, in only 4 of its 24 provinces was less than 40% of the employed male labor force still in agriculture. (See Table III.) As a country with a large agrarian sector that had been subject to rapid modernization for several decades by 1901–1910, it is not surprising that EFM was found in almost every

Table III. Population of Sweden by major economic groups and
urban versus rural distribution (%)[a]

Date	Agriculture	Industry	Trade, transport, professions, etc.	Urban (2500+) (%)
1870	72	15	13	13
1890	61	23	16	15
1900	55	27	17	21

[a] Data for percentage urban from Sundbärg (1970:68). Data for major economic groups from Sundbärg (1904:498).

province. Table IV shows that in only two provinces was EFM absent. However, the least agriculturally oriented provinces were those most likely to have low levels of EFM. Those with over 60% of their male labor force still in agriculture were most likely to have higher than average EFM.

Already in the urban sector of the Swedish population, EFM had disappeared or failed to establish itself. In Table V, it is clear that in terms of "average years to live" once a certain age had been attained, the female residents of Stockholm and Göteborg (Sweden's two largest cities) had a clear mortality advantage over males at every age that their rural sisters lacked. The larger the town, the more likely was this pattern to be found. Another familiar pattern is displayed here as well. The rural areas remained healthier for males in general, whatever their age. But for females attaining the age of 5, city life carried almost no mortality penalty, which is what would be expected if powerful economic forces were offsetting the tendency to devalue and underinvest in females (which characterized the countryside), hence overcoming the other disadvantages of urban life (overcrowding, poor sanitation, etc.).

Up to now, nothing has been said about the underlying causes of death that produced the preceding patterns. As mentioned earlier, cause-of-death data for Sweden was not modernized in form or content until after 1910. Throughout most of the nineteenth century, the parish officials responsible for providing cause-of-death data were required only to identify those deaths due to accidents and violence, or certain easily identifiable infectious diseases. Although tuberculosis was excluded from this list, it was, nevertheless, nineteenth-century Sweden's major health problem. In fact, it was the age-specific mortality pattern unique to tuberculosis that gave EFM in Sweden a pattern different from that found in India today.

Among all the major cause-of-death categories described by Preston (1976) in his seminal study of national mortality data, tuberculosis is the only cause of death that (before a cure was found for it) hit adoles-

Table IV. Excess female mortality (ages 10–14) according to the percentage of the male labor force in primary industry in 1900

Province	Mortality (means 1901–1910)		Relationship to the Swedish mean[c]	
	Level[a]	Differential[b]	Level	Differential
39.9% or less				
Sodermanland	2.81	0.37	−	−
Malmöhus	3.28	0.47	−	−
Gothenburg & Bohus	3.52	0.56	+	+
Stockholm Stad[d]	3.19	0.27	−	−
40–59.9%				
Stockholm Län				
Uppsala Län	3.15	0.47	−	−
Ostergötland	2.50	0	−	−
Jönköping	2.97	0.64	−	−
Kalmar	2.96	0.17	−	−
Blekinge	3.88	0.59	+	+
Örebro	3.17	0.88	−	+
Vastmanland	3.18	0	−	−
Kopparberg	3.76	0.56	+	+
Gälveborg	3.62	0.33	+	−
Vasternorrland	3.81	0.14	+	−
Norbotten	6.27	1.90	+	+
60% or over				
Kronoberg	3.31	0.86	−	+
Gotland	3.47	0.32	+	−
Kristianstad	3.98	0.72	+	+
Hallands	3.45	0.62	+	+
Alvsborg	2.94	0.54	−	+
Skaraborg	2.60	0.35	−	−
Värmland	2.98	0.03	−	−
Jämtland	4.52	1.00	+	+
Västerbotten	4.02	0.85	+	+
Sweden	3.40	0.48		

[a] The *level* of mortality is measured as the deaths per 1000 females aged 10–14.

[b] The male/female differential is the result of subtracting the male death rate (age 10–14) from the female death rate for the same age. If the female death rate is lower than the male death rate the differential is said to equal 0.

[c] The mean is for the Total Population. A (+) indicates above the mean, and a (−) indicates a provincial value below the Swedish mean.

[d] Includes Stad plus Stockholm Län, or "county."

Table V. Average years to live in Sweden: rural versus urban (1891–1900)[a]

Age	Rural areas		Stockholm		Göteborg (Gothenburg)	
	Male	Female	Male	Female	Male	Female
0	52.7	54.3	38.9	46.9	43.9	50.6
5	57.4	57.9	48.9	57.3	50.8	57.9
10	54.0	54.6	45.7	54.5	47.3	53.7
15	49.9	50.6	41.5	50.5	43.1	49.7
20	46.0	46.7	37.6	46.4	39.3	45.9

[a] From Sundbärg (1970:158).

cents and young adults with greater force than infants and old people. In the nineteenth century, tuberculosis of the lungs was the leading cause of death in most European countries, and Sweden was no exception. Even though the national government did not publish statistics on its incidence until after 1910, Swedish doctors were well aware of the magnitude of the problem and wrote about it frequently. In addition, special government commissions published historical and contemporary data. In 1861–1870, 12% of the deaths in Swedish cities were attributed to tuberculosis; by 1891–1900, nearly 16% of the recorded urban fatalities were attributed to its influence (Sundbärg, 1970:149). By 1900, roughly 25% of urban fatalities aged 10–14 were due to tuberculosis: Of those dying between the ages of 15 and 19, almost one-half were victims of consumption (Sundbärg, 1970:150). Because of its importance as a cause of death, the fact that more females than males died of tuberculosis was almost sufficient to account for EFM in late childhood and adolescence. The ratio of male to female deaths caused by tuberculosis in Stockholm (1890s) in the group aged 5–15 was .715, a very substantial excess of female deaths (Sundbärg, 1970:150). In the 10–15 age group, while 20% of all males dying died of tuberculosis, the figure was over 30% for females.

After 1900, Stockholm began to display a unique pattern: Above the age of 20, more males than females began to die of the disease. At the turn of the century, rural tuberculosis remained a disease to which females were particularly prone until over the age of 50. Over all ages, 11% more females than males died of tuberculosis in the rural areas of Sweden (ca. 1900); in the cities, there was a 1% excess of male deaths. In Stockholm, the total male excess was 29% (J. E. Johansson, 1977:68).

The available literature does not discuss the reasons for the observed urban/rural contrasts in any detail. Physicians knew that the incidence of tuberculosis was systematically related to climate, housing (Carls-son, 1908), and overall sanitation. But these were factors by which men and women were equally affected. The contributing influences of nutrition and other material factors were generally ignored. The only attempt to "explain" EFM from tuberculosis in the rural areas was the rather casual one of Gustaf Neander (1928). Neander attributed the unfavorable mortality patterns of adult women vis à vis men to the "stultifying" workloads of rural farm women. In addition to child-bearing, they were responsible for an unceasing round of domestic and agricultural tasks that exhausted and prematurely aged them. The workload of men, while heavy, had a more seasonal character and thus greater opportunities for leisure (Neander, 1928:19). No discussion of why younger girls should show the greatest tendency to EFM from tuberculosis was found at all.

It seems likely that nutritional factors played some role in the ten-dency of rural women to suffer from EFM through most of life. The peasant "feeding rule" required women to prepare the food but serve it first to the males of the family, senior and junior. If the rule were followed, there might not have been much food left for women and girls. Meat, in particular, might have been a scarce resource, one that was less frequently made available to females than males.

There is, at least, no evidence to counter the suggestion that by the late nineteenth-century females, particularly as young girls, were regarded as less valuable than males to the farm-family economy and were consequently less well fed and treated. Unlike Bangladesh and certain areas of India where the lesser economic value of girls leads to practices conducive to death in infancy and early childhood, Swedish parents did not actively try to rid themselves of their daughters. Rather, they did less to ensure their survival. As the benefits of development accrued to farm families in various situations, the opportunities to in-vest in the welfare of children were affected by a marked aggregate sex bias prejudicial to daughters. As the family diet improved, the last to benefit were the young girls. Because the postulated patterns of discrimination were passive rather than active, they could be ex-pected to produce a mortality pattern in which the survival chances of girls fall gradually behind boys rather than immediately as in Bangla-desh and other areas where EFM begins in infancy.

The postulated reluctance to invest family resources equally in boys and girls has a direct relevance for the EFM from tuberculosis in child-hood and adolescence. Before the 1930s, there was no specific medical cure for the disease, but a specific course of treatment for those afflicted was widely recommended. Basically, a stricken child or adult was supposed to be isolated from the rest of the family (even if it meant building a separate room), allowed to rest quietly (having been excused from all work), fed a diet that was rich in high protein (meat and milk), and kept warm and cleanly dressed. This recipe for recovery was simply one that maximized the effectiveness of the body's own defense mechanisms; but the prescribed regime required a heavy investment of time and material resources in the afflicted person. If the investment were not forthcoming, the probability of dying from tuberculosis was probably greater than if it were. This was the principle behind the spread of the sanatorium movement. Despite the building of numerous sanatoriums in the late nineteenth century, most tuberculosis cases were still treated at home. In the absence of any concrete data on how tubercular sons and daughters were treated by their parents, it can only be assumed that daughters were less likely to benefit from selective investment than sons, although to a lesser degree in the urban areas.

CONCLUSIONS

Excess female mortality in the prechildbearing years has been analyzed as a product of economic influences on parental behavior toward female children. But economic pressures that result in differential investment in sons and daughters are themselves shaped by cultural pressures operating in the context of a specific disease environment. It has been argued that the commercialization/modernization of agriculture generally causes parents to devalue daughters relative to sons more consistently than is the case in traditional agrarian regimes. Whether or not this will result in EFM depends on prevailing disease patterns interacting with specific norms and values. Biologically, cause-of-death patterns must be dominated by infectious and parasitic diseases and, therefore, life expectancy at birth be below 50. Within such a disease environment, the age pattern of EFM in childhood and adolescence will be influenced by whether or not parents are permitted to remove unwanted daughters in infancy or pressured to keep them alive while stinting them of food, clothing, and other material resources under parental control for the duration of their childhood.

The latter strategy prevailed in European countries, including Sweden. The progressive debilitation that resulted produced a pattern of EFM that only began in late childhood and peaked in adolescence. The level of EFM in nineteenth-century Europe was also influenced by the fact that tuberculosis of the lungs was the leading cause of death among teenagers and young adults. In this form, tuberculosis is a nutritionally sensitive disease; in its absence, both the pattern and level of EFM would have been much less pronounced than they were.

It was further argued that industrialization and urbanization eventually minimized the differential value of sons and daughters to the family economy, first by providing more employment opportunities for young girls and second, in their later stages, by removing child labor altogether. Ultimately as standards of living rose well above subsistence, favoritism toward sons, if it continued at all, ceased to have mortality consequences. In this case, the "natural" mortality disadvantages of males would be expected to reappear.

ACKNOWLEDGMENTS

The author wishes to thank Gene Hammel, Ken Wachter, Ronald Lee, and all of the other members of the Group in Demography at the University of California, Berkeley, as well as the members of the Stanford–Berkeley Colloquium in Historical Demography for the many helpful comments and criticisms I have received. Special thanks are due to Paul David for his criticisms, support, and encouragement.

24 A sociobiological analysis of human infanticide

Martin Daly
Margo Wilson

All organisms, including people, are products of the historical process of differential survival and reproduction that Charles Darwin called *natural selection.* This selective process is creative, producing attributes that appear to have been designed to achieve adaptive functions: digestion, clear vision, circulation of the blood, escape from predators, and so forth. But attributes are naturally selected only if they eventually contribute to reproduction, or more precisely to genetic replication, hereafter called "fitness." In evolutionary theoretical perspective, then, species-characteristic attributes must be explained in terms of their contributions to fitness. This is the "adaptationist program" that has guided most advances in biological understanding (Mayr, 1983).

This adaptationist approach is relatively straightforward when the attributes in question are morphological structures: A first question about a newly discovered organ or skeletal structure is, "What is it for?" Applying the same perspective to behavioral control mechanisms ("psyche"), however, is more problematic since a structural description of species-characteristic psyche (the thing to be explained) remains elusive. An adaptationist ("sociobiological") approach can shed considerable light on the human psyche, and we shall consider the motives and circumstances surrounding infanticide as a case in point.

Our emphasis on a psychological, rather than behavioristic, level of description is intentional and, indeed, essential. The specific act of infanticide may or may not benefit the actor's fitness, whether in an individual case or on average, but the act need not contribute to fitness for a sociobiological analysis to be illuminating. Infanticide can be viewed as one (rare) manifestation of variations in more abstract motivational states such as child-specific parental love and solicitude. Adaptation may then be sought at the level of these more abstract states. Thus, in this chapter, we shall use the proposition that parental inclination varies adaptively to generate a series of testable hypotheses about human infanticide, hypotheses that in no way demand that infanticide per se contribute to fitness.

Two very different sources of data will be used to test our hypotheses. The first is the ethnographic record, which contains descriptions of circumstances in which infanticide is allegedly common, acceptable, sometimes even obligatory, in various human societies. Scrimshaw (Chapter 22, this volume) reviews several examples. These ethnographic accounts will enable us to test whether the circumstances in which infanticide is alleged to occur in different societies correspond to circumstances in which mitigation of parental inclination can be predicted from evolutionary theory. (These predictions presuppose that there is a cross culturally consistent human psyche at some level of abstraction, in contrast to an hypothesis of extreme cultural relativism we do not expect that motives of people in one society will be totally alien to people from another.) A limitation of ethnographic sources is that they are almost devoid of quantitative information that would permit the test of more specific predictions about the probability of infanticide under different circumstances. For this purpose, we shall examine recent data on children as homicide victims in Canada.

INFANTICIDE IN THE ETHNOGRAPHIC RECORD

The adaptive functions of parental solicitude toward offspring seem obvious. Parental care makes a clear and direct contribution to parental fitness. But each episode of parental care in animals such as ourselves also involves an enormous commitment of time and resources that might have earned higher fitness returns elsewhere. Evolved mechanisms of parental motivation are therefore unlikely to be indiscriminate: Natural selection would be expected to favor those individuals whose parental effort is best allocated so as to contribute to their own fitness. Parental inclination to care for a particular child is thus expected to be determined in part by available predictors of that child's eventual contribution to parental fitness. In Richard Alexander's (1979:109) words:

> Selection should refine parental altruism as if in response to three hypothetical cost–benefit questions: (1) What is the relationship of the putative

offspring to its parents? (Is the juvenile really my own offspring?) (2) What is the need of the offspring? (More properly, what is its ability to translate parental assistance into reproduction?) (3) What alternative uses might a parent make of the resources it can invest in the offspring?

We predict here that the typologically described circumstances of infanticide in different societies will reflect parental sensitivity to each of these cost–benefit questions. A still stronger adaptationist hypothesis is this: Parentally instigated infanticide that does not make reproductive strategic sense within this framework will nowhere be described as normal or typical.

In order to test these hypotheses, ethnographic materials in the Human Relations Area Files (HRAF) for the "Probability Sample" of 60 societies described by Lagacé (1974) were examined. The HRAF consist of ethnographic materials arranged on microfiche according to various topics, one of which is infanticide (Murdock, 1976). The Probability Sample has been devised by cultural anthropologists to be independent and representative of the world's cultures, according to several criteria including geographic region and mode of subsistence. The files which we consulted contained ethnographic source material published up to 1971.

Infanticide was reported in these sources for 39 of the 60 societies in the sample, and circumstances in which infanticide allegedly occurs were described in the HRAF materials for 35 of these 39 (Table I). Often, several circumstances were noted for a single culture; Dogon (Africa), for example, were said to kill deformed infants, those conceived in adultery, those born to unwed mothers, and those whose mothers died in childbirth. Counting each such rationale in each society separately, 112 infanticidal circumstances to be noted in the sample of HRAF material (Table I) were found. Most of these are clearly related to one or more of Alexander's three cost–benefit questions.

Question 1: Is the infant the putative parent's own?
Twenty of the 112 infanticidal circumstances were explicit matters of nonpaternity. In 15 societies, adulterous conception was offered as grounds for infanticide. In three, tribal males were said to insist upon the death of any child whose features suggested a nontribal sire. And in two societies—Tikopia (Oceania) and Yanomamö (South America)— men acquiring wives with children were said to demand that those children be put to death.

Question 2: What is the infant's fitness potential?
Alexander (quoted previously) translated offspring "need" as capacity to convert parental assistance into fitness, and it is important to note this nonintuitive translation. A hopelessly deformed infant, for

Table I. Circumstances of alleged infanticide in society[a]

Society	Inappropriate paternity			Poor infant quality	Inadequate parental resource circumstance					
	Adulterous conception	Nontribal sire	Sired by mother's first husband	Deformed or very ill	Twins	Birth too soon or too many	No male support	Mother dead	Mother unwed	Economic hardship
Africa										
Dogon	X			X				X		X
Twi	X			X		X			X	
Tiv										
Baganda				X						
Masai				X			X			
Pygmies				X	X					
Azande									X	
Bemba				X						
Lozi					X					
Asia										
Central Thai				X						
Andaman		X		X	X					
Europe										
Serbs	X								X	
Lapps										
Middle East										
Somali				X					X	
North America										
Tlingit	X				X	X			X	
Copper Eskimo				X	X	X				
Blackfoot				X	X					

490

Society	1	2	3	4	5	6	7	8	9	10	11	12
Ojibwa	X					X					X	
Iroquois	X							X			X	
Klamath	X										X	
Tarahumara				X		X					X	
Oceania												
Iban	X				X						X	
Toradja	X				X			X			X	
Aranda	X	X			X			X				
Trobriands												
Lau												
Truk	X			X	X	X					X	
Tikopia	X		X		X							X
Russia												
Yakut												
Chukchee	X							X				X
South America												
Cuna	X	X			X	X					X	
Cagaba	X				X							
Aymara	X			X	X	X					X	
Ona	X				X							
Mataco	X			X	X	X		X			X	
Guarani	X			X	X							
Bororo	X			X	X							
Yanomamo	X		X	X	X						X	
Tucano	X										X	
Number of Societies	15	3	2	3	21	14	11	6	6	6	14	3

a Circumstances in which infanticide allegedly occurs in 39 out of 60 societies in a representative sample drawn from the Human Relations Area File. Listed are 95 infanticidal circumstances that make clear reproductive strategic sense for the parents; other miscellaneous rationales are discussed in the text. (A bibliography of ethnographic materials from which this table was compiled is available on request from the authors.)

example, while extremely "in need" in ordinary parlance, is not "in need" in this special evolutionary theoretical sense: Parental care is of no utility to such an infant because "utility" is here considered only with respect to fitness potential. One prediction, then, is that children of demonstrably poor phenotypic quality will be common victims of infanticide.

The killing or abandonment of deformed or very ill children at birth was noted for 21 of the 35 societies. In only one of these cases—Blackfoot (North America)—was it suggested that this practice was disapproved by the society-at-large. In several societies, deformed children were described as ghosts or demons, with the rationale for infanticide expressed in terms of a struggle with hostile supernatural forces. Whatever the expressed rationale, however, choosing not to raise a deformed child obviously serves the parents' fitness interests by avoiding the squandering of prolonged effort upon a child with poor reproductive prospects.

Question 3: What are the parent's alternatives?

This third cost–benefit consideration is perhaps the most broad-ranging of the three and must interact with the others in influencing parental inclination in any given situation. For example, an older mother with little reproductive future may be relatively willing to raise a deformed child. In general, an individual might be expected to be reluctant to invest parentally in a particular child when other channels promise better returns, whether these be already in existence or future reproductive opportunities.

Present maternal incapacity to cope with the demands of child-rearing is a prevalent class of rationales for infanticide and one that may be said to reflect sensitivity to some combination of cost–benefit Questions 2 and 3: Question 2 because poor prospects for the present child may be due to circumstance rather than to poor offspring quality; Question 3 because attempts to raise children with inadequate parental resources presumably diminish one's capacity to contribute to fitness elsewhere.

Of the 112 circumstances listed, 56 fit this category of maternal overburdening. In 14 societies, the birth of twins was cited as a circumstance necessitating infanticide. The child to be killed may be prescribed to be the second born, the weaker, the female. In only two cases—Aranda (Oceania) and Lozi (Africa)—was it claimed that both twins were killed; and in the latter case, different ethnographers contradicted one another on this point. Granzberg (1973:411) has shown that "twin infanticide is typically found in societies where mothers have a heavy workload and where they have a minimum amount of help" and is rare elsewhere. Similarly, in 11 societies in the sample, it was noted that the newborn may be killed at birth if it arrived too soon after the last child or if the mother had too many children already. A different problem of timing arises among the Copper Eskimo (North America), where children born at the wrong time of year cannot conveniently be transported and were said to have been killed at birth. In six societies, infants were said to be killed when no man would acknowledge paternity or accept an obligation to provide for the child. Perhaps similar is a case (Baganda) in which women were said to kill their infants to spite their husbands when they had quarreled severely. In another three instances, infanticide was attributed simply to poverty or hard times. And in six societies, infants were put to death when the mother herself had died in childbirth. In 14 societies, the unwed status of the mother was offered as grounds for infanticide; unwed mothers lack paternal support for their infants, but more than this, they may find the child an impediment to future marriage prospects.

Other Rationales

To this point, we have summarized 97 of 112 alleged infanticidal circumstances within the rubric of adaptive variation in parental inclinations. We predicted that considerations of parental reproductive strategy would predominate, and the prediction is clearly supported. But 15 of the 112 descriptions of alleged infanticidal circumstances remain to be enumerated.

Four (Yanomamö, Mataco, Trobriands, Tikopia) of these fifteen are cases in which the infant's sex was offered as distinct grounds for infanticide (and in four other societies—Copper Eskimo, Tlingit, Aranda, Tucano—sex was remarked as relevant to the decision in the event of twins or short birth intervals). Female-selective infanticide is, at first sight, perplexing, since daughters offer just as great a contribution to parental fitness as sons (or even more if female-selective infanticide has had the consequence of biasing population sex ratios so that the average surviving female must have more children than the average surviving male). Proximate economic goals often dictate a preference for sons (see Johansson, Chapter 23, this volume), and it is not clear whether this preference generally enhances or diminishes parental fitness. The preference for sons may yet prove to contribute to parental fitness in certain cultural milieus and certain social classes (see Chagnon, Flinn, and Melancon, 1979; Dickemann, 1979a; Hartung, 1982; Hughes, 1981).

Another possibly surprising circumstance is that of the killing of children conceived in incest, as was noted in three societies (Tarahumara, Aymara, Cuna); this might reflect an apprehension of poor offspring quality, but we might then have expected the decision to rest on overt defects. One plausible hypothesis is that these infanticides are not parental decisions but, instead, are imposed from without so that interests other than those of the parents are served. We have hitherto been concerned with variations in parental inclinations, but distantly related or unrelated individuals sometimes advance their interests by disposing of babies. Baganda (Africa) chiefs, for example, ordered the death of collateral male kin at birth with the express purpose of eliminating rival claimants to the succession (Roscoe, 1911). A more perplexing case is that of the Lau Islanders (Oceania): according to Hocart (1929:168), "the people of Wathiwathi used to destroy the children of all their women who married into Tumbou so that they should have no *rasu,* that is sister's sons to be a burden upon them." It would be interesting to know the actual genealogical links between these "mother's brothers" and their victims. Tiv (Africa) men reputedly killed babies for ritual purposes (Akiga, 1939), although nothing is reported about how the kidnapped victims were selected.

Besides the Tiv case, there were two others in which infanticide of healthy children was alleged to occur for purely magical reasons. According to Galaal (1968:30), Somali (Africa) parents used to dispose of babies born under inauspicious astrological signs "in the days before Islam came to the Somali lands." Similarly, infanticide of healthy children as "ghosts" (in contrast to such treatment of deformed babies) is said by the Trukese (Oceania) to have characterized an unspecified past (Fischer, 1963). These tales refer to a bad old time before modern morality took hold and have the air of myth. Neither report provides a convincing exception to the strong adaptationist hypothesis that parentally instigated infanticide that does not make reproductive strategic sense will nowhere be described as normal or typical.

Three cases remain. One is the Baganda chiefs who reportedly killed not just collateral kin but even their own first child if a son, stating that the birth of a boy indicated that the father would die; perhaps the concern here was again to delay a successional bid in this highly stratified and polygynous society. Another surprise is Karsten's (1932) assertion that "a Toba ['Mataco', South America] man may kill the newborn child of his married daughter if his son-in-law has incurred his dislike."

Of all the rationales for infanticide described in this ethnographic sample, the one that seems most clearly contrary to parental fitness interests comes from the Yanomamö:

> Young couples do not relish the prospect of a long period of celibacy that pregnancy and lactation taboos impose on them. From the time a woman discovers she is pregnant until the time she weans her child, she is not allowed to have sexual relations. Faced with this prospect, young couples may decide to kill their child, irrespective of its sex [Chagnon 1967:53–55].

This last rationale for infanticide is the only one that clearly contravenes the strong adaptationist hypothesis: The parents are reported to damage their own fitness in pursuit of incompatible hedonic goals. It should be noted that Chagnon cited no particular cases to illustrate this motive, in contrast to the specific infanticidal incidents he attributed to the motives of a too short birth interval and inappropriate paternity. But if this motive is genuine, then one must ask how Yanomamö society has come to be one in which the ordinary fitness-promoting human motives of sexual desire and parental love are so at odds. Who enforces such unpopular taboos and are the interests of the powerful in any way served? Certainly, the general conclusion from the ethnographic record must be that infanticide in most human societies is considered appropriate in circumstances in which it happens to be reproductively adaptive for the parties involved. We do not find accounts of infanticide according to arbitrary cultural rules or descriptions of parents willingly suffering fitness costs by sacrificing their children to some higher good. In those few cases where the parents' interests seem not to be served, we would suggest that the most promising analytic approach will be to ask, Whose are? In some cases, for example, the mothers' interests may be violated by female-selective infanticide, a practice imposed by a larger social group demanding the production of warriors. In general, the ethnographic record suggests that the goals pursued by infanticidal individuals are consistent with their fitness interests.

CHILDREN AS HOMICIDE VICTIMS IN CANADA

Contrast the situation in modern North American society with those just considered. The ethnographic record provides numerous typological descriptions of circumstances legitimizing infanticide, but there is seldom any evidence on its actual frequency. Our own society is one in which killing children for any reason is decried and is likely to bring severe punishment. Faced with these sanctions, some adults kill children anyway, and various public bodies collect information on such cases. So instead of having a prescriptive set of circumstances legitimizing infanticide and little case information, we have a general condemnation of the practice and a great deal of case information.

Statistics Canada maintains a data bank on all homicides investigated by any of the country's police departments. During the years 1961–1979, 8032 homicides were investigated; 1153 victims were minors (under the age of 18), and 1059 of these cases were solved. Of these victims, 158 were infants (less than 1 year old), and 148 of these cases were solved. (See Rodenburg [1971] for some earlier analyses of a portion of this data set.) These case reports might have permitted a further test of the correspondence between infanticidal circumstances and Alexander's "cost–benefit questions," but information on "motives" is extremely sketchy, and no tabulation of cases attributable to dubious paternity, deformity, short birth intervals or the like is possible. Instead, the data permit the testing of some more specific hypotheses about factors affecting the risk of child homicide.

Prediction 1: *The probability of child homicide by parents will be maximal with infants and will rapidly decline with the child's age, in contrast to child homicide by nonparents.* This prediction follows from the consideration that an inclination to terminate investment in dependent offspring, if adaptive, would be expected to occur early, when the child had consumed relatively little of the nurture that a complete rearing demands. Translating the hypothesis into proximate psychological terms, we would expect parents to value their children increasingly over the first few years. On the same basis, several sociobiologists have suggested that willingness to incur costs of parental activity should rise as helpless offspring approach independence, a prediction that has found support in several animal studies (e.g., Greig-Smith, 1980; Patterson, Petrinovich, and James, 1980).

Test. A major decrease in parental homicides occurs in the first year: 137 infants and 49 one year olds. (And there is reason to suspect that improved detection of infanticides among infant deaths would further elevate this difference.) Parental homicides continue to decline with increasing child age (Fig. 1). The pattern with respect to child age is very different for homicides committed by nonparents, whose "valuation" of the victims was not expected to follow parental patterns. Here, the frequency increases with age (Fig. 1). In part this difference must be attributable to increasing access of nonparents to older children, but it is noteworthy that parental and nonparental homicides differ even between infants and 1 year olds: Infants were significantly ($\chi^2_{1df} = 36.0$, $p < 0.0001$) more likely to have been killed by parents (93% of solved cases) than were 1-year-old victims (59%). Note, too, that the decline in parental homicide with child's age cannot easily be dismissed as due to a generalized decline in the child's vulnerability or annoyance value, because toddlers (still relatively defenceless in their own right) are at greater risk from nonparents than are infants and yet are at lesser risk from parents.

Prediction 2. *Infanticidal mothers will be relatively often unmarried.* As in the ethnographic sample, we suggest that a lack of paternal support damages a child's prospects, thus contributing to maternal despair and disinclination to embark on the possibly lost cause of rearing the child.

Test. Infanticidal mothers were indeed often unmarried: Birth regis-

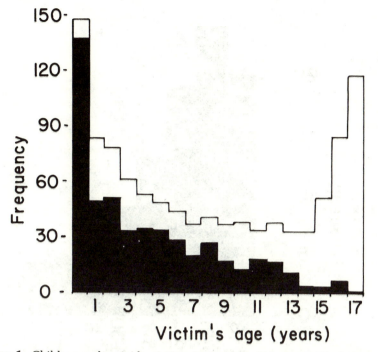

Figure 1. Children as homicide victims in Canada, 1961–1979. The histogram includes all victims under 18 years of age excluding unsolved cases. The black portion represents those children who were killed by their natural parents. (Data supplied by Statistics Canada.)

tration data for Canada from 1977 to 1979 reveal that 88.3% of babies were born to legally married mothers, but only 39.5% of 38 mothers committing infanticide during that period were legally married. The difference is highly significant ($\chi^2_{1df} = 74.6$, $p < 0.0001$).

Prediction 3. *Infanticidal mothers will be relatively young.* This prediction follows from the consideration that parental willingness to invest in present offspring, other things being equal, should increase as the parent's own expectation of future reproduction (the parent's "residual reproductive value") decreases with age (see, e.g., Pugesek, 1981).

Test. Infanticidal mothers were indeed younger than mothers in the Canadian population-at-large as is shown in Fig. 2. Of infanticidal mothers, 15.7% were 17 years old or less compared to 3.1% of all new mothers in Canada in the same period.

Prediction 4. *Children will be at greater risk of homicide in stepparent households than in natural parent households.* As noted earlier, parents may be expected to be sensitive to the biological reality of the parent–offspring relationship and to resent "parental" obligation to children not their own. We have elsewhere reported a substantial

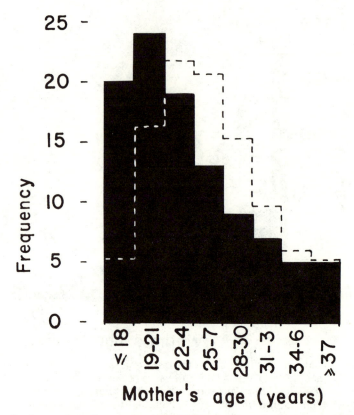

Figure 2. Ages of mothers who killed infants (less than 1 year of age) in
Canada, 1961–1979. The black histogram represents the actual distribution of ages of infanticidal mothers. The dotted histogram represents the expected distribution given the age distribution of women
giving birth in the population-at-large. The infanticidal mothers are
significantly ($X^2_{7df} = 50.7$, $p < 0.0001$) younger than new mothers
generally. (Data supplied by Statistics Canada.)

elevation of the risk of child abuse in stepparent households (Wilson,
Daly, and Weghorst, 1980) and that four of seven preschool-age homicide victims in Detroit in 1972 lived with stepfathers (Daly and Wilson,
1982a). Similarly, Scott (1973) reported that 15 of 29 British "fathers"
who killed their children under 5 years of age were not the putative
biological fathers.

Test. Table II shows that substitute parents are indeed prevalent
among "parental" homicide offenders in Canada. Of 63 cases in which
substitute parents killed minors, 15 cases were included where stepparents legally married to the natural parent were the offenders (14 stepfathers and 1 stepmother), 43 cases in which the natural parent's common-
law mate killed the stepchild (42 cases with stepfathers, in 6 of which

Table II. Children killed by parents or parent substitutes
in Canada, 1961–1979

Victim's age	(A) Number of children killed by persons "in loco parentis" to them	(B) Percentage of A in which offender was an unrelated substitute parent
0	139	1.4
1	64	23.4
2	62	17.7
3	42	21.4
4	43	18.6
5	38	9.5
6–8	79	5.1
9–11	50	4.0
12–14	37	13.5
15–17	14	21.4

the natural mother was also charged, and 1 stepmother case), and 5 cases involving foster parents (3 men, 1 woman, and 1 case in which both were charged).

We cannot say precisely how the percentages in Table II compare with the prevalence of substitute-parent situations for children in the population-at-large. Like its American counterpart (see Wilson, Daly, and Weghorst, 1980), the Canadian census bureau does not distinguish step from natural relationships. Only two infants under 1 year of age were killed by stepparents, but of course infants will rarely *have* stepparents. The probability of living with a stepparent increases as a child grows older, because the time in which marital dissolution and reconstitution might have occurred increases. In the United States in 1967, for example, Sweet (1974) estimated from survey data that 1.6% of children under 3 years of age lived with one parent and one stepparent (including common-law) compared to 5.2% of children aged 3–5, 8.3% of those aged 6–9 and 9.5% of those aged 10–13. The corresponding figures for Canada over the period covered by our homicide data must be substantially lower. The 1967 divorce rate was five times higher in the United States than in Canada (United Nations, 1977), and the Canadian rate only approached the 1967 United States rate by the late 1970s (the end of the period for which homicide data are analyzed). We surmise that overall rates of marital dissolution and reconstitution were also lower in Canada, and hence that step-relationships were less prevalent in Canada. These considerations, together with the data in Table II, strongly suggest that preschool-age children are at much higher risk of homicide by substitute parents than by natural parents.

Interestingly, this elevation of relative risk at the hands of parent substitutes appears to decline as children grow older, perhaps beyond the age of 1 and certainly beyond the age of 5 (Table II; recall that the chance expectancy for Column B, if natural and substitute parents presented equal threats to children, would rise monotonically). Perhaps the resentment of pseudoparental obligation is greatest when a prolonged period of dependency and investment is anticipated. Conflict between older children and stepparents is, of course, well known and undoubtedly severe, but it leads stepparents to homicide relatively rarely. Of course, children are more formidable in self-defense as they grow, but the important point is that the extent to which stepparents are likelier than natural parents to kill children declines. Similarly, in a study of physical abuse of American children (Wilson, Daly, and Weghorst, 1980), children under 3 years of age were 6.9 times as likely to be abused in a natural-parent–stepparent home as in a two-natural-parent home; this ratio of relative risk declined to 5.1 for ages 3–5, 3.3 for ages 6–9, 3.0 for ages 10–13, and 2.2 for ages 14–17.

Some Other Characteristics of Child Homicide

Several other aspects of the Statistics Canada data warrant discussion from a sociobiological perspective. Although information on motives is sketchy, it is interesting to note the varying prevalence of cases attributed by the reporting agency to "mental illness or retardation." Of cases with adult victims, 5.6% were attributed to this cause between 1961–1979. By contrast, 46% of parents who killed their children were so categorized (compared to 12% of other people who killed minors), including 45% of mothers and 18% of fathers who killed infants, and 84% of mothers and 26% of fathers who killed older children. If these figures can be taken at face value, the implication would seem to be that a loss of reason is more often characteristic of those who kill children than those who kill adults, of those who kill own as opposed to others' children, of those who kill their older children as opposed to their infants, of homicidal mothers than of homicidal fathers. All of these contrasts are readily predicted on sociobiological grounds, if "loss of reason" is interpreted as a breakdown of adaptive function, that is to say, a collapse (for whatever reason) of a normal, species-characteristic recognition of where one's self-interest lies (see, e.g., Essock-Vitale and McGuire, 1979).

However, it is important to note the possibility that it is the nature of the offense that is directly responsible for the diagnosis: those people who damage their own fitness may be likeliest to be called mad, more as a result of some general cultural definition of what is rational than because of any independently manifested symptoms. But even if diagnosis is indeed biased in this way, then the coincidence of culturally defined rationality with nepotistic self-interest is itself revealing. In any case, there is some evidence that those who kill close relatives exhibit delusions and other psychiatric symptoms more often than those who kill nonrelatives (Gillies, 1976; Wong and Singer, 1973; Guttmacher, 1962).

Besides the many cases of child homicide by stepfathers, it is likely that uncertain paternity is relevant to other cases in which the offender is the victim's putative father. (This need not be a matter of conscious suspicion of nonpaternity; see Daly and Wilson, 1982b.) Some differences in homicide by mothers versus fathers may be interpreted in this light. Paternal homicides decline in frequency with increasing age of victim much less sharply than do maternal homicides. This general decline was noted in parental homicides in Fig. 1 and interpreted as reflecting a growing valuation of growing offspring. In the case of mothers, this change over time is uncomplicated by changes in perceived probability of relatedness; in the case of fathers, grounds for suspicion of nonrelatedness may sometimes increase over time as the child's phenotype develops.

There are other striking differences between homicides committed by fathers and those committed by mothers, particularly with respect to multiple homicides (Table III). Fathers who killed one of their children were more than twice as likely (32.7%) as mothers (15.1%) to have killed more than one child. And whereas 54 men killed their wives and one or more children, there was not a single case of a woman killing her husband and one or more children. Women certainly killed their own children and often killed more than one. And women killed husbands too: Of the total sample of 8032 homicides, 1205 men killed their wives and 311 women killed their husbands (including common-law). What women did not do was to destroy spouse and children together. This appears to be a peculiarly male crime, and one which we suggest may be psychologically linked to men's proprietary attitude toward women and their reproductive capacity (cf. Daly, Wilson, and Weghorst, 1982). It would be most interesting to know in what propor-

Table III. Multiple victim cases among parental homicides in Canada, 1961–1979

	Victims			
Offender	One child only	More than one child (and not spouse)	One child and spouse	More than one child and spouse
Mother	203	36	0	0
Father	93	19	22	32

tion of these cases—and indeed in all paternal homicides—the putative father was not the actual sire.

CONCLUSION

Human infanticide is widespread, and a sociobiological model of the human psyche helps to make it intelligible. Ethnocentric commentators have often vilified infanticidal practices as lunatic savagery, but the ethnographic record makes clear that infanticide is nowhere taken lightly. It is condoned primarily where it makes adaptive sense for one or both parents—where the mother is overburdened, for example, or where the child is of poor quality or inappropriate paternity. In societies such as our own, where infanticide is condemned in all circumstances, cases occur nonetheless, and it appears that the infanticidal parties are sensitive to these same predictors of fitness. The act of infanticide is unlikely to enhance the fitness of a Canadian parent. The psychology that occasionally permits such drastic failures of parental inclination nevertheless exhibits an adaptive logic and is interpreted readily, therefore, as a product of natural selection.

ACKNOWLEDGMENTS

The authors thank Craig McVie and Statistics Canada for the provision of data files of Canadian homicides and the Harry Frank Guggenheim Foundation and the Natural Sciences and Engineering Research Council of Canada for financial support.

25 Ayoreo infanticide: A case study

Paul E. Bugos, Jr.
Lorraine M. McCarthy

INTRODUCTION

The Ayoreo are tribal people who live in southwestern Bolivia and northern Paraguay. Until recently infanticide was an accepted practice among them (Pérez Diez and Salzano, 1978; Bórmida and Califano, 1978; Sebag, 1964). Since the time of Carr-Sanders (1922), theoretical views of infanticide among tribal people have focused on its population regulation function and have explained infanticide from a group adaptation perspective. However, beginning with the important critique of group adaptation by Williams (1966; see Introduction) there has been a growing trend to view infanticide in terms of its effect on the reproductive interests of individuals. The issue of whether infanticide is best viewed from a group or individual adaptation perspective cannot be resolved in the absence of empirical data. However, as Daly and Wilson (Chapter 24, this volume) note, there is little quantitative information on infanticide among tribal people. During field research among the Ayoreo, from January 1980 to March 1981, we collected such information on infanticide. Our data are detailed enough to allow for the testing of some hypotheses based on these two perspectives on infanticide. Obviously, Ayoreo infanticide can only be understood in terms of the environment in which it occurred; thus before presenting our analyses of reproductive histories we will discuss some pertinent aspects of Ayoreo history and culture.

History

The area in which the Ayoreo live was explored early in the colonial history of South America. In 1717 Jesuit missionaries contacted ancestral Ayoreo, Zumocoan language family speakers, and settled them on missions. Warfare among these groups hindered the Jesuits' missionary efforts and when the Jesuit order was expelled from Paraguay in 1767 some ancestral Ayoreo groups still remained uncontacted. These latter people were the ancestors of the contemporary Ayoreo. From the 18th century until the 1950s, contact between the Ayoreo and other peoples—both indigenous and European—was rare and usually violent. As a result, the Ayoreo and their neighbors held each other in contempt.

The Chaco War between Bolivia and Paraguay, which lasted from 1932 to 1935, had indirect but nonetheless devastating effects on the Ayoreo. Major battles were fought south of Ayoreoland and there were major troop movements through Ayoreo territory. The Ayoreo avoided direct contact with the warring armies, but these efforts may have exacerbated conflicts among the Ayoreo themselves. The most devastating effect of the war was the disease brought on by the influx of thousands of people into the area. By 1935 the Ayoreo population began to decline because of infectious disease and internal and external warfare.

In 1945 construction began on a railway line that ran through Ayoreoland. This railroad supported the evangelical efforts of missionaries who sought to contact the Ayoreo by leaving gifts for them in the forest. By 1948 disease and warfare had taken such a toll on some Ayoreo bands that they decided to abandon their long-standing antagonistic policy toward foreigners and seek their aid. The first bands to contact missionaries were those in the northwest. During the next 25 years all but a few isolated groups followed suit. Figure 1 outlines the area occupied by the Ayoreo prior to 1950 and distribution and size of Ayoreo settlements in 1981; villages visited during our research are indicated by numbers. It should be noted that although the Ayoreo were few and their territory large, even in pre-Columbian times they were not the sole occupants of that territory.

Today most Ayoreo make their living as sedentary farmers and part-time laborers. The process of acculturation has been rapid and most Ayoreo now profess to be Christians. Infanticide is now socially unacceptable and rarely occurs. Missionaries have encouraged traditional adoption practices; mothers are urged to give unwanted children to someone else to raise. However, the cases of infanticide discussed in this paper occurred before the women involved were settled on

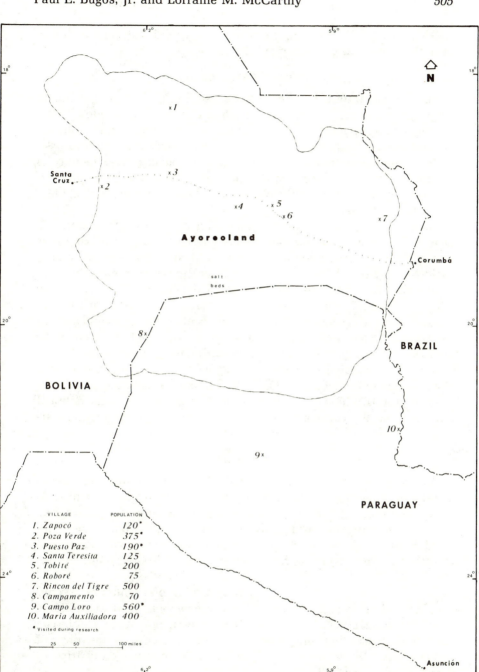

Figure 1. Map outlining the distribution of the Ayoreo in 1945 (solid line) and the location of Ayoreo settlements (numbered) in 1980.

missions, and the following description of traditional Ayoreo life is thus also based on presettlement practices.

Political Organization

The Ayoreo are a tribe only in the sense that they speak a common language and share a common culture and history. They view themselves as being divided into 25 or so politically autonomous, territorially defined bands. Each band comprises several *ogasuri,* which are the units of food production and consumption. Because matrilocality is the preferred form of postmarital residence, the core of an *ogasuri* usually is a mature couple, their single children, and married daughters and their husbands.

Each band is led by several men who are *asute.* This status is achieved by killing an Ayoreo, a foreigner or a large cat—a jaguar or a puma. Shamans, *daijnai,* also are politically important in Ayoreo society. Their role is to invoke supernatural powers to cure the sick, send sickness to enemies, and to predict the future. The Ayoreo use only supernatural means to cure and cause sickness. Although all important shaman are men, Ayoreo women also can cure and kill by supernatural means. Women, therefore, are not immune from being accused of sorcery, a common cause of feuds within Ayoreo bands.

In addition to being a member of an *ogasuri* and a band, each Ayoreo also belongs to one of seven *kucierane,* named exogamous patrilineal descent groups. The *kucierane* have important religious and political functions, but the various *kucierane* do not engage in systematic marriage exchanges.

Subsistence

Ayoreo subsistence patterns are shaped by the sharp seasonality of rainfall in the Chaco. During the rainy season, from November to April, they practice swidden horticulture. From May to October they are nomadic foragers. During this nomadic period the bands move toward salt beds in the center of Ayoreoland. They extract enough salt to season a year's worth of food and then return to their home territories.

On these treks, women carry the salt in addition to other household supplies and the young children. All Ayoreo carrying devices, clothing, rope, and cord are made of fiber from a wild pineapple plant. The collection, processing, and weaving of this material is the duty of women. In addition to these duties, the women make daily trips to gather wild plant foods.

Men make daily foraging trips in search of game or honey, a favorite food of the Ayoreo. With the exception of large game animals, men give the fruits of their day's labor to their wives. The women of an *ogasuri* partition what is available among themselves and each cooks an evening meal for her immediate family at her own hearth.

The bands return to their territories in August and await *tiho'utato*— "first rain." The Ayoreo believe the first rainfall of the year is a good predicter of the amount and location of precipitation during the upcoming rainy season. Using this information, they select a village site and the men begin to clear gardens. Most men clear two or three small gardens in locations some distance apart as insurance against patchy and unpredictable rainfall patterns.

Once the gardens are cleared and burned, the men's role in horticulture declines and the women's role increases. Wives and husbands plant gardens together, but women are responsible for harvesting when the gardens begin to produce food. Garden produce, like wild food, is considered the property of the women of an *ogasuri*. If the rains in a given year are good, if pests do not destroy the gardens and if enemies leave them in peace, bands can subsist on garden produce for 3 or 4 months and perhaps even cache some food for the dry season. However, there are years during which gardening yields very little and they are nomads the year round.

When the rains subside, fish gathered from receding streams become a mainstay of the Ayoreo diet. Entire bands participate in fish collecting. The fish are smoked on racks, rather than preserved with salt, which usually is exhausted by then. The lack of salt provides the impetus for another trek to the salt beds.

THE LIFE CYCLE

Conception, Pregnancy, and Birth

The Ayoreo believe both parents contribute substances that lead to the formation of life. Roughly translated, the father contributes white substance (bone and mother's milk) and the mother contributes red substance (blood). The reproductive organs are the sources of these substances. Repeated copulation is belived necessary for the full formation of a new human. Once pregnancy is detected, sexual relations are taboo until the new child is able to walk and talk. Coitus is thought to adversely affect the mother's milk and, hence, the health of the child.

Magico-religious practices are said to influence the sex of one's next child. These practices are used because couples desire children of both sexes. Girls are desired because at marriage they bring husbands into the household to provide for the parents in their old age. Boys are desired because they perpetuate the *kucierane*. During pregnancy the expectant mother obeys certain food taboos. We know of no proscribed behavior for the father-to-be other than the taboo on sexual relations.

When labor begins, the expectant mother moves to the nearby forest, accompanied by a party of close kinswomen. The attending women prepare the spot of earth upon which the infant will fall by softening it with water. They dig a hole near this spot to bury the afterbirth and the newborn if it is not kept. While in labor, a woman sits on or hangs from a tree branch. The attending women comfort the mother and chant therapeutic songs to ease the delivery. Ayoreo newborns are not eased into the world by human hands. The Ayoreo verb "to be born" (*basui*) also means "to fall." The women inspect the newborn for signs of deformity. If the infant is unwanted, it is pushed into the hole with a stick and buried, never touched by human hands.

If the newborn is wanted, the senior attending woman—ideally the maternal grandmother—cuts the umbilicus, applies hot ashes to the stub, bathes the infant in water warmed in her mouth, and then hands it to the mother. There is a special bond in Ayoreo society between the child and the woman who washes it—the *upurigado*—who also is responsible for naming the newborn. Once the newborn has been accepted, the relationship between infant and mother is close and prolonged. Ayoreo mothers carry infants in a sling that permits the infant to nurse on demand. Children nurse for as long as 3 or 4 years.

If the newborn is the first child or first grandchild, the parents and grandparents receive new names marking their new status. A mother takes the name of the newborn plus the suffix *-date;* the father adds the suffix *-de;* the grandmother adds the suffix *-dacode;* the grandfather adds *-dakide*. It is not unusual for the newborn to remain unnamed for several weeks or months, particularly if the infant is sickly. The reason given is that should the child die, the loss will not be so deeply felt.

Normally, male participation in the birth process is minimal, but mature married couples constitute important exceptions. Women with several children sometimes give birth assisted only by their husbands.

From the moment of birth until a child can sit he is referred to as a *caratai. Caratai* also means "jaguar" as well as "red." The multiple meanings of this word suggest something about the ontological status of newborns in Ayoreo culture. The blood of humans and jaguars contains a spiritual quality that makes it ritually polluting. The *asute* status is not achieved merely from the act of killing but as a result of successfully performing a purification ritual required to rid oneself of the dangerous effects of contact with blood. This suggests that newborns occupy an ambiguous category somewhere between humanity and that which is antithetical to humanity—pollution. An Ayoreo child is not considered a complete human being until the time he can walk and talk. This age category is called *aiuketio*. It provides the root for the word *aiuketotiguei,* which means "understanding" or "personality."

The Ayoreo today use this word to express what they feel they are losing as a result of rapid cultural change.

Marriage

The Ayoreo are somewhat unusual among tribal people in that parents do not arrange their children's marriages. We once mentioned this to an Ayoreo father who disapproved of his daughter's choice of husband; he was somewhat envious. He said Ayoreo parents hope their children will find good mates, but teenagers are strong-willed and often ignore their parents' advice. The fact that the Ayoreo word for single adult also means "insolent," "lazy" and "recalcitrant" suggests his experience is not the exception.

Sex and marriage are two very distinct things in Ayoreo culture. Both boys and girls become sexually active at puberty. Most women do not marry until the age of 18 or 20 and many men postpone marriage even longer. At puberty, an Ayoreo girl undergoes a simple ceremony: she makes an incision on her abdomen, symbolizing she is prepared to withstand the pain of childbirth. She also begins to adorn herself with decorations restricted to single women and to wear a woman's skirt. By the time girls reach this age, they have long been performing all the economic tasks of adults.

There is no puberty ritual for boys. They begin to wear a man's belt and to style their hair in the fashion of men. During this period of a young man's life, he begins to develop his reputation as an *asute*. He participates in wrestling and other contests that pit bachelors against married men, accompanies others on raids, and begins hunting. Single men contribute game to their natal *ogasui* but rarely sleep in their natal households. They sleep with the single women near a smoky fire kept burning in the center of the village to discourage mosquitoes and other pests.

Ayoreo women initiate romantic affairs. It is taboo for a man to speak directly to a woman who is not kin. But the young men are not passive participants in the process; a bachelor interested in a particular girl relies on his sisters to act as go-betweens. It is customary for young people to have a number of romantic relationships before settling on a mate.

Despite their comparatively liberal attitudes toward sexuality, the Ayoreo apply a double standard in determining acceptable behavior for women and men. If a woman changes partners too often she risks being labeled an *amunaheto*, a "wanton woman." Such women have difficulty finding husbands and are subject to harsh treatment, particularly from married women. On the other hand, young Lotharios do not meet with the same intolerant attitudes. Sexual prowess contributes to a man's *asute* status and these men are vital community members because of their ability as warriors. Nevertheless, a man can not achieve full status or become a political leader unless he is married and has children. But bachelors often avoid marriage because it requires giving up the sexual freedom of single life and moving into the wife's household and being subservient to her father.

The Ayoreo have no marriage ceremony. Ideally, the man moves into the bride's house and gives her parents a gift, but this procedure rarely is followed. Most Ayoreo say a young couple is considered married when they keep a child, thereby acquiring new names. Extramarital sex is socially unacceptable for both men and women. Adultery is a common cause of divorce and feuding.

INFANTICIDE

There are several reasons for the paucity of quantitative information on infanticide. The collection of demographic data about preliterate people largely depends on the memory of informants, who often use unsophisticated numerary techniques. Furthermore, people tend to forget unpleasant events in their lives, and even if they remember such events, they may avoid discussing them. In addition, most ethnographers and their informants have been male. Ayoreo men know less about the details of infanticide and are less comfortable discussing the subject than are Ayoreo women.

Men occasionally reported that women had killed newborns, usually in the context of failed marriages, but they rarely knew the sex of the child who was killed. When men gave us the reproductive history of a woman that did not include infanticides, we would ask if the woman had other children who died before being named. They usually did not remember, but if the woman or someone who knew her well lived in the village, the informants would check and report the information later. A number of stillbirths and miscarriages were discovered this way, but the information about infanticide was usually something like, "She may have killed one or two babies before keeping so-and-so." Once, when told of a woman in the village who had killed several babies, Bugos asked the men if they thought she would talk to him about it. They said it was not a good idea so the subject was dropped.

Men would, however, discuss infanticide in general. They clearly viewed the decision to bury a newborn at birth as a decision made by the mother and her close kinswomen. The reasons given for the practice were: the birth of an "ugly" (deformed) child, the birth of twins, the birth of a child too soon after a previous birth, the termination of the marriage because of death or divorce near the time of the birth, and the first births to young women who were not prepared to accept the responsibilities of motherhood. The logic underlying these reasons is generally practical: the Ayoreo view the chances of survival for such children as limited. The exception to this is the birth of twins. The Ayoreo view multiple births as appropriate for animals rather than humans. Ayoreo mythology includes a tale of twin brothers, one particularly good, the other particularly evil. The teaching of this myth is that both twins must be killed in order to avoid keeping the bad twin.

Data Collection and Analysis

The demographic data were collected using methods similar to those described by Chagnon (1974). We usually worked with older people, mostly men, assisted by younger, Spanish-speaking Ayoreo men who served as translators. This method was chosen because the collection of genealogical information was an important aspect of the research and older men, particularly former headmen, were by far the best Ayoreo genealogists and historians. Furthermore, because most residents of Ayoreo villages have lived together all their lives, interviews with knowledgeable informants often provided more detailed demographic information about their co-villagers than did separate direct interviews with each resident of a village.

The problem of men's lack of detailed information about the reproductive histories of women was overcome when McCarthy began interviewing women. The women told McCarthy about specific cases of infanticide, including sex of the infants and reasons for the infanticides. Typically, women only knew such information about their close kinswomen and friends and were less likely to discuss their own infanticides than those of others.

Most information was verified by asking other informants for the same information or even asking the original informant for the same information during a later session. The Ayoreo were very consistent in their reporting. If they did not know the cause of death or sex of a child, they would say so. The verification process most often yielded additional information and only rarely called the original report into question. Unless informants in several villages that were not obviously in communication conspired to mislead us, the data must be the truth to the best of our informants' knowledge.

This chapter will focus primarily on a sample of well-documented cases of infanticide in which the mother was a party to the decision to kill the child. The sample is limited to only those cases in which the sex of the infanticide victim is known. We were told of cases in which males killed children, such as men killing the children of women abducted in raids. We also observed cases of parental neglect, such

as a first-time mother refusing to breast feed an unwanted child. However, cases such as these are rare compared to the type of infanticide
discussed in this paper.

Figure 2 summarizes the reproductive and marital histories of women
known to have practiced infanticide. We lived with the Ayoreo for 6
months before we began interviewing women. We were accustomed
to seeing them walking from their gardens laboring under loads of
bananas or sitting in front of their mud houses weaving and chatting.
Like mothers everywhere they anguish when their babies are sick and
beam with joy when told their babies are beautiful.

Some of the women in the sample were our good friends. Soon after
we moved into her village, Eho welcomed us with a gift of a chicken.
She often visited us and more than once lamented that we had no
children and told us when we did they would surely be beautiful. We
were somewhat incredulous when we first heard of Eho's infanticides
from another woman. Even when trained as an anthropologist, it is
difficult to believe that someone one knows as a charming friend, devoted wife, and doting mother could do something that one's own culture deems repugnant. Yet even the most intolerant missionary among
the Ayoreo understands that there was mercy involved in the burying
of infants.

Eho also was an informant. She reported the infanticides of others,
but when verifying her own reproductive history, she omitted her infanticides, although she acknowledged being married to the men who fathered the children. McCarthy asked the translator, who originally reported the information about Eho, to ask Eho about this inconsistency,
but she declined to pose the question. The translator later told us that
the information was true but that we should not ask a woman about
her own infanticides because it will make her "sad." Acote and Doria
also were informants. Acote treated her own infanticides in the same
way Eho did. Doria mentioned hers but we did not question her about
them specifically because of our previous experience with Eho.

We were given specific reasons for 18 of the infanticides. The reasons
given most often were that the father already had left the mother or
the mother thought the father would leave. It is interesting to note
that men often attributed infanticides to women's unwillingness to accept the responsibilities of motherhood and women attributed infanticides to men's unwillingness to accept the responsibilities of father-
hood.

The large number of marriages for many women in the sample is
deceptive. Many of the early marriages were romances or trial marriages that did not work. A married couple with living children rarely
divorces. Furthermore, three of the women in the sample—Ducupie,
Nutaia and Uwo—were captured from other bands in raids. Although

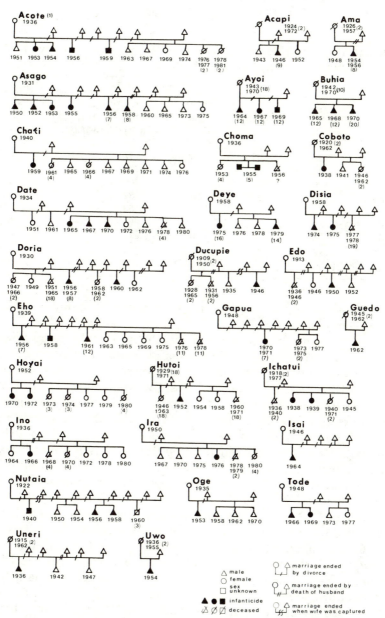

Figure 2. The marital and reproductive histories of Ayoreo women known to have practiced infanticide. (1) All names are pseudonyms. (2) Died of disease. (3) Died at birth. (4) Died in infancy. (5) Twins. (6) Stolen by non-Ayoreo. (7) Father left mother. (8) Father died before child born. (9) Marriage was polygynous and mother ended it soon after the birth. (10) Mother died in childbirth. (11) Premature birth. (12) Mother thought father was going to leave her. (14) Born too soon after older sibling. (16) Father not an Ayoreo. (17) Poisoned by non-Ayoreo. (18) Killed by other Ayoreo. (19) Mother did not want child and others talked her into giving the child to someone else. She did, but the child soon died.

Table I. Fertility and infanticide rate for a sample of Ayoreo women
known to have practiced infanticide

Age class (1)	Person years (2)	Births (3)	Infanti- cides (4)	Birth rate (3/2)	Infanti- cide rate (4/3)	Infanti- cide effect (3–4/2)
15–19	143	31	20	.217	.65	.077
20–24	131	36	18	.275	.50	.137
25–29	120	36	8	.300	.22	.233
30–34	99	18	4	.182	.22	.141
35–39	85	13	4	.153	.31	.106
40–44	74	6	0	.081	—	.081
45–50	35	1	0	.029	—	.029
Total	686	141	54	.207	.38	.126
Total fertility rate				6.185		4.02

these women were not treated cruelly, they did not enjoy full status
in their new band.

Ten of the women and many of the children in the sample were
not alive in 1981. The probable causes of death are listed in Fig. 2
and indicate the types of stresses on the Ayoreo population in recent
years. The most common cause of death was infectious disease. We
asked the Ayoreo to describe the symptoms of the disease, and in
many cases they described a severe cold or influenza. Six people were
victims of violence. The son of Choma was captured by soldiers when
he was 11. He never returned to his people and is presumed dead.
Ayoi's brother and sister told us that she died as a result of drinking
water poisoned by non-Ayoreo. Hutoi, two of her children, and the
first son of Hoyai were killed by other Ayoreo.

Alexander (1979) and Daly and Wilson (Chapter 24, this volume)
have argued that human infanticide is best viewed in terms of its long-
term effect on parental fitness. A prediction generated from this perspective is that the reproductive potential of a woman will affect her
decision to keep a child. Because reproductive potential is largely a
function of age, we can test this prediction.

Table I summarizes the number of births and infanticides for women
in the sample by 5-year age intervals and clearly shows the rate of
infanticide varies with age ($\chi^2 = 13.37$ $df = 5$, $p < .25$). Figure 3 is a
plot of rate of infanticide against age of mother and shows that infanticide rates are highest in the youngest age category and lowest in the
oldest age category, a pattern that conforms to the above prediction.

In Fig. 4, the age-specific fertility rates for the women in our sample—
all of whom were known to have practiced infanticide—are plotted
against age, grouped into five-years age classes. Also shown in this

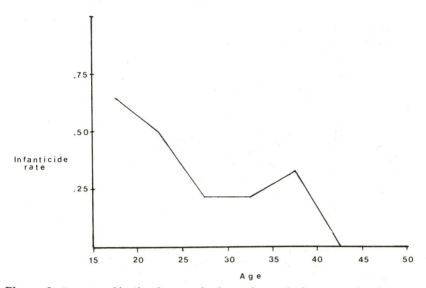

Figure 3. Percent of births that resulted in infanticide for a sample of Ayoreo women all of whom were known to have practiced infanticide. Points plotted are mean percentages calculated for 5-year age classes.

figure is an estimate of the effect of infanticide on the fertility of these women as well as estimates of age-specific fertility rates for a sample of women who are highly unlikely to have practiced infanticide. Specifically, these latter fertility rates are based on the estimated number of births experienced by a sample of acculturated Ayoreo women between the years 1970–1980. During this time period, the acculturated Ayoreo were sedentary and can be viewed as a natural fertility population (Henry, 1961); these data in our opinion thus provide the best available estimates of Ayoreo fertility rates.

Estimates of Ayoreo fertility both for acculturated women and those following traditional subsistence patterns indicate that the peak rate of reproduction falls between the ages of 25 and 29. It will be recalled that this corresponds to the age period during which the rate of infanticide was shown in Fig. 3 to decline most precipitously. The co-occurrence in the 25- to 29-year age classes of both a sharp decline in age-specific rate of infanticide and a high age-specific fertility rate again conforms to the prediction stated above.

It is important to emphasize that the infanticide rates presented in Table I and Fig. 3 at best provide an estimate of the upper bound of the true rate of infanticide among Ayoreo women. This is so because women not known to practice infanticide were specifically excluded from our sample. Obviously, calculation of an infanticide rate based

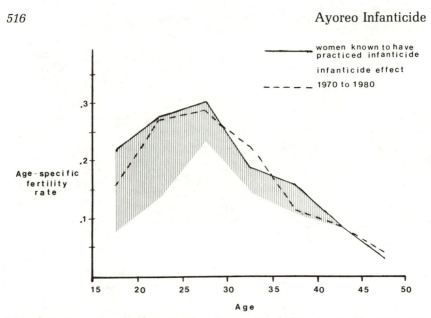

Figure 4. Age-specific fertility rates estimated from the reproductive histories of a cohort of Ayoreo women all of whom were known to have practiced infanticide. Also shown are the effect of infanticide on these rates and the age-specific fertility rates for a sample of acculturated Ayoreo women who presumably did not practice infanticide. Values plotted in figure are means for 5-year age classes. Solid line, women known to have practiced infanticide; hatched area, infanticide effect; dashed line, acculturated women.

only on a sample of women known to have practiced infanticide will yield an overestimate of the population-wide rate of infanticide. On the other hand, one could readily argue that Ayoreo infanticide is so variable in space and time that calculation of such a population-wide rate of infanticide actually would be of little value.

For example, a large proportion of the cases of infanticide in our data occurred in the late 1950s and early 1960s. During this time, the Ayoreo bands in our sample were settled on missions and we believe that rates of infanticide were unusually high during the years immediately preceding and following such settlement. While working on the age estimates in one of the older villages, we noticed there were few people between the ages of 25 and 30—those who would have been born between 1950 and 1955, when missionaries established the village. The Ayoreo explained that during that period, women were "frightened" and few kept their babies. A preliminary analysis of demographic data for this subpopulation appears to confirm that infanticide rates were indeed exceptionally high during this period in Ayoreo history. tory.

In particular, age-specific fertility rates for this subpopulation were

estimated for three 10-year time periods: 1970–1980, the most recent
interval for which we have data; 1945–1955, the period during which
contact with missionaries was made; and for reference, the immediately
preceding period, 1935–1945 (Fig. 5). The estimated fertility rates for
the 1945 to 1955 period are significantly lower than the more recent
rates. When the effect of the reported cases of infanticide is considered,
a strong argument can be made that this population was in danger
of extinction. The argument is made even stronger when the high mortality rates during this period are considered. For reasons mentioned
earlier, these estimates of fertility may be low because some of the
infanticide that occurred during this period was unreported.

There is reason to believe the actual fertility rate during the 1945–
1955 period may have been lower than it is today. During most of
this period, the Ayoreo had no access to modern medicine and the
overall health of the population was poor. Infectious disease, particularly measles, took such a toll at this time that even today some Ayoreo
will not even say the word "measles" but rather refer to it as "the
sickness that kills the Ayoreo." High rates of infectious disease probably affected fecundity and marriage stability and thus lowered the
actual fertility rate.

In addition, during most of this time, the Ayoreo were pursuing their
traditional, semi-nomadic mode of subsistence. Lee (1979, pp. 309, 330)

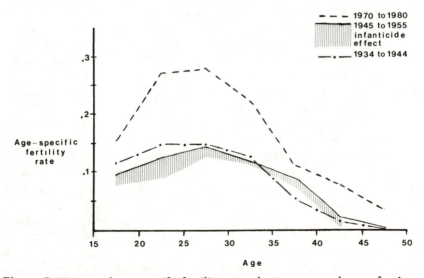

Figure 5. Estimated age-specific fertility rates, by 5-year age classes, for Ayoreo women during three 10-year periods: 1934–1944 (199 births and
1670 person years), 1945–1955 (151 births and 1402 person years)
and 1970–1980 (185 births and 913 person years). The effect of infanticide for the 1945–1955 period (24 reported cases) is also shown.

documented shorter birth intervals among acculturated !Kung who no longer practice nomadic foraging. The Ayoreo acculturation process in many ways parallels that of the !Kung. Today, sedentary Ayoreo mothers are also having children in more rapid succession.

Our method of sampling, which depended on informants' memories, also led to lower estimates of fertility for earlier time periods. However, contrary to what would be expected, the rates for the 1935–1945 period are slightly higher than those from 1945 to 1955. This suggests that "frightening" aspects of rapid culture change did affect the reproductive decisions of Ayoreo women during the 1945–1955 period. In an environment that was hostile and unpredictable, women chose to postpone reproduction. This suggests that infanticide was another factor, in addition to disease and warfare, that led to the depopulation of the Ayoreo in this century. It also may have broader implications for our understanding of depopulation and the acculturation process.

DISCUSSION

Ayoreo infanticide is highly variable and depends on two factors: (1) the physical and social condition of the infant and mother and (2) the predictability of the physical and social environment. In our opinion, the variation in the practice of infanticide among the Ayoreo can best be understood in terms of an individual adaptation. Earlier we demonstrated that Ayoreo infanticide conforms to the prediction that the likelihood of infanticide will vary with a woman's reproductive potential. A second prediction was that women will not keep infants unlikely to survive and hence reproduce. This category obviously includes twins, deformed, and premature infants. In addition, because Ayoreo women needed the economic contribution and protection of husbands in order to successfully raise children, the infanticides of women without husbands—and even those of women who feared their husbands' desertion—also must be included in this category. These latter cases of infanticide conform to the individual adaptation view of infanticide in another way: because of Ayoreo sex taboos, unwed mothers could not be sexually active and therefore could not find husbands. This would have detrimental long-range reproductive consequences.

The relationship between marriage formation and infanticide merits further attention. The marital histories and the reasons for specific cases of infanticide, presented in Fig. 2, suggest that marriage instability may be the most common cause of Ayoreo infanticide. While sanctioning premarital sex, Ayoreo culture did not discourage young people from dissolving these trial marriages if they had not yet resulted in children. In addition, although there were important political and economic dimensions to Ayoreo marriage, marriages were not arranged.

Each marriage stood on its own merits; it was not part of a nexus of overlapping economic and political obligations between kin groups. Therefore, the early dissolution of a marriage rarely had far-ranging implications for other marriages. Thus, Ayoreo women may have used infanticide or the threat of infanticide to manipulate males into investing in their children. Infanticide in this sense can be viewed as an individual adaptation to a social environment that lacked other means of establishing stable marriages.

However, infanticide as a means of securing male investment is a costly reproductive strategy. Furthermore, the social environment that fosters this behavior is largely a creation of the Ayoreo. Hence, it is tempting to use group selection arguments to answer the question of why the Ayoreo went about the process of establishing marriages in such a costly manner (cf. Schrimshaw, Chapter 22, this volume). It is difficult to reject on strictly empirical grounds the hypothesis that Ayoreo marriage formation practices were group adaptations to regulate population growth. Yet, as Williams (1966) argues, group adaptations are unlikely; group selection should be used only as an explanatory device of last resort. Furthermore, as Bates and Lees (1979:286) point out, the population regulation view of human infanticide "does not account for differential behaviors of individuals within the group." Our finding that the frequency of infanticide varies with age of mother lends strong support to this argument. Elsewhere, Bugos (in prep.) argues that Ayoreo marriage practices provide individuals with a large degree of choice, which is adaptive in an unpredictable environment.

Although larger issues of the level of selection (individual or group) cannot be resolved on the basis of Ayoreo demography alone, our data do provide strong empirical grounds for questioning one group selection view of human infanticide: the Divale and Harris (1975) warfare, male dominance, and preferential female infanticide hypothesis. Warfare was endemic among the Ayoreo and aggressive male qualities were highly valued. However, there was no evidence that the Ayoreo valued male children more than female children. The Ayoreo explicitly state that sex of offspring was not a consideration in infanticide decisions. Thus among 134 newborns, 74 were males and 54 were females, a sex ratio of 137. Among the 47 cases of infanticide in which the sex of the infant was known, there were 31 males and 16 females, a sex ratio of 194. If anything, one might conclude that Ayoreo infanticide is preferentially male but, in fact, the sex ratios of the newborns and infanticide victims do not differ. Nevertheless, one can conclusively reject the hypothesis that Ayoreo infanticide is preferentially female ($p < .022$).

In summary, our research strongly suggests that infanticide among traditional societies needs to be examined in a historical and life-historical context as well as in its cultural ecological context. Perhaps the most striking patterns to emerge from this analysis are the mother's decreasing propensity to practice infanticide with increasing age and the apparent correlation between probable male investment and maternal willingness to rear a particular child.

ACKNOWLEDGMENTS

Funds for the field research were provided by the National Geographic Society (grant number 2245-80) and the Pennsylvania State University Hill Foundation. While we were in Bolivia, representatives of the South American Mission, particularly Charles and Jean Ramsey, Joseph and Kathy Kemper, Janet Briggs and James Davidson, and representatives of the New Tribes Missions, particularly Tim and Betty Wyma, shared their hospitality and their insights into Ayoreo culture with us. In Paraguay, John Renshaw and Graciela Ocariz of the Instituto Nacional del Indigena also extended their hospitality to us. Drs. Napoleon Chagnon, Oswald Werner, William Irons, Nancy Berte, and Raymond Hames read versions of the paper and provided useful comments.

Above all, we want to thank the Ayoreo people, without whose cooperation and kindness this work could not have been done.

Bibliography

Abernathy, V. (1979). *Population pressure and cultural adjustment.* New York: Human Sciences Press.

Abramsky, Z., and C. R. Tracy. (1979). Population biology of a "noncycling" population of prairie voles and a hypothesis on the role of migration in regulating microtine cycles. *Ecology* **60**, 349–361.

Adamson, G. (1968). *Bwana game.* London: Collins.

Adler, N. T. (1981). *Neuroendocrinology of reproduction: Physiology and behavior.* New York: Plenum Press.

Adler, N. (1983). The neuroethology of reproduction. In *Advances in vertebrate neuroethology* (J. Ewert, ed.). New York: Plenum Press.

Adler, N., T. Allen, and J. Toner. (1982). Effects of hormones and behavioral stimulation in female rats. Reproductive Behavior Meeting (June), East Lansing, Michigan.

Adolf, E. F. (1931). The size of the body and the size of the environment in the growth of tadpoles. *Biological Bulletin* **61**, 350–375.

Agren, G. (1976). Social and territorial behaviour in the Mongolian gerbil (*Meriones unguiculatus*) under seminatural conditions. *Biology of Behaviour* **1**, 267–285.

Agren, G. (1980). Two laboratory experiments on inbreeding avoidance in the Mongolian gerbil. *Behavioural Processes* **6**, 291–297.

Agren, K. *et al.* (1973). *Aristocrats, farmers, proletarians: Essays in Swedish history* (Studia Historica Upsaliensia XLVII). Uppsala: Almquist and Wiksell.

Aguirre, A. Columbia. (1966). The family in Candelaria. *Studies in Family Planning* **1**, 11.

Akiga. (1939). *Akiga's story: The Tiv tribe as seen by one of its members* (R. East, trans. and ed.). London: International Institute of African Languages and Cultures.

Alcock, J. (1979). *Animal behavior: An evolutionary approach,* 2nd ed. Sunderland, Mass.: Sinauer Associates.

Aldrich-Blake, F. P. G. (1970). The ecology and behaviour of the blue monkey *Cercopithecus mitis stuhlmanni.* Unpublished Ph.D. thesis, University of Bristol, Bristol, England.

Alekseev, V. P. (1973). Paleodemography of the USSR. *Soviet Anthropology and Archeology* **12,** 51–82.

Alexander, R. D. (1974). The evolution of social behavior. *Annual Review of Ecology and Systematics* **5,** 325–383.

Alexander, R. D. (1979). *Darwinism and human affairs.* Seattle: University of Washington Press.

Alland, A. (1970). *Adaptation in cultural evolution: An approach to medical anthropology.* New York: Columbia University Press.

Allen, M. J. (1932). A survey of the amphibians and reptiles of Harrison County, Mississippi. *American Museum Novitates* **524,** 1–20.

Alm, G. (1952). Year class fluctuations and span of life of perch. *Institute of Freshwater Research Drottningholm Report* **33,** 17–38.

Altman, P. L., and D. S. Dittmer. (1972). *Biological data book,* Vol. 1, 2nd ed. Bethesda, Md.: Federation of American Societies for Experimental Biology.

Altmann, D. (1974). Beziehungen zwischen sozialer Rangordnung und Jungenaufzucht bei *Canis lupus* L. *Zoologische Garten* **44,** 235–236.

Altmann, J. (1980). *Baboon mothers and infants.* Cambridge, Mass.: Harvard University Press.

Altmann, J., S. A. Altmann, and G. Hausfater. (1978). Primate infant's effects on mother's future reproduction. *Science* **201,** 1028–1029.

Altmann, J., S. A. Altmann, G. Hausfater, and S. A. McCuskey. (1977). Life history of yellow baboons: Physical development, reproductive parameters and infant mortality. *Primates* **18,** 315–330.

Andelman, S. (1984). Ecology and reproductive strategies among vervet monkeys (*Cercopithecus aethiops*) in the Amboseli National Park, Kenya. (in prep.)

Anderson, J. D., D. D. Hassinger, and G. H. Dalrymple. (1971). Natural mortality of eggs and larvae of *Ambystoma t. tigrinum. Ecology* **52,** 1107–1112.

Anderson, P. K. (1964). Lethal alleles in *Mus musculus:* Local distribution and evidence for isolation of demes. *Science* **145,** 177–178.

Andrewartha, H. G. (1971). The concept of local population and the mechanisms of negative feedback in natural populations. In *Dynamics of Populations* (P. J. den Boer and G. R. Gradwell, eds.), pp. 189–198. Wageningen: Pudoc.

Angst, W., and D. Thommen. (1977). New data and a discussion of infant killing in Old World monkeys and apes. *Folia Primatologica* **27,** 198–229.

Ankney, C. D. (1982). Sex ratio varies with egg sequence in lesser snow geese. *Auk* **99,** 662–666.

Anonymous. (1900). Logements etroits et mortalité par tuberculose à Stockholm 1871–1900. Pamphlet in the collection of the Society for Heart and Lung Diseases Library (Kungsgatan 54), Stockholm.

Ardrey, R. (1970). *The social contract.* New York: Atheneum.

Armitage, K. B., D. Johns, and D. C. Andersen. (1979). Cannibalism among yellow-bellied marmots. *Journal of Mammalogy* **60,** 205–207.

Aron, C. (1979). Mechanisms of control of the reproductive function by olfactory stimuli in female mammals. *Physiological Reviews* **59,** 229–284.

Arvola, A., M. Ilmén, and T. Koponen. (1962). On the aggressive behaviour of the Norwegian lemming (*Lemmus lemmus*), with special reference to the sounds produced. *Archivum Societatis Zoologicae Botanicae Fennicae "Vanamo"* **17**, 80–101.

Asdell, S. A. (1964). *Patterns of mammalian reproduction,* 2nd ed. Ithaca, N.Y.: Cornell University Press.

Askew, R. (1971). *Parasitic insects.* New York: American Elsevier.

Assem, J. van den. (1967). Territory in the three-spined stickleback, *Gasterosteus aculeatus* L. *Behaviour* Suppl. **16**, 164 pp.

Austin, C. R. (1972). Fertilization. In *Reproduction in mammals,* Vol. 1: *Germ cells and fertilization* (C. R. Austin and R. V. Short, eds.), pp. 103–133. Cambridge: Cambridge University Press.

Austin, C. R., and R. G. Edwards. (1981). *Mechanisms of sex differentiation in animals and man.* New York: Academic Press.

Ayer, M. L., and J. M. Whitsett. (1980). Aggressive behaviour of female prairie deer mice in laboratory populations. *Animal Behaviour* **28**, 763–771.

Bacon, A. M. (1891). *Japanese girls and women.* New York: Gordon Press.

Badinter, E. (1980). *L'amour en plus.* Paris: Flammarion.

Baerends, G. P., and J. M. Baerends-van Roon. (1950). An introduction to the study of the ethology of cichlid fishes. *Behaviour* Suppl. **1**, 242 pp.

Bailey, E. D. (1969). Immigration and emigration as contributory regulators of populations through social disruption. *Canadian Journal of Zoology* **47**, 1213–1215.

Bailey, J. E. (1952). Life history and ecology of the sculpin *Cottus bairdi punctulatus* in southwestern Montana. *Copeia,* pp. 243–255.

Baird, Sir Dugald. (1945). Social and economic factors on stillbirths and neonatal deaths. *Journal of Obstetrics and Gynecology of the British Empire* **52**, 217–234.

Baker, A. E. M. (1981). Gene flow in house mice: Behavior in a population cage. *Behavioral Ecology and Sociobiology* **8**, 83–90.

Baker, J. R. (1938). Evolution of breeding seasons. In *Evolution: Essays on aspects of evolutionary biology* (G. R. deBeer, ed.), pp. 161–177. London: Oxford Clarendon Press.

Bakke, A. (1968). Field and laboratory studies on sex ratio in *Ips acuminatus* (Coleoptera: Scolytidae) in Norway. *Canadian Entomologist* **100**, 640–648.

Balikci, A. (1967). Female infanticide on the Arctic coast. *Man* **2**, 615–625.

Ball, S. C. (1936). The distribution and behavior of the spadefoot toad in Connecticut. *Transactions of the Connecticut Academy of Arts and Science* **32**, 351–379.

Balon, E. K. (1975a). Reproductive guilds of fishes: A proposal and definition. *Journal of the Fisheries Research Board of Canada* **32**, 821–864.

Balon, E. K. (1975b). Terminology of intervals in fish development. *Journal of the Fisheries Research Board of Canada* **32**, 1663–1670.

Banerji, S. R., and D. Prasad. (1974). Observations on reproduction and survival of *Anabas testudineus* (Bloch) in Bihar Region. *Journal of the Inland Fisheries Society of India* **6**, 6–17.

Banfield, A. W. F. (1974). *The mammals of Canada.* Toronto: University of Toronto Press.

Banks, C. J. (1956). Observations on the behaviour and mortality in Coccinellidae before dispersal from the egg shells. *Proceedings of the Royal Entomological Society of London,* **A31**, 56–60.

Bannikov, A. G. (1950). Age distribution of a population and its dynamics in *Bombina bombina* L. *Trudy Akademiia Nauk. S.S.S.R.* **70**, 101–103.

Bannikov, A. G. (1958). Die Biologie des Froschzahnmolches, *Ranodon sibiricus* Kessler. *Zoologisches Jahrbücher* **86**, 245–249.

Barbour, T., and A. Loveridge. (1928). A comparative study of the herpetological faunae of the Uluguru and Usambara Mountains, Tanganyika Territory with descriptions of new species. *Memoirs of the Museum of Comparative Zoology Harvard* **50**, 137–142.

Bardhan, P. K. (1974). On life and death questions. *Economic and Political Weekly* **9**, 1293–1304.

Barlow, G. W. (1964). Ethology of the Asian teleost *Badis badis*. V. Dynamics of fanning and other parental activities, with comments on the behavior of the larvae and postlarvae. *Zeitschrift für Tierpsychologie* **21**, 99–123.

Barlow, G. W. (1967). Social behavior of a South American leaf fish, *Polycentrus schomburgkii*, with an account of recurring pseudofemale behavior. *American Midland Naturalist* **78**, 215–234.

Barlow, G. W. (1974). Contrasts in social behavior between Central American cichlid fishes and coral-reef surgeon fishes. *American Zoologist* **14**, 9–34.

Barlow, G. W. (1976). The midas cichlid in Nicaragua. In *Investigations of the ichthyofauna of Nicaraguan lakes* (T. B. Thorson, ed.), pp. 333–358. Lincoln, Neb.: School of Life Sciences, University of Nebraska.

Barlow, G. W. (1981). Patterns of parental investment, dispersal, and size among coral-reef fishes. *Environmental Biology of Fishes* **6**, 65–85.

Bartels, J. M., and G. N. Lanier. (1974). Emergence and mating in *Scolytus multistriatus* (Coleoptera: Scolytidae). *Annals of the Entomological Society of America* **67**, 365–369.

Bartholomew, G. A. (1972). Body temperature and energy metabolism. In *Animal physiology: Principles and adaptations* (M. S. Gordon, ed.), 2nd ed., pp. 298–368. New York: Macmillan.

Bartke, A., and J. G. M. Shire. (1972). Differences between mouse strains in testicular cholesterol levels and androgen target organs. *Journal of Endocrinology* **55**, 173–184.

Bates, D. G., and S. H. Lees. (1979). The myth of population regulation. In *Evolutionary biology and human social behavior: An anthropological perspective* (N. A. Chagnon and W. Irons, eds.), pp. 273–289. North Scituate, Mass.: Duxbury Press.

Batty, J. (1978). Plasma levels of testosterone and male sexual behavior in strains of the house mouse. *Animal Behaviour* **26**, 339–348.

Baum, M. J. (1979). Differentiation of coital behavior in mammals: A comparative analysis. *Neuroscience and Biobehavioral Reviews* **3**, 265–284.

Baylis, J. R. (1981). The evolution of parental care in fishes, with reference to Darwin's rule of male sexual selection. *Environmental Biology of Fishes* **6**, 223–251.

Beard, R. L. (1964). Pathogenic stinging of housefly pupae by *Nasonia vitripennis* (Walker). *Journal of Insect Pathology* **6**, 107.

Beatty, W. (1979). Gonadal hormones and sex differences in nonreproductive behaviors in rodents: Organizational and activational influences. *Hormones and Behavior* **12**, 112–163.

Beaver, R. A. (1977). Bark and ambrosia beetles in tropical forests. *Proceedings of the Symposium of Forest Pests and Diseases in S. E. Asia. Biotropica* (Special publ.) **2**, 133–147.

Bedford, J. M. (1970). The saga of mammalian sperm from ejaculation to syngamy. In *Mammalian reproduction* (H. Gibian and E. J. Plotz, eds.), pp. 124–182. New York: Springer-Verlag.

Beecher, M. D., I. M. Beecher, and S. Lumpkin. (1981a). Parent–offspring recognition in bank swallows (*Riparia riparia*): I. Natural history. *Animal Behaviour* **29**, 86–94.

Beecher, M. D., I. M. Beecher, and S. Hahn. (1981b). Parent–offspring recognition in bank swallows (*Riparia riparia*): II. Development and acoustic basis. *Animal Behaviour* **29**, 95–101.

Bekoff, M., J. Diamond, and J. B. Milton. (1981). Life history patterns and sociality in canids: Body size, reproduction, and behavior. *Oecologia (Berlin)* **50**, 386–390.

Belisle, S., and D. Tulchinsky. (1980). Amniotic fluid hormones. In *Maternal-fetal endocrinology* (D. Tulchinsky and K. Ryan, eds.), pp. 169–195. Philadelphia: W. B. Saunders.

Bellringer, J. F., H. P. M. Pratt, and E. B. Keverne. (1980). Involvement of the vomeronasal organ and prolactin in pheromonal induction of delayed implantation in mice.

Benson, G. K., and C. R. Morris. (1971). Foetal growth and lactation in rats exposed to high temperatures during pregnancy. *Journal of Reproduction and Fertility* **27**, 369–384.

Berens von Rautenfeld, D. (1978). Bemerkungen zur Austauschbarkeit von Küken der Silbermöwe (*Larus argentatus*) nach der ersten Lebenswoche. *Zeitschrift für Tierpsychologie* **47**, 180–181.

Berger, J. (1983). Induced abortion and social factors in wild horses. *Nature (London)* **303**, 59–61.

Berle, B. B., and C. T. Javert. (1954). Stress and habitual abortion. *Obstetrics Gynecology* **3**, 298–312.

Bernds, W. P. and D. P. Barash. (1979). Early termination of parental investment in mammals, including humans. In: *Evolutionary Biology and Human social behavior.* (N. A. Chagaon and W. Irons eds.), pp. 487–506. North Scituate, Mass.: Duxbury Press.

Bernstein, I. S. (1968). The lutong of Kuala Selangor. *Behaviour* **32**, 1–16.

Berry, R. J., and M. E. Jakobson. (1974). Vagility in an island population of the house mouse. *Journal of Zoology (London)* **173**, 341–354.

Bertram, B. C. R. (1975a). Social factors influencing reproduction in wild lions. *Journal of Zoology (London)* **177**, 463–482.

Bertram, B. C. R. (1975b). The social system of lions. *Scientific American* **232**, 54–65.

Bertram, B. C. R. (1976). Kin selection in lions and evolution. In *Growing points in ethology* (P. P. G. Bateson and R. A. Hinde, eds.), pp. 281–301. Cambridge: Cambridge University Press.

Bertram, B. C. R. (1979). Ostriches recognize their own eggs and discard others. *Nature (London)* **279**, 233–234.

Biliski, F. (1921). Über den Einfluss des Lebensraumes auf des Wachtum der Kaulquappen. *Pflüger's Archiv* **188**, 254–272.

Biocca, E. (1971). *Yanoáma.* New York: E. P. Dutton.

Birdsell, J. B. (1968). Some predictions for the Pleistocene based on equilibrium systems among recent hunter-gatherers. In *Man the Hunter.* (R. B. Lee and I. DeVore, eds.), pp. 229–240. Chicago: Aldine.

Bishop, N., S. B. Hrdy, J. Teas, and J. Moore. (1981). Measures of human influence in habitats of South Asian monkeys. *International Journal of Primatology* **2**, 153–167.

Bishop, S. D. (1941). *The salamanders of New York.* New York State Museum Bulletin, University of the State of New York Publications, New York. 365 pp.

Blair, W. F. (1957). Changes in vertebrate populations under conditions of drought. *Cold Spring Harbor Symposia on Quantitative Biology* **22**, 272–275.

Blaker, D. (1969). Behaviour of the cattle egret *Ardeola ibis*. *Ostrich* **40**, 75–129.

Blanchard, F. N. (1934). Relation of the female *Hemidactylium scutatum* to her nest and eggs. *Copeia* pp. 137–139.

Blandau, R. J. (1961). Biology of eggs and implantation. In *Sex and internal secretions* (W. C. Young and G. W. Corner, eds.), pp. 797–882. Baltimore: Williams and Wilkins.

Blaustein, A. R., and R. K. O'Hara. (1982). Kin recognition in *Rana cascade* tadpoles: Maternal and paternal effects. *Animal Behaviour* **30**, 1151–1157.

Bleakney, S. (1958). Cannibalism in *Rana sylvatica* tadpoles. *Herpetologica* **14**, 34.

Bledsoe, C. H. (1983). Stealing food as a problem in demography and nutrition. Paper presented at the 82nd annual Meeting American Anthropological Association, Chicago, Illinois, Nov. 16–20.

Bloch, S., and H. I. Wyss. (1973). An anti-androgen (cyproterone acetate) inhibits the pregnancy block in mice caused by the presence of strange males (Bruce effect). *Journal of Endocrinology* **59**, 365–366.

Block, E., M. Lew, and M. Klein. (1971). Studies on the inhibition of fetal androgen formation: Testosterone synthesis by fetal and newborn mouse testes *in vitro*. *Endocrinology* **88**, 41–46.

Blumer, L. S. (1979). Male parental care in the bony fishes. *Quarterly Review of Biology* **54**, 149–161.

Blumer, L. S. (1982a). A bibliography and categorization of bony fishes exhibiting parental care. *Zoological Journal of the Linnean Society* **76**, 1–22.

Blumer, L. S. (1982b). Parental care and reproductive ecology of the North American catfish, *Ictalurus nebulosus*. Unpublished Ph.D. thesis, University of Michigan, Ann Arbor, Mich.

Blumer, L. S., and W. J. Dominey. The evolution of biparental care. Submitted ms.

Bluntschli, H. (1938). Le developpement primaire et l'implantation chez un Centetine (*Hemicentetes*). *Comptes Rendus de l'Association des Anatomistes* **44**, 39–46.

Blurton-Jones, N. G., and R. M. Sibly. (1978). Testing adaptiveness of culturally determined behavior: Do Bushman women maximize reproductive success by spacing births widely and foraging seldom? In *Human behaviour and adaptation* (Symposium No. 18 of the Society for the Study of Human Biology) (N. G. Blurton-Jones and V. Reynolds, eds.), pp. 135–157. London: Taylor and Francis.

Boersma, P. D., and N. T. Wheelwright. (1979). Egg neglect in the procellariiformes: Reproductive adaptations in the fork-tailed stormpetrel. *Condor* **81**, 157–165.

Boggess, J. E. (1976). The social behavior of the Himalayan langur (*Presbytis entellus*) in eastern Nepal. Unpublished Ph.D. thesis, University of California, Berkeley, Calif.

Boggess, J. E. (1979). Troop male membership changes and infant killing in langurs (*Presbytis entellus*). *Folia Primatologica* **32**, 65–107.

Boggess, J. E. (1980). Intermale relations and troop male membership changes in langurs (*Presbytis entellus*) in Nepal. *International Journal of Primatology* **1**, 233–274.

Boggess, J. E. (1982). Immature male and adult male interactions in bisexual langur (*Presbytis entellus*) troops. *Folia Primatologica* **38**, 19–38.

Boonstra, R. (1977). Effect of conspecifics on survival during population declines in *Microtus townsendii*. *Journal of Animal Ecology* **46**, 835–851.

Boonstra, R. (1978). Effect of adult Townsend voles (*Microtus townsendii*) on survival of young. *Ecology* **59**, 242–248.

Boonstra, R. (1980). Infanticide in microtines: Importance in natural populations. *Oecologia* (*Berlin*) **46**, 262–265.

Bórmidaa, M. and M. Califano. (1978). Los indios Ayoreo del Chaco Boreal. Buenos Aires: Fundacion para la Education, la Ciencia y la Cultura.

Boucher, D. H. (1977). On wasting parental investment. *American Naturalist* **111**, 786–788.

Bourlière, F., C. Hunkeler, and M. Bertrand. (1970). Ecology and behavior of Lowe's guenon (*Cercopithecus campbelli lowei*) in the Ivory Coast. In *Old World monkeys* (J. R. Napier and P. H. Napier, eds.), pp. 297–350. New York: Academic Press.

Boving, B. G. (1972). Spacing and orientation of blastocysts *in utero*. In *Biology of mammalian fertilization and implantation* (K. S. Moshissi and E. S. E. Hafez, eds.), pp. 357–378. Springfield, Ill.: C. C. Thomas.

Bowers, J. M., and B. K. Alexander. (1967). Mice: Individual recognition by olfactory cues. *Science* **158**, 1208–1210.

Bowles, G. T. (1953). Population control and the family in feudal and post-restoration Japan. *Kroeber Anthropological Society Papers* **8–9**, 1–19.

Bragg, A. N. (1962). Predator–prey relationships in two species of spadefoot tadpole with notes on some other features of their biology. *Wasmann Journal of Biology* **22**, 81–97.

Bragg, A. N. (1964). Further study of predation and cannibalism in spadefoot tadpoles. *Herpetologica* **20**, 12–24.

Bragg, A. N., and W. Bragg. (1959). Variation in the mouthparts in tadpoles of *Scaphiopus* (*Spea*) *bombifrons* Cope (Amphibia: Salientia). *Southwestern Naturalist* **3**, 55–59.

Brambell, F. W. R. (1948). Prenatal mortality in mammals. *Biological Reviews* **23**, 370–405.

Brame, A. H. (1967). A list of the world's recent and fossil salamanders. *Herpeton* **2**, 1–26.

Braun, B. M. (1981). Siblicide, the mechanism of brood reduction in the black-legged kittiwake, *Rissa tridactyla*. Unpublished M.S. thesis, University of California, Irvine, Calif.

Braun, B. M., and G. L. Hunt, Jr. (1983). Brood reduction in black-legged kittiwakes. *Auk* **100**, 469–476.

Breder, C. M. (1936). The reproductive habits of the North American sunfishes (Family Centrarchidae). *Zoologica* **21**, 1–48.

Breder, C. M. (1943). A note on erratic viciousness in *Astyanax mexicanus* (Phillipi). *Copeia*, pp. 82–84.

Breder, C. M., and C. W. Coates. (1932). A preliminary study of population stability and sex ratio of *Lebistes*. *Copeia*, pp. 147–155.

Breder, C. M., and D. E. Rosen. (1966). *Modes of reproduction in fishes*. Garden City, N.Y.: Natural History Press.

Breed, W. G. (1969). Oestrus and ovarian histology in the lactating vole (*Microtus agrestis*). *Journal of Reproduction and Fertility* **18**, 33–42.

Brian, M. (1965). *Social insect populations*. New York: Academic Press.

Bridges, R. S. (1975). Long-term effects of pregnancy and parturition upon maternal responsiveness in the rat. *Physiology and Behavior* **14**, 245–249.

Brockleman, W. Y. (1969). An analysis of density effects and predation in *Bufo americanus* tadpoles. *Ecology* **50**, 632–644.

Brockway, J. M., J. D. McDonald, and J. D. Pallar. (1963). The energetic cost of reproduction in sheep. *Journal of Physiology* **167**, 318–327.

Broida, J., and B. Svare. (1982). Postpartum aggression in C57BL/6J and DBA/2J mice: Experiential and environmental influences. *Behavioral and Neural Biology* **35**, 76–83.

Bronson, F. H. (1968). Pheromonal influences on mammalian reproduction. In *Reproduction and sexual behavior* (M. Diamond, ed.), pp. 341–361. Bloomington, Ind.: Indiana University Press.

Bronson, F. H. (1973). Establishment of social rank among grouped male mice: Relative effects of circulating FSH, LH, and corticosterone. *Physiology and Behavior* **10**, 947–952.

Bronson, F. H. (1979). The reproductive ecology of the house mouse. *Quarterly Review of Biology* **54**, 265–299.

Bronson, F. H. (1983). Chemical communication in house mice and deer mice: Functional roles in reproduction of wild populations. In *Advances in the study of mammalian behavior* (J. F. Eisenberg and D. G. Kleiman, eds.), pp. 198–238. Special Publication No. 7, The American Society of Mammalogists.

Bronson, F. H., and A. Coquelin. (1980). The modulation of reproduction by priming pheromones in house mice: Speculations on adaptive function. In *Chemical signals: Vertebrates and aquatic invertebrates* (D. Müller-Schwarze and R. M. Silverstein, eds.), pp. 243–265. New York: Plenum Press.

Bronson, F. H., and B. E. Eleftheriou. (1963). Influence of strange males on implantation in the deermouse. *General and Comparative Endocrinology* **3**, 515–518.

Bronson, F. H., and H. M. Marsden. (1973). The preputial gland as an indicator of social dominance in male mice. *Behavioral Biology* **9**, 625–628.

Bronson, F. H., M. H. Stetson, and M. E. Stiff. (1973). Serum FSH and LH in male mice following aggressive and non-aggressive interactions. *Physiology and Behavior* **10**, 366–372.

Bronson, F. H., and W. K. Whitten. (1968). Oestrus-accelerating pheromone of mice: Assay, androgen-dependency, and presence in bladder urine. *Journal of Reproduction and Fertility* **15**, 131–154.

Brooks, R. J. (1978). Lemming behavior: A possible parallel to strandings? In *Biology of marine mammals: Insights through strandings* (J. R. Geraci and D. J. St. Aubin, eds.), pp. 114–128. Washington, D.C.: U.S. Marine Mammal Commission.

Brooks, R. J., and E. M. Banks. (1971). Radio-tracking study of lemming home range. *Communications in Behavioral Biology* **6**, 1–5.

Brooks, R. J., and L. Schwarzkopf. (1982). Factors affecting incidence of infanticide and discrimination of related and unrelated neonates in male *Mus musculus. Behavioral and Neural Biology.* **37**, 149–161.

Brower, L. P. (1961). Experimental analyses of egg cannibalism in the Monarch and Queen butterflies, *Danaus plexippus* and *D. gilippus berenice. Physiological Zoology* **34**, 287–296.

Brown, H. D. (1972). The behaviour of newly hatched coccinellid larvae. *Journal of the Entomological Society of Southern Africa* **35**, 144–157.

Brown, J. L., and E. R. Brown. (1981). Kin selection and individual selection in babblers. In *Natural selection and social behavior* (R. D. Alexander and D. W. Tinkle, eds.), pp. 244–256. New York: Chiron Press.

Brown, L. (1942). Propagation of the spotted channel catfish *Ictalurus lacustrus punctatus. Transactions of the Kansas Academy of Science* **45**, 311–314.

Brown, L. H. (1974). A record of two young reared by Verreaux's eagle. *Ostrich* **45**, 146–147.

Brown, L. H., V. Gargett, and P. Steyn. (1977). Breeding success in some African eagles related to theories about sibling aggression and its effects. *Ostrich* **48**, 65–71.

Brown, R. Z. (1953). Social behavior, reproduction, and population changes in the house mouse (*Mus musculus* L.). *Ecological Monographs* **23**, 217–240.

Bruce, H. M. (1959). An exteroceptive block to pregnancy in the mouse. *Nature* (*London*) **184**, 105.

Bruce, H. M. (1960). A block to pregnancy in the house mouse caused by the proximity of strange males. *Journal of Reproduction and Fertility* **1**, 96–103.

Bruce, H. M. (1961a). Observations on the suckling stimulus and lactation in the rat. *Journal of Reproduction and Fertility* **2**, 17–34.

Bruce, H. M. (1961b). Time relations in the pregnancy block induced in mice by strange males. *Journal of Reproduction and Fertility* **2**, 138–142.

Bruce, H. M. (1965). The effect of castration on the reproductive pheromones of male mice. *Journal of Reproduction and Fertility* **10**, 141–143.

Bruce, H. M. (1967). Effects of olfactory stimuli on reproduction in mammals. *Ciba Foundation Study Group* **26**, 29–42.

Bruce, H. M., and D. M. V. Parrott. (1960). Role of olfactory sense in pregnancy block by strange males. *Science* **131**, 1526.

Bruce, R. C. (1972). Variation in the life cycle of the salamander *Gyrinophilus porphyriticus*. *Herpetologica* **28**, 230–245.

Bruce, R. C. (1975). Reproductive biology of the mud salamander, *Pseudotriton montanus* in western South Carolina. *Copeia*, pp. 129–137.

Bry, C., and C. Gillet. (1980). Reduction of cannibalism in pike (*Esox lucious*) fry by isolation of full-sib families. *Reproductive and Nutritional Development* **20**, 173–182.

Bryant, D. M. (1978). Establishment of weight hierarchies in the broods of house martins *Delichon urbica*. *Ibis* **120**, 16–26.

Bryden, M. M. (1969). Growth of the southern elephant seal *Mirounga leonina* (L). *Growth* **33**, 69–82.

Bryden, M. M. (1972). Growth and development of marine mammals. In *Functional anatomy of marine mammals* (R. J. Harrison, ed.), pp. 1–79. New York: Academic Press.

Buckley, T. (1982). Menstruation and the power of Yurok women: Methods in cultural reconstruction. *American Ethnologist* **9**, 47–60.

Bugos, P. In preparation. An evolutionary ecological analysis of the social organization of the Ayoreo of the Chaco Boreal. Doctoral dissertation. Department of Anthropology, Northwestern University. Evanston, Illinois.

Buhl, A. E., J. F. Hasler, M. C. Tyler, N. Goldberg, and E. M. Banks. (1978). The effects of social rank on reproductive indices in groups of male collared lemmings (*Dicrostonyx groenlandicus*). *Biology of Reproduction* **18**, 317–324.

Bujalska, G. (1970). Reproduction stabilizing elements in an island population of *Clethrionomys glareolus* (Schreber, 1780). *Acta Theriologica* **15**, 381–412.

Bujalska, G. (1973). The role of spacing behaviour among females in the regulation of reproduction in the bank vole. *Journal of Reproduction and Fertility Suppl.* **19**, 465–474.

Bulkley, R. V. (1970). Feeding interaction between adult bass and their offspring. *Transactions of the American Fisheries Society* **99**, 732–738.

Bull, J. J. (1983). *The evolution of sex determining mechanisms and sex chromosomes*. Reading, Mass.: Addison-Wesley Publishing Co.

Burger, J. (1974). Breeding adaptations of Franklin's gull (*Larus pipixcan*) to a marsh habitat. *Animal Behaviour* 22, 521–567.

Burger, J. (1978). The transition to independence and postfledging parental care in seabirds. In *Behavior of marine animals* (J. Burger, B. L. Olla, and H. E. Winn, eds.), Vol. 4, pp. 367–447. New York: Plenum Press.

Burgess, R. (1950). Development of spadefoot toad larvae under laboratory conditions. *Copeia*, pp. 49–51.

Burney, D. A. (1980). The effects of human activities on cheetahs (*Acinonyx jubatus* Schr.) in the Mara region of Kenya. Unpublished M.Sc. thesis, University of Nairobi, Nairobi, Kenya.

Burton, T. (1977). Population estimates, feeding habits, and energy relationships of *Notophthalmus viridescens* in Mirror Lake, New Hampshire. *Copeia*, pp. 139–143.

Buskirk, W. H., R. E. Buskirk, and W. J. Hamilton, III. (1974). Troop-mobilizing behavior of adult male chacma baboons. *Folia Primatologica* 22, 9–18.

Busse, C. (1980). Leopard and lion predation upon chacma baboons living in the Moremi Wildlife Reserve. *Botswana Notes and Records* 12, 15–21.

Busse, C. (1984). Triadic interactions among male and infant chacma baboons. In *Primate paternalism: An evolutionary and comparative view of male investment* (D. M. Taub, ed.), pp. 186–212. New York: Van Nostrand Reinhold.

Busse, C. and T. P. Gordon. 1983. Attacks on neonates by a male mangabey (*Cercocebus atys*). *American Journal of Primatology* 5(4), 345–356.

Busse, C., and W. J. Hamilton, III. (1981). Infant carrying by male chacma baboons. *Science* 212, 1281–1283.

Butynski, T. M. (1982). Harem-male replacement and infanticide in the blue monkey (*Cercopithecus mitis stuhlmanni*) in the Kibale Forest, Uganda. *American Journal of Primatology* 3, 1–22.

Bygott, J. D., B. C. R. Bertram, and J. P. Hanby. (1979). Male lions in large coalitions gain reproductive advantages. *Nature* (*London*) 282, 839–841.

Calef, C. W. (1973). Natural mortality of tadpoles in a population of *Rana aurora*. *Ecology* 45, 741–758.

Calhoun, J. B. (1962). Population density and social pathology. *Scientific American* 206, 139–148.

Calvert, W. H. (1913). *The further evolution of man*. London: A. C. Fifield.

Camenzind, F. J. (1978). Behavioral ecology of coyotes on the National Elk Refuge, Jackson, Wyoming. In *Coyotes: Biology, behavior, and management* (M. Bekoff, ed.), pp. 267–296. New York: Academic Press.

Campling, R. C. (1966). A preliminary study of the effect of pregnancy and of lactation on the voluntary intake of food by cows. *British Journal of Nutrition* 20, 25–39.

Carlisle, T. R. (1982). Brood success in variable environments: Implications for parental care allocation. *Animal Behaviour* 30, 824–836.

Carlsson, Sten. (1977). *Froknar, mamseller, jungfru och pigor*. Uppsala: Almquist and Wiksell.

Carlsson, Sture. (1908). *The struggle against tuberculosis in Sweden*. Stockholm: Centraltryckeriet.

Carr-Saunders, A. M. (1922). *The population problem: A study in human evolution*. London: Clarendon Press.

Case, T. J. (1978). On the evolution and significance of postnatal growth rates in the terrestrial vertebrates. *Quarterly Review of Biology* 53, 243–282.

Casida, L. E. (1968). Studies on the postpartum cow. *Wisconsin Agricultural Experiment Station Research Bulletin* **270**, 1–54.

Cassidy, C. M. (1980). Benign neglect and toddler malnutrition. In *Social and biological predictors of nutritional status, physical growth, and neurological development* (L. Greene and F. Johnston, eds.), pp. 101–131. New York: Academic Press.

Cassidy, J. D. (1975). The parasitoid wasps, *Habrobracon* and *Mormoniella*. In *Handbook of genetics* (R. C. King, ed.), Vol. 3, pp. 173–203. New York: Plenum Press.

Cecil, S., and J. Just. (1979). Survival rate, population density and development of naturally occurring anuran larvae (*Rana catesbeiana*). *Copeia* pp. 447–453.

Chabora, P. C., and D. Pimentel. (1966). Effect of host (*Musca domestica* L.) age on the pteromalid parasite (*Nasonia vitripennis* Walker). *Canadian Entomologist* **98**, 1226–1231.

Chagnon, N. A. (1967). Yanomamo warfare, social organization and marriage alliances. Unpublished Ph.D. thesis, University of Michigan, Ann Arbor, Michigan.

Chagnon, N. A. (1974). *Studying the Yanomamo*. New York: Holt, Rinehart, and Winston.

Chagnon, N. A., M. V. Flinn, and T. F. Melancon. (1979). Sex-ratio variation among the Yanomamo Indians. In *Evolutionary biology and human social behavior: An anthropological perspective* (N. A. Chagnon and W. Irons, eds.), pp. 290–320. North Scituate, Mass.: Duxbury Press.

Chandrasekhar, S. (1959). *Infant mortality in India 1901–1955*. London: Allen and Unwin.

Chang, B. D., and N. R. Liley. (1974). The effect of experience on the development of parental behavior in the blue gourami, *Trichogaster trichopterus*. *Canadian Journal of Zoology* **52**, 1499–1503.

Chapman, M. (1980). Infanticide and fertility among Eskimos: A computer simulation. *American Journal of Physical Anthropology* **53**, 317–327.

Chapman, M., and G. Hausfater. (1979). The reproductive consequences of infanticide in langurs: A mathematical model. *Behavioral Ecology and Sociobiology* **5**, 227–240.

Chapman, V. M., and F. H. Bronson. (1968). Pregnancy block capacity and inbreeding in laboratory mice. *Experientia* **4**, 199–200.

Charnov, E. L. (1982). *The theory of sex allocation* (Princeton Monograph in Population Biology No. 18). Princeton, N.J.: Princeton University Press.

Charnov, E. L., and J. P. Finerty. (1980). Vole population cycles: A case for kin-selection? *Oecologia* (*Berlin*) **45**, 1–2.

Charnov, E. L., and J. R. Krebs. (1974). On clutch size and fitness. *Ibis* **116**, 217–219.

Chen, L. et al. (1981). Sex bias and the family allocations of food and health care in rural Bangladesh. *Population and Development Review* **7**, 55–70.

Cheney, D. L., and R. M. Seyfarth. (1977). Behaviour of adult and immature male baboons during inter-group encounters. *Nature* (*London*) **269**, 404–406.

Chevalier, J. R. (1973). Cannibalism as a factor in first year survival of walleye in Oneida Lake. *Transactions of the American Fisheries Society* **102**, 739–744.

Chipman, R. K., and K. A. Fox. (1966). Oestrous synchronization and pregnancy blocking in wild house mice (*Mus musculus* L.). *Journal of Reproduction and Fertility* **12**, 233–236.

Chipman, R. K., J. A. Holt, and K. A. Fox. (1966). Pregnancy failure in laboratory mice after multiple short-term exposure to strange males. *Nature (London)* **210**, 653.

Chitty, D., and E. Phipps. (1966). Seasonal changes in survival in mixed populations of two species of vole. *Journal of Animal Ecology* **35**, 313–331.

Choudhuri, D., and R. Bagh. (1974). On the sub-social behaviour and cannibalism in *Schizodactylus monstrosus* (Orthoptera: Schizodactylidae). *Revue d'Ecologie et de Biologie du Sol* **11**, 569–573.

Christensen, M. S. (1981). A note on the breeding and growth rates of the catfish *Clarias mossambicus* in Kenya. *Aquaculture* **25**, 285–288.

Christian, J. J. (1956). Adrenal and reproductive responses to population size in mice from freely growing populations. *Ecology* **37**, 258–273.

Christian, J. J. (1963). Endocrine adaptive mechanisms and the physiologic regulation of population growth. In *Physiological mammalogy* (M. V. Mayer and R. G. Van Gelder, ed.), New York: Academic Press.

Christian, J. J. (1971). Population density and reproductive efficiency. *Biology of Reproduction* **4**, 248–294.

Clady, M. D. (1974). Food habits of yellow perch, smallmouth bass and largemouth bass in two unproductive lakes in northern Michigan. *American Midland Naturalist* **91**, 453–459.

Clark, A. B., and D. S. Wilson. (1981). Avian breeding adaptations: Hatching asynchrony, brood reduction, and nest failure. *Quarterly Review of Biology* **56**, 253–277.

Clark, C. B. (1977). A preliminary report on weaning among chimpanzees of the Gombe National Park, Tanzania. In *Primate bio-social development: Biological, social and ecological determinants* (S. Chevalier-Skolnikoff and F. E. Poirier, eds.), pp. 235–260. New York: Garland Press.

Clarke, J. R., F. V. Clulow, and F. Grieg. (1970). Ovulation in the bank vole, *Clethrionomys glareolus. Journal of Reproduction and Fertility* **23**, 531.

Clarke, Margaret R. (1983). Infant-killing and infant disappearance following male takeovers in a group of free-ranging howling monkeys (*Alouatta palliata*) in Costa Rica. *American Journal of Primatology* **5**, 241–247.

Clarke, S. F. (1880). The development of *Ambystoma punctatum. Studies in Biology from the Laboratory of Johns Hopkins University* **1**, 105–125.

Clulow, F. V., and J. R. Clarke. (1968). Pregnancy block in *Microtus agrestis* an induced ovulator. *Nature (London)* **219**, 511.

Clulow, F. V., and P. E. Langford. (1971). Pregnancy block in the meadow vole, *Microtus pennsylvanicus. Journal of Reproduction and Fertility* **24**, 275–277.

Clutton-Brock, T. H., and J. B. Gillett. (1979). A survey of forest composition in the Gombe National Park. *African Journal of Ecology* **17**, 131–158.

Clutton-Brock, T. H., F. E. Guinness, and S. D. Albon. (1982). *Red deer: Behavior and ecology of two sexes.* Chicago: University of Chicago Press.

Coale, A. J., and P. Demeny. (1966). *Regional model life tables and stable populations.* Princeton, N.J.: Princeton University Press.

Coe, M. J. (1966). The biology of *Tilapia grahami* Boulenger in Lake Magadi, Kenya. *Acta Tropica* **23**, 146–177.

Cohen, M., R. S. Malpass, and H. G. Klein. (eds.). (1980). *Biosocial mechanisms of population regulation.* New Haven: Yale University Press.

Coleman, E. (1974). L'infanticide dans le haut moyen age. *Annales: Economies, Sociétés, Civilisations* **29**, 315–335.

Coleman, E. (1976). Infanticide in the early Middle Ages. In *Women in medieval society* (S. Stuard, ed.), pp. 47–70. Philadelphia: University of Pennsylvania Press.

Coles, R. J. (1919). The large sharks of Cape Lookout, North Carolina. The white shark or maneater, tiger shark and hammerhead. *Copeia*, pp. 34–43.

Collins, L. C. (1973). *Monotremes and marsupials: A reference for zoological institutions*. Washington, D.C.: Smithsonian Institution Press.

Condran, G. A. and E. Crimmons. A description and evaluation of the mortality data in federal Censuses: 1850–1900. *Historical Methods* **12**, 1–23.

Conover, M. R., F. D. Klopfer, and D. E. Miller. (1980). Stimulus features of chicks and other factors evoking parental protective behaviour in ring-billed gulls. *Animal Behaviour* **28**, 29–41.

Constanz, G. D. (1975). Behavioral ecology of mating in the male gila topminnow, *Poeciliopsis occidentalis* (Cyprinodontiformes: Poeciliidae). *Ecology* **56**, 966–973.

Constanz, G. D. (1979). Social dynamics and parental care in the tessellated darter (Pisces: Percidae). *Proceedings of the Academy of Natural Sciences of Philadelphia* **131**, 131–138.

Cook, R. (1964). Nutrition and mortality of females under 5 years of age compared with males in the greater Syria region. *Journal of Tropical Pediatrics* **10**, 76–81.

Cook, S. F. (1946). Human sacrifice and warfare as factors in the demography of pre-colonial Mexico. *Human Biology* **18**, 81–102.

Cooke, F., and R. Harmsen. (1983). Does sex ratio vary with egg sequence in lesser snow geese? *Auk* **100**, 215–217.

Cooper, G. P. (1936). Food habits, rate of growth and cannibalism of young largemouth bass (*Aplites salmoides*) in state-operated rearing ponds in Michigan during 1935. *Transactions of the American Fisheries Society* **66**, 242–266.

Cooper, J. (1980). Fatal sibling aggression in pelicans—A review. *Ostrich* **51**, 183–186.

Corbet, G. B., and H. N. Southern. (1977). *The handbook of British animals*, 2nd ed. Oxford: Blackwell Scientific Publications.

Corbet, P. S., and A. Griffiths. (1963). Observation on the aquatic stages of two species of *Toxorhynchites* (Diptera: Culcidae) in Uganda. *Proceedings of the Royal Entomological Society of London* A**32**, 125–135.

Coulson, J. C., and E. White. (1958). The effect of age on the breeding biology of the kittiwake *Rissa tridactyla. Ibis* **100**, 40–51.

Coutts, R. R., and I. W. Rowlands. (1969). The reproductive cycle of the Skomer vole (*Clethrionomys glareolus skomerensis*). *Journal of Zoology (London)* **158**, 1–25.

Cowlishaw, G. (1978). Infanticide in aboriginal Australia. *Oceania* **48**, 262–283.

Cowlishaw, G. (1981). The determinants of fertility among Australian aborigines. *Mankind* **13**, 37–55.

Coyne, J. (1968). *Laspeyresia ingens*, a seedworm infesting cones of longleaf pine. *Annals of the Entomological Society of America* **61**, 1116–1122.

Crisp, D. T. (1962). Estimates of the annual production of *Corixa germari* (Fieb.) in an upland reservoir. *Archiv für Hydrobiologie* **58**, 210–223.

Crockett, C. M. (1984). Emigration by female red howler monkeys and the case for female competition. In *Female Primates: Studies by women primatologists*, (M. Small, ed.). New York: Alan R. Liss.

Crockett, C. M., and R. Sekulic. (1982). Gestation length in red howler monkeys. *American Journal of Primatology* **3**, 291–294.

Crockett Wilson, C., and W. L. Wilson. (1977). Behavioral and morphological variation among primate populations in Sumatra. *Yearbook of Physical Anthropology* **20**, 207–233.

Croft, B. A., and J. A. McMurtry. (1972). Comparative studies on four strains of *Typhlodromus occidentalis* Nesbitt (Acarina: Phytoseiidae). IV. Life history studies. *Acarologia* **12**, 460–470.

Crombie, A. C. (1944). On intraspecific and interspecific competition in larvae of graminivorous insects. *Journal of Experimental Biology* **20**, 135–151.

Crook, J. H. (1972). Sexual selection, dimorphism, and social organization in primates. In *Sexual selection and the descent of man 1871–1971* (B. Campbell, ed.), pp. 231–281. Chicago: Aldine Publishing Co.

Crook, J. R., and W. M. Shields. (1983). Sexually selected infanticide by male barn swallows. Abstracts of 101st Stated Meeting of American Ornithological Union, Paper No. 100, p. 23.

Cross, B. A. (1977). Comparative physiology of milk removal. *Symposia of the Zoological Society of London* **41**, 193–210.

Crossner, K. A. (1977). Natural selection and clutch size in the European starling. *Ecology* **58**, 885–892.

Crowcroft, P., and F. P. Rowe. (1957). The growth of confined colonies of the wild house mouse (*Mus musculus* L.). *Proceedings of the Zoological Society of London* **129**, 359–370.

Crowcroft, P., and F. P. Rowe. (1963). Social organization and territorial behaviour in the wild house mouse (*Mus musculus* L.). *Proceedings of the Zoological Society of London* **140**, 517–531.

Crump, M. L. (1974). Reproductive strategies in a tropical anuran community. *University of Kansas Museum of Natural History Miscellaneous Publications* **61**, 1–68.

Crump, M. L. (1983). Opportunistic cannibalism by amphibian larvae in temporary aquatic environments. *American Naturalist* **121**, 281–289.

Cuff, W. R. (1977). Initiation and control of cannibalism in larval walleyes. *Progressive Fish-Culturist* **39**, 29–32.

Cuff, W. R. (1980). Behavioral aspects of cannibalism in larval walleye, *Stizostedion vitreum*. *Canadian Journal of Zoology* **58**, 1504–1509.

Cullen, A. (1969). *Window onto wilderness*. Nairobi: East African Publishing House.

Cullen, E. (1957). Adaptations in the kittiwake to cliff-nesting. *Ibis* **99**, 275–302.

Curtin, R. A. (1977). Langur social behavior and infant mortality. *Kroeber Anthropological Society Papers* **50**, 27–36.

Curtin, R. A. (1982). Range use of langurs in highland Nepal. *Folia Primatologica* **38**, 1–18.

Curtin, R. A., and P. Dolhinow. (1978). Primate social behavior in a changing world. *American Scientist* **66**, 468–475.

Curtin, R. A., and P. Dolhinow. (1979). Infanticide among langurs: A solution to overcrowding? *Science Today* (*New Delhi*) **13**, 35–41.

Cushing, D. H. (1974). The possible density-dependence of larval mortality and adult mortality in fishes. In *The early life history of fish* (J. H. S. Blaxter, ed.), pp. 103–111. New York: Springer-Verlag.

Czaja, J. A., S. G. Eisele, and R. W. Goy. (1975). Cyclical changes in the sexual skin of female rhesus: Relationship to mating behavior and successful artificial insemination. *Federation Proceedings* **34**, 1680–1684.

Dalrymple, G. H. (1970). Caddis fly larvae feeding upon eggs of *Ambystoma t. tigrinum. Herpetologica* **26**, 128–129.

Daly, M., and M. I. Wilson. (1978). *Sex, evolution, and behavior.* North Scituate, Mass.: Duxbury Press.

Daly, M., and M. I. Wilson. (1980). Discriminative parental solicitude: A biological perspective. *Journal of Marriage and the Family* **42**, 277–278.

Daly, M., and M. I. Wilson. (1981). Abuse and neglect of children in evolutionary perspective. In *Natural selection and social behavior: Recent research and new theory* (R. D. Alexander and D. Tinkle, eds.), pp. 405–416. New York: Chiron Press.

Daly, M., and M. I. Wilson. (1982a). Homicide and kinship. *American Anthropologist* **84**, 372–378.

Daly, M., and M. I. Wilson. (1982b). Whom are newborn babies said to resemble? *Ethology and Sociobiology* **3**, 69–78.

Daly, M., M. I. Wilson, and S. J. Weghorst. (1982). Male sexual jealousy. *Ethology and Sociobiology* **3**, 11–27.

Darwin, C. R. (1859). *The origin of species by means of natural selection or the preservation of favoured races in the struggle for life.* London: John Murray.

David, G. F. X., and L. S. Ramaswami. (1969). Studies on menstrual cycles and other related phenomena in the langur (*Presbytis entellus entellus*). *Folia Primatologica* **11**, 300–313.

Davis, J. W. F., and E. K. Dunn. (1976). Intraspecific predation and colonial breeding in lesser black-backed gulls *Larus fuscus. Ibis* **118**, 65–77.

Davis, K., and J. Blake. (1956). Social structure and fertility: An analytic framework. *Economic Development and Cultural Change* **4**, 211–235.

Davis, P. G., and R. Gandelman. (1972). Pup-killing produced by the administration of testosterone propionate to adult female mice. *Hormones and Behavior* **3**, 169–173.

Davis, R. M. (1967). Parasitism by newly-transformed anadromous sea lamprey on landlocked salmon and other fishes in a coastal Maine lake. *Transactions of the American Fisheries Society* **96**, 11–16.

Dawkins, R. (1976). *The selfish gene.* New York: Oxford University Press.

Dawkins, R., and J. Brockmann. (1980). Do digger wasps commit the Concorde fallacy? *Animal Behaviour* **28**, 892–896.

Dawkins, R., and T. R. Carlisle. (1976). Parental investment, mate desertion, and a fallacy. *Nature (London)* **262**, 131–133.

Dawkins, R., and J. R. Krebs. (1979). Arms races between and within species. *Proceedings of the Royal Society of London* **B205**, 489–511.

Deag, J. M., and J. H. Crook. (1971). Social behaviour and "agonistic buffering" in the wild barbary macaque, *Macaca sylvana* L. *Folia Primatologica* **15**, 183–200.

DeAngelis, D. L., D. K. Cox, and C. C. Coutant. (1980). Cannibalism and size dispersal in young-of-the-year largemouth bass: Experiment and model. *Ecological Modelling* **8**, 133–148.

Defler, T. R. (1981). The density of *Alouatta seniculus* in the eastern llanos of Colombia. *Primates* **22**, 564–569.

DeFries, J., and G. McClearn. (1972). Social dominance and Darwinian fitness in the laboratory mouse. *American Naturalist* **104**, 408–411.

De Kock, L. L., and I. Rohn. (1972). Intra-specific behaviour during the upswing of groups of Norway lemmings, kept under semi-natural conditions. *Zeitschrift für Tierpsychologie* **30**, 405–415.

DeLong, K. T. (1966). Population ecology of feral house mice: Interference by *Microtus. Ecology* **47**, 481–484.

DeLong, K. T. (1967). Population ecology of feral house mice. *Ecology* **48**, 611–634.

DeLong, K. T. (1978). The effect of the manipulation of social structure on reproduction in house mice. *Ecology* **59**, 922–933.

DeMartini, E. E. (1976). The adaptive significance of territoriality and egg cannibalism in the painted greenling, *Oxylebius pictus* Gill, a Northeastern Pacific marine fish. Unpublished Ph.D. thesis, University of Washington, Seattle, Wash.

de Mause, L. (ed.). (1974). *The history of childhood.* New York: Harper Torchbooks.

de Montellano, B. R. O. (1978). Aztec cannibalism: An ecological necessity? *Science* **200**, 611–617.

Demos, J. (1965). Notes on life in Plymouth Colony. *William and Mary Quarterly* 3rd Ser. **22**, 264–286.

DeSteven, D. (1980). Clutch size, breeding success, and parental survival in the tree swallow (*Iridoprocne bicolor*). *Evolution* **34**, 278–291.

DeVos, A., and A. Omar. (1971). Territories and movements of Sykes monkeys (*Ceropithecus mitis kolbi*) in Kenya. *Folia Primatologica* **16**, 196–205.

Dickman, M. (1968). The effect of grazing by tadpoles on the structure of a periphyton community. *Ecology* **49**, 1188–1190.

Dickeman, M. (subsequently Dickemann). (1975). Demographic consequences of infanticide in man. *Annual Review of Ecology and Systematics* **6**, 107–137.

Dickemann, M. (1979a). Female infanticide, reproductive strategies, and social stratification: A preliminary model. In *Evolutionary biology and human social behavior: An anthropological perspective* (N. Chagnon and W. Irons, eds.), pp. 321–367. North Scituate, Mass: Duxbury Press.

Dickemann, M. (1979b). The ecology of mating systems in hypergynous dowry societies. *Social Science Information* **18**, 163–195.

Dickemann, M. (1981). Paternal confidence and dowry competition: A biocultural analysis of purdah. In *Natural selection and social behavior: Recent research and new theory* (R. D. Alexander and D. Tinkle, eds.), pp. 417–438. New York: Chiron Press.

Dickemann, M. (1984). On the search for self-control. [A review of *Biosocial mechanisms of population regulation* (M. Cohen, R. S. Malpass, and H. G. Klein eds.)]. *Revue Anthropologique* (*Paris*). In press.

Dieterlen, F. (1959). Das Verhalten des Syrischen Goldhamsters. *Zeitschrift für Tierpsychologie* **16**, 47–103.

Diez, P. A. A., and F. M. Salzano. (1978). Evolutionary implications of the ethnography and demography of Ayoreo Indians. *Journal of Human Evolution* **7**, 253–268.

Dimetry, N. A. (1974). The consequences of egg cannibalism in *Adalia bipunctata* (Coleoptera: Coccinellidae). *Entomophaga* **19**, 445–452.

Din, N. A., and S. K. Eltringham. (1974). Breeding of the pink-backed pelican *Pelecanus rufescens* in Rwenzori National Park, Uganda, with notes on a colony of marabou storks *Leptoptilos crumeniferus. Ibis* **116**, 477–493.

Dittus, W. P. J. (1975). Population dynamics of the toque monkey, *Macaca sinica.* In *Socioecology and psychology of primates* (R. H. Tuttle, ed.), pp. 125–151. The Hague: Mouton Publishers.

Dittus, W. P. J. (1977). The social regulation of population density and age-sex distribution in the toque monkey. *Behaviour* **63**, 281–322.

Dittus, W. P. J. (1979). The evolution of behaviors regulating population density and age-specific sex ratios in a primate population. *Behaviour* **69**, 265–302.

Divale, W. T., and M. Harris. (1976). Population, warfare and the male supremacist complex. *American Anthropologist* **78**, 521–538.

Dolhinow, P. (1977). Normal monkeys? *American Scientist* **65**, 266.

Dolhinow, P., and M. G. DeMay. (1982). Adoption: The importance of infant choice. *Journal of Human Evolution* **11**, 391–420.

Dominey, W. J. (1980). Female mimicry in bluegill sunfish—A genetic polymorphism? *Nature (London)* **284**, 546–548.

Dominey, W. J. (1981a). Anti-predator function of bluegill sunfish nesting colonies. *Nature (London)* **290**, 586–588.

Dominey, W. J. (1981b). The mating system of the bluegill sunfish (Centrarchidae: *Lepomis macrochirus*). Unpublished Ph.D. thesis, Cornell University, Ithaca, N.Y.

Dominey, W. J. (1981c). Maintenance of female mimicry as a reproductive strategy in bluegill sunfish (*Lepomis macrochirus*). *Environmental Biology of Fishes* **6**, 59–64.

Dominic, C. J. (1965). The origin of the pheromones causing pregnancy block in mice. *Journal of Reproduction and Fertility* **10**, 469–472.

Dominic, C. J. (1966). Observations on the reproductive pheromones of mice. II. Neuroendocrine mechanisms involved in the olfactory block to pregnancy. *Journal of Reproduction and Fertility* **11**, 415–421.

Dominic, C. J. (1976). Role of pheromones in mammalian fertility. In *Neuroendocrine regulation of fertility* (T. C. Anand-Kumar, ed.), pp. 236–245. Basel: S. Karger.

Dominic, C. J. (1978). Mammalian reproductive pheromones. *Journal of Animal Morphology and Physiology,* Silver Jubilee Volume, pp. 104–127.

Dornstreich, M. D., and G. E. B. Morren. (1974). Does New Guinea cannibalism have nutritional value? *Human Ecology* **2**, 1–12.

Dorward, E. F. (1962). Comparative biology of the white booby and brown booby *Sula* spp. at Ascension. *Ibis* **103b**, 174–220.

Doty, R. L. (ed.). (1976). *Mammalian olfaction, reproductive processes, and behavior.* New York: Academic Press.

Downhower, J. F., and L. Brown. (1980). Mate preferences of female mottled sculpins, *Cottus bairdi. Animal Behaviour* **28**, 728–734.

Droogleever Fortuyn, A. B. (1929). Prenatal death in the striped hamster (*Cricetulus griseus* M-Edw.). *Archives de Biologie* **39**, 583–606.

D'Souza, S., and L. C. Chen. (1980). Sex differentials and mortality in rural Bangladesh. *Population and Development Review* **6**, 257–270.

Dublin, L. I., A. J. Lotka, and M. Spiegelman. (1949). *Length of life: A study of the life table.* Rev. ed. New York: Ronald Press.

Duelli, P. (1981). Larval cannibalism in lacewings (Neuroptera: Chrysopidae). *Researches on Population Ecology (Kyoto)* **23**, 193–209.

Duellman, W. E. (1970). Hylid frogs of Middle America. *University of Kansas Museum of Natural History Monograph.* 753 pp.

Duellman, W. E. (1978). The biology of an equatorial herpetofauna in Amazonia, Ecuador. *University of Kansas Museum of Natural History Miscellaneous Publications* **65**, 1–352.

Ealey, E. H. M. (1963). The ecological significance of delayed implantation in a population of the hill kangaroo (*Macropus robustus*). In *Delayed implantation* (A. C. Enders, ed.), pp. 33–48. Chicago: University of Chicago Press.

Ealey, E. H. M. (1967). Ecology of the euro (*Macropus robustus* Gould) in northwest Australia. IV. Age and growth. *Commonwealth Scientific and Industrial Research Organization Wildlife Research* **12**, 67–80.
Ebersole, J. P. (1977). The adaptive significance of interspecific territoriality
in the reef fish *Eupomacentrus leucostictus. Ecology* **58**, 914–920.
Edgar, W. D. (1969). Prey and predators of the wolf spider *Lycosa lugubris.
Journal of Zoology (London)* **159**, 405–411.
Edgar, W. D. (1971). The life cycle, abundance and seasonal movement of
the wolf spider *Lycosa lugubris (Pardosa)* in central Scotland. *Journal
of Animal Ecology* **40**, 303–322.
Edgerton, R. B. (1981). Foreword. In *Child abuse and neglect: Cross-cultural
perspectives* (J. E. Korbin, ed.), pp. vii–viii. Berkeley: University of Califor-
nia Press.
Edwards, R. L. (1954). The host finding and oviposition behavior of *Mormoniella
vitripennis* (Walker) (Hymenoptera: Pteromalidae), a parasite of muscoid
flies. *Behaviour* **7**, 88–112.
Edwards, T. C., Jr. and M. W. Collopy. (1983). Obligate and facultative brood
reduction in eagles: An examination of factors that influence fratricide.
Auk **100**, 630–635.
Eickwort, K. R. (1973). Cannibalism and kin selection in *Labidomera clivicollis*
(Coleoptera: Chrysomelidae). *American Naturalist* **107**, 452–453.
Eisenberg, J. F. (1968). Behavior patterns. In *Biology of Peromyscus (Rodentia)*
(J. A. King, ed.), pp. 451–495. Stillwater, Okla.: American Society of Mam-
malogists.
Eisenberg, J. F., N. A. Muckenhirn, and R. Rudran. (1972). The relation between
ecology and social structure in primates. *Science* **176**, 863–874.
El-Badry, M. A. (1969). Higher female than male mortality in some countries
of South Asia: A digest. *Journal of the American Statistical Association*
64, 1234–1244.
Elliott, J. M. (1973). The diel activity pattern, drifting and food of the leech
Erpobdella octoculata (L.) (Hirudinea: Erpobdellidae) in a Lake District
stream. *Journal of Animal Ecology* **42**, 449–459.
Elsey, C. A. (1954). A case of cannibalism in Canada lynx (*Lynx canadensis*).
Journal of Mammalogy **35**, 129.
Elsley, F. W. H. (1971). Nutrition and lactation in the sow. In *Lactation,* (I. R.
Falconer, ed.), pp. 393–411. London: Butterworths.
Elwood, R. W. (1975a). Paternal and maternal behaviour of the Mongolian
gerbil. *Animal Behaviour* **23**, 766–772.
Elwood, R. W. (1975b). Paternal and maternal behaviour of the Mongolian
gerbil, and the development of the young. Unpublished Ph.D. thesis, Univer-
sity of Reading, Reading, England.
Elwood, R. W. (1977). Changes in the responses of male and female gerbils
(*Meriones unguiculatus*) towards test pups during the pregnancy of the
female. *Animal Behaviour* **25**, 46–51.
Elwood, R. W. (1979). Maternal and paternal behavior of the Mongolian gerbil:
A correlational study. *Behavioral and Neural Biology* **25**, 555–562.
Elwood, R. W. (1980). The development, inhibition and disinhibition of pup-
cannibalism in the Mongolian gerbil. *Animal Behaviour* **28**, 1188–1194.
Elwood, R. W. (1981). Postparturitional re-establishment of pup cannibalism
in female gerbils. *Developmental Psychobiology* **14**, 209–212.
Elwood, R. W. (1983). Paternal care in rodents. In *Parental behaviour of rodents*
(R. W. Elwood, ed.), pp. 235–257. Chichester: Wiley.

Elwood, R. W., and D. M. Broom. (1978). The influence of litter size and parental behaviour on the development of Mongolian gerbil pups. *Animal Behaviour* **26,** 438–454.

Elwood, R. W. and M. C. Ostermeyer. (1984). Does copulation inhibit infanticide in male rodents? *Animal Behaviour* **32,** 293–294.

Emlen, J. T. (1956). Juvenile mortality in a ring-billed gull colony. *Wilson Bulletin* **68,** 232–238.

Emlen, J. T., Jr., and D. E. Miller. (1975). Individual chick recognition and family integrity in the ring-billed gull. *Behaviour* **52,** 124–144.

Emlen, S. T. (1982). The evolution of helping. II. The role of behavioral conflict. *American Naturalist* **119,** 40–53.

Enders, A. C. (1963). *Delayed implantation.* Chicago: University of Chicago Press.

Erpino, M. J. (1975). Androgen-induced aggression in neonatally androgenized female mice: Inhibition by progesterone. *Hormones and Behavior* **6,** 181–188.

Essock-Vitale, S. M., and M. T. McGuire. (1979). Sociobiology and its potential usefulness to psychiatry. *McLean Hospital Journal* **3,** 69–81.

Evans, R. M. (1970). Imprinting and mobility in young ring-billed gulls, *Larus delawarensis. Animal Behaviour Monographs* **3,** 193–248.

Ewer, R. F. (1973). *The carnivores.* Ithaca, N.Y.: Cornell University Press.

Faladé, S. (1963). Women of Dakar and the surrounding urban area. In *Women of tropical Africa* (D. Paulme, ed.), pp. 217–230. Berkeley: University of California Press.

Farr, W. (1974). Mortality in mid 19th century Britain (vital statistics of the statistics of health, sickness, diseases and death, 1837). Reprinted in the *Pioneers of demography* series. London: Gregg International.

Fedorenko, A. (1975). Instar and species-specific diets in two species of *Chaoborus. Limnology and Oceanography* **20,** 238–244.

Fetterolf, P. M. (1983). Effects of investigator activity on ring-billed gull behavior and reproductive performance. *Wilson Bulletin* **95,** 23–41.

Finney, G. L., and T. W. Fisher. (1964). Culture of entomophagous insects and their hosts. In *Biological control of pests and weeds* (P. DeBach, ed.), pp. 328–353. New York: Reinhold.

Firth, R. (1957). *We, the Tikopia.* London: Allen and Unwin.

Firth, R. (1961). *Elements of social organization.* Boston: Beacon Press.

Fischer, A. (1963). Reproduction in Truk. *Ethnology* **2,** 526–540.

Fischer, Z. (1960). Cannibalism among the larvae of the dragonfly *Lestes nympha* Selys. *Ekologia Polska* **B7,** 33–39.

Fischermann, B. (1976). Los Ayoreode. In *En Busca de la Loma Santa.* (J. Reister, ed.). La Paz: Amigos del Libros.

Fisher, R. A. (1930). *The genetical theory of natural selection.* Oxford: Oxford University Press.

Fisher, R. C. (1970). Aspects of the physiology of endoparasitic Hymenoptera. *Biological Reviews* **46,** 243–278.

Fitch, J. E. (1964). A relatively unexploited population of Pismo clams, *Tivela stultorum* (Mawe 1823) (Veneridae). *Proceedings of the Malacology Society of London* **36,** 309–312.

Fjellman, S. M. (1979). Hey, you can't do that: A response to Divale and Harris' "Population, warfare and the male supremacist complex." *Behavior Science Research,* **14,** 189.

Flatt, W. P., and P. W. Moe. (1971). Partition of nutrients between lactation and body weight gain in dairy cattle. In *Lactation* (I. R. Falconer, ed.), pp. 341–347. London: Butterworths.

Fleming, A. S. (1979). Maternal nest defense in the desert woodrat *Neotoma lepida lepida*. *Behavioral and Neural Biology* **26**, 41–63.

Fleming, M. W., J. D. Harder, and J. J. Wukie. (1981). Reproductive energetics of the Virginia opossum compared with some eutherians. *Comparative Biochemistry and Physiology* **70B**, 645–648.

Flowerdew, J. R. (1974). Field and laboratory experiments on the social behaviour and population dynamics of the wood mouse (*Apodemus sylvaticus*). *Journal of Animal Ecology* **43**, 499–511.

Flynn, R. B., and R. D. Hoyt. (1979). The life history of the teardrop darter, *Etheostoma barbouri* Kuehne and Small. *American Midland Naturalist* **101**, 127–141.

Ford, C. S. (1964). *A comparative study of human reproduction* (Human Relations Area Files Press No. 32). New Haven, Conn.: Yale University Press.

Fordham, R. A. (1970). Mortality and population change of Dominican gulls in Wellington, New Zealand. *Journal of Animal Ecology* **39**, 13–27.

Forester, L. C. (1979). The adaptiveness of parental care in *Desmognathus ochrophaeus* (Urodele: Plethodontidae). *Copeia*, pp. 332–341.

Forney, J. L. (1974). Interactions between yellow perch abundance, walleye predation, and survival of alternate prey in Oneida Lake, New York. *Transactions of the American Fisheries Society* **103**, 15–24.

Forney, J. L. (1976). Year-class formation in the walleye (*Stizostedion vitreum vitreum*) population of Oneida Lake, New York, 1966–73. *Journal of the Fisheries Research Board of Canada* **33**, 783–792.

Forster, J. R. M. (1970). Further studies on the culture of the prawn *Palaemon serratus* Pennant, with emphasis on the post-larval stages. *Fisheries Investigations* **II26**, 6.

Fossey, D. (1974). Observations on the home range of one group of mountain gorillas (*Gorilla gorilla beringei*). *Animal Behaviour* **22**, 568–581.

Fossey, D. (1979). Development of the mountain gorilla (*Gorilla gorilla beringei*): The first thirty-six months. In *The great apes* (D. A. Hamburg and E. R. McCown, eds.), pp. 138–184. Menlo Park, Calif.: Benjamin/Cummings.

Fossey, D. (1981). The imperiled mountain gorilla. *National Geographic Magazine* **159**, 500–523.

Fossey, D. (1982). Reproduction among free-living mountain gorillas. *American Journal of Primatology Suppl.* **1**, 97–104.

Fowler, H. W. (1917). Some notes on the breeding habits of local catfishes. *Copeia* **1917(42)**, 32–36.

Fox, L. R. (1975a). Cannibalism in natural populations. *Annual Review of Ecology and Systematics* **6**, 87–106.

Fox, L. R. (1975b). Factors influencing cannibalism, a mechanism of population limitation in the predator *Notonecta hoffmanni*. *Ecology* **56**, 933–941.

Fox, L. R. (1975c). Some demographic consequences of food shortage for the predator, *Notonecta hoffmanni*. *Ecology* **56**, 868–880.

Frame, G. W. (1980). Cheetah social organization in the Serengeti ecosystem, Tanzania. Paper presented at the meetings of the Animal Behavior Society, Fort Collins, Colorado, 20 pp.

Frame, G. W., and L. H. Frame. (1981). *Swift and enduring*. New York: Dutton.

Frame, L. H., J. R. Malcolm, G. W. Frame, and H. van Lawick. (1979). Social organisation of African wild dogs (*Lycaon pictus*) on the Serengeti Plains, Tanzania 1967–1978. *Zeitschrift für Tierpsychologie* **50**, 225–249.

Frank, F. (1957). The causality of microtine cycles in Germany. *Journal of Wildlife Management* **21**, 113–121.

Fraser, D., and R. M. Jones. (1975). The "teat order" of suckling pigs. I. Relation to birth weight and subsequent growth. *Journal of Agricultural Science* **84**, 387–391.

Freedman, T., and D. Weir. (1983). Polluting the most vulnerable. *The Nation* **236** (109), 601.

Freeland, W. J. (1977). Dynamics of primate parasites. Unpublished Ph.D. thesis, University of Michigan, Ann Arbor, Mich.

Freeman, M. (1971). A social and economic analysis of systemic female infanticide. *American Anthropologist* **73**, 1011–1018.

Freuchen, D. (ed.). (1961). *Peter Freuchen's book of the Eskimos*. New York: World.

Frost, W. E. (1954). The food of pike, *Esox lucius* L., in Windermere. *Journal of Animal Ecology* **23**, 339–360.

Fryer, G., and T. D. Iles. (1972). *The cichlid fishes of the Great Lakes of Africa: Their biology and evolution*. Edinburgh: Oliver and Boyd.

Fuller, J. L., and W. R. Thompson. (1978). *Behavior genetics*. St. Louis: Mosby.

Gaines, M. S., R. K. Rose, and L. R. McClenaghan, Jr. (1977). The demography of *Synaptomys cooperi* populations in eastern Kansas. *Canadian Journal of Zoology* **55**, 1584–1594.

Galaal, M. H. I. (1968). *The terminology and practice of Somali weather lore, astronomy, and astrology*. Mogadishu: Published by the author.

Galat-Luong, A., and G. Galat. (1979). Consequences comportementales de perturbations sociales répétées sur une troupe due mones de Lowe *Cercopithecus campbelli lowei* de Côte-d'Ivoire. *La Terre et la Vie* **33**, 49–58.

Galdikas, B. (1980). Living with the great orange apes. *National Geographic Magazine* **157**, 830–853.

Galef, B. G. (1981). The ecology of weaning. In *Parental care in mammals* (D. J. Gubernick and P. H. Klopfer, eds.), pp. 211–241. New York: Plenum Press.

Gallepp, G. W. (1974). Behavioral ecology of *Brachycentrus occidentalis* Banks during the pupation period. *Ecology* **55**, 1283–1294.

Gandelman, R. (1972). Induction of pup killing in female mice by androgenization. *Physiology and Behavior* **9**, 101–102.

Gandelman, R. (1973). The development of cannibalism in male Rockland–Swiss albino mice and the influence of olfactory bulb removal. *Developmental Psychobiology* **6**, 159–164.

Gandelman, R., and P. G. Davis. (1973). Spontaneous and testosterone-induced pup killing in female Rockland–Swiss mice: The effect of lactation and the presence of young. *Developmental Psychobiology* **6**, 251–257.

Gandelman, R., and F. S. vom Saal. (1975). Pup-killing in mice: The effects of gonadectomy and testosterone administration. *Physiology and Behavior* **15**, 647–651.

Gandelman, R., and F. S. vom Saal. (1977). Exposure to early androgen attenuates androgen-induced pup-killing in male and female mice. *Behavioral Biology* **20**, 252–260.

Gandelman, R., M. X. Zarrow, V. H. Denenberg, and M. Myers. (1971). Olfactory bulb removal eliminates maternal behavior in the mouse. *Science* **171**, 210–211.

Gargett, V. (1977). A 13-year population study of the black eagles in the Matopos, Rhodesia, 1964–1976. *Ostrich* **48**, 17–27.

Gargett, V. (1978). Sibling aggression in the black eagle in the Matapos, Rhodesia. *Ostrich* **49**, 57–63.

Garten, C. T., Jr. (1976). Relationships between aggressive behavior and genetic heterozygosity in the oldfield mouse, *Peromyscus polionotus*. *Evolution* **30**, 59–72.

Gartlan, J. S., and S. C. Gartlan. (1973). Quelques observations sur les groupes exclusivement mâles chez *Erythrocebus patas*. *Annales de la Faculté des Sciences du Cameroun* **12**, 121–144.

Gauzer, M. E. (1981a). Socially conditioned mortality of nestlings in the *Thalasseus sandvicensis* (Laridae) colonies on the Krasnovodsk Bay islands. 1. General characteristics of juvenile mortality and its possible causes. *Zoologicheskii Zhurnal* **60**(4), 530–539. [In Russian: English summary only consulted.]

Gauzer, M. E. (1981b). Socially conditioned mortality of nestlings in the *Thalasseus sandvicensis* (Laridae) colonies on the Krasnovodsk Bay islands. 2. Role of colony structure and organization. *Zoologicheskii Zhurnal* **60**(6), 879–886. [In Russian: English summary only consulted.]

Gessain, M. (1963). Coniagui women, Guinea. In *Women in tropical Africa* (D. Paulme, ed.). Berkeley: University of California Press.

Getz, L. L. (1978). Speculation on social structure and population cycles of microtine rodents. *The Biologist* **60**, 134–147.

Ghiglieri, M. P. (1979). The socioecology of chimpanzees in Kibale Forest, Uganda. Unpublished Ph.D. thesis, University of California, Davis, Calif.

Gidley-Baird, A. A. (1981). Endocrine control of implantation and delayed implantation in rats and mice. *Journal of Reproduction and Fertility Suppl.* **29**, 97–109.

Giese, A. C. (1973). *Blepharisma.* Palo Alto, Calif.: Stanford University Press.

Gil, D. G. (1970). *Violence against children.* Cambridge, Mass.: Harvard University Press.

Gilbert, A. N. (1982). Post-partum breeding in Norway rats: the ecology of motivational conflict. Doctoral Dissertation, University of Pennsylvania.

Gilbert, J. (1980). Female polymorphism and sexual reproduction in the rotifer *Asplancha:* Evolution of their relationship and control by dietary tocopherol. *American Naturalist* **116**, 409–431.

Gillies, H. (1976). Homicide in the west of Scotland. *British Journal of Psychiatry* **128**, 105–127.

Gilmore, D., and B. Cook. (1981). *Environmental factors in mammal reproduction.* Baltimore: University Park Press.

Gipps, J. H. W., and P. A. Jewell. (1979). Maintaining populations of bank voles, *Clethrionomys glareolus*, in large outdoor enclosures, and measuring the response of population variables to the castration of males. *Journal of Animal Ecology* **48**, 535–555.

Gipps, J. H. W., M. J. Taitt, C. J. Krebs, and Z. Dundjerski. (1981). Male aggression and the population dynamics of the vole, *Microtus townsendii*. *Canadian Journal of Zoology* **59**, 147–157.

Glander, K. E. (1980). Reproduction and population growth in free-ranging mantled howling monkeys. *American Journal of Physical Anthropology* **53**, 25–36.

Glass, G. E. (1983). Some theoretical considerations of infanticide among vertebrates. Unpublished Ph.D. thesis, University of Kansas, Lawrence, Kans.

Glynn, P. (1973). Ecology of a Caribbean coral reef. The *Porites* reef-flat biotope. Part II. Plankton community with evidence for depletion. *Marine Biology* **22**, 1–21.

Godfrey, G. K. (1955). Observations on the nature of the decline in numbers of two *Microtus* populations. *Journal of Mammalogy* **36**, 209–214.

Goetsch, W. (1924). Lebensraum und Körpergrösse. *Biologisches Zentralblatt* **44**, 529–560.

Goin, C. J., O. B. Goin, and G. R. Zug. (1977). *Introduction to herpetology*, 3rd Ed. San Francisco: W. H. Freeman.

Goldman, L., and H. Swanson. (1975). Population control in confined colonies of golden hamsters (*Mesocricetus auratus* Waterhouse). *Zeitschrift für Tierpsychologie* **37**, 225–236.

Goldschmid, A., and K. Kotrschal. (1980). Feeding ecology of three populations of *Blennius incognitus* Bath 1968 (Pisces: Teleostei: Blennidae) during the reproductive period and under human influence. *Marine Ecology* (*Berlin*) **2**, 1–14.

Goodale, J. (1971). *Tiwi wives*. Seattle: University of Washington Press.

Goodall, J. van Lawick. (1968). The behaviour of free-living chimpanzees in the Gombe Stream Reserve. *Animal Behaviour Monographs* **1**, 161–311.

Goodall, J. (1977). Infant killing and cannibalism in free-living chimpanzees. *Folia Primatologica* **28**, 259–282.

Goodall, J., A. Bandora, E. Bergmann, C. Busse, H. Matama, E. Mpongo, A. Pierce, and D. Riss. (1979). Intercommunity interactions in the chimpanzee population of the Gombe National Park. In *The great apes* (D. A. Hamburg and E. R. McCown, eds.), pp. 13–53. Menlo Park, Calif.: Benjamin/Cummings.

Gorski, R. (1979). The neuroendocrinology of reproduction: An overview. *Behavioral Biology* **20**, 111–127.

Gould, F., G. Holtzman, R. Rabb, and M. Smith. (1980). Genetic variation in predatory and cannibalistic tendencies of *Heliothis virescens* strains. *Annals of the Entomological Society of America* **73**, 243–250.

Gould, S. J. (1982). The guano ring. *Natural History* **91**, 12–19.

Granzberg, G. (1973). Twin infanticide: A cross-cultural test of a materialistic explanation. *Ethos* **1**, 405–412.

Graves, J. A., and A. Whiten. (1980). Adoption of strange chicks by herring gulls, *Larus argentatus* L. *Zeitschrift für Tierpsychologie* **54**, 267–278.

Graves, P. L. (1977). Nutrition, infant behavior and maternal characteristics: A pilot study in West Bengal, India. *American Journal of Clinical Nutrition* **30**, 242.

Greeley, J. R. (1932). The spawning habits of brook, brown, and rainbow trout, and the problem of egg predators. *Transactions of the American Fisheries Society* **62**, 239–248.

Green, E. L. (1975). *Biology of the laboratory mouse*. New York: Dover.

Greenwood, P. H. (1981). Species flocks and explosive evolution. In *Chance, change, and challenge—The evolving biosphere* (P. H. Greenwood and P. L. Forey, eds.), pp. 61–74. London: Cambridge University Press.

Greer, B. J., and K. D. Wells. (1980). Territorial and reproductive behavior of the tropical American frog *Centrolenella fleischmanni*. *Herpetologica* **36**, 318–326.

Greig-Smith, P. W. (1980). Parental investment in nest defence by stonechats (*Saxicola torquata*). *Animal Behaviour* **28**, 604–619.

Griffiths, M. (1978). *The biology of monotremes*. New York: Academic Press.

Gromko, M. H., F. S. Mason, and S. J. Smith-Gill. (1973). Analysis of crowding effects in *Rana pipiens* tadpoles. *Journal of Experimental Zoology* **186**, 63–72.

Gruber, S. H., and L. J. V. Campagno. (1981). Taxonomic status and biology of the bigeye thresher, *Alopias superciliosus*. *Fishery Bulletin* **79**, 617–640.

Gunter, G. (1947). Observations on breeding of the marine catfish, *Galeichthys felis* (Linneaus). *Copeia*, pp. 217–223.

Gutierrez de Pineda, V. (1955). Causas culturales de la mortalidad infantil. *Revista Colombiana de Antropologia* **4**, 11–86.

Guttmacher, M. S. (1962). *The mind of the murderer*. New York: Strauss and Cudahy.

Hadingham, E. (1979). *Secrets of the Ice Age*. New York: Walker.

Hagen, D. R., K. B. Kephart, and P. J. Wangsness. (1980). Reproduction in domestic and feral swine. II. Interrelationships between fetal size and spacing and litter size. *Biology of Reproduction* **23**, 929–934.

Hahn, D. C. (1981). Asynchronous hatching in the laughing gull: Cutting losses and reducing rivalry. *Animal Behaviour* **29**, 421–427.

Haldar, A. K., and N. Bhattacharyya. (1969). Fertility and sex-sequence of children of Indian couples. *Sankhya* **B31**, 144.

Hallander, H. (1970). Prey, cannibalism and microhabitat selection in the wolf spiders *Pardosa chelata* (O. F. Muller) and *P. pullata* (Clerck). *Oikos* **21**, 337–340.

Hamilton, R. (1948). The egg-laying process in the tiger salamander. *Copeia*, p. 212.

Hamilton, W. D. (1964a). The genetical evolution of social behaviour, I. *Journal of Theoretical Biology* **7**, 1–16.

Hamilton, W. D. (1964b). The genetical evolution of social behaviour, II. *Journal of Theoretical Biology* **7**, 17–52.

Hamilton, W. D. (1967). Extraordinary sex ratios. *Science* **156**, 477–488.

Hamilton, W. D. (1971). Geometry for the selfish herd. *Journal of Theoretical Biology* **31**, 295–311.

Hamilton, W. D. (1979). Wingless and fighting males in fig wasps and other insects. In *Sexual selection and reproductive competition in insects* (M. S. Blum and N. A. Blum, eds.), pp. 167–220. New York: Academic Press.

Hamilton, W. J., Jr. (1953). Reproduction and young of the Florida wood rat, *Neotoma f. floridana* (Ord). *Journal of Mammalogy* **34**, 180–189.

Hamilton, W. J., III (1962). Reproductive adaptations of the red tree mouse. *Journal of Mammalogy* **43**, 486–504.

Hamilton, W. J., III, R. E. Buskirk, and W. H. Buskirk. (1976). Defense of space and resources by chacma (*Papio ursinus*) baboon troops in an African desert and swamp. *Ecology* **57**, 1264–1272.

Hamilton, W. J., III, C. Busse, and K. S. Smith. (1982). Adoption of infant orphan chacma baboons. *Animal Behaviour* **30**, 29–34.

Harcourt, A. H., and D. Fossey. (1981). The Virunga gorillas: Decline of an 'island' population. *African Journal of Ecology* **19**, 83–97.

Harcourt, A. H., D. Fossey, and J. Sabater-Pí. (1981). Demography of *Gorilla gorilla*. *Journal of Zoology* (*London*) **195**, 215–233.

Harland, R. M., P. J. Blancher, and J. S. Millar. (1979). Demography of a population of *Peromyscus leucopus*. *Canadian Journal of Zoology* **57**, 323–328.

Harlow, H. F., M. K. Harlow, R. O. Dodsworth, and G. L. Arling. (1966). Maternal behavior of rhesus monkeys deprived of mothering and peer association in infancy. *Proceedings of the American Philosophical Society* **110**, 58–66.

Harner, M. (1977). The ecological basis for Aztec sacrifice. *American Ethnologist* **4**, 117–135.

Harraway, Donna. (1983). The contest for primate nature: Daughters of man-the-hunter in the field, 1960–1980. In *The Future of American Democracy: Views from the Left* (Mark E. Kann, ed.). Philadelphia: Temple University Press.

Harris, M. (1975). *Culture, people, nature.* New York: T. Y. Crowell.

Harris, M. (1977). *Cannibals and kings: The origins of cultures.* New York: Random House.

Hart, J. L. (1973). Pacific fishes of Canada. *Bulletin of the Fisheries Research Board of Canada,* No. 180.

Hartl, D. L. (1980). *Principles of population genetics.* Sunderland, Mass.: Sinauer Associates.

Hartung, J. (1982). Polygyny and inheritance of wealth. *Current Anthropology* **23,** 1–12.

Hartung, T. G., and D. A. Dewsbury. (1979). Paternal behavior in six species of muroid rodents. *Behavioral and Neural Biology* **26,** 466–478.

Harvey, J. M., B. C. Lieff, C. D. MacInnes, and J. P. Prevett. (1968). Observations on behavior of sandhill cranes. *Wilson Bulletin* **80,** 421–425.

Hasler, J. F., and E. M. Banks. (1975). The influence of mature males on sexual maturation in female collared lemmings (*Dicrostonyx groenlandicus*). *Biology of Reproduction* **12,** 647–656.

Hasler, J. F., and A. V. Nalbandov. (1974). The effect of weaning and adult males on sexual maturation in female voles (*Microtus ochragaster*). *General and Comparative Endocrinology* **23,** 237–238.

Hastings, P. A., and S. A. Bortone. (1980). Observations on the life history of the belted sandfish, *Serranus subligarius* (Serranidae). *Environmental Biology of Fishes* **5,** 365–374.

Hauschka, T. S. (1952). Mutilation patterns and hereditary (?) cannibalism. *Journal of Heredity* **43,** 117–123.

Hausfater, G. (1975). Dominance and reproduction in baboons (*Papio cynocephalus*): A quantitative analysis. *Contributions to Primatology* **7,** 1–150.

Hausfater, G., and C. Vogel. (1982). Infanticide in langur monkeys (*Presbytis entellus*): Recent research and a review of hypotheses. In *Advanced views in primate biology* (A. B. Chiarelli and R. S. Corruccini, eds.), pp. 160–176. Berlin: Springer-Verlag.

Hausfater, G., J. Altmann, and S. Altmann. (1982a). Long-term consistency of dominance rank among female baboons (*Papio cynocephalus*). *Science* **217,** 752–755.

Hausfater, G., S. Aref, and S. J. Cairns. (1982b). Infanticide as an alternative male reproductive strategy in langurs: A mathematical model. *Journal of Theoretical Biology* **94,** 391–412.

Hayssen, V. In preparation. Aspects of the reproductive biology of marsupials. Unpublished Ph.D. thesis, Cornell University, Ithaca, N.Y.

Healey, M. C. (1967). Aggression and self-regulation of population size in deermice. *Ecology* **48,** 377–392.

Hearn, J. P. (1973). Pituitary inhibition of pregnancy. *Nature (London)* **241,** 207–208.

Helfman, G. S. (1978). Patterns of community structure in fishes: Summary and overview. *Environmental Biology of Fishes* **3,** 129–148.

Helle, W. (1967). Fertilization in the two-spotted spider mite (*Tetranychus urticae:* Acari). *Entomologia Experimentalis et Applicata* **10,** 103–110.

Helm, J. (1980). Female infanticide, European diseases, and population levels among the McKenzie Dene. *American Ethnologist* **7,** 259–285.

Heltne, P. G., and R. W. Thorington, Jr. (1976). Problems and potentials for primate biology and conservation in the New World. In *Neotropical primates: Field studies and conservation* (R. W. Thorington, Jr. and P. G. Heltne, eds.), pp. 110–124. Washington, D.C.: National Academy of Sciences.

Hemker, T. P. (1982). Population characteristics and movement patterns of cougars in southern Utah. Unpublished M.Sc. thesis, Utah State University, Logan, Utah.

Hendrickx, A. G., and D. C. Kraemer. (1969). Observations on the menstrual cycle, optimal mating time and pre-implantation embryos of the baboon, *Papio anubis* and *Papio cynocephalus. Journal of Reproduction and Fertility Suppl.* **6**, 119–128.

Henry, L. (1961). Some data on natural fertility. *Eugenics Quarterly* **8**, 81–91.

Henschen, S. E. (ed.). (1905). La lutte contre la tuberculose en Suede. *Congress International de la Tuberculosis, Paris.*

Herbert, W. (1982). The evolution of child abuse. *Science News* **122**, 24–26.

Herreid, C. F., and S. Kinney. (1966). Survival of Alaskan wood frog (*Rana sylvatica*) larvae. *Ecology* **47**, 1039–1041.

Heusser, H. (1971). Laich-Rauben und Kannibalismus bei sympatrichen Anuran-Kualquappen. *Experientia* **27**, 474–475.

Heusser, H. (1972). Intra- and Inter-spezifisch Crowding-effekte bei Kualquappen der Kreuzkrote *Bufo calamita* Laur. *Oecologia (Berlin)* **10**, 93–98.

Heyer, W. R. (1973). Ecological interactions of frog larvae at a seasonal tropical location in Thailand. *Journal of Herpetology* **7**, 337–361.

Heyer, W. R. (1979). Annual variation in larval amphibian populations within a temperate pond. *Journal of the Washington Academy of Science* **69**, 65–74.

Heyer, W. R., R. W. McDiarmid, and D. Weigmann. (1975). Tadpoles, predation and pond habits in the tropics. *Biotropica* **7**, 100–111.

Highton, R., and T. Savage. (1961). Functions of the brooding behavior in the female red-backed salamander *Plethodon cinereus. Copeia,* pp. 95–98.

Hill, L. G. (1969). Feeding and food habits of the spring cavefish, *Chologaster agassizi. American Midland Naturalist* **82**, 110–116.

Hirschfeld, L. A., J. Howe, and B. Levin. (1978). Warfare, infanticide, and statistical inference: A comment on Divale and Harris. *American Anthropologist* **80**, 110–115.

Hladik, C. M., and A. Hladik. (1972). Disponibilités alimentaires et domaines vitaux des primates à Ceylon. *La Terre et la Vie* **26**, 149–215.

Hocart, A. M. (1929). *Lau Islands, Fiji.* Honolulu: Bishop Museum.

Hoffmann, R. S. (1958). The role of reproduction and mortality in population fluctuations of voles (*Microtus*). *Ecological Monographs* **28**, 79–109.

Hofsten, E., and H. Lundstrom. (1976). *Swedish population history: Main trends from 1750 to 1970 Urval,* No. 8. Stockholm, Sweden.

Hogarth, P. J. (1978). *Biology of reproduction.* London: Blackie.

Holcik, J. (1977). Changes in fish community of Klicava Reservoir with particular reference to Eurasian perch (*Perca fluviatilis*), 1957–72. *Journal of the Fisheries Research Board of Canada* **34**, 1734–1747.

Holley, A. J. F. (1980). Naturally arising adoption in the herring gull. *Animal Behaviour* **29**, 302–303.

Holmes, H. B. (1970). Alteration of sex ratio in the parasitic wasp, *Nasonia vitripennis.* Unpublished Ph.D. thesis, University of Massachusetts, Amherst, Mass.

Holmes, H. B. (1972). Genetic evidence for fewer progeny and a higher percent males when *Nasonia vitripennis* oviposits in previously parasitized hosts. *Entomophaga* **17**, 79–88.

Holmes, W. G., and P. W. Sherman. (1983). Kin recognition in animals. *American Scientist* **71**, 46–55.

Hoppe, P. C. (1975). Genetic and endocrine studies of the pregnancy-blocking pheromone of mice. *Journal of Reproduction and Fertility* **45**, 109–115.

Hornocker, M. G. (1970). An analysis of mountain lion predation upon mule deer and elk in the Idaho primitive area. *Wildlife Monographs* **21**, 5–39.

Howe, H. F. (1976). Egg size, hatching asynchrony, sex, and brood reduction in the common grackle. *Ecology* **57**, 1195–1207.

Howe, H. F. (1978). Initial investment, clutch size, and brood reduction in the common grackle (*Quiscalus quiscula* L.). *Ecology* **59**, 1109–1122.

Howell, N. (1976). The population of the Dobe area !Kung. In *Kalahari Hunter Gatherers* (R. B. Lee and I. DeVore, eds.), pp. 137–151. Cambridge: Harvard University Press.

Howell, N. (1979). *Demography of the Dobe !Kung*. New York: Academic Press.

Howitt, A. W. (1904). *The native tribes of south-east Australia*. London: Macmillan.

Hrdy, S. Blaffer. (1974). Male–male competition and infanticide among the langurs (*Presbytis entellus*) of Abu, Rajasthan. *Folia Primatologica* **22**, 19–58.

Hrdy, S. Blaffer. (1976). The care and exploitation of nonhuman primate infants by conspecifics other than the mother. *Advances in the Study of Behavior* **6**, 101–158.

Hrdy, S. Blaffer. (1977a). Infanticide as a primate reproductive strategy. *American Scientist* **65**, 40–49.

Hrdy, S. Blaffer. (1977b). *The langurs of Abu: Female and male strategies of reproduction*. Cambridge, Mass.: Harvard University Press.

Hrdy, S. Blaffer. (1979). Infanticide among animals: A review, classification, and examination of the implications for the reproductive strategies of females. *Ethology and Sociobiology* **1**, 13–40.

Hrdy, S. Blaffer. (1981). *The woman that never evolved*. Cambridge, Mass.: Harvard University Press.

Hrdy, S. Blaffer, and D. B. Hrdy. (1976). Hierarchical relations among female Hanuman langurs (Primates: Colobinae, *Presbytis entellus*). *Science* **193**, 913–915.

Huber, M., and F. H. Bronson. (1980). Social modulation of spontaneous ejaculation in the mouse. *Behavioral and Neural Biology* **29**, 390–393.

Huck, U. W. (1982). Pregnancy block in laboratory mice as a function of male social status. *Journal of Reproduction and Fertility* **66**, 181–184.

Huck, U. W., and E. M. Banks. (1982). Male dominance status, female choice and mating success in the brown lemming, *Lemmus trimucronatus*. *Animal Behaviour* **30**, 665–675.

Huck, U. W., E. M. Banks, and S-C. Wang. (1981). Olfactory discrimination of social status in the brown lemming. *Behavioral and Neural Biology* **33**, 364–371.

Huck, U. W., C. S. Carter, and E. M. Banks. (1979). Estrogen and progesterone interactions influencing sexual and social behavior in the brown Lemming, *Lemmus trimucronatus*. *Hormones and Behavior* **12**, 40–49.

Huck, U. W., R. L. Soltis, and C. B. Coopersmith. (1982). Infanticide in male laboratory mice: Effects of social status, prior sexual experience, and basis for discrimination between related and unrelated young. *Animal Behaviour* **30**, 1158–1165.

Hughes, A. L. (1981). Female infanticide: Sex ratio manipulation in humans. *Ethology and Sociobiology* **2**, 109–111.

Hunt, B. P., and W. F. Carbine. (1951). Food of young pike, *Esox lucius* L., and associated fishes in Peterson's ditches, Houghton Lake, Michigan. *Transactions of the American Fisheries Society* **80**, 67–83.

Hunt, G. L., Jr., and M. W. Hunt. (1975). Reproductive ecology of the western gull: The importance of nest spacing. *Auk* **92**, 270–279.

Hunt, G. L., Jr., and M. W. Hunt. (1976). Gull chick survival: The significance of growth rates, timing of breeding and territory size. *Ecology* **57**, 62–75.

Hunt, G. L., Jr., and S. C. McLoon. (1975). Activity patterns of gull chicks in relation to feeding by parents and their potential significance for density-dependent mortality. *Auk* **92**, 525–527.

Hunter, J. R., and C. A. Kimbrell. (1980a). Early life history of Pacific mackerel, *Scomber japonicus*. *Fishery Bulletin* **78**, 89–101.

Hunter, J. R., and C. A. Kimbrell. (1980b). Egg cannibalism in the northern anchovy, *Engraulis mordax*. *Fishery Bulletin* **78**, 811–816.

Hussain, N., S. Akatsu, and C. El-Zahr. (1981). Spawning, egg and early larval development, and growth of *Acanthopagrus cuvieri* (Sparidae). *Aquaculture* **22**, 125–136.

Hussell, D. J. T. (1972). Factors affecting clutch size in Arctic passerines. *Ecological Monographs* **42**, 317–364.

Hynes, H. B. N. (1950). The food of fresh-water sticklebacks (*Gasterosteus aculeatus* and *Pygosteus pungitius*), with a review of methods used in studies of the food of fishes. *Journal of Animal Ecology* **19**, 36–58.

Ibsen, H. L. (1928). Prenatal growth in guinea-pigs, with special reference to environmental factors affecting weight at birth. *Journal of Experimental Zoology* **51**, 51–91.

Iersel, J. J. A. van. (1953). An analysis of parental behaviour of the male three-spined stickleback (*Gasterosteus aculeatus* L.). *Behaviour Suppl.* **3**, 159 pp.

Imhof, M. A., and S. W. Hewett. (1982). *Statpro statistical package*. Madison, Wisc.: Blue Lakes Computing.

Imler, R. L., D. T. Weber, and O. L. Fyock. (1975). Survival, reproduction, age, growth, and food habits of Sacramento perch, *Archoplites interruptus* (Girard), in Colorado. *Transactions of the American Fisheries Society* **104**, 232–236.

Ingram, C. (1959). The importance of juvenile cannibalism in the breeding biology of certain birds of prey. *Auk* **76**, 218–226.

Ingram, C. (1962). Cannibalism by nestling short-eared owls. *Auk* **79**, 715.

Itani, J. (1954). *Takasakiyama No Saru*. Tokyo: Kobunsha.

Jackman, B., and J. Scott. (1982). *The marsh lions*. London: Elm Tree Books/ Hamish Hamilton.

Jackson, R. J. (1982). The biology of *Portia fimbriata*, a web building jumping spider (*Araneae, Salticidae*) from Queensland: Intraspecific interactions. *Journal of Zoology (London)* **196**, 295–305.

Jaffe, R. B. (1969). Testosterone metabolism in target tissues: Hypothalamic and pituitary tissues of adult rat and human fetus and the immature rat epiphysis. *Steroids* **114**, 483–498.

Jain, M. K. (1975). Growing imbalance in the sex composition of India. *Demography India* **4**, 305–315.

Jainudeen, M. R., and E. S. E. Hafez. (1980). Reproductive failure in females.

In *Reproduction in farm animals* (E. S. E. Hafez, ed.), 4th ed., pp. 449–470. Philadelphia: Lea and Febiger.

Jakubowski, M., and J. Terkel. (1982). Infanticide and caretaking in non-lactating *Mus musculus:* Influence of genotype, family group and sex. *Animal Behaviour* **30**, 1029–1035.

Jay, P. (1963). Mother–infant relations in langurs. In *Maternal behavior in mammals* (H. L. Rheingold, ed.), pp. 282–304. New York: Wiley.

Jay, P. (1965). The common langur of north India. In *Primate behavior: Field studies of monkeys and apes* (I. DeVore, ed.), pp. 197–249. New York: Holt, Rinehart and Winston.

Jenness, D. (1922). *The life of the copper Eskimoes: Report on the Canadian Arctic Expedition, 1913–18.* Ottawa: F. A. Adand.

Jenni, D. (1969). A study of the ecology of four species of herons during the breeding season at Lake Alice, Alachua County, Florida. *Ecological Monographs* **39**, 245–270.

Jenssen, T. A. (1967). Food habits of the green frog *Rana clamitans* before and during metamorphosis. *Copeia*, pp. 214–218.

Jewell, E. D. (1968). SCUBA diving observations on lingcod spawning at a Seattle breakwater. *Washington State Department of Fisheries, Fisheries Research Paper* **3**, 27–36.

Johansson, S. R. (1976). Her story as his story—A theoretical approach to the study of social change and the status of women. In *Liberating women's history* (B. Carroll, ed.). Urbana: University of Illinois.

Johansson, S. R. (1977). Sex and death in Victorian England. In *A widening sphere* (M. Vicinus, ed.), pp. 163–180. Bloomington: Indiana University Press.

John, K. R., and D. Fenster. (1975). The effects of partitions on the growth rates of crowded *Rana pipiens* tadpoles. *American Midland Naturalist* **93**, 123–130.

Johnson, O. (1981). The socioeconomic context of child abuse and neglect in native South America. In *Child abuse and neglect: Cross-cultural perspectives.* (J. E. Korbin, ed.), pp. 55–70. Berkeley: University of California Press.

Johnson, R. G. (1959). Spatial distribution of *Phoronopsis viridis* Hilton. *Science* **129**, 1221.

Jonasson, P. (1971). Population studies on *Chronomus anthracinus*. In *Dynamics of populations* (P. J. den Boer and G. Gradwell, eds.), pp. 220–231. Wageningen: Pudoc.

Jones, C. B. (1980). The functions of status in the mantled howler monkey, *Alouatta palliata* Gray: Intraspecific competition for group membership in a folivorous neotropical primate. *Primates* **21**, 389–405.

Jonkel, C. (1970). Behaviour of captured North American bears. *BioScience* **20**, 1145–1147.

Jorberg, L. (1965). Structural change and economic growth: Sweden in the 19th century. *Economy and History* **8**, 1–46.

Juterbock, J. E. (1982). Is prudent brooding behavior in the dusky salamander measured by success or investment? *American Zoologist* **22**, 972.

Kaczmarski, F. (1966). Bioenergetics of pregnancy and lactation in the bank vole. *Acta Theriologica* **11**, 409–417.

Kaddou, I. K. (1960). The feeding behavior of *Hippodamia quinquesignata* (Kirby) larvae. *University of California Publications in Entomology* **16**, 181–232.

Kahl, M. P. (1964). Food ecology of the wood stork (*Mycteria americana*) in Florida. *Ecological Monographs* **34**, 97–117.

Kaku, K. (1975). Were girl babies sacrificed to a folk superstition in 1966 in Japan? *Annals of Human Biology* **2**, 391–393.

Kalela, O. (1957). Regulation of reproduction rate in subarctic populations of the vole, *Clethrionomys rufocanus* (Sund.). *Annales Academiae Scientiarum Fennicae* Ser. A-IV (*Biologia*) **34**, 1–60.

Kalvemark, A. S. (1977). The country that kept track of its population. In *Time, space and man* (J. Sundin and E. Soderlund, eds.), pp. 221–238. Umea, Sweden.

Kan, T. T., and C. E. Bond. (1981). Notes on the biology of the Miller Lake lamprey *Lampetra* (*Entosphenus*) *minima. Northwest Science* **55**, 70–74.

Kaplan, R. H., and P. W. Sherman. (1980). Intraspecific oophagy in California newts. *Journal of Herpetology* **14**, 183–185.

Karsten, R. (1932). *Indian tribes of the Argentine and Bolivian Chaco: Ethnological studies.* Helsingfors: Akademische Buchhandlung (HRAF transl.).

Kaston, B. J. (1968). Remarks on black widow spiders, with an account of some anomalies. *Entomological News* **79**, 113–124.

Kasuya, E., Y. Hibino, and Y. Ito. (1980). On "intercolonial" cannibalism in Japanese paper wasps, *Polistes chinensis antennalis* Perez and *P. jadwigae* Torre (Hymenoptera: Vespidae). *Researches on Population Ecology* (*Kyoto*) **22**, 255–262.

Kawai, A. (1978). Sibling cannibalism in the first instar larvae of *Harmonia axyridis* (Coleoptera, Coccinellidae). *Kontyu* **46**, 14–19.

Kawanaka, K. (1981). Infanticide and cannibalism in chimpanzees with special reference to the newly observed case in the Mahale Mountains. *African Studies Monograph* **1**, 69–99.

Keast, A. (1978). Trophic and spatial interrelationships in the fish species of an Ontario temperate lake. *Environmental Biology of Fishes* **3**, 7–31.

Keenleyside, M. H. A. (1972). Intraspecific intrusions into nests of spawning longear sunfish (Pisces: Centrarchidae). *Copeia,* pp. 272–278.

Keenleyside, M. H. A. (1978). Parental care behavior in fishes and birds. In *Contrasts in behavior* (E. S. Reese and F. J. Lighter, eds.), pp. 3–29. New York: Wiley.

Keenleyside, M. H. A. (1979). *Diversity and adaptation in fish behaviour.* New York: Springer-Verlag.

Kekagul, B., and J. A. McNeely. (1977). *Mammals of Thailand.* Bangkok: Kurusapha Ladprao Press.

Kellum, B. (1974). Infanticide in England in the later Middle Ages. *History of Infanticide Quarterly* **1**, 367–388.

Kempe, R. S., and H. C. Kempe. (1978). *Child abuse.* Cambridge, Mass.: Harvard University Press.

Kennedy, R., Jr. (1972). The social status of the sexes and their relative mortality in Ireland. In *Readings in population* (William Petersen, ed.), pp. 121–135. New York: Macmillan.

Kenneth, J. H., and G. R. Ritchie. (1953). *Gestation periods: A table and bibliography.* Edinburgh: Technical Communication No. 5 of the Commonwealth Bureau of Animal Breeding and Genetics.

Kenney, A. M., R. L. Evans, and D. A. Dewsbury. (1977). Postimplantation pregnancy disruption in *Microtus ochrogaster, M. pennsylvanicus,* and *Peromyscus maniculatus. Journal of Reproduction and Fertility* **49**, 365–367.

Kenny, J. S. (1969). Feeding mechanisms in anuran larvae. *Journal of Zoology* (*London*) **157**, 225–246.

Kepler, C. B. (1969). Breeding biology of the blue-faced booby *Sula dactylatra personata* on Green Island, Kure Atoll. *Publication of the Nuttall Ornithological Club*, No. 8.

Keverne, E. B., and C. de la Riva. (1982). Pheromones in mice: reciprocal interactions between the nose and brain. *Nature* (*London*) **296**, 148–50.

Keverne, E., F. Levy, P. Poindron, and D. Lindsay. (1983). Vaginal stimulation: An important determinant of maternal bonding in sheep. *Science* **219**, 81–83.

Khan, M. E. (1973). Factors affecting spacing of births. *Journal of Family Welfare* **20**, 54–67.

Kihlstrom, J. E. (1972). Periods of gestation and body weight in some placental mammals. *Comparative Biochemistry and Physiology* **43A**, 673–679.

Kiltie, R. A. (1982). Intraspecific variation in the mammalian gestation period. *Journal of Mammalogy* **63**, 646–652.

Kimmance, K. J. (1972). Failure to thrive and lactation failure in Jordanian villages in 1970. *Environmental Child Health* **18**, 313–316.

King, C. E., and P. S. Dawson. (1973). Population biology and *Tribolium* model. *Evolutionary Biology* **5**, 133–227.

King, J. A. (1963). Maternal behavior of *Peromyscus*. In (H. Rheingold, ed.). *Maternal Behavior in Mammals*. New York: Wiley.

King, J. A., J. C. Deschares, and R. Webster. (1963). Age of weaning in two subspecies of deer mice. *Science* **139**, 483–484.

King, P. E., and C. R. Hopkins. (1963). Length of life of the sexes in *Nasonia vitripennis* (Walker) (Hymenoptera: Pteromalidae) under conditions of starvation. *Journal of Experimental Biology* **40**, 751–761.

King, W. (1939). A survey of the herpetology of Great Smoky Mountains National Park. *American Midland Naturalist* **21**, 531–582.

Kingston, B. (1967). *Working plan for Kibale and Itwara Central Forest Reserves*. Entebbe, Uganda: Forest Dept.

Kipling, C., and W. E. Frost. (1970). A study of the mortality, population numbers, year class strengths, production and food consumption of pike, *Esox lucius* L., in Windermere from 1944–1962. *Journal of Animal Ecology* **39**, 115–158.

Kirkpatrick, T. H. (1968). Studies on the wallaroo. *Queensland Agricultural Journal* **94**, 362–365.

Kleiman, D. G. (1977). Monogamy in animals. *Quarterly Review of Biology* **52**, 39–69.

Kleiman, D. G. (1980). The sociobiology of captive propagation. In *Conservation biology: An evolutionary perspective* (E. Soule and B. A. Wilcox, eds.), pp. 243–261. Sunderland, Mass.: Sinauer.

Kleiman, D. G. (1981). Correlations among life history characteristics of mammalian species exhibiting two extreme forms of monogamy. In *Natural selection and social behavior: Recent research and new theory* (R. D. Alexander and D. W. Tinkle, eds.), pp. 332–344. New York: Chiron Press.

Kleiman, D. G., and J. F. Eisenberg. (1973). Comparisons of canid and felid social systems from an evolutionary perspective. *Animal Behaviour* **21**, 637–659.

Klomp, H. (1970). The determination of clutch-size in birds: A review. *Ardea* **58**, 1–124.

Kluchareva, O. A. (1956). Intraspecies relations of fishes. *Zoologicheskii Zhurnal* **35**, 275–289. [English summary.]

Kluge, A. G. (1981). The life history, social organization, and parental behavior of *Hyla rosenbergi* Boulenger, a nest building gladiator frog. *Miscellaneous Publications Museum of Zoology University of Michigan* **160**, 1–170.

Kluge, E.-H. (1978). Infanticide as the murder of persons: Infanticide and the value of life. In *Infanticide and the value of life* (M. Kohl, ed.), pp. 32–45. Buffalo: Prometheus Books.

Knopf, F. L. (1979). Spatial and temporal aspects of colonial nesting of white pelicans. *Condor* **81**, 353–363.

Kochetova, N. I. (1977). Factors determining the sex ratio in some entomophagous Hymenoptera. *Entomological Review* **56**, 1–5.

Kodric-Brown, A. (1977). Reproductive success and the evolution of breeding territories in pupfish (Cyprinodon). *Evolution* **31**, 750–766.

Koenig, W. D., R. L. Mumme, and F. A. Pitelka. (1983). Female roles in cooperatively breeding acorn woodpeckers. In *Social behavior of female vertebrates* (S. K. Wasser, ed.), pp. 235–261. New York: Academic Press.

Koester, H. (1970). Ovum transport. In *Mammalian reproduction* (H. Gibian and E. J. Plotz, eds.), pp. 189–228. New York: Springer-Verlag.

Korbin, J. E. (1981). Conclusions. In *Child abuse and neglect: Cross-cultural perspectives* (J. E. Korbin, ed.), pp. 205–210. Berkeley: University of California Press.

Kore, B. A., and M. C. Joshi. (1975). Food of the squid, *Loligo duvauceli* d'Orbigny. *Proceedings of the Indian Academy of Science* **B81**, 20–28.

Koshkina, T. V., and Y-S. Korotkov. (1975). Regulative adaptations in populations of the red vole (*Clethrionomys rutilus*) under optimum conditions of its range. *Fauna and Ecology of Rodents* **12**, 5–61.

Koster, W. J. (1936). The food of sculpins (Cottidae) in central New York. *Transactions of the American Fisheries Society* **66**, 374–382.

Kramer, D. L. (1973). Parental behaviour in the blue gourami *Trichogaster trichopterus* (Pisces, Belontiidae) and its induction during exposure to varying numbers of conspecific eggs. *Behaviour* **47**, 14–32.

Kramer, D. L., and N. R. Liley. (1971). The role of spawning behaviour and stimuli from the eggs in the induction of a parental response in the blue gourami, *Trichogaster trichopterus* (Pisces, Belontiidae). *Animal Behaviour* **19**, 87–92.

Krebs, C. J. (1966). Demographic changes in fluctuating populations of *Microtus californicus*. *Ecological Monographs* **36**, 239–273.

Krebs, C. J. (1970). *Microtus* population biology: Behavioral changes associated with the population cycle in *M. ochrogaster* and *M. pennsylvanicus*. *Ecology* **51**, 34–52.

Krebs, C. J., B. L. Keller, and R. H. Tamarin. (1969). *Microtus* population biology: Demographic changes in fluctuating populations of *M. ochrogaster* and *M. pennsylvanicus* in southern Indiana. *Ecology* **50**, 587–607.

Krebs, C. J., and J. H. Myers. (1974). Population cycles in small mammals. *Advances in Ecological Research* **8**, 267–399.

Kruuk, H. (1972). *The spotted hyena*. Chicago: University of Chicago Press.

Kruuk, H. (1975). Functional aspects of social hunting by carnivores. In *Function and evolution in behaviour* (G. Baerends, C. Beer, and A. Manning, eds.), pp. 119–141. Oxford: Clarendon Press.

Kruuk, H. (1978). Social organization and territorial behaviour of the European badger *Meles meles*. *Journal of Zoology* (*London*) **184**, 1–19.

Kryzsik, A. J. (1980). Trophic aspects of brooding behavior in *Desmognathus fuscus fuscus*. *Journal of Herpetology* **14**, 426–428.

Kryzwicki, L. (1934). *Primitive society and its vital statistics.* London: Macmillan.

Kummer, H. (1968). *Social organization of Hamadryas baboons.* Chicago: University Press.

Kummer, H., W. Goetz, and W. Angst. (1974). Triadic differentiation: An inhibitory process protecting pair bonds in baboons. *Behaviour* 49, 62–87.

Kynard, B. E. (1978). Breeding behavior of a lacustrine population of three-spined sticklebacks (*Gasterosteus aculeatus* L.). *Behaviour* 67, 178–207.

Labov, J. B. (1980). Factors influencing infanticidal behavior in wild male house mice (*Mus musculus*). *Behavioral Ecology and Sociobiology* 6, 297–303.

Labov, J. B. (1981a). Pregnancy blocking in rodents: Adaptive advantages for females. *American Naturalist* 118, 361–371.

Labov, J. B. (1981b). Male social status, physiology, and ability to block pregnancies in female house mice (*Mus musculus*). *Behavioral Ecology and Sociobiology* 8, 287–291.

Lack, D. (1947). The significance of clutch size. *Ibis* 89, 302–352.

Lack, D. (1954). *The natural regulation of animal numbers.* Oxford: Clarendon Press.

Lack, D. (1956). Further notes on the breeding biology of the swift *Apus apus. Ibis* 98, 606–619.

Lack, D. (1966). *Population studies of birds.* Oxford: Clarendon Press.

Lack, D. (1968). *Ecological adaptations for breeding in birds.* London: Methuen.

Lack, D., and E. Lack. (1951). The breeding biology of the swift *Apus apus. Ibis* 93, 501–546.

Lacy, R. C. (1978). Dynamics of t-alleles in *Mus musculus* populations: Review and speculation. *The Biologist* 60, 41–67.

Laessle, A. M. (1961). A micro-limnological study of Jamaican bromeliads. *Ecology* 42, 499–517.

Lagace, R. O. (1974). *Nature and use of the HRAF files.* New Haven: Human Relations Area Files.

Lagler, K. F. (1956). The pike, *Esox lucius* Linnaeus, in relation to waterfowl on the Seney National Wildlife Refuge, Michigan. *Journal of Wildlife Management* 20, 114–124.

Lancaster, C., and J. Lancaster. (1978). On the male supremacist complex: A reply to Divale and Harris. *American Anthropologist* 80, 115–117.

Lancaster, J. B., and R. B. Lee. (1965). The annual reproductive cycle in monkeys and apes. In *Primate behavior* (I. DeVore, ed.), pp. 486–513. New York: Holt, Rinehart and Winston.

Lande, R. (1980). Sexual dimorphism, sexual selection, and adaptation in polygenic characters. *Evolution* 34, 292–305.

Landry, M. R. (1978a). Predatory feeding behavior of a marine copepod, *Labidocera trispinosa. Limnology and Oceanography* 23, 1103–1113.

Landry, M. R. (1978b). Population dynamics and production of a planktonic marine copepod *Acartia clausii* in a small temperate lagoon on San Juan Island, Washington. *Internationale Revue der gesamten Hydrobiologie.* 63, 77–119.

Langer, W. (1974). Infanticide: A historical survey. *History of Childhood Quarterly* 1, 353–365.

Lawlor, M. (1963). Social dominance in the golden hamster. *Bulletin of the British Psychological Society* 16, 25–38.

Laws, J. V. H., and J. Laws. (1983). Social interactions among adult male langurs (*Presbytis entellus*) at Rajaji Wildlife Sanctuary. *International Journal of Primatology* 5, 31–50.

Lee, R. B. (1979). The !Kung Sun. Cambridge: Cambridge University Press.

Lee, R. B. (1980). Lactation, ovulation, infanticide and woman's work: A study of hunter-gatherer population regulation. In Biosocial Mechanisms of Population Regulation. (M. N. Cohen et al., eds.). New Haven: Yale University Press.

Leitch, L., F. E. Hytten, and W. Z. Billewicz. (1959). The maternal and neonatal weights of some mammals. Proceedings of the Zoological Society of London 133, 11–28.

Lenington, S. (1981). Child abuse: The limits of sociobiology. Ethology and Sociobiology 2, 17–29.

Leontjev, A. N. (1964). Studying Meriones unguiculatus by the method of marking. (1962). 161298 cit. from Referativnyi zhurnal. Biologiia. No. 103056.

Leshner, A. I. (1978). An introduction to behavioral endocrinology. New York: Oxford.

Lesowski, J. (1963). Two observations of cougar cannibalism. Journal of Mammalogy 44, 586.

Leutenegger, W. (1973). Maternal-fetal weight relationships in primates. Folia Primatologica 20, 283–293.

Lewontin, R. C. (1974). The genetic basis of evolutionary change. New York: Columbia University Press.

Li, S. K., and D. H. Owings. (1978). Sexual selection in the three-spined stickleback: II. Nest raiding during the courtship phase. Behaviour 64, 298–304.

Licht, L. E. (1967). Growth inhibition in crowded tadpoles: Intraspecific and interspecific effects. Ecology 48, 736–745.

Licht, L. E. (1974). Survival of embryos, tadpoles, and adults of the frogs Rana aurora aurora and Rana pretiosa pretiosa in southwestern British Columbia. Canadian Journal of Zoology 52, 613–627.

Lidicker, W. Z., Jr. (1965). Comparative study of density regulation in confined populations of four species of rodents. Researches on Population Ecology (Kyoto) 7, 57–72.

Lidicker, W. Z., Jr. (1975). The role of dispersal in the demography of small mammals. In Small mammals: Their productivity and population dynamics (F. Golley, K. Petrusewicz, and L. Ryszkowski, eds.), pp. 103–128. Cambridge: Cambridge University Press.

Lidicker, W. Z., Jr. (1976). Social behaviour and density regulation in house mice living in large enclosures. Journal of Animal Ecology 45, 677–697.

Lidicker, W. Z., Jr. (1979). Analysis of two freely-growing enclosed populations of the California vole. Journal of Mammalogy 60, 447–466.

Liebman, E. (1933). Some observations on the breeding habits of Palestine Cichlidae. Proceedings of the Zoological Society of London, pp. 85–87.

Liggins, G. C., R. J. Fairclough, S. A. Grieves, J. Z. Kendall, and B. S. Knox. (1973). The mechanism of initiation of parturition in the ewe. Recent Progress in Hormone Research 29, 111–159.

Lightcap, J. L., J. A. Kurland, and R. L. Burgess. (1982). Child abuse: A test of some predictions from evolutionary theory. Ethology and Sociobiology 3, 61–67.

Lillegraven, J. A. (1975). Biological considerations of the marsupial–placental dichotomy. Evolution 29, 707–722.

Linzey, D. W., and A. W. Linzey. (1967). Growth and development of the golden mouse Ochrotomys nuttalli nuttalli. Journal of Mammalogy 48, 445–448.

Lloyd, D. G. (1972a). Breeding systems in Cotula L. (Compositae, Anthemideae). I. The array of monoclinous and diclinous systems. New Phytologist 71, 1181–1194.

Lloyd, D. G. (1972b). Breeding systems in *Cotula* L. (Compositae, Anthemideae). II. Monoecious populations. *New Phytologist* **71**, 1195–1202.

Lloyd, J. A. (1975). Social structure and reproduction in two freely-growing populations of house mice (*Mus musculus* L.). *Animal Behaviour* **23**, 413–424.

Lloyd, J. A., and J. J. Christian. (1967). Relationship of activity and aggression to density in two confined populations of house mice (*Mus musculus*). *Journal of Mammalogy* **48**, 262–269.

Lloyd, J. A., and J. J. Christian. (1969). Reproductive activity of individual females in three experimental freely growing populations of house mice (*Mus musculus*). *Journal of Mammalogy* **50**, 49–59.

Lockie, J. D. (1955). The breeding and feeding of jackdaws and rooks with notes on carrion crows and other Corvidae. *Ibis* **97**, 341–369.

Loflin, R. K. (1982). Egg-burying behavior and intraspecific egg parasitism in smooth-billed ani (*Crotophaga ani*). Abstracts of the 100th American Ornithologists' Union Conference, Chicago, Ill.

Loiselle, P. V. (1977). Colonial breeding by an African substratum-spawning cichlid fish, *Tilapia zillii* (Gervais). *Biology of Behaviour* **2**, 129–142.

Loiselle, P. V. (1978). Prevalence of male brood care in teleosts. *Nature (London)* **276**, 98.

Loiselle, P. V. (1983). Filial cannibalism and egg recognition by males of the primitively custodial teleost *Cyprinodon macularius californiensis* Girard (Atherinomorpha: Cyprinodontidae). *Ethology and Sociobiology* **4**, 1–9.

Loiselle, P. V., and G. W. Barlow. (1978). Do fishes lek like birds? In *Contrasts in behavior* (E. S. Reese and F. J. Lighter, eds.), pp. 31–75. New York: Wiley.

Lonsdale, D., D. Heinle, and C. Siegfried. (1979). Carnivorous feeding behavior of the adult calanoid copepod *Acartia tonsa* Dana. *Journal of Experimental Marine Biology and Ecology* **36**, 235–248.

Lorenz, K. (1966). *On aggression*. New York: Harcourt, Brace and World.

Lorimer, F. (1954). *Culture and human fertility*. Zurich: UNESCO.

Lounibos, L. P. (1979). Temporal and spatial distribution, growth and predatory behavior of *Toxorhynchites brevipalpis* (Diptera: Culcidae) on the Kenya coast. *Journal of Animal Ecology* **48**, 213–236.

Loveridge, A. (1947). History and habits of the east African bullfrog. *East African Natural History Society* **19**, 95–99.

Low, B. S. (1978). Environmental uncertainty and the parental strategies of marsupials and placentals. *American Naturalist* **112**, 197–213.

Lund, R. (1980). Viviparity and intrauterine feeding in a new Holocephalan fish from the Lower Carboniferous of Montana. *Science* **209**, 697–699.

Lundberg, C.-A., and R. A. Väisänen. (1979). Selective correlation of egg size with chick mortality in the black-headed gull (*Larus ridibundus*). *Condor* **81**, 146–156.

Lundquist, J. (1944). *Tuberkulosie och des Behampande*. Stockholm: Albert Forlag.

Lutz, B. (1947). Trends toward non-aquatic and direct development. *Copeia*, pp. 242–252.

Lynn, G. W., and H. Edleman. (1936). Crowding and metamorphosis in the tadpole. *Ecology* **17**, 104–109.

Lyons, A., and T. Spight. (1973). Diversity of feeding mechanisms among embryos of Pacific Northwest *Thais*. *Veliger* **16**, 189–194.

McCauley, D. E., and M. J. Wade. (1980). Group selection: The genetic and demographic basis for the phenotypic differentiation of small populations of *Tribolium castaneum*. *Evolution* **34**, 813–821.

McClintock, M. K. (1981). Social control of the ovarian cycle and the function of estrous synchrony. *American Zoologist* **21**, 243–256.

McClintock, M. K. (1983). Pheromonal control of the ovarian cycle: Enhancement, suppression, and synchrony. In *Pheromones in mammalian reproduction* (J. G. Vandenbergh, ed.). New York: Academic Press. In press.

McClure, P. A. (1981). Sex-biased litter reduction in food-restricted wood rats (*Neotoma floridana*). *Science* **211**, 1058–1060.

McClure, P. A., and J. C. Randolph. (1980). Relative allocation of energy to growth and development of homeothermy in the eastern wood rat (*Neotoma floridana*) and hispid cotton rat (*Sigmodon hispidus*). *Ecological Monographs* **50**, 199–219.

McCormack, J. C. (1965). Observations on the perch population of Ullswater. *Journal of Animal Ecology* **34**, 463–478.

McCormack, J. C. (1970). Observations on the food of perch (*Perca fluviatilis* L.) in Windermere. *Journal of Animal Ecology* **39**, 255–267.

McDiarmid, R. W. (1978). Evolution of parental care in frogs. In *The development of behavior* (G. M. Burghardt and M. Bekoff, eds.), pp. 127–147. New York: Garland STPM Press.

Macdonald, D. W. (1978). "Helpers" in fox society. *Nature (London)* **282**, 69–71.

Macdonald, D. W. (1979). The flexible social system of the golden jackal, *Canis aureus*. *Behavioral Ecology and Sociobiology* **5**, 17–38.

Macdonald, D. W. and Moehlman, P. D. (1982). Cooperation, altruism, and restraint in the reproduction of carnivores. In *Perspectives in Ethology, Vol. 5: Ontogeny.* (P. P. G. Bateson and P. Klopfer, eds.), pp. 433–467, New York: Plenum Press.

MacDonald, P. C., J. C. Porter, B. E. Schwarz, and J. M. Johnson. (1978). Initiation of parturition in the human female. *Seminars in Perinatology* **2**, 273–286.

McEnroe, W. D. (1969). Spreading and inbreeding in the spider mite. *Journal of Heredity* **60**, 343–345.

McGill, T. (1970). Induction of luteal activity in female house mice. *Hormones and Behavior* **1**, 211–222.

McGill, T., and R. Coughlin. (1970). Ejaculatory reflex and luteal activity induction in *Mus musculus*. *Journal of Reproduction and Fertility* **21**, 215–220.

Mack, D. (1978). Final report. Unpublished manuscript.

McKaye, K. R., and G. W. Barlow. (1976a). Chemical recognition of young by the midas cichlid, *Cichlasoma citrinellum*. *Copeia*, pp. 276–282.

McKaye, K. R., and G. W. Barlow. (1976b). Competition between color morphs of the midas cichlid, *Cichlasoma citrinellum*, in Lake Jiloa, Nicaragua. In *Investigations of the ichthyofauna of Nicaraguan lakes* (T. B. Thorson, ed.), pp. 465–475. Lincoln, Nebr.: School of Life Sciences, University of Nebraska.

McKaye, K. R., and N. M. McKaye. (1977). Communal care and kidnapping of young by parental cichlids. *Evolution* **31**, 674–681.

McKaye, K. R., D. J. Weiland, and T. M. Lim. (1979). Comments on the breeding biology of *Gobiomorus dormitor* (Osteichthyes: Eleotridae) and the advantage of schooling behavior to its fry. *Copeia*, pp. 542–544.

McKee, L. (1982). Preferential care and child mortality differentials. Paper presented at Symposium on Indirect Infanticide and sex differentials in Children's Treatment, 81st Annual Meeting of the American Anthropological Association, Washington, D.C., December 3–7, 1982.

McKinney, T. D., and C. Desjardins. (1973a). Postnatal development of the testis, fighting behavior, and fertility in house mice. *Biology of Reproduction* **9**, 279–294.

McKinney, T. D., and C. Desjardins. (1973b). Intermale stimuli and testicular function in adult and immature house mice. *Biology of Reproduction* **9**, 370–378.

McLaren, A. (1965). Genetic and environmental effects on foetal and placental growth in mice. *Journal of Reproduction and Fertility* **9**, 79–98.

McLaren, A. (1972). The embryo. In *Reproduction in mammals,* Vol. 2: *Embryonic and fetal development* (C. R. Austin and R. V. Short, eds.), pp. 1–42. Cambridge: Cambridge University Press.

McLaren, A. (1980). Fertilization, cleavage and implantation. In *Reproduction in farm animals,* 4th ed., ed. E. S. E. Hafez, pp. 226–246. Philadelphia: Lea and Febiger.

McLean, I. G. (1982). The association of female kin in the Arctic ground squirrel, *Spermophilus parryii. Behavioral Ecology and Sociobiology* **10**, 91–99.

McLean, I. G. (1983). Paternal behaviour and killing of young in Arctic ground squirrels. *Animal Behaviour* **31**, 32–44.

McLoughlin, V. L. (1980). The effects of the social and physical environments on the behaviour of gerbil families. Unpublished Ph.D. thesis, University of Reading, Reading, England.

McNab, B. K. (1980). Food habits, energetics, and the population biology of mammals. *American Naturalist* **16**, 106–124.

Macnair, M. R., and G. A. Parker. (1979). Models of parent–offspring conflict. III. Intra-brood conflict. *Animal Behaviour* **27**, 1202–1209.

Macpherson, A. H. (1969). *The dynamics of Canadian Arctic fox populations* (Canadian Wildlife Service Report Series 8). Ottawa: Queens Printer.

McQueen, D. J. (1969). Reduction of zooplankton standing stocks by predaceous *Cyclops bicuspidatus thomasi* in Marion Lake, British Columbia. *Journal of the Fisheries Research Board of Canada* **26**, 1605–1618.

Macrides, F., A. Bartke, and S. Dalterio. (1975). Strange females increase plasma testosterone levels in male mice. *Science* **189**, 1104–1106.

Madigan, F. C. (1957). Are sex mortality differentials biologically caused? *Milbank Memorial Fund Quarterly* **35**, 202–223.

Madison, D. M. (1980a). Space use and social structure in meadow voles, *Microtus pennsylvanicus. Behavioral Ecology and Sociobiology* **7**, 65–71.

Madison, D. M. (1980b). An integrated view of the social biology of *Microtus pennsylvanicus. The Biologist* **62**, 20–33.

Makwana, S. C. (1979). Infanticide and social change in two groups of the Hanuman langur, *Presbytis entellus,* at Jodhpur. *Primates* **20**, 293–300.

Makwana, S. C., and R. Advani. (1981). Social changes in the Hanuman langur, *Presbytis entellus,* around Jodhpur. *Journal of the Bombay Natural History Society* **78**, 1–3.

Mallory, F. F. (1979). Reproductive strategies and population dynamics of small mammals: The collared lemming, *Dicrostonyx groenlandicus* and laboratory mouse, *Mus musculus.* Unpublished Ph.D. thesis, University of Guelph, Guelph, Ontario, Canada.

Mallory, F. F., and R. J. Brooks. (1978). Infanticide and other reproductive strategies in the collared lemming, *Dicrostonyx groenlandicus. Nature (London)* **273**, 144–146.

Mallory, F. F., and R. J. Brooks. (1980). Infanticide and pregnancy failure: Reproductive strategies in the female collared lemming (*Dicrostonyx groenlandicus*). *Biology of Reproduction* **22**, 192–196.

Mallory, F. F., and F. V. Clulow. (1977). Evidence of pregnancy failure in the wild meadow vole, *Microtus pennsylvanicus. Canadian Journal of Zoology* **55**, 1–17.

Mann, M. A., C. Kinsley, J. Broida, and B. Svare. (1983). Infanticide exhibited by female mice: Genetic, developmental and hormonal influences. *Physiology and Behavior.* **30**, 697–702.

Mann, R. H. K. (1982). The annual food consumption and prey preferences of pike (*Esox lucius*) in the River Frome, Dorset. *Journal of Animal Ecology* **51**, 81–95.

Mantelenakis, S., and M. Ketchell. (1966). Frequency and extent of delayed implantation in lactating rats and mice. *Journal of Reproduction and Fertility* **12**, 391–394.

Marchlewska-Koj, A. (1977). Pregnancy block elicited by urinary proteins of male mice. *Biology of Reproduction* **17**, 729–732.

Marchlewska-Koj, A. (1980). Partial isolation of pregnancy block pheromone in mice. In *Chemical signals, vertebrates and aquatic invertebrates* (D. Müller-Schwarze and R. M. Silverstein, eds.), pp. 413–414. New York: Plenum.

Marques, D. M., and E. S. Valenstein. (1976). Another hamster paradox: More males carry pups and fewer kill and cannibalize young than do females. *Journal of Comparative and Physiological Psychology* **90**, 653–657.

Marques, D. M., and E. S. Valenstein. (1977). Individual differences in aggressiveness of female hamsters: Response to intact and castrated males and to females. *Animal Behaviour* **25**, 131–139.

Marsden, H. M., and F. H. Bronson. (1965). The synchrony of oestrus in mice: Relative roles of the male and female environments. *Journal of Endocrinology* **32**, 313–319.

Marsh, C. W. (1979). Comparative aspects of social organization in the Tana River red colobus, *Colobus badius rufomitratus. Zeitschrift für Tierpsychologie* **51**, 337–362.

Martin, A. A. (1968). The biology of tadpoles. *Australian Natural History* **15**, 326–330.

Martin, E. P. (1956). A population study of the prairie vole (*Microtus ochrogaster*) in northeastern Kansas. *University of Kansas Museum of Natural History Miscellaneous Publications* **8**, 361–416.

Martinius, S. (1977). *Peasant destinies, the history of 552 Swedes born 1810–12* (Stockholm Studies in Economic History). Stockholm: Almquist and Wiksell.

Martof, B. S. (1956). Growth and development of the green frog, *Rana clamitans* under natural conditions. *American Midland Naturalist* **55**, 101–117.

Massey, A., and J. G. Vandenbergh. (1980). Puberty delay by a urinary cue from female house mice in feral populations. *Science* **209**, 821–822.

Massey, A., and J. G. Vandenbergh. (1981). Puberty acceleration by a urinary cue from male mice in feral populations. *Biology of Reproduction* **24**, 523–527.

Matray, P. F. (1974). Broad-winged hawk behavior and ecology. *Auk* **91**, 307–324.

Mavrogenis, A. P., and O. W. Robison. (1976). Factors affecting puberty in swine. *Journal of Animal Science* **42**, 1251–1255.

Mayden, R. L., and B. M. Burr. (1981). Life history of the slender madtom,

Noturus exilis, in southern Illinois (Pisces: Ictaluridae). *Occasional Papers University of Kansas Museum of Natural History* No. 93, 64 pp.

Mayr, E. (1983). How to carry out the adaptationist program? *American Naturalist* **121**, 324–334.

Mebs, T. (1964). Zur biologie und populations dynamik des maussebussards (*Buteo buteo*). *Journal für Ornithologie* **105**, 247–306. [English summary only consulted.]

Meffe, G. K., and R. C. Vrijenhoek. (1981). Starvation stress and intraovarian cannibalism in livebearers (Atheriniformes: Poeciliidae). *Copeia,* pp. 702–705.

Mentis, M. T. (1972). A review of some life history features of the large herbivores of Africa. *The Lammergeyer* **16**, 1–89.

Merrell, D. J. (1968). A comparison of the estimated size and the "effective" size of breeding populations of the leopard frog, *Rana pipiens. Evolution* **22**, 274–283.

Mertz, D. B. (1969). Age-distribution and abundance in populations of flour beetles. I. Experimental studies. *Ecological Monographs* **39**, 1–31.

Metzelaar, J. (1929). The food of the trout in Michigan. *Transactions of the American Fisheries Society* **59**, 146–152.

Meyburg, B.-U. (1974). Sibling aggression and mortality among nestling eagles. *Ibis* **116**, 224–228.

Meyburg, B.-U. (1977). Sibling aggression and cross-fostering of eagles. In *Endangered birds* (S. A. Temple, ed.), pp. 195–200. Madison: University of Wisconsin Press.

Michael, R. P., and E. B. Keverne. (1968). Pheromones in the communication of sexual status in primates. *Nature (London)* **218**, 746–749.

Michener, G. R. (1982a). Infanticide in ground squirrels. *Animal Behaviour* **30**, 936–938.

Michener, G. R. (1982b). Kin identification, matriarchies, and the evolution of sociality in ground-dwelling sciurids. In *Advances in the study of mammalian behavior* (J. F. Eisenberg and D. G. Kleiman, eds.), pp. 528–572. Special Publication No. 7, American Society of Mammalogists.

Migula, P. (1969). Bioenergetics of pregnancy and lactation in European common vole. *Acta Theriologica* **14**, 167–179.

Millar, J. S. (1977). Adaptive features of mammalian reproduction. *Evolution* **31**, 370–386.

Millar, J. S. (1978). Energetics of reproduction in *Peromyscus leucopus:* The cost of lactation. *Ecology* **59**, 1055–1061.

Millar, J. S. (1981). Pre-partum reproductive characteristics of eutherian mammals. *Evolution* **35**, 1149–1163.

Miller, B. D. (1981). *The endangered sex.* Ithaca, N.Y.: Cornell University Press.

Miller, D. E., and J. T. Emlen, Jr. (1975). Individual chick recognition and family integrity in the ring-billed gull. *Behaviour* **52**, 124–144.

Miller, N. (1909). The American toad (*Bufo lentiginosus americanus* Leconte). II. A study in dynamic biology. *American Naturalist* **43**, 641–730.

Miller, R. J. (1964). Studies on the social behavior of the blue gourami, *Trichogaster trichopterus* (Pisces: Belontiidae). *Copeia,* pp. 469–496.

Miller, R. S. (1973). The brood size of cranes. *Wilson Bulletin* **85**, 436–441.

Milligan, S. R. (1976). Pregnancy blocking in the vole, *Microtus agrestis.* I. Effect of the social environment. *Journal of Reproduction and Fertility* **46**, 91–95.

Milligan, S. R. (1979). Pregnancy blockage and the memory of the stud male in the vole (*Microtus agrestis*). *Journal of Reproduction and Fertility* **57**, 223–225.

Milligan, S. R. (1980). Pheromones and rodent reproductive physiology. *Symposium of the Zoological Society of London* **45**, 251–275.

Mills, M. G. L. (1978). The comparative socio-ecology of the Hyaenidae. *Carnivore* **1**, 1–7.

Minturn, L., and J. Shastak. (1983). Infanticide as a terminal abortion procedure. *Behavior Science Research* **17**, 70–90.

Mitchell, R. (1972). The sex ratio of the spider mite, *Tetranychus urticae*. *Entomologia Experimentalis et Applicata* **15**, 299–304.

Mitchell, R. (1973). Growth and population dynamics of a spider mite (*Tetranychus urticae*; Acarina: Tetranychidae). *Ecology* **54**, 1349–1355.

Mitchell, R. (1975). The evolution of oviposition tactics in the bean weevil, *Callosobrauchus maculatus* (F.). *Ecology* **56**, 696–702.

Moehlman, P. D. (1979). Jackal helpers and pup survival. *Nature* (*London*) **277**, 382–383.

Moehlman, P. D. (1982). Socioecology of silverbacked and golden jackals, *Canis mesomelas* and *C. aureus*. In *Recent Advances in the Study of Mammalian Behavior* (J. F. Eisenberg and D. G. Kleiman, eds.), Special Publication No. 7, American Society of Mammalogists.

Mohnot, S. M. (1971a). Some aspects of social changes and infant-killing in the hanuman langur, *Presbytis entellus* (Primates: Cercopithecidae), in Western India. *Mammalia* **35**, 175–198.

Mohnot, S. M. (1971b). Ecology and behavior of the hanuman langur, *Presbytis entellus* (Primates: Cercopithecidae) invading field, gardens and orchards around Jodhpur western India. *Tropical Ecology* **12**, 237–249.

Mohnot, S. M. (1974). Ecology and behaviour of the common Indian langur, *Presbytis entellus entellus* Dufresne. Unpublished Ph.D. thesis, University of Jodhpur, India.

Mohnot, S. M. (1978). Peripheralization of weaned male juveniles in *Presbytis entellus*. In *Recent advances in primatology*, Vol. 1: *Behaviour* (D. J. Chivers and J. Herbert, eds.), pp. 87–91. London: Academic Press.

Mohnot, S. M., M. Gadgil, and S. C. Makwana. (1981). On the dynamics of the hanuman langur populations of Jodhpur (Rajasthan, India). *Primates* **22**, 182–191.

Montag, B. A., and T. W. Montag. (1979). Infanticide: A historical perspective. *Minnesota Medicine* (May), pp. 368–372.

Moore, J. (1983). Where the boys are. Paper presented at Annual Meeting of the Animal Behavior Society, June 1983.

Mori, A. (1979). Analysis of population change by measurement of body weight in the Koshima troop of Japanese monkeys. *Primates* **20**, 371–398.

Morris, D. (1952). Homosexuality in the ten-spined stickleback (*Pygosteus pungitius* L.). *Behaviour* **4**, 233–261.

Morse, J. L. (1963). *Funk and Wagnalls Encyclopedia*, Vol. 21. New York: Standard Reference Works Publishing Co.

Mugford, R. A., and N. W. Nowell. (1970). Pheromones and their effect on aggression in mice. *Nature* (*London*) **226**, 967–968.

Mumme, R. L., W. D. Koenig, and F. A. Pitelka. (1983). Reproductive competition in the communal acorn woodpecker: sisters destroy each other's eggs. *Nature* (London) **306**, 583–584.

Murdoch, W. W., and A. Sih. (1978). Age-dependent interference in a predatory insect. *Journal of Animal Ecology* **47**, 581–592.

Murdock, G. P. (1976). *Outline of world cultures*, 5th Ed. New Haven: Human Relations Area Files.

Murphy, M. R. (1971). Natural history of the Syrian golden hamster: A reconnaissance expedition. *American Zoologist* **11**, 632.

Murphy, M. R. (1976). A review of the behavior of the Syrian golden hamster. In *Inbred and genetically defined strains of laboratory animals*, part 2, (P. L. Altman and D. D. Katz, eds.), pp. 455–465. Bethesda, Md.: Federal Society for Experimental Biology.

Murphy, M. R. (1977). Intraspecific sexual preferences of female hamsters. *Journal of Comparative and Physiological Psychology* **91**, 1337–1346.

Murray, K. G., K. Winnett-Murray, Z. A. Eppley, G. L. Hunt, Jr., and D. B. Schwartz. (1983). Breeding biology of the xantus' murrelet. *Condor* **85**, 12–21.

Myers, K., and W. E. Poole. (1961). A study of the biology of the wild rabbit, *Oryctolagus cuniculus* (L.), in confined populations. II. The effects of season and population increase on behaviour. *Commonwealth Scientific and Industrial Research Organization Wildlife Research*, **6**, 1–41.

Mykytowycz, R. (1960). Social behaviour in an experimental colony of wild rabbits, *Oryctolagus cuniculus* (L.). III. Second breeding season. *Commonwealth Scientific and Industrial Research Organization Wildlife Research* **5**, 1–20.

Mykytowycz, R., and E. R. Hesterman. (1975). An experimental study of aggression in captive European rabbits, *Oryctolagus cuniculus* (L). *Behaviour* **52**, 104–123.

Myllymäki, A. (1977). Demographic mechanisms in the fluctuating populations of the field vole *Microtus agrestis*. *Oikos* **29**, 468–493.

Nalbandov, A. V. (1964). *Reproductive physiology*, 2nd Ed. San Francisco: Freeman.

Napier, J. R., and P. H. Napier. (1967). *A handbook of living primates*. New York: Academic Press.

Nathanielsz, P. W. (1978). Parturition in rodents. *Seminars in Perinatology* **2**, 223–234.

Neander, G. (1928). L'establissement de Halsan dans le Norrbotten: Centraltryckeriet, Stockholm. Pamphlets in the collection of the Hjartoch Lungsjukdomar Society, Stockholm, Sweden.

Needham, P. R. (1961). Observations on the natural spawning of eastern brook trout. *California Fish and Game* **47**, 27–40.

Neel, J. V. (1970). Lessons from a "primitive" people. *Science* **170**, 815–822.

Nelson, B. (1957). Propagation of channel catfish in Arkansas. *Annual Conference Southeastern Association Game and Fish Commissioners Proceedings* **10**, 165–168.

Nelson, J. B. (1966). The behaviour of the young gannet. *British Birds* **59**, 393–419.

Nelson, J. B. (1978). *The Sulidae*. Oxford: Oxford University Press.

Nelson, J. S. (1976). *Fishes of the world*. New York: Wiley.

Newcombe, H. (1965). Environmental versus genetic interpretations of birth order effects. *Eugenics Quarterly* **12**, 90–101.

Newton, I. (1977). Breeding strategies in birds of prey. *Living Bird* **16**, 51–82.

Nikolsky, G. V. (1963). *The ecology of fishes* (trans. L. Birkett). New York: Academic Press.

Ninth Annual Report of the Registrar-General of England and Wales, 1845.

Nisbet, I. C. T. (1973). Courtship-feeding, egg size and breeding success in common terns. *Nature (London)* **241**, 141–142.

Nisbet, I. C. T. (1978). Dependence of fledging success on egg-size, parental performance, and egg composition among common and roseate terns, *Sterna hirundo* and *S. dougallii. Ibis* **120**, 207–215.

Nisbet, I. C. T., and M. Cohen. (1975). Asynchronous hatching in common and roseate terns, *Sterna hirundo* and *S. dougallii. Ibis* **117**, 374–379.

Nisbet, I. C. T., K. J. Wilson, and W. A. Broad. (1978). Common terns raise young after death of their mates. *Condor* **80**, 106–109.

Nishida, T. (1979). The social structure of chimpanzees of the Mahale Mountains. In *The great apes* (D. A. Hamburg and E. R. McCown, eds.), pp. 72–191. Menlo Park, Calif.: Benjamin/Cummings.

Nishida, T., S. Uehara, and R. Nyundo. (1979). Predatory behavior among wild chimpanzees of the Mahale Mountains. *Primates* **20**, 1–20.

Noakes, D. L. G., and G. W. Barlow. (1973). Ontogeny of parent-contacting behavior in young *Cichlasoma citrinellum* (Pisces: Cichlidae). *Behaviour* **45**, 221–225.

Noble, G. K. (1927). The value of life history data in the study of the evolution of amphibia. *Annals of the New York Academy of Science* **30**, 31–128.

Noble, G. K. (1929). The adaptive modifications of the arboreal tadpoles of *Hoplophryne* and the torrent tadpoles *Staurois. Bulletin of the American Museum of Natural History* **58**, 291–334.

Noble, G. K. (1931). *The biology of amphibia.* New York: McGraw-Hill.

Norris, M. L., and C. E. Adams. (1971). Delayed implantation in the Mongolian gerbil (*Meriones unguiculatus*). *Journal of Reproduction and Fertility* **27**, 486–487.

Norris, M. L., and C. E. Adams. (1979). Exteroceptive factors and pregnancy block in the Mongolian gerbil, *Meriones unguiculatus. Journal of Reproduction and Fertility* **57**, 401–404.

Nuechterlein, G. L. (1981). Asynchronous hatching and sibling competition in western grebe broods. *Canadian Journal of Zoology* **59**, 994–998.

Nuechterlein, G. L., and A. Johnson. (1981). The downy young of the hooded grebe. *Living Bird* **19**, 69–71.

Nygren, J. (1980). Allozyme variation in natural populations of field vole (*Microtus agrestis* L.). III. Survey of a cyclically density-varying population. *Hereditas* **93**, 125–136.

Oakshott, J. (1974). Social dominance, aggressiveness and mating success among male house mice (*Mus musculus*). *Oecologia (Berlin)* **15**, 143–158.

Oates, J. F. (1977). The social life of a black-and-white colobus monkey, *Colobus guereza. Zeitschrift für Tierpsychologie* **45**, 1–60.

O'Connor, R. J. (1978). Brood reduction in birds: Selection for fratricide, infanticide, and suicide? *Animal Behaviour* **26**, 79–96.

O'Gara, B. W. (1969). Unique aspects of reproduction in the female pronghorn (*Antilocapra americana* Ord). *American Journal of Anatomy* **125**, 217–231.

O'Hara, R. K., and A. R. Blaustein. (1981). An investigation of sibling recognition in *Rana cascade* tadpoles. *Animal Behaviour* **29**, 1121–1126.

Omran, A. R. (1971). *The health theme in family planning.* Chapel Hill: Carolina Population Center Monograph no. 16.

Oppenheimer, J. R. (1970). Mouthbreeding in fishes. *Animal Behaviour* **18**, 493–503.

Oppenheimer, J. R. (1977). *Presbytis entellus,* the hanuman langur. In *Primate conservation* (HSH Prince Rainier III of Monaco and G. H. Bourne, eds.), pp. 469–512. New York: Academic Press.

Orians, G. H. (1969). Age and hunting success in the brown pelican (*Pelecanus occidentalis*). *Animal Behaviour* **17**, 316–319.

Orians, G. H., and D. H. Janzen. (1974). Why are embryos so tasty? *American Naturalist* **108**, 581–592.

Orton, G. L. (1957). The bearing of larval evolution on some problems in frog classification. *Systematic Zoology* **6**, 79–81.

Ostermeyer, M. C. (1983). Maternal aggression. In *Parental behaviour of rodents* (R. W. Elwood, ed.), pp. 151–179. Chichester: Wiley.

Ostermeyer, M. C. and R. W. Elwood. (In press). Helpers (?) at the nest in the Mongolian gerbil. *Behaviour.*

Osterud, N., and J. Fulton. (1979). Family limitation and age at marriage: Fertility decline in Sturbridge, Massachusetts. In *American Historical Demography* (M. Vinovskis, ed.), pp. 399–412. New York: Academic Press.

Owen, D. F. (1955). The food of the heron *Ardea cinerea* in the breeding season. *Ibis* **97**, 276–295.

Owen, D. F. (1960). The nesting success of the heron *Ardea cinerea* in relation to the availability of food. *Proceedings of the Zoological Society of London* **133**, 597–617.

Owens, D. D., and M. J. Owens. (1979). Communal denning and clan associations in brown hyenas (*Hyaena brunnea*, Thurberg) of the central Kalahari desert. *African Journal of Ecology* **17**, 35–44.

Oxhorn, H. (1955). Hazards of grand multiparity. *Obstetrics and Gynecology* **5**, 150–156.

Packer, C. (1979a). Inter-troop transfer and inbreeding avoidance in *Papio anubis*. *Animal Behaviour* **27**, 1–36.

Packer, C. (1979b). Male dominance and reproductive activity in *Papio anubis*. *Animal Behaviour* **27**, 37–45.

Packer, C. (1980). Male care and exploitation of infants in *Papio anubis*. *Animal Behaviour* **28**, 512–520.

Packer, C., and A. E. Pusey. (1982). Cooperation and competition within coalitions of male lions: Kin selection or game theory? *Nature (London)* **296**, 740–742.

Packer, C., and A. E. Pusey. (1983a). Male takeovers and female reproductive parameters: A simulation of oestrous synchrony in lions (*Panthera leo*). *Animal Behaviour* **31**, 334–340.

Packer, C., and A. E. Pusey. (1983b). Adaptations of female lions to infanticide by incoming males. *American Naturalist* **121**, 716–728.

Padden, R. C. (1967). *The hummingbird and the hawk: Conquest and sovereignty in the Valley of Mexico*, pp. 1503–1541. New York: Harper and Row.

Padykula, H. A., and J. M. Taylor. (1976). Ultrastructural evidence for loss of the trophoblastic layer in the chorioallantoic placenta of Australian bandicoots (Marsupialia: Peramelidae). *Anatomical Record* **186**, 357–386.

Parâtre, R. (1894). Notes sur *Salamandra maculosa*, sa présence aux environs immédiats de Paris: Remarques sur sa réproduction, époque de sa partruition, développement de la larvae. *Memoires de la Société Zoologique de France* **10**, 132–160.

Parker, G. A., and M. R. Macnair. (1979). Models of parent–offspring conflict. IV. Suppression: Evolutionary retaliation by the parent. *Animal Behaviour* **27**, 1210–1235.

Parker, P. J. (1977). An ecological comparison of marsupial and placental patterns of reproduction. In *The biology of marsupials* (B. Stonehouse and D. Gilmore, eds.), pp. 273–286. Baltimore: University Park Press.

Parkes, A. S., and H. M. Bruce. (1961). Olfactory stimuli in mammalian reproduction. *Science* **134**, 1049–1054.

Parkes, A. S., and H. M. Bruce. (1962). Pregnancy block in female mice placed in boxes soiled by males. *Journal of Reproduction and Fertility* **4**, 303–308.

Parks, M. (1983). Peking moving to curb killing of baby girls. *Los Angeles Times*, April 17.

Parmelee, D. F., H. A. Stephens, and R. H. Schmidt. (1967). The birds of southeastern Victoria Island and adjacent small islands. *National Museum of Canada Bulletin*, No. 222.

Parsons, J. (1970). Relationship between egg size and post-hatching chick mortality in the herring gull (*Larus argentatus*). *Nature (London)* **228**, 1221–1222.

Parsons, J. (1971). Cannibalism in herring gulls. *British Birds* **64**, 528–537.

Parsons, J. (1975). Asynchronous hatching and chick mortality in the herring gull, *Larus argentatus*. *Ibis* **117**, 517–520.

Parsons, J. (1976). Factors determining the number and size of eggs laid by the herring gull. *Condor* **78**, 481–492.

Parthasarathy, M. D., and H. Rahaman. (1974). Infant-killing and dominance assertion among the hanuman langur. *Abstracts of the Fifth Congress of the International Primatological Society, August 21–24, 1974*, Nagoya, Japan, p. 35.

Patriquin, D. G. (1967). Biology of *Gadus morhua* in Ogac Lake, a landlocked fiord on Baffin Island. *Journal of the Fisheries Research Board of Canada* **24**, 2573–2594.

Patterson, T. L., L. Petrinovich, and D. K. James. (1980). Reproductive value and appropriateness of response to predators by white-crowned sparrows. *Behavioral Ecology and Sociobiology* **7**, 227–231.

Paul, L., and J. Kupferschmidt. (1975). Killing of conspecific and mouse young by male rats. *Journal of Comparative and Physiological Psychology* **88**, 755–763.

Payman, B. C., and H. H. Swanson. (1980). Social influence on sexual maturation and breeding in the female Mongolian gerbil (*Meriones unguiculatus*). *Animal Behaviour* **28**, 528–535.

Payne, A. P., and H. H. Swanson. (1970). Agnostic behaviour between pairs of hamsters of the same and opposite sex in a neutral observation area. *Behaviour* **36**, 259–269.

Pearre, S. (1982). Feeding by Chaetognatha: Aspects of inter- and intraspecific predation. *Marine Ecology in Progress* **7**, 33–45.

Pedersen, R. D. (1979). The seasonal cycle of body composition in the mottled sculpin, *Cottus bairdi*. Unpublished M.S. thesis, Ohio State University, Columbus, Ohio.

Pereira, M. E. (1983). Abortion following the immigration of an adult male baboon (*Papio cynocephalus*). *American Journal of Primatology* **4**, 93–98.

Pérez Diez, A. A., and Salzano, F. M. (1978). Evolutionary implications of the ethnography and demography of Ayoreo Indians. *Journal Human Evolution* **7**, 253–268.

Perrins, C. M. (1965). Population fluctuations and clutch size in the Great Tit, *Parus major*. *Journal of Animal Ecology* **34**, 601–647.

Perrone, M., Jr., and T. M. Zaret. (1979). Parental care patterns of fishes. *American Naturalist* **113**, 351–361.

Perry, J. S., and J. G. Rowell. (1969). Variations in fetal weight and vascular supply along uterine horns of the pig. *Journal of Reproduction and Fertility* **19**, 527–534.

Perry, R. (1966). *The world of the polar bear*. London: Cox and Wyman.

Pettingill, O. S. (1939). History of one hundred nests of Arctic tern. *Auk* **56**, 420–428.

Pfaff, D. W., and C. Pfaffman. (1969). Olfactory and hormonal influences on the basal forebrain of the male rat. *Brain Research* **15**, 137–156.

Picman, J. (1977). Intraspecific nest destruction in the long-billed marsh wren (*Telmatodytes palustris palustris*). *Canadian Journal of Zoology* **55**, 1997–2003.

Pierce, B. A., J. Mitton, and F. Rose. (1981). Allozyme variation among large, small, and cannibal morphs of the tiger salamander inhabiting the Llano Estacado of west Texas. *Copeia*, pp. 590–595.

Pierotti, R. (1980). Spite and altruism in gulls. *American Naturalist* **115**, 290–300.

Pierotti, R. (1981). Why do gull chicks run? Abstracts of the 99th American Ornithologists' Union Conference, Edmonton, Alberta.

Piersol, W. H. (1910). The habits and larval state of *Plethodon cinereus erythanthus*. *Transactions of the Royal Canadian Institute* **8**, 469–493.

Pilz, W. R., and L. K. Siebert. (1978). Fratricide and cannibalism in Swainson's hawk. *Auk* **95**, 584–585.

Poffenberger, T. (1981). Childrearing and social structure in rural India: Toward a cross-cultural definition of child abuse and neglect. In *Child abuse and neglect: Cross-cultural perspectives* (J. E. Korbin, ed.), pp. 71–95. Berkeley: University of California Press.

Polgar, S., J. F. Marshall, and S. Marshall. (1976). The search for culturally acceptable fertility regulating mechanisms. In *Culture, natality and family planning* (J. F. Marshall and S. Polgar, eds.), pp. 204–220. North Carolina: Carolina Population Center.

Poliakov, L. (1979). *Harvest of hate: The Nazi program for the destruction of the Jews of Europe*, Rev. Ed. New York: The Holocaust Library.

Polis, G. A. (1980). The effect of cannibalism on the demography and activity of a natural population of desert scorpions. *Behavioral Ecology and Sociobiology* **7**, 25–35.

Polis, G. A. (1981). The evolution and dynamics of intraspecific predation. *Annual Review of Ecology and Systematics* **12**, 225–251.

Pollard, S. D. In press. Egg guarding by *Clubiona cambridgei* (Araneae, Clubionidae) against conspecific predators. *Journal of Arachnology*.

Pomeroy, L. V. (1981). Developmental polymorphism in the tadpoles of the spadefoot toad, *Scaphiopus multiplicatus*. Unpublished Ph.D. thesis, University of California, Riverside, Calif.

Pommerenke, W. T., H. F. Haney, and W. J. Meek. (1930). The energy metabolism of pregnant rabbits. *American Journal of Physiology* **93**, 249–257.

Poole, A. (1979). Sibling aggression among nestling ospreys in Florida Bay. *Auk* **96**, 415–416.

Poole, A. (1982). Brood reduction in temperate and sub-tropical ospreys. *Oecologia (Berlin)* **53**, 111–119.

Poole, T. B., and H. D. R. Morgan. (1973). Differences in aggressive behaviour between male mice (*Mus musculus* L.) in colonies of different sizes. *Animal Behaviour* **21**, 788–795.

Popova, O. A., and L. A. Sytina. (1977). Food and feeding relations of Eurasian perch (*Perca fluviatilis*) and pikeperch (*Stizostedion lucioperca*) in various waters of the USSR. *Journal of the Fisheries Research Board of Canada* **34**, 1559–1570.

Porter, R. D., and S. W. Wiemeyer. (1970). Propagation of captive American kestrels. *Journal of Wildlife Management* **34**, 594–604.

Potter, D. A. (1978). Functional sex ratio in the carmine spider mite. *Annals of the Entomological Society of America* **71**, 218–222.

Potter, D. A. (1979). Reproductive behavior and sexual selection in tetranychine mites. *Recent Advances in Acarology* **1**, 137–145.

Potter, D. A., D. L. Wrensch, and D. E. Johnston. (1976a). Guarding, aggressive behavior and mating success in male two-spotted spider mites. *Annals of the Entomological Society of America* **69**, 707–711.

Potter, D. A., D. L. Wrensch, and D. E. Johnston. (1976b). Aggression and mating success in male spider mites. *Science* **193**, 160–161.

Poulson, T. L. (1963). Cave adaptations in amblyopsid fishes. *American Midland Naturalist* **70**, 257–290.

Pourbagher, N. (1969). Étude experimentale de l'effete de groupe chez le tetards de batraciens. *Revue du Comportement Animal* **3**, 75–119.

Powers, J. H. (1907). Morphological variation and its causes in *Ambystoma tigrinum* (Green). *Studies University of Michigan* **7**, 197–274.

Prakash, I. (1962). Ecology of the gerbils of the Rajasthan desert. *Mammalia* **26**, 311–331.

Preston, S. H. (1941). *Mortality patterns in national populations*. New York: Academic Press.

Preston, S. H. (1970). *Older male mortality and cigarette smoking: A demographic analysis*. Westport, Conn.: Greenwood Press.

Preston, S. H. (1976). *Mortality patterns in national populations*. New York: Academic Press.

Procter, D. L. C. (1975). The problem of chick loss in the south polar skua *Catharacta maccormicki*. *Ibis* **117**, 452–459.

Puffer, R. R., and C. V. Serrano. (1973). Patterns of mortality in childhood. *PAHO Scientific Publication* No. 262.

Pugesek, B. H. (1981). Increased reproductive effort with age in the California gull (*Larus californicus*). *Science* **212**, 822–823.

Puget, A., and C. Gouarderes. (1974). Weight gain of the Afghan pika (*Ochotona rufescens rufescens*) from birth to 19 weeks of age, and during gestation. *Growth* **38**, 117–129.

Pusey, A. E. (1980). Inbreeding avoidance in chimpanzees. *Animal Behaviour* **28**, 543–552.

Qasim, S. Z. (1956). The spawning habits and embryonic development of the shanny (*Blennius pholis* L.). *Proceedings of the Zoological Society of London* **127**, 79–93.

Qasim, S. Z. (1957). The biology of *Blennius pholis* L. (Teleostein). *Proceedings of the Zoological Society of London* **128**, 161–208.

Quanstrom, W. R. (1968). Some aspects of the ethoecology of Richardson's ground squirrel in eastern North Dakota. Unpublished Ph.D. thesis, University of Oklahoma, Norman, Okla.

Rabb, G. B., J. H. Woolpy, and B. E. Ginsburg. (1967). Social relationships in a group of captive wolves. *American Zoologist* **7**, 305–311.

Radbill, S. X. (1974). A history of child abuse and infanticide. In *The battered child* (R. E. Helfer and C. H. Kempe, eds.). Chicago: University of Chicago Press.

Radovic, P. (1966). Frequent and high parity as a medical and social problem. *American Journal of Obstetrics and Gynecology* **94**, 583–585.

Radovich, J. (1962). Effects of sardine spawning stock size and environment on year–class production. *California Fish and Game* **48**, 123–140.

Ramaswami, L. S. (1975). Some aspects of the reproductive biology of the langur monkey *Presbytis entellus entellus* Dufresne. *Proceedings of the Indian National Science Academy* **B41**, 1–30.

Randolph, P. A., J. C. Randolph, K. Mattingly, and M. M. Foster. (1977). Energy costs of reproduction in the cotton rat, *Sigmodon hispidus*. *Ecology* **58**, 31–45.

Ransom, T. W. (1981). *Beach troop of the Gombe.* Lewisburg, Penn.: Bucknell University Press.

Ransom, T. W., and B. S. Ransom. (1971). Adult male–infant relations among baboons (*Papio anubis*). *Folia Primatologica* **16**, 179–195.

Rasa, O. A. E. (1979). The effects of crowding on the social relationships and behaviour of the dwarf mongoose (*Helogale undulata rufula*). *Zeitschrift für Tierpsychologie* **49**, 317–329.

Rausher, M. (1979). Egg recognition: Its advantage to a butterfly. *Animal Behaviour* **27**, 1034–1040.

Rawson, D. S., and C. A. Elsey. (1950). Reduction in the longnose sucker population of Pyramid Lake, Alberta, in an attempt to improve angling. *Transactions of the American Fisheries Society* **78**, 13–31.

Recher, H. F., and J. A. Recher. (1969). Comparative foraging efficiency of adult and immature little blue herons. *Animal Behaviour* **17**, 320–322.

Redfield, J. A., M. J. Taitt, and C. J. Krebs. (1978). Experimental alteration of sex ratios in populations of *Microtus townsendii*, a field vole. *Canadian Journal of Zoology* **56**, 17–27.

Reimer, J. D., and M. L. Petras. (1967). Breeding structure of the house mouse, *Mus musculus*, in a population cage. *Journal of Mammalogy* **48**, 88–99.

Reimer, J. D., and M. L. Petras. (1968). Some aspects of commensal populations of *Mus musculus* in southwestern Ontario. *Canadian Field Naturalist* **82**, 32–42.

Reimer, S. *et al.* (1941). *Population movements and industrialization, Swedish countries, 1895–1930,* 2 vols. London: P. S. King and Sons.

Reite, M., and N. Caine (eds.). (1983). *Child abuse: The nonhuman primate data.* New York: Alan R. Liss.

Renfree, M. B., and J. H. Calaby. (1981). Background to delayed implantation and embryonic diapause. *Journal of Reproduction and Fertility Suppl.* **29**, 1–9.

Rhine, R. J., G. W. Norton, W. J. Roertgen, and H. D. Klein. (1980). The brief survival of free-ranging baboon infants (*Papio cynocephalus*) after separation from their mothers. *International Journal of Primatology* **1**, 401–409.

Rhodes, W., and J. V. Merriner. (1973). A preliminary report on closed system rearing of striped bass sac fry to fingerling size. *Progressive Fish-Culturist* **35**, 199–201.

Richards, C. M. (1968). The inhibition of growth in crowded *Rana pipiens*. *Physiological Zoology* **31**, 138–151.

Richards, C. M. (1962). The control of tadpole growth by alga-like cells. *Physiological Zoology* **35**, 285–296.

Richards, M. P. M. (1966a). Maternal behaviour in virgin female golden hamsters

(*Mesocricetus auratus* Waterhouse): The role of the age of the test pup. *Animal Behaviour* **14**, 303–309.

Richards, M. P. M. (1966b). Maternal behaviour in the golden hamster: Responsiveness to young in virgin, pregnant, and lactating females. *Animal Behaviour* **14**, 310–313.

Richdale, L. E. (1957). *A population study of penguins.* London: Oxford University Press.

Riches, D. (1974). The Netsilik Eskimo: A special case of selective female infanticide. *Ethnology* **13**, 351–362.

Richmond, M. E., and R. A. Stehn. (1976). Olfaction and reproductive behavior in microtine rodents. In *Mammalian olfaction, reproductive processes and behavior* (R. L. Doty, ed.), pp. 198–214. New York: Academic Press.

Ricker, W. E. (1954). Stock and recruitment. *Journal of the Fisheries Research Board of Canada* **11**, 559–623.

Ricklefs, R. E. (1965). Brood reduction in the curve-billed thrasher. *Condor* **67**, 505–510.

Ricklefs, R. E. (1967). An analysis of nesting mortality in birds. *Smithsonian Contributions to Zoology* **9**, 1–48.

Ridley, M. (1978). Paternal care. *Animal Behaviour* **26**, 904–932.

Rijksen, H. D. (1981). Infant killing: A possible consequence of a disputed leader role. *Behaviour* **78**, 138–168.

Ripley, S. (1970). Leaves and leaf-monkeys: The social organization of foraging in gray langurs, *Presbytis entellus thersites.* In *Old World monkeys* (J. R. Napier and P. H. Napier, eds.), pp. 481–509. New York: Academic Press.

Ripley, S. (1980). Infanticide in langurs and man: Adaptive advantage or social pathology? In *Biosocial mechanisms of population regulation* (M. N. Cohen, R. S. Malpass, and H. G. Klein, eds.), pp. 349–390. New Haven: Yale University Press.

Ritchie, J., and J. Ritchie. (1981). Child rearing and child abuse: The Polynesian context. In *Child abuse and neglect: Cross-cultural perspectives* (J. E. Korbin, ed.), pp. 186–204. Berkeley: University of California Press.

Roberts, C., and C. Lowe. (1975). Where have all the conceptions gone? *Lancet* **1**, 498–499.

Roberts, D. F., and R. E. S. Tanner. (1963). Effects of parity on birth weight and other variables in a Tanganyika Bantu sample. *British Journal of Preventive and Social Medicine* **17**, 309–315.

Robinette, W. L., J. S. Gashwiler, and O. W. Morris. (1961). Notes on cougar productivity and life history. *Journal of Mammalogy* **42**, 204–217.

Robinson, H. P., and J. S. Caines. (1977). Sonar evidence of early pregnancy failure in patients with twin conceptions. *British Journal of Obstetrics and Gynaecology* **84**, 22–25.

Rodenburg, M. (1971). Child murder by depressed parents. *Canadian Psychiatric Association Journal* **16**, 41–48.

Rogers, J. G., and G. K. Beauchamp. (1976). Some ecological implications of primer chemical stimuli in rodents. In *Mammalian olfaction, reproductive processes, and behavior* (R. L. Doty, ed.), pp. 181–195. New York: Academic Press.

Rohrbach, C. (1982). Investigation of the Bruce effect in the Mongolian gerbil (*Meriones unguiculatus*). *Journal of Reproduction and Fertility* **65**, 411–417.

Rohwer, S. (1978). Parent cannibalism of offspring and egg raiding as a courtship strategy. *American Naturalist* **112**, 429–440.

Romanoff, A. L., and J. A. Romanoff. (1949). *The avian egg.* New York: Wiley and Chapman.

Rood, J. P. (1980). Mating relationships and breeding suppression in the dwarf mongoose. *Animal Behaviour* **28**, 143–150.

Roonwal, M. L., and S. M. Mohnot. (1977). *Primates of South Asia: Ecology, sociobiology and behavior.* Cambridge, Mass.: Harvard University Press.

Root, R. B., and S. Chaplin. (1976). The life-styles of tropical milkweed bugs, *Oncopeltus* (Hemiptera: Lygaeidae) utilizing the same hosts. *Ecology* **57**, 132–140.

Rosahn, P. D., and H. S. N. Greene. (1936). The influence of intrauterine factors on the fetal weight of rabbits. *Journal of Experimental Medicine* **63**, 901–921.

Roscoe, J. (1911). *The Baganda: An account of their native customs and beliefs.* London: Macmillan.

Rose, F. L., and D. Armentrout. (1976). Adaptive strategies of *Ambystoma tigrinum* inhabiting the Llano Estacado of west Texas. *Journal of Animal Ecology* **45**, 713–730.

Rose, S. M. (1959). Population control in guppies. *American Midland Naturalist* **62**, 474–481.

Rose, S. M. (1960). A feedback mechanism of growth control in tadpoles. *Ecology* **41**, 188–199.

Rose, S. M., and F. C. Rose. (1961). Growth controlling exudates of tadpoles. *Symposium of the Society for Experimental Biology* **15**, 407–411.

Rosenberg, K. M., and G. F. Sherman. (1975). The role of testosterone in the organization, maintenance and activation of pup killing in the male rat. *Hormones and Behavior* **6**, 173–179.

Rosenblatt, J. S., and H. I. Siegel. (1983). Physiological and behavioural changes during pregnancy and parturition underlying the onset of maternal behaviour in rodents. In *Parental behaviour of rodents* (R. W. Elwood, ed.), pp. 23–66. Chichester: Wiley.

Rosenblatt, J., H. Siegel, and A. Mayer. (1979). Progress in the study of maternal behavior in the rat: Hormonal, nonhormonal, sensory, and developmental aspects. In *Advances in the Study of Behavior* (J. Rosenblatt, R. Hinde, C. Beer, and M. Busnel, eds.), Vol. 10, pp. 225–311. New York: Academic Press.

Rosenson, L. M., and A. K. Asheroff. (1975). Maternal aggression in CD-1 mice: Influence of the hormonal condition of the intruder. *Behavioral Biology* **15**, 219–224.

Rothstein, S. I. (1979). Gene frequencies and selection for inhibitory traits, with special emphasis on the adaptiveness of territoriality. *American Naturalist* **113**, 317–331.

Rowe, E. G. (1947). The breeding biology of *Aquila verreauxi* Lesson. *Ibis* **89**, 576–606.

Rowell, T. E. (1961a). Maternal behaviour in non-lactating golden hamsters. *Animal Behaviour* **9**, 11–15.

Rowell, T. E. (1961b). The family group in hamsters: Its formation and break-up. *Behaviour* **17**, 81–94.

Rowell, T. E. (1970a). Baboon menstrual cycles affected by social environment. *Journal of Reproduction and Fertility* **21**, 133–141.

Rowell, T. E. (1970b). Reproductive cycles of two *Cercopithecus* monkeys. *Journal of Reproduction and Fertility* **22**, 321–338.

Rowley, M. H., and J. J. Christian. (1976). Intraspecific aggression of *Peromyscus leucopus. Behavioral Biology* **17**, 249–253.

Royce, W. F. (1951). Breeding habits of lake trout in New York. *Fishery Bulletin* **52**, 59–76.

Rudnai, J. (1973). Reproductive biology of lions (*Panthera leo massaica* Neumann) in Nairobi National Park. *East African Wildlife Journal* **11**, 241–253.

Rudran, R. (1973). Adult male replacement in one-male troops of purple-faced langurs (*Presbytis senex senex*) and its effect on population structure. *Folia Primatologica* **19**, 166–192.

Rudran, R. (1978). Socioecology of the blue monkeys (*Cercopithecus mitis stuhlmanni*) of the Kibale Forest, Uganda. *Smithsonian Contributions to Zoology* No. 249, iv + 88 pp.

Rudran, R. (1979). The demography and social mobility of a red howler (*Alouatta seniculus*) population in Venezuela. In *Vertebrate ecology in the northern Neotropics* (J. F. Eisenberg, ed.), pp. 107–126. Washington, D.C.: Smithsonian Institution Press.

Rugh, R. (1968). *The mouse, its reproduction and development.* Minneapolis: Burgess.

Russell, E. M. (1982). Parental investment and desertion of young in marsupials. *American Naturalist* **119**, 744–748.

Russell, J. K. (1981). Exclusion of adult male coatis from social groups: Protection from predation. *Journal of Mammalogy* **62**, 206–208.

Rutman, D., and A. H. Rutman. Of agues and fevers: Malaria in the early Chesapeake. *William and Mary Quarterly* 3rd ser. **33**, 31–60.

Ryden, O., and H. Bengsston. (1980). Differential begging and locomotory behaviour by early and late hatched nestlings affecting the distribution of food in asynchronously hatched broods of altricial birds. *Zeitschrift für Tierpsychologie* **53**, 209–224.

Ryder, J. P. (1983). Sex ratio and egg sequence in ring-billed gulls. *Auk* **100**, 726–728.

Saayman, G. S. (1971). Behaviour of the adult males in a troop of free-ranging chacma baboons (*Papio ursinus*). *Folia Primatologica* **15**, 36–57.

Sacher, G. A., and E. Staffeldt. (1974). Relation of gestation time to brain weight for placental mammals: Implications for the theory of vertebrate growth. *American Midland Naturalist* **108**, 593–615.

Sadleir, R. M. F. S. (1965). The relationship between agonistic behavior and population changes in the deermouse, *Peromyscus maniculatus* (Wagner). *Journal of Animal Ecology* **34**, 331–352.

Sadleir, R. M. F. S. (1969). *The ecology of reproduction in wild and domestic mammals.* London: Methuen.

Safriel, U. N. (1981). Social hierarchy among siblings in broods of the oystercatcher *Haematopus ostralegus. Behavioral Ecology and Sociobiology* **9**, 59–63.

Salt, G. (1961). Competition among insect parasitoids. *Symposium of the Society for Experimental Biology* **15**, 96–119.

Salthe, S. N. (1969). Reproductive modes and the numbers and sizes of ova in urodeles. *American Midland Naturalist* **81**, 467–490.

Salthe, S. N., and W. E. Duellman. (1973). Quantitative restraints associated with reproductive mode in anurans. In *Evolutionary biology of the anurans* (J. Vial, ed.), pp. 229–250. Columbia: University of Missouri Press.

Salthe, S. N., and J. S. Mecham. (1974). Reproduction and courtship patterns. In *Physiology of the Amphibia* (B. Lofts, ed.), pp. 309–521. New York: Academic Press.

Samuels, O., G. Jason, M. Mann, and B. Svare. (1981). Pup-killing behavior in mice: Suppression by early androgen exposure. *Physiology and Behavior* **26**, 473–477.

Sankhala, K. S. (1967). Breeding behaviour of the tiger, *Panthera tigris*, in Rajasthan. *International Zoo Yearbook* **7**, 133–147.

Sauer, R. (1978). Infanticide and abortion in nineteenth century Britain. *Population Studies* **32**, 81–93.

Savage, R. M. (1952). Ecological, physiological, and anatomical observations of some species of anuran tadpoles. *Proceedings of the Zoological Society of London* **122**, 467–514.

Savage, R. M. (1963). A speculation of the pallid tadpoles of *Xenopus laevis*. *British Journal of Herpetology* **3**, 74–76.

Savidge, I. R. (1974). Social factors in dispersal of deer mice (*Peromyscus maniculatus*) from their natal site. *American Midland Naturalist* **91**, 395–405.

Saylor, A., and M. Salmon. (1971). An ethological analysis of communal nursing by the house mouse (*Mus musculus*). *Behaviour* **40**, 62–85.

Schadler, M. H. (1981). Post implantation abortion in pine voles (*Microtus pinetorum*) induced by strange males and pheromones of strange males. *Biology of Reproduction* **25**, 295–297.

Schaller, G. B. (1963). *The mountain gorilla: Ecology and behavior.* Chicago: University of Chicago Press.

Schaller, G. B. (1967). *The deer and the tiger.* Chicago: Chicago University Press.

Schaller, G. B. (1972). *The Serengeti lion.* Chicago: University of Chicago Press.

Scharf, W. C., and E. Balfour. (1971). Growth and development of nestling hen harriers. *Ibis* **113**, 323–329.

Schrire, C., and W. L. Steiger. (1974). A matter of life and death: An investigation into the practice of female infanticide in the Arctic. *Man* **9**, 161–184.

Schrire, C., and W. L. Steiger. (1981). Arctic infanticide revisited. *Etudes/Inuit/Studies* **5**, 111–117.

Schubert, G. (1982). Infanticide by usurper hanuman langur males: A sociobiological myth. *Social Science Information* **21**, 199–244.

Schüz, E. (1957). Das verschlingen eigener junger ("Kronismus") bei vögeln und seine bedeutung. *Vögelwarte* **19**, 1–15.

Schwagmeyer, P. L. (1979). The Bruce effect: An evaluation of male/female advantages. *American Naturalist* **114**, 932–938.

Scott, N. J., and A. Starrett. (1974). An unusual breeding aggregation of frogs with notes on the ecology of *Agalychnis spurelli* (Anura: Hylidae). *Bulletin of the Southern California Academy of Sciences* **73**, 86–94.

Scott, P. D. (1973). Fatal battered baby cases. *Medicine, Science, and the Law* **13**, 197–206.

Scott, W. B., and E. J. Crossman. (1973). Freshwater fishes of Canada. *Bulletin of the Fisheries Research Board of Canada* No. 184.

Scrimshaw, S. C. M. (1978). Infant mortality and behavior in the regulation of family size. *Population and Development Review* **4**, 383–403.

Scrimshaw, S. C. M. (1983). Infanticide as deliberate fertility regulation. In *Determinants of fertility in developing countries: A summary of knowledge* (R. Lee and R. Bulatao, eds.), pp. 714–731. New York: Academic Press.

Seale, D. B. (1982). Physical factors influencing oviposition by the woodfrog *Rana sylvatica* in Pennsylvania. *Copeia*, pp. 627–635.

Sebag, L. (1964). Compte rendu de mission chez Ayoré. *L'Homme* **IV**(2), 126–130.

Sebag, L. (1965). Compte rendu de mission chez les indiens Ayoré du Paraguay et de Bolvie. L'Homme, pp. 126–127.

Sekulic, R. (1982a). Behavior and ranging patterns of a solitary female red howler (Alouatta seniculus). Folia Primatologica 38, 217–232.

Sekulic, R. (1982b). Daily and seasonal patterns of roaring and spacing in four red howler (Alouatta seniculus) troops. Folia Primatologica 39, 22–48.

Sekulic, R. (1982c). The function of howling in red howler monkeys (Alouatta seniculus). Behaviour 81, 38–54.

Sekulic, R. (1982d). Birth in free-ranging howler monkeys, Alouatta seniculus. Primates 23, 580–582.

Sekulic, R. (1983a). Male relationships and infant deaths in red howler monkeys (Alouatta seniculus). Zeitschrift für Tierpsychologie 61, 185–202.

Sekulic, R. (1983b). The effect of female call on male howling in red howler monkeys (Alouatta seniculus). International Journal of Primatology. In press.

Selmanoff, M. K., E. Abreu, B. D. Goldman, and B. E. Ginsburg. (1977a). Manipulation of aggressive behavior in adult DBA/2Bg and C57BL/10Bg male mice implanted with testosterone and silastic tubing. Hormones and Behavior 8, 377–390.

Selmanoff, M. K., B. D. Goldman, S. C. Maxson, and B. E. Ginsburg. (1977b). Correlated effect of Y-chromosome of mice on developmental changes in testosterone levels and intermale aggression. Life Sciences 20, 359–366.

Semb-Johansson, A., R. Wiger, and C. E. Engh. (1979). Dynamics of freely growing, confined populations of the Norwegian lemming Lemmus lemmus. Oikos 33, 246–260.

Semler, D. E. (1971). Some aspects of adaptation in a polymorphism for breeding colours in the threespine stickleback (Gasterosteus aculeatus). Journal of Zoology (London) 165, 291–302.

Shah, M. K. (1956). Reciprocal egg transplantations to study the embryo–uterine relationship in heat-induced failure of pregnancy in rabbits. Nature (London) 177, 1134–1135.

Sharman, G. B., and P. J. Berger. (1969). Embryonic diapause in marsupials. Advances in Reproductive Physiology 4, 211–240.

Shaw, R. F., and J. D. Mohler. (1953). The selective advantage of the sex ratio. American Naturalist 87, 337–342.

Sherman, P. W. (1981). Reproductive competition and infanticide in Belding's ground squirrels and other animals. In Natural selection and social behavior: Recent research and new theory (R. D. Alexander and D. W. Tinkle, eds.), pp. 311–331. New York: Chiron Press.

Sholiton, L. J., and E. E. Work. (1969). The less polar metabolites produced by incubation of testosterone-14-14C with rat and bovine brain. Acta Endocrinologica 61, 641–648.

Shoop, C. R. (1974). Yearly variation in larval survival of Ambystoma maculatum. Ecology 55, 440–444.

Shopland, J. M. (1982). An intergroup encounter with fatal consequences in yellow baboons (Papio cynocephalus). American Journal of Primatology 3, 263–266.

Shorter, E. (1977). The making of the modern family. New York: Basic Books.

Shorter, E. (1982). A history of women's bodies. New York: Basic Books.

Shostak, M. (1981). Nisa: The life and words of a !Kung woman. Cambridge, Mass.: Harvard University Press.

Shrivastava, N. P., and V. R. Desai. (1979). A case of cannibalism observed in *Glossogobius giuris* (Hamilton) from Rihand Reservoir (Uttar Pradesh). *Journal of the Inland Fisheries Society of India* **11**, 134–135.

Sieber, B. (1981). Breeding of Sykes and blue monkeys in captivity. *Institute of Primate Research Annual Report, Tigoni Kenya,* p. 22.

Siegfried, W. R. (1968). Breeding season, clutch, and brood sizes in Verreaux's eagle. *Ostrich* **39**, 139–145.

Siegfried, W. R. (1972). Breeding success and reproductive output of the cattle egret. *Ostrich* **43**, 43–55.

Silk, J. (1983). Local resource competition and facultative adjustment of sex ratios in relation to competitive abilities. *American Naturalist* **121**, 56–66.

Simmons, G. B., C. Smuker, S. Bernstein, and E. Jenson. (1908). Post-neonatal mortality in rural India: Implications of an economic model. Paper presented to the Annual Meeting of the American Public Health Association, Detroit.

Simon, M. P. (1980). Adaptive significance of nest guarding in a microhylid frog from New Guinea. *American Zoologist* **20**, 728. (Abstr.).

Simon, M. P. (1982). The evolution and ecology of parental care in a terrestrial breeding frog from New Guinea. Unpublished Ph.D. thesis, University of California, Davis, Calif.

Simon, N. G. (1979). The genetics of intermale aggressive behavior in mice: Recent research and alternative strategies. *Neuroscience and Biobehavioral Reviews* **3**, 97–107.

Simpson, M. J. A., and A. E. Simpson. (1982). Birth sex ratios and social rank in rhesus monkey mothers. *Nature (London)* **300**, 440–441.

Singh, S., J. E. Gordon, and J. B. Wyon. (1965). Cause of death at different ages by sex and by season in a rural population of the Punjab 1957–1959: A field study. *Indian Journal of Medical Research* **53**, 906–917.

Skeet, W. W., and C. O. Blagden. (1906). *Pagan races of the Malay Peninsula,* Vol. 2. London.

Skinner, S. W. (1982). Maternally inherited sex ratio in the parasitoid wasp, *Nasonia vitripennis. Science* **215**, 1133–1134.

Skreslet, S. (1973). The ecosystem of the Arctic lake Nordlaguna, Jan Mayen Island. III. Ecology of the Arctic char, *Salvelinus alpinus* (L.). *Astarte* **6**, 43–54.

Skutch, A. F. (1967). Adaptive limitation of the reproductive rate of birds. *Ibis* **109**, 579–599.

Smith, B. G. (1907). The life history and habits of *Cryptobranchus alleganiensis. Biological Bulletin* **13**, 5–39.

Smith, B. G. (1911). Notes on the natural history of *Ambystoma jeffersonianum, Ambystoma punctatum,* and *Ambystoma tigrinum. Bulletin of the Wisconsin Natural History Society* **9**, 14–47.

Smith, H. M., and L. G. Harron. (1904). Breeding habits of the yellow cat-fish. *United States Fish Commission Bulletin* **22** (1902), 149–154.

Smith, J. L. D. In preparation. Ph.D. thesis, University of Minnesota, Minneapolis, Minn.

Smith, T. C. (1977). *Nakahara: Family farming and population in a Japanese village, 1717–1830.* Stanford: Stanford University Press.

Smith-Gill, S. J., and K. A. Berven. (1979). Predicting amphibian metamorphosis. *American Naturalist* **113**, 563–585.

Smith-Gill, S. J., and D. E. Gill. (1978). Curvilinearities in the competition equations: An experiment with ranid tadpoles. *American Naturalist* **112**, 557–570.

Smuts, B. B. (1982). Special relationships between adult male and female olive baboons (*Papio anubis*). Unpublished Ph.D. thesis, Stanford University, Stanford, Calif.

Smyly, W. J. P. (1952). Observations on the food of the fry of perch (*Perca fluviatilis* Linn.) in Windermere. *Proceedings of the Zoological Society of London* **122**, 407–416.

Smyth, M. (1968). The effects of the removal of individuals from a population of bank voles *Clethrionomys glareolus*. *Journal of Animal Ecology* **37**, 167–183.

Snow, B. (1960). The breeding biology of the shag *Phalacrocorax aristotelis* on the Island of Lundy, Bristol Channel. *Ibis* **102**, 554–575.

Snow, D. W. (1958). The breeding of the blackbird *Turdus merula* at Oxford. *Ibis* **100**, 1–30.

Sod-Moriah, U. A. (1971). Reproduction in the heat-acclimatized female rat as affected by high ambient temperature. *Journal of Reproduction and Fertility* **26**, 209–218.

Sokal, O. M. (1962). The tadpole of *Hymenochirus boettgeri*. *Copeia*, pp. 272–284.

Sokal, R. R., and F. J. Rohlf. (1969). *Biometry*. San Francisco: Freeman.

Sommer, V. In press. Kindestötung bei indischen Langurenaffen (*Presbytis entellus*)—eine männliche Reproduktionsstrategie? *Anthropologischer Anzeiger* **3**.

Southern, H. N. (1970). The natural control of a population of tawny owls (*Strix aluco*). *Journal of Zoology (London)* **162**, 197–285.

Southwick, C. H. (1955a). The population dynamics of confined house mice supplied with unlimited food. *Ecology* **36**, 212–225.

Southwick, C. H. (1955b). Regulatory mechanisms of house mouse populations: Social behavior affecting litter survival. *Ecology* **36**, 627–634.

Spellerberg, I. F. (1971a). Breeding behaviour of the McCormick skua *Catharacta maccormicki* in Antarctica. *Ardea* **59**, 189–230.

Spellerberg, I. F. (1971b). Aspects of McCormick skua breeding biology. *Ibis* **113**, 357–363.

Spencer-Booth, Y. (1971). The relationships between mammalian young and conspecifics other than mothers and peers: A review. In *Advances in the Study of Behavior* (D. S. Lehrman, J. S. Rosenblatt, R. A. Hinde, and E. Shaw, eds.), pp. 120–194. New York: Academic Press.

Spitz, F. (1974). Démographie du campagnol des champs *Microtus arvalis* en vendée. *Annales de Zoologie–Écologie Animale* **6**, 259–312.

Springer, S. (1948). Oviphagous embryos of the sand shark, *Carcharias taurus*. *Copeia*, pp. 153–157.

Sprunt, A., Jr. (1948). The tern colonies of the Dry Tortugas Keys. *Auk* **65**, 1–19.

Stacey, P. B., and T. C. Edwards, Jr. (1983). Possible cases of infanticide by immigrant females in a group-breeding bird. *Auk.* **100**, 731–733.

Stamp, N. (1980). Egg deposition patterns in butterflies: Why do some species cluster their eggs rather than deposit them singly? *American Naturalist* **115**, 367–380.

Stamps, J. A., and R. A. Metcalf. (1980). Parent–offspring conflict. In *Sociobiology: Beyond Nature–Nurture?* (AAAS Selected Symposium no. 35) (G. W. Barlow and J. Silverberg, eds.), pp. 589–618. Boulder, Colo.: Westview Press.

Staples, G. V. (1980). The function of male parental care in the mottled sculpin, *Cottus bairdi*. Unpublished M.S. thesis, Ohio State University, Columbus, Ohio.

Starrett, P. (1960). Descriptions of tadpoles of middle American frogs. *Miscellaneous Publications Museum of Zoology University of Michigan* **110**, 5–37.

Statistiska Centralbyran. (1917). *Befolkningsrorelsen Oversikt for Aren 1901–10.* Stockholm.

Stebbins, R. C. (1954). Natural history of the salamanders of the plethodontid genus *Ensatina*. *University of California Publications in Zoology* **54**, 377–512.

Stehn, R. A., and F. J. Jannett, Jr. (1981). Male-induced abortion in various microtine rodents. *Journal of Mammalogy* **62**, 369–372.

Stehn, R. A., and M. E. Richmond. (1975). Male-induced pregnancy termination in the prairie vole, *Microtus ochrogaster*. *Science* **187**, 1211–1213.

Stein, D. M. (1981). The nature and function of social interactions between infant and adult male yellow baboons (*Papio cynocephalus*). Unpublished Ph.D. thesis, University of Chicago, Chicago, Ill.

Steiner, A. L. (1972). Mortality resulting from intraspecific fighting in some ground squirrel populations. *Journal of Mammalogy* **53**, 601–603.

Steinwascher, K. F. (1978). Interference and exploitation competition among tadpoles of *Rana utriculcaria*. *Ecology* **59**, 1039–1046.

Steinwascher, K. F. (1979). Host–parasite interaction as a potential population-regulating mechanism. *Ecology* **60**, 884–890.

Stepanova, Z. L. (1974). The chemical nature of the products of metabolism of amphibian larvae, excreted into the water. *Soviet Journal of Ecology* **5**, 148–149.

Stephens, M. L. (1984). Mate takeover and possible infanticide by a female northern jacana (*Jacana spinosa*). *Animal Behaviour* **30**, 1253–1254.

Stephens, M. L. (1983). Intraspecific distraction displays in the polyandrous northern jacana, *Jacana spinosa*. *Ibis.* **126**, 70–72.

Stinson, C. H. (1979). On the selective advantage of fratricide in raptors. *Evolution* **33**, 1219–1225.

Stinson, C. H. (1980). Weather-dependent foraging success and sibling aggression in red-tailed hawks in central Washington. *Condor* **82**, 76–80.

Stirling, I. (1974). Midsummer observations on the behavior of wild polar bears (*Ursus maritimus*). *Canadian Journal of Zoology* **52**, 1191–1198.

Stoeckle, M. Y. (1974). Some selected aspects of the breeding biology of the common tern *Sterna hirundo*. Unpublished B.A. thesis, Harvard College, Cambridge, Mass.

Stolnitz, G. (1956). A century of international mortality trends, II. *Population Studies* **10**, 17–42.

Storm, R. M. (1947). Eggs and young of *Aneides ferreus*. *Herpetologica* **4**, 60–62.

Strong, R. M. (1914). On the habits and behavior of the herring gull, *Larus argentatus* Pont. *Auk* **31**, 22–49, 178–199.

Struhsaker, T. T. (1969). Correlates of ecology and social organization among African cercopithecines. *Folia Primatologica* **11**, 80–118.

Struhsaker, T. T. (1975). *The red colobus monkey.* Chicago: University of Chicago Press.

Struhsaker, T. T. (1977). Infanticide and social organization in the redtail monkey (*Cercopithecus ascanius schmidti*) in the Kibale forest. *Zeitschrift für Tierpsychologie* **45**, 75–84.

Struhsaker, T. T. (1978a). Food habits of five monkey species in the Kibale Forest, Uganda. In *Recent Advances in Primatology,* Vol. 1: *Behavior* (D. Chivers and J. Herbert, eds.), pp. 225–248. New York: Academic Press.

Struhsaker, T. T. (1978b). Infanticide in the redtailed monkey (*Cercopithecus ascanius schmidti*). In *Recent Advances in Primatology*, Vol. 1: *Behavior* (D. Chivers and J. Herbert, eds.), pp. 591–592. New York: Academic Press.

Struhsaker, T. T. (1980). Comparison of the behavior and ecology of red colobus and redtail monkeys in the Kibale Forest, Uganda. *African Journal of Ecology* **18**, 33–51.

Struhsaker, T. T., and L. Leland. (1979). Socioecology of five sympatric monkey species in the Kibale Forest, Uganda. *Advances in the Study of Behavior* **9**, 159–228.

Strum, S. C. (1975). Life with the Pumphouse Gang. *National Geographic Magazine* **147**, 673–691.

Studier, E. H., V. L. Lysengen, and M. J. O'Farrell. (1973). Biology of *Myotis thysanodes* and *M. lucifugus* (Chiroptera: Vespertilionidae). II. Bioenergetics of pregnancy and lactation. *Comparative Biochemistry and Physiology* **44A**, 467–471.

Sugiyama, Y. (1964). Group composition, population density, and some sociological observations of hanuman langurs (*Presbytis entellus*). *Primates* **5**, 7–37.

Sugiyama, Y. (1965a). Behavioral development and social structure in two troops of hanuman langurs (*Presbytis entellus*). *Primates* **6**, 213–247.

Sugiyama, Y. (1965b). On the social change of hanuman langurs (*Presbytis entellus*) in their natural condition. *Primates* **6**, 381–418.

Sugiyama, Y. (1966). An artificial social change in a hanuman langur troop (*Presbytis entellus*). *Primates* **7**, 41–72.

Sugiyama, Y. (1967). Social organization of hanuman langurs. In *Social communication among primates* (S. Altmann, ed.), pp. 221–236. Chicago: University of Chicago Press.

Sugiyama, Y. (1976a). Characteristics of the ecology of the Himalayan langurs. *Journal of Human Evolution* **5**, 249–277.

Sugiyama, Y. (1976b). Life history of male Japanese monkeys. *Advances in the Study of Behavior* **7**, 255–284.

Sugiyama, Y., and H. Ohsawa. (1982). Population dynamics of Japanese monkeys with special reference to the effect of artificial feeding. *Folia Primatologica* **39**, 238–263.

Sugiyama, Y., and M. D. Parthasarathy. (1969). A brief account in the life of hanuman langurs. *Proceedings of the National Institute of Science India* **35**, 306–319.

Sugiyama, Y., and M. D. Parthasarathy. (1979). Population change of the hanuman langur (*Presbytis entellus*), 1961–1976, in Dharwar area, India. *Journal of the Bombay Natural History Society* **75**, 860–867.

Sugiyama, Y., K. Yoshiba, and M. D. Parthasarathy. (1965). Home-range, breeding season, male group, and inter-troop relations in hanuman langurs (*Presbytis entellus*). *Primates* **6**, 73–106.

Sundbärg, G. (1970). Behvölkerungsstatistik Schwedens 1750–1900. *Urval* No. 3. Stockholm: Statistiska Centralbyran.

Sundbärg, G. (ed.). (1904). *Sweden: Its people and its industry*. Stockholm: Government Printing Office.

Sunquist, M. E. (1981). The social organization of tigers (*Panthera tigris*) Royal Chitawan National Park, Nepal. *Smithsonian Contributions to Zoology* No. 336.

Suomi, S. J., and C. Ripp. (1983). A history of motherless mother monkey mothering at the University of Wisconsin Primate Laboratory. In *Child abuse:*

The nonhuman primate data (M. Reite and N. Caine, eds.), pp. 49–78. New York: Alan R. Liss.

Surface, H. A. (1913). First report on the economic features of the amphibians of Pennsylvania. *Zoological Bulletin of the Division of Zoology at the Pennsylvania Department of Agriculture* **3**, 68–152.

Sussman, G. D. (1975). The wet-nursing business in nineteenth century France. *French Historical Studies* **9**, 304–328.

Sussman, G. D. (1977). Parisian infants and Norman wet nurses in the early nineteenth century: A statistical study. *Journal of Interdisciplinary History* **7**, 637–653.

Suzuki, A. (1971). Carnivority and cannibalism among forest-living chimpanzees. *Journal of the Anthropological Society of Nippon* **79**, 30–48.

Svare, B. (1979). Steroidal influences on pup-killing behavior in mice. *Hormones and Behavior* **13**, 153–164.

Svare, B. (1981). Maternal aggression in mammals. In *Parental care in mammals* (P. Klopfer and D. Gubernick, eds.), pp. 179–210. New York: Plenum Press.

Svare, R., and A. Bartke. (1978). Food deprivation induces conspecific pup-killing in mice. *Aggressive Behavior* **4**, 253–261.

Svare, B., and J. Broida. (1982). Genotypic influences on infanticide in mice: Environmental, situational, and experimental determinants. *Physiology and Behavior* **28**, 171–175.

Svare, B., and R. Gandelman. (1976). Postpartum aggression in mice: The influence of suckling stimulation. *Hormones and Behavior* **7**, 407–416.

Svare, B., and M. Mann. (1981). Infanticide: Genetic, developmental and hormonal influences in mice. *Physiology and Behavior* **27**, 921–927.

Svare, B., A. Bartke, and R. Gandelman. (1977). Individual differences in the maternal behavior of male mice: No evidence for a relationship to circulating testosterone levels. *Hormones and Behavior* **8**, 372–376.

Svare, B., A. Bartke, and F. Macrides. (1978). Juvenile male mice: An attempt to accelerate testis function by exposure to female stimuli. *Physiology and Behavior* **21**, 1009–1013.

Svare, B., M. A. Mann, C. Kinsley, and J. Broida. In press. Infanticide: Accounting for genetic variation. *Physiology and Behavior*.

Swanson, H. H. (1967). Alteration of sex-typical behavior of hamsters in open field and emergence tests by neonatal administration of androgen or oestrogen. *Animal Behaviour* **15**, 209–216.

Sweet, J. A. (1974). *The family living arrangements of children.* Working paper 74-28, University of Wisconsin Center for Demography and Ecology.

Swenson, W. A., and L. L. Smith. (1976). Influence of food competition, predation, and cannibalism on walleye (*Stizostedion vitreum vitreum*) and sauger (*S. canadense*) populations in Lake of the Woods, Minnesota. *Journal of the Fisheries Research Board of Canada* **33**, 1946–1954.

Taborsky, M., and D. Limberger. (1981). Helpers in fish. *Behavioral Ecology and Sociobiology* **8**, 143–145.

Tabutin, D. (1978). Le surmortalité feminine en Europe avant 1940. *Population* **10**, 121–148.

Taigen, T. L., H. Pough, and M. M. Stewart. (1984). Water balance of terrestrial anuran (*Eleutherodactylus coqui*) eggs: Importance of parental care. *Ecology* **65**, 248–255.

Tait, D. E. N. (1980). Abandonment as a tactic in grizzly bears. *American Naturalist* **115**, 800–808.

Tamarin, R. H., M. Sheridan, and C. K. Levy. (1983). Determining matrilineal kinship in natural populations of rodents using radionuclides. *Canadian Journal of Zoology* **61**, 271–274.

Tanimoto, K. (1943). Studies on mammals in relation to bubonic plague in Manchuria. *Zoological Magazine (Tokyo)* **55**, 117–127.

Tarby, M. J. (1974). Characteristics of yellow perch cannibalism in Oneida Lake and the relation to first year survival. *Transactions of the American Fisheries Society* **103**, 462–471.

Teitelbaum, M. S. (1970). Factors affecting the sex ratio in large populations. *Journal of Biosocial Science Suppl.* **2**, 61–71.

Terman, C. R. (1965). A study of population growth and control exhibited in the laboratory by prairie deermice. *Ecology* **46**, 890–895.

Terman, C. R. (1969). Pregnancy failure in prairie deermice related to parity and social environment. *Animal Behaviour* **17**, 104–108.

Thibault, R. E. (1974). Genetics of cannibalism in a viviparous fish and its relationship to population density. *Nature (London)* **251**, 138–140.

Thiessen, D. D. (1968). The roots of territorial markings in the Mongolian gerbil: A problem of species-common topography. *Behavior Research Methods Instrumentation* **1**, 70–76.

Thorburn, G. D., and J. R. G. Challis. (1979). Endocrine control of parturition. *Physiological Reviews* **59**, 863–918.

Tietze, C., J. Bongaarts, and S. B. Schearer. (1976). Mortality associated with a control of fertility. *Family Planning Perspectives* **8**, 6–14.

Tilley, S. G. (1972). Aspects of parental care and embryonic development in *Desmognathus ochrophaeus*. *Copeia*, pp. 532–540.

Tinbergen, N. (1953). *The herring gull's world.* New York: Basic Books.

Tinley, K. L. (1973). *An ecological reconnaissance of the Moremi Wildlife Reserve, Botswana.* Gaborones, Botswana: Okavango Wildlife Society.

Tomich, P. Q. (1962). The annual cycle of the California ground squirrel *Citellus beecheyi*. *University of California Publications in Zoology* **65**, 213–282.

Townsend, D. S., M. M. Stewart, and F. H. Pough. (1984). Male parental care and its adaptive significance in a neotropical frog. *Animal Behaviour, In Press.*

Trail, P. W., S. D. Strahl, and J. L. Brown. (1981). Infanticide in relation to individual and flock histories in a communally breeding bird, the Mexican jay (*Aphelocoma ultramarina*). *American Naturalist* **118**, 72–82.

Travis, J. (1980). Phenotypic variation and the outcome of interspecific competition in hylid tadpoles. *Evolution* **34**, 40–50.

Travis, J. (1981). Control of larval growth variation in a population of *Pseudoacris triseriata* (Anura: Hylidae). *Evolution* **35**, 423–432.

Trexler, R. (1973a). Infanticide in Florence: New sources and first results. *History of Childhood Quarterly* **1**, 98–116.

Trexler, R. (1973b). The foundlings of Florence 1395–1455. *History of Childhood Quarterly* **1**, 259–284.

Tripp, H. R. H. (1971). Reproduction in elephant-shrews (Macroscelididae) with special reference to ovulation and implantation. *Journal of Reproduction and Fertility* **26**, 149–159.

Trivers, R. L. (1972). Parental investment and sexual selection. In *Sexual selection and the descent of man 1871–1971* (B. Campbell, ed.), pp. 136–179. Chicago: Aldine.

Trivers, R. L. (1974). Parent–offspring conflict. *American Zoologist* **14**, 249–264.

Trivers, R. L., and D. E. Willard. (1973). Natural selection of parental ability to vary the sex ratio of offspring. *Science* **179**, 90–92.

Troisi, Alfonso, Francesca R. D'Amato, Roberto Fuccillo, and Stefano Scucchi. (1982). Infant abuse by a wild-born group-living Japanese macaque mother. *Journal of Abnormal Psychology* **91**, 451–456.

Troth, R. G. (1979). Vegetational types on a ranch in the central llanos of Venezuela. In *Vertebrate ecology in the northern Neotropics* (J. F. Eisenberg, ed.), pp. 17–30. Washington, D.C.: Smithsonian Institution Press.

Troyer, W. A., and R. J. Hensel. (1962). Cannibalism in brown bear. *Animal Behaviour* **10**, 231.

Trpis, M. (1973). Interaction between the predator *Toxorhynchites brevipalpis* and its prey *Aedes aegypti*. *Bulletin. World Health Organization* **49**, 359–365.

Tschinkel, W. (1978). Dispersal behavior of the larval tenebrionid beetle *Zophobas rugipes*. *Physiological Zoology* **51**, 300–313.

Turnbull, C. (1972). *The mountain people*. New York: Simon and Shuster.

Turner, B. N., and S. L. Iverson. (1973). The annual cycle of aggression in male *Microtus pennsylvanicus*, and its relation to population parameters. *Ecology* **54**, 967–981.

Turner, C. L. (1947). Viviparity in teleost fishes. *Science Monthly* **65**, 508–518.

Turner, F. B. (1960). Population structure and dynamics of the western spotted frog, *Rana p. pretiosa*, Baird and Girard, in Yellowstone Park. *Ecological Monographs* **30**, 251–278.

Turner, F. B. (1962). The demography of frogs and toads. *Quarterly Review of Biology* **37**, 303–314.

Turner, M. (1979). Diet and feeding phenology of the green lynx spider, *Peucetia viridans* (Araneae: Oxyopidae). *Journal of Arachnology* **7**, 149–154.

Tyler, M. J. (1963). A taxonomic study of amphibians and reptiles of the Central Highlands of New Guinea, with notes of their ecology and biology: 1. Anura, Microhylidae. *Transactions of the Royal Society of South Australia* **36**, 11–34.

Tyler, M. J., A. A. Martin, and M. Davies. (1979). Biology and systematics of a new Limnodynastine genus (Anura: Leptodactylidae) from northwestern Australia. *Australian Journal of Zoology* **27**, 135–150.

Tyndale-Biscoe, C. H. (1973). *Life of marsupials*. New York: Elsevier.

Tyndale-Biscoe, C. H., and J. C. Rodger. (1978). Differential transport of spermatozoa into the two sides of the genital tract of a monovular marsupial, the tammer wallaby (*Macropus eugenii*). *Journal of Reproduction and Fertility* **52**, 37–43.

Ulberg, L. C., and L. A. Sheean. (1973). Early development of mammalian embryos in elevated ambient temperatures. *Journal of Reproduction and Fertility Suppl.* **19**, 155–161.

Ullyette, G. C. (1950). Competition for food and allied phenomena in sheep blowfly populations. *Philosophical Transactions of the Royal Society of London* **234**, 77–174.

United Nations. (1962). *The situation and recent trends of mortality in the world*. New York: United Nations.

United Nations. (1977). *U. N. demographic yearbook 1976*. New York: U.N.

Utida, S. (1942). Studies on experimental population of the Azuki bean weevil, *Callobruchus chinensis* (L.). VII. Analysis of the density effect in the preimaginal stage. *Memoirs of the College of Agriculture Kyoto University* **53**, 19–31.

Valerio, C. (1974). Feeding on eggs by spiderlings of *Achaearanea tepidariorum*

(Araneae: Theridiidae), and the significance of quiescent instar in spiders. *Journal of Arachnology* **2**, 57–63.

Vandenbergh, J. G. (1967). Effect of the presence of a male on the sexual maturation of female mice. *Endocrinology* **81**, 345–349.

Vandenbergh, J. G. (1976). Acceleration of sexual maturation in female rats by male stimulation. *Journal of Reproduction and Fertility* **45**, 451–453.

van der Horst, C. J., and J. Gillman. (1941). The number of eggs and surviving embryos in *Elephantulus*. *Anatomical Record* **80**, 443–452.

van der Horst, C. J., and J. Gillman. (1942). Pre-implantation phenomena in the uterus of *Elephantulus*. *South African Journal of Medical Science* **7**, 47–71.

van Lawick, H. (1974). *Solo.* London: Collins.

van Lawick, H., and J. van Lawick-Goodall. (1971). *Innocent killers.* London: Collins.

Vannini, M., A. Ugolini, and C. Marucelli. (1978). Notes on the mother–young relationship in some *Euscorpius* (Scorpiones: Chactidae). *Monitore Zoologico Italiano* [N.S.] **12**, 143–154.

Van Orsdol, K. G. (1981). Lion predation in Rwenzori National Park, Uganda. Unpublished Ph.D. thesis, Cambridge University, England.

Van Someren, V. G. L., and G. R. C. Van Someren. (1945). Evacuated weaver colonies and notes on the breeding ecology of *Euodice cantans* Gmelin and *Amadina fasciata* Gmelin. *Ibis* **87**, 33–44.

Varma, T. R. (1979). Ultrasound evidence of early pregnancy failure in patients with multiple conceptions. *British Journal of Obstetrics and Gynecology* **86**, 290–292.

Vehrencamp, S. L. (1977). Relative fecundity and parental effort in communally nesting anis, *Crotophaga sulcirostris*. *Science* **197**, 403–405.

Velthuis, H. H. W., F. M. Velthuis-Kluppel, and G. A. H. Bossink. (1965). Some aspects of the biology and population dynamics of *Nasonia vitripennis* (Walker) (Hymenoptera: Pteromalidae). *Entomologia Experimentalis et Applicata* **8**, 205–227.

Vermeer, K. (1970). Breeding biology of California and ring-billed gulls: A study of ecological adaptation to the inland habitat. *Canadian Wildlife Service. Report Series* No. 12, 52 p.

Verner, J. (1977). On the adaptive significance of territoriality. *American Naturalist* **111**, 769–775.

Vesey-Fitzgerald, D. (1957). The breeding of the white pelican *Pelecanus onocrotalus* in the Rukwa Valley, Tanganyika. *Bulletin of the British Ornithologists' Club* **77**, 127–129.

Viitala, J. (1977). Social organization in cyclic subarctic populations of the voles *Clethrionomys rufocanus* (Sund.) and *Microtus agrestis* (L.). *Annales Zoologici Fennici* **14**, 53–93.

Viktorov, G. A. (1968). Effect of population density on sex ratio in *Trissolcus grandis* Thoms. (Hymenoptera, Scelionidae). *Zoologicheskii Zhurnal* **47**, 1035–1039.

Viktorov, G. A., and N. I. Kochetova. (1973a). The role of trace pheromones in regulating the sex ratio in *Trissolcus grandis* (Hymenoptera, Scelionidae). *Zhurnal Obshchei Biologii* **34**, 559–562.

Viktorov, G. A., and N. I. Kochetova. (1973b). On the regulation of the sex ratio in *Dahlbominus fuscipennis* Zett. (Hymenoptera, Eulophidae). *Entomologicheskoe Obozrenie* **52**, 651–657.

Vinovskis, M. (1972). Mortality rates and trends in Massachusetts before 1860. *Journal of Economic History* **32**, 184–213.

Vogel, C. (1976). *Okologie, Lebensweise und Sozialverhalten der grauen Languren in verschiedenen Biotropen Indiens* (Advances in Ethology No. 17, supplement to *Zeitschrift für Tierpsychologie*). Berlin: Verlag Paul Parey.

Vogel, C. (1977). Ecology and sociology of *Presbytis entellus*. In *Use of nonhuman primates in biomedical research* (M. R. D. Prasad and T. C. Anand Kumar, eds.), pp. 24–45. New Delhi: Indian National Science Academy.

Vogel, C. (1979). Der Hanuman-Langur (*Presbytis entellus*), ein Parade-Exempel für die theoretischen Konzepte der "Soziobiologie"? In *Verhandlungen der Deutschen Zoologischen Gesellschaft 1979 in Regensburg* (W. Rathmayer, ed.), pp. 73–89. Stuttgart: Gustav Fischer Verlag.

vom Saal, F. S. (1979). Prenatal exposure to androgen influences morphology and aggressive behavior of male and female mice. *Hormones and Behavior* **12**, 1–11.

vom Saal, F. S. (1981). Variations in phenotype due to random intrauterine positioning of male and female fetuses in rodents. *Journal of Reproduction and Fertility* **62**, 633–650.

vom Saal, F. S. (1983a). Intrauterine position influences aggression and population dynamics in mice. In *Biological perspectives on aggression* (C. Blanchard, K. Flannelly, and R. Blanchard, eds.). New York: Alan R. Liss.

vom Saal, F. S. (1983b). Models of early hormonal effects on intrasex aggression in mice. In *Hormones and aggressive behavior* (B. Svare, ed.), pp. 197–222. New York: Plenum.

vom Saal, F. S. (1983c). Variation in infanticide and parental behavior in male mice due to prior intrauterine proximity to female fetuses: Elimination by prenatal stress. *Physiology and Behavior* **30**, 675–681.

vom Saal, F. S. (1983d). The interaction of circulating estrogens and androgens in regulating mammalian sexual differentiation. In *Hormones and behavior in higher vertebrates* (J. Balthazart, E. Prove, and R. Giles, eds.), pp. 159–177. New York: Springer-Verlag.

vom Saal, F. S. In press. Time-contingent change in behavior toward young induced by ejaculation in male mice. *Physiology Behavior*.

vom Saal, F. S., and F. H. Bronson. (1978). In utero proximity of female mouse fetuses to males: Effect on reproductive performance during later life. *Biology of Reproduction* **19**, 842–853.

vom Saal, F. S., and F. H. Bronson. (1980a). Sexual characteristics of adult female mice are correlated with their blood testosterone levels during prenatal development. *Science* **208**, 597–599.

vom Saal, F. S., and F. H. Bronson. (1980b). Variation in length of the estrous cycle in mice due to former intrauterine proximity to male fetuses. *Biology of Reproduction* **22**, 777–780.

vom Saal, F. S., and L. S. Howard (1982). The regulation of infanticide and parental behavior: Implications for reproductive success in male mice. *Science* **215**, 1270–1272.

vom Saal, F. S., S. Pryor, and F. H. Bronson. (1981). Change in oestrous cycle length during adolescence in mice is influenced by prior intrauterine position and housing. *Journal of Reproduction and Fertility* **62**, 33–37.

vom Saal, F. S., W. Grant, C. McMullen, and K. Laves. (1983). High fetal estrogen concentrations: Correlation with increased adult sexual performance and decreased aggression in male mice. *Science* **220**, 1306–1308.

Waage, J. K. (1982). Sib-mating and sex ratio strategies in scelionid wasps. *Ecological Entomology* **7**, 103–112.

Wade, M. J. (1978). A critical review of the models of group selection. *Quarterly Review of Biology* **53**, 101–114.

Wade, M. J. (1980). An experimental study of kin selection. *Evolution* **34**, 844–855.

Wade, M. J., and D. E. McCauley. (1980). Group selection: The phenotypic and genotypic differentiation of small populations. *Evolution* **34**, 799–812.

Wagley, C. (1969). Cultural influences on population: A comparison of two Tupi tribes. In *Environment and cultural behavior* (A. P. Vayda, ed.), pp. 268–280. New York: The Natural History Press.

Wagley, C. (1977). *Welcome of tears: The Tapirapé Indians of central Brazil.* New York: Oxford University Press.

Wake, M. H. (1977). The reproductive biology of caecilians: An evolutionary perspective. In *The reproductive biology of amphibians* (D. H. Taylor and S. S. Guttman, eds.), pp. 73–102. New York: Plenum.

Wake, M. H. (1980). Reproduction, growth, and population structure of the Central American caecilian, *Dermophis mexicanus. Herpetologica* **36**, 244–256.

Waldman, B., and K. Adler. (1979). Toad tadpoles associate preferentially with siblings. *Nature (London)* **282**, 611–613.

Walker, I. (1967). Effect of population density on the viability and fecundity in *Nasonia vitripennis* Walker (Hymenoptera, Pteromalidae). *Ecology* **48**, 294–301.

Walker, K. Z., and C. H. Tyndale-Biscoe. (1978). Immunological aspects of gestation in the tammar wallaby, *Macropus eugenii. Australian Journal of Biological Sciences* **31**, 173–182.

Wall, Richard. (1981). Inferring differential neglect of females from mortality data. *Annales de Demographie Historique*, pp. 9–140.

Wallace, P., K. Owen, and D. D. Thiessen. (1973). The control and function of maternal scent marking in the Mongolian gerbil (*Meriones unguiculatus*). *Physiology and Behavior* **10**, 463–466.

Wallis, S. J. (1978). The socioecology of *Cercocebus albigena johnstoni* (Lyddeker): An arboreal, rain forest monkey. Unpublished Ph.D. thesis, University of London.

Ward, H. L. (1906). Why do herring gulls kill their young? *Science* **24**, 593–594.

Ward, J. A., and J. I. Samarakoon. (1981). Reproductive tactics of the Asian cichlids of the genus *Etroplus* in Sri Lanka. *Environmental Biology of Fishes* **6**, 95–103.

Ward, P. (1965). The breeding biology of the black-faced dioch *Quelea quelea* in Nigeria. *Ibis* **107**, 326–344.

Ware, H. (1977). The relationship between infant mortality and fertility: Replacement and insurance effects. In *Proceedings of the international population conference*, vol. 1. Liege, Belgium: International Union for the Scientific Study of Population.

Ware, H. (1981). *Women, demography and development.* Canberra: The Australian National University, Development Studies Center Demography Teaching Notes.

Warham, J. (1975). The crested penguins. In *The biology of penguins* (B. Stonehouse, ed.), pp. 189–269. Baltimore: University Park Press.

Warner, R. R., D. R. Robertson, and E. G. Leigh, Jr. (1975). Sex change and sexual selection. *Science* **190**, 633–638.

Waser, P. M. (1974). Intergroup interaction in a forest monkey: The mangabey *Cercocebus albigena*. Unpublished Ph.D. thesis, Rockefeller University, New York City, N.Y.

Waser, P. M. (1981). Sociality or territorial defense? The influence of resource renewal. *Behavioral Ecology and Sociobiology* **8**, 231–237.

Wasser, S. K. (1982). Reciprocity and the trade-off between associate quality and relatedness. *American Naturalist* **119**, 720–731.

Wasser, S. K. (1983). Reproductive competition and cooperation among female yellow baboons. In *Social behavior of female vertebrates* (S. K. Wasser, ed.), pp. 349–390. New York: Academic Press.

Wasser, S. K., and D. P. Barash (1983). Reproductive suppression among female mammals: Implications for biomedicine and sexual selection theory. *Quarterly Review of Biology*, **58**, 513–538.

Wassersug, R. J. (1975). The adaptive significance of the tadpole stage with comments on the maintenance of complex life cycles in anurans. *American Zoologist* **15**, 405–417.

Wassersug, R. J., and E. A. Seibert. (1975). Behavioral response of amphibian larvae to variation in dissolved oxygen. *Copeia*, pp. 86–103.

Wassersug, R. J., K. J. Frogners, and R. F. Inger. (1981). Adaptations for life in tree holes by rhacophorid tadpoles from Thailand. *Journal of Herpetology* **15**, 41–52.

Watson, R. M. (1965). Observations on the behaviour of young spotted hyaena (*Crocuta crocuta*) in the burrow. *East African Wildlife Journal* **3**, 122–123.

Watts, C. H. S. (1970). A field experiment on intraspecific interactions in the red-backed vole, *Clethrionomys gapperi*. *Journal of Mammalogy* **51**, 341–347.

Watts, C. H. S., and H. J. Aslin. (1981). *The rodents of Australia*. Sydney: Angus and Robertson.

Watts, R., and S. Smith. (1978). Oogenesis in *Toxorhynchites rutilus* (Diptera: Culicidae). *Canadian Journal of Zoology* **56**, 136–139.

Weber, W. J. (1975). Notes on cattle egret breeding. *Auk* **92**, 111–117.

Webster, A. B., and R. J. Brooks. (1981). Social behavior of *Microtus pennsylvanicus* in relation to seasonal changes in demography. *Journal of Mammalogy* **62**, 738–751.

Webster, A. B., R. G. Gartshore, and R. J. Brooks. (1981). Infanticide in the meadow vole, *Microtus pennsylvanicus*: Significance in relation to social system and population cycling. *Behavioral and Neural Biology* **31**, 342–347.

Weinberg, E. (1978). Iron and infection. *Microbiological Review* **42**, 45–66.

Weir, B. J. (1971). The reproductive organs of the female plains viscacha, *Lagostomus maximus*. *Journal of Reproduction and Fertility* **25**, 365–373.

Weir, B. J. (1974). Reproductive characteristics of hystricomorph rodents. *Symposium of the Zoological Society of London* **34**, 265–301.

Weisz, J., and I. Ward. (1980). Plasma testosterone and progesterone titers of pregnant rats, their male and female fetuses, and neonatal offspring. *Endocrinology* **106**, 306–316.

Welch, F. (1974). *Sex of children, prior uncertainty, and subsequent fertility behavior*. Santa Monica, Calif.: Rand Corporation R-1510-RF.

Welch, S. M. (1979). The application of simulation models to mite pest management. *Recent Advances in Acarology* **1**, 31–40.

Welcomme, R. L. (1967). The relationship between fecundity and fertility in the mouthbrooding cichlid fish *Tilapia leucosticta*. *Journal of Zoology (London)* **151**, 453–468.

Wells, K. D. (1978). Courtship and parental behavior in a Panamanian poison arrow frog (*Dendrobates auratus*). *Herpetologica* **34**, 148–155.

Wells, K. D. (1981). Parental behavior of male and female frogs. In *Natural selection and social behavior* (R. D. Alexander and D. W. Tinkle, eds.), pp. 184–197. New York: Chiron Press.

Wells, R. (1975). *The population of the British colonies in America before 1776*. Princeton, N.J.: Princeton University Press.

Welty, J. C. (1975). *The life of birds*, 3rd Ed. Philadelphia: W. B. Saunders.

Werner, D. I. (1978). On the biology of *Tropidurus delanonis*, Baur (Iguanidae). *Zeitschrift für Tierpsychologie* **47**, 337–395.

Werren, J. H. (1980a). Sex ratio adaptations to local mate competition in a parasitic wasp. *Science* **208**, 1157–1159.

Werren, J. H. (1980b). Studies in the evolution of sex ratios. Unpublished Ph.D. thesis, University of Utah, Salt Lake City, Utah.

Werren, J. H. (1983). Sex ratio evolution under local mate competition in a parasitic wasp. *Evolution* **37**, 116–124.

Werren, J. H., S. W. Skinner, and E. L. Charnov. (1981). Paternal inheritance of a daughterless sex ratio factor. *Nature (London)* **293**, 467–468.

Werschkul, D. F. (1979). Nestling mortality and the adaptive significance of early locomotion in the little blue heron. *Auk* **96**, 116–130.

West, L. B. (1960). The nature of the inhibitory material from crowded *Rana pipiens* tadpoles. *Physiological Zoology* **33**, 232–239.

Western, D. (1979). Size, life history and ecology in mammals. *African Journal of Ecology* **17**, 185–204.

Weyer, E. M. (1932). *The Eskimos: Their environment and folkways*. New Haven: Yale University Press.

Weygoldt, P. (1980). Complex brood care and reproductive behavior in captive poison arrow frogs, *Dendrobates pumilio* Schmidt. *Behavioral Ecology and Sociobiology* **7**, 329–332.

Wheeler, A. (1975). *Fishes of the world*. New York: Macmillan.

White, H. C. (1930). Some observations on the eastern brook trout (*S. fontinalis*) of Prince Edward Island. *Transactions of the American Fisheries Society* **60**, 101–108.

Whitehead, L. (1968). Altitude, fertility and mortality in Andean countries. *Population Studies* **22**, 335–346.

Whiting, A. R. (1967). The biology of the parasitic wasp, *Mormoniella vitripennis*. *Quarterly Review of Biology* **42**, 333–406.

Whiting, J., P. Bogucki, W-Y. Kwong, and J. Nigro. (1977). Infanticide. *Society for Cross-Cultural Research Newsletter*, No. 5 (September).

Whitney, P. (1976). Population ecology of two sympatric species of subarctic microtine rodents. *Ecological Monographs* **46**, 85–104.

Whitsett, J. M., L. E. Gray, and G. M. Bediz. (1979). Gonadal hormones and aggression toward juvenile conspecifics in prairie deer mice. *Behavioral Ecology and Sociobiology* **6**, 165–168.

Whitten, W. K. (1966). Pheromones and mammalian reproduction. *Advances in Reproductive Physiology* **1**, 155–177.

Widen, L. (1975). Mortality and causes of death in Sweden during the 18th century. *Statistisk Tidskrift* **13**, 93–104.

Wiesner, B. P., and M. M. Sheard. (1933). *Maternal behaviour of the rat.* Edinburgh: Oliver and Boyd.

Wilbur, H. M. (1972). Competition, predation, and the structure of the *Ambystoma-Rana sylvatica* community. *Ecology* **53**, 3–21.

Wilbur, H. M. (1976). Density-dependent aspects of metamorphosis in *Ambystoma* and *Rana sylvatica. Ecology* **57**, 1289–1296.

Wilbur, H. M. (1977). Interactions of food level and population density in *Rana sylvatica. Ecology* **58**, 206–209.

Wilbur, H. M. (1980). Complex life cycles. *Annual Review of Ecology and Systematics* **11**, 67–93.

Wilbur, H. M., and J. P. Collins. (1973). Ecological aspects of amphibian metamorphosis. *Science* **182**, 1305–1314.

Wilkenson, R. G. (1973). *Poverty and progress.* London: Methuen.

Williams, A. J., and A. E. Burger. (1979). Aspects of the breeding biology of the imperial cormorant, *Phalacrocorax atriceps,* at Marion Island. *Le Gerfaut* **69**, 407–423.

Williams, G. C. (1966). *Adaptation and natural selection: A critique of some current evolutionary thought.* Princeton, N.J.: Princeton University Press.

Williams, G. C. (1979). The question of adaptive sex ratio in outcrossed vertebrates. *Proceedings of the Royal Society of London* **B205**, 567–580.

Williams, G. C. (1980). Huxley's evolution and ethics in sociobiological perspective. Lecture delivered at the University of Kentucky, October 6, 1980.

Williamson, L. (1978). Infanticide: An anthropological analysis. In *Infanticide and the value of life* (M. Kohl, ed.), pp. 61–75. Buffalo, N.Y.: Prometheus Books.

Wills, C. (1981). *Genetic variability.* Oxford: Clarendon Press.

Wilson, D. S. (1979). *The natural selection of populations and communities.* Menlo Park, Calif.: Benjamin/Cummings.

Wilson, E. O. (1971). *The insect societies.* Cambridge, Mass.: Harvard University Press.

Wilson, E. O. (1975). *Sociobiology: The new synthesis.* Cambridge, Mass.: Harvard University Press.

Wilson, M. I., M. Daly, and S. J. Weghorst. (1980). Household composition and the risk of child abuse and neglect. *Journal of Biosocial Science* **12**, 333–340.

Wimsatt, W. A. (1942). Survival of spermatozoa in the female reproductive tract of the bat. *Anatomical Record* **83**, 299–307.

Wimsatt, W. A. (1945). Notes on breeding behavior, pregnancy, and parturition in some vespertilionid bats of the eastern United States. *Journal of Mammalogy* **26**, 23–33.

Wimsatt, W. A. (1975). Some comparative aspects of implantation. *Biology of Reproduction* **12**, 1–40.

Wimsatt, W. A., and A. C. Enders. (1980). Structure and morphogenesis of the uterus, placenta, and paraplacental organs of the Neotropical discwinged bat *Thyroptera tricolor spix* (Microchiroptera: Thyropteridae). *American Journal of Anatomy* **159**, 209–243.

Winberg, C. (1975). *Folkokning och Prolketarisering.* Göteborg, Sweden: Meddelanden Fran Historiska Institutionen.

Wing, L. D., and I. O. Buss. (1970). Elephants and forests. *Wildlife Monographs* No. 19.

Winkler, P. (1981). Zur Etho-Ökologie freilebender Hanuman-Languren (*Presbytis entellus entellus* Dufresne, 1797) in Jodhpur (Rajasthan), Indien. Unpublished Ph.D. thesis, University of Göttingen, Federal Republic of Germany.

Winter, J., K. Fujieda, C. Faiman, F. Reyes, and J. Thliveris. (1980). Control of steroidogenesis by human fetal adrenal cells in tissue culture. In *Adrenal androgens* (A. Genazzani, J. Thijssen, and P. Siiteri, eds.), pp. 55–61. New York: Raven Press.

Wirtz, P. (1978). The behavior of the Mediterranean *Tripterygion* species (Pisces, Blennioidei). *Zeitschrift für Tierpsychologie* **48**, 142–174.

Wise, D. A. (1974). Aggression in the female golden hamster: Effects of reproductive state and social isolation. *Hormones and Behavior* **5**, 235–250.

Wolf, K. E. (1980). Social change and male reproductive strategy in silvered leaf-monkeys, *Presbytis cristata*, in Kuala Selangor, peninsular Malaysia. Paper presented at the 49th annual meeting of physical anthropologists, Niagra Falls, April 17–19.

Wolf, K., and J. Fleagle. (1977). Adult male replacement in a group of silvered leaf-monkeys (*Presbytis cristata*) at Kuala Selangor, Malasia. *Primates* **18**, 949–955.

Wolfers, D., and S. C. M. Scrimshaw. (1975). Child survival and intervals between pregnancies in Guayaquil, Ecuador. *Population Studies* **29**, 479–496.

Wong, M., and K. Singer. (1973). Abnormal homicide in Hong Kong. *British Journal of Psychiatry* **123**, 295–298.

Wood, J. T., and R. F. Clarke. (1955). The dusky salamander: Oophagy in nesting sites. *Herpetologica* **11**, 150–151.

Wood, J. T., and F. E. Wood. (1955). Notes on the nests and nesting of the Carolina mountain dusky salamander in Tennessee and Virginia. *Journal of the Tennessee Academy of Science* **30**, 36–39.

Woodin, S. A. (1974). Polychaete abundance patterns in a marine soft-sediment environment: The importance of biological interactions. *Ecological Monographs* **44**, 171–187.

Woodin, S. A. (1976). Adult–larval interactions in dense infaunal assemblages: Patterns of abundance. *Journal of Marine Research* **34**, 25–41.

Woodruff, D. S. (1976). Embryonic mortality in *Pseudophryne* (Anura: Leptodactylidae). *Copeia,* pp. 445–449.

Woodruff, D. S. (1977). Male postmating brooding behavior in three Australian *Pseudophryne* (Anura: Leptodactylidae). *Herpetologica* **33**, 296–303.

Wootton, R. J. (1971). A note on the nest-raiding behavior of male sticklebacks. *Canadian Journal of Zoology* **49**, 960–962.

Wootton, R. J. (1976). *The biology of the sticklebacks.* New York: Academic Press.

Wourms, J. P. (1977). Reproduction and development in chondrichthyan fishes. *American Zoologist* **17**, 379–410.

Wourms, J. P. (1981). Viviparity: The maternal–fetal relationship in fishes. *American Zoologist* **21**, 473–515.

Wourms, J. P., W. C. Hamlet, and M. D. Stribling. (1981). Embryonic oophagy and adelphophagy in sharks. Abstract No. 606. *American Zoologist* **21**, 1019.

Wrangham, R. W. (1974a). Artificial feeding of chimpanzees and baboons in their natural habitat. *Animal Behaviour* **22**, 83–93.

Wrangham, R. W. (1974b). The behavioural ecology of chimpanzees in Gombe National Park, Tanzania. Unpublished Ph.D. thesis, University of Cambridge.

Wray, J., and A. Aguirre. (1969). Protein caloric malnutrition in Candelaria, Columbia. I. Prevalence, social and demographic causal factors. *Journal of Tropical Pediatrics* **15**, 91, 93–97.

Wrensch, D. L. (1979). Components of reproductive success in spider mites. *Recent Advances in Acarology* **1**, 155–164.

Wrensch, D. L., and S. S. Y. Young. (1978). Effects of density and host quality on rate of development, survivorship and sex ratio in the carmine spider mite. *Environmental Entomology* **7**, 499–501.

Wright, J. K. (1976). Inter- and intraspecific relationships of the anabantoid fish *Trichogaster trichopterus* (Pallas). Unpublished manuscript, as cited in Loiselle and Barlow, 1978.

Wrigley, E. A. (1978). Fertility strategy for the individual and the group. In *Historical studies of changing fertility* (C. Tilly, ed.), pp. 135–154. Princeton, N.J.: Princeton University Press.

Wrigley, E., and Schofield (1981). *The population history of England 1541–1871.* Cambridge, Mass.: Harvard University Press.

Wu, D. Y. H. (1981). Child abuse in Taiwan. In *Child abuse: Cross-cultural perspectives* (J. E. Korbin, ed.), pp. 139–165. Berkeley: University of California Press.

Wylie, H. G. (1958). Factors that affect host finding by *Nasonia vitripennis* (Walker) (Hymenoptera: Pteromalidae). *Canadian Entomologist* **90**, 597–608.

Wylie, H. G. (1963). Some effects of host age on parasitism by *Nasonia vitripennis* (Walker) (Hymenoptera: Pteromalidae). *Canadian Entomologist* **95**, 881–886.

Wylie, H. G. (1965). Some factors that reduce the reproductive rate of *Nasonia vitripennis* (Walk.) at high adult population densities. *Canadian Entomologist* **97**, 970–977.

Wylie, H. G. (1966). Some mechanisms that affect the sex ratio of *Nasonia vitripennis* (Walk.) (Hymenoptera: Pteromalidae) reared from superparasitized housefly pupae. *Canadian Entomologist* **98**, 645–653.

Wynne-Edwards, V. C. (1962). *Animal dispersion in relation to social behaviour.* Edinburgh: Oliver and Boyd.

Wyon, J., and J. Gordon. (1971). *The Khanna study: Population problems in rural Punjab.* Cambridge, Mass.: Harvard University Press.

Yeates, N. T. M. (1958). Foetal dwarfism in sheep: An effect of high atmospheric temperature during gestation. *Journal of Agricultural Science* **51**, 84–89.

Yom-Tov, Y. (1974). The effect of food and predation on breeding density and success, clutch size and laying date of the crow (*Corvus corone* L.). *Journal of Animal Ecology* **43**, 479–498.

Yom-Tov, Y. (1976). Recognition of eggs and young by the carrion crow (*Corvus cornone*). *Behaviour* **59**, 247–251.

Yoshiba, K. (1967). An ecological study of Hanuman langurs (*Presbytis entellus*). *Primates* **8**, 127–154.

Yoshiba, K. (1968). Local and intertroop variability in ecology and social behavior of common Indian langurs. In *Primates* (P. Jay, ed.), pp. 217–242. New York: Holt, Rinehart and Winston.

Young, E. C. (1963). The breeding behaviour of the South Polar skua, *Catharacta maccormicki*. *Ibis* **105**, 203–233.

Young, H. (1963). Age-specific mortality in the eggs and chicks of blackbirds. *Auk* **80**, 145–155.

Young, S. P. (1927). Mountain lion eats its kittens. *Journal of Mammalogy* **8**, 158–160.

Yung, E. (1885). Influence du nombre des individus contenus dans un même vase, et de la forme de ce vase, sur la développement des larves de grenouille. *Comptes Rendus de l'Academie des Sciences* **101**, 1018–1020.

Zaher, M. A., K. K. Shehata, and H. El-Khatib. (1979). Population density effects on biology of *Tetranychus arabicus,* the common spider mite in Egypt. *Recent Advances in Acarology* **1**, 507–509.

Zarbock, W. M. (1951). Life history of the Utah sculpin, *Cottus bairdi semiscaber* (Cope), in Logan River, Utah. *Transactions of the American Fisheries Society* **81**, 249–259.

Zaret, T. M. (1977). Inhibition of cannibalism in *Cichla ocellaris* and hypothesis of predator mimicry among South American fishes. *Evolution* **31**, 421–437.

Zaret, T. M. (1980). *Predation and freshwater communities.* New Haven: Yale University Press.

Zeveloff, S. I., and M. S. Boyce. (1980). Parental investment and mating systems in mammals. *Evolution* **34**, 973–982.

Zimen, E. (1976). On the regulation of pack size in wolves. *Zeitschrift für Tierpsychologie* **40**, 300–341.

Zimmermann, H., and E. Zimmermann. (1981). Sozialverhalten Fortpflanzungverhalten und Zucht de Farberfroche, *Dendrobates histrionicus* und *D. lehamanni* sowie einiger anderer Dendrobatiden. *Zeitschrift des Kolner Zoo* **24**, 83–89.

Zuckerman, S. (1932). *The social life of monkeys and apes.* New York: Harcourt and Brace.

Subject Index